# AN ESSAY
# CONCERNING
# HUMAN
# UNDERSTANDING

# AN ESSAY
# CONCERNING
# HUMAN
# UNDERSTANDING

## JOHN
## LOCKE

GREAT BOOKS IN PHILOSOPHY

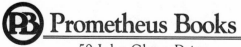
Prometheus Books

59 John Glenn Drive
Amherst, NewYork 14228-2197

Published 1995 by Prometheus Books

59 John Glenn Drive, Amherst, New York 14228-2197.
716-691-0133. FAX: 716-691-0137.

Library of Congress Cataloging-in-Publication Data

Locke, John, 1632–1704.
    An essay concerning human understanding / John Locke.
        p.        cm. — (Great books in philosophy)
    Previously published : London : George Routledge and Sons Limited;
New York : E. P. Dutton and Co., [1910]
    Includes index.
    ISBN 0-87975-917-8 (pbk. : alk. paper)
    1. Knowledge, Theory of—Early works to 1800. I. Title. II. Series.
B1290      1994
121—dc20                                                          94-32887
                                                                          CIP

# Additional Titles on
## Metaphysics and Epistemology in
## Prometheus's Great Books in Philosophy Series

Aristotle
*De Anima*

Aristotle
*The Metaphysics*

George Berkeley
*Three Dialogues Between
Hylas and Philonous*

René Descartes
*Discourse on Method*
and *The Meditations*

John Dewey
*How We Think*

Epicurus
*The Essential Epicurus: Letters, Principal
Doctrines, Vatican Sayings, and Fragments*

Sidney Hook
*The Quest for Being*

David Hume
*An Enquiry Concerning
Human Understanding*

David Hume
*Treatise of Human Nature*

William James
*Pragmatism*

Immanuel Kant
*Critique of Pure Reason*

Gottfried Wilhelm Leibniz
*Discourse on Metaphysics*
and *The Monadology*

Plato
*The Euthyphro, Apology, Crito,*
and *Phaedo*

Bertrand Russell
*The Problems of Philosophy*

Sextus Empiricus
*Outlines of Pyrrhonism*

See the back of this volume for a complete list of titles in
Prometheus's Great Books in Philosophy and Great Minds series.

JOHN LOCKE was born August 29, 1632, in Somerset, England, the son of landed English gentry. He entered Christ Church, Oxford, in 1652 and passed through the academic ranks quite uneventfully, later assuming a teaching post at the university. To escape ordination in the Church of England—a natural bureaucratic step toward university promotion—Locke took up the study of medicine and was transported into a new world of "natural philosophy" in which he associated with powerful scientific minds like that of Robert Boyle.

It was through his concern for the authority of the state in religious matters and the Natural Law used to support it that Locke became interested in the role of Natural Law in experience—a curiosity that led him to philosophy, and more particularly, to epistemology, as an avocation. Add to his interest in Natural Law the sociopolitical climate of seventeenth-century England—steeped in violent civil war, counter-revolution, deposition of the monarchy and the subsequent Parliamentary rule, and the eventual restoration of the monarchy late in the century—along with an intellectual stage dominated by the authoritarianism of Thomas Hobbes's *Leviathan,* and one can begin to sense the pressures at work on Locke.

After accepting a brief diplomatic mission to Madrid in 1665, Locke retreated to his teaching and medical experiments. His real political education was to come quite by accident as a result of an association with the first Earl of Shaftesbury, a wealthy and extremely powerful figure who had survived the vicissitudes of England's political turbulence. Initially employed as the Earl's medical advisor, Locke later became a permanent member of the household. It was here under the skillful tutelage of Shaftesbury that Locke matured as a social philosopher. The political intrigues in which the Earl was engaged caused Locke to be exiled, though he later returned to England after the Glorious Revolution that saw William and Mary placed on the English throne in 1688.

Locke's famous *Two Treatises of Government,* of which the second is more widely read, are an outgrowth of his original political proclivities, the sociopolitical chaos plaguing England during his lifetime, and his association with the Earl of Shaftesbury. Locke's dedication to individual liberty, government by consent, the social contract, and the right to revolt against governments that endanger the rights of citizens, has made him one of the most important political thinkers of the past four centuries. His legacy will live on as long as there are people fighting for freedom. He died in Oates, England, on October 28, 1704.

Some of John Locke's major works include: *A Letter Concerning Toleration* (1689), *Two Treatises of Government* (1690), *An Essay Concerning Human Understanding* (1693), *Some Thoughts Concerning Education* (1693), and *The Reasonableness of Christianity* (1695).

# CONTENTS.

--◆--

## BOOK I.

### OF INNATE NOTIONS.

## BOOK II.

### OF IDEAS.

## BOOK III.

### OF WORDS.

## BOOK IV.

### OF KNOWLEDGE AND OPINION.

TO THE RIGHT HONOURABLE

# THOMAS, EARL OF PEMBROKE AND MONTGOMERY,

BARON HERBERT OF CARDIFF, LORD ROSS OF KENDAL, PAR, FITZHUGH,
MARMION, ST. QUINTIN AND SHURLAND; LORD PRESIDENT OF
HIS MAJESTY'S MOST HONOURABLE PRIVY COUNCIL, AND LORD
LIEUTENANT OF THE COUNTY OF WILTS, AND OF SOUTH WALES.

MY LORD,

THIS treatise, which is grown up under your lordship's eye, and has ventured into the world by your order, does now, by a natural kind of right, come to your lordship for that protection which you several years since promised it. It is not that I think any name, how great soever, set at the beginning of a book, will be able to cover the faults that are to be found in it. Things in print must stand and fall by their own worth, or the reader's fancy. But, there being nothing more to be desired for truth than a fair unprejudiced hearing, nobody is more likely to procure me that than your lordship, who are allowed to have got so intimate an acquaintance with her in her more retired recesses. Your lordship is known to have so far advanced your speculations in the most abstract and general knowledge of things, beyond the ordinary reach or common methods, that your allowance and approbation of the design of this treatise will at least preserve it from being condemned without reading; and will prevail to have those parts a little weighed which might otherwise, perhaps, be thought to deserve no consideration, for being somewhat out of the common road. The imputation of novelty is a terrible charge amongst those who judge of men's heads, as they do of their perukes, by the fashion; and can allow none to be right but the received doctrines. Truth scarce ever yet carried it by vote any where at its first appearance; new opinions are always suspected, and usually opposed, without any other reason but because they are not already common. But truth, like gold, is not the less so for being newly brought out of the mine. It is trial and examination must give it price, and not any antique fashion; and though it be not yet current by the public stamp, yet it may, for all that, be as old as nature, and is certainly not the less genuine. Your lordship can give great and convincing instances of this, whenever you please to oblige the public with some of those large and comprehensive discoveries you have made of truths hitherto unknown, unless to some few, to whom your lordship has been pleased not wholly to conceal them. This alone were a sufficient reason, were there no other, why I should dedicate this Essay to your lordship; and its having some little correspondence with some parts of that nobler and vast system of the sciences your lordship has made so new, exact, and instructive a draught of, I think it glory enough if your lordship permit me to boast that here and there I have fallen into some thoughts not wholly different from yours. If your lordship think fit, that, by your encouragement, this should appear in the world, I hope it may be a reason, some time or other, to lead your lordship farther; and you will allow me to say, that you here give the world an earnest of something, that, if they can bear with this, will be truly worth their expectation. This, my lord, shows what a present I here make to your lordship; just such as the poor man does to his rich and great neighbour, by whom the basket of flowers or fruit is not ill taken, though he has more plenty of his own growth, and in much greater perfection. Worthless things receive a value when they are made the offerings of respect, esteem, and gratitude; these you have given me so mighty and peculiar reasons to have in the highest degree for your lordship, that if they can add a price to what they go along with proportionable to their own greatness, I can with confidence brag, I here make your lordship the richest present you ever received. This I am sure, I am under the greatest obligation to seek all occasions to acknowledge a long train of favours I have received from your lordship; favours, though great and important in themselves, yet made much more so by the forwardness, concern, and kindness, and other obliging circumstances, that never failed to accompany them. To all this, you are pleased to add that which gives yet more weight and relish to all the rest; you vouchsafe to continue me in some degrees of your esteem, and allow me a place in your good thoughts, I had almost said friendship. This, my lord, your words and actions so constantly show on all occasions, even to others when I am absent, that it is not vanity in me to mention what every body knows; but it would be want of good manners not to acknowledge what so many are witnesses of, and every day tell me I am indebted to your lordship for. I wish they could as easily assist my gratitude, as they convince me of the great and growing engagements it has to your lordship. This I am sure, I should write of the UNDERSTANDING without having any, if I were not extremely sensible of them, and did not lay hold on this opportunity to testify to the world how much I am obliged to be, and how much I am,

MY LORD,

Your lordship's most humble and

most obedient servant,

JOHN LOCKE.

*Dorset Court, May 24, 1689.*

# THE EPISTLE TO THE READER.

READER,

I HERE put into thy hands what has been the diversion of some of my idle and heavy hours; if it has the good-luck to prove so of any of thine, and thou hast but half so much pleasure in reading as I had in writing it, thou wilt as little think thy money, as I do my pains, ill bestowed. Mistake not this for a commendation of my work; nor conclude, because I was pleased with the doing of it, that therefore I am fondly taken with it now it is done. He that hawks at larks and sparrows, has no less sport, though a much less considerable quarry, than he that flies at nobler game: and he is little acquainted with the subject of this treatise, the Understanding, who does not know, that as it is the most elevated faculty of the soul, so it is employed with a greater and more constant delight than any of the other. Its searches after truth are a sort of hawking and hunting, wherein the very pursuit makes a great part of the pleasure. Every step the mind takes in its progress towards knowledge makes some discovery, which is not only new, but the best, too, for the time at least.

For the understanding, like the eye, judging of objects only by its own sight, cannot but be pleased with what it discovers, having less regret for what has escaped it, because it is unknown. Thus he who has raised himself above the alms-basket, and not content to live lazily on scraps of begged opinions, sets his own thoughts on work, to find and follow truth, will (whatever he lights on) not miss the hunter's satisfaction; every moment of his pursuit will reward his pains with some delight, and he will have reason to think his time not ill spent, even when he cannot much boast of any great acquisition.

This, reader, is the entertainment of those who let loose their own thoughts, and follow them in writing; which thou oughtest not to envy them, since they afford thee an opportunity of the like diversion, if thou wilt make use of thy own thoughts in reading. It is to them, if they are thy own, that I refer myself; but if they are taken upon trust from others, it is no great matter what they are, they not following truth, but some meaner consideration; and it is not worth while to be concerned what he says or thinks, who says or thinks only as he is directed by another. If thou judgest for thyself, I know thou wilt judge

candidly; and then I shall not be harmed or offended, whatever
be thy censure.  For, though it be certain that there is nothing
in this treatise of the truth whereof I am not fully persuaded,
yet I consider myself as liable to mistakes as I can think thee;
and know that this book must stand or fall with thee, not by any
opinion I have of it, but thy own.  If thou findest little in it new
or instructive to thee, thou art not to blame me for it.  It was
not meant for those that had already mastered this subject, and
made a thorough acquaintance with their own understandings,
but for my own information, and the satisfaction of a few friends,
who acknowledged themselves not to have sufficiently considered
it.  Were it fit to trouble thee with the history of this Essay, I
should tell thee, that five or six friends, meeting at my chamber,
and discoursing on a subject very remote from this, found themselves quickly at a stand by the difficulties that rose on every
side.  After we had awhile puzzled ourselves, without coming
any nearer a resolution of those doubts which perplexed us, it
came into my thoughts, that we took a wrong course; and that,
before we set ourselves upon inquiries of that nature, it was
necessary to examine our own abilities, and see what objects
our understandings were or were not fitted to deal with.  This I
proposed to the company, who all readily assented; and thereupon
it was agreed, that this should be our first inquiry.  Some hasty
and undigested thoughts, on a subject I had never before
considered, which I set down against our next meeting, gave the
first entrance into this discourse, which, having been thus begun
by chance, was continued by entreaty; written by incoherent
parcels; and, after long intervals of neglect, resumed again, as
my humour or occasions permitted; and at last, in a retirement,
where an attendance on my health gave me leisure, it was
brought into that order thou now seest it.
    This discontinued way of writing may have occasioned, besides
others, two contrary faults; viz., that too little and too much
may be said in it.  If thou findest any thing wanting, I shall be
glad, that what I have writ gives thee any desire that I should
have gone farther: if it seems too much to thee, thou must blame
the subject; for when I first put pen to paper, I thought all I
should have to say on this matter would have been contained in
one sheet of paper; but the farther I went, the larger prospect
I had: new discoveries led me still on, and so it grew insensibly
to the bulk it now appears in.  I will not deny but possibly it
might be reduced to a narrower compass than it is; and that
some parts of it might be contracted; the way it has been writ
in, by catches, and many long intervals of interruption, being
apt to cause some repetitions.  But, to confess the truth, I am
now too lazy or too busy to make it shorter.
    I am not ignorant how little I herein consult my own reputa-
tion, when I knowingly let it go with a fault so apt to disgust the

most judicious, who are always the nicest readers. But they who know sloth is apt to content itself with any excuse, will pardon me, if mine has prevailed on me where I think I have a very good one. I will not, therefore, allege in my defence, that the same notion, having different respects, may be convenient or necessary to prove or illustrate several parts of the same discourse; and that so it has happened in many parts of this: but, waving that, I shall frankly avow, that I have sometimes dwelt long upon the same argument, and expressed it different ways, with a quite different design. I pretend not to publish this Essay for the information of men of large thoughts and quick apprehensions; to such masters of knowledge, I profess myself a scholar, and therefore warn them beforehand not to expect any thing here but what, being spun out of my own coarse thoughts, is fitted to men of my own size, to whom, perhaps, it will not be unacceptable that I have taken some pains to make plain and familiar to their thoughts some truths, which established prejudice or the abstractness of the ideas themselves, might render difficult. Some objects had need be turned on every side; and when the notion is new, as I confess some of these are to me, or out of the ordinary road, as I suspect they will appear to others, it is not one simple view of it that will gain it admittance into every understanding, or fix it there with a clear and lasting impression. There are few, I believe, who have not observed in themselves or others, that what in one way of proposing was very obscure, another way of expressing it has made very clear and intelligible; though afterward the mind found little difference in the phrases, and wondered why one failed to be understood more than the other. But every thing does not hit alike upon every man's imagination. We have our understandings no less different than our palates; and he that thinks the same truth shall be equally relished by every one in the same dress, may as well hope to feast every one with the same sort of cookery; the meat may be the same, and the nourishment good, yet every one not be able to receive it with that seasoning; and it must be dressed another way, if you will have it go down with some even of strong constitutions. The truth is, those who advised me to publish it, advised me, for this reason, to publish it as it is; and since I have been brought to let it go abroad, I desire it should be understood by whoever gives himself the pains to read it. I have so little affection to be in print, that if I were not flattered this Essay might be of some use to others, as I think it has been to me, I should have confined it to the view of some friends, who gave the first occasion to it. My appearing therefore in print being on purpose to be as useful as I may, I think it necessary to make what I have to say as easy and intelligible to all sorts of readers as I can. And I had much rather the speculative and quick-sighted should complain of my being in

some parts tedious, than that any one, not accustomed to
abstract speculations, or prepossessed with different notions,
should mistake or not comprehend my meaning.

It will possibly be censured as a great piece of vanity or insolence in me, to pretend to instruct this our knowing age, it
amounting to little less when I own that I publish this Essay
with hopes that it may be useful to others.  But if it may be
permitted to speak freely of those who, with a feigned modesty,
condemn as useless what they themselves write, methinks it
savours much more of vanity or insolence to publish a book for
any other end; and he fails very much of that respect he owes
the public, who prints, and consequently expects that men should
read, that wherein he intends not they should meet with any
thing of use to themselves or others: and should nothing else be
found allowable in this treatise, yet my design will not cease to
be so; and the goodness of my intention ought to be some
excuse for the worthlessness of my present.  It is that chiefly
which secures me from the fear of censure, which I expect not to
escape more than better writers.  Men's principles, notions,
and relishes are so different, that it is hard to find a book which
pleases or displeases all men.  I acknowledge the age we live in
is not the least knowing, and therefore not the most easy to be
satisfied.  If I have not the good-luck to please, yet nobody
ought to be offended with me.  I plainly tell all my readers,
except half a dozen, this treatise was not at first intended for
them; and therefore they need not be at the trouble to be of
that number.  But yet if any one thinks fit to be angry, and
rail at it, he may do it securely; for I shall find some better
way of spending my time than in such kind of conversation.  I
shall always have the satisfaction to have aimed sincerely at
truth and usefulness, though in one of the meanest ways.  The
commonwealth of learning is not at this time without master-
builders, whose mighty designs in advancing the sciences will
leave lasting monuments to the admiration of posterity: but
every one must not hope to be a Boyle or a Sydenham; and in
an age that produces such masters as the great Huygenius, and
the incomparable Mr. Newton, with some other of that strain,
it is ambition enough to be employed as an under-labourer in
clearing ground a little, and removing some of the rubbish that
lies in the way to knowledge; which certainly had been very
much more advanced in the world, if the endeavours of ingenious
and industrious men had not been much cumbered with the
learned but frivolous use of uncouth, affected, or unintelligible
terms introduced into the sciences, and there made an art of to
that degree, that philosophy, which is nothing but the true
knowledge of things, was thought unfit or uncapable to be
brought into well-bred company and polite conversation.  Vague
and insignificant forms of speech, and abuse of language, have

so long passed for mysteries of science; and hard or misapplied words, with little or no meaning, have, by prescription, such a right to be mistaken for deep learning and height of speculation; that it will not be easy to persuade either those who speak or those who bear them, that they are but the covers of ignorance, and hinderance of true knowledge. To break in upon the sanctuary of vanity and ignorance, will be, I suppose, some service to human understanding: though so few are apt to think they deceive or are deceived in the use of words, or that the language of the sect they are of has any faults in it which ought to be examined or corrected, that I hope I shall be pardoned if I have in the third book dwelt long on this subject; and endeavoured to make it so plain, that neither the inveterateness of the mischief, nor the prevalency of the fashion, shall be any excuse for those who will not take care about the meaning of their own words, and will not suffer the significancy of their expressions to be inquired into.

I have been told that a short epitome of this treatise, which was printed 1688, was by some condemned without reading, because innate ideas were denied in it; they too hastily concluding, that if innate ideas were not supposed, there would be little left either of the notion or proof of spirits. If any one take the like offence at the entrance of this treatise, I shall desire him to read it through; and then I hope he will be convinced, that the taking away false foundations is not to the prejudice, but advantage, of truth, which is never injured or endangered so much as when mixed with or built on falsehood. In the second edition I added as followeth:—

The bookseller will not forgive me, if I say nothing of this second edition, which he has promised, by the correctness of it, shall make amends for the many faults committed in the former. He desires, too, that it should be known, that it has one whole new chapter concerning identity, and many additions and amendments in other places. These, I must inform my reader, are not all new matter, but most of them either farther confirmation of what I had said, or explications to prevent others being mistaken in the sense of what was formerly printed, and not any variation in me from it: I must only except the alterations I have made in book ii. chap. xxi.

What I had there writ concerning "liberty" and the "will," I thought deserved as accurate a review as I was capable of: those subjects having in all ages exercised the learned part of the world with questions and difficulties that have not a little perplexed morality and divinity, those parts of knowledge that men are most concerned to be clear in. Upon a closer inspection into the working of men's minds, and a stricter examination of those motives and views they are turned by, I have found reason somewhat to alter the thoughts I formerly had concerning that which gives the last determination to the will in all voluntary actions. This I cannot forbear to acknowledge to the world, with as much freedom and readiness as I at first published what then seemed to me to be right; thinking myself more concerned to quit and renounce any opinion of my own, than oppose that of another, when truth appears against it. For it is truth alone I seek, and that will always be welcome to me, when or from whence soever it comes.

But what forwardness soever I have to resign any opinion I have, or to recede from any thing I have writ, upon the first evidence of any error in it; yet this I must own, that I have not had the good-luck to receive any light from those exceptions I have met with in print against any part of my book; nor have, from any thing has been urged against it, found reason to alter my sense in any of the points have been questioned. Whether the subject I have in hand requires often more thought and attention than cursory readers, at least such as are prepossessed, are willing to allow; or whether any obscurity in my expressions casts a cloud over it, and these notions are made difficult to others' apprehension in my way of treating them; so it is, that my meaning, I find, is often mistaken, and I have not the good-luck to be every where rightly understood. There are so many instances of this, that I think it justice to my reader and myself to conclude, that either my book is plainly enough written to be rightly understood by those who peruse it with that attention and indifferency which every one, who will give himself the pains to read, ought to employ in reading; or else that I have writ mine so obscurely, that it is in vain to go about to mend it. Whichever of these be that truth, it is myself only am affected thereby; and therefore I shall be far from troubling my reader with what I think might be said in answer to those several objections I have met with to passages here and there of my book; since I persuade myself, that he who thinks them of moment enough to be concerned whether they are true or false, will be able to see, that what is said is either not well-founded, or else not contrary to my doctrine, when I and my opposer come both to be well understood.

If any (careful that none of their good thoughts should be lost) have published their censures of my Essay, with this honour done to it, that they will not suffer it to be an Essay, I leave it to the public to value the obligation they have to their critical pens, and shall not waste my reader's time in so idle or ill-natured an employment of mine, as to lessen the satisfaction any one has in himself, or gives to others, in so hasty a confutation of what I have written.

The booksellers, preparing for the fourth edition of my Essay, gave me notice of it, that I might, if I had leisure, make any additions or alterations I should think fit. Whereupon I thought it convenient to advertise the reader, that besides several corrections I had made here and there, there was one alteration which it was necessary to mention, because it ran through the whole book, and is of consequence to be rightly understood. What I thereupon said, was this:—

"Clear and distinct ideas" are terms which, though familiar and frequent in men's mouths, I have reason to think every one who uses does not perfectly understand. And possibly it is but here and there one who gives himself the trouble to consider them so far as to know what he himself or others precisely mean by them. I have therefore, in most places, chose to put "determinate" or "determined," instead of "clear" and "distinct," as more likely to direct men's thoughts to my meaning in this matter. By those denominations, I mean some object in the mind, and consequently determined, *i. e.*, such as it is there seen and perceived to be. This, I think, may fitly be called a "determinate" or "determined" idea, when such as it is at any time objectively in the mind, and so determined there, it is annexed, and without variation determined, to a name or articulate sound which is to be steadily the sign of that very same object of the mind, or determinate idea.

To explain this a little more particularly: By "determinate," when applied to a simple idea, I mean that simple appearance which the mind has in its view, or perceives in itself, when that idea is said to be in it. By "determinate," when applied to a complex idea, I mean such an one as consists of a determinate number of certain simple or less complex ideas, joined in such a proportion and situation as the mind has before its view, and sees in itself, when that idea is present in it, or should be present in it when a man gives a name to it. I say "should be;" because it is not every one, nor perhaps any one, who is so careful of his language as to use no word till he views in his mind the precise determined idea which he resolves to make it the sign of. The want of this is the cause of no small obscurity and confusion in men's thoughts and discourses.

I know there are not words enough in any language to answer all the variety of ideas that enter into men's discourses and reasonings. But this hinders not but that when any one uses any term, he may have in his mind a determined idea which he makes it the sign of, and to which he should keep it steadily annexed during that present discourse. Where he does not or cannot do this, he in vain pretends to clear or distinct ideas: it is plain his are not so; and therefore there can be expected nothing but obscurity and confusion, where such terms are made use of which have not such a precise determination.

Upon this ground I have thought "determined ideas" a way of speaking less liable to mistake than "clear and distinct:" and where men have got such determined ideas of all that they reason, inquire, or argue about, they will find a great part of their doubts and disputes at an end. The greatest part of the questions and controversies that perplex mankind, depending on the doubtful and uncertain use of words, or (which is the same) indetermined ideas, which they are made to stand for: I have made choice of these terms to signify, 1. Some immediate object of the mind, which it perceives and has before it, distinct from the sound it uses as a sign of it. 2. That this idea, thus determined, *i. e.*, which the mind has in itself, and knows and sees there, be determined without any change to that name, and that name determined to that precise idea. If men had such determined ideas in their inquiries and discourses, they would both discern how far their own inquiries and discourses went, and avoid the greatest part of the disputes and wranglings they have with others.

Besides this, the bookseller will think it necessary I should advertise the reader, that there is an addition of two chapters wholly new; the one of the Association of Ideas, the other of Enthusiasm. These, with some other larger additions never before printed, he has engaged to print by themselves after the same manner, and for the same purpose, as was done when this Essay had the second impression.

In this sixth edition there is very little added or altered, the greatest part of what is new is contained in the twenty-first chapter of the second book, which any one, if he thinks it worth the while, may, with a very little labour, transcribe into the margin of the former edition.

# OF
# HUMAN UNDERSTANDING.

## BOOK I.

### CHAPTER I.

#### INTRODUCTION.

**1.** *An inquiry into the understanding, pleasant and useful.*—
Since it is the understanding that sets man above the rest of
sensible beings, and gives him all the advantage and dominion
which he has over them, it is certainly a subject, even for its
nobleness, worth our labour to inquire into. The understanding,
like the eye, whilst it makes us see and perceive all other things,
takes no notice of itself; and it requires art and pains to set it at
a distance, and make it its own object. But whatever be the
difficulties that lie in the way of this inquiry, whatever it be that
keeps us so much in the dark to ourselves, sure I am that all the
light we can let in upon our own minds, all the acquaintance
we can make with our own understandings, will not only be very
pleasant, but bring us great advantage in directing our thoughts
in the search of other things.

2. *Design.*—This therefore being my purpose, to inquire into
the original, certainty, and extent of human knowledge, together
with the grounds and degrees of belief, opinion, and assent, I
shall not at present meddle with the physical consideration of the
mind, or trouble myself to examine wherein its essence consists,
or by what motions of our spirits, or alterations of our bodies, we
come to have any sensation by our organs, or any ideas in our
understandings; and whether those ideas do, in their formation,
any or all of them, depend on matter or no : these are speculations which, however curious and entertaining, I shall decline, as
lying out of my way in the design I am now upon. It shall
suffice to my present purpose, to consider the discerning faculties
of a man as they are employed about the objects which they have
to do with; and I shall imagine I have not wholly misemployed
myself in the thoughts I shall have on this occasion, if, in this
historical, plain method, I can give any account of the ways

whereby our understandings come to attain those notions of things we have, and can set down any measures of the certainty of our knowledge, or the grounds of those persuasions which are to be found amongst men, so various, different, and wholly contradictory; and yet asserted somewhere or other with such assurance, and confidence, that he that shall take a view of the opinions of mankind, observe their opposition, and at the same time consider the fondness and devotion wherewith they are embraced, the resolution and eagerness wherewith they are maintained, may perhaps have reason to suspect that either there is no such thing as truth at all, or that mankind hath no sufficient means to attain a certain knowledge of it.

3. *Method.*—It is therefore worth while to search out the bounds between opinion and knowledge, and examine by what measures, in things whereof we have no certain knowledge, we ought to regulate our assent, and moderate our persuasions. In order whereunto, I shall pursue this following method :—

First. I shall inquire into the original of those ideas, notions, or whatever else you please to call them, which a man observes, and is conscious to himself he has in his mind, and the ways whereby the understanding comes to be furnished with them.

Secondly. I shall endeavour to show what knowledge the understanding hath by those ideas, and the certainty, evidence, and extent of it.

Thirdly. I shall make some inquiry into the nature and grounds of faith or opinion ; whereby I mean, that assent which we give to any proposition as true, of whose truth yet we have no certain knowledge : and here we shall have occasion to examine the reasons and degrees of assent.

4. *Useful to know the extent of our comprehension.*—If by this inquiry into the nature of the understanding, I can discover the powers thereof, how far they reach, to what things they are in any degree proportionate, and where they fail us, I suppose it may be of use to prevail with the busy mind of man to be more cautious in meddling with things exceeding its comprehension, to stop when it is at the utmost extent of its tether, and to sit down in a quiet ignorance of those things which, upon examination, are found to be beyond the reach of our capacities. We should not then, perhaps, be so forward, out of an affectation of an universal knowledge, to raise questions, and perplex ourselves and others with disputes, about things to which our understandings are not suited, and of which we cannot frame in our minds any clear or distinct perceptions, or whereof (as it has, perhaps, too often happened) we have not any notions at all. If we can find out how far the understanding can extend its view, how far it has faculties to attain certainty, and in what cases it can only judge and guess, we may learn to content ourselves with what is attainable by us in this state.

**5.** *Our capacity suited to our state and concerns.*—For though
the comprehension of our understandings comes exceeding short
of the vast extent of things, yet we shall have cause enough to
magnify the bountiful Author of our being for that portion * and
degree of knowledge he has bestowed on us, so far above all the
rest of the inhabitants of this our mansion. Men have reason
to be well satisfied with what God hath thought fit for them,
since he has given them, as St. Peter says, πάντα πρὸς ζωὴν καὶ
εὐσέβειαν, "whatsoever is necessary for the conveniences of life,
and information of virtue;" and has put within the reach of their
discovery the comfortable provision for this life, and the way that
leads to a better. How short soever their knowledge may come
of an universal or perfect comprehension of whatsoever is, it yet
secures their great concernments that they have light enough to
lead them to the knowledge of their Maker, and the sight of
their own duties. Men may find matter sufficient to busy their
heads and employ their hands with variety, delight, and satisfaction, if they will not boldly quarrel with their own constitution,
and throw away the blessings their hands are filled with,
because they are not big enough to grasp everything. We shall
not have much reason to complain of the narrowness of our
minds, if we will but employ them about what may be of use to
us; for of that they are very capable; and it will be an unpardonable as well as childish peevishness, if we undervalue the
advantages of our knowledge, and neglect to improve it to the
ends for which it was given us, because there are some things
that are set out of the reach of it. It will be no excuse to an idle
and untoward servant, who would not attend his business by
candlelight, to plead that he had not broad sunshine. The candle
that is set up in us shines bright enough for all our purposes.
The discoveries we can make with this ought to satisfy us; and
we shall then use our understandings right, when we entertain
all objects in that way and proportion that they are suited to our
faculties, and upon those grounds they are capable of being proposed to us; and not peremptorily or intemperately require
demonstration, and demand certainty, where probability only is
to be had, and which is sufficient to govern all our concernments.
If we will disbelieve everything because we cannot certainly
know all things, we shall do much-what as wisely as he who
would not use his legs, but sit still and perish because he had no
wings to fly.

**6.** *Knowledge of our capacity a cure of scepticism and idleness.*
—When we know our own strength, we shall the better know
what to undertake with hopes of success; and when we have well
surveyed the powers of our own minds, and made some estimate
what we may expect from them, we shall not be inclined either

---

* The reading of the ninth edition is "proportion."—EDIT.

to sit still, and not set our thoughts on work at all, in despair of
knowing anything; nor, on the other side, question everything,
and disclaim all knowledge, because some things are not to be
understood. It is of great use to the sailor to know the length
of his line, though he cannot with it fathom all the depths of
the ocean; it is well he knows that it is long enough to reach
the bottom at such places as are necessary to direct his voyage,
and caution him against running upon shoals that may ruin him.
Our business here is not to know all things, but those which
concern our conduct. If we can find out those measures whereby
a rational creature, put in that state which man is in in this world,
may and ought to govern his opinions and actions depending
thereon, we need not be troubled that some other things escape
our knowledge.

7. *Occasion of this Essay.*—This was that which gave the first
rise to this Essay concerning the Understanding. For I thought
that the first step towards satisfying several inquiries the mind
of man was very apt to run into, was, to take a survey of our own
understandings, examine our own powers, and see to what things
they were adapted. Till that was done, I suspected we began at
the wrong end, and in vain sought for satisfaction in a quiet and
sure possession of truths that most concerned us, whilst we let
loose our thoughts into the vast ocean of being; as if all that
boundless extent were the natural and undoubted possession of
our understandings, wherein there was nothing exempt from its
decisions, or that escaped its comprehension. Thus men, extending their inquiries beyond their capacities, and letting their
thoughts wander into those depths where they can find no sure
footing, it is no wonder that they raise questions and multiply
disputes, which, never coming to any clear resolution, are proper
only to continue and increase their doubts, and to confirm
them at last in perfect scepticism. Whereas, were the capacities
of our understandings well considered, the extent of our knowledge once discovered, and the horizon found which sets the
bounds between the enlightened and dark parts of things—
between what is and what is not comprehensible by us—men
would, perhaps, with less scruple, acquiesce in the avowed ignorance of the one, and employ their thoughts and discourse with
more advantage and satisfaction in the other.

8. *What "idea" stands for.*—Thus much I thought necessary
to say concerning the occasion of this inquiry into human understanding. But, before I proceed on to what I have thought on
this subject, I must here, in the entrance, beg pardon of my
reader for the frequent use of the word "idea" which he will
find in the following treatise. It being that term which, I think,
serves best to stand for whatsoever is the object of the understanding when a man thinks, I have used it to express whatever is
meant by phantasm, notion, species, or whatever it is which the

mind can be employed about in thinking; and I could not avoid frequently using it.*

I presume it will be easily granted me, that there are such *ideas* in men's minds. Every one is conscious of them in himself; and men's words and actions will satisfy him that they are in others.

Our first inquiry, then, shall be, how they come into the mind.

* See Note at the end of this Chapter.

## NOTE.

THIS modest apology of our author could not procure him the free use of the word "idea." But great offence has been taken at it; and it has been censured as of dangerous consequence: to which you may here see what he answers. "The world," saith the Bishop of Worcester, "hath been strangely amused with ideas of late; and we have been told that strange things might be done by the help of ideas; and yet these ideas, at last, come to be only common notions of things, which we must make use of in our reasoning. You" (that is, the author of the Essay concerning Human Understanding) "say in that chapter about the Existence of God, you thought it most proper to express yourself in the most usual and familiar way, by common words and expressions. I would you had done so quite through your book; for then you had never given that occasion to the enemies of our faith, to take up your new way of ideas as an effectual battery, as they imagined, against the mysteries of the Christian faith. But you might have enjoyed the satisfaction of your ideas long enough before I had taken notice of them, unless I had found them employed about doing mischief."*

To which our author replies:† "It is plain that that which your lordship apprehends in my book 'may be of dangerous consequence to the article which your lordship has endeavoured to defend,' is my introducing new terms; and that which your lordship instances in, is that of ideas. And the reason your lordship gives, in every of these places, why your lordship has such an apprehension of ideas, as that they may be of dangerous consequence to that article of faith which your lordship has endeavoured to defend, is because they have been applied to such purposes. And 'I might,' your lordship says, 'have enjoyed the satisfaction of my ideas long enough before you had taken notice of them, unless your lordship had found them employed in doing mischief.' Which, at last, as I humbly conceive, amounts to thus much, and no more; viz., that your lordship fears ideas (that is, the term 'ideas') may, some time or other, prove of very dangerous consequence to what your lordship has endeavoured to defend, because they have been made use of in arguing against it. For, I am sure, your lordship does not mean, that you apprehend the things signified by 'ideas' may be of dangerous consequence to the article of faith

* Answer to Mr. Locke's First Letter, p. 93.
† In his Second Letter to the Bishop of Worcester, p. 63, &c.

your lordship endeavours to defend, because they have been made use of against it : for (besides that your lordship mentions 'terms') that would be to expect, that those who oppose that article should oppose it without any thoughts ; for the thing signified by 'ideas' is nothing but the immediate objects of our minds in thinking ; so that, unless anyone can oppose the article your lordship defends without thinking on something, he must use the things signified by 'ideas ;' for he that thinks, must have some immediate object of his mind in thinking—that is, must have ideas.

" But whether it be the name or the thing—ideas in sound, or ideas in signification—that your lordship apprehends 'may be of dangerous consequence to that article of faith which your lordship endeavours to defend ;' it seems to me, I will not say, a new way of reasoning (for that belongs to me), but were it not your lordship's I should think it a very extraordinary way of reasoning, to write against a book wherein your lordship acknowledges they are not used to bad purposes, nor employed to do mischief ; only because you find that ideas are, by those who oppose your lordship, 'employed to do mischief ;' and so apprehend, 'they may be of dangerous consequence to the article your lordship has engaged in the defence of.' For whether ideas as terms, or ideas as the immediate objects of the mind signified by those terms, may be, in your lordship's apprehension, of 'dangerous consequence to that article,' I do not see how your lordship's writing against the notion of ideas as stated in my book, will at all hinder your opposers 'from employing them in doing mischief,' as before.

"However, be that as it will, so it is, that your lordship apprehends these new terms, these 'ideas with which the world hath of late been so strangely amused' (though, 'at last, they come to be only common notions of things,' as your lordship owns), 'may be of dangerous consequence to that article.'

" My lord, if any, in their answer to your lordship's sermons, and in their other pamphlets, wherein your lordship complains they have talked so much of ideas, have been troublesome to your lordship with that term, it is not strange that your lordship should be tired of that sound ; but how natural soever it be to our weak constitutions to be offended with any sound wherewith an importunate din hath been made about our ears, yet, my lord, I know your lordship has a better opinion of the articles of our faith, than to think any of them can be overturned, or so much as shaken, with a breath formed into any sound or term whatsoever.

"Names are but the arbitrary marks of conceptions ; and, so they be sufficiently appropriated to them in their use, I know no other difference any of them have in particular, but as they are of easy or difficult pronunciation, and of a more or less pleasant sound ; and what particular antipathies there may be in men to some of them upon that account, is not easy to be foreseen. This I am sure, no term whatsoever in itself bears, one more than another, any opposition to truth of any kind ; they are only propositions that do or can oppose the truth of any article or doctrine : and thus no term is privileged from being set in opposition to truth.

"There is no word to be found which may not be brought into a proposition, wherein the most sacred and most evident truths may be opposed; but that is not a fault in the term, but him that uses it. And, therefore, I cannot easily persuade myself (whatever your lordship hath said in the heat of your concern) that you have bestowed so much pains upon my book because the word 'idea' is so much used there. For though, upon my saying, in my chapter about the Existence of God, that 'I scarce used the word *idea* in that whole chapter,' your lordship wishes that 'I had done so quite through my book;' yet I must rather look upon that as a compliment to me, wherein your lordship wished that my book had been all through suited to vulgar readers, not used to that and the like terms, than that your lordship has such an apprehension of the word 'idea,' or that there is any such harm in the use of it, instead of the word 'notion' (with which your lordship seems to take it to agree in signification), that your lordship would think it worth your while to spead any part of your valuable time and thoughts about my book for having the word 'idea' so often in it; for this would be to make your lordship to write only against an impropriety of speech. I own to your lordship, it is a great condescension in your lordship to have done it, if that word have such a share in what your lordship has writ against my book, as some expressions would persuade one; and I would, for the satisfaction of your lordship, change the term of 'idea' for a better, if your lordship, or anyone, could help me to it. For that 'notion' will not so well stand for every immediate object of the mind in thinking, as 'idea' does, I have, as I guess, somewhere given a reason in my book, by showing that the term 'notion' is more peculiarly appropriated to a certain sort of those objects, which I call mixed 'modes;' and, I think, it would not sound altogether so well to say, 'the *notion* of red,' and 'the *notion* of a horse,' as 'the *idea* of red,' and 'the *idea* of a horse.' But if anyone thinks it will, I contend not; for I have no fondness for, no antipathy to, any particular articulate sounds; nor do I think there is any spell or fascination in any of them.

"But be the word 'idea' proper or improper, I do not see how it is the better or the worse because ill men have made use of it, or because it has been made use of to bad purposes; for if that be a reason to condemn or lay it by, we must lay by the terms 'scripture,' 'reason,' 'perception,' 'distinct,' 'clear,' &c. Nay, the name of God himself will not escape; for I do not think any one of these, or any other term, can be produced, which has not been made use of by such men and to such purposes. And therefore if the Unitarians, 'in their late pamphlets, have talked very much of and strangely amused the world with ideas,' I cannot believe your lordship will think that word one jot the worse or the more dangerous because they use it; any more than, for their use of them, you will think 'reason' or 'scripture' terms ill or dangerous. And, therefore, what your lordship says in the bottom of this 93rd page, that 'I might have enjoyed the satisfaction of my ideas long enough before your lordship had taken notice of them, unless you had found them employed in doing mischief,' will, I presume, when your lordship has considered again of this matter, prevail with your lordship to let me 'enjoy still the satisfaction I take in my ideas;' that is, as much satisfaction as I can take in so small a matter as is the using of a proper term, notwithstanding it 'should be employed by others in doing mischief.'

"For, my lord, if I should leave it wholly out of my book, and substitute the word 'notion' everywhere in the room of it, and everybody else do so too (though your lordship does not, I suppose, suspect that I have the vanity to think they would follow my example), my book would, it seems, be the more to your lordship's liking; but I do not see how this would one jot abate the 'mischief' your lordship complains of, for the Unitarians might as much employ notions as they do now ideas, to do mischief; unless they are such fools as to think they can conjure with this notable word 'idea,' and that the force of what they say lies in the sound, and not in the signification, of their terms.

"This I am sure of, that the truths of the Christian religion can be no more battered by one word than another; nor can they be beaten down or endangered by any sound whatsoever. And I am apt to flatter myself that your lordship is satisfied, there is no harm in the word 'ideas,' because you say, 'you should not have taken any notice of my ideas, if the enemies of our faith had not taken up my new way of ideas as an effectual battery against the mysteries of the Christian faith.' In which place, by 'new way of ideas,' nothing, I think, can be construed to be meant but my expressing myself by that of ideas, and not by other more common words, and of ancienter standing in the English language."

As to the objection of the author's way by ideas being "a new way," he thus answers: "'My new way of ideas,' or 'my way by ideas,' which often occurs in your lordship's letter, is, I confess, a very large and doubtful expression: and may, in the full latitude, comprehend my whole Essay; because treating in it of the understanding, which is nothing but the faculty of thinking, I could not well treat of that faculty of the mind which consists in thinking, without considering the immediate objects of the mind in thinking, which I call ideas; and therefore, in treating of the understanding, I guess it will not be thought strange that the greatest part of my book has been taken up in considering what these objects of the mind in thinking are, whence they come, what use the mind makes of them in its several ways of thinking, and what are the outward marks whereby it signifies them to others, or records them for its own use. And this, in short, is 'my way by ideas,' that which your lordship calls 'my new way by ideas;' which, my lord, if it be new, it is but a new history of an old thing. For, I think, it will not be doubted, that men always performed the actions of thinking, reasoning, believing, and knowing, just after the same manner that they do now; though whether the same account has heretofore been given of the way how they performed these actions, or wherein they consisted, I do not know. Were I as well read as your lordship, I should have been safe from that gentle reprimand of your lordship's for thinking 'my way of ideas new, for want of looking into other men's thoughts, which appear in their books.'

"Your lordship's words, as an acknowledgment of your instructions in the case, and as a warning to others who will be so bold adventurers as 'to spin anything barely out of their own thoughts,' I shall set down at large; and they run thus: 'Whether you took this way of ideas from the modern philosopher mentioned by you, is not at all material; but I intended no reflection upon you in it, (for that you mean by my commending you as a scholar of so great a master ;) I never meant to take from you the honour of your own inventions : and I do believe you when you say that you wrote from your own thoughts, and the ideas you had there. But many things may seem new to one that converses only with his own thoughts, which really are not so ; as he may find when he looks into the thoughts of other men, which appear in their books. And therefore, although I have a just esteem for the invention of such who can spin volumes barely out of their own thoughts, yet I am apt to think they would oblige the world more if, after they have thought so much themselves, they would examine what thoughts others have had before them concerning the same things, that so those may not be thought their own inventions which are common to themselves and others. If a man should try all the magnetical experiments himself, and publish them as his own thoughts, he might take himself to be the inventor of them ; but he that examines and compares with them what Gilbert and others have done before him, will not diminish the praise of his diligence, but may wish he had compared his thoughts with other men's ; by which the world would receive greater advantage, although he lost the honour of being an original.'

"To alleviate my fault herein, I agree with your lordship that 'many things may seem new to one that converses only with his own thoughts, which really are not so ;' but I must crave leave to suggest to your lordship, that if, in the spinning of them out of his own thoughts, they seem new to him, he is certainly the inventor of them ; and they may as justly be thought his own invention as anyone's, and he is as certainly the inventor of them as anyone who thought on them before him : the distinction of invention or not invention lying not in thinking first or not first, but in borrowing or not borrowing your thoughts from another ; and he to whom, spinning them out of his own thoughts, they seem new, could not certainly borrow them from another. So he truly invented printing in Europe, who, without any communication with the Chinese, spun it out of his own thoughts ; though it were ever so true that the Chinese had the use of printing, nay, of printing in the very same way, among them many ages before him. So that he that spins anything out of his own thoughts, that seems new to him, cannot cease to think it his own invention ; should he 'examine' ever so far 'what thoughts others have had before him concerning the same thing ;' and should find, by examining, that they had the same thoughts too.

"But what great obligation this would be to the world, or weighty cause of turning over and looking into books, I confess I do not see. The great end to me, in conversing with my own or other men's thoughts, in matters of speculation, is to find truth, without being much concerned whether my own spinning of it out of mine, or their spinning of it out of their own thoughts, helps me to it. And how little I affect the honour of an original, may be seen in that place of my book where, if anywhere, that itch of vain-glory was likeliest to have shown itself, had I been so overrun with it as to need a cure. It is where I speak of certainty, in these following words, taken notice of by your lordship in another place : 'I think I have shown wherein it is that certainty, real certainty, consists ; which, whatever it was to others, was, I confess, to me heretofore, one of those *desiderata* which I found great want of.'

"Here, my lord, however new this seemed to me, and the more so because possibly I had in vain hunted for it in the 'books of others,' yet I spoke of it as new only to myself; leaving others in the undisturbed possession of what, either by invention or reading, was theirs before, without assuming to myself any other honour but that of my own ignorance, till that time, if others before had shown wherein certainty lay. And yet, my lord, if I had upon this occasion been forward to assume to myself the honour of an original, I think I had been pretty safe in it; since I should have had your lordship for my guarantee and vindicator in that point, who are pleased to call it *new*, and, as such, to write against it.

"And truly, my lord, in this respect, my book has had very unlucky stars; since it hath had the misfortune to displease your lordship with many things in it, for their novelty; as, 'new way of reasoning,' 'new hypothesis about reason,' 'new sort of certainty,' 'new terms,' 'new way of ideas,' 'new method of certainty,' &c. And yet, in other places, your lordship seems to think it worthy in me of your lordship's reflection, for saying but what others have said before. As where I say, 'In the different make of men's tempers, and application of their thoughts, some arguments prevail more on one and some on another, for the confirmation of the same truth; your lordship asks, 'What is this different from what all men of understanding have said?' Again, I take it, your lordship meant not these words for a commendation of my book, where you say: 'But if no more be meant by the simple ideas that come by sensation or reflection and their being the foundation of our knowledge, but that our notions of things come in either from our senses, or the exercise of our minds; as there is nothing extraordinary in the discovery,' so your lordship is far enough from opposing that wherein you think all mankind are agreed.

"And again: 'But what need all this great noise about ideas and certainty, true and real certainty by ideas, if, after all, it comes only to this—that our ideas only represent to us such things, from whence we bring arguments to prove the truth of things?'

"But 'the world hath been strangely amused with ideas of late; and we have been told, that strange things might be done by the help of ideas; and yet these ideas, at last, come to be only common notions of things which we must make use of in our reasoning.' And to the like pr .pose in other places.

"Whether, therefore, at last, your lordship will resolve that it is new or no, or more faulty by its being new, must be left to your lordship. This I find by it, that my book cannot avoid being condemned on the one side or the other; nor do I see a possibility to help it. If there be readers that like only new thoughts; or, on the other side, others that can bear nothing but what can be justified by received authorities in print; I must desire them to make themselves amends, in that part which they like, for the displeasure they receive in the other: but if any should be so exact as to find fault with both, truly I know not well what to say to them. The case is a plain case; the book is all over naught; and there is not a sentence in it that is not, either from

its antiquity a novelty, to be condemned ; and so there is a short end
of it. From your lordship, indeed, in particular, I can hope for something better ; for your lordship thinks the 'general design of it so
good,' that that, I flatter myself, would prevail on your lordship to
preserve it from the fire.

"But as to the way your lordship thinks I should have taken to
prevent the 'having it thought my invention, when it was common to
me with others, it unluckily so fell out, in the subject of my Essay of
Human Understanding, that I could not look into the thoughts of
other men to inform myself : for my design being, as well as I could,
to copy nature, and to give an account of the operations of the mind
in thinking, I could look into nobody's understanding but my own to
see how it wrought ; nor have a prospect into other men's minds, to
view their thoughts there, and observe what steps and motions they
took, and by what gradations they proceeded in their acquainting
themselves with truth, and their advance to knowledge. What we
find of their thoughts in books, is but the result of this, and not the
progress and working of their minds in coming to the opinions or conclusions they set down and published.

"All therefore that I can say of my book is, that it is a copy of my
own mind in its several ways of operation. And all that I can say
for the publishing of it is, that I think the intellectual faculties are
made, and operate, alike in most men ; and that some that I showed
it to before I published it, liked it so well that I was confirmed in
that opinion. And therefore, if it should happen that it should not
be so, but that some men should have ways of thinking, reasoning,
or arriving at certainty, different from others, and above those that
I find my mind to use and acquiesce in, I do not see of what use
my book can be to them. I can only make it my humble request,
in my own name, and in the name of those that are of my size, who
find their minds work, reason, and know in the same low way that
mine does, that those men of a more happy genius would show us
the way of their nobler flights, and particularly would discover to us
their shorter or surer way to certainty than by ideas, and the observing their agreement or disagreement.

"Your lordship adds : ' But now, it seems, nothing is intelligible
but what suits with the new way of ideas.' My lord, ' the new way of
ideas,' and the old way of speaking intelligibly, was always, and ever
will be, the same ; and, if I may take the liberty to declare my sense
of it, herein it consists :—1. That a man use no words but such as he
makes the signs of certain determined objects of his mind in thinking,
which he can make known to another. 2. Next, that he use the same
word steadily, for the sign of the same immediate object of his mind
in thinking. 3. That he join those words together in propositions,
according to the grammatical rules of that language he speaks in.
4. That he unite those sentences in a coherent discourse. Thus, and
thus only, I humbly conceive, anyone may preserve himself from the
confines and suspicion of jargon, whether he pleases to call those
immediate objects of his mind which his words do or should stand for,
*ideas* or no."*

* Mr. Locke's Third Letter to the Bishop of Worcester, p. 353, &c.

## CHAPTER II

### NO INNATE PRINCIPLES IN THE MIND.

**1.** *The way shown how we come by any knowledge, sufficient to prove it not innate.*—It is an established opinion among some men, that there are in the understanding certain innate principles ; some primary notions, κοιναὶ ἔννοιαι, characters, as it were, stamped upon the mind of man, which the soul receives in its very first being, and brings into the world with it. It would be sufficient to convince unprejudiced readers of the falseness of this supposition, if I should only show (as I hope I shall in the following parts of this discourse) how men, barely by the use of their natural faculties, may attain to all the knowledge they have, without the help of any innate impressions, and may arrive at certainty without any such original notions or principles. For I imagine, anyone will easily grant, that it would be impertinent to suppose the ideas of colours innate in a creature to whom God hath given sight, and a power to receive them by the eyes from external objects : and no less unreasonable would it be to attribute several truths to the impressions of nature and innate characters, when we may observe in ourselves faculties fit to attain as easy and certain knowledge of them as if they were originally imprinted on the mind.

But because a man is not permitted without censure to follow his own thoughts in the search of truth, when they lead him ever so little out of the common road, I shall set down the reasons that made me doubt of the truth of that opinion as an excuse for my mistake, if I be in one ; which I leave to be considered by those who, with me, dispose themselves to embrace truth wherever they find it.

**2.** *General assent the great argument.*—There is nothing more commonly taken for granted, than that there are certain principles, both speculative and practical (for they speak of both), universally agreed upon by all mankind ; which therefore, they argue, must needs be constant impressions which the souls of men receive in their first beings, and which they bring into the world with them, as necessarily and really as they do any of their inherent faculties.

**3.** *Universal consent proves nothing innate.*—This argument, drawn from universal consent, has this misfortune in it, that if it were true in matter of fact, that there were certain truths wherein all mankind agreed, it would not prove them innate, if there can be any other way shown, how men may come to that universal agreement in the things they do consent in ; which I presume may be done.

**4.** "*What is, is;*" *and,* "*It is impossible for the same thing to be, and not to be,*" *not universally assented to.*—But, which is worse, this argument of universal consent, which is made use of to prove innate principles, seems to me a demonstration that there are none such; because there are none to which all mankind give an universal assent. I shall begin with the speculative, and instance in those magnified principles of demonstration: "Whatsoever is, is;" and, "It is impossible for the same thing to be, and not to be," which, of all others, I think, have the most allowed title to innate. These have so settled a reputation of maxims universally received, that it will, no doubt, be thought strange if anyone should seem to question it. But yet I take liberty to say, that these propositions are so far from having an universal assent, that there are a great part of mankind to whom they are not so much as known.

**5.** *Not on the mind naturally imprinted, because not known to children, idiots, &c.*—For, first, it is evident, that all children and idiots have not the least apprehension or thought of them; and the want of that is enough to destroy that universal assent, which must needs be the necessary concomitant of all innate truths: it seeming to me near a contradiction to say, that there are truths imprinted on the soul which it perceives or understands not; imprinting, if it signify anything, being nothing else but the making certain truths to be perceived. For to imprint anything on the mind, without the mind's perceiving it, seems to me hardly intelligible. If therefore children and idiots have souls, have minds, with those impressions upon them, they must unavoidably perceive them, and necessarily know and assent to these truths; which since they do not, it is evident that there are no such impressions. For if they are not notions naturally imprinted, how can they be innate? And if they are notions imprinted, how can they be unknown? To say, a notion is imprinted on the mind, and yet at the same time to say that the mind is ignorant of it, and never yet took notice of it, is to make this impression nothing. No proposition can be said to be in the mind which it never yet knew, which it was never yet conscious of. For if any one may, then, by the same reason, all propositions that are true, and the mind is capable ever of assenting to, may be said to be in the mind, and to be imprinted; since if any one can be said to be in the mind, which it never yet knew, it must be only because it is capable of knowing it; and so the mind is of all truths it ever shall know. Nay, thus truths may be imprinted on the mind which it never did, nor ever shall, know: for a man may live long, and die at last in ignorance of many truths which his mind was capable of knowing, and that with certainty. So that if the capacity of knowing be the natural impression contended for, all the truths a man ever comes to know will, by this account, be every one of them innate: and this great point will amount to no more, but only to a very improper way of speaking; which, whilst it pretends to assert the contrary, says nothing different from those who deny innate principles. For nobody, I think, ever denied that the mind was capable of knowing several truths. The capacity, they say, is innate; the knowledge acquired. But then, to what end such contest for certain innate maxims? If truths can be imprinted on the understanding without being perceived, I can see no difference there can be between any truths the mind is capable of knowing in respect of their original: they must all be innate, or all adventitious; in vain shall a man go about to distinguish them. He therefore that talks of innate notions in the understanding, cannot (if he intend thereby any distinct sort of truths) mean such truths to be in the understanding as it never perceived, and is yet wholly ignorant of. For if these words ("to be in the understanding") have any propriety, they signify to be understood. So that, to be in the understanding, and not to be understood; to be in the mind, and never to be perceived; is all one as to say, any thing is, and is not, in the mind or understanding. If therefore these two propositions: "Whatsoever is, is;" and, "It is impossible for the same thing to be, and not to be," are by nature imprinted, children cannot be ignorant of them; infants, and all that have souls, must necessarily have them in their understandings, know the truth of them, and assent to it.

·6. *That men know them when they come to the use of reason, answered.*—To avoid this, it is usually answered, that all men know and assent to them, when they come to the use of reason; and this is enough to prove them innate. I answer,

7. Doubtful expressions, that have scarce any signification, go for clear reasons to those who, being prepossessed, take not the pains to examine even what they themselves say. For, to apply this answer with any tolerable sense to our present purpose, it must signify one of these two things; either, that, as soon as men come to the use of reason, these supposed native inscriptions come to be known and observed by them; or else, that the use and exercise of men's reasons assists them in the discovery of these principles, and certainly makes them known to them.

8. *If reason discovered them, that would not prove them innate.* —If they mean that by the use of reason men may discover these principles, and that this is sufficient to prove them innate, their way of arguing will stand thus: viz., That, whatever truths reason can certainly discover to us, and make us firmly assent to, those are all naturally imprinted on the mind; since that universal assent which is made the mark of them, amounts to no more but this—that by the use of reason we are capable to come to a certain knowledge of, and assent to, them; and by this means there will be no difference between the maxims of

the mathematicians and theorems they deduce from them: all must be equally allowed innate, they being all discoveries made by the use of reason, and truths that a rational creature may certainly come to know, if he apply his thoughts rightly that way.

9. *It is false that reason discovers them.*—But how can these men think the use of reason necessary to discover principles that are supposed innate, when reason (if we may believe them) is nothing else but the faculty of deducing unknown truths from principles or propositions that are already known? That certainly can never be thought innate which we have need of reason to discover, unless, as I have said, we will have all the certain truths that reason ever teaches us to be innate. We may as well think the use of reason necessary to make our eyes discover visible objects, as that there should be need of reason, or the exercise thereof, to make the understanding see what is originally engraven in it, and cannot be in the understanding before it be perceived by it. So that to make reason discover those truths thus imprinted, is to say, that the use of reason discovers to a man what he knew before; and if* men have those innate impressed truths originally, and before the use of reason, and yet are always ignorant of them till they come to the use of reason, it is in effect to say that men know, and know them not, at the same time.

10. It will here perhaps be said, that mathematical demonstrations, and other truths that are not innate, are not assented to, as soon as proposed, wherein they are distinguished from these maxims and other innate truths. I shall have occasion to speak of assent upon the first proposing, more particularly by and by. I shall here only, and that very readily, allow, that these maxims and mathematical demonstrations are in this different—that the one has need of reason, using of proofs, to make them out and to gain our assent; but the other, as soon as understood, are, without any the least reasoning, embraced and assented to. But I withal beg leave to observe, that it lays open the weakness of this subterfuge which requires the use of reason for the discovery of these general truths, since it must be confessed, that in their discovery there is no use made of reasoning at all. And I think those who give this answer will not be forward to affirm, that the knowledge of this maxim, "That it is impossible for the same thing to be, and not to be," is a deduction of our reason. For this would be to destroy that bounty of nature they seem so fond of, whilst they make the knowledge of those principles to depend on the labour of our thoughts; for all reasoning is search and casting about, and requires pains and application. And how can it with any tolerable sense be supposed, that what was im-

printed by nature, as the foundation and guide of our reason,
should need the use of reason to discover it?

11. Those who will take the pains to reflect with a little
attention on the operations of the understanding, will find that
this ready assent of the mind to some truths, depends not either
on native inscription, or the use of reason ; but on a faculty of
the mind quite distinct from both of them, as we shall see hereafter. Reason therefore having nothing to do in procuring our
assent to these maxims, if by saying, that "men know and
assent to them when they come to the use of reason," be meant
that the use of reason assists us in the knowledge of these
maxims, it is utterly false ; and, were it true, would prove them
not to be innate.

12. *The coming to the use of reason, not the time we come to
know these maxims.*—If by knowing and assenting to them,
" when we come to the use of reason," be meant, that this is the
time when they come to be taken notice of by the mind ; and
that as soon as children come to the use of reason, they come
also to know and assent to these maxims ; this also is false and
frivolous. First, it is *false;* because it is evident these maxims
are not in the mind so early as the use of reason, and therefore
the coming to the use of reason is falsely assigned as the time of
their discovery. How many instances of the use of reason may
we observe in children, a long time before they have any knowledge of this maxim, " That it is impossible for the same thing
to be, and not to be "! And a great part of illiterate people and
savages pass many years, even of their rational age, without ever
thinking on this and the like general propositions. I grant, men
come not to the knowledge of these general and more abstract
truths, which are thought innate, till they come to the use of
reason; and I add, nor then neither. Which is so, because till
after they come to the use of reason, those general abstract ideas
are not framed in the mind, about which those general maxims
are, which are mistaken for innate principles, but are indeed
discoveries made, and verities introduced, and brought into the
mind by the same way, and discovered by the same steps, as
several other propositions which nobody was ever so extravagant
as to suppose innate. This I hope to make plain in the sequel of
this discourse. I allow therefore a necessity that men should
come to the use of reason before they get the knowledge of those
general truths ; but deny, that men's coming to the use of reason
is the time of their discovery.

13. *By this they are not distinguished from other knowable
truths.*—In the meantime it is observable, that this saying,
" That men know and assent to these maxims when they come to
the use of reason," amounts, in reality of fact, to no more but this :
That they are never known nor taken notice of before the use of
reason, but may possibly be assented to some time after during

a man's life; but when, is uncertain: and so may all other knowable truths as well as these; which therefore have no advantage nor distinction from others, by this note of being known when we come to the use of reason; nor are thereby proved to be innate, but quite the contrary.

14. *If coming to the use of reason were the time of their discovery, it would not prove them innate.*—But, secondly, were it true that the precise time of their being known and assented to were when men come to the use of reason, neither would that prove them innate. This way of arguing is as *frivolous* as the supposition of* itself is false. For by what kind of logic will it appear that any notion is originally by nature imprinted in the mind in its first constitution, because it comes first to be observed and assented to when a faculty of the mind, which has quite a distinct province, begins to exert itself? And therefore the coming to the use of speech, if it were supposed the time that these maxims are first assented to (which it may be with as much truth as the time when men come to the use of reason), would be as good a proof that they were innate, as to say they are innate because men assent to them when they come to the use of reason. I agree, then, with these men of innate principles, that there is no knowledge of these general and self-evident maxims in the mind till it comes to the exercise of reason; but I deny that the coming to the use of reason is the precise time when they are first taken notice of; and if that were the precise time, I deny that it would prove them innate. All that can, with any truth, be meant by this proposition, "That men assent to them when they come to the use of reason," is no more but this—That the making of general abstract ideas, and the understanding of general names, being a concomitant of the rational faculty, and growing up with it, children commonly get not those general ideas, nor learn the names that stand for them, till, having for a good while exercised their reason about familiar and more particular ideas, they are, by their ordinary discourse and actions with others, acknowledged to be capable of rational conversation. If assenting to these maxims, when men come to the use of reason, can be true in any other sense, I desire it may be shown; or, at least, how in this, or any other sense, it proves them innate.

15. *The steps by which the mind attains several truths.*—The senses at first let in particular ideas, and furnish the yet empty cabinet : and the mind by degrees growing familiar with some of them, they are lodged in the memory, and names got to them. Afterwards the mind, proceeding farther, abstracts them, and by degrees learns the use of general names. In this manner the mind comes to be furnished with ideas and language, the materials about which to exercise its discursive faculty; and the use of reason becomes daily more visible, as these materials, that give

* The ninth edition omits "of."—EDIT.

it employment, increase. But though the having of general ideas, and the use of general words and reason, usually grow together, yet I see not how this any way proves them innate. The knowledge of some truths, I confess, is very early in the mind ; but in a way that shows them not to be innate. For, if we will observe, we shall find it still to be about ideas not innate, but acquired ; it being about those first, which are imprinted by external things, with which infants have earliest to do, which make the most frequent impressions on their senses. In ideas thus got, the mind discovers that some agree, and others differ, probably as soon as it has any use of memory, as soon as it is able to retain and receive distinct ideas. But whether it be then or no, this is certain, it does so long before it has the use of words, or comes to that which we commonly call " the use of reason." For a child knows as certainly, before it can speak, the difference between the ideas of sweet and bitter, (that is, that sweet is not bitter,) as it knows afterwards, when it comes to speak, that wormwood and sugarplums are not the same thing.

16. A child knows not that three and four are equal to seven till he comes to be able to count to seven, and has got the name and idea of equality ; and then, upon explaining those words, he presently assents to, or rather perceives the truth of that proposition. But neither does he then readily assent because it is an innate truth, nor was his assent wanting till then because he wanted the use of reason ; but the truth of it appears to him as soon as he has settled in his mind the clear and distinct ideas that these names stand for ; and then he knows the truth of that proposition upon the same grounds, and by the same means, that he knew before, that a rod and cherry are not the same thing ; and upon the same grounds also, that he may come to know afterwards, " that it is impossible for the same thing to be, and not to be," as shall be more fully shown hereafter : so that the later it is before anyone comes to have those general ideas about which those maxims are, or to know the signification of those general terms that stand for them, or to put together in his mind the ideas they stand for ; the later also will it be before he comes to assent to those maxims, whose terms, with the ideas they stand for, being no more innate than those of a cat or a weasel, he must stay till time and observation have acquainted him with them ; and then he will be in a capacity to know the truth of these maxims, upon the first occasion that shall make him put together those ideas in his mind, and observe whether they agree or disagree, according as is expressed in those propositions. And therefore it is that a man knows that eighteen and nineteen are equal to thirty-seven, by the same self-evidence that he knows one and two to be equal to three ; yet a child knows this not so soon as the other ; not for want of the use of reason, but because the ideas the words eighteen, nineteen, and thirty-seven stand

for, are not so soon got, as those which are signified by one,
two, and three.

17. *Assenting as soon as proposed and understood, proves them
not innate.*—This evasion therefore of general assent when men
come to the use of reason, failing as it does, and leaving no difference between those supposed innate and other truths that are
afterwards acquired and learnt, men have endeavoured to secure
an universal assent to those they call maxims, by saying, they
are generally assented to as soon as proposed and the terms
they are proposed in understood : seeing all men, even children,
as soon as they hear and understand the terms, assent to these
propositions, they think it is sufficient to prove them innate.
For, since men never fail, after they have once understood the
words, to acknowledge them for undoubted truths, they would
infer, that certainly these propositions were first lodged in the
understanding, which, without any teaching, the mind, at the
very first proposal, immediately closes with, and assents to, and
after that never doubts again.

18. *If such an assent be a mark of innate, then, that one and two
are equal to three, that sweetness is not bitterness, and a thousand
the like, must be innate.*—In answer to this, I demand whether
ready assent, given to a proposition upon first hearing and understanding the terms, be a certain mark of an innate principle ? If
it be not, such a general assent is in vain urged as a proof of
them : if it be said, that it is a mark of innate, they must then
allow all such propositions to be innate which are generally
assented to as soon as heard ; whereby they will find themselves
plentifully stored with innate principles. For, upon the same
ground, viz., of assent at first hearing and understanding the
terms, that men would have those maxims pass for innate, they
must also admit several propositions about numbers to be innate ;
and thus, that "one and two are equal to three," that "two and
two are equal to four," and a multitude of other the like propositions in numbers that everybody assents to at first hearing and
understanding the terms, must have a place amongst these innate
axioms.    Nor is this the prerogative of numbers alone, and propositions made about several of them ; but even natural
philosophy, and all the other sciences, afford propositions, which
are sure to meet with assent as soon as they are understood.
That "two bodies cannot be in the same place " is a truth that
nobody any more sticks at than at this maxim, that "it is impossible for the same thing to be and not to be," that "white is
not black," that a "square is not a circle," that "yellowness is
not sweetness ": these and a million of other such propositions,
as many at least as we have distinct ideas, every man in his wits
at first hearing, and knowing what the names stand for, must
necessarily assent to.    If these men will be true to their own
rule, and have " assent at first hearing and understanding the

terms " to be a mark of innate, they must allow not only as many
innate propositions as men have distinct ideas, but as many as men
can make propositions wherein different ideas are denied one or
another : since every proposition, wherein one different idea is
denied of another, will as certainly find assent at first hearing and
understanding the terms, as this general one, " It is impossible
for the same to be and not to be "; or that which is the foundation of it, and is the easier understood of the two, "The same is
not different": by which account they will have legions of innate
propositions of this one sort, without mentioning any other. But
since no proposition can be innate, unless the ideas about which
it is be innate, this will be to suppose all our ideas of colours,
sounds, tastes, figure, etc., innate : than which there cannot be
anything more opposite to reason and experience. Universal
and ready assent upon hearing and understanding the terms, is,
I grant, a mark of self-evidence: but self-evidence, depending not
on innate impressions, but on something else (as we shall show
hereafter), belongs to several propositions, which nobody was yet
so extravagant as to pretend to be innate.

19. *Such less general propositions known before these universal
maxims.*—Nor let it be said, that those more particular self-
evident propositions which are assented to at first hearing, as,
that "one and two are equal to three," that "green is not red,"
etc., are received as the consequences of those more universal
propositions, which are looked on as innate principles ; since anyone who will but take the pains to observe what passes in the
understanding will certainly find that these and the like less
general propositions are certainly known and firmly assented to
by those who are utterly ignorant of those more general maxims ;
and so, being earlier in the mind than those (as they are called)
first principles, cannot owe to them the assent wherewith they
are received at first hearing.

20. *One and one equal to two, etc., not general nor useful,
answered.*—If it be said, that these propositions, viz., "Two and
two are equal to four," " Red is not blue," etc., are not general
maxims, nor of any great use ; I answer, That makes nothing to
the argument of universal assent, upon hearing and understanding. For, if that be the certain mark of innate, whatever proposition can be found that receives general assent, as soon as
heard and understood, that must be admitted for an innate proposition, as well as this maxim, "that it is impossible for the
same thing to be and not to be," they being upon this ground equal.
And as to the difference of being more general, that makes this
maxim more remote from being innate; those general and
abstract ideas being more strangers to our first apprehensions
than those of* more particular self-evident propositions; and
therefore it is longer before they are admitted and assented to

* The ninth edition omits "of."—EDIT.

by the growing understanding. And as to the usefulness of these magnified maxims, that perhaps will not be found so great as is generally conceived, when it comes to* its due place to be more fully considered.

21. *These maxims not being known sometimes till proposed, proves them not innate.*—But we have not yet done with "assenting to propositions at first hearing and understanding their terms:" it is fit we first take notice, that this, instead of being a mark that they are innate, is a proof of the contrary; since it supposes that several who understand and know other things, are ignorant of these principles till they are proposed to them, and that one may be unacquainted with these truths till he hears them from others. For if they were innate, what need they be proposed in order to gaining assent; when, by being in the understanding, by a natural and original impression (if there were any such), they could not but be known before? Or doth the proposing them print them clearer in the mind than nature did? If so, then the consequence will be, that a man knows them better after he has been thus taught them than he did before. Whence it will follow, that these principles may be made more evident to us by others' teaching than nature has made them by impression; which will ill agree with the opinion of innate principles, and give but little authority to them; but, on the contrary, makes them unfit to be the foundations of all our other knowledge, as they are pretended to be. This cannot be denied, that men grow first acquainted with many of these self-evident truths, upon their being proposed; but it is clear that whosoever does so, finds in himself that he then begins to know a proposition which he knew not before; and which, from thenceforth, he never questions; not because it was innate, but because the consideration of the nature of the things contained in those words would not suffer him to think otherwise, how or whensoever he is brought to reflect on them. And if whatever is assented to at first hearing and understanding the terms, must pass for an innate principle, every well-grounded observation drawn from particulars into a general rule must be innate; when yet it is certain, that not all but only sagacious heads light at first on these observations, and reduce them into general propositions; not innate, but collected from a preceding acquaintance and reflection on particular instances. These, when observing men have made them, unobserving men when they are proposed to them, cannot refuse their assent to.

22. *Implicitly known before proposing, signifies that the mind is capable of understanding them, or else signifies nothing.*—If it be said, "The understanding hath an implicit knowledge of these principles, but not an explicit, before this first hearing," (as they must who will say that they are in the understanding before they are known,) it will be hard to conceive what is meant by a prin-

* The ninth has "in" instead of "to."—EDIT.

ciple imprinted on the understanding implicitly ; unless it be this, that the mind is capable of understanding and assenting firmly to such propositions.  And thus all mathematical demonstrations, as well as first principles, must be received as native impressions on the mind : which I fear they will scarce allow them to be who find it harder to demonstrate a proposition than assent to it when demonstrated.  And few mathematicians will be forward to believe, that all the diagrams they have drawn were but copies of those innate characters which nature had engraven upon their minds.

23. *The argument of assenting on first hearing, is upon a false supposition of no precedent teaching.*—There is, I fear, this farther weakness in the foregoing argument, which would persuade us that therefore those maxims are to be thought innate which men admit at first hearing, because they assent to propositions which they are not taught nor do receive from the force of any argument or demonstration, but a bare explication or understanding of the terms.  Under which there seems to me to lie this fallacy : that men are supposed not to be taught, nor to learn anything *de novo;* when in truth they are taught and do learn something they were ignorant of before.  For, first, it is evident they have learned the terms and their signification ; neither of which was born with them.  But this is not all the acquired knowledge in the case; the ideas themselves, about which the proposition is, are not born with them no more than their names, but got afterwards.  So that in all propositions that are assented to at first hearing, the terms of the proposition, their standing for such ideas, and the ideas themselves that they stand for, being neither of them innate, I would fain know what there is remaining in such propositions that is innate.  For I would gladly have anyone name that proposition whose terms or ideas were either of them innate.  We by degrees get ideas and names, and learn their appropriated connexion one with another; and then to propositions, made in such terms whose signification we have learnt, and wherein the agreement or disagreement we can perceive in our ideas when put together is expressed, we at first hearing assent ; though to other propositions, in themselves as certain and evident, but which are concerning *ideas* not so soon or so easily got, we are at the same time no way capable of assenting.  For though a child quickly assents to this proposition, that " an apple is not fire," when, by familiar acquaintance, he has got the ideas of those two different things distinctly imprinted on his mind, and has learnt that the names " apple " and " fire " stand for them ; yet it will be some years after, perhaps, before the same child will assent to this proposition, that " it is impossible for the same thing to be and not to be," because that, though perhaps the words are as easy to be learnt, yet the signification of them being more large, comprehensive, and abstract

than of the names annexed to those sensible things the child
hath to do with, it is longer before he learns their precise meaning, and it requires more time plainly to form in his mind those
general ideas they stand for. Till that be done, you will in vain
endeavour to make any child assent to a proposition made up of
such general terms; but as soon as ever he has got those ideas,
and learned their names, he forwardly closes with the one as well
as the other of the forementioned propositions, and with both for
the same reason, viz., because he finds the ideas he has in his
mind to agree or disagree, according as the words standing for
them are affirmed or denied one of another in the proposition.
But if propositions be brought to him in words which stand for
ideas he has not yet in his mind; to such propositions, however
evidently true or false in themselves, he affords neither assent
nor dissent, but is ignorant. For words being but empty sounds,
any farther than they are signs of our ideas, we cannot but
assent to them as they correspond to those ideas we have, but
no farther than that. But the showing by what steps and ways
knowledge comes into our minds, and the grounds of several
degrees of assent being the business of the following discourse,
it may suffice to have only touched on it here, as one reason that
made me doubt of those innate principles.

24. *Not innate, because not universally assented to.*—To conclude this argument of universal consent, I agree with these
defenders of innate principles, that if they are innate, they must
needs have universal assent. For, that a truth should be innate
and yet not assented to, is to me as unintelligible as for a man to
know a truth and be ignorant of it at the same time. But then,
by these men's own confession, they cannot be innate; since they
are not assented to by those who understand not the terms, nor
by a great part of those who do understand them, but have yet
never heard nor thought of those propositions, which, I think, is
at least one-half of mankind. But were the number far less, it
would be enough to destroy universal assent, and thereby show
these propositions not to be innate, if children alone were ignorant
of them.

25. *These maxims not the first known.*—But that I may not be
accused to argue from the thoughts of infants, which are unknown
to us, and to conclude from what passes in their understandings,
before they express it, I say next, that these two general propositions are not the truths that first possess the minds of children,
nor are antecedent to all acquired and adventitious notions,
which, if they were innate, they must needs be. Whether we
can determine it or no, it matters not; there is certainly a time
when children begin to think, and their words and actions do
assure us that they do so. When therefore they are capable of
thought, of knowledge, of assent, can it rationally be supposed
they can be ignorant of those notions that nature has imprinted

were there any such ? Can it be imagined, with any appearance of reason, that they perceive the impressions from things without, and be at the same time ignorant of those characters which nature itself has taken care to stamp within ? Can they receive and assent to adventitious notions, and be ignorant of those which are supposed woven into the very principles of their being, and imprinted there in indelible characters, to be the foundation and guide of all their acquired knowledge and future reasonings ? This would be to make nature take pains to no purpose, or, at least, to write very ill; since its characters could not be read by those eyes which saw other things very well : and those are very ill supposed the clearest parts of truth and the foundations of all our knowledge, which are not first known, and without which the undoubted knowledge of several other things may be had. The child certainly knows that the nurse that feeds it is neither the cat it plays with, nor the Blackmoor it is afraid of ; that the worm seed or mustard it refuses is not the apple or sugar it cries for; this it is certainly and undoubtedly assured of : but will anyone say, it is by virtue of this principle, that "it is impossible for the same thing to be and not to be," that it so firmly assents to these and other parts of its knowledge ? or that the child has any notion or apprehension of that proposition at an age wherein yet, it is plain, it knows a great many other truths ? He that will say, " Children join these general abstract speculations with their sucking-bottles and their rattles," may perhaps, with justice, be thought to have more passion and zeal for his opinion, but less sincerity and truth, than one of that age.

26. *And so not innate.*—Though therefore there be several general propositions that meet with constant and ready assent as soon as proposed to men grown up, who have attained the use of more general and abstract ideas, and names standing for them; yet they not being to be found in those of tender years, who nevertheless know other things, they cannot pretend to universal assent of intelligent persons, and so by no means can be supposed innate; it being impossible that any truth which is innate (if there were any such) should be unknown, at least to anyone who knows anything else : since, if they are innate truths, they must be innate thoughts; there being nothing a truth in the mind that it has never thought on. Whereby it is evident if there be any innate truths,* they must necessarily be the first of any thought on, the first that appear there.

27. *Not innate, because they appear least where what is innate shows itself clearest.*—That the general maxims we are discoursing of are not known to children, idiots, and a great part of mankind, we have already sufficiently proved ; whereby it is evident, they have not an universal assent, nor are general impressions. But

* The ninth adds here, *in the mind.*—Edit

there is this farther argument in it against their being innate : that these characters, if they were native and original impressions, should appear fairest and clearest in those persons in whom yet we find no footsteps of them ; and it is, in my opinion, a strong presumption that they are not innate, since they are least known to those in whom, if they were innate, they must needs exert themselves with most force and vigour. For children, idiots, savages, and illiterate people, being of all others the least corrupted by custom or borrowed opinions ; learning and education having not cast their native thoughts into new moulds, nor by superinducing foreign and studied doctrines confounded those fair characters nature had written there; one might reasonably imagine that in their minds these innate notions should lie open fairly to everyone's view, as it is certain the thoughts of children do. It might very well be expected that these principles should be perfectly known to naturals ; which, being stamped immediately on the soul (as these men suppose), can have no dependence on the constitutions or organs of the body, the only confessed difference between them and others. One would think, according to these men's principles, that all these native beams of light (were there any such) should in those who have no reserves, no arts of concealment, shine out in their full lustre, and leave us in no more doubt of their being there than we are of their love of pleasure and abhorrence of pain. But, alas! amongst children, idiots, savages, and the grossly illiterate, what general maxims are to be found? what universal principles of knowledge? Their notions are few and narrow, borrowed only from those objects they have had most to do with, and which have made upon their senses the frequentest and strongest impressions. A child knows his nurse and his cradle, and, by degrees, the playthings of a little more advanced age; and a young savage has perhaps his head filled with love and hunting, according to the fashion of his tribe. But he that from a child untaught, or a wild inhabitant of the woods, will expect these abstract maxims and reputed principles of sciences, will, I fear, find himself mistaken. Such kind of general propositions are seldom mentioned in the huts of Indians ; much less are they to be found in the thoughts of children, or any impressions of them on the minds of naturals. They are the language and business of the schools and academies of learned nations, accustomed to that sort of conversation or learning where disputes are frequent : these maxims being suited to artificial argumentation and useful for conviction; but not much conducing to the discovery of truth or advancement of knowledge. But of their small use for the improvement of knowledge, I shall have occasion to speak more at large, book iv. chap. 7.

28. *Recapitulation.*—I know not how absurd this may seem to the masters of demonstration : and probably it will hardly go down

with anybody at first hearing. I must therefore beg a little truce with prejudice and the forbearance of censure till I have been heard out in the sequel of this discourse, being very willing to submit to better judgments. And since I impartially search after truth, I shall not be sorry to be convinced that I have been too fond of my own notions; which, I confess, we are all apt to be when application and study have warmed our heads with them.

Upon the whole matter, I cannot see any ground to think these two famed speculative maxims innate, since they are not universally assented to; and the assent they so generally find is no other than what several propositions, not allowed to be innate, equally partake in with them; and since the assent that is given them is produced another way, and comes not from natural inscription, as I doubt not but to make appear in the following discourse. And if these first principles of knowledge and science are found not to be innate, no other speculative maxims can, I suppose, with better right pretend to be so.

---

## CHAPTER III.

### NO INNATE PRACTICAL PRINCIPLES.

1. *No moral principles so clear and so generally received as the fore-mentioned speculative maxims.*—If those speculative maxims whereof we discoursed in the foregoing chapter, have not an actual universal assent from all mankind, as we there proved, it is much more visible concerning practical principles, that they come short of an universal reception; and I think it will be hard to instance any one moral rule which can pretend to so general and ready an assent as, "What is, is," or to be so manifest a truth as this, "That it is impossible for the same thing to be, and not to be." Whereby it is evident that they are farther removed from a title to be innate; and the doubt of their being native impressions on the mind is stronger against these moral principles than the other. Not that it brings their truth at all in question. They are equally true, though not equally evident. Those speculative maxims carry their own evidence with them; but moral principles require reasoning and discourse, and some exercise of the mind, to discover the certainty of their truth. They lie not open as natural characters engraven on the mind; which if any such were, they must needs be visible by them-selves, and by their own light be certain and known to everybody. But this is no derogation to their truth and certainty; no more than it is to the truth or certainty of the three angles of a triangle being equal to two right ones, because it is not so evident as, "The whole is bigger than a part," nor so apt to be assented to at first hearing. It may suffice that these moral

rules are capable of demonstration; and therefore it is our own fault if we come not to a certain knowledge of them. But the ignorance wherein many men are of them, and the slowness of assent wherewith others receive them, are manifest proofs that they are not innate, and such as offer themselves to their view without searching.

2. *Faith and justice not owned as principles by all men.*— Whether there be any such moral principles wherein all men do agree, I appeal to any who have been but moderately conversant in the history of mankind, and looked abroad beyond the smoke of their own chimneys. Where is that practical truth that is universally received without doubt or question, as it must be if innate? Justice, and keeping of contracts, is that which most men seem to agree in. This is a principle which is thought to extend itself to the dens of thieves, and the confederacies of the greatest villains; and they who have gone farthest towards the putting off of humanity itself, keep faith and rules of justice one with another. I grant, that outlaws themselves do this one amongst another; but it is without receiving these as the innate laws of nature. They practise them as rules of convenience within their own communities; but it is impossible to conceive that he embraces justice as a practical principle who acts fairly with his fellow-highwayman, and at the same time plunders or kills the next honest man he meets with. Justice and truth are the common ties of society; and therefore even outlaws and robbers, who break with all the world besides, must keep faith and rules of equity amongst themselves, or else they cannot hold together. But will anyone say, that those that live by fraud and rapine have innate principles of truth and justice, which they allow and assent to?

3. *Objection.* "*Though men deny them in their practice, yet they admit them in their thoughts,*" *answered.*—Perhaps it will be urged, that the tacit assent of their minds agrees to what their practice contradicts. I answer, First, I have always thought the actions of men the best interpreters of their thoughts; but since it is certain that most men's practice, and some men's open professions, have either questioned or denied these principles, it is impossible to establish an universal consent (though we should look for it only amongst grown men); without which it is impossible to conclude them innate. Secondly, It is very strange and unreasonable to suppose innate practical principles that terminate only in contemplation. Practical principles derived from nature are there for operation, and must produce conformity of action, not barely speculative assent to their truth, or else they are in vain distinguished from speculative maxims. Nature, I confess, has put into man a desire of happiness, and an aversion to misery; these, indeed, are innate practical principles, which, as practical principles ought, do continue constantly

to operate and influence all our actions without ceasing: these may be observed in all persons and all ages, steady and universal; but these are inclinations of the appetite to good, not impressions of truth on the understanding. I deny not that there are natural tendencies imprinted on the minds of men; and that, from the very first instances of sense and perception, there are some things that are grateful and others unwelcome to them; some things that they incline to, and others that they fly: but this makes nothing for innate characters on the mind, which are to be the principles of knowledge, regulating our practice. Such natural impressions on the understanding are so far from being confirmed hereby, that this is an argument against them; since if there were certain characters imprinted by nature on the understanding, as the principles of knowledge, we could not but perceive them constantly operate in us and influence our knowledge, as we do those others on the will and appetite; which never cease to be the constant springs and motives of all our actions, to which we perpetually feel them strongly impelling us.

4. *Moral rules need a proof; ergo, not innate.*—Another reason that makes me doubt of any innate principles, is, that I think there cannot any one moral rule be proposed whereof a man may not justly demand a reason; which would be perfectly ridiculous and absurd, if they were innate, or so much as self-evident; which every innate principle must needs be, and not need any proof to ascertain its truth, nor want any reason to gain it approbation. He would be thought void of common sense who asked on the one side, or on the other side, when* to give a reason, why it is impossible for the same thing to be, and not to be. It carries its own light and evidence with it, and needs no other proof; he that understands the terms assents to it for its own sake, or else nothing will ever be able to prevail with him to do it. But should that most unshaken rule of morality, and foundation of all social virtue, "That one should do as he would be done unto," be proposed to one who never heard it before, but yet is of capacity to understand its meaning; might he not without any absurdity ask a reason why? and were not he that proposed it bound to make out the truth and reasonableness of it to him? which plainly shows it not to be innate; for if it were, it could neither want nor receive any proof, but must needs (at least as soon as heard and understood) be received and assented to as an unquestionable truth, which a man can by no means doubt of. So that the truth of all these moral rules plainly depends upon some other antecedent to them, and from which they must be deduced, which could not be if either they were innate, or so much as self-evident.

* In the ninth edition *when* is entirely omitted; and in the fourth (folio) this reading occurs: "He would be thought void of common sense, who asked on the one side, or on the other side went to give, a reason why it is," &c —EDIT.

**5.** *Instance in keeping compacts.*—That men should keep their compacts, is certainly a great and undeniable rule in morality; but yet, if a Christian, who has the view of happiness and misery in another life, be asked why a man must keep his word, he will give this as a reason: "Because God, who has the power of eternal life and death, requires it of us." But if an Hobbist be asked why, he will answer, "Because the public requires it, and the Leviathan will punish you if you do not." And if one of the old heathen philosophers had been asked, he would have answered, "Because it was dishonest, below the dignity of a man, and opposite to virtue, the highest perfection of human nature, to do otherwise."

**6.** *Virtue generally approved, not because innate, but because profitable.*—Hence naturally flows the great variety of opinions concerning the moral rules, which are to be found among men according to the different sorts of happiness they have a prospect of, or propose to themselves; which could not be, if practical principles were innate, and imprinted in our minds immediately by the hand of God. I grant the existence of God is so many ways manifest, and the obedience we owe him so congruous to the light of reason, that a great part of mankind give testimony to the law of nature; but yet I think it must be allowed, that several moral rules may receive from mankind a very general approbation, without either knowing or admitting the true ground of morality; which can only be the will and law of a God, who sees men in the dark, has in his hand rewards and punishments, and power enough to call to account the proudest offender. For God having, by an inseparable connexion, joined virtue and public happiness together, and made the practice thereof necessary to the preservation of society, and visibly beneficial to all with whom the virtuous man has to do; it is no wonder that everyone should not only allow, but recommend and magnify those rules to others, from whose observance of them he is sure to reap advantage to himself. He may, out of interest, as well as conviction, cry up that for sacred, which, if once trampled on and profaned, he himself cannot be safe nor secure. This, though it takes nothing from the moral and eternal obligation which these rules evidently have, yet it shows that the outward acknowledgment men pay to them in their words proves not that they are innate principles: nay, it proves not so much as that men assent to them inwardly in their own minds, as the inviolable rules of their own practice; since we find that self-interest and the conveniences of this life make many men own an outward profession and approbation of them, whose actions sufficiently prove that they very little consider the Lawgiver that prescribed these rules, nor the hell he has ordained for the punishment of those that transgress them.

**7.** *Men's actions convince us, that the rule of virtue is not their*

*internal principle.*—For, if we will not in civility allow too much
sincerity to the professions of most men, but think their actions
to be the interpreters of their thoughts, we shall find that they
have no such internal veneration for these rules, nor so full a
persuasion of their certainty and obligation. The great principle
of morality, "To do as one would be done to," is more com-
mended than practised. But the breach of this rule cannot be a
greater vice, than to teach others that it is no moral rule nor
obligatory, would be thought madness, and contrary to that
interest men sacrifice to when they break it themselves. Perhaps conscience will be urged as checking us for such breaches,
and so the internal obligation and establishment of the rule be
preserved.

8. *Conscience no proof of any innate moral rule.*—To which
I answer, that I doubt not but, without being written on their
hearts, many men, may, by the same way that they come to the
knowledge of other things, come to assent to several moral rules,
and be convinced of their obligation. Others also may come to be
of the same mind, from their education, company, and customs of
their country; which persuasion, however got, will serve to set
conscience on work, which is nothing else but our own opinion or
judgment of the moral rectitude or pravity of our own actions.
And if conscience be a proof of innate principles, contraries may
be innate principles; since some men, with the same bent of
conscience prosecute what others avoid.

9. *Instances of enormities practised without remorse.*—But I
cannot see how any men should ever transgress those moral rules
with confidence and serenity, were they innate and stamped upon
their minds. View but an army at the sacking of a town, and
see what observation or sense of moral principles, or what touch
of conscience, for all the outrages they do. Robberies, murders,
rapes, are the sports of men set at liberty from punishment and
censure. Have there not been whole nations, and those of the
most civilized people, amongst whom the exposing their children,
and leaving them in the fields, to perish by want or wild beasts,
has been the practice, as little condemned, or scrupled as the
begetting them? Do they not still, in some countries, put them
into the same graves with their mothers, if they die in child-
birth; or despatch them if a pretended astrologer declares them
to have unhappy stars? and are there not places where, at a
certain age, they kill or expose their parents without any remorse
at all? In a part of Asia, the sick, when their case comes to be
thought desperate, are carried out and laid on the earth before
they are dead, and left there, exposed to wind and weather, to
perish without assistance or pity.* It is familiar among the
Mingrelians, a people professing Christianity, to bury their

---

* Gruber *apud* Thevenot, part iv. p. 13.

children alive without scruple.* There are places where they eat their own children.† The Caribbs were wont to geld their children, on purpose to fat and eat them.‡ And Garcilasso de la Vega tells us of a people in Peru, which were wont to fat and eat the children they got on their female captives, whom they kept as concubines for that purpose; and when they were past breeding, the mothers themselves were killed too and eaten.§ The virtues whereby the Tououpinambos believed they merited Paradise, were revenge, and eating abundance of their enemies. They have not so much as the name for God, no acknowledgment of any God, no religion, no worship.‖ The saints who are canonized amongst the Turks, lead lives which one cannot with modesty relate. A remarkable passage to this purpose, out of the Voyage of Baumgarten, which is a book not every day to be met with, I shall set down at large, in the language it is published in. *Ibi (sc. prope Belbes in Ægypto) vidimus sanctum unum Saracenicum inter arenarum cumulos, ita ut ex utero matris prodiit, nudum sedentem. Mos est, ut didicimus, Mahometistis, ut eos qui amentes et sine ratione sunt, pro sanctis colant et venerentur. Insuper et eos qui cum diu vitam egerint inquinatissimam, voluntariam demum pœnitentiam et paupertatem, sanctitate venerandos deputant. Ejusmodi verò genus hominum libertatem quandam effrænem habent, domos quas volunt intrandi, edendi, bibendi, et quod majus est, concumbendi; ex quo concubitu si proles secuta fuerit, sancta similiter habetur. His ergò hominibus, dum vivunt, magnos exhibent honores; mortuis verò vel templa vel monumenta extruunt amplissima, eosque contingere ac sepelire maximæ fortunæ ducunt loco. Audivimus hæc dicta et dicenda per interpretem à Mucrelo nostro. Insuper sanctum illum, quem eo loco vidimus, publicitus apprimè commendari, eum esse hominem sanctum, divinum, ac integritate præcipuum; eo quod, nec fœminarum unquam esset, nec puerorum, sed tantummodo asellarum concubitor atque mularum!* ¶ More of the same kind, concerning these precious saints among the Turks, may be seen in Pietro della Valle, in his letter of the 25th of January, 1616. Where then are those innate principles of justice, piety, gratitude, equity, chastity? Or, where is that universal consent, that assures us there are such inbred rules? Murders in duels, when fashion has made them honourable, are committed without remorse of conscience: nay, in many places, innocence in this case is the greatest ignominy. And if we look abroad to take a view of men as they are, we shall find that they have remorse in one place for doing or omitting that which others, in another place, think they merit by.

10. *Men have contrary practical principles.*—He that will carefully peruse the history of mankind, and look abroad into the

---

\* LAMBERT *apud* THEVENOT, p. 38.  † VOSSIUS *de Nili Origine*, cap. 18, 19.
‡ P. MART, *Dec.* 1.  § *Hist. des Incas*, lib. i. cap. 12.
‖ LERY, cap. xvi. pp. 216, 231.  ¶ BAUMGARTEN, *Peregrin*, lib. ii. cap. 1, p. 73

several tribes of men, and with indifferency survey their actions, will be able to satisfy himself that there is scarce that principle of morality to be named, or rule of virtue to be thought on (those only excepted that are absolutely necessary to hold society together, which commonly, too, are neglected betwixt distinct societies), which is not, somewhere or other, slighted and condemned by the general fashion of whole societies of men, governed by practical opinions and rules of living quite opposite to others.

11. *Whole nations reject several moral rules.*—Here, perhaps, it will be objected, that it is no argument, that the rule is not known, because it is broken. I grant the objection good where men, though they transgress yet disown not, the law; where fear of shame, censure, or punishment carries the mark of some awe it has upon them. But it is impossible to conceive, that a whole nation of men should all publicly reject and renounce what every one of them, certainly and infallibly, knew to be a law; for so they must who have it naturally imprinted on their minds. It is possible men may sometimes own rules of morality which, in their private thoughts, they do not believe to be true, only to keep themselves in reputation and esteem amongst those who are persuaded of their obligation. But it is not to be imagined, that a whole society of men should publicly and professedly disown and cast off a rule which they could not, in their own minds, but be infallibly certain was a law; nor be ignorant, that all men they should have to do with knew it to be such: and therefore must every one of them apprehend from others all the contempt and abhorrence due to one who professes himself void of humanity; and one who, confounding the known and natural measures of right and wrong, cannot but be looked on as the professed enemy of their peace and happiness. Whatever practical principle is innate, cannot but be known to everyone to be just and good. It is therefore little less than a contradiction to suppose, that whole nations of men should, both in their professions and practice, unanimously and universally give the lie to what, by the most invincible evidence, every one of them knew to be true, right, and good. This is enough to satisfy us, that no practical rule which is anywhere universally, and with public approbation and allowance, transgressed, can be supposed innate. But I have something farther to add in answer to this objection.

12. The breaking of a rule, say you, is no argument that it is unknown. I grant it; but the generally allowed breach of it anywhere, I say, is a proof that it is not innate. For example: let us take any of these rules, which, being the most obvious deductions of human reason, and comfortable to the natural inclination of the greatest part of men, fewest people have had the impudence to deny, or inconsideration to doubt of. If any can be thought to be naturally imprinted, none, I think, can have a fairer pretence to be innate than this: "Parents, preserve and

cherish your children." When therefore you say that this is an
innate rule, what do you mean? Either that it is an innate
principle which, upon all occasions, excites and directs the actions
of all men; or else that it is a truth which all men have imprinted
on their minds, and which, therefore, they know and assent to.
But in neither of these senses is it innate. First,—That it is not
a principle which influences all men's actions, is what I have
proved by the examples before cited: nor need we seek so far as
Mingrelia or Peru to find instances of such as neglect, abuse,
nay, and destroy, their children; or look on it only as the more
than brutality of some savage and barbarous nations, when we
remember that it was a familiar and uncondemned practice
amongst the Greeks and Romans to expose, without pity or
remorse, their innocent infants. Secondly,—That it is an innate
truth known to all men, is also false: for, "Parents, preserve
your children," is so far from an innate truth, that it is no truth
at all; it being a command, and not a proposition; and so not
capable of truth or falsehood. To make it capable of being
assented to as true, it must be reduced to some such proposition
as this: "It is the duty of parents to preserve their children."
But what duty is, cannot be understood without a law; nor a
law be known, or supposed, without a lawmaker, or without
reward and punishment; so that it is impossible that this or any
other practical principle should be innate (that is, be imprinted
on the mind as a duty), without supposing the ideas of God, of
law, of obligation, of punishment, of a life after this, innate. For
that punishment follows not in this life the breach of this rule,
and, consequently, that it has not the force of a law in countries
where the generally allowed practice runs counter to it, is in itself
evident. But these ideas (which must be all of them innate,
if anything as a duty be so) are so far from being innate, that it
is not every studious or thinking man, much less everyone that
is born, in whom they are to be found clear and distinct; and
that one of them which of all others seems most likely to be innate,
is not so (I mean, the idea of God), I think, in the next chapter,
will appear very evident to any considering man.

13. From what has been said, I think we may safely conclude,
that, whatever practical rule is, in any place, generally, and with
allowance broken, cannot be supposed innate; it being impossible
that men should without shame or fear, confidently and serenely
break a rule which they could not but evidently know that Gɔd
had set up, and would certainly punish the breach of (which they
must, if it were innate) to a degree to make it a very ill bargain
to the transgressor. Without such a knowledge as this, a man
can never be certain that anything is his duty. Ignorance or
doubt of the law, hopes to escape the knowledge or power of the
lawmaker, or the like, may make men give way to a present
appetite. But let anyone see the fault, and the rod by it, and

with the transgression, a fire ready to punish it; a pleasure tempting, and the hand of the Almighty visibly held up and prepared to take vengeance (for this must be the case where any duty is imprinted on the mind); and then tell me, whether it be possible for people with such a prospect, such a certain knowledge as this, wantonly, and without scruple, to offend against a law which they carry about them in indelible characters, and that stares them in the face whilst they are breaking it; whether men, at the same time that they feel in themselves the imprinted edicts of an omnipotent Lawmaker, can, with assurance and gaiety, slight and trample under foot his most sacred injunctions; and, lastly, whether it be possible that, whilst a man thus openly bids defiance to this innate law and supreme Lawgiver, all the bystanders, yea, even the governors and rulers of the people, full of the same sense both of the law and Lawmaker, should silently connive without testifying their dislike, or laying the least blame on it? Principles of actions, indeed, there are lodged in men's appetites; but these are so far from being innate moral principles, that, if they were left to their full swing, they would carry men to the overturning of all morality. Moral laws are sent as a curb and restraint to these exorbitant desires, which they cannot be but by rewards and punishments that will overbalance the satisfaction anyone shall propose to himself in the breach of the law. If therefore anything be imprinted on the mind of all men as a law, all men must have a certain and unavoidable knowledge that certain and unavoidable punishment will attend the breach of it. For if men can be ignorant or doubtful of what is innate, innate principles are insisted on and urged to no purpose; truth and certainty (the things pretended) are not at all secured by them; but men are in the same uncertain, floating estate with as without them. An evident, indubitable knowledge of unavoidable punishment, great enough to make the transgression very uneligible, must accompany an innate law; unless with an innate law they can suppose an innate gospel too. I would not be here mistaken, as if, because I deny an innate law, I thought there were none but positive laws. There is a great deal of difference between an innate law and a law of nature; between something imprinted on our minds in this very original, and something that we, being ignorant of, may attain to the knowledge of by the use and due application of our natural faculties. And, I think, they equally forsake the truth who, running into the contrary extremes, either affirm an innate law, or deny that there is a law knowable by the light of nature; that is, without the help of positive revelation.

14. *Those who maintain innate practical principles, tell us not what they are.*—The difference there is amongst men, in their practical principles, is so evident, that, I think, I need say no more to evince that it will be impossible to find any innate moral rules

by this mark of general assent. And it is enough to make one
suspect, that the supposition of such innate principles is but an
opinion taken up at pleasure; since those who talk so confidently
of them are so sparing to tell us which they are. This might
with justice be expected from those men who lay stress upon
this opinion; and it gives occasion to distrust either their knowledge or charity, who, declaring that God has imprinted on the
minds of men the foundations of knowledge and the rules of
living, are yet so little favourable to the information of their
neighbours, or the quiet of mankind, as not to point out to them
which they are, in the variety men are distracted with. But, in
truth, were there any such innate principles, there would be no
need to teach them. Did men find such innate propositions
stamped on their minds, they would easily be able to distinguish
them from other truths that they afterwards learned and deduced
from them; and there would be nothing more easy than to
know what and how many they were. There could be no more
doubt about their number, than there is about the number of our
fingers; and it is like, then, every system would be ready to give
them us by tale. But since nobody that I know has ventured
yet to give a catalogue of them, they cannot blame those who
doubt of the innate principles; since even they who require men
to believe that there are such innate propositions, do not tell us
what they are. It is easy to foresee, that if different men, of
different sects, should go about to give us a list of those innate
practical principles, they would set down only such as suited
their distinct hypotheses, and were fit to support the doctrines
of their particular schools or churches; a plain evidence that
there are no such innate truths. Nay, a great part of men are
so far from finding any such innate moral principles in themselves
that, by denying freedom to mankind, and thereby making men
no other than bare machines, they take away not only innate,
but all moral, rules whatsoever, and leave not a possibility to
believe any such to those who cannot conceive how anything
can be capable of a law that is not a free agent; and upon that
ground they must necessarily reject all principles of virtue, who
cannot put morality and mechanism together, which are not very
easy to be reconciled, or made consistent.

15. *Lord Herbert's innate principles examined.*—When I had
writ this, being informed that my Lord Herbert had, in his books
*De Veritate*, assigned these innate principles, I presently consulted him; hoping to find, in a man of so great parts, something
that might satisfy me in this point, and put an end to my inquiry.
In his chapter *De Instinctu naturali*, p. 76, edit. 1656, I met
with these six marks of his *notitiæ communes*: (1.) *Prioritas.*
(2.) *Independentia.* (3.) *Universalitas.* (4.) *Certitudo.* (5.) *Necessitas; i.e.*, as he explains it, *Faciunt ad hominis conserva-
tionem.** (6.) *Modus conformationis;* that is, *Assensus nullâ*

* The ninth and some subsequent editions have the erroneous reading of
*conversationem.*—EDIT.

*interposita morâ.* And at the latter end of his little treatise, *De Religione Laici,* he says this of these innate principles : *Adeò ut non uniuscujusvis religionis confinio arctentur quæ ubique vigent veritates. Sunt enim in ipsâ mente cælitùs descriptæ, nullisque traditionibus, sive scriptis, sive non scriptis, obnoxiæ.* (P. 3.) And, *Veritates nostræ catholicæ, quæ tanquam indubia Dei effata in foro interiori descripta.* Thus, having given the marks of the innate principles, or common notions, and asserted their being imprinted on the minds of men by the hand of God, he proceeds to set them down; and they are these : (1.) *Esse aliquod supremum numen.* (2.) *Numen illud coli debere.* (3.) *Virtutem cum pietate conjunctam optimam esse rationem cultûs divini.* (4.) *Resipiscendum esse a peccatis.* (5.) *Dari præmium vel pœnam post hanc vitam transactam.* Though I allow these to be clear truths, and such as, if rightly explained, a rational creature can hardly avoid giving his assent to; yet, I think, he is far from proving them innate impressions *in foro interiori descriptæ :* for I must take leave to observe,

16. **First.** That these five propositions are either not all, or more than all, those common notions writ on our minds by the finger of God, if it were reasonable to believe any at all to be so written; since there are other propositions which, even by his own rules, have as just a pretence to such an original, and may be as well admitted for innate principles, as, at least, some of these five he enumerates: viz., " Do as thou wouldst be done unto;" and perhaps some hundreds of others when well considered.

17. **Secondly.** That all his marks are not to be found in each of his five propositions; viz., his first, second, and third marks agree perfectly to neither of them; and the first, second, third, fourth, and sixth marks agree but ill to his third, fourth, and fifth propositions. For, besides that we are assured from history of many men, nay, whole nations, who doubt or disbelieve some or all of them; I cannot see how the third, viz., that " virtue joined with piety is the best worship of God," can be an innate principle, when the name or sound, virtue, is so hard to be understood, liable to so much uncertainty in its signification, and the thing it stands for so much contended about, and difficult to be known. And therefore this can be but a very uncertain rule of human practice, and serve but very little to the conduct of our lives, and is therefore very unfit to be assigned as an innate practical principle.

18. For let us consider this proposition as to its meaning, (for it is the sense and not sound that is and must be the principle or common notion;) viz., " Virtue is the best worship of God ;" *i.e.,* is the most acceptable to him ; which, if virtue be taken, as most commonly it is, for those actions which, according to the different opinions of several countries, are accounted laudable,

will be a proposition so far from being certain, that it will not be
true. If virtue be taken for actions conformable to God's will,
or to the rule prescribed by God, which is the true and only
measure of virtue, when virtue is used to signify what is in its
own nature right and good; then this proposition, that " virtue
is the best worship of God," will be most true and certain, but of
very little use in human life; since it will amount to no more
but this, viz., that " God is pleased with the doing of what he
commands;" which a man may certainly know to be true, without knowing what it is that God doth command, and so be as
far from any rule or principle of his actions as he was before;
and I think very few will take a proposition which amounts to
no more than this, viz., that " God is pleased with the doing of
what he himself commands," for an innate moral principle writ
on the minds of all men (however true and certain it may be),
since it teaches so little. Whosoever does so, will have reason
to think hundreds of propositions innate principles, since there
are many which have as good a title as this to be received for
such, which nobody yet ever put into that rank of innate
principles.
19. Nor is the fourth proposition (viz. " Men must repent
of their sins ") much more instructive, till what those actions are
that are meant by sins be set down. For the word *peccata*, or
" sins," being put, as it usually is, to signify in general ill actions
that will draw on punishment upon the doers; what great principle of morality can that be, to tell us we should be sorry, and
cease to do that which will bring mischief upon us, without
knowing what those particular actions are that will do so?
Indeed, this is a very true proposition, and fit to be inculcated
on and received by those who are supposed to have been taught
what actions in all kinds are sins; but neither this nor the
former can be imagined to be innate principles, nor to be of any
use if they were innate, unless the particular measures and
bounds of all virtues and vices were engraven in men's minds,
and were innate principles also, which, I think, is very much to
be doubted. And therefore, I imagine, it will scarce seem
possible that God should engrave principles in men's minds in
words of uncertain signification, such as " virtues " and " sins,"
which amongst different men stand for different things: nay, it
cannot be supposed to be in words at all, which, being in most
of these principles very general names, cannot be understood but
by knowing the particulars comprehended under them. And if
the practical instances, the measures must be taken from the
knowledge of the actions themselves, and the rules of them abstracted from words, and antecedent to the knowledge of names;
which rules a man must know, what language soever he chance
to learn, whether English or Japan, or if he should learn no
language at all, or never should understand the use of words, as

happens in the case of dumb and deaf men. When it shall be made out, that men ignorant of words, or untaught by the laws and customs of their country, know that it is part of the worship of God not to kill another man ; not to know more women than one; not to procure abortion ; not to expose their children ; not to take from another what is his though we want it ourselves, but, on the contrary, relieve and supply his wants ; and, whenever we have done the contrary, we ought to repent, be sorry, and resolve to do so no more ;—when, I say, all men shall be proved actually to know and allow all these and a thousand other such rules, all which come under these two general words made use of above, viz. *virtutes et peccata*, "virtues and sins," there will be more reason for admitting these and the like for common notions and practical principles ; yet, after all, universal consent (were there any in moral principles) to truths, the knowledge whereof may be attained otherwise, would scarce prove them to be innate, which is all I contend for.

20. *Objection.* "*Innate principles may be corrupted,*" *answered.*—Nor will it be of much moment here to offer that very ready but not very material answer, (viz.) that the innate principles of morality may, by education and custom, and the general opinion of those amongst whom we converse, be darkened, and at last quite worn out of the minds of men. Which assertion of theirs, if true, quite takes away the argument of universal consent by which this opinion of innate principles is endeavoured to be proved ; unless those men will think it reasonable that their private persuasions, or that of their party, should pass for universal consent—a thing not unfrequently done when men, presuming themselves to be the only masters of right reason, cast by the votes and opinions of the rest of mankind as not worthy of reckoning. And then their argument stands thus : " The principles which all mankind allow for true are innate ; those that men of right reason admit are the principles allowed by all mankind ; we, and those of our mind, are men of reason ; therefore, we agreeing, our principles are innate ;" which is a very pretty way of arguing, and a short cut to infallibility. For otherwise it will be very hard to understand how there be some principles which all men do acknowledge and agree in ; and yet there are none of those principles which are not, by depraved custom and ill education, blotted out of the minds of many men ; which is to say, that all men admit, but yet many men do deny and dissent from, them. And indeed the supposition of such first principles will serve us to very little purpose, and we shall be as much at a loss with as without them, if they may by any human power, such as is the will of our teachers, or opinions of our companions, be altered or lost in us; and, notwithstanding all this boast of first principles and innate light, we shall be as much in the dark and uncertainty as if there were no such

thing at all; it being all one to have no rule, and one that will warp
any way; or, amongst various and contrary rules, not to know
which is the right. But concerning innate principles, I desire
these men to say whether they can or cannot, by education and
custom, be blurred and blotted out; if they cannot, we must find
them in all mankind alike, and they must be clear in everybody;
and, if they may suffer variation from adventitious notions, we
must then find them clearest and most perspicuous nearest the
fountain, in children and illiterate people, who have received least
impression from foreign opinions. Let them take which side
they please, they will certainly find it inconsistent with visible
matter of fact and daily observation.

21. *Contrary principles in the world.*—I easily grant that there
are great numbers of opinions which, by men of different countries, educations, and tempers, are received and embraced as
first and unquestionable principles; many whereof, both for
their absurdity as well as opposition one to another, it is impossible should be true. But yet all those propositions, how
remote soever from reason, are so sacred somewhere or other,
that men even of good understanding in other matters will
sooner part with their lives, and whatever is dearest to them,
than suffer themselves to doubt, or others to question, the truth
of them.

22. *How men commonly come by their principles.*—This, however strange it may seem, is that which every day's experience
confirms: and will not, perhaps, appear so wonderful if we
consider the ways and steps by which it is brought about, and
how really it may come to pass, that doctrines that have been
derived from no better original than the superstition of a nurse,
or the authority of an old woman, may, by length of time and
consent of neighbours, grow up to the dignity of principles in
religion or morality. For such who are careful (as they call it)
to principle children well (and few there be who have not a set
of those principles for them which they believe in), instil into the
unwary, and as yet unprejudiced, understanding (for white paper
receives any characters) those doctrines they would have them
retain and profess. These—being taught them as soon as they
have any apprehension, and still as they grow up confirmed to
them, either by the open profession or tacit consent of all they
have to do with; or at least by those of whose wisdom, knowledge, and piety they have an opinion, who never suffer those
propositions to be otherwise mentioned but as the basis and
foundation on which they build their religion or manners—come,
by these means, to have the reputation of unquestionable, self-
evident, and innate truths.

23. To which we may add, that when men so instructed are
grown up and reflect on their own minds, they cannot find anything more ancient there than those opinions which were taught

them before their memory began to keep a register of their
actions, or date the time when any new thing appeared to them;
and therefore make no scruple to conclude that those propositions, of whose knowledge they can find in themselves no original,
were certainly the impress of God and nature upon their minds,
and not taught them by anyone else. These they entertain and
submit to, as many do to their parents, with veneration; not
because it is natural, nor do children do it where they are not so
taught; but because, having been always so educated, and having
no remembrance of the beginning of this respect, they think it
is natural.

24. This will appear very likely, and almost unavoidably to
come to pass, if we consider the nature of mankind and the constitution of human affairs; wherein most men cannot live without employing their time in the daily labours of their callings,
nor be at quiet in their minds without some foundation or principles to rest their thoughts on. There is scarce anyone so
floating and superficial in his understanding who hath not some
reverenced propositions, which are to him the principles on
which he bottoms his reasonings, and by which he judgeth of
truth and falsehood, right and wrong; which some wanting skill
and leisure, and others the inclination, and some being taught
that they ought not, to examine, there are few to be found who
are not exposed, by their ignorance, laziness, education, or precipitancy, to take them upon trust.

25. This is evidently the case of all children and young folks;
and custom, a greater power than nature, seldom failing to make
them worship for divine what she hath inured them to bow their
minds and submit their understandings to, it is no wonder that
grown men, either perplexed in the necessary affairs of life, or hot
in the pursuit of pleasures, should not seriously sit down to examine their own tenets; especially when one of their principles is,
that principles ought not to be questioned. And, had men
leisure, parts, and will, who is there almost that dare shake the
foundations of all his past thoughts and actions, and endure to
bring upon himself the shame of having been a long time wholly
in mistake and error? Who is there hardy enough to contend
with the reproach which is everywhere prepared for those who
dare venture to dissent from the received opinions of their
country or party? And where is the man to be found that can
patiently prepare himself to bear the name of whimsical, sceptical,
or atheist, which he is sure to meet with who does in the least
scruple any of the common opinions? And he will be much more
afraid to question those principles when he shall think them, as
most men do, the standards set up by God in his mind to be the
rule and touchstone of all other opinions. And what can hinder
him from thinking them sacred when he finds them the earliest
of all his own thoughts, and the most reverenced by others?

26. It is easy to imagine how, by these means, it comes to pass, that men worship the idols that have been set up in their minds, grow fond of the notions they have been long acquainted with there, and stamp the characters of divinity upon absurdities and errors, become zealous votaries to bulls and monkeys; and contend, too, fight, and die in defence of their opinions. *Dum solos credit habendos esse Deos, quos ipse colit.* For since the reasoning faculties of the soul, which are almost constantly (though not always warily nor wisely) employed, would not know how to move for want of a foundation and footing in most men, who through laziness or avocation, do not—or for want of time, or true helps, or for other causes, cannot—penetrate into the principles of knowledge, and trace truth to its fountain and original, it is natural for them, and almost unavoidable, to take up with some borrowed principles; which, being reputed and presumed to be the evident proofs of other things, are thought not to need any other proof themselves. Whoever shall receive any of these into his mind, and entertain them there with the reverence usually paid to principles, never venturing to examine them, but accustoming himself to believe them because they are to be believed, may take up from his education and the fashions of his country any absurdity for innate principles; and by long poring on the same objects, so dim his sight as to take monsters lodged in his own brain for the images of the Deity, and the workmanship of his hands.

27. *Principles must be examined.*—By this progress how many there are who arrive at principles which they believe innate, may be easily observed in the variety of opposite principles held and contended for by all sorts and degrees of men. And he that shall deny this to be the method wherein most men proceed to the assurance they have of the truth and evidence of their principles, will, perhaps, find it a hard matter any other way to account for the contrary tenets, which are firmly believed, confidently asserted, and which great numbers are ready at any time to seal with their blood. And, indeed, if it be the privilege of innate principles to be received upon their own authority, without examination, I know not what may not be believed, or how anyone's principles can be questioned. If they may and ought to be examined and tried, I desire to know how first and* innate principles can be tried; or at least it is reasonable to demand the marks and characters whereby the genuine innate principles may be distinguished from others; that so, amidst the great variety of pretenders, I may be kept from mistakes in so material a point as this. When this is done, I shall be ready to embrace such welcome and useful propositions; and till then I may with modesty doubt, since I fear universal consent (which is the only one produced) will scarce prove a sufficient mark to

* The ninth edition and some others have *any* instead of *and.*—EDIT.

direct my choice, and assure me of any innate principles. From
what has been said, I think it past doubt, that there are no
practical principles wherein all men agree, and therefore none
innate.

---

## CHAPTER IV.

### OTHER CONSIDERATIONS CONCERNING INNATE PRINCIPLES BOTH SPECULATIVE AND PRACTICAL.

1. *Principles not innate, unless their ideas be innate.*—Had
those who would persuade us that there are innate principles,
not taken them together in gross, but considered separately the
parts out of which those propositions are made, they would not,
perhaps, have been so forward to believe they were innate;
since, if the ideas which made up those truths were not, it was
impossible that the propositions made up of them should be,
innate, or our knowledge of them be born with us. For if the
ideas be not innate, there was a time when the mind was
without those principles; and then they will not be innate, but
be derived from some other original: for where the ideas themselves are not, there can be no knowledge, no assent, no mental
or verbal propositions about them.

2. *Ideas, especially those belonging to principles, not born with
children.*—If we will attentively consider new-born children, we
shall have little reason to think that they bring many ideas into
the world with them: for, bating, perhaps, some faint ideas of
hunger, and thirst, and warmth, and some pains which they may
have felt in the womb, there is not the least appearance of any
settled ideas at all in them; especially of ideas answering the
terms which make up those universal propositions that are
esteemed innate principles. One may perceive how, by degrees,
afterwards, ideas come into their minds; and that they get no
more, nor no other, than what experience, and the observation
of things that come in their way, furnish them with; which
might be enough to satisfy us that they are not original characters
stamped on the mind.

3. "It is impossible for the same thing to be, and not to be,"
is certainly (if there be any such) an innate principle. But can
anyone think, or will anyone say, that impossibility and identity
are two innate ideas? Are they such as all mankind have, and
bring into the world with them? And are they those that are
the first in children, and antecedent to all acquired ones? If
they are innate, they must needs be so. Hath a child an idea of
impossibility and identity before it has of white or black, sweet
or bitter? And is it from the knowledge of this principle that
it concludes, that wormwood rubbed on the nipple hath not the

same taste that it used to receive from thence ? Is it the actual knowledge of *Impossibile est idem esse, et non esse*, that makes a child distinguish between its mother and a stranger; or that makes it fond of the one and fly the other? Or does the mind regulate itself, and its assent, by ideas that it never yet had? or the understanding draw conclusions from principles which it never yet knew or understood? The names " impossibility " and "identity" stand for two ideas so far from being innate, or born with us, that, I think, it requires great care and attention to form them right in our understandings : they are so far from being brought into the world with us, so remote from the thoughts of infancy and childhood, that, I believe, upon examination, it will be found that many grown men want them.

4. *Identity, an idea not innate.*—If identity (to instance in that alone) be a native impression, and, consequently, so clear and obvious to us that we must needs know it even from our cradles, I would gladly be resolved, by one of seven or seventy years old, whether a man being a creature consisting of soul and body, be the same man when his body is changed; whether Euphorbus and Pythagoras, having had the same soul, were the same man, though they lived several ages asunder; nay, whether the cock, too, which had the same soul, were not the same with both of them? Whereby, perhaps, it will appear, that our idea of sameness is not so settled and clear as to deserve to be thought innate in us. For if those innate ideas are not clear and distinct, so as to be universally known and naturally agreed on, they cannot be subjects of universal and undoubted truths, but will be the unavoidable occasion of perpetual uncertainty. For, I suppose, everyone's idea of identity will not be the same that Pythagoras and thousands others of his followers have ; and which, then, shall be the true? which innate? or are there two different ideas of identity, both innate ?

5. Nor let anyone think that the questions I have here proposed, about the identity of man, are bare, empty speculations; which if they were, would be enough to show that there was in the understandings of men no innate idea of identity. He that shall, with a little attention, reflect on the resurrection, and consider that Divine Justice shall bring to judgment, at the last day, the very same persons, to be happy or miserable in the other, who did well or ill in this, life, will find it, perhaps, not easy to resolve with himself what makes the same man, or wherein identity consists ; and will not be forward to think he and everyone, even children themselves, have naturally a clear idea of it.

6. *Whole and part, not innate ideas.*—Let us examine that principle of mathematics, viz., that the "whole is bigger than a part." This, I take it, is reckoned amongst innate principles. I am sure it has as good a title as any to be thought so; which yet nobody can think it to be, when he considers the ideas it compre-

hends in it, whole and part, are perfectly relative; but the positive ideas to which they properly and immediately belong are extension and number, of which alone whole and part are relations. So that if whole and part are innate ideas, extension and number must be so too; it being impossible to have an idea of a relation, without having any at all of the thing to which it belongs, and in which it is founded. Now, whether the minds of men have naturally imprinted on them the ideas of extension and number, I leave to be considered by those who are the patrons of innate principles.

7. *Idea of worship not innate.*—That "God is to be worshipped," is, without doubt, as great a truth as any can enter into the mind of man, and deserves the first place amongst all practical principles; but yet it can by no means be thought innate, unless the ideas of God and worship are innate. That the idea the term "worship" stands for is not in the understanding of children, and a character stamped on the mind in its first original, I think, will be easily granted by anyone that considers how few there be, amongst grown men, who have a clear and distinct notion of it. And, I suppose, there cannot be anything more ridiculous than to say, that children have this practical principle innate,— that "God is to be worshipped;" and yet that they know not what that worship of God is, which is their duty. But, to pass by this:

8. *Idea of God not innate.*—If any idea can be imagined innate, the idea of God may, of all others, for many reasons, be thought so; since it is hard to conceive how there should be innate moral principles without an innate idea of a Deity: without a notion of a law-maker, it is impossible to have a notion of a law, and an obligation to observe it. Besides the atheists taken notice of amongst the ancients, and left branded upon the records of history, hath not navigation discovered, in these later ages, whole nations, at the Bay of Soldania,* in Brazil,† in Boranday,‡ and the Carribee Islands, &c., amongst whom there was to be found no notion of a God, no religon? Nicholaus del Techo *in Literis, ex Paraquariâ de Caaiguarum Conversione*, has these words: *Reperi eam gentem nullum nomen habere, quod Deum et hominis animam significet: nulla sacra habet, nulla idola.§* These are instances of nations where uncultivated nature has been left to itself, without the help of letters and discipline, and the improvements of arts and sciences. But there are others to be found, who have enjoyed these in a very great measure, who yet for want of a due application of their thoughts this way, want the idea and knowledge of God. It will, I doubt not, be a surprise to others

---

* ROE *apud* THEVENOT, p. 2.   † JO. DE LERY, cap. xvi.
‡ MARTINIERE, $\frac{201}{322}$; TERRY, $\frac{17}{545}$; OVINGTON, $\frac{489}{608}$.
§ *Relatio triplex de Rebus Indicis Caaiguarum*, $\frac{9}{8}$.

as it was to me, to find the Siamites, of this number; but for
this, let them consult the king of France's late envoy thither,*
who gives no better account of the Chinese themselves.† And
if we will not believe La Loubere, the missionaries of China, even
the Jesuits themselves, the great encomiasts of the Chinese, do
all to a man agree, and will convince us, that the sect of the
*Literati*, or " Learned," keeping to the old religion of China, and
the ruling party there, are all of them atheists. (*Vid.* Nava-
rette, in the Collection of Voyages, vol. i.; and *Historia Cultûs
Sinensium*.) And, perhaps, if we should with attention mind the
lives and discourses of people not so far off, we should have too
much reason to fear that many, in more civilized countries, have
no very strong and clear impressions of a Deity upon their
minds; and that the complaints of atheism made from the pulpit
are not without reason. And though only some profligate wretches
own it too barefacedly now; yet, perhaps, we should hear more
than we do of it from others, did not the fear of the magistrate's
sword, or their neighbour's censure, tie up people's tongues,
which, were the apprehensions of punishment or shame taken
away, would as openly proclaim their atheism as their lives do.‡
9. But had all mankind everywhere a notion of a God (whereof
yet history tells us the contrary), it would not from thence follow
that the idea of him was innate. For though no nation were to
be found without a name and some few dark notions of him, yet
that would not prove them to be natural impressions on the
mind, no more than the names of "fire," or the "sun," "heat,"
or "number," do prove the ideas they stand for to be innate,
because the names of those things, and the ideas of them, are so
universally received and known amongst mankind. Nor, on the
contrary, is the want of such a name, or the absence of such a
notion out of men's minds, any argument against the being of a
God, any more than it would be a proof that there was no loadstone in the world, because a great part of mankind had neither
a notion of any such thing, nor a name for it; or be any show
of argument to prove, that there are no distinct and various
species of angels, or intelligent beings above us, because we have
no ideas of such distinct species or names for them. For men,
being furnished with words by the common language of their own
countries, can scarce avoid having some kind of ideas of those
things whose names those they converse with have occasion frequently to mention to them: and if it carry with it the notion of
excellency, greatness, or something extraordinary; if apprehension and concernment accompany it; if the fear of absolute and
irresistible power set it on upon the mind; the idea is likely to
sink the deeper and spread the farther; especially if it be such

* La Loubrre, *Du Royaume de Siam*, tom. i. cap. ix. sect. xv. &c.; cap. xx.
sect. xxii. &c.; cap. xxii. sect. vi.
† *Ibid.*, tom. i. cap. xx. sect. iv. &c.; cap. xxiii.
‡ See the Note at the end of this chapter, p. 57.—Edit.

an idea as is agreeable to the common light of reason, and naturally deducible from every part of our knowledge, as that of a God is. For the visible marks of extraordinary wisdom and power appear so plainly in all the works of the creation, that a rational creature who will but seriously reflect on them, cannot miss the discovery of a Deity; and the influence that the discovery of such a Being must necessarily have on the minds of all that have but once heard of it is so great, and carries such a weight of thought and communication with it, that it seems stranger to me that a whole nation of men should be anywhere found so brutish as to want the notion of a God, than that they should be without any notion of numbers, or fire.

10. The name of God being once mentioned in any part of the world, to express a superior, powerful, wise, invisible Being, the suitableness of such a notion to the principles of common reason, and the interest men will always have to mention it often, must necessarily spread it far and wide, and continue it down to all generations; though yet the general reception of this name, and some imperfect and unsteady notions conveyed thereby to the unthinking part of mankind, prove not the idea to be innate; but only that they who made the discovery had made a right use of their reason, thought maturely of the causes of things, and traced them to their original; from whom other less considering people having once received so important a notion, it could not easily be lost again.

11. This is all could be inferred from the notion of a God, were it to be found universally in all the tribes of mankind, and generally acknowledged by men grown to maturity in all countries. For the generality of the acknowledging of a God, as I imagine, is extended no farther than that; which, if it be sufficient to prove the idea of God innate, will as well prove the idea of fire innate; since, I think, it may truly be said, that there is not a person in the world who has a notion of a God, who has not also the idea of fire. I doubt not but if a colony of young children should be placed in an island where no fire was, they would certainly neither have any notion of such a thing nor name for it, how generally soever it were received and known in all the world besides; and perhaps, too, their apprehensions would be as far removed from any name or notion of a God, till some one amongst them had employed his thoughts, to inquire into the constitution and causes of things, which would easily lead him to the notion of a God; which having once taught to others, reason and the natural propensity of their own thoughts would afterwards propagate and continue amongst them.

12. "*Suitable to God's goodness, that all men should have an idea of him, therefore naturally imprinted by him,*" answered.— Indeed it is urged that it is suitable to the goodness of God to imprint upon the minds of men characters and notions of himself,

and not to leave them in the dark and doubt in so grand a concernment; and also by that means to secure to himself the homage and veneration due from so intelligent a creature as man; and therefore he has done it.

This argument, if it be of any force, will prove much more than those who use it in this case expect from it. For if we may conclude that God hath done for men all that men shall judge is best for them, because it is suitable to his goodness so to do, it will prove not only that God has imprinted on the minds of men an idea of himself, but that he hath plainly stamped there, in fair characters, all that men ought to know or believe of him, all that they ought to do in obedience to his will; and that he hath given them a will and affections conformable to it. This, no doubt, everyone will think it better for men, than that they should, in the dark, grope after knowledge, as St. Paul tells us, all nations did after God (Acts xvii. 27); than that their wills should clash with their understandings, and their appetites cross their duty. The Romanists say, it is best for men, and so suitable to the goodness of God, that there should be an infallible judge of controversies on earth; and therefore there is one. And I, by the same reason, say, it is better for men that every man himself should be infallible. I leave them to consider, whether by the force of this argument they shall think that every man is so. I think it a very good argument to say, "The infinitely wise God hath made it so, and therefore it is best." But it seems to me a little too much confidence of our own wisdom to say, "I think it best, and therefore God hath made it so;" and in the matter in hand, it will be in vain to argue from such a topic that God hath done so, when certain experience shows us that he hath not. But the goodness of God hath not been wanting to men without such original impressions of knowledge, or ideas stamped on the mind; since he hath furnished man with those faculties which will serve for the sufficient discovery of all things requisite to the end of such a being; and I doubt not but to show that a man, by the right use of his natural abilities, may, without any innate principles, attain the knowledge of a God, and other things that concern him. God, having endued man with those faculties of knowing which he hath, was no more obliged by his goodness to implant those innate notions in his mind, than that, having given him reason, hands, and materials, he should build him bridges or houses; which some people in the world, however of good parts, do either totally want, or are but ill provided of, as well as others are wholly without ideas of God, and principles of morality; or, at least, have but very ill ones: the reason in both cases being, that they never employed their parts, faculties, and powers industriously that way, but contented themselves with the opinions, fashions, and things of their country as they found them, without looking any farther,

Had you or I been born at the Bay of Soldania, possibly our
thoughts and notions had not exceeded those brutish ones of the
Hottentots that inhabit there; and had the Virginian king
Apochancana been educated in England, he had, perhaps, been
as knowing a divine, and as good a mathematician, as any in it;
the difference between him and a more improved Englishman
lying barely in this, that the exercise of his faculties was bounded
within the ways, modes, and notions of his own country, and
never directed to any other, or farther inquiries; and if he had
not any idea of a God, it was only because he pursued not those
thoughts that would have led him to it.

13. *Ideas of God various in different men.*—I grant, that if
there were any ideas to be found imprinted on the minds of men,
we have reason to expect it should be the notion of his Maker,
as a mark God set on his own workmanship, to mind man of his
dependence and duty; and that herein should appear the first
instances of human knowledge. But how late is it before any
such notion is discoverable in children! and when we find it
there, how much more does it resemble the opinion and notion of
the teacher, than represent the true God! He that shall observe
in children the progress whereby their minds attain the knowledge they have, will think that the objects they do first and
most familiarly converse with, are those that make the first
impressions on their understandings; nor will he find the least
footsteps of any other. It is easy to take notice how their
thoughts enlarge themselves only as they come to be acquainted
with a greater variety of sensible objects, to retain the ideas of
them in their memories, and to get the skill to compound and
enlarge them, and several ways put them together. How by
these means they come to frame in their minds an idea men have
of a Deity, I shall hereafter show.

14. Can it be thought, that the ideas men have of God are the
characters and marks of himself, engraven in their minds by his
own finger; when we see, that in the same country, under one
and the same name, men have far different, nay, often contrary
and inconsistent ideas and conceptions of him? Their agreeing
in a name or sound will scarce prove an innate notion of him.

15. What true or tolerable notion of a Deity could they have
who acknowledged and worshipped hundreds? Every deity
that they owned above one was an infallible evidence of their
ignorance of him, and a proof that they had no true notion of
God, where unity, infinity, and eternity were excluded. To
which if we add their gross conceptions of corporeity, expressed
in their images, and representations of their deities, the amours,
marriages, copulations, lusts, quarrels, and other mean qualities
attributed by them to their gods, we shall have little reason to
think that the heathen world, *i.e.*, the greatest part of mankind,
had such ideas of God in their minds, as he himself, out of care

that they should not be mistaken about him, was author of. And this universality of consent, so much argued, if it prove any native impressions, it will be only this: That God imprinted on the minds of all men, speaking the same language, a name for himself, but not any idea; since those people who agreed in the name, had, at the same time, far different apprehensions about the thing signified. If they say, that the variety of deities worshipped by the heathen world were but figurative ways of expressing the several attributes of that incomprehensible Being, or several parts of his providence; I answer, What they might be in their original, I will not here inquire; but that they were so in the thoughts of the vulgar, I think nobody will affirm; and he that will consult the Voyage of the Bishop of Beryte, cap. xiii. (not to mention other testimonies,) will find that the theology of the Siamites professedly owns a plurality of gods; or, as the Abbé de Choisy more judiciously remarks, in his Journal *du Voyage de Siam*, $\frac{107}{177}$, it consists properly in acknowledging no God at all.

15. If it be said that wise men of all nations came to have true conceptions of the unity and infinity of the Deity, I grant it. But then this,

First, excludes universality of consent in anything but the name; for those wise men being very few, perhaps one of a thousand, this universality is very narrow.

Secondly, it seems to me plainly to prove, that the truest and best notions men had of God were not imprinted, but acquired by thought and meditation, and a right use of their faculties; since the wise and considerate men of the world, by a right and careful employment of their thoughts and reason, attained true notions in this as well as other things; whilst the lazy and in-considerate part of men, making the far greater number, took up their notions, by chance, from common tradition and vulgar conceptions, without much beating their heads about them. And if it be a reason to think the notion of God innate because all wise men had it, virtue, too, must be thought innate; for that also wise men have always had.

16. This was evidently the case of all Gentilism: nor hath, even amongst Jews, Christians, and Mahometans, who acknow-ledge but one God, this doctrine, and the care* taken in those nations to teach men to have true notions of a God, prevailed so far as to make men to have the same and true ideas of him. How many, even amongst us, will be found, upon inquiry, to fancy him in the shape of a man, sitting in heaven; and to have many other absurd and unfit conceptions of him! Christians, as well as Turks, have had whole sects owning and contending earnestly for it, that the Deity was corporeal, and of human

* This is the reading of the fourth folio. The sixth and subsequent editions in 8vo. insert *is* after *care.*—EDIT.

shape: and though we find few amongst us who profess themselves anthropomorphites (though some I have met with that
own it), yet, I believe, he that will make it his business may find,
amongst the ignorant and uninstructed Christians, many of that
opinion. Talk but with country-people almost of any age, or
young people almost of any condition, and you shall find, that
though the name of God be frequently in their mouths, yet the
notions they apply this name to are so odd, low, and pitiful, that
nobody can imagine they were taught by a rational man, much
less that they were characters writ by the finger of God himself.
Nor do I see how it derogates more from the goodness of God,
that he has given us minds unfurnished with these ideas of himself, than that he hath sent us into the world with bodies unclothed,
and that there is no art or skill born with us. For being fitted
with faculties to attain these, it is want of industry and consideration in us, and not of bounty in him, if we have them not. It is
as certain that there is a God, as that the opposite angles, made
by the intersection of two straight lines, are equal. There was
never any rational creature, that set himself sincerely to examine
the truth of these propositions, that could fail to assent to them;
though yet it be past doubt that there are many men, who, having
not applied their thoughts that way, are ignorant both of the
one and the other. If anyone think fit to call this (which is the
utmost of its extent) universal consent, such an one I easily
allow; but such an universal consent as this proves not the idea
of God, no more than it does the idea of such angles, innate.

17. *If the idea of God be not innate, no other can be supposed
innate.*—Since, then, though the knowledge of a God be the most
natural discovery of human reason, yet the idea of him is not
innate, as, I think, is evident from what has been said; I imagine
there will be scarce any other idea found that can pretend to it;
since, if God had set any impression, any character, on the understanding of men, it is most reasonable to expect it should have
been some clear and uniform idea of himself, as far as our weak
capacities were capable to receive so incomprehensible and infinite
an object. But our minds being at first void of that idea which
we are most concerned to have, it is a strong presumption against
all other innate characters. I must own, as far as I can observe,
I can find none, and would be glad to be informed by any
other.

18. *Ideas of substance not innate.*—I confess there is another
idea which would be of general use for mankind to have, as it is
of general talk as if they had it; and that is the idea of substance,
which we neither have nor can have by sensation or reflection.
If nature took care to provide us any idea, we might well expect
it should be such as by our own faculties we cannot procure to
ourselves: but we see on the contrary, that, since by those ways
whereby other ideas are brought into our minds this is not, we

have no such clear idea at all, and therefore signify nothing by the word "substance," but only an uncertain supposition of we know not what (*i.e.*, of something whereof we have no particular, distinct, positive idea), which we take to be the *substratum*, or support of those ideas we do know.

19. *No propositions can be innate since no ideas are innate.*— Whatever, then, we talk of innate, either speculative or practical, principles, it may with as much probability be said, that a man hath £100 sterling in his pocket, and yet denied that he hath either penny, shilling, crown, or any other coin out of which the sum is to be made up; as to think, that certain propositions are innate, when the ideas about which they are can by no means be supposed to be so. The general reception and assent that is given doth not at all prove that the ideas expressed in them are innate; for in many cases, however the ideas came there, the assent to words expressing the agreement or disagreement of such ideas will necessarily follow. Everyone that hath a true idea of God and worship, will assent to this proposition, that "God is to be worshipped," when expressed in a language he understands; and every rational man that hath not thought on it to-day, may be ready to assent to this proposition to-morrow; and yet millions of men may be well supposed to want one or both of those ideas to-day. For if we will allow savages and most country people to have ideas of God and worship (which conversation with them will not make one forward to believe), yet, I think, few children can be supposed to have those ideas, which therefore they must begin to have some time or other; and then they will also begin to assent to that proposition, and make very little question of it ever after. But such an assent upon hearing no more proves the ideas to be innate, than it does that one born blind (with cataracts which will be couched to-morrow) had the innate ideas of the sun or light, or saffron or yellow, because, when his sight is cleared, he will certainly assent to this proposition, that "the sun is lucid," or that "saffron is yellow;" and therefore if such an assent upon hearing cannot prove the ideas innate, it can much less the propositions made up of those ideas. If they have any innate ideas, I would be glad to be told what and how many they are.

20. *No innate ideas in the memory.*—To which let me add : If there be any innate ideas, any ideas in the mind which the mind does not actually think on, they must be lodged in the memory, and from thence must be brought into view by remembrance; *i.e.*, must be known, when they are remembered, to have been perceptions in the mind before, unless remembrance can be without remembrance. For to remember is to perceive anything with memory, or with a consciousness that it was known or perceived before: without this, whatever idea comes into the mind is new and not remembered; this consciousness of its

having been in the mind before, being that which distinguishes
remembering from all other ways of thinking. Whatever idea
was never perceived by the mind, was never in the mind. Whatever idea is in the mind, is either an actual perception, or else,
having been an actual perception, is so in the mind, that by the
memory it can be made an actual perception again. Whenever
there is the actual perception of an idea without memory, the
idea appears perfectly new and unknown before to the understanding. Whenever the memory brings any idea into actual
view, it is with a consciousness that it had been there before,
and was not wholly a stranger to the mind. Whether this be
not so, I appeal to everyone's observation; and then I desire an
instance of an idea, pretended to be innate, which (before any
impression of it by ways hereafter to be mentioned) anyone
could revive and remember as an idea he had formerly known;
without which consciousness of a former perception there is no
remembrance; and whatever idea comes into the mind without
that consciousness, is not remembered, or comes not out of the
memory, nor can be said to be in the mind before that appearance. For what is not either actually in view or in the memory,
is in the mind no way at all, and is all one as if it never had been
there. Suppose a child had the use of his eyes till he knows
and distinguishes colours; but then cataracts shut the windows,
and he is forty or fifty years perfectly in the dark, and in that
time perfectly loses all memory of the ideas of colours he once
had. This was the case of a blind man I once talked with, who
lost his sight by the small-pox when he was a child, and had no
more notion of colours than one born blind. I ask whether anyone can say this man had then any ideas of colours in his mind
any more than one born blind? And I think nobody will say,
that either of them had in his mind any idea of colours at all.
His cataracts are couched, and then he has the ideas (which he
remembers not) of colours, *de novo*, by his restored sight conveyed to his mind, and that without any consciousness of a
former acquaintance. And these now he can revive, and call to
mind in the dark. In this case all these ideas of colours which,
when out of view can be revived, with a consciousness of a former
acquaintance, being thus in the memory, are said to be in the
mind. The use I make of this is, that whatever idea, being not
actually in view, is in the mind, is there only by being in the
memory; and if it be not in the memory, it is not in the mind;
and if it be in the memory it cannot by the memory be brought
into actual view, without a perception that it comes out of the
memory; which is this, that it had been known before, and is
now remembered. If, therefore, there be any innate ideas, they
must be in the memory, or else nowhere in the mind; and if they
be in the memory, they can be revived without any impression from without; and whenever they are brought into the

mind, they are remembered, *i.e.*, they bring with them a perception of their not being wholly new to it : this being a constant and distinguishing difference between what is, and what is not in the memory or in the mind—that what is not in the memory, whenever it appears there, appears perfectly new and unknown before ; and what is in the memory or in the mind, whenever it is suggested by the memory, appears not to be new, but the mind finds it in itself, and knows it was there before. By this it may be tried, whether there be any innate ideas in the mind before impression from sensation or reflection. I would fain meet with the man who, when he came to the use of reason, or at any other time remembered any of them ; and to whom, after he was born, they were never new. If anyone will say, there are ideas in the mind that are not in the memory, I desire him to explain himself, and make what he says intelligible.

21. *Principles not innate, because of little use or little certainty.*—Besides what I have already said, there is another reason why I doubt that neither these nor any other principles are innate. I that am fully persuaded that the infinitely wise God made all things in perfect wisdom, cannot satisfy myself why he should be supposed to print upon the minds of men some universal principles, whereof those that are pretended innate and concern speculation are of no great use, and those that concern practice not self-evident, and neither of them distinguishable from some other truths not allowed to be innate. For to what purpose should characters be graven on the mind by the finger of God, which are not clearer there than those which are afterwards introduced, or cannot be distinguished from them ? If anyone thinks there are such innate ideas and propositions, which by their clearness and usefulness are distinguishable from all that is adventitious in the mind and acquired, it will not be a hard matter for him to tell us which they are, and then everyone will be a fit judge whether they be so or no : since, if there be such innate ideas and impressions, plainly different from all other perceptions and knowledge, everyone will find it true in himself. Of the evidence of these supposed innate maxims I have spoken already ; of their usefulness I shall have occasion to speak more hereafter.

22. *Difference of men's discoveries depends upon the different application of their faculties.*—To conclude : some ideas forwardly offer themselves to all men's understandings ; some sorts of truths result from any ideas as soon as the mind puts them into propositions ; other truths require a train of ideas placed in order, a due comparing of them, and deductions made with attention, before they can be discovered and assented to. Some of the first sort, because of their general and easy reception, have been mistaken for innate ; but the truth is, ideas and notions are no more born with us than arts and sciences ; though some of them, indeed, offer themselves to our faculties more readily than others, and

therefore are more generally received; though that, too, be according as the organs of our bodies and powers of our minds happen to be employed; God having fitted men with faculties and means to discover, receive, and retain truths accordingly as they are employed. The great difference that is to be found in the notions of mankind is, from the different use they put their faculties to: whilst some (and those the most), taking things upon trust, misemploy their power of assent, by lazily enslaving their minds to the dictates and dominion of others, in doctrines which it is their duty carefully to examine, and not blindly, with an implicit faith, to swallow; others, employing their thoughts only about some few things, grow acquainted sufficiently with them, attain great degrees of knowledge in them, and are ignorant of all other, having never let their thoughts loose in the search of other inquiries. Thus, that the three angles of a triangle are equal to two right ones, is a truth as certain as anything can be, and I think more evident than many of those propositions that go for principles; and yet there are millions, however expert in other things, who know not this at all, because they never set their thoughts on work about such angles; and he that certainly knows this proposition may yet be utterly ignorant of the truth of other propositions in mathematics itself, which are as clear and evident as this, because, in his search of those mathematical truths, he stopped his thoughts short, and went not so far. The same may happen concerning the notions we have of the being of a Deity; for though there be no truth which a man may more evidently make out to himself than the existence of a God, yet he that shall content himself with things as he finds them in this world, as they minister to his pleasures and passions, and not make inquiry a little farther into their causes, ends, and admirable contrivances, and pursue the thoughts thereof with diligence and attention, may live long without any notion of such a Being: and if any person hath, by talk, put such a notion into his head, he may, perhaps, believe it; but if he hath never examined it, his knowledge of it will be no perfecter than his who, having been told that the three angles of a triangle are equal to two right ones, takes it upon trust, without examining the demonstration, and may yield his assent as a probable opinion, but hath no knowledge of the truth of it; which yet his faculties, if carefully employed, were able to make clear and evident to him. But this only by the by, to show how much our knowledge depends upon the right use of those powers nature hath bestowed upon us, and how little upon such innate principles as are in vain supposed to be in all mankind for their direction; which all men could not but know, if they were there, or else they would be there to no purpose; and which since all men do not know, nor can distinguish from other adventitious truths, we may well conclude there are no such.

**23.** *Men must think and know for themselves.*—What censure doubting thus of innate principles may deserve from men who will be apt to call it "pulling up the old foundations of knowledge and certainty," I cannot tell; I persuade myself, at least, that the way I have pursued, being conformable to truth, lays those foundations surer. This I am certain, I have not made it my business either to quit or follow any authority in the ensuing discourse: truth has been my only aim ; and wherever that has appeared to lead, my thoughts have impartially followed, without minding whether the footsteps of any other lay that way or no. Not that I want a due respect to other men's opinions; but, after all, the greatest reverence is due to truth; and I hope it will not be thought arrogance to say, that perhaps we should make greater progress in the discovery of rational and contemplative knowledge, if we sought it in the fountain, in the consideration of things themselves, and made use rather of our own thoughts than other men's to find it : for, I think, we may as rationally hope to see with other men's eyes as to know by other men's understandings. So much as we ourselves consider and comprehend of truth and reason, so much we possess of real and true knowledge. The floating of other men's opinions in our brains makes us not one jot the more knowing, though they happen to be true. What in them was science is in us but opiniatrety, whilst we give up our assent only to reverend names, and do not, as they did, employ our own reason to understand those truths which gave them reputation. Aristotle was certainly a knowing man; but nobody ever thought him so because he blindly embraced and confidently vented the opinions of another. And if the taking up of another's principles without examining them made not him a philosopher, I suppose it will hardly make anyone else so. In the sciences, everyone has so much as he really knows and comprehends; what he believes only, and takes upon trust, are but shreds; which, however well* in the whole piece, make no considerable addition to his stock who gathers them. Such borrowed wealth, like fairy money, though it'were gold in the hand from which he received it, will be but leaves and dust when it comes to use.

**24.** *Whence the opinion of innate principles.*—When men have found some general propositions that could not be doubted of as soon as understood, it was, I know, a short and easy way to conclude them innate. This being once received, it eased the lazy from the pains of search, and stopped the inquiry of the doubtful, concerning all that was once styled innate; and it was of no small advantage to those who affected to be masters and teachers, to make this the principle of principles,—that principles must not be questioned; for, having once established this tenet,—

---

* The fourth folio edition has this curious reading : "which, however, will, in the whole piece, make no," &c.—EDIT.

that there are innate principles, it put their followers upon a necessity of receiving some doctrines as such; which was to take them off from the use of their own reason and judgment, and put them upon believing and taking them upon trust, without farther examination; in which posture of blind credulity, they might be more easily governed by, and made useful to, some sort of men who had the skill and office to principle and guide them. Nor is it a small power it gives one man over another, to have the authority to be the dictator of principles, and teacher of unquestionable truths; and to make a man swallow that for an innate principle which may serve to his purpose who teacheth them. Whereas had they examined the ways whereby men came to the knowledge of many universal truths, they would have found them to result in the minds of men from the being of things themselves, when duly considered; and that they were discovered by the application of those faculties that were fitted by nature to receive and judge of them, when duly employed about them.

25. *Conclusion.*—To show how the understanding proceeds herein, is the design of the following discourse; which I shall proceed to, when I have first premised, that hitherto, to clear my way to those foundations which I conceive are the only true ones whereon to establish those notions we can have of our own knowledge, it hath been necessary for me to give an account of the reasons I had to doubt of innate principles: and since the arguments which are against them, do, some of them, rise from common received opinions, I have been forced to take several things for granted, which is hardly avoidable to anyone whose task it is to show the falsehood or improbability of any tenet; it happening in controversial discourses, as it does in assaulting of towns; where, if the ground be but firm whereon the batteries are erected, there is no further inquiry of whom it is borrowed, nor whom it belongs to, so it affords but a fit rise for the present purpose. But in the future part of this discourse, designing to raise an edifice uniform and consistent with itself, as far as my own experience and observation will assist me, I hope to erect it on such a basis, that I shall not need to shore it up with props and buttresses, leaning on borrowed or begged foundations; or, at least, if mine prove a castle in the air, I will endeavour it shall be all of a piece, and hang together. Wherein I warn the reader not to expect undeniable cogent demonstrations, unless I may be allowed the privilege, not seldom assumed by others, to take my principles for granted; and then, I doubt not, but I can demonstrate too. All that I shall say for the principles I proceed on, is, that I can only appeal to men's own unprejudiced experience and observation, whether they be true or no; and this is enough for a man who professes no more than to lay down candidly and freely his own conjectures concerning a

subject lying somewhat in the dark, without any other design than an unbiassed inquiry after truth.

---

## NOTE.—Page 45.

On this reasoning of the author against innate ideas, great blame hath been laid ; because it seems to invalidate an argument commonly used to prove the being of a God ; viz., universal consent ; to which our author answers :* " I think that the *universal consent* of mankind, as to the being of a God, amounts to thus much,—that the vastly greater majority of mankind have, in all ages of the world, actually believed a God ; that the majority of the remaining part have not actually disbelieved it ; and, consequently, those who have actually opposed the belief of a God have truly been very few. So that, comparing those that have actually disbelieved, with those who have actually believed, a God, their number is so inconsiderable, that, in respect of this incomparably greater majority of those who have owned the belief of a God, it may be said to be the universal consent of mankind.

" This is all the universal consent which truth or matter of fact will allow ; and therefore all that can be made use of to prove a God. But if anyone would extend it farther, and speak deceitfully for God ; if this universality should be urged in a strict sense, not for much the majority, but for a general consent of everyone, even to a man, in all ages and countries ; this would make it either no argument, or a perfectly useless and unnecessary one. For if anyone deny a God, such a perfect universality of consent is destroyed ; and if nobody does deny a God, what need of arguments to convince atheists ?

" I would crave leave to ask your lordship, Were there ever in the world any atheists or no ? If there were not, what need is there of raising a question about the being of a God, when nobody questions it ? What need of provisional arguments against a fault from which mankind are so wholly free ; and which, by an universal consent, they may be presumed to be secure from ? If you say (as I doubt not but you will), that there have been atheists in the world, then your lordship's universal consent reduces itself to only a great majority ; and then make that majority as great as you will, what I have said in the place quoted by your lordship leaves it in its full force ; and I have not said one word that does in the least 'invalidate this argument' for a God. The argument I was upon there, was to show that the idea of a God was not innate ; and to my purpose it was sufficient, if there were but a less number found in the world who had no idea of God, than your lordship will allow there have been of professed atheists ; for whatsoever is innate must be universal in the strictest sense : one exception is a sufficient proof against it. So that all that I said, and which was quite to another purpose, did not at all tend, nor can be made use of, to 'invalidate the argument' for a Deity, grounded on such an universal consent as your lordship, and all that build on it, must own ; which is only a very disproportioned majority : such an universal consent my argument there neither affirms nor requires to be less than you will

* In his Third Letter to the Bishop of Worcester, p. 447, &c.

be pleased to allow it.  Your lordship, therefore, might, without any
prejudice to those declarations of good-will and favour you have for
the author of the Essay of Human Understanding, have spared the
mentioning his quoting authors that are in print, for matters of fact, to
quite another purpose, 'as going about to invalidate the argument for
a Deity from the universal consent of mankind ;' since he leaves that
universal consent as entire and as large as you yourself do, or can own
or suppose it.  But here I ' have no reason to be sorry that' your lordship ' has given me this occasion for the vindication of this passage of
my book ;' if there should be anyone besides your lordship who should
so far mistake it, as to think it in the least 'invalidates the argument
for a God from the universal consent of mankind.'

"But, because you question the credibility of those authors I have
quoted, which, you say, 'were very ill chosen,' I will crave leave to say,
that he whom I relied on for his testimony concerning the Hottentots
of Soldania, was no less a man than an ambassador from the King of
England to the Great Mogul.  Of whose relation Monsieur Thevenot
(no ill judge in the case) has so great an esteem, that he was at the
pains to translate it into French, and publish it in his (which is
accounted no injudicious) Collection of Travels.  But to intercede with
your lordship for a little more favourable allowance of credit to Sir
Thomas Roe's relation : Coore, an inhabitant of the country, who
could speak English, assured Mr. Terry that they of Soldania had no
God.*  But if he, too, have the ill luck to find no credit with you, I
hope you will be a little more favourable to a divine of the church of
England, now living, and admit of his testimony in confirmation of Sir
Thomas Roe's.  This worthy gentleman, in the relation of his voyage
to Surat, printed but two years since, speaking of the same people, has
these words: ' They are sunk even below idolatry ; are destitute of both
priest and temple ; and, saving a little show of rejoicing, which is made
at the full and new moon, have lost all kinds of religious devotion.
Nature has so richly provided for their convenience in this life, that
they have drowned all sense of the God of it, and are grown quite
careless of the next.'†

"But, to provide against the clearest evidence of atheism in these
people, you say, that ' the account given of them makes them not fit
to be a standard for the sense of mankind.'  This, I think, may pass
for nothing, till somebody be found "that makes them to be a standard
for the sense of mankind.'  All the use I made of them was to show,
that there were men in the world that had no innate idea of a God.
But, to keep something like an argument going, (for what will not that
do ?) you go near denying those Caffers to be men.  What else do
these words signify ?—' A people so strangely bereft of common sense,
that they can hardly be reckoned among mankind ? as appears by the
best accounts of the Caffers of Soldania,' &c.  I hope if any of them
were called Peter, James, or John, it would be past scruple that they
were men : however Courwee, Wewena, and Cousheda, and those
others who had names that had no places in your nomenclator, would
hardly pass muster with your lordship.

"My lord, I should not mention this, but that what you yourself say
here may be a motive to you to consider, that what you have laid such

stress on, concerning 'the general nature of man,' as 'a real being,
and the subject of properties,' amounts to nothing for the distinguishing of species ; since you yourself own that there may be 'individuals
wherein there is a common nature, with a particular subsistence proper
to each of them,' whereby you are so little able to know of which of
the ranks or sorts they are, into which, you say, 'God has ordered
beings,' and which he 'hath distinguished by essential properties,'
that you are in doubt whether 'they ought to be reckoned among
mankind or no.'"

# BOOK II.

## CHAPTER I.

### OF IDEAS IN GENERAL, AND THEIR ORIGINAL.

**1.** *Idea is the object of thinking.*—Every man being conscious
to himself, that he thinks, and that which his mind is applied
about, whilst thinking, being the ideas that are there, it is past
doubt that men have in their mind several ideas, such as are
those expressed by the words, " whiteness, hardness, sweetness,
thinking, motion, man, elephant, army, drunkenness," and others.
It is in the first place then to be inquired, How he comes by
them ? I know it is a received doctrine, that men have native
ideas and original characters stamped upon their minds in their
very first being. This opinion I have at large examined already ;
and, I suppose, what I have said in the foregoing book will be
much more easily admitted, when I have shown whence the
understanding may get all the ideas it has, and by what ways and
degrees they may come into the mind ; for which I shall appeal
to every one's own observation and experience.

**2.** *All ideas come from sensation or reflection.*—Let us then
suppose the mind to be, as we say, white paper, void of all characters, without any ideas ; how comes it to be furnished ? Whence
comes it by that vast store, which the busy and boundless fancy
of man has painted on it with an almost endless variety ? Whence
has it all the materials of reason and knowledge ? To this I
answer, in one word, From experience : in that all our knowledge
is founded, and from that it ultimately derives itself. Our observation, employed either about external sensible objects, or
about the internal operations of our minds, perceived and reflected
on by ourselves, is that which supplies our understandings with
all the materials of thinking. These two are the fountains of
knowledge, from whence all the ideas we have, or can naturally
have, do spring.

**3.** *The object of sensation one source of ideas.*—First. Our
senses, conversant about particular sensible objects, do convey into
the mind several distinct perceptions of things, according to those

various ways wherein those objects do affect them ; and thus we
come by those ideas we have of yellow, white, heat, cold, soft,
hard, bitter, sweet, and all those which we call sensible qualities ;
which when I say the senses convey into the mind, I mean, they
from external objects convey into the mind what produces there
those perceptions. This great source of most of the ideas we have,
depending wholly upon our senses, and derived by them to the
understanding, I call " sensation."

4. *The operations of our minds the other source of them.*—
Secondly. The other fountain, from which experience furnisheth
the understanding with ideas, is the perception of the operations
of our own minds within us, as it is employed about the ideas it
has got ; which operations, when the soul comes to reflect on and
consider, do furnish the understanding with another set of ideas
which could not be had from things without ; and such are perception, thinking, doubting, believing, reasoning, knowing, willing,
and all the different actings of our own minds ; which we, being
conscious of, and observing in ourselves, do from these receive
into our understanding as distinct ideas, as we do from bodies
affecting our senses. This source of ideas every man has wholly
in himself ; and though it be not sense as having nothing to do
with external objects, yet it is very like it, and might properly
enough be called " internal sense." But as I call the other
" sensation," so I call this " reflection," the ideas it affords being
such only as the mind gets by reflecting on its own operations
within itself. By reflection, then, in the following part of this
discourse, I would be understood to mean that notice which the
mind takes of its own operations, and the manner of them, by
reason whereof there come to be ideas of these operations in the
understanding. These two, I say, viz., external material things
as the objects of sensation, and the operations of our own minds
within as the objects of reflection, are, to me, the only originals
from whence all our ideas take their beginnings. The term
" operations " here, I use in a large sense, as comprehending not
barely the actions of the mind about its ideas, but some sort of
passions arising sometimes from them, such as is the satisfaction
or uneasiness arising from any thought.

5. *All our ideas are of the one or the other of these.*—The understanding seems to me not to have the least glimmering of any
ideas which it doth not receive from one of these two. External
objects furnish the mind with the ideas of sensible qualities, which
are all those different perceptions they produce in us ; and the
mind furnishes the understanding with ideas of its own operations.

These, when we have taken a full survey of them, and their
several modes, combinations, and relations, we shall find to contain all our whole stock of ideas ; and that we have nothing in
our minds which did not come in one of these two ways. Let
any one examine his own thoughts, and thoroughly search into

his understanding, and then let him tell me, whether all the
original ideas he has there, are any other than of the objects of
his senses, or of the operations of his mind considered as objects
of his reflection; and how great a mass of knowledge soever he
imagines to be lodged there, he will, upon taking a strict view,
see that he has not any idea in his mind but what one of these
two hath imprinted, though perhaps with infinite variety compounded and enlarged by the understanding, as we shall see
hereafter.

6. *Observable in children.*—He that attentively considers the
state of a child at his first coming into the world, will have little
reason to think him stored with plenty of ideas that are to be the
matter of his future knowledge. It is by degrees he comes to be
furnished with them; and though the ideas of obvious and familiar
qualities imprint themselves before the memory begins to keep a
register of time and order, yet it is often so late before some
unusual qualities come in the way, that there are few men that
cannot recollect the beginning of their acquaintance with them;
and, if it were worth while, no doubt a child might be so ordered
as to have but a very few even of the ordinary ideas till he were
grown up to a man. But all that are born into the world being
surrounded with bodies that perpetually and diversely affect
them, variety of ideas whether care be taken about it, or no, are
imprinted on the minds of children. Light and colours are busy
at hand everywhere when the eye is but open; sounds and some
tangible qualities fail not to solicit their proper senses, and force
an entrance to the mind; but yet I think it will be granted easily,
that if a child were kept in a place where he never saw any other
but black and white till he were a man, he would have no more
ideas of scarlet or green, than he that from his childhood never
tasted an oyster or a pine-apple has of those particular relishes.

7. *Men are differently furnished with these according to the
different objects they converse with.*—Men then come to be furnished with fewer or more simple ideas from without, according
as the objects they converse with afford greater or less variety;
and from the operations of their minds within, according as they
more or less reflect on them. For, though he that contemplates
the operations of his mind cannot but have plain and clear ideas
of them; yet, unless he turn his thoughts that way, and considers
them attentively, he will no more have clear and distinct ideas
of all the operations of his mind, and all that may be observed
therein, than he will have all the particular ideas of any land-
scape, or of the parts and motions of a clock, who will not turn
his eyes to it, and with attention heed all the parts of it. The
picture or clock may be so placed that they may come in his
way every day; but yet he will have but a confused idea of all
the parts they are made of, till he applies himself with attention
to consider them each in particular.

**8. *Ideas of reflection later, because they need attention.*—And** hence we see the reason why it is pretty late before most children get ideas of the operations of their own minds; and some have not any very clear or perfect ideas of the greatest part of them all their lives:—because, though they pass there continually, yet like floating visions, they make not deep impressions enough to leave in the mind clear, distinct, lasting ideas, till the understanding turns inwards upon itself, reflects on its own operations, and makes them the object of its own contemplation. Children, when they come first into it, are surrounded with a world of new things, which, by a constant solicitation of their senses, draw the mind constantly to them, forward to take notice of new, and apt to be delighted with the variety of changing objects. Thus the first years are usually employed and diverted in looking abroad. Men's business in them is to acquaint themselves with what is to be found without; and so, growing up in a constant attention to outward sensations, seldom make any considerable reflection on what passes within them till they come to be of riper years; and some scarce ever at all.

**9. *The soul begins to have ideas when it begins to perceive.*—To** ask, at what time a man has first any ideas, is to ask when he begins to perceive; having ideas, and perception, being the same thing. I know it is an opinion, that the soul always thinks; and that it has the actual perception of ideas within itself constantly, as long as it exists; and that actual thinking is as inseparable from the soul, as actual extension is from the body: which, if true, to inquire after the beginning of a man's ideas is the same as to inquire after the beginning of his soul. For, by this account, soul and its ideas, as body and its extension, will begin to exist both at the same time.

**10. *The soul thinks not always; for this wants proofs.*—But** whether the soul be supposed to exist antecedent to, or coeval with, or some time after, the first rudiments or organization, or the beginnings of life in the body, I leave to be disputed by those who have better thought of that matter. I confess myself to have one of those dull souls that doth not perceive itself always to contemplate ideas; nor can conceive it any more necessary for the soul always to think, than for the body always to move; the perception of ideas being, as I conceive, to the soul, what motion is to the body; not its essence, but one of its operations; and, therefore, though thinking be supposed never so much the proper action of the soul, yet it is not necessary to suppose that it should be always thinking, always in action: that, perhaps, is the privilege of the infinite Author and Preserver of things, "who never slumbers nor sleeps;" but it is not competent to any finite being, at least not to the soul of man. We know certainly, by experience, that we sometimes think; and thence draw this infallible consequence,—that there is something in us that has a power to think; but whether that substance perpetually thinks, or no, we can be no farther assured than experience informs us. For to say that actual thinking is essential to the soul and inseparable from it, is to beg what is in question, and not to prove it by reason; which is necessary to be done, if it be not a self-evident proposition. But whether this—that " the soul always thinks," be a self-evident proposition, that everybody assents to on first hearing, I appeal to mankind. It is doubted whether I thought all last night, or no; the question being about a matter of fact, it is begging it to bring as a proof for it an hypothesis which is the very thing in dispute; by which way one may prove anything; and it is but supposing that all watches, whilst the balance beats, think, and it is sufficiently proved, and past doubt, that my watch thought all last night. But he that would not deceive himself ought to build his hypothesis on matter of fact, and make it out by sensible experience, and not presume on matter of fact because of his hypothesis; that is, because he supposes it to be so; which way of proving amounts to this,—that I must necessarily think all last night because another supposes I always think, though I myself cannot perceive that I always do so.

But men in love with their opinions may not only suppose what is in question, but allege wrong matter of fact. How else could anyone make it an inference of mine, that a thing is not, because we are not sensible of it in our sleep? I do not say there is no soul in a man because he is not sensible of it in his sleep; but I do say, he cannot think at any time, waking or sleeping, without being sensible of it. Our being sensible of it is not necessary to anything but to our thoughts; and to them it is, and to them it will always be, necessary, till we can think without being conscious of it.

11. *It is not always conscious of it.*—I grant that the soul in a waking man is never without thought, because it is the condition of being awake; but whether sleeping without dreaming be not an affection of the whole man, mind as well as body, may be worth a waking man's consideration; it being hard to conceive that any thing should think and not be conscious of it. If the soul doth think in a sleeping man without being conscious of it, I ask, whether, during such thinking, it has any pleasure or pain, or be capable of happiness or misery? I am sure the man is not, no more than the bed or earth he lies on. For to be happy or miserable without being conscious of it, seems to me utterly inconsistent and impossible. Or if it be possible that the soul can, whilst the body is sleeping, have its thinking, enjoyments, and concerns, its pleasure or pain, apart, which the man is not conscious of, nor partakes in, it is certain that Socrates asleep, and Socrates awake, is not the same person; but his soul when he sleeps, and Socrates the man, consisting of body and soul,

when he is waking, are two persons; since waking Socrates has no knowledge of, or concernment for that happiness or misery of his soul which it enjoys alone by itself whilst he sleeps, without perceiving anything of it, no more than he has for the happiness or misery of a man in the Indies, whom he knows not. For if we take wholly away all consciousness of our actions and sensations, especially of pleasure and pain, and the concernment that accompanies it, it will be hard to know wherein to place personal identity.

12. *If a sleeping man thinks without knowing it, the sleeping and waking man are two persons.*—"The soul, during sound sleep, thinks," say these men. Whilst it thinks and perceives, it is capable, certainly, of those of delight or trouble, as well as any other perceptions; and it must necessarily be conscious of its own perceptions. But it has all this apart. The sleeping man, it is plain, is conscious of nothing of all this. Let us suppose, then, the soul of Castor, whilst he is sleeping, retired from his body; which is no impossible supposition for the men I have here to do with, who so liberally allow life without a thinking soul to all other animals. These men cannot, then, judge it impossible, or a contradiction, that the body should live without the soul; nor that the soul should subsist and think, or have perception, even perception of happiness or misery, without the body. Let us, then, as I say, suppose the soul of Castor separated, during his sleep, from his body, to think apart. Let us suppose, too, that it chooses for its scene of thinking the body of another man, v. g. Pollux, who is sleeping without a soul: for if Castor's soul can think whilst Castor is asleep, what Castor is never conscious of, it is no matter what place it chooses to think in. We have here, then, the bodies of two men with only one soul between them, which we will suppose to sleep and wake by turns; and the soul still thinking in the waking man, whereof the sleeping man is never conscious, has never the least perception. I ask, then, whether Castor and Pollux, thus, with only one soul between them, which thinks and perceives in one what the other is never conscious of, nor is concerned for, are not two as distinct persons as Castor and Hercules, or as Socrates and Plato, were? and whether one of them might not be very happy and the other very miserable? Just by the same reason they make the soul and the man two persons, who make the soul think apart what the man is not conscious of. For, I suppose, nobody will make identity of persons to consist in the soul's being united to the very same numerical particles of matter; for if that be necessary to identity, it will be impossible, in that constant flux of the particles of our bodies, that any man should be the same person two days or two moments together.

13. *Impossible to convince those that sleep without dreaming that they think.*—Thus, methinks, every drowsy nod shakes their

doctrine who teach that their soul is always thinking. Those, at least, who do at any time sleep without dreaming can never be convinced that their thoughts are sometimes for hours busy without their knowing of it; and if they are taken in the very act, waked in the middle of that sleeping·contemplation, can give no manner of account of it.

14. *That men dream without remembering it, in vain urged.* —It will perhaps be said, that the soul thinks even in the soundest sleep, but the memory retains it not. That the soul in a sleeping man should be this moment busy a-thinking, and the next moment in a waking man not remember, nor be able to recollect one jot of all those thoughts, is very hard to be conceived, and would need some better proof than bare assertion to make it be believed. For who can without any more ado but being barely told so, imagine that the greatest part of men do, during all their lives, for several hours every day think of something which, if they were asked even in the middle of these thoughts, they could remember nothing at all of? Most men, I think, pass a great part of their sleep without dreaming. I once knew a man that was bred a scholar, and had no bad memory, who told me, he had never dreamed in his life till he had that fever he was then newly recovered of, which was about the five-or-six-and-twentieth year of his age. I suppose the world affords more such instances; at least, every one's acquaintance will furnish him with examples enough of such as pass most of their nights without dreaming.

15. *Upon this hypothesis, the thoughts of a sleeping man ought to be most rational.*—To think often and never to retain it so much as one moment, is a very useless sort of thinking; and the soul, in such a state of thinking, does very little if at all excel that of a looking-glass, which constantly receives a variety of images, or ideas, but retains none; they disappear and vanish, and there remain no footsteps of them; the looking-glass is never the better for such ideas, nor the soul for such thoughts. Perhaps it will be said, "that in a waking man the materials of the body are employed and made use of in thinking; and that the memory of thoughts is retained by the impressions that are made on the brain, and the traces there left after such thinking; but that in the thinking of the soul which is not perceived in a sleeping man, there the soul thinks apart, and, making no use of the organs of the body, leaves no impressions on it and consequently no memory of such thoughts." Not to mention again the absurdity of two distinct persons, which follows from this supposition, I answer farther, that whatever ideas the mind can receive and contemplate without the help of the body, it is reasonable to conclude it can retain without the help of the body too; or else the soul, or any separate spirit, will have but little advantage by thinking. If it has no memory of its own thoughts;

if it cannot lay them up for its use, and be able to recall them upon occasion; if it cannot reflect upon what is past, and make use of its former experiences, reasonings, and contemplations; to what purpose does it think? They who make the soul a thinking thing, at this rate will not make it a much more noble being than those do whom they condemn for allowing it to be nothing but the subtilest parts of matter. Characters drawn on dust that the first breath of wind effaces, or impressions made on a heap of atoms or animal spirits, are altogether as useful, and render the subject as noble, as the thoughts of a soul that perish in thinking; that, once out of sight, are gone for ever, and leave no memory of themselves behind them. Nature never makes excellent things for mean or no uses; and it is hardly to be conceived that our infinitely wise Creator should make so admirable a faculty as the power of thinking, that faculty which comes nearest the excellency of his own incomprehensible being, to be so idly and uselessly employed, at least a fourth part of its time here, as to think constantly without remembering any of those thoughts, without doing any good to itself or others, or being any way useful to any other part of the creation. If we will examine it, we shall not find, I suppose, the motion of dull and senseless matter anywhere in the universe made so little use of, and so wholly thrown away.

16. *On this hypothesis, the soul must have ideas not derived from sensation or reflection, of which there is no appearance.*— It is true, we have sometimes instances of perception whilst we are asleep, and retain the memory of those thoughts: but how extravagant and incoherent for the most part they are, how little conformable to the perfection and order of a rational being, those who are acquainted with dreams need not be told. This I would willingly be satisfied in: Whether the soul, when it thinks thus apart, and as it were separate from the body, acts less rationally than when conjointly with it, or no? If its separate thoughts be less rational, then these men must say that the soul owes the perfection of rational thinking to the body; if it does not, it is a wonder that our dreams should be for the most part so frivolous and irrational, and that the soul should retain none of its more ra ional soliloquies and meditations.

17. *If I think when I know it not, nobody else can know it.* —Those who so confidently tell us, that the soul always actually thinks, I would they would also tell us what those ideas are that are in the soul of a child before or just at the union with the body, before it hath received any by sensation. The dreams of sleeping men are, as I take it, all made up of the waking man's ideas, though for the most part oddly put together. It is strange, if the soul has ideas of its own that it derived not from sensation or reflection (as it must have, if it thought before it received any impression from the body), that it should never in

its private thinking (so private, that the man himself perceives
it not)), retain any of them the very moment it wakes out of
them, and then make the man glad with new discoveries. Who
can find it reasonable that the soul should in its retirement, during
sleep, have so many hours' thoughts, and yet never light on any
of those ideas it borrowed not from sensation or reflection, or at
least preserve the memory of none but such which, being occasioned from the body, must needs be less natural to a spirit?
It is strange the soul should never once in a man's whole life
recall over any of its pure, native thoughts, and those ideas it
had before it borrowed anything from the body; never bring
into the waking man's view any other ideas but what have a
tang of the cask, and manifestly derive their original from that
union. If it always thinks, and so had ideas before it was
united, or before it received any from the body, it is not to be
supposed but that during sleep it recollects its native ideas
and during that retirement from communicating with the body,
whilst it thinks by itself, the ideas it is busied about should be,
sometimes at least, those more natural and congenial ones which
it had in itself, underived from the body, or its own operations
about them; which since the waking man never remembers, we
must from this hypothesis conclude, either that the soul remembers something that the man does not, or else that memory
belongs only to such ideas as are derived from the body, or the
mind's operations about them.

18. *How knows anyone that the soul always thinks?  For if it
be not a self-evident proposition, it needs proof.*—I would be glad
also to learn from these men, who so confidently pronounce that
the human soul, or, which is all one, that a man, always thinks,
how they come to know it; nay, how they come to know that they
themselves think, when they themselves do not perceive it? This,
I am afraid, is to be sure without proofs, and to know without
perceiving. It is, I suspect, a confused notion taken up to serve
an hypothesis; and none of those clear truths that either their
own evidence forces us to admit, or common experience makes
it impudence to deny. For the most that can be said of it is,
that it is possible the soul may always think, but not always
retain it in memory; and I say, it is as possible that the soul
may not always think, and much more probable that it should
sometimes not think, than that it should often think, and that
a long while together, and not be conscious to itself, the next
moment after, that it had thought.

19. *That a man should be busy in thinking, and yet not retain it
the next moment, very improbable.*—To suppose the soul to think,
and the man not to perceive it, is, as has been said, to make two
persons in one man; and if one considers well these men's way of
speaking, one should be led into a suspicion that they do so. For
they who tell us that the soul always thinks, do never, that I

remember, say, that a man always thinks. Can the soul think, and not the man? or a man think, and not be conscious of it? This perhaps would be suspected of jargon in others. If they say, "The man thinks always, but is not always conscious of it," they may as well say, his body is extended without having parts. For it is altogether as intelligible to say, that a body is extended without parts, as that anything thinks without being conscious of it, or perceiving that it does so. They who talk thus may, with as much reason, if it be necessary to their hypothesis, say, that a man is always hungry, but that he does not always feel it: whereas hunger consists in that very sensation, as thinking consists in being conscious that one thinks. If they say, that a man is always conscious to himself of thinking, I ask how they know it? Consciousness is the perception of what passes in a man's own mind. Can another man perceive that I am conscious of any thing, when I perceive it not myself? No man's knowledge here can go beyond his experience. Wake a man out of a sound sleep, and ask him what he was that moment thinking on. If he himself be conscious of nothing he then thought on, he must be a notable diviner of thoughts that can assure him that he was thinking: may he not with more reason assure him he was not asleep? This is something beyond philosophy; and it cannot be less than revelation that discovers to another thoughts in my mind when I can find none there myself: and they must needs have a penetrating sight who can certainly see that I think, when I cannot perceive it myself, and when I declare that I do not; and yet can see that dogs or elephants do not think, when they give all the demonstration of it imaginable, except only telling us that they do so. This some may suspect to be a step beyond the Rosicrucians; it seeming easier to make one's self invisible to others than to make another's thoughts visible to me, which are not visible to himself. But it is but defining the soul to be a substance that always thinks, and the business is done. If such definition be of any authority, I know not what it can serve for, but to make many men suspect that they have no souls at all, since they find a good part of their lives pass away without thinking. For no definitions that I know, no suppositions of any sect, are of force enough to destroy constant experience; and perhaps it is the affectation of knowing beyond what we perceive that makes so much useless dispute and noise in the world.

20. *No ideas but from sensation or reflection evident, if we observe children.*—I see no reason therefore to believe that the soul thinks before the senses have furnished it with ideas to think on; and as those are increased and retained, so it comes by exercise to improve its faculty of thinking in the several parts of it; as well as afterwards, by compounding those ideas and reflecting on its own operations, it increases its stock, as well as

facility in remembering, imagining, reasoning, and other modes of thinking.

21. He that will suffer himself to be informed by observation and experience, and not make his own hypothesis the rule of nature, will find few signs of a soul accustomed to much thinking in a new-born child, and much fewer of any reasoning at all. And yet it is hard to imagine, that the rational soul should think so much and not reason at all.  And he that will consider that infants newly come into the world, spend the greatest part of their time in sleep, and are seldom awake, but when either hunger calls for the teat, or some pain (the most importunate of all sensations), or some other violent impression on the body, forces the mind to perceive and attend to it:—he, I say, who considers this will, perhaps, find reason to imagine, that a fœtus in the mother's womb differs not much from the state of a vegetable ; but passes the greatest part of its time without perception or thought, doing very little but sleep in a place where it needs not seek for food, and is surrounded with liquor always equally soft, and near of the same temper; where the eyes have no light, and the ears so shut up are not very susceptible of sounds ; and where there is little or no variety or change of objects to move the senses.

22. Follow a child from its birth, and observe the alterations that time makes, and you shall find, as the mind by the senses comes more and more to be furnished with ideas, it comes to be more and more awake, thinks more the more it has matter to think on.  After some time it begins to know the objects which, being most familiar with it, have made lasting impressions. Thus it comes by degrees to know the persons it daily converses with, and distinguish them from strangers; which are instances and effects of its coming to retain and distinguish the ideas the senses convey to it : and so we may observe how the mind, by degrees, improves in these, and advances to the exercise of those other faculties of enlarging, compounding, and abstracting its ideas, and of reasoning about them, and reflecting upon all these ; of which I shall have occasion to speak more hereafter.

23. If it shall be demanded, then, when a man begins to have any ideas ? I think, the true answer is, When he first has any sensation.  For since there appear not to be any ideas in the mind before the senses have conveyed any in, I conceive that ideas in the understanding are coeval with sensation; which is such an impression or motion made in some part of the body as produces some perception in the understanding.  It is about these impressions made on our senses by outward objects, that the mind seems first to employ itself in such operations as we call " perception, remembering, consideration, reasoning," &c.

24. *The original of all our knowledge.*—In time the mind comes to reflect on its own operations about the ideas got by sensation,

and thereby stores itself with a new set of ideas, which I call
"ideas of reflection." These are the impressions that are made
on our senses by outward objects, that are extrinsical to the
mind; and its own operations, proceeding from powers intrinsical
and proper to itself, which, when reflected on by itself, become
also objects of its contemplation, are, as I have said, the original
of all knowledge. Thus the first capacity of human intellect is,
that the mind is fitted to receive the impressions made on it,
either through the senses by outward objects, or by its own
operations when it reflects on them. This is the first step a man
makes towards the discovery of anything, and the ground-work
whereon to build all those notions which ever he shall have
naturally in this world. All those sublime thoughts which tower
above the clouds, and reach as high as heaven itself, take their
rise and footing here : in all that great extent wherein the mind
wanders in those remote speculations it may seem to be elevated
with, it stirs not one jot beyond those ideas which sense or reflection have offered for its contemplation.

25. *In the reception of simple ideas, the understanding is for
the most part passive.*—In this part the understanding is merely
passive ; and whether or no it will have these beginnings and, as
it were, materials of knowledge, is not in its own power. For the
objects of our senses do many of them obtrude their particular
ideas upon our minds, whether we will or no ; and the operations
of our minds will not let us be without at least some obscure
notions of them. No man can be wholly ignorant of what he
does when he thinks. These simple ideas, when offered to the
mind, the understanding can no more refuse to have, nor alter
when they are imprinted, nor blot them out and make new ones
itself, than a mirror can refuse, alter or obliterate the images or
ideas, which the objects set before it do therein produce. As
the bodies that surround us do diversely affect our organs, the
mind is forced to receive the impressions, and cannot avoid the
perception of those ideas that are annexed to them.

## CHAPTER II.

### OF SIMPLE IDEAS.

1. *Uncompounded appearances.*—The better to understand the
nature, manner, and extent of our knowledge, one thing is carefully to be observed concerning the ideas we have ; and that is,
that some of them are simple, and some complex.

Though the qualities that affect our senses are, in the things
themselves, so united and blended that there is no separation, no
distance between them ; yet it is plain the ideas they produce in
the mind enter by the senses simple and unmixed. For though
the sight and touch often take in from the same object at the

same time different ideas—as a man sees at once motion and colour, the hand feels softness and warmth in the same piece of wax—yet the simple ideas thus united in the same subject are as perfectly distinct as those that come in by different senses; the coldness and hardness which a man feels in a piece of ice being as distinct ideas in the mind as the smell and whiteness of a lily, or as the taste of sugar and smell of a rose: and there is nothing can be plainer to a man than the clear and distinct perception he has of those simple ideas; which, being each in itself uncompounded, contains in it nothing but one uniform appearance or conception in the mind, and is not distinguishable into different ideas.

2. *The mind can neither make nor destroy them.*—These simple ideas, the materials of all our knowledge, are suggested and furnished to the mind only by those two ways above mentioned, viz., sensation and reflection.* When the understanding is once stored with these simple ideas, it has the power to repeat, compare, and unite them, even to an almost infinite variety, and so can make at pleasure new complex ideas. But it is not in the power of the most exalted wit or enlarged understanding, by any quickness or variety of thoughts, to invent or frame one new simple idea in the mind, not taken in by the ways before mentioned; nor can any force of the understanding destroy those that are there: the dominion of man in this little world of his own understanding, being much-what the same as it is in the great world of visible things, wherein his power, however managed by art and skill, reaches no farther than to compound and divide the materials that are made to his hand but can do nothing towards the making the least particle of new matter, or destroying one atom of what is already in being. The same inability will everyone find in himself, who shall go about to fashion in his understanding any simple idea not received in by his senses from external objects, or by reflection from the operations of his own mind about them. I would have anyone try to fancy any taste which had never affected his palate, or frame the idea of a scent he had never smelt; and when he can do this, I will also conclude, that a blind man hath *ideas* of colours, and a deaf man true, distinct notions of sounds.

8. This is the reason why, though we cannot believe it impossible to God to make a creature with other organs, and more ways to convey into the understanding the notice of corporeal things than those five as they are usually counted, which he has given to man; yet I think it is not possible for anyone to imagine any other qualities in bodies, howsoever constituted, whereby they can be taken notice of, besides sounds, tastes, smells, visible and tangible qualities. And had mankind been made with but four senses, the qualities then which are the objects of the fifth sense, had been

* See the Note at the end of this chapter, p. 72.—EDIT.

as far from our notice, imagination, and conception, as now any
belonging to a sixth, seventh, or eighth sense, can possibly be:
which, whether yet some other creatures, in some other parts of
this vast and stupendous universe, may not have, will be a great
presumption to deny. He that will not set himself proudly at the
top of all things, but will consider the immensity of this fabric,
and the great variety that is to be found in this little and inconsiderable part of it which he has to do with, may be apt to think,
that in other mansions of it there may be other and different intelligible beings, of whose faculties he has as little knowledge or
apprehension, as a worm shut up in one drawer of a cabinet hath
of the senses or understanding of a man; such variety and excellency being suitable to the wisdom and power of the Maker. I
have here followed the common opinion of man's having but five
senses, though perhaps there may be justly counted more; but
either supposition serves equally to my present purpose.

---

### NOTE.—Page 71.

AGAINST this—that the materials of all our knowledge are suggested
and furnished to the mind only by sensation and reflection, the Bishop
of Worcester makes use of the idea of substance in these words : " If
the idea of substance be grounded upon plain and evident reason, then
we must allow an idea of substance which comes not in by sensation
or reflection; so we may be certain of something which we have not
by those ideas."

To which our author answers :* "These words of your lordship's
contain nothing that I see in them against me; for I never said, that
the general idea of substance comes in by sensation and reflection, or
that it is a simple idea of sensation or reflection, though it be ultimately founded in them; for it is a complex idea made up of the
general idea of some thing or being with the relation of a support to
accidents. For general ideas come not into the mind by sensation or
reflection, but are the creatures or inventions of the understanding, as
I think I have shown ;† and also how the mind makes them from
ideas which it has got by sensation and reflection; and as to the ideas
of relation, how the mind forms them, and how they are derived from,
and ultimately terminate in, ideas of sensation and reflection, I have
likewise shown.

"But that I may not be mistaken what I mean when I speak of
ideas of sensation and reflection as the materials of all our knowledge, give me leave, my lord, to set down here a place or two out of
my book to explain myself; as I thus speak of ideas of sensation and
reflection :

"That these, when we have taken a full survey of them and their
several modes, and the compositions made out of them, we shall find
to contain all our whole stock of ideas, and we have nothing in our

---

* In his First Letter to the Bishop of Worcester, p. 85, &c.
† Book iii. chap. iii. ; book ii. chap. xxv. &c. xxviii. sect. 18.

minds which did not come in one of those two ways.'* This thought
in another place I express thus :

"'These simple ideas, the materials of all our knowledge, are suggested and furnished to the mind, only by those two ways above mentioned, viz., sensation and reflection.'† And again,

"'These are the most considerable of those simple ideas which
the mind has, and out of which is made all its other knowledge ; all
which it receives by the two fore-mentioned ways of sensation and
reflection.'‡ And,

"'Thus I have in a short draught given a view of our original
ideas, from whence all the rest are derived, and of which they are
made up.'§

"This and the like, said in other places, is what I have thought
concerning ideas of sensation and reflection, as the foundation and
materials of all our ideas, and consequently of all our knowledge :
I have set down these particulars out of my book, that the reader,
having a full view of my opinion herein, may the better see what in
it is liable to your lordship's reprehension.  For that your lordship is
not very well satisfied with it, appears not only by the words under
consideration, but by these also : 'But we are still told that our
understanding can have no other ideas but either from sensation or
reflection.'

"Your lordship's argument, in the passage we are upon, stands thus :
'If the general idea of substance be grounded upon plain and evident
reason, then we must allow an idea of substance which comes not in
by sensation or reflection.'  This is a consequence which, with submission, I think will not hold, because it is founded upon a supposition
which I think will not hold ; viz. that reason and ideas are inconsistent : for if that supposition be not true, then the general idea of
substance may be grounded on plain and evident reason ; and yet it
will not follow from thence that it is not ultimately grounded on and
derived from ideas 'which come in by sensation or reflection,' and so
cannot be said to come in by sensation or reflection.

"To explain myself, and clear my meaning in this matter.  All the
ideas of all the sensible qualities of a cherry come into my mind by
sensation ; the ideas of perceiving, thinking, reasoning, knowing, &c.,
come into my mind by reflection.  The ideas of these qualities and
actions or powers are perceived by the mind to be by themselves
inconsistent with existence ; or, as your lordship well expresses it,
'we find that we can have no true conception of any modes or accidents, but we must conceive a substratum or subject wherein they are;'
*i.e.*, that they cannot exist or subsist of themselves.  Hence the mind
perceives the necessary connection with inherence or being supported,
which being a relative idea superadded to the red colour in a cherry,
or to thinking in a man, the mind frames the correlative idea of a support.  For I never denied that the mind could frame to itself ideas of
relation, but have showed the quite contrary in my chapters about
relation.  But because a relation cannot be founded in nothing, or be
the relation of nothing, and the thing here related as a supporter or
a support is not represented to the mind by any clear and distinct

* Book ii. chap. i. sect. 5.    † Book ii. chap. ii. sect. 2.
‡ Book ii. chap. vii. sect. 10.    § Book ii. chap. xxi. sect. 73.

idea, therefore the obscure, indistinct, vague idea of thing or something is all that is left to be the positive idea which has the relation of a support or substratum to modes or accidents ; and that general, indetermined idea of something is, by the abstraction of the mind, derived also from the simple ideas of sensation and reflection : and thus the mind, from the positive, simple ideas got by sensation and reflection, comes to the general, relative idea of substance, which, without these positive, simple ideas, it would never have.

"This your lordship (without giving by retail all the particular steps of the mind in this business) has well expressed in this more familiar way : 'We find we can have no true conception of any modes or accidents, but we must conceive a substratum or subject wherein they are ; since it is a repugnancy to our conceptions of things, that modes or accidents should subsist by themselves.'

" Hence your lordship calls it 'the rational idea of substance ;' and says, 'I grant that by sensation and reflection we come to know the powers and properties of things ; but our reason is satisfied that there must be something beyond these, because it is impossible that they should subsist by themselves ;' so that if this be that which your lordship means by 'the rational idea of substance,' I see nothing there is in it against what I have said, that it is founded on simple ideas of sensation or reflection, and that it is a very obscure idea.

" Your lordship's conclusion from your foregoing words is, 'And so we may be certain of some things which we have not by those ideas ;' which is a proposition whose precise meaning your lordship will forgive me if I profess, as it stands there, I do not understand. For it is uncertain to me whether your lordship means, we may certainly know the existence of something 'which we have not by those ideas,' or certainly know the distinct properties of something 'which we have not by those ideas,' or certainly know the truth of some proposition 'which we have not by those ideas ;' for to be certain of something may signify either of these : but in whichsoever of these it be meant I do not see how I am concerned in it."

## CHAPTER III.

### OF IDEAS OF ONE SENSE.

1. *Division of simple ideas.*—The better to conceive the ideas we receive from sensation, it may not be amiss for us to consider them in reference to the different ways whereby they make their approaches to our minds, and make themselves perceivable by us.

First, then, there are some which come into our minds by one sense only.

Secondly. There are others that convey themselves into the mind by more senses than one.

Thirdly. Others that are had from reflection only.

Fourthly. There are some that make themselves way, and are suggested to the mind, by all the ways of sensation and reflection.

We shall consider them apart under these several heads.

1. There are some ideas which have admittance only through one sense, which is peculiarly adapted to receive them. Thus light and colours, as white, red, yellow, blue, with their several degrees or shades and mixtures, as green, scarlet, purple, sea-green, and the rest, come in only by the eyes; all kinds of noises, sounds, and tones, only by the ears; the several tastes and smells, by the nose and palate. And if these organs, or the nerves which are the conduits to convey them from without to their audience in the brain, the mind's presence-room, (as I may so call it,) are, any of them, so disordered as not to perform their functions, they have no postern to be admitted by, no other way to bring themselves into view, and be received by the understanding.

The most considerable of those belonging to the touch are heat, and cold, and solidity; all the rest – consisting almost wholly in the sensible configuration, as smooth and rough; or else more or less firm adhesion of the parts, as hard and soft, tough and brittle—are obvious enough.

2. I think it will be needless to enumerate all the particular simple ideas belonging to each sense. Nor indeed is it possible if we would, there being a great many more of them belonging to most of the senses than we have names for. The variety of smells, which are as many almost, if not more, than species of bodies in the world, do most of them want names. *Sweet* and *stinking* commonly serve our turn for these ideas, which in effect is little more than to call them pleasing or displeasing; though the smell of a rose and violet, both sweet, are certainly very distinct ideas. Nor are the different tastes that by our palates we receive ideas of, much better provided with names. *Sweet, bitter, sour, harsh,* and *salt,* are almost all the epithets we have to denominate that numberless variety of relishes which are to be found distinct, not only in almost every sort of creatures, but in the different parts of the same plant, fruit, or animal. The same may be said of colours and sounds. I shall therefore, in the account of simple ideas I am here giving, content myself to set down only such as are most material to our present purpose, or are in themselves less apt to be taken notice of, though they are very frequently the ingredients of our complex ideas; amongst which I think I may well account " solidity," which therefore I shall treat of in the next chapter.

## CHAPTER IV

### OF SOLIDITY.

**1. *We receive this idea from touch*.**—The idea of solidity we receive by our touch; and it arises from the resistance which we find in body to the entrance of any other body into the place it possesses, till it has left it. There is no idea which we receive more constantly from sensation than solidity. Whether we move or rest, in what posture soever we are, we always feel something under us that supports us, and hinders our farther sinking downwards; and the bodies which we daily handle make us perceive that whilst they remain between them, they do, by an insurmountable force, hinder the approach of the parts of our hands that press them. That which thus hinders the approach of two bodies, when they are moving one towards another, I call "solidity." I will not dispute whether this acceptation of the word "solid" be nearer to its original signification than that which mathematicians use it in; it suffic s that, I think, the common notion of "solidity," will allow, if not justify, this use of it; but if anyone think it better to call it "impenetrability," he has my consent. Only I have thought the term "solidity" the more proper to express this idea, not only because of its vulgar use in that sense, but also because it carries something more of positive in it than "impenetrability," which is negative, and is perhaps, more a consequence of solidity than solidity itself. This, of all other, seems the idea most intimately connected with and essential to body, so as nowhere else to be found or imagined but only in matter; and though our senses take no notice of it but in masses of matter, of a bulk sufficient to cause a sensation in us; yet the mind, having once got this idea from such grosser sensible bodies, traces it farther and considers it, as well as figure, in the minutest particle of matter that can exist, and finds it inseparably inherent in body, wherever or however modified.

**2. *Solidity fills space*.**—This is the idea belongs to body, whereby we conceive it to fill space. The idea of which filling of space is, that where we imagine any space taken up by a solid substance, we conceive it so to possess it that it excludes all other solid substances, and will for ever hinder any two other bodies, that move towards one another in a straight line, from coming to touch one another, unless it removes from between them in a line not parallel to that which they move in. This idea of it, the bodies which we ordinary handle sufficiently furnish us with.

**3. *Distinct from space*.**—This resistance, whereby it keeps

other bodies out of the space which it possesses, is so great
that no force, how great soever, can surmount it. All the
bodies in the world, pressing a drop of water on all sides, will
never be able to overcome the resistance which it will make,
as soft as it is, to their approaching one another, till it
be removed out of their way : whereby our idea of solidity is
distinguished both from pure space, which is capable neither
of resistance nor motion, and from the ordinary idea of
hardness. For a man may conceive two bodies at a distance
so as they may approach one another without touching or displacing any solid thing till their superficies come to meet;
whereby, I think, we have the clear idea of space without
solidity. For, (not to go so far as annihilation of any particular
body,) I ask, whether a man cannot have the idea of the motion
of one single body alone, without any other succeeding immediately into its place ? I think it is evident he can : the idea
of motion in one body no more including the idea of motion in
another, than the idea of a square figure in one body includes
the idea of a square figure in another. I do not ask, whether
bodies do so exist, that the motion of one body cannot really
be without the motion of another ? To determine this either
way is to beg the question for or against a *vacuum*. But
my question is, whether one cannot have the idea of one body
moved, whilst others are at rest ? And I think this no one will
deny : if so, then the place it deserted gives us the idea of
pure space without solidity, whereinto another body may
enter without either resistance or protrusion of anything.
When the sucker in a pump is drawn, the space it filled in the
tube is certainly the same, whether any other body follows the
motion of the sucker or no : nor does it imply a contradiction
that upon the motion of one body, another that is only contiguous
to it should not follow it. The necessity of such a motion is
built only on the supposition, that the world is full, but not on
the distinct ideas of space and solidity ; which are as different
as resistance and not-resistance, protrusion and not-protrusion.
And that men have ideas of space without body, their very disputes about a *vacuum* plainly demonstrate, as is showed in
another place. As,

4. *From hardness.*—Solidity is hereby also differenced from
hardness, in that solidity consists in repletion, and so an utter
exclusion of other bodies out of the space it possesses ; but
hardness, in a firm cohesion of the parts of matter, making up
masses of a sensible bulk, so that the whole does not easily
change its figure. And, indeed, *hard* and *soft* are names that
we give to things only in relation to the constitutions of our
own bodies ; that being generally called " hard " by us which
will put us to pain sooner than change figure by the pressure of
any part of our bodies : and that, on the contrary, " soft " which

changes the situation of its parts upon an easy and unpainful
touch.

But this difficulty of changing the situation of the sensible
parts amongst themselves, or of the figure of the whole, gives
no more solidity to the hardest body in the world than to the
softest; nor is an adamant one jot more solid than water. For
though the two flat sides of two pieces of marble will more
easily approach each other, between which there is nothing but
water or air, than if there be a diamond between them; yet it
is not that the parts of the diamond are more solid than those
of water, or resist more, but because the parts of water being
more easily separable from each other, they will by a side-motion
be more easily removed and give way to the approach of two
pieces of marble : but if they could be kept from making place
by that side-motion, they would eternally hinder the approach of
these two pieces of marble as much as the diamond ; and it
would be as impossible by any force to surmount their resistance,
as to surmount the resistance of the parts of a diamond. The
softest body in the world will as invincibly resist the coming
together of any two other bodies, if it be not put out of the way,
but remain between them, as the hardest that can be found or
imagined. He that shall fill a yielding soft body well with air
or water will quickly find its resistance : and he that thinks that
nothing but bodies that are hard can keep his hands from approaching one another, may be pleased to make a trial with the air
enclosed in a foot-ball. The experiment I have been told was
made at Florence, with a hollow globe of gold filled with water,
and exactly closed, farther shows the solidity of so soft a body
as water. For, the golden globe thus filled being put into a
press which was driven by the extreme force of screws, the
water made itself way through the pores of that very close
metal, and, finding no room for a nearer approach of its particles
within, got to the outside, where it rose like a dew, and so fell
in drops before the sides of the globe could be made to yield to
the violent compression of the engine that squeezed it.

5. *On solidity depends impulse, resistance, and protrusion.*—
By this idea of solidity is the extension of body distinguished from
the extension of space : the extension of body being nothing but
the cohesion or continuity of solid, separable, movable parts ;
and the extension of space, the continuity of unsolid, inseparable, and immovable parts. Upon the solidity of bodies also
depends their mutual impulse, resistance, and protrusion. Of
pure space, then, and solidity, there are several (amongst which
I confess myself one) who persuade themselves they have clear
and distinct ideas : and that they can think on space without anything in it that resists or is protruded by body. This is the idea
of pure space, which they think they have as clear as any idea
they can have of the extension of body ; the idea of the distance

between the opposite parts of a concave superficies being equally
as clear without as with the idea of any solid parts between;
and on the other side they persuade themselves that they have,
distinct from that of pure space, the idea of something that fills
space, that can be protruded by the impulse of other bodies, or
resist their motion. If there be others that have not these two
ideas distinct, but confound them, and make but one of them, I
know not how men who have the same idea under different
names, or different ideas under the same name, can in that case
talk with one another, any more than a man who, not being
blind or deaf, has distinct ideas of the colour of scarlet and the
sound of a trumpet, would discourse concerning scarlet-colour
with the blind man I mention in another place, who fancied that
the idea of scarlet was like the sound of a trumpet.

6. *What it is.*—If anyone asks me, what this solidity is, I send
him to his senses to inform him: let him put a flint or a foot-
ball between his hands, and then endeavour to join them, and he
will know. If he thinks this not a sufficient explanation of solidity,
what it is, and wherein it consists, I promise to tell him what it is,
and wherein it consists, when he tells me what thinking is, or
wherein it consists; or explains to me what extension or motion
is, which perhaps seems much easier. The simple ideas we have
are such as experience teaches them us; but if, beyond that, we
endeavour by words to make them clearer in the mind, we shall
succeed no better than if we went about to clear up the darkness
of a blind man's mind by talking, and to discourse into him the
ideas of light and colour. The reason of this I shall show in
another place.

## CHAPTER V.

### OF SIMPLE IDEAS OF DIVERS SENSES.

THE ideas we get by more than one sense are of space or extension, figure, rest and motion: for these make perceivable
impressions both on the eyes and touch ; and we can receive and
convey into our minds the ideas of our extension, figure, motion,
and rest of bodies, both by seeing and feeling. But having
occasion to speak more at large of these in another place, I here
only enumerate them.

## CHAPTER VI.

### OF SIMPLE IDEAS OF REFLECTION.

**1.** *Simple ideas of reflection are the operations of the mind about its other ideas.*—The mind, receiving the ideas mentioned in the foregoing chapters from without, when it turns its view inward upon itself, and observes its own actions about those ideas it has, takes from thence other ideas, which are as capable to be the objects of its contemplation as any of those it received from foreign things.

**2.** *The idea of perception, and idea of willing, we have from reflection.*—The two great and principal actions of the mind, which are most frequently considered, and which are so frequent that everyone that pleases may take notice of them in himself, are these two: perception or thinking, and volition or willing. The power of thinking is called "the understanding," and the power of volition is called "the will;" and these two powers or abilities in the mind are denominated "faculties." Of some of the modes of these simple ideas of reflection, such as are remembrance, discerning, reasoning, judging, knowledge, faith, &c., I shall have occasion to speak hereafter.

## CHAPTER VII.

### OF SIMPLE IDEAS OF BOTH SENSATION AND REFLECTION.

**1.** *Pleasure and pain.*—There be other simple ideas which convey themselves into the mind by all the ways of sensation and reflection; viz., pleasure or delight, and its opposite, pain or uneasiness; power, existence, unity.

**2.** Delight or uneasiness, one or other of them, join themselves to almost all our ideas both of sensation and reflection; and there is scarce any affection of our senses from without, any retired thought of our mind within, which is not able to produce in us pleasure or pain. By "pleasure" and "pain," I would be understood to signify whatsoever delights or molests us; whether it arises from the thoughts of our minds, or anything operating on our bodies. For whether we call it "satisfaction, delight, pleasure, happiness," &c., on the one side; or "uneasiness, trouble, pain, torment, anguish, misery," &c., on the other; they are still but different degrees of the same thing, and belong to the ideas of pleasure and pain, delight or uneasiness; which are the names I shall most commonly use for those two sorts of ideas.

**3.** The infinitely wise Author of our being—having given us the power over several parts of our bodies. to move or keep them at rest as we think fit, and also by the motion of them to move ourselves and other* contiguous bodies, in which consist all the actions of † body; having also given a power to our minds, in several instances, to choose amongst its ideas which it will think on, and to pursue the inquiry of this or that subject with consideration and attention—to excite us to these actions of thinking and motion that we are capable of, has been pleased to join to several thoughts and several sensations a perception of *delight*. If this were wholly separated from all our outward sensations and inward thoughts, we should have no reason to prefer one thought or action to another, negligence to attention, or motion to rest: and so we should neither stir our bodies, nor employ our minds; but let our thoughts (if I may so call it) run adrift, without any direction or design; and suffer the ideas of our minds, like unregarded shadows, to make their appearances there as it happened, without attending to them : in which state man, however furnished with the faculties of understanding and will, would be a very idle, unactive creature, and pass his time only in a lazy, lethargic dream. It has therefore pleased our wise Creator to annex to several objects, and to the ideas which we receive from them, as also to several of our thoughts, a concomitant pleasure, and that in several objects to several degrees, that those faculties which he had endowed us with might not remain wholly idle and unemployed by us.

4. *Pain* has the same efficacy and use to set us on work that pleasure has, we being as ready to employ our faculties to avoid that, as to pursue this: only this is worth our consideration—that pain is often produced by the same objects and ideas that produce pleasure in us. This their near conjunction, which makes us often feel pain in the sensations where we expected pleasure, gives us new occasion of admiring the wisdom and goodness of our Maker, who, designing the preservation of our being, has annexed pain to the application of many things to our bodies, to warn us of the harm that they will do, and as advices to withdraw from them. But He, not designing our preservation barely, but the preservation of every part and organ in its perfection, hath in many cases annexed pain to those very ideas which delight us. Thus heat, that is very agreeable to us in one degree, by a little greater increase of it proves no ordinary torment; and the most pleasant of all sensible objects, light itself, if there be too much of it, if increased beyond a due proportion to our eyes, causes a very painful sensation : which is wisely and favourably so ordered by nature, that when any object does by the vehemency of its operation disorder the instruments of sensation, whose structures cannot but be very nice and delicate, we might by the pain be

* The sixth and ninth editions 8vo, have *our* instead of *other;* the latter being the reading of the fourth edition, in folio.—EDIT.

† This is the reading of the sixth. Many of the later editions erroneously insert *our* before "body."—EDIT.

warned to withdraw before the organ be quite put out of order, and so be unfitted for its proper functions for the future. The consideration of those objects that produce it may well persuade us, that this is the end or use of pain; for though great light be insufferable to our eyes, yet the highest degree of darkness does not at all disease them, because the causing no disorderly motion in it leaves that curious organ unharmed in its natural state. But yet excess of cold as well as heat pains us because it is equally destructive to that temper which is necessary to the preservation of life, and the exercise of the several functions of the body, and which consists in a moderate degree of warmth, or, if you please, a motion of the insensible parts of our bodies confined within certain bounds.

5. Beyond all this, we may find another reason why God hath scattered up and down several degrees of pleasure and pain in all the things that environ and affect us, and blended them together in almost all that our thoughts and senses have to do with; that we, finding imperfection, dissatisfaction, and want of complete happiness in all the enjoyments which the creatures can afford us, might be led to seek it in the enjoyment of Him " with whom there is fulness of joy, and at whose right hand are pleasures for evermore."

6. *Pleasure and pain.*—Though what I have here said may not perhaps make the ideas of pleasure and pain clearer to us than our own experience does, which is the only way that we are capable of having them; yet the consideration of the reason why they are annexed to so many other ideas, serving to give us due sentiments of the wisdom and goodness of the Sovereign Disposer of all things, may not be unsuitable to the main end of these inquiries: the knowledge and veneration of Him being the chief end of all our thoughts, and the proper business of all our understandings.

7. *Existence and unity.*—Existence and unity are two other ideas that are suggested to the understanding by every object without, and every idea within. When ideas are in our minds, we consider them as being actually there, as well as we consider things to be actually without us: which is, that they exist, or have existence: and whatever we can consider as one thing, whether a real being or idea, suggests to the understanding the idea of unity.

8. *Power.*—Power also is another of those simple ideas which we receive from sensation and reflection. For, observing in ourselves that we can at pleasure move several parts of our bodies which were at rest, the effects also that natural bodies are able to produce in one another occurring every moment to our senses, we both these ways get the idea of power.

9. *Succession.*—Besides these there is another idea, which though suggested by our senses yet is more constantly offered

us by what passes in our own minds; and that is the idea of succession. For if we look immediately into ourselves, and reflect on what is observable there, we shall find our ideas always, whilst we are awake or have any thought, passing in train, one going and another coming without intermission.

10. *Simple ideas the materials of all our knowledge.*—These, if they are not all, are at least (as I think) the most considerable of those simple ideas which the mind has, and out of which is made all its other knowledge : all of which it receives only by the two fore-mentioned ways of sensation and reflection.

Nor let anyone think these too narrow bounds for the capacious mind of man to expatiate in, which takes its flight farther than the stars, and cannot be confined by the limits of the world; that extends its thoughts often even beyond the utmost expansion of matter, and makes excursions into that incomprehensible inane. I grant all this; but desire anyone to assign any simple idea which is not received from one of those inlets before mentioned, or any complex idea not made out of those simple ones. Nor will it be so strange to think these few simple ideas sufficient to employ the quickest thought or largest capacity, and to furnish the materials of all that various knowledge and more various fancies and opinions of all mankind, if we consider how many words may be made out of the various composition of twenty-four letters; or if, going one step farther, we will but reflect on the variety of combinations may be made with barely one of the above-mentioned ideas, viz., number, whose stock is inexhaustible and truly infinite ; and what a large and immense field doth extension alone afford the mathematicians !

## CHAPTER VIII.

### SOME FARTHER CONSIDERATIONS CONCERNING OUR SIMPLE IDEAS.

1. *Positive ideas from privative causes.*—Concerning the simple ideas of sensation it is to be considered, that whatsoever is so constituted in nature as to be able by affecting our senses to cause any perception in the mind, doth thereby produce in the understanding a simple idea; which, whatever be the external cause of it, when it comes to be taken notice of by our discerning faculty, it is by the mind looked on and considered there to be a real positive idea in the understanding, as much as any other whatsoever; though perhaps the cause of it be but a privation in the subject.

2. Thus the ideas of heat and cold, light and darkness, white and black, motion and rest, are equally clear and positive ideas in the mind; though perhaps some of the causes which produce them are barely privations in those subjects from whence our

senses derive those ideas. These the understanding, in its view
of them, considers all as distinct positive ideas without taking
notice of the causes that produce them; which is an inquiry
not belonging to the idea as it is in the understanding, but
to the nature of the thing existing without us. These are
two very different things, and carefully to be distinguished; it
being one thing to perceive and know the idea of white or black,
and quite another to examine what kind of particles they must
be, and how ranged in the superficies, to make any object appear
white or black.

8. A painter or dyer who never inquired into their causes,
hath the ideas of white and black and other colours as clearly,
perfectly, and distinctly in his understanding, and perhaps more
distinctly than the philosopher who hath busied himself in considering their natures, and thinks he knows how far either of
them is in its cause positive or privative; and the idea of black
is no less positive in his mind than that of white, however the
cause of that colour in the external object may be only a privation.

4. If it were the design of my present undertaking to inquire
into the natural causes and manner of perception, I should offer
this as a reason why a privative cause might, in some cases at
least, produce a positive idea, viz., that all sensation being produced in us only by different degrees and modes of motion in our
animal spirits, variously agitated by external objects, the abatement of any former motion must as necessarily produce a new
sensation as the variation or increase of it; and so introduce a
new idea, which depends only on a different motion of the animal
spirits in that organ.

5. But whether this be so or no I will not here determine, but
appeal to everyone's own experience, whether the shadow of a
man, though it consists of nothing but the absence of light (and
the more the absence of light is, the more discernible is the
shadow), does not, when a man looks on it, cause as clear and
positive an idea in his mind as a man himself, though covered
over with clear sunshine! And the picture of a shadow is a
positive thing. Indeed, we have negative names, which stand
not directly for positive ideas, but for their absence, such as
*insipid, silence, nihil,* &c., which words denote positive ideas,
*v. g., taste, sound, being,* with a signification of their absence.

6. *Positive ideas from privative causes.*—And thus one may
truly be said to see darkness. For, supposing a hole perfectly
dark, from whence no light is reflected, it is certain one may see
the figure of it, or it may be painted; or whether the ink I
write with make any other idea, is a question. The privative
causes I have here assigned of positive ideas are according to
the common opinion; but, in truth, it will be hard to determine
whether there be really any ideas from a privative cause, till

It be determined whether rest be any more a privation than motion.

7. *Ideas in the mind, qualities in bodies.*—To discover the nature of our ideas the better, and to discourse of them intelligibly, it will be convenient to distinguish them, as they are ideas or perceptions in our minds, and as they are modifications of matter in the bodies that cause such perceptions in us; that so we may not think (as perhaps usually is done) that they are exactly the images and resemblances of something inherent in the subject; most of those of sensation being in the mind no more the likeness of something existing without us than the names that stand for them are the likeness of our ideas, which yet upon hearing they are apt to excite in us.

8. Whatsoever the mind perceives in itself, or is the immediate object of perception, thought, or understanding, that I call "idea"; and the power to produce any idea in our mind, I call "quality" of the subject wherein that power is. Thus a snowball having the power to produce in us the ideas of white, cold, and round, the powers to produce those ideas in us as they are in the snowball, I call "qualities"; and as they are sensations or perceptions in our understandings, I call them "ideas"; which ideas, if I speak of them sometimes as in the things themselves, I would be understood to mean those qualities in the objects which produce them in us.

9. *Primary qualities.*—Qualities thus considered in bodies are, First, such as are utterly inseparable from the body, in what estate soever it be; such as, in all the alterations and changes it suffers, all the force can be used upon it, it constantly keeps; and such as sense constantly finds in every particle of matter which has bulk enough to be perceived, and the mind finds inseparable from every particle of matter, though less than to make itself singly be perceived by our senses; *v.g.*, take a grain of wheat, divide it into two parts, each part has still solidity, extension, figure, and mobility; divide it again, and it retains still the same qualities: and so divide it on till the parts become insensible, they must retain still each of them all those qualities. For, division (which is all that a mill or pestle or any other body does upon another, in reducing it to insensible parts) can never take away either solidity, extension, figure, or mobility from any body, but only makes two or more distinct separate masses of matter of that which was but one before; all which distinct masses, reckoned as so many distinct bodies, after division, make a certain number. These I call *original* or *primary* qualities of body, which I think we may observe to produce simple ideas in us, viz., solidity, extension, figure, motion or rest, and number.

10. *Secondary qualities.* Secondly. Such qualities, which in truth are nothing in the objects themselves, but powers to produce various sensations in us by their primary qualities, *i.e.*, by

the bulk, figure, texture, and motion of their insensible parts, as colours, sounds, tastes, &c., these I call *secondary* qualities. To these might be added a third sort, which are allowed to be barely powers, though they are as much real qualities in the subject as those which I, to comply with the common way of speaking, call qualities, but, for distinction, *secondary* qualities. For, the power in fire to produce a new colour or consistence in wax or clay by its primary qualities, is as much a quality in fire as the power it has to produce in me a new idea or sensation of warmth or burning, which I felt not before, by the same primary qualities, viz., the bulk, texture, and motion of its insensible parts.

11. *How primary qualities produce their ideas.*—The next thing to be considered is, how bodies produce ideas in us; and that is manifestly by impulse, the only way which we can conceive bodies operate in.

12. If, then, external objects be not united to our minds when they produce ideas in it, and yet we perceive these original qualities in such of them as singly fall under our senses, it is evident that some motion must be thence continued by our nerves or animal spirits, by some parts of our bodies, to the brain or the seat of sensation, there to produce in our minds the particular ideas we have of them. And since the extension, figure, number, and motion of bodies of an observable bigness, may be perceived at a distance by the sight, it is evident some singly imperceptible bodies must come from them to the eyes, and thereby convey to the brain some motion which produces these ideas which we have of them in us.

13. *How secondary.*—After the same manner that the ideas of these original qualities are produced in us, we may conceive that the ideas of secondary qualities are also produced, viz., by the operation of insensible particles on our senses. For it being manifest that there are bodies, and good store of bodies, each whereof are so small that we cannot by any of our senses discover either their bulk, figure, or motion (as is evident in the particles of the air and water, and other extremely smaller than those, perhaps as much smaller than the particles of air or water as the particles of air or water are smaller than pease or hailstones): let us suppose at present that the different motions and figures, bulk and number, of such particles, affecting the several organs of our senses, produce in us those different sensations which we have from the colours and smells of bodies, *v.g.*, that a violet, by the impulse of such insensible particles of matter of peculiar figures and bulks, and in different degrees and modifications of their motions, causes the ideas of the blue colour and sweet scent of that flower to be produced in our minds; it being no more impossible to conceive that God should annex such ideas to such motions with which they have no similitude, than that he should annex the idea of pain to the

motion of a piece of steel dividing our flesh, with which that idea hath no resemblance.

14. What I have said concerning colours and smells may be understood also of tastes and sounds, and other the like sensible qualities; which, whatever reality we by mistake attribute to them, are in truth nothing in the objects themselves, but powers to produce various sensations in us, and depend on those primary qualities, viz., bulk, figure, texture, and motion of parts, as I have said.

15. *Ideas of primary qualities are resemblances; of secondary, not.*—From whence I think it is easy to draw this observation, that the ideas of primary qualities of bodies are resemblances of them, and their patterns do really exist in the bodies themselves; but the ideas produced in us by these secondary qualities have no resemblance of them at all. There is nothing like our ideas existing in the bodies themselves. They are, in the bodies we denominate from them, only a power to produce those sensations in us; and what is sweet, blue, or warm in idea, is but the certain bulk, figure, and motion of the insensible parts in the bodies themselves, which we call so.

16. Flame is denominated *hot* and *light*; snow, *white* and *cold*; and manna, *white* and *sweet*, from the ideas they produce in us, which qualities are commonly thought to be the same in those bodies that those ideas are in us, the one the perfect resemblance of the other, as they are in a mirror; and it would by most men be judged very extravagant, if one should say otherwise. And yet he that will consider that the same fire that at one distance produces in us the sensation of warmth, does at a nearer approach produce in us the far different sensation of pain, ought to bethink himself what reason he has to say, that his idea of warmth which was produced in him by the fire, is actually in the fire, and his idea of pain which the same fire produced in him the same way is not in the fire. Why is whiteness and coldness in snow and pain not, when it produces the one and the other idea in us, and can do neither but by the bulk, figure, number, and motion of its solid parts?

17. The particular bulk, number, figure, and motion of the parts of fire or snow are really in them, whether anyone's senses perceive them or no; and therefore they may be called *real* qualities, because they really exist in those bodies. But light, heat, whiteness, or coldness, are no more really in them than sickness or pain is in manna. Take away the sensation of them; let not the eyes see light or colours, nor the ears hear sounds; let the palate not taste, nor the nose smell; and all colours, tastes, odours and sounds, as they are such particular ideas, vanish and cease, and are reduced to their causes, *i.e.*, bulk, figure, and motion of parts.

18. A piece of manna of a sensible bulk is able to produce in

us the idea of a round or square figure; and, by being removed
from one place to another, the idea of motion. This idea of
motion represents it as it really is in the manna moving; a
circle or square are the same, whether in idea or existence, in
the mind or in the manna; and this both motion and figure are
really in the manna, whether we take notice of them or no: this
everybody is ready to agree to. Besides, manna, by the bulk,
figure, texture, and motion of its parts, has a power to produce
the sensations of sickness, and sometimes of acute pains or grip-
ings, in us. That these ideas of sickness and pain are not in the
manna, but effects of its operations on us, and are nowhere when
we feel them not; this also everyone readily agrees to. And
yet men are hardly to be brought to think that sweetness and
whiteness are not really in manna, which are but the effects of
the operations of manna by the motion, size, and figure of its
particles on the eyes and palate; as the pain and sickness caused
by manna, are confessedly nothing but the effects of its operations on the stomach and guts by the size, motion, and figure of
its insensible parts (for by nothing else can a body operate, as has
been proved); as if it could not operate on the eyes and palate,
and thereby produce in the mind particular distinct ideas which
in itself it has not, as well as we allow it can operate on the guts
and stomach, and thereby produce distinct ideas which in itself
it has not. These ideas being all effects of the operations of
manna on several parts of our bodies, by the size, figure, number,
and motion of its parts, why those produced by the eyes and
palate should rather be thought to be really in the manna than
those produced by the stomach and guts: or why the pain and
sickness, ideas that are the effects of manna, should be thought
to be nowhere when they are not felt; and yet the sweetness
and whiteness, effects of the same manna on other parts of the
body, by ways equally as unknown, should be thought to exist
in the manna, when they are not seen nor tasted; would need
some reason to explain.

19. *Ideas of primary qualities are resemblances; of secondary, not.*—Let us consider the red and white colours in porphyry;
hinder light but from striking on it, and its colours vanish; it no
longer produces any such ideas in us. Upon the return of light,
it produces these appearances on us again. Can anyone think
any real alterations are made in the porphyry by the presence
or absence of light, and that those ideas of whiteness and redness are really in porphyry in the light, when it is plain it has
no colour in the dark? It has indeed such a configuration of
particles, both night and day, as are apt, by the rays of light
rebounding from some parts of that hard stone, to produce in us
the idea of redness, and from others the idea of whiteness. But
whiteness or redness are not in it at any time, but such a texture
that hath the power to produce such a sensation in us.

20. Pound an almond, and the clear white colour will be altered into a dirty one, and the sweet taste into an oily one. What real alteration can the beating of the pestle make in any body, but an alteration of the texture of it?

21. Ideas being thus distinguished and understood, we may be able to give an account how the same water, at the same time, may produce the idea of cold by one hand, and of heat by the other; whereas it is impossible that the same water, if those ideas were really in it, should at the same time be both hot and cold. For if we imagine warmth as it is in our hands, to be nothing but a certain sort and degree of motion in the minute particles of our nerves or animal spirits, we may understand how it is possible that the same water may at the same time produce the sensation of heat in one hand, and cold in the other; which yet figure never does, that never producing the idea of a square by one hand which has produced the idea of a globe by another. But if the sensation of heat and cold be nothing but the increase or diminution of the motion of the minute parts of our bodies, caused by the corpuscles of any other body, it is easy to be understood that if that motion be greater in one hand than in the other, if a body be applied to the two hands, which has in its minute particles a greater motion than in those of one of the hands and a less than in those of the other, it will increase the motion of the one hand, and lessen it in the other, and so cause the different sensations of heat and cold that depend thereon.

22. I have, in what just goes before, been engaged in physical inquiries a little farther than perhaps I intended. But it being necessary to make the nature of sensation a little understood, and to make the difference between the qualities in bodies and the ideas produced by them in the mind to be distinctly conceived, without which it were impossible to discourse intelligibly of them, I hope I shall be pardoned this little excursion into natural philosophy, it being necessary in our present inquiry to distinguish the primary and real qualities of bodies, which are always in them, (viz., solidity, extension, figure, number, and motion or rest, and are sometimes perceived by us, viz., when the bodies they are in are big enough singly to be discerned,) from those secondary and imputed qualities, which are but the powers of several combinations of those primary ones, when they operate without being distinctly discerned; whereby we also may come to know what ideas are, and what are not, resemblances of something really existing in the bodies we denominate from them.

23. *Three sorts of qualities in bodies.*—The qualities then that are in bodies, rightly considered, are of three sorts:

First. The bulk, figure, number, situation, and motion or rest of their solid parts; those are in them, whether we perceive them or no; and when they are of that size that we can discover them, we have by these an idea of the thing as it is in itself, as is plain in artificial things. These I call *primary* qualities.

Secondly. The power that is in any body by reason of its insensible primary qualities, to operate after a peculiar manner on any of our senses, and thereby produce in us the different ideas of several colours, sounds, smells, tastes, &c. These are usually called *sensible* qualities.

Thirdly. The power that is in any body, by reason of the particular constitution of its primary qualities, to make such a change in the bulk, figure, texture, and motion of another body, as to make it operate on our senses differently from what it did before. Thus the sun has a power to make wax white, and fire, to make lead fluid. These are usually called "powers."

The first of these, as has been said, I think may be properly called real, original, or primary qualities, because they are in the things themselves, whether they are perceived or no; and upon their different modifications it is that the secondary qualities depend.

The other two are only powers to act differently upon other things, which powers result from the different modifications of those primary qualities.

24. *The first are resemblances; the second thought resemblances, but are not; the third neither are, nor are thought so.*—But though these two latter sorts of qualities are powers barely, and nothing but powers, relating to several other bodies, and resulting from the different modifications of the original qualities, yet they are generally otherwise thought of. For the second sort, viz., the powers to produce several ideas in us by our senses, are looked upon as real qualities in the things thus affecting us; but the third sort are called and esteemed barely powers. *V. g.*, the idea of heat or light which we receive by our eyes or touch from the sun, are commonly thought real qualities existing in the sun, and something more than mere powers in it. But when we consider the sun in reference to wax, which it melts or blanches, we look upon the whiteness and softness produced in the wax, not as qualities in the sun, but effects produced by powers in it: whereas, if rightly considered, these qualities of light and warmth, which are perceptions in me when I am warmed or enlightened by the sun, are no otherwise in the sun than the changes made in the wax, when it is blanched or melted, are in the sun. They are all of them equally powers in the sun, depending on its primary qualities, whereby it is able in the one case so to alter the bulk, figure, texture, or motion of some of the insensible parts of my eyes or hands as thereby to produce in me the idea of light or heat, and in the other it is able so to alter the bulk, figure, texture, or motion of the insensible parts of the wax as to make them fit to produce in me the distinct ideas of white and fluid.

25. The reason why the one are ordinarily taken for real quali-

ties, and the other only for bare powers, seems to be because the ideas we have of distinct colours, sounds, &c., containing nothing at all in them of bulk, figure, or motion, we are not apt to think them the effects of these primary qualities which appear not to our senses to operate in their production, and with which they have not any apparent congruity, or conceivable connexion. Hence it is that we are so forward to imagine that those ideas are the resemblances of something really existing in the objects themselves, since sensation discovers nothing of bulk, figure, or motion of parts, in their production, nor can reason show how bodies by their bulk, figure, and motion, should produce in the mind the ideas of blue or yellow, &c. But, in the other case, in the operations of bodies changing the qualities one of another, we plainly discover that the quality produced hath commonly no resemblance with anything in the thing producing it; wherefore we look on it as a bare effect of power. For though, receiving the idea of heat or light from the sun, we are apt to think it is a perception and resemblance of such a quality in the sun, yet when we see wax or a fair face receive change of colour from the sun, we cannot imagine that to be the perception or resemblance of anything in the sun, because we find not those different colours in the sun itself: for, our senses being able to observe a likeness or unlikeness of sensible qualities in two different external objects, we forwardly enough conclude the production of any sensible quality in any subject to be an effect of bare power, and not the communication of any quality which was really in the efficient, when we find no such sensible quality in the thing that produced it. But our senses not being able to discover any unlikeness between the idea produced in us and the quality of the object producing it, we are apt to imagine that our ideas are resemblances of something in the objects, and not the effects of certain powers placed in the modification of their primary qualities, with which primary qualities the ideas produced in us have no resemblance.

26. *Secondary qualities twofold: first, immediately perceivable; secondly, mediately perceivable.*—To conclude: Besides those before-mentioned primary qualities in bodies, viz., bulk, figure, extension, number, and motion of their solid parts, all the rest whereby we take notice of bodies, and distinguish them one from another, are nothing else but several powers in them depending on those primary qualities, whereby they are fitted, either by immediately operating on our bodies, to produce several different ideas in us; or else by operating on other bodies, so to change their primary qualities as to render them capable of producing ideas in us different from what before they did. The former of these, I think, may be called secondary qualities immediately perceivable; the latter, secondary qualities mediately perceivable.

## CHAPTER IX.

### OF PERCEPTION.

**1.** *Perception the first simple idea of reflection.*—Perception, as it is the first faculty of the mind exercised about our ideas, so it is the first and simplest idea we have from reflection, and is by some called " thinking " in general. Though thinking, in the propriety of the English tongue, signifies that sort of operation of the mind about its ideas wherein the mind is active ; where it, with some degree of voluntary attention, considers anything : for in bare, naked perception, the mind is, for the most part, only passive, and what it perceives it cannot avoid perceiving.

**2.** *Is only when the mind receives the impression.*—What perception is, everyone will know better by reflecting on what he does himself, when he sees, hears, feels, &c., or thinks, than by any discourse of mine. Whoever reflects on what passes in his own mind, cannot miss it ; and if he does not reflect, all the words in the world cannot make him have any notion of it.

**3.** This is certain, that whatever alterations are made in the body, if they reach not the mind ; whatever impressions are made on the outward parts, if they are not taken notice of within ; there is no perception. Fire may burn our bodies with no other effect than it does a billet, unless the motion be continued to the brain, and there the sense of heat or idea of pain be produced in the mind, wherein consists actual perception.

**4.** How often may a man observe in himself, that whilst his mind is intently employed in the contemplation of some objects, and curiously surveying some ideas that are there, it takes no notice of impressions of sounding bodies made upon the organ of hearing with the same alteration that uses to be for the producing the idea of sound ! A sufficient impulse there may be on the organ ; but it not reaching the observation of the mind, there follows no perception : and though the motion that uses to produce the idea of sound be made in the ear, yet no sound is heard. Want of sensation in this case is not through any defect in the organ, or that the man's ears are less affected than at other times when he does hear : but that which uses to produce the idea, though conveyed in by the usual organ, not being taken notice of in the understanding, and so imprinting no idea on the mind, there follows no sensation. So that wherever there is sense or perception, there some idea is actually produced, and present in the understanding.

**5.** *Children, though they have ideas in the womb, have none innate.*—Therefore, I doubt not but children, by the exercise of their senses about objects that affect them in the womb, receive

some few ideas before they are born, as the unavoidable effects
either of the bodies that environ them, or else of those wants or
diseases they suffer; amongst which (if one may conjecture concerning things not very capable of examination) I think the ideas
of hunger and warmth are two, which probably are some of the
first that children have, and which they scarce ever part with
again.

6. But though it be reasonable to imagine that children receive
some ideas before they come into the world, yet these simple ideas
are far from those innate principles which some contend for, and
we above have rejected. These here mentioned, being the effects
of sensation, are only from some affections of the body which
happen to them there, and so depend on something exterior to the
mind; no otherwise differing in their manner of production from
other ideas derived from sense, but only in the precedency of
time; whereas those innate principles are supposed to be quite
of another nature, not coming into the mind by any accidental
alterations in or operations on the body; but, as it were, original
characters impressed upon it in the very first moment of its
being and constitution.

7. *Which ideas first, is not evident.*—As there are some ideas
which we may reasonably suppose may be introduced into the
minds of children in the womb, subservient to the necessities of
their life and being there; so after they are born those ideas are
the earliest imprinted which happen to be the sensible qualities
which first occur to them: amongst which, light is not the least
considerable, nor of the weakest efficacy. And how covetous the
mind is to be furnished with all such ideas as have no pain
accompanying them, may be a little guessed by what is observable in children new born, who always turn their eyes to
that part from whence the light comes, lay them how you please.
But the ideas that are most familiar at first being various,
according to the divers circumstances of children's first entertainment in the world, the order wherein the several ideas come
at first into the mind is very various and uncertain also, neither
is it much material to know it.

8. *Ideas of sensation often changed by the judgment.*—We
are farther to consider concerning perception, that the ideas we
receive by sensation are often in grown people altered by the
judgment without our taking notice of it. When we set before
our eyes a round globe of any uniform colour, *v.g.*, gold, alabaster,
or jet, it is certain that the idea thereby imprinted in our mind
is of a flat circle variously shadowed, with several degrees of
light and brightness coming to our eyes. But we having by use
been accustomed to perceive what kind of appearance convex
bodies are wont to make in us, what alterations are made in the
reflections of light by the difference of the sensible figures of
bodies, the judgment presently, by an habitual custom, alters the

appearances into their causes: so that, from that which truly is variety of shadow or colour collecting the figure, it makes it pass for a mark of figure, and frames to itself the perception of a convex figure and an uniform colour ; when the idea we receive from thence is only a plane variously coloured, as is evident in painting. To which purpose I shall here insert a problem of that very ingenious and studious promoter of real knowledge, the learned and worthy Mr. Molineux, which he was pleased to send me in a letter some months since: and it is this : " Suppose a man born blind, and now adult, and taught by his touch to distinguish between a cube and a sphere of the same metal, and nighly of the same bigness, so as to tell, when he felt one and the other, which is the cube, which the sphere. Suppose then the cube and sphere placed on a table, and the blind man to be made to see; query, Whether by his sight, before he touched them, he could now distinguish and tell which is the globe, which the cube ?" To which the acute and judicious proposer answers : "Not. For though he has obtained the experience of how a globe, how a cube, affects his touch ; yet he has not yet attained the experience, that what affects his touch so or so, must affect his sight so or so ; or that a protuberant angle in the cube, that pressed his hand unequally, shall appear to his eye as it does in the cube." I agree with this thinking gentleman, whom I am proud to call my friend, in his answer to this his problem ; and am of opinion, that the blind man, at first sight, would not be able with certainty to say which was the globe, which the cube, whilst he only saw them ; though he could unerringly name them by his touch, and certainly distinguish them by the difference of their figures felt. This I have set down, and leave with my reader, as an occasion for him to consider how much he may be beholden to experience, improvement, and acquired notions, where he thinks he has not the least use or help from them ; and the rather, because this observing gentleman farther adds, that having upon the occasion of my book proposed this to divers very ingenious men, he hardly ever met with one that at first gave the answer to it which he thinks true, till by hearing his reasons they were convinced.

9. But this is not, I think, usual in any of our ideas but those received by sight ; because sight, the most comprehensive of all our senses, conveying to our minds the ideas of light and colours, which are peculiar only to that sense ; and also the far different ideas of space, figure and motion, the several varieties whereof change the appearances of its proper objects, viz., light and colours ; we bring ourselves by use to judge of the one by the other. This, in many cases, by a settled habit in things whereof we have frequent experience, is performed so constantly and so quick, that we take that for the perception of our sensation which is an idea formed by our judgment ; so that one, viz., that

of sensation, serves only to excite the other, and is scarce taken notice of itself; as a man who reads or hears with attention and understanding, takes little notice of the characters or sounds, but of the ideas that are excited in him by them.

10. Nor need we wonder that this is done with so little notice, if we consider how very quick the actions of the mind are performed: for as itself is thought to take up no space, to have no extension, so its actions seem to require no time, but many of them seem to be crowded into an instant. I speak this in comparison to the actions of the body. Anyone may easily observe this in his own thoughts who will take the pains to reflect on them. How, as it were in an instant, do our minds with one glance see all the parts of a demonstration, which may very well be called a long one, if we consider the time it will require to put it into words, and step by step show it another! Secondly. We shall not be so much surprised that this is done in us with so little notice, if we consider how the facility which we get of doing things, by a custom of doing, makes them often pass in us without our notice. Habits, especially such as are begun very early, come at last to produce actions in us which often escape our observation. How frequently do we in a day cover our eyes with our eye-lids, without perceiving that we are at all in the dark! Men, that by custom have got the use of a by-word, do almost in every sentence pronounce sounds which, though taken notice of by others, they themselves neither hear nor observe. And therefore it is not so strange that our mind should often change the idea of its sensation into that of its judgment, and make one serve only to excite the other, without our taking notice of it.

11. *Perception puts the difference between animals and inferior beings.*—This faculty of perception seems to me to be that which puts the distinction betwixt the animal kingdom and the inferior parts of nature. For however vegetables have, many of them, some degrees of motion, and, upon the different application of other bodies to them, do very briskly alter their figures and motions, and so have obtained the name of "sensitive plants" from a motion which has some resemblance to that which in animals follows upon sensation; yet I suppose it is all bare mechanism, and no otherwise produced than the turning of a wild oat-beard by the insinuation of the particles of moisture, or the shortening of a rope by the affusion of water. All which is done without any sensation in the subject, or the having or receiving any ideas.

12. Perception, I believe, is in some degree in all sorts of animals; though in some possibly the avenues provided by nature for the reception of sensations are so few, and the perception they are received with so obscure and dull, that it comes extremely short of the quickness and variety of sensations which

is in other animals : but yet it is sufficient for and wisely adapted
to the state and condition of that sort of animals who are thus
made; so that the wisdom and goodness of the Maker plainly
appears in all the parts of this stupendous fabric, and all the
several degrees and ranks of creatures in it.

13. We may, I think, from the make of an oyster or cockle,
reasonably conclude that it has not so many nor so quick senses
as a man, or several other animals; nor, if it had, would it, in
that state and incapacity of transferring itself from one place to
another, be bettered by them. What good would sight and
hearing do to a creature that cannot move itself to or from the
objects wherein at a distance it perceives good or evil? And
would not quickness of sensation be an inconvenience to an
animal that must lie still where chance has once placed it, and
there receive the afflux of colder or warmer, clean or foul, water,
as it happens to come to it?

14. But yet I cannot but think there is some small dull perception whereby they are distinguished from perfect insensibility.
And that this may be so, we have plain instances even in mankind itself. Take one in whom decrepit old age has blotted out
the memory of his past knowledge, and clearly wiped out the
ideas his mind was formerly stored with; and has, by destroying
his sight, hearing, and smell quite, and his taste to a great degree,
stopped up almost all the passages for new ones to enter; or if
there be some of the inlets yet half open, the impressions made
are scarce perceived, or not at all retained. How far such an
one (notwithstanding all that is boasted of innate principles) is
in his knowledge and intellectual faculties above the condition
of a cockle or an oyster, I leave to be considered. And if a man
had passed sixty years in such a state, as it is possible he might
as well as three days, I wonder what difference there would have
been, in any intellectual perfections, between him and the lowest
degree of animals.

15. *Perception the inlet of knowledge.*—Perception, then, being
the first step and degree towards knowledge, and the inlet of
all the materials of it, the fewer senses any man as well as any
other creature hath, and the fewer and duller the impressions
are that are made by them, and the duller the faculties are that
are employed about them, the more remote are they from that
knowledge which is to be found in some men. But this, being
in great variety of degrees (as may be perceived amongst men),
cannot certainly be discovered in the several species of animals,
much less in their particular individuals. It suffices me only to
have remarked here, that perception is the first operation of all
our intellectual faculties, and the inlet of all knowledge into our
minds. And I am apt, too, to imagine that it is perception in
the lowest degree of it which puts the boundaries between
animals and the inferior ranks of creatures. But this I mention

only as my conjecture by the by, it being indifferent to the matter in hand which way the learned shall determine of it.

---

## CHAPTER X.

### OF RETENTION.

**1.** *Contemplation.*—The next faculty of the mind, whereby it makes a farther progress towards knowledge, is that which I call retention or the keeping of those simple ideas which from sensation or reflection it hath received. This is done two ways. First, by keeping the idea which is brought into it for some time actually in view, which is called contemplation.

**2.** *Memory.*—The other way of retention is the power to revive again in our minds those ideas which after imprinting have disappeared, or have been as it were laid aside out of sight; and thus we do, when we conceive heat or light, yellow or sweet, the object being removed. This is memory, which is, as it were, the storehouse of our ideas. For the narrow mind of man, not being capable of having many ideas under view and consideration at once, it was necessary to have a repository to lay up those ideas, which at another time it might have use of. But our ideas being nothing but actual perceptions in the mind, which cease to be anything when there is no perception of them, this laying up of our ideas in the repository of the memory signifies no more but this,—that the mind has a power, in many cases, to revive perceptions which it has once had, with this additional perception annexed to them,—that it has had them before. And in this sense it is that our ideas are said to be in our memories, when indeed they are actually nowhere, but only there is an ability in the mind when it will to revive them again, and, as it were, paint them anew on itself, though some with more, some with less, difficulty; some more lively, and others more obscurely. And thus it is by the assistance of this faculty that we are said to have all those ideas in our understandings, which though we do not actually contemplate, yet we can bring in sight, and make appear again and be the objects of our thoughts, without the help of those sensible qualities which first imprinted them there.

**3.** *Attention, repetition, pleasure, and pain fix ideas.*—Attention and repetition help much to the fixing any ideas in the memory; but those which naturally at first make the deepest and most lasting impression, are those which are accompanied with pleasure or pain. The great business of the senses being to make us take notice of what hurts or advantages the body, it is wisely ordered by nature (as has been shown) that pain should accompany the reception of several ideas; which, supplying the place of consideration and reasoning in children, and acting quicker than consideration in grown men, makes both the young and old avoid painful objects with that haste which is necessary for their preservation, and in both settles in the memory a caution for the future.

4. *Ideas fade in the memory.*—Concerning the several degrees of lasting wherewith ideas are imprinted on the memory, we may observe, that some of them have been produced in the understanding by an object affecting the senses once only, and no more than once : others, that have more than once offered themselves to the senses, have yet been little taken notice of : the mind, either heedless as in children, or otherwise employed as in men, intent only on one thing, not setting the stamp deep into itself; and in some, where they are set on with care and repeated impressions, either through the temper of the body or some other default, the memory is very weak. In all these cases, ideas in the mind quickly fade, and often vanish quite out of the understanding, leaving no more footsteps or remaining characters of themselves, than shadows do flying over fields of corn: and the mind is as void of them as if they never had been there.

5. Thus many of those ideas which were produced in the minds of children in the beginning of their sensation (some of which perhaps, as of some pleasures and pains, were before they were born, and others in their infancy), if in the future course of their lives they are not repeated again, are quite lost, without the least glimpse remaining of them. This may be observed in those who by some mischance have lost their sight when they were very young, in whom the ideas of colours, having been but slightly taken notice of, and ceasing to be repeated, do quite wear out; so that some years after there is no more notion nor memory of colours left in their minds, than in those of people born blind. The memory in some men, it is true, is very tenacious, even to a miracle; but yet there seems to be a constant decay of all our ideas, even of those which are struck deepest, and in minds the most retentive ; so that if they be not sometimes renewed by repeated exercise of the senses, or reflection on those kinds of objects which at first occasioned them, the print wears out, and at last there remains nothing to be seen. Thus the ideas, as well as children, of our youth often die before us ; and our minds represent to us those tombs to which we are approaching; where though the brass and marble remain, yet the inscriptions are effaced by time, and the imagery moulders away. The pictures drawn in our minds are laid in fading colours; and if not sometimes refreshed, vanish and disappear. How much the constitution of our bodies, and the make of our animal spirits, are concerned in this; and whether the temper of the brain makes this difference, that in some it retains the characters drawn on it like marble, in others like free-stone, and in

others little better than sand, I shall not here inquire: though it may seem probable that the constitution of the body does sometimes influence the memory; since we oftentimes find a disease quite strip the mind of all its ideas, and the flames of a fever in a few days calcine all those images to dust and confusion, which seemed to be as lasting as if graved in marble.

6. *Constantly repeated ideas can scarce be lost.*—But concerning the ideas themselves it is easy to remark, that those that are oftenest refreshed (amongst which are those that are conveyed into the mind by more ways than one) by a frequent return of the objects or actions that produce them, fix themselves best in the memory, and remain clearest and longest there: and therefore those which are of the original qualities of bodies, viz., solidity, extension, figure, motion, and rest; and those that almost constantly affect our bodies, as heat and cold; and those which are the affections of all kinds of beings, as existence, duration, and number, which almost every object that affects our senses, every thought which employs our minds, bring along with them: these, I say, and the like ideas, are seldom quite lost whilst the mind retains any ideas at all.

7. *In remembering, the mind is often active.*—In this secondary perception, as I may so call it, or viewing again the ideas that are lodged in the memory, the mind is oftentimes more than barely passive; the appearances of those dormant pictures depending sometimes on the will. The mind very often sets itself on work in search of some hidden idea, and turns, as it were, the eye of the soul upon it; though sometimes too they start up in our minds of their own accord, and offer themselves to the understanding, and very often are roused and tumbled out of their dark cells into open daylight by some turbulent and tempestuous passion; our affections bringing ideas to our memory which had otherwise lain quiet and unregarded. This farther is to be observed concerning ideas lodged in the memory, and upon occasion revived by the mind,—that they are not only (as the word "revive" imports) none of them new ones, but also that the mind takes notice of them as of a former impression, and renews its acquaintance with them as with ideas it had known before. So that though ideas formerly imprinted are not all constantly in view, yet in remembrance they are constantly known to be such as have been formerly imprinted, *i.e.*, in view, and taken notice of before by the understanding.

8. *Two defects in the memory, oblivion and slowness.*— Memory, in an intellectual creature, is necessary in the next degree to perception. It is of so great moment, that where it is wanting all the rest of our faculties are in a great measure useless; and we in our thoughts, reasonings, and knowledge, could not proceed beyond present objects, were it not for the assistance of our memories, wherein there may be two defects,

First, That it loses the idea quite; and so far it produces perfect ignorance. For since we can know nothing further than we have the idea of it, when that is gone we are in perfect ignorance.

Secondly, That it moves slowly, and retrieves not the ideas that it has, and are laid up in store, quick enough to serve the mind upon occasions. This, if it be to a great degree, is stupidity; and he who through this default in his memory has not the ideas that are really preserved there ready at hand when need and occasion calls for them, were almost as good be without them quite, since they serve him to little purpose. The dull man who loses the opportunity whilst he is seeking in his mind for those ideas that should serve his turn, is not much more happy in his knowledge than one that is perfectly ignorant. It is the business therefore of the memory to furnish to the mind those dormant ideas which it has present occasion for; in the having them ready at hand on all occasions, consists that which we call invention, fancy, and quickness of parts.

9. These are defects we may observe in the memory of one man compared with another. There is another defect which we may conceive to be in the memory of man in general, compared with some superior created intellectual beings, which in this faculty may so far excel man, that they may have constantly in view the whole sense of all their former actions, wherein no one of the thoughts they have ever had may slip out of their sight. The omniscience of God, who knows all things, past, present, and to come, and to whom the thoughts of men's hearts always lie open, may satisfy us of the possibility of this. For who can doubt but God may communicate to those glorious spirits, his immediate attendants, any of his perfections in what proportion he pleases, as far as created finite beings can be capable? It is reported of that prodigy of parts, Monsieur Pascal, that, till the decay of his health had impaired his memory, he forgot nothing of what he had done, read, or thought in any part of his rational age. This is a privilege so little known to most men, that it seems almost incredible to those who, after the ordinary way, measure all others by themselves; but yet, when considered, may help us to enlarge our thoughts towards greater perfections of it in superior ranks of spirits. For this of Mr. Pascal was still with the narrowness that human minds are confined to here—of having great variety of ideas only by succession, not all at once: whereas the several degrees of angels may probably have larger views, and some of them be endowed with capacities able to retain together and constantly set before them, as in one picture, all their past knowledge at once. This, we may conceive, would be no small advantage to the knowledge of a thinking man, if all his past thoughts and reasonings could be always present to him; and therefore we may suppose it one of those

ways wherein the knowledge of separate spirits may exceedingly surpass ours.

10. *Brutes have memory.*—This faculty of laying up and retaining the ideas that are brought into the mind, several other animals seem to have to a great degree, as well as man. For to pass by other instances, birds' learning of tunes, and the endeavours one may observe in them to hit the notes right, put it past doubt with me that they have perception, and retain ideas in their memories, and use them for patterns. For it seems to me impossible that they should endeavour to conform their voices to notes (as it is plain they do) of which they had no ideas. For though I should grant sound may mechanically cause a certain motion of the animal spirits in the brains of those birds whilst the tune is actually playing, and that motion may be continued on to the muscles of the wings, and so the bird mechanically be driven away by certain noises, because this may tend to the bird's preservation; yet that can never be supposed a reason why it should cause mechanically either whilst the tune was playing, much less after it has ceased, such a motion in the organs of the bird's voice as should conform it to the notes of a foreign sound, which imitation can be of no use to the bird's preservation. But, which is more, it cannot with any appearance of reason be supposed (much less proved) that birds without sense and memory can approach their notes, nearer and nearer by degrees, to a tune played yesterday; which if they have no idea of it in their memory is now nowhere, nor can be a pattern for them to imitate, or which any repeated essays can bring them nearer to; since there is no reason why the sound of a pipe should leave traces in their brains, which not at first, but by their after endeavours, should produce the like sounds; and why the sounds they make themselves should not make traces which they should follow, as well as those of the pipe, is impossible to conceive.

## CHAPTER XI.

### OF DISCERNING, AND OTHER OPERATIONS OF THE MIND.

1. *No knowledge without discerning.*—Another faculty we may take notice of in our minds, is that of discerning and distinguishing between the several ideas it has. It is not enough to have a confused perception of something in general: unless the mind had a distinct perception of different objects and their qualities, it would be capable of very little knowledge; though the bodies that affect us were as busy about us as they are now, and the mind were continually employed in thinking. On this faculty of distinguishing one thing from another, depends the evidence and certainty of several even very general propositions, which

have passed for innate truths; because men, overlooking the
true cause why those propositions find universal assent, impute
it wholly to native uniform impressions: whereas it in truth
depends upon this clear discerning faculty of the mind, whereby
it perceives two ideas to be the same or different. But of this
more hereafter.

2. *The difference of wit and judgment.*—How much the imperfection of accurately discriminating ideas one from another lies
either in the dulness or faults of the organs of sense, or want of
acuteness, exercise, or attention in the understanding, or hasti-
ness and precipitancy natural to some tempers, I will not here
examine; it suffices to take notice, that this is one of the operations that the mind may reflect on and observe in itself. It is of
that consequence to its other knowledge, that so far as this
faculty is in itself dull, or not rightly made use of for the distinguishing one thing from another, so far our notions are confused,
and our reason, and judgment disturbed or misled. If in having
our ideas in the memory ready at hand consists quickness of
parts; in this of having them unconfused, and being able nicely
to distinguish one thing from another where there is but the
least difference, consists in a great measure the exactness of
judgment and clearness of reason which is to be observed in one
man above another. And hence, perhaps, may be given some
reason of that common observation—that men who have a great
deal of wit and prompt memories, have not always the clearest
judgment or deepest reason. For, wit lying most in the assemblage of ideas, and putting those together with quickness and
variety wherein can be found any resemblance or congruity,
thereby to make up pleasant pictures and agreeable visions in
the fancy; judgment, on the contrary, lies quite on the other
side, in separating carefully one from another ideas wherein can
be found the least difference, thereby to avoid being misled by
similitude and by affinity to take one thing for another. This is
a way of proceeding quite contrary to metaphor and illusion,
wherein for the most part lies that entertainment and pleasantry
of wit which strikes so lively on the fancy, and therefore so
acceptable to all people; because its beauty appears at first sight,
and there is required no labour of thought to examine what
truth or reason there is in it. The mind, without looking any
farther, rests satisfied with the agreeableness of the picture and
the gaiety of the fancy: and it is a kind of an affront to go
about to examine it by the severe rules of truth and good reason:
whereby it appears that it consists in something that is not perfectly conformable to them.

3. *Clearness alone hinders confusion.*—To the well distinguishing our ideas, it chiefly contributes that they be clear and determinate; and when they are so, it will not breed any confusion
or mistake about them, though the senses should (as sometimes

they do) convey them from the same object differently on different occasions, and so seem to err. For though a man in a fever should from sugar have a bitter taste, which at another time would produce a sweet one, yet the idea of bitter in that man's mind would be as clear and distinct from the idea of sweet, as if he had tasted only gall. Nor does it make any more confusion between the two ideas of sweet and bitter, that the same sort of body produces at one time one and at another time another idea by the taste, than it makes a confusion in two ideas of white and sweet, or white and round, that the same piece of sugar produces them both in the mind at the same time. And the ideas of orange-colour and azure that are produced in the mind by the same parcel of the infusion of *lignum nephriticum*, are no less distinct ideas than those of the same colours taken from two very different bodies.

4. *Comparing.*—The comparing them one with another, in respect of extent, degrees, time, place, or any other circumstances, is another operation of the mind about its ideas, and is that upon which depends all that large tribe of ideas, comprehended under relation; which of how vast an extent it is, I shall have occasion to consider hereafter.

5. *Brutes compare, but imperfectly.*—How far brutes partake in this faculty is not easy to determine; I imagine they have it not in any great degree : for though they probably have several ideas distinct enough, yet it seems to me to be the prerogative of human understanding, when it has sufficiently distinguished any ideas so as to perceive them to be perfectly different, and so consequently two, to cast about and consider in what circumstances they are capable to be compared. And therefore, I think, beasts compare not their ideas farther than some sensible circumstances annexed to the objects themselves. The other power of comparing which may be observed in men, belonging to general ideas, and useful only to abstract reasonings, we may probably conjecture beasts have not.

6. *Compounding.*—The next operation we may observe in the mind about its ideas is composition; whereby it puts together several of those simple ones it has received from sensation and reflection, and combines them into complex ones. Under this of composition may be reckoned also that of enlarging; wherein though the composition does not so much appear as in more complex ones, yet it is nevertheless a putting several ideas together, though of the same kind. Thus, by adding several units together we make the idea of a dozen, and putting together the repeated ideas of several perches we frame that of a furlong.

7. *Brutes compound but little.*—In this also I suppose brutes come far short of men. For though they take in and retain together several combinations or simple ideas (as possibly the

shape, smell, and voice of his master, make up the complex idea a dog has of him, or rather, are so many distinct marks whereby he knows him); yet I do not think they do of themselves ever compound them and make complex ideas. And perhaps even where we think they have complex ideas, it is only one simple one that directs them in the knowledge of several things, which possibly they distinguish less by their sight than we imagine. For I have been credibly informed that a bitch will nurse, play with, and be fond of young foxes, as much as and in place of her puppies, if you can but get them once to suck her so long that her milk may go through them. And those animals which have a numerous brood of young ones at once, appear not to have any knowledge of their number; for though they are mightily concerned for any of their young that are taken from them whilst they are in sight or hearing, yet if one or two of them be stolen from them in their absence or without noise, they appear not to miss them, or to have any sense that their number is lessened.

8. *Naming.*—When children have by repeated sensations got ideas fixed in their memories, they begin by degrees to learn the use of signs. And when they have got the skill to apply the organs of speech to the framing of articulate sounds, they begin to make use of words to signify their ideas to others. These verbal signs they sometimes borrow from others, and sometimes make themselves, as one may observe among the new and unusual names children often give to things in their first use of language.

9. *Abstracting.*—The use of words then being to stand as outward marks of our internal ideas, and those ideas being taken from particular things, if every particular idea that we take in should have a distinct name, names must be endless. To prevent this, the mind makes the particular ideas, received from particular objects, to become general; which is done by considering them as they are in the mind such appearances separate from all other existences, and the circumstances of real existence, as time, place, or any other concomitant ideas. This is called "abstraction," whereby ideas taken from particular beings become general representatives of all of the same kind; and their names, general names, applicable to whatever exists conformable to such abstract ideas. Such precise, naked appearances in the mind, without considering how, whence, or with what others they came there, the understanding lays up (with names commonly annexed to them) as the standards to rank real existences into sorts, as they agree with these patterns, and to denominate them accordingly. Thus, the same colour being observed to-day in chalk or snow, which the mind yesterday received from milk, it considers that appearance alone, makes it a representative of all of that kind, and, having given it the name

" whiteness," it by that sound signifies the same quality wheresoever to be imagined or met with; and thus universals, whether
ideas or terms, are made.

10. *Brutes abstract not.*—If it may be doubted whether beasts
compound and enlarge their ideas that way to any degree, this,
I think, I may be positive in, that the power of abstracting is
not at all in them, and that the having of general ideas is that
which puts a perfect distinction between man and brutes, and is
an excellency which the faculties of brutes do by no means
attain to. For it is evident we observe no footsteps in them of
making use of general signs for universal ideas; from which we
have reason to imagine, that they have not the faculty of abstracting or making general ideas, since they have no use of words or
any other general signs.

11. Nor can it be imputed to their want of fit organs to frame
articulate sounds, that they have no use or knowledge of general
words : since many of them, we find, can fashion such sounds
and pronounce words distinctly enough, but never with any such
application. And, on the other side, men who, through some
defect in the organs, want words, yet fail not to express their
universal ideas by signs, which serve them instead of general
words; a faculty which we see beasts come short in. And
therefore, I think, we may suppose that it is in this that the
species of brutes are discriminated from man; and it is that
proper difference wherein they are wholly separated, and which
at last widens to so vast a distance. For if they have any
ideas at all, and are not bare machines (as some would have
them), we cannot deny them to have some reason. It seems
as evident to me that they do, some of them, in certain instances,
reason, as that they have sense; but it is only in particular
ideas, just as they received them from their senses. They are,
the best of them, tied up within those narrow bounds, and have
not (as I think) the faculty to enlarge them by any kind of
abstraction.

12. *Idiots and madmen.*—How far idiots are concerned in the
want of weakness of any or all of the foregoing faculties, an
exact observation of their several ways of faltering would no
doubt discover. For those who either perceive but dully, or
retain the ideas that come into their minds but ill, who cannot
readily excite or compound them, will have little matter to think
on. Those who cannot distinguish, compare, and abstract, would
hardly be able to understand and make use of language, or
judge, or reason, to any tolerable degree; but only a little and
imperfectly about things present and very familiar to their
senses. And indeed any of the fore-mentioned faculties, if
wanting or out of order, produce suitable defects in men's
understandings and knowledge.

13. In fine, the defect in naturals seems to proceed from want

of quickness, activity, and motion in the intellectual faculties, whereby they are deprived of reason ; whereas madmen, on the other side, seem to suffer by the other extreme. For they do not appear to me to have lost the faculty of reasoning ; but, having joined together some ideas very wrongly, they mistake them for truths, and they err as men do that argue right from wrong principles. For by the violence of their imaginations having taken their fancies for realities, they make right deductions from them. Thus you shall find a distracted man, fancying himself a king, with a right inference, require suitable attendance, respect, and obedience ; others, who have thought themselves made of glass, have used the caution necessary to preserve such brittle bodies. Hence it comes to pass, that a man who is very sober and of a right understanding in all other things, may in one particular be as frantic as any in Bedlam ; if either by any sudden very strong impression, or long fixing his fancy upon one sort of thoughts, incoherent ideas have been cemented together so powerfully as to remain united. But there are degrees of madness, as of folly; the disorderly jumbling ideas together is in some more and some less. In short, herein seems to lie the difference between idiots and madmen, that madmen put wrong ideas together, and so make wrong propositions, but argue and reason right from them ; but idiots make very few or no propositions, and reason scarce at all.

14. *Method.*—These, I think, are the first faculties and operations of the mind which it makes use of in understanding; and though they are exercised about all its ideas in general, yet the instances I have hitherto given have been chiefly in simple ideas ; and I have subjoined the explication of these faculties of the mind to that of simple ideas, before I come to what I have to say concerning complex ones, for these following reasons :—

First, Because, several of these faculties being exercised at first principally about simple ideas, we might, by following nature in its ordinary method, trace and discover them in their rise, progress, and gradual improvements.

Secondly, Because, observing the faculties of the mind, how they operate about simple ideas, which are usually in most men's minds much more clear, precise, and distinct than complex ones, we may the better examine and learn how the mind abstracts, denominates, compares, and exercises its other operations about those which are complex, wherein we are much more liable to mistake.

Thirdly, Because these very operations of the mind about ideas received from sensation are themselves, when reflected on, another set of ideas, derived from that other source of our knowledge which I call "reflection;" and therefore fit to be considered in this place after the simple ideas of sensation. Of compounding, comparing, abstracting, &c., I have but just spoken, having occasion to treat of them more at large in other places.

15. *These are the beginnings of human knowledge.*—And thus I have given a short and, I think, true history of the first beginnings of human knowledge, whence the mind has its first objects, and by what steps it makes its progress to the laying in and storing up those ideas out of which is to be framed all the knowledge it is capable of; wherein I must appeal to experience and observation whether I am in the right: the best way to come to truths being to examine things as really they are, and not to conclude they are as we fancy of ourselves, or have been taught by others to imagine.

16. *Appeal to experience.*—To deal truly, this is the only way that I can discover whereby the ideas of things are brought into the understanding: if other men have either innate ideas or infused principles, they have reason to enjoy them; and if they are sure of it, it is impossible for others to deny them the privilege that they have above their neighbours. I can speak but of what I find in myself, and is agreeable to those notions which, if we will examine the whole course of men in their several ages, countries, and educations, seem to depend on those foundations which I have laid, and to correspond with this method in all the parts and degrees thereof.

17. *Dark room.*—I pretend not to teach, but to inquire; and therefore cannot but confess here again, that external and internal sensation are the only passages that I can find of knowledge to the understanding. These alone, as far as I can discover, are the windows by which light is let into this dark room. For methinks the understanding is not much unlike a closet wholly shut from light, with only some little opening left to let in external visible resemblances or ideas of things without: would the pictures coming into such a dark room but stay there, and lie so orderly as to be found upon occasion, it would very much resemble the understanding of a man in reference to all objects of sight, and the ideas of them.

These are my guesses concerning the means whereby the understanding comes to have and retain simple ideas and the modes of them, with some other operations about them. I proceed now to examine some of these simple ideas and their modes a little more particularly.

## CHAPTER XII

### OF COMPLEX IDEAS.

**1.** *Made by the mind out of simple ones.*—We have hitherto
considered those ideas, in the reception whereof the mind is only
passive, which are those simple ones received from sensation and
reflection before mentioned, whereof the mind cannot make one
to itself, nor have any idea which does not wholly consist of them.
But as the mind is wholly passive in the reception of all its simple
ideas, so it exerts several acts of its own, whereby out of its
simple ideas, as the materials and foundations of the rest, the
other are framed. The acts of the mind wherein it exerts its
power over its simple ideas are chiefly these three: (1.) Combining several simple ideas into one compound one ; and thus all
complex ideas are made. (2.) The second is bringing two ideas,
whether simple or complex, together, and setting them by one
another, so as to take a view of them at once, without uniting
them into one; by which it gets all its ideas of relations. (3.)
The third is separating them from all other ideas that accompany them in their real existence; this is called "abstraction:"
and thus all its general ideas are made. This shows man's power
and its way of operation to be much-what the same in the material
and intellectual world. For, the materials in both being such
as he has no power over, either to make or destroy, all that man
can do is either to unite them together, or to set them by one
another, or wholly separate them. I shall here begin with the
first of these in the consideration of complex ideas, and come
to the other two in their due places. As simple ideas are
observed to exist in several combinations united together, so
the mind has a power to consider several of them united together as one idea; and that not only as they are united in
external objects, but as itself has joined them. Ideas thus
made up of several simple ones put together I call "complex;"
such as are beauty, gratitude, a man, an army, the universe;
which, though complicated of various simple ideas or complex
ideas made up of simple ones, yet are, when the mind pleases,
considered each by itself as one entire thing, and signified by
one name.

**2.** *Made voluntarily.*—In this faculty of repeating and joining
together its ideas, the mind has great power in varying and multiplying the objects of its thoughts infinitely beyond what sensation or reflection furnished it with; but all this still confined to
those simple ideas which it received from those two sources, and
which are the ultimate materials of all its compositions. For,
simple ideas are all from things themselves; and of these the

mind ean have no more nor other than what are suggested to it. It can have no other ideas of sensible qualities than what come from without by the senses, nor any ideas of other kind of operations of a thinking substance than what it finds in itself; but when it has once got these simple ideas, it is not confined barely to observation, and what offers itself from without; it can, by its own power, put together those ideas it has, and make new complex ones which it never received so united.

3. *Are either modes, substances, or relations.*—Complex ideas, however compounded and decompounded, though their number be infinite, and the variety endless wherewith they fill and entertain the thoughts of men, yet I think they may be all reduced under these three heads: 1. Modes. 2. Substances. 8. Relations.

4. *Modes.*—First. "Modes" I call such complex ideas which, however compounded, contain not in them the supposition of subsisting by themselves, but are considered as dependencies on or affections of substances; such are the ideas signified by the words, "triangle, gratitude, murder," &c. And if in this I use the word "mode" in somewhat a different sense from its ordinary signification, I beg pardon; it being unavoidable in discourses differing from the ordinary received notions, either to make new words or to use old words in somewhat a new signification : the latter whereof, in our present case, is perhaps the more tolerable of the two.

5. *Simple and mixed modes.*—Of these modes there are two sorts which deserve distinct consideration. First. There are some which are only variations or different combinations of the same simple idea, without the mixture of any other, as a dozen, or score; which are nothing but the ideas of so many distinct units added together: and these I called "simple modes," as being contained within the bounds of one simple idea. Secondly. There are others compounded of simple ideas, of several kinds, put together to make one complex one; v.g., beauty, consisting of a certain composition of colour and figure, causing delight in the beholder; theft, which, being the concealed change of the possession of anything, without the consent of the proprietor, contains, as is visible, a combination of several ideas of several kinds; and these I call "mixed modes."

6. *Substances single or collective.*—Secondly. The ideas of substances are such combinations of simple ideas as are taken to represent distinct particular things subsisting by themselves, in which the supposed or confused idea of substance, such as it is, is always the first and chief. Thus, if to substance be joined the simple idea of a certain dull, whitish colour, with certain degrees of weight, hardness, ductility, and fusibility, we have the idea of lead; and a combination of the ideas of a certain sort of figure, with the powers of motion, thought, and reasoning,

joined to substance, make the ordinary idea of a man. Now of substances also there are two sorts of ideas, one of single substances, as they exist separately, as of a man or a sheep; the other of several of those put together, as an army of men or flock of sheep; which collective ideas of several substances thus put together, are as much each of them one single idea as that of a man or an unit.

7. *Relation.*—Thirdly. The last sort of complex ideas is that we call "Relation," which consists in the consideration and comparing one idea with another. Of these several kinds we shall treat in their order.

8. *The abstrusest ideas from the two sources.*—If we will trace the progress of our minds, and with attention observe how it repeats, adds together, and unites its simple ideas received from sensation or reflection, it will lead us farther than at first perhaps we should have imagined. And I believe we shall find, if we warily observe the originals of our notions, that even the most abstruse ideas, how remote soever they may seem from sense, or from any operation of our own minds, are yet only such as the understanding frames to itself, by repeating and joining together ideas that it had either from objects of sense, or from its own operations about them; so that those even large and abstract ideas are derived from sensation or reflection, being no other than what the mind, by the ordinary use of its own faculties, employed about ideas received from objects of sense, or from the operations it observes in itself about them, may and does attain unto. This I shall endeavour to show in the ideas we have of space, time, and infinity, and some few other that seem the most remote from those originals.

---

# CHAPTER XIII.

## OF SIMPLE MODES; AND FIRST, OF THE SIMPLE MODES OF SPACE.

1. *Simple modes.*—Though in the foregoing part I have often mentioned simple ideas, which are truly the materials of all our knowledge; yet, having treated of them there rather in the way that they come into the mind than as distinguished from others more compounded, it will not be perhaps amiss to take a view of some of them again under this consideration, and examine those different modifications of the same idea, which the mind either finds in things existing, or is able to make within itself, without the help of any extrinsical object, or any foreign suggestion.

Those modifications of any one simple idea (which, as has been said, I call "simple modes"), are as perfectly different and distinct ideas in the mind as those of the greatest distance or contrariety; for the idea of two is as distinct from that of one as blueness from heat, or either of them from any number; and yet it is made up only of that simple idea of an unit repeated; and repetitions of this kind joined together make those distinct simple modes of a dozen, a gross, a million.

2. *Idea of space.*—I shall begin with the simple idea of space. I have showed above (chap. iv.) that we get the idea of space both by our sight and touch: which I think is so evident that it would be as needless to go to prove that men perceive by their sight a distance between bodies of different colours, or between the parts of the same body, as that they see colours themselves; nor is it less obvious that they can do so in the dark by feeling and touch.

3. *Space and extension.*—This space considered barely in length between any two beings, without considering anything else between them, is called " distance ;" if considered in length, breadth, and thickness, I think it may be called " capacity ;" the term " extension " is usually applied to it, in what manner soever considered.

4. *Immensity.*—Each different distance is a different modification of space, and each idea of any different distance or space is a simple mode of this idea. Men, for the use and by the custom of measuring, settle in their minds the ideas of certain stated lengths, such as are an inch, foot, yard, fathom, mile, diameter of the earth, &c., which are so many distinct ideas made up only of space. When any such stated lengths or measures of space are made familiar to men's thoughts, they can in their minds repeat them as often as they will, without mixing or joining to them the idea of body or anything else, and frame to themselves the ideas of long, square, or cubic feet, yards, or fathoms, here amongst the bodies of the universe, or else beyond the utmost bounds of all bodies; and, by adding these still one to another, enlarge their idea of space as much as they please. This power of repeating or doubling any idea we have of any distance, and adding it to the former as often as we will, without being ever able to come to any stop or stint, let us enlarge it as much as we will, is that which gives us the idea of immensity.

5. *Figure.*—There is another modification of this idea, which is nothing but the relation which the parts of the termination of extension or circumscribed space have amongst themselves. This the touch discovers in sensible bodies, whose extremities come within our reach; and the eye takes both from bodies and colours, whose boundaries are within its view: where, observing how the extremities terminate either in straight lines which meet at discernible angles, or in crooked lines wherein no angles can be perceived, by considering these as they relate to one another, in all parts of the extremities of any body or space, it has that idea we call " figure," which affords to the

mind infinite variety. For, besides the vast number of different figures that do really exist in the coherent masses of matter, the stock that the mind has in its power by varying the idea of space, and thereby making still new compositions, by repeating its own ideas and joining them as it pleases, is perfectly inexhaustible; and so it can multiply figures *in infinitum*.

6. For, the mind having a power to repeat the idea of any length directly stretched out, and join it to another in the same direction, which is to double the length of that straight line, or else join it to another with what inclination it thinks fit, and so make what sort of angle it pleases; and being able also to shorten any lines it imagines, by taking from it one-half, or one-fourth, or what part it pleases, without being able to come to an end of any such divisions, it can make an angle of any bigness: so also the lines that are its sides, of what length it pleases; which joining again to other lines of different lengths and at different angles, till it has wholly enclosed any space, it is evident that it can multiply figures both in their shape and capacity *in infinitum;* all which are but so many different simple modes of space.

The same that it can do with straight lines, it can do also with crooked, or crooked and straight together; and the same it can do in lines, it can also in superficies; by which we may be led into farther thoughts of the endless variety of figures that the mind has a power to make, and thereby to multiply the simple modes of space.

7 *Place.*—Another idea coming under this head and belonging to this tribe, is that we call "place." As in simple space we consider the relation of distance between any two bodies or points, so in our idea of place we consider the relation of distance betwixt anything and any two or more points, which are considered as keeping the same distance one with another, and so considered as at rest: for when we find anything at the same distance now which it was yesterday from any two or more points, which have not since changed their distance one with another, and with which we then compared it, we say it hath kept the same place; but if it hath sensibly altered its distance with either of those points, we say it hath changed its place; though, vulgarly speaking in the common notion of place, we do not always exactly observe the distance from precise points, but from large portions of sensible objects to which we consider the thing placed to bear relation, and its distance from which we have some reason to observe.

8. Thus a company of chess-men, standing on the same squares of the chess-board where we left them, we say they are all in the same place, or unmoved,—though perhaps the chess-board hath been in the meantime carried out of one room into another,—because we compared them only to the parts of the chess-board

which keep the same distance one with another. The chess-board, we also say, is in the same place it was, if it remain in the same part of the cabin, though perhaps the ship which it is in sails all the while; and the ship is said to be in the same place, supposing it kept the same distance with the parts of the neighbouring land, though perhaps the earth had turned round, and so both chess-men, and board, and ship have every one changed place, in respect of remoter bodies, which have kept the same distance one with another. But yet the distance from certain parts of the board being that which determines the place of the chess-men, and the distance from the fixed parts of the cabin (with which we made the comparison) being that which determined the place of the chess-board, and the fixed parts of the earth that by which we determined the place of the ship; these things may be said properly to be in the same place in those respects; though their distance from some other things, which in this matter we did not consider, being varied, they have undoubtedly changed place in that respect: and we our-selves shall think so when we have occasion to compare them with those other.

9. By this modification of distance we call "place" being made by men, for their common use, that by it they might be able to design the particular position of things, where they had occasion for such designation; men consider and determine of this place by reference to those adjacent things which best served to their present purpose, without considering other things which to another purpose would better determine the place of the same thing. Thus in the chess-board the use of the designation of the place of each chess-man being determined only within that chequered piece of wood, it would cross that purpose to measure it by anything else: but when these very chess-men are put up in a bag, if anyone should ask where the Black King is, it would be proper to determine the place by the parts of the room it was in, and not by the chess-board, there being another use of designing the place it is now in than when in play it was on the chess-board, and so must be deter-mined by other bodies. So, if anyone should ask in what place are the verses which report the story of Nisus and Euryalus, it would be very improper to determine this place by saying, they were in such a part of the earth, or in Bodley's library; but the right designation of the place would be by the parts of Virgil's works, and the proper answer would be, that these verses were about the middle of the ninth book of his Æneids, and that they have been always constantly in the same place ever since Virgil was printed: which is true, though the book itself hath moved a thousand times; the use of the idea of place here being to know only in what part of the book that story is, that so upon occasion we may know where to find it, and have recourse to it for our use.

10. That our idea of place is nothing else but such a relative position of anything as I have before mentioned, I think is plain, and will be easily admitted when we consider that we can have no idea of the place of the universe, though we can of all the parts of it; because beyond that we have not the idea of any fixed, distinct, particular beings, in reference to which we can imagine it to have any relation of distance: but all beyond it is one uniform space or expansion, wherein the mind finds no variety, no marks. For to say that the world is somewhere, means no more than that it does exist: this, though a phrase borrowed from place, signifying only its existence, not location; and when one can find out and frame in his mind clearly and distinctly the place of the universe, he will be able to tell us whether it moves or stands still in the undistinguishable inane of infinite space : though it be true that the word "place" has sometimes a more confused sense, and stands for that space which any body takes up; and so the universe is in a place. The idea therefore of place we have by the same means that we get the idea of space (whereof this is but a particular limited consideration), viz., by our sight and touch, by either of which we receive into our minds the ideas of extension or distance.

11. *Extension and body not the same.*—There are some that would persuade us that body and extension are the same thing; who either change the signification of words, which I would not suspect them of, they having so severely condemned the philosophy of others because it hath been too much placed in the uncertain meaning or deceitful obscurity of doubtful or insignificant terms. If therefore they mean by body and extension the same that other people do, viz., by body, something that is solid and extended, whose parts are separable and moveable different ways; and by extension, only the space that lies between the extremities of those solid coherent parts, and which is possessed by them, they confound very different ideas one with another. For I appeal to every man's own thoughts, whether the idea of space be not as distinct from that of solidity, as it is from the idea of scarlet colour? It is true, solidity cannot exist without extension, neither can scarlet colour exist without extension ; but this hinders not but that they are distinct ideas. Many ideas require others as necessary to their existence or conception, which yet are very distinct ideas. Motion can neither be, nor be conceived, without space ; and yet motion is not space, nor space motion; space can exist without it, and they are very distinct ideas ; and so, I think, are those of space and solidity. Solidity is so inseparable an idea from body, that upon that depends its filling of space, its contact, impulse, and communication of motion upon impulse. And if it be a reason to prove that spirit is different from body, because thinking includes not the idea of extension in it, the same reason will be as valid. I sup-

pose, to prove that space is not body, because it includes not the idea of solidity in it; space and solidity being as distinct ideas as thinking and extension, and as wholly separable in the mind one from another. Body, then, and extension, it is evident, are two distinct ideas. For,

12. First. Extension includes no solidity nor resistance to the motion of body, as body does.

13. Secondly. The parts of pure space are inseparable one from the other; so that the continuity cannot be separated, neither really nor mentally. For I demand of anyone to remove any part of it from another with which it is continued, even so much as in thought. To divide and separate actually, is as I think, by removing the parts one from another, to make two superfices, where before there was a continuity : and to divide mentally, is to make in the mind two superficies, where before there was a continuity, and consider them as removed one from the other; which can only be done in things considered by the mind as capable of being separated; and, by separation, of acquiring new distinct superficies, which they then have not, but are capable of ; but neither of these ways of separation, whether real or mental, is, as I think, compatible to pure space.

It is true, a man may consider so much of such a space as is answerable or commensurate to a foot, without considering the rest; which is indeed a partial consideration, but not so much as mental separation or division; since a man can no more mentally divide without considering two superficies separate one from the other, than he can actually divide without making two superficies disjoined one from the other; but a partial consideration is not separating. A man may consider light in the sun without its heat, or mobility in body without its extension, without thinking of their separation. One is only a partial consideration, ter-minating in one alone; and the other is a consideration of both, as existing separately.

14. Thirdly. The parts of pure space are immovable, which follows from their inseparability; motion being nothing but change of distance between any two things: but this cannot be between parts that are inseparable; which therefore must needs be at perpetual rest one amongst another.

Thus the determined idea of simple space distinguishes it plainly and sufficiently from body, since its parts are inseparable, immovable, and without resistance to the motion of body.

15. *The definition of extension explains it not.*—If anyone ask me, what this space I speak of is, I will tell him when he tells me what his extension is. For to say, as is usually done, that extension is to have *partes extra partes*, it is to say only that extension is extension; for what am I the better informed in the nature of extension, when I am told, that extension is to have parts that are extended, exterior to parts that are extended, *i.e.*,

extension consists of extended parts ? As if, one asking what a
fibre was, I should answer him, that it was a thing made up of
several fibres; would he hereby be enabled to understand what
a fibre was better than he did before ? Or rather, would he not
have reason to think that my design was to make sport with
him, rather than seriously to instruct him ?

16. *Division of beings into bodies and spirits, proves not space
and body the same.*—Those who contend that space and body are
the same, bring this dilemma : Either this space is something or
nothing; if nothing be between two bodies, they must necessarily
touch ; if it be allowed to be something, they ask, whether it be
body or spirit ? To which I answer by another question, Who
told them that there was, or could be, nothing but solid beings
which could not think, and thinking beings that were not extended? which is all they mean by the terms "body" and "spirit."

17. *Substance which we know not, no proof against space
without body.*—If it be demanded (as usually it is), whether this
space, void of body, be substance or accident, I shall readily
answer, I know not; nor shall be ashamed to own my ignorance,
till they that ask show me a clear distinct idea of substance.

18. I endeavour, as much as I can, to deliver myself from those
fallacies which we are apt to put upon ourselves by taking words
for things. It helps not our ignorance to feign a knowledge
where we have none, by making a noise with sounds without
clear and distinct significations. Names made at pleasure neither
alter the nature of things, nor make us understand them but as
they are signs of and stand for determined ideas. And I desire
those who lay so much stress on the sound of these two syllables,
*sub-stance*, to consider whether, applying it as they do to the
infinite incomprehensible God, to finite spirit, and to body, it be
in the same sense; and whether it stands for the same idea, when
each of those three so different beings are called substances ? If
so, whether it will not thence follow, that God, spirits, and body,
agreeing in the same common nature of substance, differ not anÿ
otherwise than in a bare different modification of that substance ;
as a tree and a pebble, being in the same sense body, and agreeing
in the common nature of body, differ only in a bare modification
of that common matter ? which will be a very harsh doctrine.
If they say that they apply it to God, finite spirits, and matter,
in three different significations, and that it stands for one idea
when God is said to be a substance, for another when the soul is
called substance, and for a third when a body is called so : if the
name " substance " stands for three several distinct ideas, they
would do well to make known those distinct ideas, or at least to
give three distinct names to them, to prevent, in so important a
notion, the confusion and errors that will naturally follow from
the promiscuous use of so doubtful a term ; which is so far from
being suspected to have three distinct, that in ordinary use it has

scarce one clear distinct signification; and if they can thus make three distinct ideas of substance, what hinders why another may not make a fourth ?

19. *Substance and accidents of little use in philosophy.*—They who first ran into the notion of accidents, as a sort of real beings that needed something to inhere in, were forced to find out the word " substance " to support them. Had the poor Indian philosopher (who imagined that the earth also wanted something to bear it up) but thought of this word " substance," he needed not to have been at the trouble to find an elephant to support it, and a tortoise to support his elephant ; the word " substance " would have done it effectually. And he that inquired, might have taken it for as good an answer from an Indian philosopher, that substance, without knowing what it is, is that which supports the earth, as we take it for a sufficient answer and good doctrine from our European philosophers, that substance, without knowing what it is, is that which supports accidents. So that of substance we have no idea of what it is, but only a confused obscure one of what it does.

20. Whatever a learned man may do here, an intelligent American, who inquired into the nature of things, would scarce take it for a satisfactory account, if, desiring to learn our architecture, he should be told that a pillar was a thing supported by a basis, and a basis something that supported a pillar. Would he not think himself mocked, instead of taught, with such an account as this ? And a stranger to them would be very liberally instructed in the nature of books, and the things they contained, if he should be told that all learned books consisted of paper and letters, and that letters were things inhering in paper, and paper a thing that held forth letters: a notable way of having clear ideas of letters and paper ! But were the Latin words *inhærentia* and *substantia* put into the plain English ones that answer them, and were called " sticking on " and " under-propping ;" they would better discover to us the very great clearness there is in the doctrine of substance and accidents, and show of what use they are in deciding of questions in philosophy.

21. *A vacuum beyond the utmost bounds of body.*—But, to return to our idea of space : If body be not supposed infinite, which I think no one will affirm, I would ask, whether, if God placed a man at the extremity of corporeal beings, he could not stretch his hand beyond his body ? If he could, then he would put his arm where there was before space without body ; and if there he spread his fingers, there would still be space between them without body. If he could not stretch out his hand, it must be because of some external hindrance (for we suppose him alive, with such a power of moving the parts of his body that he hath now ; which is not in itself impossible if God so pleased to have it, or at least it is not impossible for God so to

move him); and then I ask, whether that which hinders his
hand from moving outwards, be substance or accident, something
or nothing? And when they have resolved that, they will be
able to resolve themselves what that is which is, or may be,
between two bodies at a distance, that is not body, and has no
solidity. In the meantime the argument is at least as good,
that where nothing hinders (as beyond the utmost bounds of all
bodies), a body put into motion may move on, as where there is
nothing between, there two bodies must necessarily touch; for
pure space between is sufficient to take away the necessity of
mutual contact; but bare space in the way is not sufficient to
stop motion. The truth is, these men must either own that
they think body infinite, though they are loath to speak it out,
or else affirm that space is not body. For I would fain meet
with that thinking man, that can in his thoughts set any bounds
to space, more than he can to duration; or, by thinking, hope
to arrive at the end of either: and therefore if his idea of eternity
be infinite, so is his idea of immensity; they are both finite or
infinite alike.

22. *The power of annihilation proves a* vacuum.—Farther,
those who assert the impossibility of space existing without
matter, must not only make body infinite, but must also deny a
power in God to annihilate any part of matter. No one, I
suppose, will deny that God can put an end to all motion that is
in matter, and fix all the bodies of the universe in a perfect quiet
and rest, and continue them so as long as he pleases. Whoever
then will allow that God can, during such a general rest, annihilate either this book or the body of him that reads it, must
necessarily admit the possibility of a *vacuum;* for it is evident
that the space that was filled by the parts of the annihilated
body will still remain, and be a space without body. For, the
circumambient bodies, being in perfect rest, are a wall of adamant, and in that state make it a perfect impossibility for any
other body to get into that space. And indeed the necessary
motion of one particle of matter into the place from whence
another particle of matter is removed, is but a consequence from
the supposition of plenitude, which will therefore need some
better proof than a supposed matter of fact, which experiment
can never make out; our own clear and distinct ideas plainly
satisfying us, that there is no necessary connexion between
space and solidity, since we can conceive the one without the
other. And those who dispute for or against a *vacuum,* do
thereby confess they have distinct ideas of *vacuum* and *plenum,*
*i.e.,* that they have an idea of extension void of solidity,
though they deny its existence; or else they dispute about
nothing at all. For they who so much alter the signification
of words, as to call extension "body," and consequently make
the whole essence of body to be nothing but pure extension

without solidity, must talk absurdly whenever they speak of *vacuum*, since it is impossible for extension to be without extension. For *vacuum*, whether we affirm or deny its existence, signifies space without body; whose very existence no one can deny to be possible who will not make matter infinite, and take from God a power to annihilate any particle of it.

23. *Motion proves a* vacuum.—But not to go so far as beyond the utmost bounds of body in the universe, nor appeal to God's omnipotency to find a *vacuum*, the motion of bodies that are in our view and neighbourhood seems to me plainly to evince it. For I desire anyone so to divide a solid body, of any dimension he pleases, as to make it possible for the solid parts to move up and down freely every way within the bounds of that superficies, if there be not left in it a void space as big as the least part into which he has divided the said solid body. And if, where the least particle of the body divided is as big as a mustard seed, a void space equal to the bulk of a mustard-seed be requisite to make room for the free motion of the parts of the divided body within the bounds of its superficies, where the particles of matter are 100,000,000 times less than a mustard-seed, there must also be a space void of solid matter as big as 100,000,000th part of a mustard-seed; for if it hold in one, it will hold in the other, and so on *in infinitum*. And let this void space be as little as it will, it destroys the hypothesis of plenitude. For if there can be a space void of body, equal to the smallest separate particle of matter now existing in nature, it is still space without body, and makes as great a difference between space and body, as if it were μέγα χάσμα, a distance as wide as any in nature. And therefore, if we suppose not the void space necessary to motion equal to the least parcel of the divided solid matter, but to one-tenth or one-thousandth of it, the same consequence will always follow of space without matter.

24. *The ideas of space and body distinct.*—But the question being here, whether the idea of space or extension be the same with the idea of body, it is not necessary to prove the real existence of a *vacuum*, but the idea of it; which it is plain men have when they inquire and dispute whether there be a *vacuum* or no. For if they had not the idea of space without body, they could not make a question about its existence; and if their idea of body did not include in it something more than the bare idea of space, they could have no doubt about the plenitude of the world; and it would be as absurd to demand whether there were space without body, as whether there were space without space, or body without body, since these were but different names of the same idea.

25. *Extension being inseparable from body, proves it not the same.*—It is true, the idea of extension joins itself so inseparably with all visible and most tangible qualities, that it suffers us to see

no one, or feel very few external objects, without taking in impressions of extension too. This readiness of extension to make itself be taken notice of so constantly with other ideas, has been the occasion, I guess, that some have made the whole essence of body to consist in extension; which is not much to be wondered at, since some have had their minds by their eyes and touch (the busiest of all our senses) so filled with the idea of extension, and, as it were, wholly possessed with it, that they allowed no existence to anything that had not extension. I shall not now argue with those men who take the measure and possibility of all being only from their narrow and gross imaginations; but having here to do only with those who conclude the essence of body to be extension, because they say they cannot imagine any sensible quality of any body without extension, I shall desire them to consider, that had they reflected on their ideas of tastes and smells as much as on those of sight and touch; nay, had they examined their ideas of hunger and thirst, and several other pains, they would have found that they included in them no idea of extension at all; which is but an affection of body, as well as the rest, discoverable by our senses, which are scarce acute enough to look into the pure essences of things.

26. If those ideas which are constantly joined to all others must therefore be concluded to be the essence of those things which have constantly those ideas joined to them, and are inseparable from them, then unity is, without doubt, the essence of everything; for there is not any object of sensation or reflection which does not carry with it the idea of one; but the weakness of this kind of argument we have already shown sufficiently.

27. *Ideas of space and solidity distinct.*—To conclude : Whatever men shall think concerning the existence of a *vacuum*, this is plain to me—that we have as clear an idea of space distinct from solidity, as we have of solidity distinct from motion, or motion from space. We have not any two more distinct ideas ; and we can as easily conceive space without solidity, as we can conceive body or space without motion, though it be ever so certain that neither body nor motion can exist without space. But whether anyone will take space to be only a relation resulting from the existence of other beings at a distance, or whether they will think the words of the most knowing king Solomon, " The heaven and the heaven of heavens cannot contain thee," or those more emphatical ones of the inspired philosopher, St. Paul, " In him we live, move, and have our being," are to be understood in a literal sense, I leave everyone to consider : only our idea of space is, I think, such as I have mentioned, and distinct from that of body. ´ For whether we consider in matter itself the distance of its coherent solid parts, and call it in respect of those solid parts " extension ;" or whether, considering it as lying

between the extremities of any body in its several dimensions, we call it " length, breadth, and thickness;" or else, considering it as lying between any two bodies or positive beings, without any consideration whether there be any matter or no between, we call it " distance;" however named or considered, it is always the same uniform, simple idea of space, taken from objects about which our senses have been conversant, whereof having settled ideas in our minds, we can revive, repeat, and add them one to another as often as we will, and consider the space or distance so imagined either as filled with solid parts, so that another body cannot come there without displacing and thrusting out the body that was there before, or else as void of solidity, so that a body of equal dimensions to that empty or pure space may be placed in it without the removing or expulsion of anything that was there. But to avoid confusion in discourses concerning this matter, it were possibly to be wished that the name " extension " were applied only to matter, or the distance of the extremities of particular bodies, and the term "expansion" to space in general, with or without solid matter possessing it ; so as to say, " Space is expanded, and body extended." But in this everyone has his liberty: I propose it only for the more clear and distinct way of speaking.

28. *Men differ little in clear simple ideas.*—The knowing precisely what our words stand for would, I imagine, in this as well as a great many other cases, quickly end the dispute. For I am apt to think that men, when they come to examine them, find their simple ideas all generally to agree, though in discourse with one another they perhaps confound one another with different names. I imagine that men who abstract their thoughts, and do well examine the ideas of their own minds, cannot much differ in thinking, however they may perplex themselves with words, according to the way of speaking of the several schools or sects they have been bred up in; though amongst unthinking men, who examine not scrupulously and carefully their own ideas, and strip them not from the marks men use for them, but confound them with words, there must be endless dispute, wrangling, and jargon ; especially if they be learned, bookish men, devoted to some sect, and accustomed to the language of it, and have learned to talk after others. But if it should happen that any two thinking men should really have different ideas, I do not see how they could discourse or argue one with another. Here I must not be mistaken, to think that every floating imagination in men's brains is presently of that sort of ideas I speak of. It is not easy for the mind to put off those confused notions and prejudices it has imbibed from custom, inadvertency, and common conversation : it requires pains and assiduity to examine its ideas, till it resolves them into those clear and distinct simple ones out of which they are compounded, and

to see which amongst its simple ones have or have not a necessary connexion and dependence one upon another. Till a man doth this in the primary and original notions of things, he builds upon floating and uncertain principles, and will often find himself at a loss.

## CHAPTER XIV.
### OF DURATION, AND ITS SIMPLE MODES.

**1.** *Duration is fleeting extension.*—There is another sort of distance or length, the idea whereof we get not from the permanent parts of space, but from the fleeting and perpetually perishing parts of succession : this we call "duration," the simple modes whereof are any different lengths of it whereof we have distinct ideas, as hours, days, years, &c., time, and eternity.

**2.** *Its idea from reflection on the train of our ideas.*—The answer of a great man to one who asked what time was, *Si non rogas intelligo* (which amounts to this : "The more I set myself to think of it the less I understand it,") might perhaps persuade one that time, which reveals all other things, is itself not to be discovered. Duration, time, and eternity are not without reason thought to have something very abstruse in their nature. But however remote these may seem from our comprehension, yet if we trace them right to their originals, I doubt not but one of those sources of all our knowledge, viz., sensation and reflection, will be able to furnish us with these ideas as clear and distinct as many other which are thought much less obscure; and we shall find that the idea of eternity itself is derived from the same common original with the rest of our ideas.

**3.** To understand time and eternity aright, we ought with attention to consider what idea it is we have of duration, and how we came by it. It is evident to anyone who will but observe what passes in his own mind, that there is a train of ideas which constantly succeed one another in his understanding as long as he is awake. Reflection on these appearances of several ideas one after another in our minds, is that which furnishes us with the idea of succession; and the distance between any parts of that succession, or between the appearance of any two ideas in our minds, is that we call duration. For whilst we are thinking, or whilst we receive successively several ideas in our minds, we know that we do exist; and so we call the existence or the continuation of the existence of ourselves, or anything else commensurate to the succession of any ideas in our minds, the duration of ourselves, or any such other thing co-existing with our thinking.

**4.** That we have our notion of succession and duration from this original, viz., from reflection on the train of ideas which we

find to appear one after another in our own minds, seems plain
to me, in that we have no perception of duration but by considering the train of ideas that take their turns in our understandings. When that succession of ideas ceases, our perception of
duration ceases with it; which everyone clearly experiments in
himself whilst he sleeps soundly, whether an hour or a day, or
a month, or a year; of which duration of things whilst he sleeps
or thinks not he has no perception at all, but it is quite lost to
him; and the moment wherein he leaves off to think till the
moment he begins to think again, seems to him to have no
distance. And so I doubt not it would be to a waking man, if it
were possible for him to keep only one idea in his mind without
variation and the succession of others; and we see that one who
fixes his thoughts very intently on one thing, so as to take but
little notice of the succession of ideas that pass in his mind
whilst he is taken up with that earnest contemplation, lets slip
out of his account a good part of that duration and thinks the
time shorter than it is. But if sleep commonly unites the distant parts of duration, it is because during that time we have
no succession of ideas in our minds. For if a man during his
sleep dreams, and variety of ideas make themselves perceptible
in his mind one after another, he hath then, during such a
dreaming, a sense of duration, and of the length of it: by which it
is to me very clear that men derive their ideas of duration from
their reflection on the train of the ideas they observe to succeed
one another in their own understandings; without which observation they can have no notion of duration, whatever may happen
in the world.

5. *The idea of duration applicable to things whilst we sleep.*
—Indeed, a man having, from reflection on the succession and
number of his own thoughts, got the notion or idea of duration,
he can apply that notion to things which exist while he does not
think; as he that has got the idea of extension from bodies by
his sight or touch, can apply it to distances where no body is
seen or felt. And therefore, though a man has no perception
of the length of duration which passed whilst he slept or thought
not, yet, having observed the revolution of days and nights, and
found the length of their duration to be in appearance regular
and constant, he can, upon the supposition that that revolution
has proceeded after the same manner whilst he was asleep or
thought not, as it used to do at other times,—he can, I say,
imagine and make allowance for the length of duration whilst
he slept. But if Adam and Eve (when they were alone in the
world), instead of their ordinary night's sleep, had passed the
whole twenty-four hours in one continued sleep, the duration of
that twenty-four hours had been irrecoverably lost to them, and
been for ever left out of their account of time.

6. *The idea of succession not from motion.*—Thus, by reflect-

ing on the appearance of various ideas one after another in our understandings, we get the notion of succession; which if anyone should think we did rather get from our observation of motion by our senses, he will perhaps be of my mind, when he considers that even motion produces in his mind an idea of succession no otherwise than as it produces there a continued train of distinguishable ideas. For, a man, looking upon a body really moving, perceives yet no motion at all, unless that motion produces a constant train of successive ideas; *v. g.*, a man becalmed at sea, out of sight of land, in a fair day may look on the sun, or sea, or ship, a whole hour together, and perceive no motion at all in either; though it be certain that two, and perhaps all of them, have moved during that time a great way; but as soon as he perceives either of them to have changed distance with some other body, as soon as this motion produces any new idea in him, then he perceives that there has been motion. But wherever a man is with all things at rest about him, without perceiving any motion at all, if during this hour of quiet he has been thinking, he will perceive the various ideas of his own thoughts in his own mind appearing one after another, and thereby observe and find succession where he could observe no motion.

7. And this, I think, is the reason why motions very slow, though they are constant, are not perceived by us : because, in their remove from one sensible part towards another, their change of distance is so slow that it causes no new ideas in us but a good while one after another; and so, not causing a constant train of new ideas to follow one another immediately in our minds, we have no perception of motion, which, consisting in a constant succession, we cannot perceive that succession without a constant succession of varying ideas arising from it.

8. On the contrary, things that move so swift as not to affect the senses distinctly with several distinguishable distances of their motion, and so cause not any train of ideas in the mind, are not also perceived to move. For anything that moves round about in a circle in less time than our ideas are wont to succeed one another in our minds, is not perceived to move, but seems to be a perfect, entire circle of that matter or colour, and not a part of a circle in motion.

9. *The train of ideas has a certain degree of quickness.*—Hence I leave it to others to judge, whether it be not probable that our ideas do, whilst we are awake, succeed one another in our minds at certain distances, not much unlike the images in the inside of a lantern, turned round by the heat of a candle. This appearance of theirs in train, though perhaps it may be sometimes faster and sometimes slower, yet, I guess, varies not very much in a waking man : there seem to be certain bounds to the quickness and slowness of the succession of those ideas one to another in our minds, beyond which they can neither delay nor hasten.

**10.** The reason I have for this odd conjecture is from observing that, in the impressions made upon any of our senses, we can but to a certain degree perceive any succession; which if exceeding quick, the sense of succession is lost, even in cases where it is evident that there is a real succession. Let a cannon-bullet pass through a room, and in its way take with it any limb or fleshy parts of a man, it is as clear as any demonstration can be that it must strike successively the two sides of the room; it is also evident that it must touch one part of the flesh first, and another after, and so on in succession: and yet I believe nobody who ever felt the pain of such a shot, or heard the blow against the two distant walls, could perceive any succession either in the pain or sound of so swift a stroke. Such a part of duration as this, wherein we perceive no succession, is that which we may call an instant, and is that which takes up the time of only one idea in our minds without the succession of another, wherein therefore we perceive no succession at all.

**11.** This also happens where the motion is so slow as not to supply a constant train of fresh ideas to the senses, as fast as the mind is capable of receiving new ones into it; and so other ideas of our own thoughts having room to come into our minds between those offered to our senses by the moving body, there the sense of motion is lost; and the body, though it really moves, yet not changing perceivable distance with some other bodies as fast as the ideas of our own minds do naturally follow one another in train, the thing seems to stand still, as is evident in the hands of clocks and shadows of sundials, and other constant but slow motions; where, though after certain intervals we perceive by the change of distance that it hath moved, yet the motion itself we perceive not.

**12.** *This train the measure of other successions.*—So that to me it seems, that the constant and regular succession of ideas in a waking man is, as it were, the measure and standard of all other successions; whereof if any one either exceeds the place of our ideas,—as where two sounds or pains, &c., take up in their succession the duration of but one idea, or else where any motion or succession is so slow that it keeps not pace with the ideas in our minds, or the quickness in which they take their turns; as when any one or more ideas in their ordinary course come into our mind between those which are offered to the sight by the different perceptible distances of a body in motion, or between sounds or smells following one another,—there also the sense of a constant, continued succession is lost, and we perceive it not but with certain gaps of rest between.

**18.** *The mind cannot fix long on one invariable idea.*—If it be so, that the ideas of our minds, whilst we have any there, do constantly change and shift in a continual succession, it would be impossible, may anyone say, for a man to think long of any one thing: by which if it be meant that a man may have one self-same single idea a long time alone in his mind, without any variation at all, I think, in matter of fact, it is not possible: for which (not knowing how the ideas of our minds are framed, of what materials they are made, whence they have their light, and how they come to make their appearances) I can give no other reason but experience; and I would have anyone try whether he can keep one unvaried, single idea in his mind, without any other, for any considerable time together.

14. For trial, let him take any figure, any degree of light or whiteness, or what other he pleases; and he will, I suppose, find it difficult to keep all other ideas out of his mind; but that some, either of another kind, or various consideration of that idea (each of which considerations is a new idea), will constantly succeed one another in his thoughts, let him be as wary as he can.

15. All that is in a man's power in this case, I think, is only to mind and observe what the ideas are, that take their turns in his understanding, or else to direct the sort, and call in such as he hath a desire or use of; but hinder the constant succession of fresh ones I think he cannot, though he may commonly choose whether he will heedfully observe and consider them.

16. *Ideas, however made, include no sense of motion.*—Whether these several ideas in a man's mind be made by certain motions, I will not here dispute; but this I am sure, that they include no idea of motion in their appearance; and if a man had not the idea of motion otherwise, I think he would have none at all; which is enough to my present purpose; and sufficiently shows, that the notice we take of the ideas of our minds, appearing there one after another, is that which gives us the idea of succession and duration, without which we should have no such ideas at all. It is not then motion, but the constant train of ideas in our minds, whilst we are waking, that furnishes us with the idea of duration, whereof motion no otherwise gives us any perception than as it causes in our minds a constant succession of ideas, as I have before showed: and we have as clear an idea of succession and duration, by the train of other ideas succeeding one another in our minds without the idea of any motion, as by the train of ideas caused by the uninterrupted sensible change of distance between two bodies which we have from motion; and therefore we should as well have the idea of duration, were there no sense of motion at all.

17. *Time is duration set out by measures.*—Having thus got the idea of duration, the next thing natural for the mind to do is, to get some measure of this common duration, whereby it might judge of its different lengths, and consider the distinct order wherein several things exist: without which a great part of our knowledge would be confused, and a great part of history be rendered very useless. This consideration of duration, as set out

by certain periods, and marked by certain measures or epochs, is
that, I think, which most properly we call " time."

18. *A good measure of time must divide its whole duration into
equal periods.*—In the measuring of extension there is nothing
more required but the application of the standard or measure we
make use of to the thing of whose extension we would be informed.
But in the measuring of duration this cannot be done, because no
two different parts of succession can be put together to measure
one another : and nothing being a measure of duration but duration, as nothing is of extension but extension, we cannot keep by
us any standing unvarying measure of duration, which consists in a
constant fleeting succession, as we can of certain lengths of extension, as inches, feet, yards, &c., marked out in permanent parcels
of matter. Nothing then could serve well for a convenient
measure of time but what has divided the whole length of its
duration into apparently equal portions by constantly repeated
periods. What portions of duration are not distinguished or
considered as distinguished and measured by such periods come
not so properly under the notion of time, as appears by such
phrases as these, viz., " before all time," and " when time shall
be no more."

19. *The revolutions of the sun and moon the properest measures
of time.*—The diurnal and annual revolutions of the sun, as having
been from the beginning of nature, constant, regular, and universally observable by all mankind, and supposed equal to one
another, have been with reason made use of for the measure of
duration. But the distinction of days and years having depended
on the motion of the sun, it has brought this mistake with it,—
that it has been thought that motion and duration were the
measure one of another. For men in the measuring of the length
of time having been accustomed to the ideas of minutes, hours,
days, months, years, &c., which they found themselves upon any
mention of time or duration presently to think on (all which
portions of time were measured out by the motion of those
heavenly bodies), they were apt to confound time and motion, or
at least to think that they had a necessary connexion one with
another ; whereas any constant periodical appearance or alteration of ideas in seemingly equidistant spaces of duration, if constant and universally observable, would have as well distinguished
the intervals of time as those that have been made use of. For
supposing the sun, which some have taken to be a fire, had been
lighted up at the same distance of time that it now every day
comes about to the same meridian, and then gone out again about
twelve hours after, and that in the space of an annual revolution
it had sensibly increased in brightness and heat, and so decreased
again ; would not such regular appearances serve to measure out
the distances of duration to all that could observe it, as well
without as with motion ? For if the appearances were constant,

universally observable, and in equidistant periods, they would
serve mankind for measure of time as well were the motion away.

20. *But not by their motion, but periodical appearances.*—For
the freezing of water or the blowing of a plant, returning at equidistant periods in all parts of the earth, would as well serve men
to reckon their years by as the motion of the sun; and in effect
we see that some people in America counted their years by the
coming of certain birds amongst them at their certain seasons,
and leaving them at others. For a fit of an ague, the sense of
hunger or thirst, a smell, or a taste, or any other idea returning
constantly at equidistant periods, and making itself universally be
taken notice of, would not fail to measure out the course of succession, and distinguish the distances of time. Thus we see, that
men born blind count time well enough by years, whose revolutions yet they cannot distinguish by motions that they perceive
not : and I ask, whether a blind man who distinguished his years
either by heat of summer, or cold of winter, by the smell of any
flower of the spring, or taste of any fruit of the autumn, would
not have a better measure of time than the Romans had before
the reformation of their calendar by Julius Cæsar, or many other
people, whose years, notwithstanding the motion of the sun,
which they pretend to make use of, are very irregular ? And it
adds no small difficulty to chronology, that the exact lengths of
the years that several nations counted by are hard to be known,
they differing very much one from another, and, I think I may
say, all of them from the precise motion of the sun. And if the
sun moved from the creation to the flood constantly in the equator,
and so equally dispersed its light and heat, to all the habitable
parts of the earth in days all of the same length, without its
annual variations to the tropics, as a late ingenious author supposes,* I do not think it very easy to imagine that (notwithstanding the motion of the sun) men should in the antediluvian world
from the beginning count by years, or measure their time by
periods that had no sensible marks very obvious to distinguish
them by.

21. *No two parts of duration can be certainly known to be equal.*
—But perhaps it will be said, "Without a regular motion, such as
of the sun or some other, how could it ever be known that such
periods were equal ?" To which I answer, the equality of any
other returning appearances might be known by the same way
that that of days was known, or presumed to be so at first : which
was only by judging of them by the train of ideas that had passed
in men's minds in the intervals : by which train of ideas discovering inequality in the natural days, but none in the artificial
days, the " artificial days," or νυχθήμερα, were guessed to be equal,
which was sufficient to make them serve for a measure. Though
exacter search has since discovered inequality in the diurnal

* DR. THOMAS BURNET'S "Theory of the Earth."

revolutions of the sun, and we know not whether the annual also be not unequal; these, yet, by their presumed and apparent equality, serve as well to reckon time by (though not to measure the parts of duration exactly), as if they could be proved to be exactly equal. We must therefore carefully distinguish betwixt duration itself and the measures we make use of to judge of its length. Duration in itself is to be considered as going on in one constant, equal, uniform course. But none of the measures of it which we make use of can be known to do so: nor can we be assured that their assigned parts or periods are equal in duration one to another; for two successive lengths of duration, however measured, can never be demonstrated to be equal. The motion of the sun, which the world used so long and so confidently for an exact measure of duration, has, as I said, been found in its several parts unequal; and though men have of late made use of a pendulum as a more steady and regular motion than that of the sun or (to speak more truly) of the earth; yet if anyone should be asked how he certainly knows that the two successive swings of a pendulum are equal, it would be very hard to satisfy himself that they are infallibly so; since we cannot be sure that the cause of that motion which is unknown to us shall always operate equally, and we are sure that the medium in which the pendulum moves is not constantly the same: either of which varying may alter the equality of such periods, and thereby destroy the certainty and exactness of the measure by motion, as well as any other periods of other appearances; the notion of duration still remaining clear, though our measures of it cannot any of them be demonstrated to be exact. Since, then, no two portions of succession can be brought together, it is impossible ever certainly to know their equality. All that we can do for a measure of time, is to take such as have continual successive appearances at seemingly equidistant periods; of which seeming equality we have no other measure but such as the train of our own ideas have lodged in our memories, with the concurrence of other probable reasons, to persuade us of their equality.

22. *Time not the measure of motion.*—One thing seems strange to me, that whilst all men manifestly measured time by the motion of the great and visible bodies of the world, time yet should be defined to be the measure of motion; whereas it is obvious to everyone who reflects ever so little on it, that, to measure motion, space is as necessary to be considered as time; and those who look a little farther, will find also the bulk of the thing moved necessary to be taken into the computation by anyone who will estimate or measure motion so as to judge right of it. Nor indeed does motion any otherwise conduce to the measuring of duration, than as it constantly brings about the return of certain sensible ideas in seeming equidistant periods. For if the motion of the sun were as unequal as of a ship driven

by unsteady winds, sometimes very slow, and at others irregu-
larly very swift ; or if being constantly equally swift, it yet was
not circular, and produced not the same appearances ; it would
not at all help us to measure time any more than the seeming
unequal motion of a comet does.

23. *Minutes, hours, days, and years not necessary measures
of duration.*—Minutes, hours, days, and years are, then, no more
necessary to time or duration than inches, feet, yards, and miles
marked out in any matter are to extension. For though we in
this part of the universe, by the constant use of them, as of
periods set out by the revolutions of the sun, or as known parts
of such periods have fixed the ideas of such lengths of duration
in our minds which we apply to all parts of time whose lengths
we would consider ; yet there may be other parts of the universe
where they no more use these measures of ours than in Japan
they do our inches, feet, or miles ; but yet something analogous
to them there must be. For without some regular periodical
returns, we could not measure ourselves or signify to others the
length of any duration, though at the same time the world were
as full of motion as it is now, but no part of it disposed into
regular and apparently equidistant revolutions. But the different measures that may be made use of for the account of
time do not at all alter the notion of duration, which is the
thing to be measured, no more than the different standards of a
foot and a cubit alter the notion of extension to those who make
use of those different measures.

25. *Our measures of time applicable to duration before time.*
—The mind, having once got such a measure of time as the
annual revolution of the sun, can apply that measure to duration wherein that measure itself did not exist, and with which
in the reality of its being it had nothing to do : for should
one say that Abraham was born in the 2712th year of the
Julian period, it is altogether as intelligible as reckoning from
the beginning of the world, though there were, so far back, no
motion of the sun, nor any other motion at all. For though
the Julian period be supposed to begin several hundred years
before there were really either days, nights, or years marked
out by any revolutions of the sun, yet we reckon as right, and
thereby measure durations as well, as if really at that time the
sun had existed, and kept the same ordinary motion it doth
now. The idea of duration equal to an annual revolution of the
sun is as easily applicable in our thoughts to duration, where no
sun nor motion was, as the idea of a foot or yard taken from
bodies here can be applied in our thoughts to distances beyond
the confines of the world, where are no bodies at all.

26. For, supposing it were 5639 miles, or millions of miles,
from this place to the remotest body of the universe (for, being
facts, it must be at a certain distance), as we suppose it to be

5639 years from this time to the first existence of any body in
the beginning of the world; we can in our thoughts apply this
measure of a year to duration before the creation, or beyond
the duration of bodies or motion, as we can this measure of a
mile to space beyond the utmost bodies; and by the one measure
duration where there was no motion, as well as by the other
measure space in our thoughts where there is no body.

27. If it be objected to me here, that in this way of explaining
of time I have begged what I should not, viz., that the world
is neither eternal nor infinite, I answer, that to my present purpose it is not needful in this place to make use of arguments to
evince the world to be finite both in duration and extension; but
it being at least as conceivable as the contrary, I have certainly
the liberty to suppose it, as well as anyone hath to suppose the
contrary: and I doubt not but that everyone that will go about
it may easily conceive in his mind the beginning of motion,
though not of all duration, and so may come to a stop and *non
ultra* in his consideration of motion. So also in his thoughts he
may set limits to body, and the extension belonging to it, but
not to space where no body is; the utmost bounds of space and
duration being beyond the reach of thought, as well as the
utmost bounds of number are beyond the largest comprehension of the mind; and all for the same reason, as we shall see in
another place.

28. *Eternity.*—By the same means, therefore, and from the
same original, that we come to have the idea of time, we have
also that idea which we call "eternity," viz., having got the idea
of succession and duration, by reflecting on the train of our own
ideas, caused in us either by the natural appearances of those
ideas coming constantly of themselves into our waking thoughts,
or else caused by external objects successively affecting our
senses; and having from the revolutions of the sun got the ideas
of certain lengths of duration, we can in our thoughts add such
lengths of duration to one another as often as we please, and
apply them, so added, to durations past or to come: and this
we can continue to do on, without bounds or limits, and proceed *in infinitum*, and apply thus the length of the annual
motion of the sun to duration, supposed before the sun's or any
other motion had its being; which is no more difficult or
absurd than to apply the notion I have of the moving of a
shadow one hour to-day upon the sun-dial to the duration of
something last night; *v. g.*, the burning of a candle, which is
now absolutely separate from all actual motion; and it is as
impossible for the duration of that flame for an hour last
night to co-exist with any motion that now is, or for ever shall
be, as for any part of duration that was before the beginning
of the world to co-exist with the motion of the sun now. But
yet this hinders not but that, having the idea of the length of

the motion of the shadow on a dial between the marks of two
hours, I can as distinctly measure in my thoughts the duration
of that candle-light last night as I can the duration of anything
that does now exist; and it is no more than to think, that had
the sun shone then on the dial, and moved after the same rate it
doth now, the shadow on the dial would have passed from one
hour-line to another whilst that flame of the candle lasted.

29. The notion of an hour, day, or year, being only the idea
I have of the length of certain periodical regular motions
(neither of which motions do ever all at once exist, but only
in the ideas I have of them in my memory, derived from my
senses or reflection), I can with the same ease and for the same
reason apply it in my thoughts to duration antecedent to all
manner of motion, as well as to anything that is but a minute
or a day antecedent to the motion that at this very moment
the sun is in. All things past are equally and perfectly at
rest; and to this way of consideration of them are all one,
whether they were before the beginning of the world, or but
yesterday: the measuring of any duration by some motion
depending not at all on the real co-existence of that thing to
that motion, or any other periods of revolution; but the having
a clear idea of the length of some periodical known motion or
other intervals of duration in my mind, and applying that to the
duration of the thing I would measure.

30. Hence we see that some men imagine the duration of the
world from its first existence to this present year 1689, to
have been 5639 years, or equal to 5639 annual revolutions of
the sun, and others a great deal more; as the Egyptians of
old, who, in the time of Alexander, counted 23,000 years from
the reign of the sun; and the Chinese now, who account the
world 3,269,000 years old, or more: which longer duration of
the world, according to their computation, though I should not
believe to be true, yet, I can equally imagine it with them, and
as truly understand and say one is longer than the other, as I
understand that Methuselah's life was longer than Enoch's.
And if the common reckoning of 5639 should be true (as it
may be, as well as any other assigned), it hinders not at all
my imagining what others mean when they make the world
1000 years older, since everyone may with the same facility
imagine (I do not say believe) the world to be 50,000 years
old as 5639, and may as well conceive the duration of 50,000
years as 5639. Whereby it appears, that, to the measuring the
duration of anything by time, it is not requisite that that thing
should be co-existent to the motion we measure by, or any
other periodical revolution; but it suffices to this purpose, that
we have the idea of the length of any regular periodical appearances, which we can in our minds apply to duration, with which
the motion or appearance never co-existed.

81. For as, in the history of the creation delivered by Moses, I can imagine that light existed three days before the sun was or had any motion, barely by thinking that the duration of light before the sun was created was so long as (if the sun had moved then as it doth now) would have been equal to three of his diurnal revolutions; so by the same way I can have an idea of the chaos or angels being created before there was either light or any continued motion, a minute, an hour, a day, a year, or one thousand years. For if I can but consider duration equal to one minute, before either the being or motion of any body, I can add one minute more till I come to sixty; and by the same way of adding minutes, hours, or years (*i.e.*, such or such parts of the sun's revolution, or any other period whereof I have the idea), proceed *in infinitum*, and supposing a duration exceeding as many such periods as I can reckon, let me add whilst I will: which I think is the notion we have of eternity, of whose infinity we have no other notion than we have of the infinity of number, to which we can add for ever without end.

82. And thus I think it is plain, that from those two fountains of all knowledge before mentioned, (viz.) reflection and sensation, we get the ideas of duration, and the measures of it.

For, First, by observing what passes in our minds, how our ideas there in train constantly some vanish, and others begin to appear, we come by the idea of succession.

Secondly. By observing a distance in the parts of this succession, we get the idea of duration.

Thirdly. By sensation observing certain appearances, at certain regular and seeming equidistant periods, we get the ideas of certain lengths or measures of duration, as minutes, hours, days, years, &c.

Fourthly. By being able to repeat those measures of time, or ideas of stated length of duration in our minds, as often as we will, we can come to imagine duration where nothing does really endure or exist; and thus we imagine to-morrow, next year, or seven years hence.

Fifthly. By being able to repeat any such idea of any length of time, as of a minute, a year, or an age, as often as we will in our own thoughts, and add them one to another, without ever coming to the end of such addition, any nearer than we can to the end of number, to which we can always add, we come by the idea of eternity, as the future eternal duration of our souls, as well as the eternity of that infinite Being which must necessarily have always existed.

Sixthly. By considering any part of infinite duration, as set out by periodical measures, we come by the idea of what we call " time " in general.

## CHAPTER XV.

### OF DURATION AND EXPANSION CONSIDERED TOGETHER.

1. *Both capable of greater and less.*—Though we have in the precedent chapters dwelt pretty long on the considerations of space and duration, yet they being ideas of general concernment, that have something very abstruse and peculiar in their nature, the comparing them one with another may perhaps be of use for their illustration; and we may have the more clear and distinct conception of them by taking a view of them together. Distance or space, in its simple abstract conception, to avoid confusion, I call "expansion," to distinguish it from extension, which by some is used to express this distance only as it is in the solid parts of matter, and so includes, or at least intimates, the idea of body; whereas, the idea of pure distance includes no such thing. I prefer also the word "expansion" to "space," because space is often applied to distance of fleeting successive parts, which never exist together, as well as to those which are permanent. In both these (viz. expansion and duration) the mind has this common idea of continued lengths, capable of greater or less quantities; for a man has as clear an idea of the difference of the length of an hour and a day as of an inch and a foot.

2. *Expansion not bounded by matter.*—The mind having got the idea of the length of any part of expansion, let it be a span, or a pace, or what length you will, can, as has been said, repeat that idea; and so adding it to the former, enlarge its idea of length, and make it equal to two spans, or two paces, and so, as often as it will, till it equals the distance of any parts of the earth one from another, and increase thus till it amounts to the distance of the sun or remotest star. By such a progression as this, setting out from the place where it is, or any other place, it can proceed and pass beyond all those lengths, and find nothing to stop its going on, either in or without body. It is true we can easily in our thoughts come to the end of solid extension; the extremity and bounds of all body, we have no difficulty to arrive at: but when the mind is there, it finds nothing to hinder its progress into this endless expansion: of that it can neither find nor conceive any end. Nor let anyone say, that beyond the bounds of body there is nothing at all, unless he will confine God within the limits of matter. Solomon, whose understanding was filled and enlarged with wisdom, seems to have other thoughts, when he says, "Heaven and the heaven of heavens cannot contain thee." And he, I think, very much magnifies to himself the capacity of his own understanding who persuades himself that he can extend his thoughts farther than God exists, or imagine any expansion where he is not.

3. *Nor duration by motion.*—Just so is it in duration. The

mind, having got the idea of any length of duration, can double, multiply, and enlarge it, not only beyond its own, but beyond the existence of all corporeal beings and all the measures of time, taken from the great bodies of the world and their motions. But yet everyone easily admits, that though we make duration bound-less, as certainly it is, we cannot yet extend it beyond all being. God, everyone easily allows, fills eternity; and it is hard to find a reason why anyone should doubt that he likewise fills immen-sity. His infinite being is certainly as boundless one way as another; and methinks it ascribes a little too much to matter to say, "Where there is no body, there is nothing."

4. *Why men more easily admit infinite duration, than infinite expansion.*—Hence I think we may learn the reason why every-one familiarly, and without the least hesitation, speaks of and supposes eternity, and sticks not to ascribe infinity to duration; but it is with more doubting and reserve that many admit or suppose the infinity of space. The reason whereof seems to me to be this, that duration and extension being used as names of affections belonging to other beings, we easily conceive in God infinite duration, and we cannot avoid doing so: but not attri-buting to him extension, but only to matter, which is finite, we are apter to doubt of the existence of expansion without matter; of which alone we commonly suppose it an attribute. And there-fore when men pursue their thoughts of space, they are apt to stop at the confines of body; as if space were there at an end, too, and reached no farther. Or if their ideas upon consideration carry them farther, yet they term what is beyond the limits of the universe, "imaginary space;" as if it were nothing, because there is no body existing in it. Whereas duration, antecedent to all body, and to the motions which it is measured by, they never term "imaginary;" because it is never supposed void of some other real existence. And if the names of things may at all direct our thoughts towards the originals of men's ideas, (as I am apt to think they may very much,) one may have occasion to think by the name "duration," that the continuation of exist-ence, with a kind of resistance to any destructive force, and the continuation of solidity (which is apt to be confounded with, and if we will look into the minute anatomical parts of matter, is little different from, hardness), were thought to have some analogy, and gave occasion to words so near of kin as *durare* and *durum esse.* And that *durare* is applied to the idea of hardness, as well as that of existence, we see in HORACE, epod. xvi. *Ferro duravit secula.* But be that as it will, this is certain, whoever pursues his own thoughts, will find them sometimes launch out beyond the extent of body, into the infinity of space or expansion; the idea whereof is distinct and separate from body and all other things: which may (to those who please) be a subject of farther meditation.

**5.** *Time to duration, is as place to expansion.*—Time in general is to duration as place to expansion. They are so much of those boundless oceans of eternity and immensity, as is set out and distinguished from the rest as it were by land-marks; and so are made use of to denote the position of finite real beings, in respect one to another, in those uniform infinite oceans of duration and space. These, rightly considered, are nothing but ideas of determinate distances, from certain known points fixed in distinguishable sensible things, and supposed to keep the same distance one from another. From such points fixed in sensible beings we reckon, and from them we measure our portions of those infinite quantities; which, so considered, are that which we call "time" and "place." For duration and space being in themselves uniform and boundless, the order and position of things without such known settled points would be lost in them; and all things would lie jumbled in an incurable confusion.

**6.** *Time and place are taken for so much of either, as are set out by the existence and motion of bodies.*—Time and place taken thus for determinate distinguishable portions of those infinite abysses of space and duration, set out, or supposed to be distinguished from the rest, by marks and known boundaries, have each of them a twofold acceptation.

First. Time in general is commonly taken for so much of infinite duration, as is measured out by and co-existent with the existence and motions of the great bodies of the universe, as far as we know anything of them; and in this sense, time begins and ends with the frame of this sensible world, as in these phrases before mentioned, "before all time," or "when time shall be no more." Place likewise is taken sometimes for that portion of infinite space which is possessed by and comprehended within the material world, and is thereby distinguished from the rest of expansion; though this may more properly be called "extension" than "place." Within these two are confined, and by the observable parts of them are measured and determined, the particular time or duration, and the particular extension and place, of all corporeal beings.

**7.** *Sometimes for so much of either, as we design by measures taken from the bulk or motion of bodies.*—Secondly. Sometimes the word "time" is used in a larger sense, and is applied to parts of that infinite duration, not that were really distinguished and measured out by this real existence and periodical motions of bodies that were appointed from the beginning to be for signs, and for seasons, and for days, and years, and are accordingly our measures of time; but such other portions, too, of that infinite uniform duration which we upon any occasion do suppose equal to certain lengths of measured time; and so consider them as bounded and determined. For if we should suppose the creation or fall of the angels was at the beginning of the Julian period,

we should speak properly enough, and should be understood, if
we said, "It is a longer time since the creation of angels than
the creation of the world, by 764 years:" whereby we would
mark out so much of that undistinguished duration as we supposed equal to, and would have admitted, 764 annual revolutions
of the sun, moving at the rate it now does. And thus likewise
we sometimes speak of place, distance, or bulk in the great inane
beyond the confines of the world, when we consider so much of
that space as is equal to or capable to receive a body of any
assigned dimensions, as a cubic-foot, or do suppose a point in it
at such a certain distance from any part of the universe.

8. *They belong to all beings.*—WHERE and WHEN are questions
belonging to all finite existences, and are by us always reckoned
from some known parts of this sensible world, and from some
certain epochs marked out to us by the motions observable in it.
Without some such fixed parts or periods, the order of things
would be lost to our finite understandings in the boundless, invariable oceans of duration and expansion; which comprehend
in them all finite beings, and in their full extent belong only to
the Deity. And therefore we are not to wonder that we comprehend them not, and do so often find our thoughts at a loss,
when we would consider them either abstractedly in themselves,
or as any way attributed to the first incomprehensible Being.
But when applied to any particular finite beings, the extension
of any body is so much of that infinite space as the bulk of that
body takes up. And place is the position of any body, when
considered at a certain distance from some other. As the idea
of the particular duration of anything is an idea of that portion
of infinite duration which passes during the existence of that
thing, so the time when the thing existed is the idea of that
space of duration which passed between some known and fixed
period of duration, and the being of that thing. One shows the
distance of the extremities of the bulk or existence of the same
thing, as that it is a foot square, or lasted two years; the other
shows the distance of it in place or existence from other fixed
points of space or duration; as that it was in the middle of
Lincoln's-Inn-Fields, or the first degree of *Taurus*, and in the
year of our Lord 1671, or the 1000th year of the Julian period:
all of which distances we measure by preconceived ideas of certain lengths of space and duration, as inches, feet, miles, and
degrees; and in the other, minutes, days, and years, &c.

9. *All the parts of extension are extension; and all the parts of
duration are duration.*—There is one thing more wherein space
and duration have a great conformity; and that is, though they
are justly reckoned amongst our simple ideas, yet none of the
distinct ideas we have of either is without all manner of composition;* it is the very nature of both of them to consist of parts:

* See the Note at the end of this chapter, p. 140.—EDIT.

but their parts, being all of the same kind, and without the
mixture of any other idea, hinder them not from having a place
amongst simple ideas. Could the mind, as in number, come to
so small a part of extension or duration as excluded divisibility,
that would be, as it were, the indivisible unit or idea; by repetition of which, it would make its more enlarged ideas of
extension and duration. But since the mind is not able to frame
an idea of any space without parts, instead thereof it makes use
of the common measures, which by familiar use in each country
have imprinted themselves on the memory : (as inches, and feet;
or cubits, and parasangs ; and so seconds, minutes, hours, days,
and years in duration:) the mind makes use, I say, of such ideas
as these, as simple ones ; and these are the component parts of
larger ideas, which the mind, upon occasion, makes by the addition of such known lengths which it is acquainted with. On
the other side, the ordinary smallest measure we have of either,
is looked on as an unit in number, when the mind by division
would reduce them into less fractions. Though on both sides,
both in addition and division, either of space or duration, when
the idea under consideration becomes very big or very small, its
precise bulk becomes very obscure and confused; and it is the
number of its repeated additions or divisions, that alone remains
clear and distinct ; as will easily appear to anyone who will let
his thoughts loose in the vast expansion of space, or divisibility
of matter. Every part of duration is duration too; and every
part of extension is extension; both of them capable of addition
or division *in infinitum*. But the least portions of either of them,
whereof we have clear and distinct ideas, may perhaps be fittest
to be considered by us as the simple ideas of that kind, out of
which our complex modes of space, extension, and duration are
made up, and into which they can again be distinctly resolved.
Such a small part in duration may be called a "moment," and
is the time of one idea in our minds, in the train of their ordinary
succession there. The other, wanting a proper name, I know not
whether I may be allowed to call " a sensible point," meaning
thereby the least particle of matter or space we can discern,
which is ordinarily about a minute, and to the sharpest eyes
seldom less than thirty seconds, of a circle whereof the eye is
the centre.

10. *Their parts inseparable.*—Expansion and duration have
this farther agreement, that though they are both considered by
us as having parts, yet their parts are not separable one from
another, no, not even in thought; though the parts of bodies
from whence we take our measure of the one, and the parts of
motion, or rather the succession of ideas in our minds, from
whence we take the measure of the other, may be interrupted
and separated, as the one is often by rest, and the other is by
sleep, which we call rest too.

**11.** *Duration is as a line, expansion as a solid.*—But yet there is this manifest difference between them, that the ideas of length which we have of expansion are turned every way, and so make figure, and breadth, and thickness; but duration is but as it were the length of one straight line extended *in infinitum*, not capable of multiplicity, variation, or figure, but is one common measure of all existence whatsoever, wherein all things, whilst they exist, equally partake. For this present moment is common to all things that are now in being, and equally comprehends that part of their existence as much as if they were all but one single being; and we may truly say, they all exist in the same moment of time. Whether angels and spirits have any analogy to this in respect of expansion is beyond my comprehension; and perhaps for us, who have understandings and comprehensions suited to our own preservation and the ends of our own being, but not to the reality and extent of all other beings, it is near as hard to conceive any existence, or to have an idea of any real being, with a perfect negation of all manner of expansion, as it is to have the idea of any real existence with a perfect negation of all manner of duration: and therefore what spirits have to do with space, or how they communicate in it, we know not. All that we know is, that bodies do each singly possess its proper portion of it, according to the extent of its solid parts; and thereby exclude all other bodies from having any share in that particular portion of space whilst it remains there.

**12.** *Duration has never two parts together, expansion all together.*—Duration and time, which is a part of it, is the idea we have of perishing distance, of which no two parts exist together, but follow each other in succession; as expansion is the idea of lasting distance, all whose parts exist together, and are not capable of succession. And, therefore, though we cannot conceive any duration without succession, nor can put it together in our thoughts that any being does now exist to-morrow, or possess at once more than the present moment of duration; yet we can conceive the eternal duration of the Almighty far different from that of man, or any other finite being; because man comprehends not in his knowledge or power all past or future things: his thoughts are but of yesterday, and he knows not what to-morrow will bring forth. What is once past he can never recall; and what is yet to come he cannot make present. What I say of man I say of all finite beings, who, though they may far exceed man in knowledge and power, yet are no more than the meanest creature in comparison with God himself. Finite, of any magnitude, holds not any proportion to infinite. God's infinite duration being accompanied with infinite knowledge and infinite power, he sees all things past and to come; and they are no more distant from his knowledge, no farther removed from his sight, than the present: they all lie under the same view: and there is nothing which he cannot make exist each moment he pleases.  For, the existence of all things depending upon his good pleasure, all things exist every moment that he thinks fit to have them exist.  To conclude : expansion and duration do mutually embrace and comprehend each other ; every part of space being in every part of duration, and every part of duration in every part of expansion.  Such a combination of two distinct ideas is, I suppose, scarce to be found in all that great variety we do or can conceive, and may afford matter to farther speculation.

---

### NOTE.—Page 137.

It has been objected to Mr. Loçke, that if space consists of parts, as it is confessed in this place, he should not have reckoned it in the number of simple ideas ; because it seems to be inconsistent with what he says elsewhere, that "a simple idea is uncompounded, and contains in it nothing but one uniform appearance or conception of the mind, and is not distinguishable into different ideas." (Page 70.)  It is farther objected, that Mr. Locke has not given in the eleventh chapter of the second book, where he begins to speak of simple ideas, an exact definition of what he understands by the word "simple ideas."  To these difficulties Mr. Locke answers thus : To begin with the last, he declares, that he has not treated his subject in an order perfectly scholastic, having not had much familiarity with those sort of books during the writing of his, and not remembering at all the method in which they are written ; and therefore his readers ought not to expect definitions regularly placed at the beginning of each new subject.  Mr. Locke contents himself to employ the principal terms that he uses, so that from his use of them the reader may easily comprehend what he means by them.  But with respect to the term "simple idea," he has had the good luck to define that in the place cited in the objection ; and therefore there is no reason to supply that defect.  The question then is to know, whether the idea of extension agrees with this definition? which will effectually agree to it, if it be understood in the sense which Mr. Locke had principally in his view : for that composition which he designed to exclude in that definition, was a composition of different ideas in the mind, and not a composition of the same kind in a thing whose essence consists in having parts of the same kind, where you can never come to a part entirely exempted from this composition.  So that if the idea of extension consists in having *partes extra partes* (as the schools speak), it is always, in the sense of Mr. Locke, a simple idea ; because the idea of having *partes extra partes*, cannot be resolved into two other ideas.  For the remainder of the objection made to Mr. Locke, with respect to the nature of extension, Mr. Locke was aware of it, as may be seen in sect. 9, chap. xv. of the second book, where he says, that "the least portion of space or extension, whereof we have a clear and distinct idea, may perhaps be the fittest to be considered by us as a simple idea of that kind, out of which our complex modes of space and extension are made up."  So that, according to Mr. Locke, it may very fitly be called a simple idea, since it is the least idea of space that the mind can form to itself, and that cannot be divided by the mind into any less whereof it has in itself any determined perception. From whence it follows, that it is to the mind one simple idea; and that is sufficient to take away this objection : for it is not the design of Mr. Locke in this place to discourse of anything but concerning the ideas of the mind. But if this is not sufficient to clear the difficulty, Mr. Locke hath nothing more to add, but that if the idea of extension is so peculiar that it cannot exactly agree with the definition that he has given of those simple ideas, so that it differs in some manner from all others of that kind, he thinks it is better to leave it there exposed to this difficulty than to make a new division in his favour. It is enough for Mr. Locke that his meaning can be understood. It is very common to observe intelligible discourses spoiled by too much subtilty in nice divisions. We ought to put things together as well as we can, *doctrinæ causâ ;* but, after all, several things will not be bundled up together under our terms and ways of speaking.

---

## CHAPTER XVI.

### OF NUMBER.

1. *Number, the simplest and most universal idea.*—Amongst all the ideas we have, as there is none suggested to the mind by more ways, so there is none more simple, than that of unity, or one. It has no shadow of variety of composition in it; every object our senses are employed about, every idea in our understandings, every thought of our minds, brings this idea along with it : and therefore it is the most intimate to our thoughts, as well as it is, in its agreement to all other things, the most universal idea we have. For number applies itself to men, angels, actions, thoughts, —everything that either doth exist or can be imagined.

2. *Its modes made by addition.*—By repeating this idea in our minds, and adding the repetitions together, we come by the complex ideas of the modes of it. Thus by adding one to one we have the complex idea of a couple : by putting twelve units together we have the complex idea of a dozen; and a score, or a million, or any other number.

3. *Each mode distinct.*—The simple modes of number are of all other the most distinct ; every the least variation which is an unit, making each combination as clearly different from that which approacheth nearest to it, as the most remote : two being as distinct from one as two hundred; and the idea of two as distinct from the idea of three, as the magnitude of the whole earth is from that of a mite. This is not so in other simple modes, in which it is not so easy, nor perhaps possible, for us to distinguish betwixt two approaching ideas, which yet are really different. For who will undertake to find a difference between the white of this paper and that of the next degree to it ? or can form distinct ideas of every the least excess in extension ?

*4. Therefore demonstrations in numbers the most precise.*—
The clearness and distinctness of each mode of number from all
others, even those that approach nearest, makes me apt to think
that demonstrations in numbers, if they are not more evident and
exact than in extension, yet they are more general in their use,
and more determinate in their application. Because the ideas of
numbers are more precise and distinguishable than in extension,
where every equality and excess are not so easy to be observed
or measured; because our thoughts cannot in space arrive at any
determined smallness beyond which it cannot go, as an unit; and
therefore the quantity or proportion of any of the least excess cannot be discovered: which is clear otherwise in number, where,
as has been said, 91 is as distinguishable from 90 as from 9000,
though 91 be the next immediate excess to 90. But it is not so
in extension, where whatsoever is more than just a foot, or an
inch, is not distinguishable from the standard of a foot, or an
inch; and in lines which appear of an equal length, one may be
longer than the other by innumerable parts; nor can anyone
assign an angle which shall be the next biggest to a right one.

*5. Names necessary to numbers.*—By the repeating, as has
been said, of the idea of an unit, and joining it to another unit,
we make thereof one collective idea, marked by the name "two."
And whosoever can do this and proceed on, still adding one more
to the last collective idea which he had of any number, and give
a name to it, may count, or have ideas for several collections of
units, distinguished one from another, as far as he hath a series
of names for following numbers, and a memory to retain that
series with their several names; all numeration being but still
the adding of one unit more, and giving to the whole together,
as comprehended in one idea, a new or distinct name or sign,
whereby to know it from those before and after, and distinguish
it from every smaller or greater multitude of units. So that he
that can add one to one, and so to two, and so go on with his
tale, taking still with him the distinct names belonging to every
progression; and so again by subtracting an unit from each collection, retreat and lessen them; is capable of all the ideas of
numbers within the compass of his language, or for which he
hath names, though not perhaps of more. For, the several simple
modes of numbers being in our minds but so many combinations
of units, which have no variety, nor are capable of any other
difference but more or less, names or marks for each distinct
combination seem more necessary than in any other sort of ideas.
For without such names or marks we can hardly well make use
of numbers in reckoning, especially where the combination is
made up of any great multitudes of units; which, put together
without a name or mark to distinguish that precise collection,
will hardly be kept from being a heap in confusion.

6. This I think to be the reason why some Americans I have

spoken with (who were otherwise of quick and rational parts
enough) could not, as we do, by any means count to one thousand,
nor had any distinct idea of that number, though they could
reckon very well to twenty ; because their language being scanty,
and accommodated only to the few necessaries of a needy, simple
life, unacquainted either with trade or mathematics, had no
words in it to stand for one thousand; so that when they were
discoursed with of those great numbers, they would show the
hairs of their head, to express a great multitude which they
could not number: which inability, I suppose, proceeded from
their want of names. The Tououpinambos had no names for
numbers above five ; any number beyond that they made out by
showing their fingers, and the fingers of others who were present :*
and I doubt not but we ourselves might distinctly number in
words a great deal farther than we usually do, would we find out
but some fit denominations to signify them by : whereas in the
way we take now to name them by millions of millions of millions,
&c., it is hard to go beyond eighteen, or at most four-and-twenty,
decimal progressions without confusion. But to show how much
distinct names conduce to our well reckoning, or having useful
ideas of numbers, let us set all these following figures as the
marks of one number ; *v. g.*

| Nonillions. | Octillions. | Septillions. | Sextillions. | Quintrillions. |
|---|---|---|---|---|
| 857324 | 162486 | 345896 | 437916 | 423147 |

| Quatrillions. | Trillions. | Billions. | Millions. | Units. |
|---|---|---|---|---|
| 248106 | 235421 | 261734 | 368149 | 623137 |

The ordinary way of naming this number in English will be the
often repeating of millions, of millions, of millions, of millions,
of millions, of millions, of millions, of millions, which is the
denomination of the second six figures. In which way it will be
very hard to have any distinguishing notions of this number :
but whether, by giving every six figures a new and orderly
denomination, these, and perhaps a great many more figures in
progression, might not easily be counted distinctly, and ideas of
them both got more easily to ourselves, and more plainly signified
to others, I leave it to be considered. This I mention only to
show how necessary distinct names are to numbering, without
pretending to introduce new ones of my invention.

7. *Why children number not earlier.*—Thus children, either
for want of names to mark the several progressions of numbers,
or not having yet the faculty to collect scattered ideas into complex ones, and range them in a regular order, and so retain them
in their memories as is necessary to reckoning, do not begin to
number very early, nor proceed in it very far or steadily, till a
good while after they are well furnished with good store of other

* *Histoire d'un Voyage fait en la Terre du Brasil, par* JEAN DE LERY, cap. **xx**
**147**.

ideas; and one may often observe them discourse and reason pretty well, and have very clear conceptions of several other things, before they can tell twenty. And some, through the default of their memories, who cannot retain the several combinations of numbers, with their names annexed in their distinct orders, and the dependence of so long a train of numeral progressions, and their relation one to another, are not able all their lifetime to reckon or regularly go over any moderate series of numbers. For he that will count twenty, or have any idea of that number, must know that nineteen went before, with the distinct name or sign of every one of them, as they stand marked in their order; for wherever this fails, a gap is made, the chain breaks, and the progress in numbering can go no farther. So that to reckon right it is required, (1.) That the mind distinguish carefully two ideas which are different one from another only by the addition or subtraction of one unit. (2.) That it retain in memory the names or marks of the several combinations from an unit to that number; and that not confusedly, and at random; but in that exact order that the numbers follow one another: in either of which, if it trips, the whole business of numbering will be disturbed, and there will remain only the confused idea of multitude; but the ideas necessary to distinct numeration will not be attained to.

8. *Number measures all measurables.*—This farther is observable in number, that it is that which the mind makes use of in measuring all things that by us are measurable, which principally are expansion and duration; and our idea of infinity even when applied to those seems to be nothing but the infinity of number. For what else are our ideas of eternity and immensity, but the repeated additions of certain ideas of imagined parts of duration and expansion, with the infinity of number, in which we can come to no end of addition? For such an inexhaustible stock, number, of all our other ideas, most clearly furnishes us with, as is obvious to everyone. For let a man collect into one sum as great a number as he pleases, this multitude, how great soever, lessens not one jot the power of adding to it, or brings him any nearer the end of the inexhaustible stock of number, where still there remains as much to be added as if none were taken out. And this endless addition or addibility (if anyone like the word better) of numbers, so apparent to the mind, is that, I think, which gives us the clearest and most distinct idea of infinity; of which more in the following chapter.

# CHAPTER XVII.

## OF INFINITY.

**1.** *Infinity, in its original intention, attributed to space, duration and number.*—He that would know what kind of idea it is to which we give the name of "infinity," cannot do it better than by considering to what infinity is by the mind more immediately attributed, and then how the mind comes to frame it.

Finite and infinite seem to me to be looked upon by the mind as the modes of quantity, and to be attributed primarily in their first designation only to those things which have parts, and are capable of increase or diminution by the addition or subtraction of any the least part; and such are the ideas of space, duration, and number, which we have considered in the foregoing chapters. It is true that we cannot but be assured that the great God, of whom and from whom are all things, is incomprehensibly infinite: but yet when we apply to that first and supreme Being our idea of infinite, in our weak and narrow thoughts, we do it primarily in respect of his duration and ubiquity; and, I think, more figuratively to his power, wisdom, and goodness, and other attributes, which are properly inexhaustible and incomprehensible, &c. For when we call them infinite, we have no other idea of this infinity but what carries with it some reflection on and intimation of that number or extent of the acts or objects of God's power, wisdom, and goodness, which can never be supposed so great or so many, which these attributes will not always surmount and exceed, let us multiply them in our thoughts as far as we can, with all the infinity of endless number. I do not pretend to say how these attributes are in God, who is infinitely beyond the reach of our narrow capacities; they do, without doubt, contain in them all possible perfection: but this, I say, is our way of conceiving them, and these our ideas of their infinity.

**2.** *The idea of finite easily got.*—Finite then and infinite being by the mind looked on as modifications of expansion and duration, the next thing to be considered is, how the mind comes by them. As for the idea of finite, there is no great difficulty. The obvious portions of extension that affect our senses carry with them into the mind the idea of finite; and the ordinary periods of succession whereby we measure time and duration, as hours, days and years, are bounded lengths. The difficulty is, how we come by those boundless ideas of eternity and immensity, since the objects which we converse with come so much short of any approach or proportion to that largeness.

**8.** *How we come by the idea of infinity.*—Everyone that has any idea of any stated lengths of space, as a foot, finds that he can repeat that idea; and, joining it to the former, make the idea of two feet, and, by the addition of a third, three feet, and so on, without ever coming to an end of his additions, whether of the same idea of a foot, or, if he pleases, of doubling it, or any other idea he has of any length, as a mile, or diameter of the earth, or of the *orbis magnus;* for, whichsoever of these he takes, and how often soever he doubles or any otherwise multiplies it, he finds that, after he has continued this doubling in his thoughts and enlarged his idea as much as he pleases, he has no more reason to stop, nor is one jot nearer the end of such addition than he was at first setting out: the power of enlarging his idea of space by farther additions remaining still the same, he hence takes the idea of infinite space.

4. *Our idea of space boundless.*—This, I think, is the way whereby the mind gets the idea of infinite space. It is a quite different consideration to examine whether the mind has the idea of such a boundless space actually existing, since our ideas are not always proofs of the existence of things; but yet, since this comes here in our way, I suppose I may say that we are apt to think that space in itself is actually boundless, to which imagination the idea of space or expansion of itself naturally leads us. For, it being considered by us either as the extension of body, or as existing by itself, without any solid matter taking it up (for of such a void space we have not only the idea, but I have proved, as I think, from the motion of body, its necessary existence), it is impossible the mind should be ever able to find or suppose any end of it, or be stopped anywhere in its progress in this space, how far soever it extends its thoughts. Any bounds made with body, even adamantine walls, are so far from putting a stop to the mind in its farther progress in space and extension, that it rather facilitates and enlarges it: for so far as that body reaches, so far no one can doubt of extension; and when we are come to the utmost extremity of body, what is there that can there put a stop, and satisfy the mind that it is at the end of space, when it perceives it is not; nay, when it is satisfied that body itself can move into it? For if it be necessary for the motion of body that there should be an empty space, though never so little, here amongst bodies; and it be possible for body to move in or through that empty space (nay, it is impossible for any particle of matter to move but into an empty space); the same possibility of a body's moving into a void space beyond the utmost bounds of body, as well as into a void space interspersed amongst bodies, will always remain clear and evident; the idea of empty pure space, whether within or beyond the confines of all bodies, being exactly the same, differing not in nature, though in bulk; and there being nothing to hinder body from moving into it: so that wherever the mind places itself by any thought, either amongst or remote from all

bodies, it can, in this uniform idea of space, nowhere find any
bounds, any end; and so must necessarily conclude it, by the
very nature and idea of each part of it, to be actually infinite.

5. *And so of duration.*—As, by the power we find in ourselves
of repeating as often as we will any idea of space, we get the idea
of immensity; so, by being able to repeat the idea of any length
of duration we have in our minds, with all the endless addition of
number, we come by the idea of eternity. For we find in ourselves, we can no more come to an end of such repeated ideas
than we can come to the end of number; which everyone perceives he cannot. But here again it is another question, quite
different from our having an idea of eternity, to know whether
there were any real being whose duration has been eternal.
And as to this, I say, he that considers something now existing
must necessarily come to something eternal. But having spoke
of this in another place, I shall say here no more of it, but proceed on to some other considerations of our idea of infinity.

6. *Why other ideas are not capable of infinity.*—If it be so,
that our idea of infinity be got from the power we observe in ourselves of repeating without end our own ideas, it may be demanded,
why we do not attribute infinity to other ideas, as well as those
of space and duration; since they may be as easily and as often
repeated in our minds as the other; and yet nobody ever thinks
of infinite sweetness or infinite whiteness, though he can repeat
the idea of sweet or white as frequently as those of a yard or a
day? To which I answer, All the ideas that are considered as
having parts, and are capable of increase by the addition of any
equal or less parts, afford us, by their repetition, the idea of
infinity: because with this endless repetition there is continued
an enlargement, of which there can be no end. But in other
ideas it is not so; for to the largest idea of extension or duration
that I at present have, the addition of any the least part makes
an increase; but to the perfectest idea I have of the whitest
whiteness, if I add another of a less or equal whiteness (and of a
whiter than I have, I cannot add the idea), it makes no increase,
and enlarges not my idea at all; and therefore the different ideas
of whiteness, &c., are called "degrees." For those ideas that
consist of parts are capable of being augmented by every addition
of the least part; but if you take the idea of white which one
parcel of snow yielded yesterday to your sight, and another idea
of white from another parcel of snow you see to-day, and put
them together in your mind, they embody, as it were, and run
into one, and the idea of whiteness is not at all increased; and
if we add a less degree of whiteness to a greater, we are so far
from increasing that we diminish it. Those ideas that consist
not of parts cannot be augmented to what proportion men please,
or be stretched beyond what they have received by their senses;
but space, duration, and number, being capable of increase by

repetition, leave in the mind an idea of an endless room for more ; nor can we conceive anywhere a stop to a farther addition or progression : and so those ideas alone lead our minds towards the thought of infinity.

7. *Difference between infinity of space and space infinite.*— Though our idea of infinity arise from the contemplation of quantity, and the endless increase the mind is able to make in quantity, by the repeated additions of what portions thereof it pleases ; yet, I guess, we cause great confusion in our thoughts when we join infinity to any supposed idea of quantity the mind can be thought to have, and so discourse or reason about an infinite quantity (viz.), an infinite space or an infinite duration. For our idea of infinity being, as I think, an endless growing idea, but the idea of any quantity the mind has being at that time terminated in that idea (for be it as great as it will, it can be no greater than it is), to join infinity to it, is to adjust a standing measure to a growing bulk; and therefore I think it is not an insignificant subtilty if I say that we are carefully to distinguish between the idea of *the infinity of space* and the idea of *a space infinite* : the first is nothing but a supposed endless progression of the mind over what repeated ideas of space it pleases ; but to have actually in the mind the idea of a space infinite, is to suppose the mind already passed over, and actually to have a view of all those repeated ideas of space which an endless repetition can never totally represent to it ; which carries in it a plain contradiction.

8. *We have no idea of infinite space.*—This, perhaps, will be a little plainer if we consider it in numbers. The infinity of numbers, to the end of whose addition everyone perceives there is no approach, easily appears to anyone that reflects on it : but how clear soever this idea of the infinity of number be, there is nothing yet more evident than the absurdity of the actual idea of an infinite number. Whatsoever positive ideas we have in our minds of any space, duration, or number, let them be never so great, they are still finite; but when we suppose an inexhaustible remainder, from which we remove all bounds, and wherein we allow the mind an endless progression of thought, without ever completing the idea, there we have our idea of infinity ; which though it seems to be pretty clear when we consider nothing else in it but the negation of an end, yet when we would frame in our minds the idea of an infinite space or duration, that idea is very obscure and confused, because it is made up of two parts very different, if not inconsistent. For let a man frame in his mind an idea of any space or number, as great as he will, it is plain the mind rests and terminates in that idea; which is contrary to the idea of infinity, which consists in a supposed endless progression. And therefore I think it is that we are so easily confounded when we come to argue and reason about infinite space or duration, &c. Because the parts of such an idea not being perceived to be, as

they are, inconsistent, the one side or other always perplexes whatever consequences we draw from the other; as an idea of *motion not passing on* would perplex anyone who should argue from such an idea, which is not better than an idea of *motion at rest;* and such another seems to me to be the idea of a space or (which is the same thing) a number infinite, *i.e.*, of a space or number which the mind actually has, and so views and terminates in, and of a space or number which, in a constant and endless enlarging and progression, it can in thought never attain to. For how large soever an idea of space I have in my mind, it is no larger than it is that instant that I have it, though I be capable the next instant to double it, and so on *in infinitum :* for that alone is infinite which has no bounds, and that the idea of infinity in our thoughts can find none.

9. *Number affords us the clearest idea of infinity.*—But of all other ideas, it is number, as I have said, which, I think, furnishes us with the clearest and most distinct idea of infinity we are capable of. For even in space and duration, when the mind pursues the idea of infinity, it there makes use of the ideas and repetitions of numbers, as of millions of millions of miles or years, which are so many distinct ideas kept best by number from running into a confused heap, wherein the mind loses itself; and when it has added together as many millions, &c., as it pleases of known lengths of space or duration, the clearest idea it can get of infinity is, the confused, incomprehensible remainder of endless addible numbers, which affords no prospect of stop or boundary.

10. *Our different conception of the infinity of number, duration, and expansion.*—It will, perhaps, give us a little farther light into the idea we have of infinity, and discover to us that it is nothing but the infinity of number applied to determinate parts, of which we have in our minds the distinct ideas, if we consider that number is not generally thought by us infinite, whereas duration and extension are apt to be so; which arises from hence, that in number we are at one end as it were: for there being in number nothing less than an unit, we there stop, and are at an end; but in addition or increase of number, we can set no bounds: and so it is like a line, whereof one end terminating with us, the other is extended still forwards beyond all that we can conceive; but in space and duration it is otherwise. For in duration we consider it as if this line of number were extended both ways to an unconceivable, undeterminate, and infinite length; which is evident to anyone that will but reflect on what consideration he hath of eternity; which, I suppose, he will find to be nothing else but the turning this infinity of number both ways, *à parte ante* and *à parte post*, as they speak. For when we would consider eternity *à parte ante*, what do we but, beginning from ourselves and the present time we are in, repeat in our minds the ideas of years, or ages, or any other assignable portion of duration past,

with a prospect of proceeding in such addition with all the infinity of number? and when we would consider eternity *à parte post*, we just after the same rate begin from ourselves, and reckon by multiplied periods yet to come, still extending that line of number as before: and these two being put together are that infinite duration we call "eternity;" which, as we turn our view either way, forwards or backwards, appears infinite, because we still turn that way the infinite end of number, *i.e.*, the power still of adding more.

11. The same happens also in space, wherein conceiving ourselves to be as it were in the centre, we do on all sides pursue those indeterminable lines of number; and reckoning any way from ourselves a yard, mile, diameter of the earth, or *orbis magnus*, by the infinity of number, we add others to them as often as we will; and having no more reason to set bounds to those repeated ideas than we have to set bounds to number, we have that indeterminable idea of immensity.

12. *Infinite divisibility.*—And since in any bulk of matter our thoughts can never arrive at the utmost divisibility, therefore there is an apparent infinity to us also in that which has the infinity also of number, but with this difference,—that in the former considerations of the infinity of space and duration, we only use addition of numbers; whereas this is like the division of an unit into its fractions, wherein the mind also can proceed *in infinitum*, as well as in the former additions, it being indeed but the addition still of new numbers; though in the addition of the one we can have no more the positive idea of a space infinitely great, than in the division of the other we can have the idea of a body infinitely little; our idea of infinity being, as I may so say, a growing and fugitive idea, still in a boundless progression, that can stop nowhere.

13. *No positive idea of infinite.*—Though it be hard, I think, to find anyone so absurd as to say he has the positive idea of an actual infinite number, the infinity whereof lies only in a power still of adding any combination of units to any former number, and that as long and as much as one will; the like also being in the infinity of space and duration, which power leaves always to the mind room for endless additions; yet there be those who imagine they have positive ideas of infinite duration and space. It would, I think, be enough to destroy any such positive idea of infinite to ask him that has it, whether he could add to it or no? which would easily show the mistake of such a positive idea. We can, I think, have no positive idea of any space or duration which is not made up of, and commensurate to, repeated numbers of feet or yards, or days and years; which are the common measures whereof we have the idea in our minds, and whereby we judge of the greatness of these sort of quantities. And therefore, since an idea of infinite space or duration must

needs be made up of infinite parts, it can have no other infinity than that of number, capable still of farther addition; but
not an actual positive idea of a number infinite. For, I think,
it is evident that the addition of finite things together (as are
all lengths whereof we have the positive ideas) can never otherwise produce the idea of infinite than as number does; which,
consisting of additions of finite units one to another, suggests
the idea of infinite only by a power we find we have of still
increasing the sum, and adding more of the same kind, without
coming one jot nearer the end of such progression.

14. They who would prove their idea of infinite to be positive, seem to me to do it by a pleasant argument, taken from the
negation of an end; which being negative, the negation of it is
positive. He that considers that the end is, in body, but the
extremity or superficies of that body, will not, perhaps, be forward to grant, that the end is a bare negative: and he that perceives the end of his pen is black or white, will be apt to think
that the end is something more than a pure negation. Nor is it,
when applied to duration, the bare negation of existence, but
more properly the last moment of it. But if they will have the
end to be nothing but the bare negation of existence, I am sure
they cannot deny but that the beginning is the first instant of
being, and is not by anybody conceived to be a bare negation;
and therefore, by their own argument, the idea of eternal *à
parte ante*, or of a duration without a beginning, is but a negative
idea.

15. *What is positive, what negative, in our idea of infinite.*—
The idea of infinite has, I confess, something of positive in all those
things we apply it to. When we would think of infinite space
or duration, we at first step usually make some very large idea,
as, perhaps, of millions of ages or miles, which possibly we double
and multiply several times. All that we thus amass together in
our thoughts is positive, and the assemblage of a great number
of positive ideas of space or duration. But what still remains
beyond this, we have no more a positive, distinct notion of, than
a mariner has of the depth of the sea, where, having let down a
large portion of his sounding-line, he reaches no bottom: whereby
he knows the depth to be so many fathoms, and more; but how
much that *more* is, he hath no distinct notion at all: and could he
always supply new line, and find the plummet always sink without ever stopping, he would be something in the posture of the
mind reaching after a complete and positive idea of infinity. In
which case, let this line be ten or ten thousand fathoms long,
it equally discovers what is beyond it; and gives only this confused and comparative idea, that this is not all, but one may yet
go farther. So much as the mind comprehends of any space, it
has a positive idea of: but in endeavouring to make it infinite,
it being always enlarging, always advancing, the idea is still im-

perfect and incomplete. So much space as the mind takes a view of, in its contemplation of greatness, is a clear picture, and positive in the understanding: but infinite is still greater. (1.) Then the idea of so much, is positive and clear. (2.) The idea of greater, is also clear, but it is but a comparative idea. (3.) The idea of so much greater as cannot be comprehended; and this is plain negative, not positive. For he has no positive, clear idea, of the largeness of any extension (which is that sought for in the idea of infinite), that has not a comprehensive idea of the dimensions of it: and such nobody, I think, pretends to in what is infinite. For, to say a man has a positive, clear idea of any quantity, without knowing how great it is, is as reasonable as to say, he has the positive, clear idea of the number of the sands on the sea-shore, who knows not how many they be, but only that they are more than twenty. For just such a perfect and positive idea has he of an infinite space or duration who says it is larger than the extent or duration of ten, a hundred, a thousand, or any other number of miles or years, whereof he has or can have a positive idea; which is all the idea, I think, we have of infinite. So that what lies beyond our positive idea towards infinity lies in obscurity, and has the undeterminate confusion of a negative idea; wherein I know I neither do nor can comprehend all I would, it being too large for a finite and narrow capacity: and that cannot but be very far from a positive complete idea, wherein the greatest part of what I would comprehend is left out, under the undeterminate intimation of being still greater. For to say, that having in any quantity measured so much, or gone so far, you are not yet at the end, is only to say that that quantity is greater. So that the negation of an end in any quantity, is, in other words, only to say, that it is bigger: and a total negation of an end, is but the carrying this *bigger* still with you in all the progressions your thoughts shall make in quantity, and adding this idea of *still greater* to all the ideas you have or can be supposed to have of quantity. Now, whether such an idea as that be positive, I leave anyone to consider.

16. *We have no positive idea of an infinite duration.*—I ask those who say they have a positive idea of eternity, whether their idea of duration includes in it succession or not? If it does not, they ought to show the difference of their notion of duration, when applied to an eternal being, and to a finite; since, perhaps, there may be others, as well as I, who will own to them their weakness of understanding in this point; and acknowledge that the notion they have of duration forces them to conceive, that whatever has duration is of a longer continuance to-day than it was yesterday. If to avoid succession in eternal existence, they recur to the *punctum stans* of the schools, I suppose they will thereby very little mend the matter, or help us to a more clear and positive idea of infinite duration, there being nothing more

inconceivable to me than duration without succession. Besides
that *punctum stans*, if it signify anything, being not *quantum*,
finite or infinite cannot belong to it. But if our weak apprehensions cannot separate succession from any duration whatsoever,
our idea of eternity can be nothing but of infinite succession of
moments of duration wherein anything does exist; and whether
anyone has or can have a positive idea of an actual infinite
number, I leave him to consider, till his infinite number be so
great that he himself can add no more to it: and as long as he
can increase it, I doubt, he himself will think the idea he hath
of it a little too scanty for positive infinity.

17. I think it unavoidable for every considering rational
creature, that will but examine his own or any other existence,
to have the notion of an eternal wise Being, who had no beginning: and such an idea of infinite duration I am sure I have.
But this negation of a beginning, being but the negation of a
positive thing, scarce gives me a positive idea of infinity; which
whenever I endeavour to extend my thoughts to, I confess myself
at a loss, and find I cannot attain any clear comprehension of it.

18. *No positive idea of infinite space.*—He that thinks he has a
positive idea of infinite space will, when he considers it, find that
he can no more have a positive idea of the greatest than he has
of the least space. For in this latter, which seems the easier of
the two, and more within our comprehension, we are capable only
of a comparative idea of smallness, which will always be less than
any one whereof we have the positive idea. All our positive ideas
of any quantity, whether great or little, have always bounds;
though our comparative idea, whereby we can always add to the
one, and take from the other, hath no bounds. For that which
remains, either great or little, not being comprehended in that
positive idea which we have, lies in obscurity : and we have no
other idea of it, but of the power of enlarging the one, and
diminishing the other, without ceasing. A pestle and mortar
will as soon bring any particle of matter to indivisibility, as the
acutest thought of a mathematician : and a surveyor may as soon
with his chain measure out infinite space as a philosopher by the
quickest flight of mind reach it, or by thinking comprehend it;
which is to have a positive idea of it. He that thinks on a cube
of an inch diameter, has a clear and positive idea of it in his
mind, and so can frame one of a half, a quarter, and an eighth,
and so on, till he has the idea in his thoughts of something very
little; but yet reaches not the idea of that incomprehensible
littleness which division can produce. What remains of smallness is as far from his thoughts as when he first began; and
therefore he never comes at all to have a clear and positive idea
of that smallness which is consequent to infinite divisibility.

19. *What is positive, what negative, in our idea of infinite.*—
Everyone that looks towards infinity does, as I have said, at first

glance make some very large idea of that which he applies it to,
let it be space or duration; and possibly he wearies his thoughts
by multiplying in his mind that first large idea: but yet by that
he comes no nearer to the having a positive clear idea of what
remains to make up a positive infinite, than the country-fellow
had of the water which was yet to come, and pass the channel of
the river where he stood:—

> *Rusticus expectat dum transeat amnis; at ille*
> *Labitur, et labetur in omne volubilis ævum.*

20. *Some think they have a positive idea of eternity, and not
of infinite space.*—There are some I have met with that put
so much difference between infinite duration and infinite space,
that they persuade themselves that they have a positive idea of
eternity, but that they have not nor can have any idea of infinite
space.   The reason of which mistake I suppose to be this, that
finding by a due contemplation of causes and effects that it is
necessary to admit some eternal Being, and so to consider the
real existence of that Being as taking up and commensurate to
their idea of eternity: but, on the other side, not finding it
necessary, but, on the contrary, apparently absurd, that body
should be infinite, they forwardly conclude they can have
no idea of infinite space, because they can have no idea of
infinite matter.   Which consequence, I conceive, is very ill
collected; because the existence of matter is no ways necessary
to the existence of space, no more than the existence of motion
or the sun is necessary to duration, though duration uses to be
measured by it: and I doubt not but a man may have the idea
of ten thousand miles square without any body so big, as well
as the idea of ten thousand years without any body so old.
It seems as easy to me to have the idea of space empty of body,
as to think of the capacity of a bushel without corn, or the
hollow of a nut-shell without a kernel in it: it being no more
necessary that there should be existing a solid body infinitely
extended because we have an idea of the infinity of space, than
it is necessary that the world should be eternal because we have
an idea of infinite duration: and why should we think our idea
of infinite space requires the real existence of matter to support
it, when we find that we have as clear an idea of infinite duration
to come, as we have of infinite duration past? though, I suppose,
nobody thinks it conceivable that anything does or has existed
in that future duration.   Nor is it possible to join our idea of
future duration with present or past existence, any more than it
is possible to make the ideas of yesterday, to-day, and to-morrow
to be the same; or bring ages past and future together, and
make them contemporary.   But if these men are of the mind,
that they have clearer ideas of infinite duration than of infinite
space, because it is past doubt that God has existed from all
ternity, but there is no real matter co-extended with infinite

space; yet those philosophers who are of opinion that infinite space is possessed by God's infinite omnipresence, as well as in finite duration by his eternal existence, must be allowed to have as clear an idea of infinite space as of infinite duration; though neither of them, I think, has any positive idea of infinity in either case. For, whatsoever positive ideas a man has in his mind of any quantity, he can repeat it, and add it to the former, as easily as he can add together the ideas of two days, or two paces (which are positive ideas of lengths he has in his mind), and so on, as long as he pleases: whereby, if a man had a positive idea of infinite, either duration or space, he could add two infinities together; nay, make one infinite infinitely bigger than another: absurdities too gross to be confuted!

21. *Supposed positive ideas of infinity cause of mistakes.*—But yet, if after all this there be men who persuade themselves that they have clear, positive, comprehensive ideas of infinity, it is fit they enjoy their privilege; and I should be very glad (with some others that I know who acknowledge they have none such) to be better informed by their communication. For I have been hitherto apt to think that the great and inextricable difficulties which perpetually involve all discourses concerning infinity, whether of space, duration, or divisibility, have been the certain marks of a defect in our ideas of infinity, and the disproportion the nature thereof has to the comprehension of our narrow capacities. For whilst men talk and dispute of infinite space or duration as if they had as complete and positive ideas of them as they have of the names they use for them, or as they have of a yard, or an hour, or any other determinate quantity; it is no wonder if the incomprehensible nature of the thing they discourse of or reason about leads them into perplexities and contradictions, and their minds be overlaid by an object too large and mighty to be surveyed and managed by them.

22. *All these ideas from sensation and reflection.*—If I have dwelt pretty long on the considerations of duration, space, and number, and what arises from the contemplation of them, infinity, it is possibly no more than the matter requires, there being few simple ideas whose modes give more exercise to the thoughts of men than these do. I pretend not to treat of them in their full latitude; it suffices to my design to show how the mind receives them, such as they are, from sensation and reflection; and how even the idea we have of infinity, how remote soever it may seem to be from any object of sense of operation of our mind, has nevertheless, as all our other ideas, its original there. Some mathematicians, perhaps, of advanced speculations, may have other ways to introduce into their minds ideas of infinity; but this hinders not but that they themselves, as well as all other men, got the first ideas which they had of infinity from sensation and reflection, in the method we have here set down.

## CHAPTER XVIII.

### OF OTHER SIMPLE MODES.

1. *Modes of motion.*—Though I have in the foregoing chapters shown how, from simple ideas taken in by sensation the mind comes to extend itself even to infinity; which, however it may of all others seem most remote from any sensible perception, yet at last hath nothing in it but what is made out of simple ideas received into the mind by the senses, and afterwards there put together by the faculty the mind has to repeat its own ideas: though, I say, these might be instances enough of simple modes of the simple ideas of sensation, and suffice to show how the mind comes by them; yet I shall, for method's sake, though briefly, give an account of some few more, and then proceed to more complex ideas.

2. To *slide, roll, tumble, walk, creep, run, dance, leap, skip,* and abundance of others that might be named, are words which are no sooner heard but everyone who understands English has presently in his mind distinct ideas which are all but the different modifications of motion. Modes of motion answer those of extension: *swift* and *slow* are two different ideas of motion, the measures whereof are made of the distances of time and space put together; so they are complex ideas comprehending time and space with motion.

3. *Modes of sounds.*—The like variety have we in sounds. Every articulate word is a different modification of sound; by which we see that, from the sense of hearing, by such modifications, the mind may be furnished with distinct ideas to almost an infinite number. Sounds, also, besides the distinct cries of birds and beasts, are modified by diversity of notes of different length put together, which make that complex idea called a "tune," which a musician may have in his mind when he hears or makes no sound at all, by reflecting on the ideas of those sounds so put together silently in his own fancy.

4. *Modes of colours.*—Those of colours are also very various; some we take notice of, as the different degrees, or, as they are termed "shades," of the same colour. But since we very seldom make assemblages of colours either for use or delight but figure is taken in also, and has its parts in it, as in painting, weaving, needle-works, &c., those which are taken notice of do most commonly belong to mixed modes, as being made up of ideas of divers kinds, viz., figure and colour, such as beauty, rainbow, &c.

5. *Modes of tastes.*—All compounded tastes and smells are also modes made up of these simple ideas of those senses. But they, being such as generally we have no names for, are less taken notice of, and cannot be set down in writing; and therefore

must be left without enumeration to the thoughts and experience of my reader.

6. *Some simple modes have no names.*—In general it may be observed that those simple modes which are considered but as different degrees of the same simple idea, though they are in themselves, many of them, very distinct ideas, yet have ordinarily no distinct names, nor are much taken notice of as distinct ideas where the difference is but very small between them. Whether men have neglected these modes, and given no names to them, as wanting measures nicely to distinguish them; or because, when they were so distinguished, that knowledge would not be of general or necessary use; I leave it to the thoughts of others: it is sufficient to my purpose to show, that all our simple ideas come to our minds only by sensation and reflection; and that when the mind has them, it can variously repeat and compound them, and so make new complex ideas. But though white, red, or sweet, &c., have not been modified or made into complex ideas by several combinations, so as to be named, and thereby ranked into species; yet some others of the simple ideas (viz., those of unity, duration, motion, &c., above instanced in, as also power and thinking) have been thus modified to a great variety of complex ideas with names belonging to them.

7. *Why some modes have and others have not names.*—The reason whereof, I suppose, has been this, that the great concernment of men being with men one amongst another, the knowledge of men and their actions and the signifying of them to one another was most necessary; and therefore they made ideas of action very nicely modified, and gave those complex ideas names that they might the more easily record and discourse of those things they were daily conversant in without long ambages and circumlocutions; and that the things they were continually to give and receive information about might be the easier and quicker understood. That this is so, and that men in framing different complex ideas, and giving them names, have been much governed by the end of speech in general (which is a very short and expedite way of conveying their thoughts one to another), is evident in the names which in several arts have been found out and applied to several complex ideas of modified actions belonging to their several trades, for despatch sake, in their direction or discourses about them. Which ideas are not generally framed in the minds of men not conversant about these operations. And hence the words that stand for them by the greatest part of men of the same language are not understood. *V. g., Colshire,*\* *drilling, filtration, cohobation,* are words standing for certain complex ideas, which being seldom in the minds of any but those few whose particular employments do at every turn suggest them to

\* A word compounded of *coulter* and *share*, which is sometimes written *coultshare.*—EDIT.

their thoughts, those names of them are not generally understood but by smiths and chemists; who, having framed the complex ideas which these words stand for, and having given names
to them or received them from others, upon hearing of these
names in communication readily conceive those ideas in their
minds; as by *cohobation*, all the simple ideas of distilling, and
the pouring the liquor distilled from anything back upon the remaining matter, and distilling it again. Thus we see that there
are great varieties of simple ideas, as of tastes and smells, which
have no names; and of modes many more. Which either not
having been generally enough observed, or else not being of any
great use to be taken notice of in the affairs and converse of men,
they have not had names given to them, and so pass not for
species. This we shall have occasion hereafter to consider more
at large when we come to speak of words.

---

## CHAPTER XIX.

### OF THE MODES OF THINKING.

**1. *Sensation, remembrance, contemplation, &c.***—When the
mind turns its view inwards upon itself, and contemplates its own
actions, thinking is the first that occurs. In it the mind observes
a great variety of modifications, and from thence receives distinct
ideas. Thus the perception which actually accompanies and is
annexed to any impression on the body made by an external
object, being distinct from all other modifications of thinking,
furnishes the mind with a distinct idea which we call "sensation;" which is, as it were, the actual entrance of any idea into
the understanding by the senses. The same idea, when it again
recurs without the operation of the like object on the external
sensory, is "remembrance:" if it be sought after by the mind,
and with pain and endeavour found, and brought again in view,
it is "recollection:" if it be held there long under attentive consideration, it is "contemplation:" when ideas float in our mind
without any reflection or regard of the understanding, it is that
which the French call *réverie;* our language has scarce a name
for it: when the ideas that offer themselves (for, as I have
observed in another place, whilst we are awake there will always
be a train of ideas succeeding one another in our minds) are taken
notice of, and, as it were, registered in the memory, it is "attention:" when the mind with great earnestness, and of choice,
fixes its view on any idea, considers it on all sides, and will not
be called off by the ordinary solicitation of other ideas, it is that
we call "intention," or "study:" "sleep" without dreaming is
rest from all these: and "dreaming" itself is the having of ideas
(whilst the outward senses are stopped, so that they receive not

outward objects with their usual quickness) in the mind not suggested by any external objects or known occasion, nor under any
choice or conduct of the understanding at all; and whether that
which we call " ecstasy " be not dreaming with the eyes open, I
leave to be examined.

2. These are some few instances of those various modes of thinking which the mind may observe in itself, and so have as distinct
ideas of as it hath of white and red, a square or a circle.  I do
not pretend to enumerate them all, nor to treat at large of this
set of ideas which are got from reflection ; that would be to make
a volume.  It suffices to my present purpose to have shown here,
by some few examples, of what sort these ideas are, and how the
mind comes by them; especially since I shall have occasion hereafter to treat more at large of reasoning, judging, volition, and
knowledge, which are some of the most considerable operations
of the mind, and modes of thinking.

3. *The various attention of the mind in thinking.*—But perhaps it may not be an unpardonable digression, nor wholly impertinent to our present design, if we reflect here upon the different
state of the mind in thinking which those instances of attention,
*reverie*, and dreaming, &c., before mentioned, naturally enough
suggest.  That there are ideas, some or other, always present in
the mind of a waking man, everyone's experience convinces him ;
though the mind employs itself about them with several degrees
of attention.  Sometimes the mind fixes itself with so much
earnestness on the contemplation of some objects, that it turns
their ideas on all sides, remarks their relations and circumstances,
and views every part so nicely, and with such intension, that it
shuts out all other thoughts, and takes no notice of the ordinary
impressions made then on the senses, which at another season
would produce very sensible perceptions ; at other times, it barely
observes the train of ideas that succeed in the understanding
without directing and pursuing any of them; and at other times
it lets them pass almost quite unregarded, as faint shadows that
make no impression.

4. *Hence it is probable that thinking is the action, not essence, of
the soul.*—This difference of intension and remission of the mind
in thinking, with a great variety of degrees between earnest study
and very near minding nothing at all, everyone, I think, has
experimented in himself.  Trace it a little farther, and you find
the mind in sleep retired, as it were, from the senses, and out of
the reach of those motions made on the organs of sense, which at
other times produce very vivid and sensible ideas.  I need not,
for this, instance in those who sleep out whole stormy nights
without hearing the thunder, or seeing the lightning, or feeling
the shaking of the house, which are sensible enough to those who
are waking.  But in this retirement of the mind from the senses,
it often retains a yet more loose and incoherent manner of

thinking, which we call "dreaming;" and, last of all, sound sleep closes the scene quite, and puts an end to all appearances. This, I think, almost everyone has experience of in himself, and his own observation without difficulty leads him thus far, That which I would farther conclude from hence is, that since the mind can sensibly put on, at several times, several degrees of thinking; and be sometimes even in a waking man so remiss as to have thoughts dim and obscure, to that degree that they are very little removed from none at all; and at last, in the dark retirements of sound sleep, loses the sight perfectly of all ideas whatsoever: since, I say, this is evidently so in matter of fact and constant experience, I ask, whether it be not probable, that thinking is the action and not the essence of the soul? since the operations of agents will easily admit of intension and remission; but the essences of things are not conceived capable of any such variation. But this by the by.

## CHAPTER XX.

### ON MODES OF PLEASURE AND PAIN.

1. *Pleasure and pain simple ideas.* — Amongst the simple ideas which we receive both from sensation and reflection, pain and pleasure are two very considerable ones. For as in the body there is sensation barely in itself, or accompanied with pain or pleasure; so the thought or perception of the mind is simply so, or else accompanied also with pleasure or pain, delight or trouble, call it how you please. These, like other simple ideas, cannot be described, nor their names defined : the way of knowing them is, as of the simple ideas of the senses, only by experience. For to define them by the presence of good or evil, is no otherwise to make them known to us than by making us reflect on what we feel in ourselves, upon the several and various operations of good and evil upon our minds, as they are differently applied to or considered by us.

2. *Good and evil, what.*—Things then are good or evil only in reference to pleasure or pain. That we call "good," which is apt to cause or increase pleasure, or diminish pain, in us ; or else to procure or preserve us the possession of any other good, or absence of any evil. And, on the contrary, we name that "evil," which is apt to produce or increase any pain, or diminish any pleasure, in us ; or else to procure us any evil, or deprive us of any good. By "pleasure" and "pain," I must be understood to mean of body or mind, as they are commonly distinguished; though, in truth, they be only different constitutions of the mind, sometimes occasioned by disorder in the body, sometimes by thoughts in the mind.

**3.** *Our passions moved by good and evil.*—Pleasure and pain, and that which causes them, good and evil, are the hinges on which our passions turn : and if we reflect on ourselves, and observe how these, under various considerations, operate in us, —what modifications or tempers of mind, what internal sensations (if I may so call them) they produce in us,—we may thence form to ourselves the ideas of our passions.

**4.** *Love.*—Thus anyone reflecting upon the thought he has of the delight which any present or absent thing is apt to produce in him, has the idea we call "love." For when a man declares in autumn, when he is eating them, or in spring, when there are none, that he loves grapes, it is no more but that the taste of grapes delights him : let an alteration of health or constitution destroy the delight of their taste, and he then can be said to love grapes no longer.

**5.** *Hatred.*—On the contrary, the thought of the pain which anything present or absent is apt to produce in us, is what we call "hatred." Were it my business here to inquire any further than into the bare ideas of our passions, as they depend on different modifications of pleasure and pain, I should remark, that our love and hatred of inanimate, insensible beings is commonly founded on that pleasure and pain which we receive from their use and application anyway to our senses, though with their destruction ; but hatred or love to beings capable of happiness or misery, is often the uneasiness or delight which we find in ourselves, arising from a consideration of their very being or happiness. Thus the being and welfare of a man's children or friends producing constant delight in him, he is said constantly to love them. But it suffices to note, that our ideas of love and hatred are but the dispositions of the mind in respect of pleasure and pain in general, however caused in us.

**6.** *Desire.*—The uneasiness a man finds in himself upon the absence of anything whose present enjoyment carries the idea of delight with it, is that we call " desire," which is greater or less as that uneasiness is more or less vehement. Where, by the by, it may perhaps be of some use to remark, that the chief, if not only, spur to human industry and action is uneasiness : for, whatever good is proposed, if its absence carries no displeasure nor pain with it, if a man be easy and content without it, there is no desire of it, nor endeavour after it ; there is no more but a bare *velleity,*—the term used to signify the lowest degree of desire, and that which is next to none at all, when there is so little uneasiness in the absence of anything, that it carries a man no farther than some faint wishes for it, without any more effectual or vigorous use of the means to attain it. Desire also is stopped or abated by the opinion of the impossibility or unattainableness of the good proposed, as far as the uneasiness is cured or allayed by that consideration. This might carry our thoughts farther, were it seasonable in this place.

7. *Joy.*—Joy is a delight of the mind from the consideration of the present or assured approaching possession of a good ; and we are then possessed of any good, when we have it so in our power that we can use it when we please. Thus a man almost starved has a joy at the arrival of relief, even before he has the pleasure of using it ; and a father in whom the very well-being of his children causes delight is always, as long as his children are in such a state, in the possession of that good; for he needs but to reflect on it to have that pleasure.

8. *Sorrow.*—Sorrow is uneasiness in the mind upon the thought of a good lost, which might have been enjoyed longer; or the sense of a present evil.

9. *Hope.*—Hope is that pleasure in the mind which everyone finds in himself, upon the thought of a profitable future enjoyment of a thing which is apt to delight him.

10. *Fear.*—Fear is an uneasiness of the mind, upon the thought of future evil likely to befall us.

11. *Despair.*—Despair is the thought of the unattainableness of any good, which works differently in men's minds; sometimes producing uneasiness or pain, sometimes rest and indolency.

12. *Anger.*—Anger is uneasiness or discomposure of the mind upon the receipt of any injury, with a present purpose of revenge.

13. *Envy.*—Envy is an uneasiness of mind caused by the consideration of a good we desire, obtained by one we think should not have had it before us.

14. *What passions all men have.*—These two last, "envy" and "anger," not being caused by pain and pleasure simply in themselves, but having in them some mixed considerations of ourselves and others, are not therefore to be found in all men, because those other parts of valuing their merits, or intending revenge, are wanting in them; but all the rest, terminated purely in pain and pleasure, are, I think, to be found in all men. For we love, desire, rejoice and hope, only in respect of pleasure; we hate, fear, and grieve, only in respect of pain ultimately: in fine, all these passions are moved by things only as they appear to be the causes of pleasure and pain, or to have pleasure or pain some way or other annexed to them. Thus we extend our hatred usually to the subject (at least, if a sensible or voluntary agent) which has produced pain in us, because the fear it leaves is a constant pain; but we do not so constantly love what has done us good, because pleasure operates not so strongly on us as pain, and because we are not so ready to have hope it will do so again. But this by the by.

15. *Pleasure and pain, what.*—By "pleasure" and "pain," "delight" and "uneasiness," I must all along be understood (as I have above intimated) to mean, not only bodily pain and plea-

sure, but whatsoever delight or uneasiness is felt by us, whether arising from any grateful or unacceptable sensation or reflection.

16. It is farther to be considered, that, in reference to the passions, the removal or lessening of a pain is considered and operates as a pleasure; and the loss or diminishing of a pleasure, as a pain.

17. *Shame.*—The passions, too, have most of them, in most persons, operations on the body, and cause various changes in it; which not being always sensible, do not make a necessary part of the idea of each passion. For shame, which is an uneasiness of the mind upon the thought of having done something which is indecent, or will lessen the valued esteem which others have for us, has not always blushing accompanying it.

18. *These instances do show how our ideas of the passions are got from sensation and reflection.*—I would not be mistaken here, as if I meant this as a discourse of the passions; they are many more than those I have here named: and those I have taken notice of would each of them require a much larger and more accurate discourse. I have only mentioned these here, as so many instances of modes of pleasure and pain resulting in our minds from various considerations of good and evil. I might, perhaps, have instanced in other modes of pleasure and pain more simple than these; as the pain of hunger and thirst, and the pleasure of eating and drinking to remove them; the pain of tender eyes, and the pleasure of music; pain from captious, un-instructive wrangling, and the pleasure of rational conversation with a friend, or of well-directed study in the search and dis-covery of truth. But the passions being of much more concern-ment to us, I rather made choice to instance in them, and show how the ideas we have of them are derived from sensation and reflection.

## CHAPTER XXI.

### OF POWER.

1. *This idea how got.*—The mind being every day informed, by the senses, of the alteration of those simple ideas it observes in things without, and taking notice how one comes to an end and ceases to be, and another begins to exist which was not before; reflecting also, on what passes within itself, and observing a con-stant change of its ideas, sometimes by the impression of outward objects on the senses, and sometimes by the determination of its own choice; and concluding, from what it has so constantly observed to have been, that the like changes will for the future be made in the same things by like agents, and by the like ways; considers in one thing the possibility of having any of its simple ideas changed, and in another the possibility of making that

change; and so comes by that idea which we call "power." Thus we say, fire has a power to melt gold; *i.e.*, to destroy the consistency of its insensible parts, and consequently its hardness, and make it fluid; and gold has a power to be melted: that the sun has a power to blanch wax; and wax a power to be blanched by the sun, whereby the yellowness is destroyed, and whiteness made to exist in its room. In which and the like cases, the power we consider is in reference to the change of perceivable ideas: for we cannot observe any alteration to be made in, or operation upon, anything, but by the observable change of its sensible ideas: nor conceive any alteration to be made, but by conceiving a change of some of its ideas.

2. *Power active and passive.*—Power thus considered is two-fold; viz., as able to make, or able to receive, any change: the one may be called "active," and the other "passive," power. Whether matter be not wholly destitute of active power, as its author, God, is truly above all passive power; and whether the intermediate state of created spirits be not that alone which is capable of both active and passive power, may be worth consideration. I shall not now enter into that inquiry; my present business being not to search into the original of power, but how we come by the idea of it. But since active powers make so great a part of our complex ideas of natural substances (as we shall see hereafter), and I mention them as such, according to common apprehension; yet they being not, perhaps, so truly active powers as our hasty thoughts are apt to represent them, I judge it not amiss, by this intimation, to direct our minds to the consideration of God and spirits, for the clearest idea of active power.

8. *Power includes relation.*—I confess power includes in it some kind of relation,—a relation to action or change; as, indeed, which of our ideas, of what kind soever, when attentively considered, does not? For our ideas of extension, duration, and number, do they not all contain in them a secret relation of the parts? Figure and motion have something relative in them much more visibly. And sensible qualities, as colours and smells, &c., what are they but the powers of different bodies in relation to our perception? &c. And if considered in the things themselves, do they not depend on the bulk, figure, texture, and motion of the parts? All which include some kind of relation in them. Our idea therefore of power, I think, may well have a place amongst other simple ideas, and be considered as one of them, being one of those that make a principal ingredient in our complex ideas of substances, as we shall hereafter have occasion to observe.

4. *The clearest idea of active power had from spirit.*—We are abundantly furnished with the idea of passive power, by almost all sorts of sensible things. In most of them we cannot avoid

observing their sensible qualities, nay, their very substances, to
be in a continual flux: and therefore with reason we look on
them as liable still to the same change. Nor have we of active
power (which is the more proper signification of the word
"power") fewer instances; since, whatever change is observed,
the mind must collect a power somewhere, able to make that
change, as well as a possibility in the thing itself to receive it.
But yet, if we will consider it attentively, bodies, by our senses,
do not afford us so clear and distinct an idea of active power, as
we have from reflection on the operations of our minds. For,
all power relating to action, and there being but two sorts of
action whereof we have any idea, viz., thinking and motion, let us
consider whence we have the clearest ideas of the powers which
produce these actions. (1.) Of thinking, body affords us no idea
at all: it is only from reflection that we have that. (2.) Neither
have we from body any idea of the beginning of motion. A body
at rest affords us no idea of any active power to move; and when
it is set in motion itself, that motion is rather a passion than an
action in it. For when the ball obeys the stroke of a billiard-
stick, it is not any action of the ball, but bare passion: also when
by impulse it sets another ball in motion that lay in its way, it
only communicates the motion it had received from another, and
loses in itself so much as the other received; which gives us but
a very obscure idea of an active power moving in body, whilst we
observe it only to transfer but not produce any motion. For it is
but a very obscure idea of power, which reaches not the production
of the action, but the continuation of the passion. For so is motion,
in a body impelled by another: The continuation of the alteration made in it from rest to motion being little more an action,
than the continuation of the alteration of its figure by the same
blow is an action. The idea of the beginning of motion we have
only from reflection on what passes in ourselves, where we find
by experience, that, barely by willing it, barely by a thought of
the mind, we can move the parts of our bodies which were before
at rest. So that it seems to me, we have, from the observation
of the operation of bodies by our senses, but a very imperfect,
obscure, idea of active power, since they afford us not any idea
in themselves of the power to begin any action, either motion or
thought. But if from the impulse bodies are observed to make
one upon another, anyone thinks he has a clear idea of power,
it serves as well to my purpose, sensation being one of those ways
whereby the mind comes by its ideas: only I thought it worth
while to consider here by the way, whether the mind doth not
receive its idea of active power clearer from reflection on its own
operations, than it doth from any external sensation.

5. *Will and understanding two powers.*—This at least I think
evident, that we find in ourselves a power to begin or forbear,
continue or end, several actions of our minds and motions of our

bodies, barely by a thought or preference of the mind ordering, or, as it were, commanding the doing or not doing such or such a particular action. This power which the mind has thus to order the consideration of any idea, or the forbearing to consider it, or to prefer the motion of any part of the body to its rest, and *vice versâ*, in any particular instance, is that which we call "the will." The actual exercise of that power, by directing any particular action or its forbearance, is that which we call "volition" or "willing." The forbearance of that action consequent to such order or command of the mind, is called "voluntary;" and whatsoever action is performed without such a thought of the mind, is called "involuntary." The power of perception is that which we call "the understanding." Perception, which we make the act of the understanding, is of three sorts: (1.) The perception of ideas in our minds. (2.) The perception of the signification of signs. (8.) The perception of the connexion or repugnancy, agreement or disagreement, that there is between any of our ideas. All these are attributed to the understanding, or perceptive power, though it be the two latter only that use allows us to say we understand.

6. *Faculties.*—These powers of the mind, viz., of perceiving and of preferring, are usually called by another name: and the ordinary way of speaking, is that the understanding and will are two faculties of the mind; a word proper enough, if it be used, as all words should be, so as not to breed any confusion in men's thoughts by being supposed (as I suspect it has been) to stand for some real beings in the soul, that performed those actions of understanding and volition. For when we say, the will is the commanding and superior faculty of the soul; that it is or is not free; that it determines the inferior faculties; that it follows the dictates of the understanding, &c.; though these and the like expressions, by those that carefully attend to their own ideas, and conduct their thoughts more by the evidence of things than the sound of words, may be understood in a clear and distinct sense: yet I suspect, I say, that this way of speaking of faculties has misled many into a confused notion of so many distinct agents in us, which had their several provinces and authorities, and did command, obey, and perform several actions, as so many distinct beings; which has been no small occasion of wrangling, obscurity, and uncertainty in questions relating to them.

7. *Whence the ideas of liberty and necessity.*—Everyone, I think, finds in himself a power to begin or forbear, continue or put an end to, several actions in himself. From the consideration of the extent of this power of the mind over the actions of the man, which everyone finds in himself, arise the ideas of liberty and necessity.

8. *Liberty, what.*—All the actions that we have any idea of, reducing themselves, as has been said, to these two, viz., thinking

and motion, so far as a man has a power to think or not to think, to move or not to move, according to the preference or direction of his own mind, so far is a man free. Wherever any performance or forbearance are not equally in a man's power, wherever doing or not doing will not equally follow upon the preference of his mind directing it, there he is not free, though perhaps the action may be voluntary. So that the idea of liberty is the idea of a power in any agent to do or forbear any particular action, according to the determination or thought of the mind, whereby either of them is preferred to the other; where either of them is not in the power of the agent, to be produced by him according to his volition, there he is not at liberty, that agent is under necessity. So that liberty cannot be where there is no thought, no volition, no will; but there may be thought, there may be will, there may be volition, where there is no liberty. A little consideration of an obvious instance or two may make this clear.

9. *Supposes the understanding and will.*—A tennis-ball, whether in motion by the stroke of a racket, or lying still at rest, is not by anyone taken to be a free agent. If we inquire into the reason, we shall find it is, because we conceive not a tennis-ball to think, and consequently not to have any volition, or preference of motion to rest, or *vice versâ;* and therefore has not liberty, is not a free agent; but all its both motion and rest come under our idea of necessary, and are so called. Likewise a man falling into the water (a bridge breaking under him) has not herein liberty, is not a free agent. For though he has volition, though he prefers his not falling to falling; yet the forbearance of that motion not being in his power, the stop or cessation of that motion follows not upon his volition; and therefore therein he is not free. So a man striking himself or his friend, by a convulsive motion of his arm, which it is not in his power, by volition or the direction of his mind, to stop or forbear, nobody thinks he has, in this, liberty; everyone pities him, as acting by necessity and restraint.

10. *Belongs not to volition.*—Again: Suppose a man be carried, whilst fast asleep, into a room, where is a person he longs to see and speak with, and be there locked fast in, beyond his power to get out; he awakes, and is glad to find himself in so desirable company, which he stays willingly in, *i.e.*, prefers his stay to going away. I ask, is not this stay voluntary? I think nobody will doubt it; and yet, being locked fast in, it is evident he is not at liberty not to stay, he has not freedom to be gone. So that liberty is not an idea belonging to volition, or preferring; but to the person having the power of doing, or forbearing to do, according as the mind shall choose or direct. Our idea of liberty reaches as far as that power, and no farther. For wherever restraint comes to check that power, or compulsion takes

away that indifferency of ability on either side to act, or to forbear acting, there liberty, and our notion of it, presently ceases.

11. *Voluntary opposed to involuntary, not to necessary.*—We
have instances enough, and often more than enough, in our own
bodies. A man's heart beats, and the blood circulates, which is
not in his power by any thought or volition to stop ; and therefore, in respect of these motions, where rest depends not on his
choice, nor would follow the determination of his mind, if it
should prefer it, he is not a free agent. Convulsive motions
agitate his legs, so that, though he wills it never so much, he
cannot by any power of his mind stop their motion (as in that
odd disease called *chorea sancti Viti*), but he is perpetually
dancing: he is not at liberty in this action, but under as much
necessity of moving as a stone that falls or a tennis-ball struck
with a racket. On the other side, a palsy or the stocks hinder
his legs from obeying the determination of his mind, if it would
thereby transfer his body to another place. In all these there is
want of freedom, though the sitting still even of a paralytic,
whilst he prefers it to a removal, is truly voluntary. Voluntary,
then, is not opposed to necessary, but to involuntary. For a man
may prefer what he can do, to what he cannot do ; the state he
is in, to its absence or change, though necessity has made it in
itself unalterable.

12. *Liberty, what.*—As it is in the motions of the body, so it
is in the thoughts of our minds: where any one is such, that we
have power to take it up, or lay it by, according to the preference
of the mind, there we are at liberty. A waking man, being
under the necessity of having some ideas constantly in his mind,
is not at liberty to think, or not to think, no more than he is at
liberty, whether his body shall touch any other or no: but
whether he will remove his contemplation from one idea to
another, is many times in his choice ; and then he is, in respect
of his ideas, as much at liberty as he is in respect of bodies he
rests on: he can at pleasure remove himself from one to another.
But yet some ideas to the mind, like some motions to the body,
are such as in certain circumstances it cannot avoid, nor obtain
their absence by the utmost effort it can use. A man on the
rack is not at liberty to lay by the idea of pain, and divert himself with other contemplations: and sometimes a boisterous
passion hurries our thoughts, as a hurricane does our bodies,
without leaving us the liberty of thinking on other things, which
we would rather choose. But as soon as the mind regains the
power to stop or continue, begin or forbear any of these motions
of the body without, or thoughts within, according as it thinks
fit to prefer either to the other, we then consider the man as a
free agent again.

13. *Necessity, what.*—Wherever thought is wholly wanting, or
the power to act or forbear according to the direction of thought,

there necessity takes place. This, in an agent capable of volition, when the beginning or continuation of any action is contrary to that preference of his mind, is called " compulsion:" when the hindering or stopping any action is contrary to this volition, it is called "restraint." Agents that have no thought, no volition at all, are in everything necessary agents.

14. *Liberty belongs not to the will.*—If this be so (as I imagine it is), I leave it to be considered, whether it may not help to put an end to that long agitated, and I think unreasonable, because unintelligible question, viz., Whether man's will be free or no? For, if I mistake not, it follows, from what I have said, that the question itself is altogether improper; and it is as insignificant to ask whether man's will be free, as to ask whether his sleep be swift, or his virtue square : liberty being as little applicable to the will, as swiftness of motion is to sleep, or squareness to virtue. Everyone would laugh at the absurdity of such a question as either of these; because it is obvious that the modifications of motion belong not to sleep, nor the difference of figure to virtue: and when anyone well considers it, I think he will as plainly perceive, that liberty, which is but a power, belongs only to agents, and cannot be an attribute or modification of the will, which is also but a power.

15. *Volition.*—Such is the difficulty of explaining and giving clear notions of internal actions by sounds, that I must here warn my reader that " ordering, directing, choosing, preferring," &c., which I have made use of, will not distinctly enough express volition, unless he will reflect on what he himself does when he wills. For example: " Preferring," which seems perhaps best to express the act of volition, does it not precisely. For though a man would prefer flying to walking, yet who can say he ever wills it ? Volition, it is plain, is an act of the mind knowingly exerting that dominion it takes itself to have over any part of the man, by employing it in or withholding it from any particular action. And what is the will, but the faculty to do this ? And is that faculty anything more in effect than a power,—the power of the mind to determine its thought to the producing, continuing, or stopping any action, as far as it depends on us? For, can it be denied, that whatever agent has a power to think on its own actions, and to prefer their doing or omission either to other, has that faculty called " will?" Will then is nothing but such a power. Liberty, on the other side, is the power a man has to do or forbear doing any particular action, according as its doing or forbearance has the actual preference in the mind ; which is the same thing as to say, according as he himself wills it.

16. *Powers belong to agents.*—It is plain then that the will is nothing but one power or ability, and freedom another power or ability : so that to ask whether the will has freedom, is to ask whether one power has another power, one ability another

ability ? a question at first sight too grossly absurd to make a
dispute, or need an answer.  For who is it that sees not, that
powers belong only to agents, and are attributes only of substances, and not of powers themselves ?  So that this way of
putting the question, viz., Whether the will be free ? is in effect
to ask, Whether the will be a substance, an agent ? or at least to
suppose it, since freedom can properly be attributed to nothing
else.   If freedom can with any propriety of speech be applied to
power, it may be attributed to the power that is in a man to
produce or forbear producing motions in parts of his body, by
choice or preference ; which is that which denominates him free,
and is freedom itself. But if any one should ask whether freedom
were free, he would be suspected not to understand well what
he said ; and he would be thought to deserve Midas's ears, who,
knowing that "rich " was a denomination from the possession of
riches, should demand whether riches themselves were rich.

17. However the name "faculty" which men have given to
this power called the " will," and whereby they have been led
into a way of talking of the will as acting, may, by an appropriation that disguises its true sense, serve a little to palliate the
absurdity ; yet the will, in truth, signifies nothing but a power
or ability to prefer or choose; and when the will, under the name
of a " faculty," is considered as it is, barely as an ability to do
something, the absurdity in saying it is free or not free, will
easily discover itself.  For if it be reasonable to suppose and
talk of faculties as distinct beings that can act (as we do when
we say, " The will orders," and " The will is free,") it is fit that
we should make a speaking faculty, and a walking faculty, and a
dancing faculty, by which those actions are produced, which are
but several modes of motion ; as well as we make the will and
understanding to be faculties by which the actions of choosing and
perceiving are produced, which are but several modes of thinking ; and we may as properly say, that it is the singing faculty
sings, and the dancing faculty dances, as that the will chooses, or
that the understanding conceives; or, as is usual, that the will
directs the understanding, or the understanding obeys or obeys
not the will : it being altogether as proper and intelligible to say,
that the power of speaking directs the power of singing, or the
power of singing obeys or disobeys the power of speaking.

18. This way of talking, nevertheless, has prevailed, and, as I
guess, produced great confusion.  For, these being all different
powers in the mind or in the man to do several actions, he exerts
them as he thinks fit: but the power to do one action is not
operated on by the power of doing another action.  For the
power of thinking operates not on the power of choosing, nor
the power of choosing on the power of thinking; no more than
the power of dancing operates on the power of singing, or the
power of singing on the power of dancing: as anyone who

reflects on it will easily perceive : and yet this is it which we say
when we thus speak, that the will operates on the understanding,
or the understanding on the will.

19. I grant that this or that actual thought may be the occasion of volition, or exercising the power a man has to choose ; or
the actual choice of the mind, the cause of actual thinking on this
or that thing ; as the actual singing of such a tune may be the
occasion of dancing such a dance ; and the actual dancing of such
a dance, the occasion of singing such a tune.   But in all these it
is not one power that operates on another ; but it is the mind
that operates and exerts these powers ; it is the man that does
the action, it is the agent that has power, or is able to do.   For
powers are relations, not agents : and that which has the power
or not the power to operate, is that alone which is or is not free,
and not the power itself : for freedom, or not freedom, can belong
to nothing but what has or has not a power to act.

20. *Liberty belongs not to the will.*—The attributing to faculties
that which belonged not to them, has given occasion to this way
of talking ; but the introducing into discourses concerning the
mind, with the name of faculties, a notion of their operating, has,
I suppose, as little advanced our knowledge in that part of ourselves, as the great use and mention of the like invention of
faculties in the operations of the body has helped us in the knowledge of physic.   Not that I deny there are faculties, both in the
body and mind : they both of them have their powers of operating, else neither the one nor the other could operate.   For nothing
can operate that is not able to operate ; and that is not able to
operate that has no power to operate.   Nor do I deny that those
words, and the like, are to have their place in the common use
of languages that have made them current.   It looks like too much
affectation wholly to lay them by ; and philosophy itself, though
it likes not a gaudy dress, yet when it appears in public, must
have so much complacency as to be clothed in the ordinary fashion
and language of the country, so far as it can consist with truth
and perspicuity.   But the fault has been that faculties have been
spoken of and represented as so many distinct agents.   For it
being asked, what it was that digested the meat in our stomachs ?
it was a ready, and very satisfactory answer, to say, that it was
the digestive faculty.   " What was it that made anything come
out of the body ?"   The expulsive faculty.   " What moved ?"
The motive faculty : and so in the mind, the intellectual faculty,
or the understanding, understood ; and the elective faculty, or
the will, willed or commanded : which is, in short, to say that
the ability to digest, digested ; and the ability to move, moved ;
and the ability to understand, understood.   For " faculty, ability,
and power," I think, are but different names of the same things :
which ways of speaking, when put into more intelligible words,
will, I think, amount to thus much ; that digestion is performed

by something that is able to digest; motion, by something able
to move; and understanding, by something able to understand.
And in truth it would be very strange, if it should be otherwise;
as strange as it would be for a man to be free without being
able to be free.

21. *But to the agent or man.*—To return, then, to the inquiry
about liberty, I think the question is not proper, whether the
will be free, but whether a man be free. Thus, I think,

(1.) That so far as anyone can, by the direction or choice of
his mind preferring the existence of any action to the non-
existence of that action, and *vice versâ*, make it to exist or not
exist, so far he is free. For if I can by a thought directing the
motion of my finger make it move when it was at rest, or *vice
versâ*, it is evident that, in respect of that, I am free; and if I
can, by a like thought of my mind preferring one to the other,
produce either words or silence, I am at liberty to speak or hold
my peace: and as far as this power reaches, of acting or not
acting, by the determination of his own thought preferring either,
so far is a man free. For how can we think anyone freer than
to have the power to do what he will? And so far as anyone
can, by preferring any action to its not being, or rest to any
action, produce that action or rest, so far can he do what he will.
For such a preferring of action to its absence, is the willing of it;
and we can scarce tell how to imagine any being freer than to be
able to do what he wills. So that, in respect of actions within
the reach of such a power in him, a man seems as free as it is
possible for freedom to make him.

22. *In respect of willing a man is not free.*—But the inquisitive mind of man, willing to shift off from himself, as far as
he can, all thoughts of guilt, though it be by putting himself into
a worse state than that of fatal necessity, is not content with
this: freedom, unless it reaches farther than this, will not serve
the turn: and it passes for a good plea, that a man is not free at
all, if he be not as free to will as he is to act what he wills.
Concerning a man's liberty, there yet therefore is raised this
farther question, whether a man be free to will? which, I think,
is what is meant, when it is disputed whether the will be free.
And as to that I imagine,

23. (2.) That willing or volition being an action, and freedom
consisting in a power of acting or not acting, a man, in respect of
willing or the act of volition, when any action in his power is
once proposed to his thoughts, as presently to be done, cannot be
free. The reason whereof is very manifest: for it being unavoidable that the action depending on his will should exist or not
exist, and its existence or not existence following perfectly the
determination and preference of his will, he cannot avoid willing
the existence or not existence of that action; it is absolutely
necessary that he will the one or the other, *i.e.*, prefer the one

to the other; since one of them must necessarily follow; and that which does follow, follows by the choice and determination of his mind; that is, by his willing it; for if he did not will it, it would not be. So that, in respect of the act of willing, a man in such a case is not free: liberty consisting in a power to act or not to act, which, in regard of volition, a man upon such a proposal has not. For it is unavoidably necessary to prefer the doing or forbearance of an action in a man's power, which is once so proposed to his thoughts; a man must necessarily will the one or the other of them: upon which preference or volition, the action or its forbearance certainly follows, and is truly voluntary. But the act of volition, or preferring one of the two, being that which he cannot avoid, a man, in respect of that act of willing, is under a necessity, and so cannot be free; unless necessity and freedom can consist together, and a man can be free and bound at once.¹

24. This, then, is evident, that, in all proposals of present action, a man is not at liberty to will or not to will, because he cannot forbear willing; liberty consisting in a power to act, or to forbear acting, and in that only. For a man that sits still is said yet to be at liberty, because he can walk if he wills it. But if a man sitting still has not a power to remove himself, he is not at liberty; so likewise a man falling down a precipice, though in motion, is not at liberty, because he cannot stop that motion if he would. This being so, it is plain that a man that is walking, to whom it is proposed to give off walking, is not at liberty whether he will determine himself to walk or give off walking, or no: he must necessarily prefer one or the other of them, walking or not walking; and so it is in regard of all other actions in our power so proposed, which are the far greater number. For, considering the vast number of voluntary actions that succeed one another every moment that we are awake in the course of our lives, there are but few of them that are thought on or proposed to the will, till the time they are to be done: and in all such actions, as I have shown, the mind, in respect of willing, has not a power to act or not to act, wherein consists liberty. The mind in that case has not a power to forbear willing; it cannot avoid some determination concerning them. Let the consideration be as short, the thought as quick, as it will, it either leaves the man in the state he was before thinking, or changes it; continues the action, or puts an end to it. Whereby it is manifest, that it orders and directs one in preference to or with neglect of the other, and thereby either the continuation or change becomes unavoidably voluntary.

25. *The will determined by something without it.*—Since, then, it is plain that in most cases a man is not at liberty whether he will *will* or no; the next thing demanded is, whether a man be at liberty to will which of the two he pleases, motion or rest?

This question carries the absurdity of it so manifestly in itself, that one might thereby sufficiently be convinced that liberty concerns not the will. For to ask, whether a man be at liberty to will either motion or rest, speaking or silence, which he pleases? is to ask, whether a man can will what he wills, or be pleased with what he is pleased with? a question which, I think, needs no answer: and they who can make a question of it, must suppose one will to determine the acts of another, and another to determine that; and so on *in infinitum*.

26. To avoid these and the like absurdities, nothing can be of greater use than to establish in our minds determined ideas of the things under consideration. If the ideas of liberty and volition were well fixed in our understandings, and carried along with us in our minds, as they ought, through all the questions that are raised about them, I suppose a great part of the difficulties that perplex men's thoughts and entangle their understandings would be much easier resolved; and we should perceive where the confused signification of terms, or where the nature of the thing, caused the obscurity.

27. *Freedom.*—First, then, it is carefully to be remembered, that freedom consists in the dependence of the existence or not existence of any action upon our volition of it, and not in the dependence of any action, or its contrary, on our preference. A man standing on a cliff is at liberty to leap twenty yards downwards into the sea, not because he has a power to do the contrary action, which is to leap twenty yards upwards, for that he cannot do; but he is therefore free, because he has a power to leap or not to leap. But if a greater force than his either holds him fast, or tumbles him down, he is no longer free in that case: because the doing or forbearance of that particular action is no longer in his power. He that is a close prisoner in a room twenty feet square, being at the north side of his chamber, is at liberty to walk twenty feet southward, because he can walk or not walk it: but is not at the same time at liberty to do the contrary; *i.e.*, to walk twenty feet northward.

In this, then, consists freedom, viz., in our being able to act, or not to act, according as we shall choose or will.

28. *Volition what.*—Secondly. We must remember that volition, or willing, is an act of the mind directing its thought to the production of any action, and thereby exerting its power to produce it. To avoid multiplying of words, I would crave leave here, under the word "action," to comprehend the forbearance, too, of any action proposed; sitting still, or holding one's peace, when walking or speaking are proposed, though mere forbearances, requiring as much the determination of the will, and being often as weighty in their consequences, as the contrary actions, may, on that consideration, well enough pass for actions too: but this I say that I may not be mistaken, if for brevity's sake I speak thus.

**29.** *What determines the will.*—Thirdly. The will being nothing but a power in the mind to direct the operative faculties of a man to motion or rest, as far as they depend on such direction; to the question, "What is it determines the will?" the true and proper answer is, The mind. For that which determines the general power of directing to this or that particular direction, is nothing but the agent itself exercising the power it has that particular way. If this answer satisfies not, it is plain the meaning of the question, "What determines the will?" is this, "What moves the mind in every particular instance to determine its general power of directing to this or that particular motion or rest?" And to this I answer, The motive for continuing in the same state or action is only the present satisfaction in it; the motive to change is always some uneasiness; nothing setting us upon the change of state, or upon any new action, but some uneasiness. This is the great motive that works on the mind to put it upon action, which for shortness' sake we will call "determining of the will;" which I shall more at large explain.

**30.** *Will and desire must not be confounded.*—But, in the way to it, it will be necessary to premise, that though I have above endeavoured to express the act of volition by "choosing, preferring," and the like terms, that signify desire as well as volition, for want of other words to mark that act of the mind whose proper name is "willing" or "volition;" yet it being a very simple act, whosoever desires to understand what it is, will better find it by reflecting on his own mind, and observing what it does when it wills, than by any variety of articulate sounds whatsoever. This caution of being careful not to be misled by expressions that do not enough keep up the difference between the will and several acts of the mind that are quite distinct from it, I think the more necessary, because I find the will often confounded with several of the affections, especially desire; and one put for the other, and that by men who would not willingly be thought not to have had very distinct notions of things, and not to have writ very clearly about them. This, I imagine, has been no small occasion of obscurity and mistake in this matter, and therefore is as much as may be to be avoided; for he that shall turn his thoughts inwards upon what passes in his mind when he wills, shall see that the will or power of volition is conversant about nothing but that particular determination of the mind whereby, barely by a thought, the mind endeavours to give rise, continuation, or stop to any action which it takes to be in its power. This, well considered, plainly shows that the will is perfectly distinguished from desire, which in the very same action may have a quite contrary tendency from that which our will sets us upon. A man, whom I cannot deny, may oblige me to use persuasions to another, which, at the same time I am speaking, I may wish may not prevail on him. In this case, it is plain the

will and desire run counter. I will the action that tends one
way, whilst my desire tends another, and that the direct contrary.
A man who, by a violent fit of the gout in his limbs, finds a
doziness in his head or a want of appetite in his stomach removed,
desires to be eased too of the pain of his feet or hands (for
wherever there is pain there is a desire to be rid of it), though
yet, whilst he apprehends that the removal of the pain may
translate the noxious humour to a more vital part, his will is
never determined to any one action that may serve to remove
this pain. Whence it is evident that desiring and willing are two
distinct acts of the mind, and consequently that the will, which
is but the power of volition, is much more distinct from desire.

81. *Uneasiness determines the will.*—To return, then, to the
inquiry, "What is it that determines the will in regard to our
actions?" And that upon second thoughts I am apt to imagine,
is not, as is generally supposed, the greater good in view, but
some (and, for the most part, the most pressing) uneasiness a
man is at present under. This is that which successively determines the will, and sets us upon those actions we perform. This
uneasiness we may call, as it is, "desire;" which is an uneasiness
of the mind for want of some absent good. All pain of the
body, of what sort soever, and disquiet of the mind, is uneasiness;
and with this is always joined desire equal to the pain or uneasiness felt, and is scarce distinguishable from it. For, desire being
nothing but an uneasiness in the want of an absent good, in
reference to any pain felt, ease is that absent good; and till that
ease be attained, we may call it desire, nobody feeling pain that
he wishes not to be eased of with a desire equal to that pain, and
inseparable from it. Besides this desire of ease from pain, there
is another of absent positive good; and here also the desire and
uneasiness are equal. As much as we desire any absent good, so
much are we in pain for it. But here all absent good does not,
according to the greatness it has, or is acknowledged to have,
cause pain equal to that greatness; as all pain causes desire
equal to itself: because the absence of good is not always a pain,
as the presence of pain is. And therefore absent good may be
looked on and considered without desire. But so much as there
is anywhere of desire, so much there is of uneasiness.

82. *Desire is uneasiness.*—That desire is a state of uneasiness,
everyone who reflects on himself will quickly find. Who is there
that has not felt in desire what the wise man says of hope (which
is not much different from it), that it being deferred makes the
heart sick? and that still proportionable to the greatness of the
desire, which sometimes raises the uneasiness to that pitch that
it makes people cry out, "Give me children," give me the thing
desired, "or I die"? Life itself, and all its enjoyments, is a
burden cannot be borne under the lasting and unremoved pressure
of such an uneasiness.

**33.** *The uneasiness of desire determines the will.*—Good and evil, present and absent, it is true, work upon the mind; but that which immediately determines the will, from time to time, to every voluntary action, is the uneasiness of desire, fixed on some absent good, either negative, as indolency to one in pain, or positive, as enjoyment of pleasure. That it is this uneasiness that determines the will to the successive voluntary actions whereof the greatest part of our lives is made up, and by which we are conducted through different courses to different ends, I shall endeavour to show both from experience and the reason of the thing.

**34.** *This the spring of action.*—When a man is perfectly content with the state he is in, which is when he is perfectly without any uneasiness, what industry, what action, what will is there left, but to continue in it? Of this every man's observation will satisfy him. And thus we see our all-wise Maker, suitable to our constitution and frame, and knowing what it is that determines the will, has put into man the uneasiness of hunger and thirst, and other natural desires, that return at their seasons, to move and determine their wills, for the preservation of themselves and the continuation of their species. For I think we may conclude, that if the bare contemplation of these good ends to which we are carried by these several uneasinesses, had been sufficient to determine the will, and set us on work, we should have had none of these natural pains, and perhaps in this world little or no pain at all. " It is better to marry than to burn," says St. Paul; where we may see what it is that chiefly drives men into the enjoyments of a conjugal life. A little burning felt pushes us more powerfully than greater pleasures in prospect draw or allure.

**35.** *The greatest positive good determines not the will, but uneasiness.*—It seems so established and settled a maxim, by the general consent of all mankind, that good, the greater good, determines the will, that I do not at all wonder that, when I first published my thoughts on this subject, I took it for granted; and I imagine, that by a great many I shall be thought more excusable for having then done so, than that now I have ventured to recede from so received an opinion. But yet upon a stricter inquiry, I am forced to conclude that good, the greater good, though apprehended and acknowledged to be so, does not determine the will until our desire, raised proportionably to it, makes us uneasy in the want of it. Convince a man never so much that plenty has its advantages over poverty; make him see and own that the handsome conveniences of life are better than nasty penury; yet as long as he is content with the latter, and finds no uneasiness in it, he moves not; his will is never determined to any action that shall bring him out of it. Let a man be never so well persuaded of the advantages of virtue, that it is as necessary to a man who has any great aims in this world or hopes in the next, as food to life: yet till he " hungers and thirsts after righteousness," till he feels an uneasiness in the want of it, his will will not be determined to any action in pursuit of this confessed greater good; but any other uneasiness he feels in himself shall take place and carry his will to other actions. On the other side, let a drunkard see that his health decays, his estate wastes; discredit and diseases, and the want of all things, even of his beloved drink, attends him in the course he follows: yet the returns of uneasiness to miss his companions, the habitual thirst after his cups, at the usual time, drives him to the tavern, though he has in his view the loss of health and plenty, and perhaps the joys of another life: the least of which is no inconsiderable good, but such as he confesses is far greater than the tickling of his palate with a glass of wine, or the idle chat of a soaking club. It is not for want of viewing the greater good; for he sees and acknowledges it, and in the intervals of his drinking hours will take resolutions to pursue the greater good; but when the uneasiness to miss his accustomed delight returns, the greater acknowledged good loses its hold, and the present uneasiness determines the will to the accustomed action; which thereby gets stronger footing to prevail against the next occasion, though he at the same time makes secret promises to himself that he will do so no more; this is the last time he will act against the attainment of those greater goods. And thus he is, from time to time, in the state of that unhappy complainer, *Video meliora proboque, deteriora sequor:* which sentence, allowed for true, and made good by constant experience, may this (and possibly no other) way be easily made intelligible.

86. *Because the removal of uneasiness is the first step to happiness.*—If we inquire into the reason of what experience makes so evident in fact, and examine why it is uneasiness alone operates on the will, and determines it in its choice, we shall find that we being capable but of one determination of the will to one action at once, the present uneasiness that we are under does naturally determine the will in order to that happiness which we all aim at in all our actions: forasmuch as whilst we are under any uneasiness, we cannot apprehend ourselves happy, or in the way to it: pain and uneasiness being by everyone concluded and felt to be inconsistent with happiness, spoiling the relish even of those good things which we have; a little pain serving to mar all the pleasure we rejoiced in. And therefore that which of course determines the choice of our will to the next action, will always be the removing of pain, as long as we have any left, as the first necessary step towards happiness.

87. *Because uneasiness alone is present.*—Another reason why it is uneasiness alone determines the will may be this: because that alone is present, and it is against the nature of things that

what is absent should operate where it is not. It may be said, that absent good may, by contemplation, be brought home to the mind, and made present. The idea of it indeed may be in the mind, and viewed as present there; but nothing will be in the mind as a present good, able to counterbalance the removal of any uneasiness which we are under, till it raises our desire, and the uneasiness of that has the prevalency in determining the will. Till then the idea in the mind of whatever good, is there only like other ideas, the object of unactive speculation, but operates not on the will, nor sets us on work: the reason whereof I shall show by and by. How many are to be found that have had lively representations set before their minds of the unspeakable joys of heaven, which they acknowledge both possible and probable too, who yet would be content to take up with their happiness here! and so the prevailing uneasiness of their desires, let loose after the enjoyments of this life, take their turns in the determining their wills, and all that while they take not one step, are not one jot moved, towards the good things of another life, considered as never so great.

88. *Because all who allow the joys of heaven possible, pursue them not.*—Were the will determined by the views of good, as it appears in contemplation greater or less to the understanding, which is the state of all absent good, and that which in the received opinion the will is supposed to move to and to be moved by, I do not see how it could ever get loose from the infinite eternal joys of heaven, once proposed and considered as possible. For all absent good, by which alone, barely proposed and coming in view, the will is thought to be determined, and so to set us on action, being only possible, but not infallibly certain, it is unavoidable that the infinitely greater possible good should regularly and constantly determine the will in all the successive actions it directs; and then we should keep constantly and steadily in our course towards heaven, without ever standing still, or directing our actions to any other end: the eternal condition of a future state infinitely outweighing the expectation of riches, or honour, or any other worldly pleasure which we can propose to ourselves, though we should grant these the more probable to be attained: for nothing future is yet in possession, and so the expectation even of these may deceive us. If it were so, that the greater good in view determines the will, so great a good once proposed could not but seize the will, and hold it fast to the pursuit of this infinitely greatest good, without ever letting it go again: for the will having a power over and directing the thoughts, as well as other actions, would, if it were so, hold the contemplation of the mind fixed to that good.

*But any great uneasiness is never neglected.*—This would be the state of the mind, and regular tendency of the will in all its determinations, were it determined by that which is considered and in view the greater good; but that it is not so, is visible in experience; the infinitely greatest confessed good being often neglected, to satisfy the successive uneasiness of our desires pursuing trifles. But though the greatest allowed, even ever-lasting unspeakable, good, which has sometimes moved and affected the mind, does not steadfastly hold the will, yet we see any very great and prevailing uneasiness, having once laid hold on the will, lets it not go; by which we may be convinced what it is that determines the will. Thus any vehement pain of the body, the ungovernable passion of a man violently in love, or the impatient desire of revenge, keeps the will steady and intent; and the will, thus determined, never lets the under-standing lay by the object, but all the thoughts of the mind and powers of the body are uninterruptedly employed that way, by the determinations of the will, influenced by that topping uneasiness as long as it lasts: whereby it seems to me evident, that the will, or power of setting us upon one action in pre-ference to all other, is determined in us by uneasiness: and whether this be not so, I desire everyone to observe in himself.

89. *Desire accompanies all uneasiness.*—I have hitherto chiefly instanced in the uneasiness of desire, as that which determines the will; because that is the chief and most sensible; and the will seldom orders any action, nor is there any voluntary action performed without some desire accompanying it; which, I think, is the reason why the will and desire are so often con-founded. But yet we are not to look upon the uneasiness which makes up, or at least accompanies, most of the other passions, as wholly excluded in the case. Aversion, fear, anger, envy, shame, &c., have each their uneasiness too, and thereby influence the will. These passions are scarce any of them in life and practice simple and alone, and wholly unmixed with others; though usually, in discourse and contemplation, that carries the name which operates strongest and appears most in the present state of the mind. Nay, there is, I think, scarce any of the passions to be found without desire joined with it. I am sure, wherever there is uneasiness, there is desire: for we constantly desire happiness; and whatever we feel of uneasiness, so much, it is certain, we want of happiness, even in our own opinion, let our state and condition otherwise be what it will. Besides, the present moment not being our eternity, whatever our enjoyment be, we look beyond the present, and desire goes with our foresight, and that still carries the will with it. So that even in joy itself, that which keeps up the action whereon the enjoyment depends, is the desire to continue it, and fear to lose it; and whenever a greater uneasiness than that takes place in the mind, the will presently is by that determined to some new action, and the present delight neglected.

40. *The most pressing uneasiness naturally determines the*

*will.*—But we being in this world beset with sundry uneasinesses, distracted with different desires, the next inquiry naturally will be, which of them has the precedency in determining the will to the next action? And to that the answer is, That, ordinarily, which is the most pressing of those that are judged capable of being then removed. For the will being the power of directing our operative faculties to some action for some end, cannot at any time be moved towards what is judged at that time unattainable: that would be to suppose an intelligent being designedly to act for an end, only to lose its labour; for so it is to act for what is judged not attainable: and therefore very great uneasinesses move not the will when they are judged not capable of a cure: they, in that case, put us not upon endeavours. But these set apart, the most important and urgent uneasiness we at that time feel, is that which ordinarily determines the will successively in that train of voluntary actions which make up our lives. The greatest present uneasiness is the spur to action that is constantly felt, and for the most part determines the will in its choice of the next action. For this we must carry along with us, that the proper and only object of the will is some action of ours, and nothing else; for we producing nothing by our willing it, but some action in our power, it is there the will terminates, and reaches no farther.

41. *All desire happiness.*—If it be farther asked, what it is moves desire? I answer, Happiness, and that alone. "Happiness" and "misery" are the names of two extremes, the utmost bounds whereof we know not: it is what "eye hath not seen, ear hath not heard, nor hath it entered into the heart of man to conceive." But of some degrees of both we have very lively impressions, made by several instances of delight and joy on the one side, and torment and sorrow on the other; which, for shortness' sake, I shall comprehend under the names of "pleasure" and "pain," there being pleasure and pain of the mind as well as the body: "With him is fulness of joy, and pleasure for evermore:" or, to speak truly, they are all of the mind; though some have their rise in the mind from thought, others in the body from certain modifications of motion.

42. *Happiness, what.*—Happiness, then, in its full extent, is the utmost pleasure we are capable of, and misery the utmost pain; and the lowest degree of what can be called "happiness" is so much ease from all pain, and so much present pleasure, as without which anyone cannot be content. Now, because pleasure and pain are produced in us by the operation of certain objects either on our minds or our bodies, and in different degrees, therefore what has an aptness to produce pleasure in us is that we call "good," and what is apt to produce pain in us we call "evil;" for no other reason but for its aptness to produce pleasure and pain in us, wherein consists our happiness and misery. Farther

though what is apt to produce any degree of pleasure be in itself good, and what is apt to produce any degree of pain be evil, yet it often happens that we do not call it so when it comes in competition with a greater of its sort; because when they come in competition, the degrees also of pleasure and pain have justly a preference. So that if we will rightly estimate what we call " good" and " evil," we shall find it lies much in comparison : for the cause of every less degree of pain, as well as every greater degree of pleasure, has the nature of good and *vice versâ.*

43. *What good is desired, what not.*—Though this be that which is called " good " and " evil," and all good be the proper object of desire in general, yet all good, even seen and confessed to be so, does not necessarily move every particular man's desire; but only that part, or so much of it, as is considered and taken to make a necessary part of his happiness. All other good, however great in reality or appearance, excites not a man's desires, who looks not on it to make a part of that happiness wherewith he, in his present thoughts, can satisfy himself. Happiness, under this view, everyone constantly pursues, and desires what makes any part of it : other things acknowledged to be good he can look upon without desire; pass by, and be content without. There is nobody, I think, so senseless as to deny that there is pleasure in knowledge; and for the pleasures of sense, they have too many followers to let it be questioned whether men are taken with them or no. Now, let one man place his satisfaction in sensual pleasures, another in the delight of knowledge : though each of them cannot but confess there is great pleasure in what the other pursues, yet neither of them making the other's delight a part of his happiness, their desires are not moved, but each is satisfied without what the other enjoys; and so his will is not determined to the pursuit of it. But yet, as soon as the studious man's hunger and thirst makes him uneasy, he whose will was never determined to any pursuit of good cheer, poignant sauces, delicious wine, by the pleasant taste he has found in them, is, by the uneasiness of hunger and thirst, presently determined to eating and drinking, though possibly with great indifferency, what wholesome food comes in his way. And on the other side, the epicure buckles to study when shame, or the desire to recommend himself to his mistress, shall make him uneasy in the want of any sort of knowledge. Thus how much soever men are in earnest and constant in pursuit of happiness, yet they may have a clear view of good, great and confessed good, without being concerned for it, or moved by it, if they think they can make up their happiness without it. Though as to pain, *that* they are always concerned for; they can feel no uneasiness without being moved. And therefore, being uneasy in the want of whatever is judged necessary to their happiness, as soon as any good appears to make a part of their portion of happiness, they begin to desire it.

**44.** *Why the greatest good is not always desired.*—This, I think, anyone may observe in himself and others, that the greater visible good does not always raise men's desires in proportion to the greatness it appears and is acknowledged to have; though every little trouble moves us, and sets us on work to get rid of it: the reason whereof is evident from the nature of our happiness and misery itself. All present pain, whatever it be, makes a part of our present misery; but all absent good does not at any time make a necessary part of our present happiness, nor the absence of it make a part of our misery: if it did, we should be constantly and infinitely miserable; there being infinite degrees of happiness which are not in our possession. All uneasiness therefore being removed, a moderate portion of good serves at present to content men; and some few degrees of pleasure in a succession of ordinary enjoyments make up a happiness wherein they can be satisfied. If this were not so, there could be no room for those indifferent and visibly trifling actions to which our wills are so often determined, and wherein we voluntarily waste so much of our lives; which remissness could by no means consist with a constant determination of will or desire to the greatest apparent good. That this is so, I think few people need go far from home to be convinced. And, indeed, in this life there are not many whose happiness reaches so far as to afford them a constant train of moderate, mean pleasures, without any mixture of uneasiness; and yet they could be content to stay here for ever; though they cannot deny but that it is possible there may be a state of eternal, durable joys after this life, far surpassing all the good that is to be found here. Nay, they cannot but see that it is more possible than the attainment and continuation of that pittance of honour, riches, or pleasure which they pursue, and for which they neglect that eternal state; but yet, in full view of this difference, satisfied of the possibility of a perfect, secure, and lasting happiness in a future state, and under a clear conviction that it is not to be had here whilst they bound their happiness within some little enjoyment or aim of this life, and exclude the joys of heaven from making any necessary part of it, their desires are not moved by this greater apparent good, nor their wills determined to any action or endeavour for its attainment.

**45.** *Why, not being desired, it moves not the will.*—The ordinary necessities of our lives fill a great part of them with the uneasiness of hunger, thirst, heat, cold, weariness with labour, and sleepiness, in their constant returns, &c., to which if, besides accidental harms, we add the fantastical uneasiness (as itch after honour, power, or riches, &c.) which acquired habits by fashion, example, and education have settled in us, and a thousand other irregular desires which custom has made natural to us, we shall find that a very little part of our life is so vacant from these uneasinesses as to leave us free to the attraction of remoter absent good. We are seldom at ease, and free enough from the solicita-tion of our natural or adopted desires, but a constant succession of uneasinesses, out of that stock which natural wants or acquired habits have heaped up, take the will in their turns; and no sooner is one action despatched, which by such a determination of the will we are set upon, but another uneasiness is ready to set us on work. For the removing of the pains we feel, and are at present pressed with, being the getting out of misery, and consequently the first thing to be done in order to happiness, absent good, though thought on, confessed, and appearing to be good, not making any part of this unhappiness, in its absence is justled out, to make way for the removal of those uneasinesses we feel, till due and repeated contemplation has brought it nearer to our mind, given some relish of it, and raised in us some desire; which, then beginning to make a part of our present uneasiness, stands upon fair terms with the rest to be satisfied, and so, according to its greatness and pressure, comes in its turn to determine the will.

46. *Due consideration raises desire.*—And thus, by a due con-sideration, and examining any good proposed, it is in our power to raise our desires in a due proportion to the value of that good whereby, in its turn and place, it may come to work upon the will, and be pursued. For good, though appearing and allowed ever so great, yet till it has raised desires in our minds, and thereby made us uneasy in its want, it reaches not our wills, we are not within the sphere of its activity; our wills being under the determination only of those uneasinesses which are present to us, which (whilst we have any) are always soliciting, and ready at hand to give the will its next determination; the balancing, when there is any in the mind, being only, which desire shall be next satisfied, which uneasiness first removed. Whereby it comes to pass, that as long as any uneasiness, any desire, remains in our mind, there is no room for good, barely as such, to come at the will, or at all to determine it. Because, as has been said, the first step in our endeavours after happiness being to get wholly out of the confines of misery and to feel no part of it, the will can be at leisure for nothing else till every uneasiness we feel be perfectly removed; which, in the multitude of wants and desires we are beset with in this imperfect state, we are not like to be ever freed from in this world.

47. *The power to suspend the prosecution of any desire, makes way for consideration.*—There being in us a great many uneasi-nesses always soliciting, and ready to determine, the will, it is natural, as I have said, that the greatest and most pressing should determine the will to the next action; and so it does for the most part, but not always. For the mind having in most cases, as is evident in experience, a power to suspend the execution and satis-faction of any of its desires, and so all, one after another, is at

liberty to consider the objects of them, examine them on all sides, and weigh them with others.  In this lies the liberty man has; and from the not using of it right, comes all that variety of mistakes, errors, and faults which we run into in the conduct of our lives, and our endeavours after happiness; whilst we precipitate the determination of our wills, and engage too soon before due examination.  To prevent this, we have a power to suspend the prosecution of this or that desire, as everyone daily may experiment in himself.  This seems to me the source of all liberty; in this seems to consist that which is (as I think improperly) called " free-will."  For during this suspension of any desire, before the will be determined to action, and the action (which follows that determination) done, we have opportunity to examine, view, and judge of the good or evil of what we are going to do; and when upon due examination we have judged, we have done our duty, all that we can or ought to do in pursuit of our happiness; and it is not a fault but a perfection of our nature to desire, will and act, according to the last result of a fair examination.

48. *To be determined by our own judgment, is no restraint to liberty.*—This is so far from being a restraint or diminution of freedom, that it is the very improvement and benefit of it; it is not an abridgment, it is the end and use, of our liberty; and the farther we are removed from such a determination, the nearer we are to misery and slavery.  A perfect indifferency in the mind, not determinable by its last judgment of the good or evil that is thought to attend its choice, would be so far from being an advantage and excellency of an intellectual nature, that it would be as great an imperfection, as the want of indifferency to act or not to act till determined by the will, would be an imperfection on the other side.  A man is at liberty to lift up his hand to his head, or let it rest quiet: he is perfectly indifferent in either; and it would be an imperfection in him if he wanted that power, if he were deprived of that indifferency.  But it would be as great an imperfection, if he had the same indifferency, whether he would prefer the lifting up his hand, or its remaining in rest, when it would save his head or eyes from a blow he sees coming: it is as much a perfection that desire, or the power of preferring, should be determined by good, as that the power of acting should be determined by the will; and the certainer such determination is, the greater is the perfection.  Nay, were we determined by any thing but the last result of our own minds judging of the good or evil of any action, we were not free; the very end of our freedom being, that we may attain the good we choose.  And therefore every man is put under a necessity by his constitution, as an intelligent being, to be determined in willing, by his own thought and judgment, what is best for him to do: else he would be under the determination of some other than himself, which is want of liberty.  And to deny that a man's will, in every determination,

follows his own judgment, is to say, that a man wills and acts for
an end that he would not have, at the time that he wills and acts
for it. For if he prefers it in his present thoughts before any
other, it is plain he then thinks better of it, and would have it
before any other, unless he can have and not have it, will and
not will it, at the same time; a contradiction too manifest to be
admitted.

49. *The freest agents are so determined.*—If we look upon those
superior beings above us who enjoy perfect happiness, we shall
have reason to judge, that they are more steadily determined in
their choice of good than we; and yet we have no reason to think
they are less happy or less free than we are. And if it were fit
for such poor finite creatures as we are to pronounce what
infinite wisdom and goodness could do, I think we might say
that God himself cannot choose what is not good; the freedom of the Almighty hinders not his being determined by what
is best.

50. *A constant determination to a pursuit of happiness, no
abridgment of liberty.*—But, to give a right view of this mistaken
part of liberty, let me ask, Would anyone be a changeling because he is less determined by wise considerations than a wise
man? Is it worth the name of freedom to be at liberty to play
the fool, and draw shame and misery upon a man's self? If to
break loose from the conduct of reason, and to want that restraint
of examination and judgment which keeps us from choosing or
doing the worst, be liberty, true liberty, madmen and fools are
the only freemen: but yet, I think, nobody would choose to be
mad for the sake of such liberty, but he that is mad already.
The constant desire of happiness, and the constraint it puts upon
us to act for it, nobody, I think, accounts an abridgment of
liberty, or at least an abridgment of liberty to be complained of.
God Almighty himself is under the necessity of being happy;
and the more any intelligent being is so the nearer is its approach
to infinite perfection and happiness. That in this state of ignorance we short-sighted creatures might not mistake true felicity,
we are endowed with a power to suspend any particular desire,
and keep it from determining the will, and engaging us in action.
This is *standing still*, where we are not sufficiently assured of the
way: examination is *consulting a guide*. The determination of
the will upon inquiry, is *following the direction of that guide:* and
he that has a power to act, or not to act, according as such determination directs, is a free agent; such determination abridges
not that power wherein liberty consists. He that has his chains
knocked off, and the prison doors set open to him, is perfectly at
liberty, because he may either go or stay, as he best likes;
though his preference be determined to stay, by the darkness of
the night, or illness of the weather, or want of other lodging.
He ceases not to be free; though the desire of some convenience,

to be had there, absolutely determines his preference, and makes him stay in his prison.

51. *The necessity of pursuing true happiness, the foundation of all liberty.*—As therefore the highest perfection of intellectual nature lies in a careful and constant pursuit of true and solid happiness, so the care of ourselves, that we mistake not imaginary for real happiness, is the necessary foundation of our liberty. The stronger ties we have to an unalterable pursuit of happiness in general, which is our greatest good, and which, as such, our desires always follow, the more are we free from any necessary determination of our will, to any particular action, and from a necessary compliance with our desire set upon any particular and then appearing preferable good, till we have duly examined whether it has a tendency to or be inconsistent with our real happiness: and therefore till we are as much informed upon this inquiry as the weight of the matter and the nature of the case demands, we are, by the necessity of preferring and pursuing true happiness as our greatest good, obliged to suspend the satisfaction of our desire in particular cases.

52. *The reason of it.*—This is the hinge on which turns the liberty of intellectual beings in their constant endeavours after and a steady prosecution of true felicity, that they can suspend this prosecution in particular cases till they have looked before them, and informed themselves whether that particular thing which is then proposed or desired lie in the way to their main end, and make a real part of that which is their greatest good; for the inclination and tendency of their nature to happiness is an obligation and motive to them, to take care not to mistake or miss it; and so necessarily puts them upon caution, deliberation, and wariness in the direction of their particular actions, which are the means to obtain it. Whatever necessity determines to the pursuit of real bliss, the same necessity, with the same force, establishes suspense, deliberation, and scrutiny of each successive desire, whether the satisfaction of it does not interfere with our true happiness, and mislead us from it. This, as seems to me, is the great privilege of finite intellectual beings; and I desire it may be well considered, whether the great inlet and exercise of all the liberty men have, are capable of, or can be useful to them, and that whereon depends the turn of their actions, does not lie in this, that they can suspend their desires, and stop them from determining their wills to any action, till they have duly and fairly examined the good and evil of it, as far forth as the weight of the thing requires. This we are able to do; and when we have done it, we have done our duty, and all that is in our power, and indeed all that needs. For, since the will supposes knowledge to guide its choice, all that we can do is to hold our wills undetermined till we have examined the good and evil of what we desire. What follows after that, follows in a chain of conse-

quences linked one to another, all depending on the last determination of the judgment; which, whether it shall be upon an
hasty and precipitate view, or upon a due and mature examination, is in our power; experience showing us, that in most cases
we are able to suspend the present satisfaction of any desire.

53. *Government of our passions, the right improvement of
liberty.*—But if any extreme disturbance (as sometimes it
happens) possesses our whole mind, as when the pain of the
rack, an impetuous uneasiness, as of love, anger, or any other
violent passion, running away with us, allows us not the liberty
of thought, and we are not masters enough of our own minds to
consider thoroughly and examine fairly; God, who knows our
frailty, pities our weakness, and requires of us no more than we
are able to do, and sees what was and what was not in our power,
will judge as a kind and merciful Father. But the forbearance
of a too hasty compliance with our desires, the moderation and
restraint of our passions, so that our understandings may be free
to examine, and reason unbiassed gives its judgment, being that
whereon a right direction of our conduct to true happiness
depends; it is in this we should employ our chief care and
endeavours. In this we should take pains to suit the relish of
our minds to the true intrinsic good or ill that is in things, and
not permit an allowed or supposed possible great and weighty
good to slip out of our thoughts without leaving any relish, any
desire of itself there, till, by a due consideration of its true worth,
we have formed appetites in our minds suitable to it, and made
ourselves uneasy in the want of it, or in the fear of losing it. And
how much this is in everyone's power, by making resolutions to
himself such as he may keep, is easy for everyone to try. Nor
let anyone say, he cannot govern his passions, nor hinder them
from breaking out, and carrying him into action; for what he
can do before a prince, or a great man, he can do alone, or in
the presence of God, if he will.

54. *How men come to pursue different courses.*\*—From what
has been said, it is easy to give account how it comes to pass,
that though all men desire happiness, yet their wills carry them
so contrarily, and consequently some of them to what is evil. And
to this I say, that the various and contrary choices that men
make in the world do not argue that they do not all pursue
good, but that the same thing is not good to every man alike.
This variety of pursuits shows that everyone does not place his
happiness in the same thing, or choose the same way to it. Were
all the concerns of man terminated in this life, why one followed
study and knowledge, and another hawking and hunting; why
one chose luxury and debauchery, and another sobriety and
riches; would not be because every one of these did not aim at
his own happiness, but because their happiness was placed in

\* The fourth folio edition has *counsels.*—EDIT.

different things. And therefore it was a right answer of the physician to his patient that had sore eyes: "If you have more pleasure in the taste of wine than in the use of your sight, wine is good for you; but if the pleasure of seeing be greater to you than that of drinking, wine is naught."

55. The mind has a different relish, as well as the palate; and you will as fruitlessly endeavour to delight all men with riches or glory (which yet some men place their happiness in), as you would to satisfy all men's hunger with cheese or lobsters; which, though very agreeable and delicious fare to some, are to others extremely nauseous and offensive: and many people would with reason prefer the griping of an hungry belly to those dishes which are a feast to others. Hence it was, I think, that the philosophers of old did in vain inquire, whether *summum bonum* consisted in riches, or bodily delights, or virtue, or contemplation? And they might have as reasonably disputed, whether the best relish were to be found in apples, plums, or nuts; and have divided themselves into sects upon it. For as pleasant tastes depend not on the things themselves, but their agreeableness to this or that particular palate, wherein there is great variety; so the greatest happiness consists in the having those things which produce the greatest pleasure, and in the absence of those which cause any disturbance, any pain. Now, these to different men are very different things. If therefore men in this life only have hope, if in this life they can only enjoy, it is not strange nor unreasonable that they should seek their happiness by avoiding all things that disease them here, and by pursuing all that delight them; wherein it will be no wonder to find variety and difference. For if there be no prospect beyond the grave, the inference is certainly right, "Let us eat and drink," let us enjoy what we delight in, "for to-morrow we shall die." This, I think, may serve to show us the reason, why, though all men's desires tend to happiness, yet they are not moved by the same object. Men may choose different things, and yet all choose right, supposing them only like a company of poor insects, whereof some are bees, delighted with flowers and their sweetness; others beetles, delighted with other kind of viands; which having enjoyed for a season, they should cease to be, and exist no more for ever.

56. *How men come to choose ill.*—These things, duly weighed, will give us, as I think, a clear view into the state of human liberty. Liberty, it is plain, consists in a power to do or not to do, to do or forbear doing, as we will. This cannot be denied. But this seeming to comprehend only the actions of a man consecutive to volition, it is farther inquired, whether he be at liberty to will or no? And to this it has been answered, that in most cases a man is not at liberty to forbear the act of volition; he must exert an act of his will, whereby the action proposed is made to exist, or not to exist. But yet there is a case wherein a

man is at liberty in respect of willing; and that is the choosing of a remote good as an end to be pursued. Here a man may suspend the act of his choice from being determined for or against the thing proposed, till he has examined whether it be really of a nature in itself and consequences to make him happy or no. For when he has once chosen it, and thereby it has become a part of his happiness, it raises desire; and that proportionably gives him uneasiness, which determines his will, and sets him at work in pursuit of his choice on all occasions that offer. And here we may see how it comes to pass, that a man may justly incur punishment, though it be certain that in all the particular actions that he wills, he does, and necessarily does, will that which he then judges to be good. For though his will be always determined by that which is judged good by his understanding, yet it excuses him not : because by a too hasty choice of his own making, he has imposed on himself wrong measures of good and evil; which, however false and fallacious, have the same influence on all his future conduct as if they were true and right. He has vitiated his own palate, and must be answerable to himself for the sickness and death that follows from it. The eternal law and nature of things must not be altered to comply with his ill-ordered choice. If the neglect or abuse of the liberty he had to examine what would really and truly make for his happiness, misleads him, the miscarriages that follow on it must be imputed to his own election. He had a power to suspend his determination : it was given him, that he might examine and take care of his own happiness, and look that he were not deceived. And he could never judge that it was better to be deceived than not, in a matter of so great and near concernment.

What has been said may also discover to us the reason why men in this world prefer different things, and pursue happiness by contrary courses. But yet, since men are always constant and in earnest in matters of happiness and misery, the question still remains, how men come often to prefer the worse to the better, and to choose that which, by their own confession, has made them miserable?

57. To account for the various and contrary ways men take, though all aim at being happy, we must consider whence the various uneasinesses that determine the will in the preference of each voluntary action, have their rise.

(1.) *From bodily pain.*—Some of them come from causes not in our power, such as are often the pains of the body from want, disease, or outward injuries, as the rack, &c., which, when present, and violent, operate for the most part forcibly on the will, and turn the courses of men's lives from virtue, piety, and religion, and what before they judged to lead to happiness; everyone not endeavouring, or, through disuse, not being able, by the contemplation of remote and future good, to raise in himself desires of them strong enough to counterbalance the uneasiness he feels in those bodily torments, and to keep his will steady in the choice of those actions which lead to future happiness. A neighbour country has been of late a tragical theatre, from which we might fetch instances, if there needed any, and the world did not in all countries and ages furnish examples enough, to confirm that received observation, *Necessitas cogit ad turpia;* and therefore there is great reason for us to pray, "Lead us not into temptation."

(2.) *From wrong desires arising from wrong judgment.*—Other uneasinesses arise from our desires of absent good; which desires always bear proportion to and depend on the judgment we make, and the relish we have, of any absent good; in both which we are apt to be variously misled, and that by our own fault.

58. *Our judgment of present good or evil always right.*—In the first place I shall consider the wrong judgments men make of future good and evil, whereby their desires are misled. For as to present happiness and misery, when that alone comes in consideration, and the consequences are quite removed, a man never chooses amiss; he knows what best pleases him, and that he actually prefers. Things in their present enjoyment are what they seem; the apparent and real good are, in this case, always the same. For the pain or pleasure being just so great and no greater than it is felt, the present good or evil is really so much as it appears. And therefore were every action of ours concluded within itself, and drew no consequences after it, we should undoubtedly never err in our choice of good; we should always infallibly prefer the best. Were the pains of honest industry, and of starving with hunger and cold set together before us, nobody would be in doubt which to choose: were the satisfaction of a lust, and the joys of heaven, offered at once to anyone's present possession, he would not balance or err in the determination of his choice.

59. But since our voluntary actions carry not all the happiness and misery that depend on them along with them in their present performance, but are the precedent causes of good and evil, which they draw after them, and bring upon us when they themselves are past and cease to be; our desires look beyond our present enjoyments, and carry the mind out to absent good, according to the necessity which we think there is of it to the making or increase of our happiness. It is our opinion of such a necessity that gives it its attraction: without that, we are not moved by absent good. For in this narrow scantling of capacity which we are accustomed to and sensible of here, wherein we enjoy but one pleasure at once, which, when all uneasiness is away, is, whilst it lasts, sufficient to make us think ourselves happy; it is not all remote and even apparent good that affects us. Because the indolency and enjoyment we have sufficing for our present

happiness, we desire not to venture the change: since we judge
that we are happy already, being content, and that is enough.
For who is content, is happy. But as soon as any new uneasiness comes, this happiness is disturbed, and we are set afresh on
work in the pursuit of happiness.

60. *From a wrong judgment of what makes a necessary part
of their happiness.*—Their aptness therefore to conclude that they
can be happy without it, is one great occasion that men often
are not raised to the desire of the greatest absent good. For
whilst such thoughts possess them, the joys of a future state
move them not; they have little concern or uneasiness about
them; and the will, free from the determination of such desires,
is left to the pursuit of nearer satisfactions, and to the removal
of those uneasinesses which it then feels in its want of and long-
ings after them. Change but a man's view of these things; let
him see that virtue and religion are necessary to his happiness;
let him look into the future state of bliss or misery, and see their
God the righteous Judge ready to " render to every man according to his deeds; to them who by patient continuance in well-
doing seek for glory, and honour, and immortality, eternal life;
but unto every soul that doth evil, indignation and wrath, tribu-
lation and anguish;" to him, I say, who hath a prospect of the
different state of perfect happiness or misery that attends all
men after this life, depending on their behaviour here, the
measures of good and evil that govern his choice are mightily
changed. For, since nothing of pleasure and pain in this life
can bear any proportion to endless happiness or exquisite misery
of an immortal soul hereafter, actions in his power will have
their preference, not according to the transient pleasure or pain
that accompanies or follows them here, but as they serve to
secure that perfect durable happiness hereafter.

61. *A more particular account of wrong judgments.*—But, to
account more particularly for the misery that men often bring
on themselves, notwithstanding that they do all in earnest
pursue happiness, we must consider how things come to be represented to our desires under deceitful appearances; and that
is by the judgment pronouncing wrongly concerning them. To
see how far this reaches, and what are the causes of wrong
judgment, we must remember that things are judged good or
bad in a double sense.

First. That which is properly good or bad, is nothing but
barely pleasure or pain.

Secondly. Because not only present pleasure and pain, but
that also which is apt by its efficacy or consequences to bring it
upon us at a distance, is a proper object of our desires, and apt
to move a creature that has foresight; therefore, things also that
draw after them pleasure and pain are considered as good and
evil.

62. The wrong judgment that misleads us, and makes the will often fasten on the worst side, lies in misreporting upon the various comparisons of these. The wrong judgment I am here speaking of, is not what one man may think of the determination of another, but what every man himself must confess to be wrong. For, since I lay it for a certain ground, that every intelligent being really seeks happiness, which consists in the enjoyment of pleasure, without any considerable mixture of uneasiness; it is impossible anyone should willingly put into his own draught any bitter ingredient, or leave out anything in his power that would tend to his satisfaction and the completing of his happiness, but only by wrong judgment. 'I shall not here speak of that mistake which is the consequence of invincible error, which scarce deserves the name of wrong judgment; but of that wrong judgment which every man himself must confess to be so.

63. *In comparing present and future.*—I. Therefore, as to present pleasure and pain, the mind, as has been said, never mistakes that which is really good or evil; that which is the greater pleasure or the greater pain is really just as it appears. But though present pleasure and pain show their difference and degrees so plainly as not to leave room for mistake, yet when we compare present pleasure or pain with future (which is usually the case in the most important determinations of the will), we often make wrong judgments of them, taking our measures of them in different positions of distance. Objects near our view are apt to be thought greater than those of a larger size that are more remote: and so it is with pleasures and pains: the present is apt to carry it, and those at a distance have the disadvantage in the comparison. Thus most men, like spendthrift heirs, are apt to judge a little in hand better than a great deal to come; and so, for small matters in possession, part with great ones in reversion. But that this is a wrong judgment, everyone must allow, let his pleasure consist in whatever it will : since that which is future will certainly come to be present; and then, having the same advantage of nearness, will show itself in its full dimensions, and discover his wilful mistake who judged of it by unequal measures. Were the pleasure of drinking accompanied, the very moment a man takes off his glass, with that sick stomach and aching head which, in some men, are sure to follow not many hours after, I think nobody, whatever pleasure he had in his cups, would, on these conditions, ever let wine touch his lips; which yet he daily swallows, and the evil side comes to be chosen only by the fallacy of a little difference in time. But if pleasure or pain can be so lessened only by a few hours' removal, how much more will it be so, by a farther distance, to a man that will not by a right judgment do what time will, *i.e.*, bring it home to himself, and consider it as

present, and there take its true dimensions! This is the way we usually impose on ourselves, in respect of bare pleasure and pain, or the true degrees of happiness or misery : the future loses its just proportion, and what is present obtains the preference as the greater. I mention not here the wrong judgment whereby the absent are not only lessened, but reduced to perfect nothing ; when men enjoy what they can in present, and make sure of that, concluding amiss that no evil will hence follow. For that lies not in comparing the greatness of future good and evil, which is that we are here speaking of ; but in another sort of wrong judgment, which is concerning good or evil, as it is considered to be the cause and procurement of pleasure or pain that will follow from it.

64. *Causes of this.*—The cause of our judging amiss when we compare our present pleasure or pain with future, seems to me to be the weak and narrow constitution of our minds. We cannot well enjoy two pleasures at once, much less any pleasure almost whilst pain possesses us. The present pleasure, if it be not very languid and almost none at all, fills our narrow souls, and so takes up the whole mind that it scarce leaves any thought of things absent : or if among our pleasures there are some which are not strong enough to exclude the consideration of things at a distance, yet we have so great an abhorrence of pain that a little of it extinguishes all our pleasures : a little bitter mingled in our cup leaves no relish of the sweet. Hence it comes that, at any rate, we desire to be rid of the present evil, which we are apt to think nothing absent can equal ; because under the present pain we find not ourselves capable of any the least degree of happiness. —Men's daily complaints are a loud proof of this : the pain that anyone actually feels is still of all other the worst ; and it is with anguish they cry out, "Any rather than this ! nothing can be so intolerable as what I now suffer !" And therefore our whole endeavours and thoughts are intent to get rid of the present evil, before all things, as the first necessary condition to our happiness, let what will follow. Nothing, as we passionately think, can exceed or almost equal the uneasiness that sits so heavy upon us. And because the abstinence from a present pleasure that offers itself is a pain, nay, oftentimes a very great one, the desire being inflamed by a near and tempting object ; it is no wonder that that operates after the same manner pain does, and lessens in our thoughts what is future ; and so forces us, as it were, blindfolded into its embraces.

65. Add to this, that absent good, or, which is the same thing, future pleasure, especially if of a sort which we are unacquainted with, seldom is able to counterbalance any uneasiness, either of pain or desire, which is present. For its greatness being no more than what shall be really tasted when enjoyed, men are apt enough to lessen that, to make it give place to any present desire : and

conclude with themselves, that when it comes to trial it may possibly not answer the report or opinion that generally passes of it, they having often found that not only what others have magnified, but even what they themselves have enjoyed with great pleasure and delight at one time, has proved insipid or nauseous at another; and therefore they see nothing in it for which they should forego a present enjoyment. But that this is a false way of judging when applied to the happiness of another life, they must confess, unless they will say, God cannot make those happy he designs to be so. For that being intended for a state of happiness, it must certainly be agreeable to everyone's wish and desire: could we suppose their relishes as different there as they are here, yet the manna in heaven will suit everyone's palate. Thus much of the wrong judgment we make of present and future pleasure and pain, when they are compared together, and so the absent considered as future.

66. *In considering consequences of actions.*—II. As to things good or bad in their consequences, and by the aptness is in them to procure us good or evil in the future, we judge amiss several ways.

(1.) When we judge that so much evil does not really depend on them, as in truth there does.

(2.) When we judge, that though the consequence be of that moment, yet it is not of that certainty but that it may otherwise fall out or else by some means be avoided, as by industry, address, change, repentance, &c. That these are wrong ways of judging were easy to show, in every particular, if I would examine them at large singly: but I shall only mention this in general, viz., that it is a very wrong and irrational way of proceeding, to venture a greater good for a less upon uncertain guesses, and before a due examination be made, proportionable to the weightiness of the matter, and the concernment it is to us not to mistake. This, I think, everyone must confess, especially if he considers the usual causes of this wrong judgment, whereof these following are some.

67. *Causes of this.*—I. *Ignorance :* He that judges without informing himself to the utmost that he is capable, cannot acquit himself of judging amiss.

II. *Inadvertency :* When a man overlooks even that which he does know. This is an affected and present ignorance, which misleads our judgments as much as the other. Judging is, as it were, balancing an account, and determining on which side the odds lie. If, therefore, either side be huddled up in haste, and several of the sums that should have gone into the reckoning be overlooked and left out, this precipitancy causes as wrong a judgment as if it were a perfect ignorance. That which most commonly causes this, is the prevalency of some present pleasure or pain, heightened by our feeble passionate nature, most strongly wrought on by what is present. To check this pre-

cipitancy, our understanding and reason was given us, if we will
make a right use of it to search and see, and then judge thereupon.  Without liberty, the undertanding would be to no purpose : and without understanding, liberty (if it could be) would
signify nothing.  If a man sees what would do him good or
harm, what would make him happy or miserable, without being
able to move himself one step towards or from it, what is he the
better for seeing ?  And he that is at liberty to ramble in perfect
darkness, what is his liberty better than if he were driven up
and down as a bubble by the force of the wind ?  The being
acted by a blind impulse from without or from within, is little
odds.  The first, therefore, and great use of liberty is, to hinder
blind precipitancy ; the principal exercise of freedom is, to stand
still, open the eyes, look about, and take a view of the consequence of what we are going to do, as much as the weight of the
matter requires.  How much sloth and negligence, heat and
passion, the prevalency of fashion, or acquired indispositions, do
severally contribute on occasion to these wrong judgments, I
shall not here farther inquire.  I shall only add one other false
judgment, which I think necessary to mention, because, perhaps,
it is little taken notice of, though of great influence.

68.  *Wrong judgment of what is necessary to our happiness.*—
All men desire happiness, that is past doubt : but, as has been
already observed, when they are rid of pain, they are apt to take
up with any pleasure at hand, or that custom has endeared to
them, to rest satisfied in that ; and so being happy, till some
new desire, by making them uneasy, disturbs that happiness,
and shows them that they are not so, they look no farther ; nor
is the will determined to any action in pursuit of any other
known or apparent good.  For, since we find that we cannot
enjoy all sorts of good, but one excludes another ; we do not fix
our desires on every apparent greater good, unless it be judged
to be necessary to our happiness : if we think we can be happy
without it, it moves us not.  This is another occasion to men of
judging wrong, when they take not that to be necessary to their
happiness which really is so.  This mistake misleads us both in
the choice of the good we aim at, and very often in the means to
it, when it is a remote good.  But, which way ever it be, either
by placing it where really it is not, or by neglecting the means
as not necessary to it, when a man misses his great end, happiness, he will acknowledge he judgeth not right.  That which
contributes to this mistake, is the real or supposed unpleasant-
ness of the actions, which are the way to this end ; it seeming so
preposterous a thing to men to make themselves unhappy in
order to happiness, that they do not easily bring themselves to it.

69.  *We can change the agreeableness or disagreeableness in
things.*—The last inquiry, therefore, concerning this matter is,
Whether it be in a man's power to change the pleasantness and un-

pleasantness that accompanies any sort of action? And, as to that, it is plain in many cases he can. Men may and should correct their palates, and give a relish to what either has, or they suppose has, none. The relish of the mind is as various as that of the body, and like that, too, may be altered; and it is a mistake to think that men cannot change the displeasingness or indifferency that is in actions into pleasure and desire, if they will do but what is in their power. A due consideration will do it in some cases; and practice, application, and custom in most. Bread or tobacco may be neglected, where they are shown to be useful to health, because of an indifferency or disrelish to them; reason and consideration at first recommends and begins their trial, and use finds or custom makes them pleasant. That this is so in virtue, too, is very certain. Actions are pleasing or displeasing, either in themselves, or considered as a means to a greater and more desirable end. The eating of a well-seasoned dish, suited to a man's palate, may move the mind by the delight itself that accompanies the eating, without reference to any other end: to which the consideration of the pleasure there is in health and strength (to which that meat is subservient) may add a new gusto, able to make us swallow an ill-relished potion. In the latter of these, any action is rendered more or less pleasing only by the contemplation of the end, and the being more or less persuaded of its tendency to it, or necessary connection with it: but the pleasure of the action itself is best acquired or increased by use and practice. Trials often reconcile us to that which at a distance we looked on with aversion, and by repetitions wear us into a liking of what possibly in the first essay displeased us. Habits have powerful charms, and put so strong attractions of easiness and pleasure into what we accustom ourselves to, that we cannot forbear to do, or at least be easy in the omission of, actions which habitual practice has suited, and thereby recommends to us. Though this be very visible, and everyone's experience shows him he can do so; yet it is a part in the conduct of men towards their happiness neglected to a degree, that it will be possibly entertained as a paradox, if it be said, that men can make things or actions more or less pleasing to themselves; and thereby remedy that to which one may justly impute a great deal of their wandering. Fashion and the common opinion having settled wrong notions, and education and custom ill habits, the just values of things are misplaced, and the palates of men corrupted. Pains should be taken to rectify these; and contrary habits change our pleasures, and give a relish to that which is necessary or conducive to our happiness. This everyone must confess he can do; and when happiness is lost, and misery overtakes him, he will confess he did amiss in neglecting it, and condemn himself for it: and I ask everyone whether he has not often done so?

**70.** *Preference of vice to virtue, a manifest wrong judgment.*
—I shall not enlarge any farther on the wrong judgments, and
neglect of what is in their power, whereby men mislead themselves. This would make a volume, and is not my business. But
whatever false notions or shameful neglect of what is in their
power, may put men out of their way to happiness, and distract
them, as we see, into so different courses of life, this yet is certain,
that morality, established upon its true foundations, cannot but
determine the choice in anyone that will but consider: and he
that will not be so far a rational creature, as to reflect seriously
upon infinite happiness and misery, must needs condemn himself
as not making that use of his understanding he should.   The
rewards and punishments of another life, which the Almighty
has established as the enforcements of his law, are of weight
enough to determine the choice against whatever pleasure or
pain this life can show, when the eternal state is considered but
in its bare possibility, which nobody can make any doubt of.
He that will allow exquisite and endless happiness to be but the
possible consequence of a good life here, and the contrary state
the possible reward of a bad one, must own himself to judge
very much amiss if he does not conclude, that a virtuous life,
with the certain expectation of everlasting bliss which may
come, is to be preferred to a vicious one, with the fear of that
dreadful state of misery which it is very possible may overtake
the guilty, or at best the terrible uncertain hope of annihilation.
This is evidently so, though the virtuous life here had nothing
but pain, and the vicious continual pleasure: which yet is, for
the most part, quite otherwise, and wicked men have not much
the odds to brag of even in their present possession; nay, all
things rightly considered, have, I think, even the worst part
here.   But when infinite happiness is put in one scale, against
infinite misery in the other; if the worst that comes to the pious
man if he mistakes, be the best that the wicked can attain to if
he be in the right, who can without madness run the venture?
Who in his wits would choose to come within a possibility of
infinite misery, which if he miss, there is yet nothing to be got
by that hazard! Whereas, on the other side, the sober man
ventures nothing against infinite happiness to be got, if his expectation comes to pass.   If the good man be in the right, he is
eternally happy; if he mistakes, he is not miserable, he feels
nothing.   On the other side, if the wicked be in the right, he is
not happy; if he mistakes, he is infinitely miserable.   Must it
not be a most manifest wrong judgment, that does not presently
see to which side, in this case, the preference is to be given?   I
have forborne to mention anything of the certainty or probability
of a future state, designing here to show the wrong judgment
that anyone must allow he makes upon his own principles, laid
how he pleases, who prefers the short pleasures of a vicious

life upon any consideration, whilst he knows, and cannot but be
certain, that a future life is at least possible.

71. *Recapitulation.*—To conclude this inquiry into human
liberty, which, as it stood before, I myself from the beginning
fearing, and a very judicious friend of mine since the publication
suspecting, to have some mistake in it, though he could not
particularly show it me, I was put upon a stricter review of this
chapter: wherein lighting upon a very easy and scarce observable slip I had made in putting one seemingly indifferent word
for another, that discovery opened to me this present view, which
here, in this second edition, I submit to the learned world,
and which, in short, is this: Liberty is a power to act or not to
act, according as the mind directs. A power to direct the operative faculties to motion or rest in particular instances, is that
which we call the "will." That which in the train of our
voluntary actions determines the will to any change of operation,
is some present uneasiness, which is, or at least is always accompanied with, that of desire. Desire is always moved by evil, to
fly it; because a total freedom from pain always makes a
necessary part of our happiness: but every good, nay, every
greater good, does not constantly move desire, because it may
not make, or may not be taken to make, any necessary part of our
happiness. For all that we desire is only to be happy. But though
this general desire of happiness operates constantly and invariably,
yet the satisfaction of any particular desire can be suspended
from determining the will to any subservient action, till we have
maturely examined whether the particular apparent good, which
we then desire, makes a part of our real happiness, or be consistent or inconsistent with it. The result of our judgment upon
that examination, is what ultimately determines the man, who
could not be free if his will were determined by anything but
his own desire, guided by his own judgment. I know that liberty
by some is placed in an indifferency of the man, antecedent to
the determination of his will. I wish they who lay so much stress
on such an "antecedent indifferency," as they call it, had told us
plainly whether this supposed indifferency be antecedent to the
thought and judgment of the understanding, as well as to the
decree of the will. For it is pretty hard to state it between
them; *i.e.*, immediately after the judgment of the understanding,
and before the determination of the will; because the determination of the will immediately follows the judgment of the understanding: and to place liberty in an indifferency antecedent to the
thought and judgment of the understanding, seems to me to place
liberty in a state of darkness, wherein we can neither see nor say
anything of it; at least it places it in a subject incapable of it,
no agent being allowed capable of liberty, but in consequence of
thought and judgment. I am not nice about phrases, and
therefore consent to say, with these that love to speak so, that

liberty is placed in indifferency; but it is in an indifferency that remains after the judgment of the understanding; yea, even after the determination of the will: and that is an indifferency not of the man; (for after he has once judged which is best, viz., to do, or forbear, he is no longer indifferent;) but an indifferency of the operative powers of the man, which, remaining equally able to operate or to forbear operating after as before the decree of the will, are in a state which, if one pleases, may be called "indifferency;" and as far as this indifferency reaches, a man is free, and no farther. *V. g.*, I have the ability to move my hand, or to let it rest; that operative power is indifferent to move or not to move my hand: I am, then, in that respect perfectly free. My will determines that operative power to rest: I am yet free, because the indifferency of that my operative power to act or not to act still remains; the power of moving my hand is not at all impaired by the determination of my will, which at present orders rest; the indifferency of that power to act or not to act, is just as it was before, as will appear if the will puts it to the trial, by ordering the contrary. But if during the rest of my hand it be seized by a sudden palsy, the indifferency of that operative power is gone, and with it my liberty; I have no longer freedom in that respect, but am under a necessity of letting my hand rest. On the other side, if my hand be put into motion by a convulsion, the indifferency of that operative faculty is taken away by that motion, and my liberty in that case is lost: for I am under a necessity of having my hand move. I have added this, to show in what sort of indifferency liberty seems to me to consist, and not in any other, real or imaginary.

72. True notions concerning the nature and extent of liberty are of so great importance, that I hope I shall be pardoned this digression, which my attempt to explain it has led me into. The ideas of will, volition, liberty, and necessity, in this chapter of power, came naturally in my way. In a former edition of this treatise, I gave an account of my thoughts concerning them, according to the light I then had: and now, as a lover of truth, and not a worshipper of my own doctrines, I own some change of my opinion, which I think I have discovered ground for. In what I first writ, I with an unbiassed indifferency followed truth whither I thought she led me. But neither being so vain as to fancy infallibility, nor so disingenuous as to dissemble my mistakes for fear of blemishing my reputation, I have, with the same sincere design for truth only, not been ashamed to publish what a severer inquiry has suggested. It is not impossible but that some may think my former notions right, and some (as I have already found) these later, and some neither. I shall not at all wonder at this variety in men's opinions; impartial deductions of reason in controverted points being so very rare, and exact ones in abstract notions not so very easy, especially if of any length.

And therefore I should think myself not a little beholden to anyone, who would upon these or any other grounds, fairly clear this
subject of liberty from any difficulties that may yet remain.

Before I close this chapter, it may perhaps be to our purpose,
and help to give us clearer conceptions about power, if we make
our thoughts take a little more exact survey of action. I have
said above, that we have ideas but of two sorts of action, viz.,
motion and thinking. These, in truth, though called and counted
" actions," yet, if nearly considered, will not be found to be
always perfectly so. For, if I mistake not, there are instances
of both kinds, which, upon due consideration, will be found rather
passions than actions, and consequently so far the effects barely
of passive powers in those subjects which yet on their account
are thought agents. For in these instances the substance that
hath motion or thought receives the impression, whereby it is
put into that action, purely from without, and so acts merely by
the capacity it has to receive such an impression from some external agent; and such a power is not properly an active power,
but a mere passive capacity in the subject. Sometimes the substance or agent puts itself into action by its own power; and
this is properly active power. Whatsoever a modification a substance has whereby it produces any effect, that is called " action;"
*v. g.*, a solid substance by motion operates on or alters the sensible
ideas of another substance, and therefore this modification of
motion we call " action." But yet this motion in that solid substance is, when rightly considered, but a passion, if it received it
only from some external agent. So that the active power of
motion is in no substance which cannot begin motion in itself, or
in another substance when at rest. So likewise in thinking, a
power to receive ideas or thoughts from the operation of any
external substance, is called " a power of thinking:" but this is
but a passive power or capacity. But to be able to bring into
view ideas out of sight at one's own choice, and to compare which
of them one thinks fit, this is an active power. This reflection
may be of some use to preserve us from mistakes about powers
and actions, which grammar and the common frame of languages
may be apt to lead us into: since what is signified by verbs that
grammarians call " active," does not always signify action;
*v. g.*, this proposition, " I see the moon or a star," or, " I feel
the heat of the sun," though expressed by a verb active, does
not signify any action in me whereby I operate on those substances; but the reception of the ideas of light, roundness, and
heat, wherein I am not active, but barely passive, and cannot,
in that position of my eyes or body, avoid receiving them. But
when I turn my eyes another way, or remove my body out of
the sunbeams, I am properly active; because of my own choice,
by a power within myself, I put myself into that motion. Such
an action is the product of active power.

**78.** And thus I have, in a short draught, given a view of our original ideas, from whence all the rest are derived, and of which they are made up; which if I would consider as a philosopher, and examine on what causes they depend, and of what they are made, I believe they all might be reduced to these very few primary and original ones, viz., extension, solidity, mobility, or the power of being moved; which by our senses we receive from body: perceptivity, or the power of perception, or thinking; motivity, or the power of moving; which by reflection we receive from our minds. I crave leave to make use of these two new words, to avoid the danger of being mistaken in the use of those which are equivocal. To which if we add existence, duration, number, which belong both to the one and the other, we have perhaps all the original ideas on which the rest depended. For by these, I imagine, might be explained the nature of colours, sounds, tastes, smells, and all other ideas we have, if we had but faculties acute enough to perceive the severally-modified extensions and motions of these minute bodies which produce those several sensations in us. But my present purpose being only to inquire into the knowledge the mind has of things by those ideas and appearances which God has fitted it to receive from them, and how the mind comes by that knowledge, rather than into their causes or manner of production, I shall not, contrary to the design of this essay, set myself to inquire philosophically into the pecular constitution of bodies and the configuration of parts, whereby they have the power to produce in us the ideas of their sensible qualities. I shall not enter any farther into that disquisition, it sufficing to my purpose to observe that gold or saffron has a power to produce in us the idea of yellow; and snow or milk, the idea of white; which we can only have by our sight, without examining the texture of the parts of those bodies, or the particular figures or motion of the particles which rebound from them, to cause in us that particular sensation: though when we go beyond the bare ideas in our minds, and would inquire into their causes, we cannot conceive anything else to be in any sensible object whereby it produces different ideas in us, but the different bulk, figure, number, texture, and motion of its insensible parts.

---

# CHAPTER XXII.

## OF MIXED MODES.

**1.** *Mixed modes, what.*—Having treated of simple modes in the foregoing chapters, and given several instances of some of the most considerable of them, to show what they are, and how we come by them: we are now, in the next place, to consider those

we call "mixed modes:" such are the complex ideas we mark
by the names "obligation," "drunkenness," "a lie," &c., which,
consisting of several combinations of simple ideas of different
kinds, I have called "mixed modes," to distinguish them from
the more simple modes, which consist only of simple ideas of the
same kind. These mixed modes, being also such combinations of
simple ideas as are not looked upon to be characteristical marks
of any real beings that have a steady existence, but scattered
and independent ideas put together by the mind, are thereby
distinguished from the complex ideas of substances.

2. *Made by the mind.*—That the mind, in respect of its simple
ideas, is wholly passive, and receives them all from the existence
and operations of things, such as sensation or reflection offers
them, without being able to make any one idea, experience
shows us. But if we attentively consider these ideas I call
"mixed modes" we are now speaking of, we shall find their
original quite different. The mind often exercises an active
power in making these several combinations: for, it being once
furnished with simple ideas, it can put them together in several
compositions, and so make variety of complex ideas, without examining whether they exist so together in nature. And hence,
I think, it is that these ideas are called "notions;" as if they
had their original and constant existence more in the thoughts
of men, than in the reality of things; and to form such ideas it
sufficed that the mind put the parts of them together, and that
they were consistent in the understanding, without considering
whether they had any real being: though I do not deny but
several of them might be taken from observation, and the existence of several simple ideas so combined as they are put
together in the understanding. For the man who first framed
the idea of hypocrisy, might have either taken it at first from
the observation of one who made show of good qualities which
he had not; or else have framed that idea in his mind without
having any such pattern to fashion it by. For it is evident that,
in the beginning of languages and societies of men, several of
those complex ideas, which were consequent to the constitutions
established amongst them, must needs have been in the minds
before they existed anywhere else; and that many names that
stood for such complex ideas were in use, and so those ideas
framed, before the combinations they stood for ever existed.

3. *Sometimes got by the explication of their names.*—Indeed,
now that languages are made, and abound with words standing
for such combinations, an usual way of getting these complex
ideas is by the explication of those terms that stand for them.
For, consisting of a company of simple ideas combined, they may,
by words standing for those simple ideas, be represented to the
mind of one who understands those words, though that complex
combination of simple ideas were never offered to his mind by

the real existence of things.   Thus a man may come to have the
idea of sacrilege or murder, by enumerating to him the simple
ideas which these words stand for, without ever seeing either of
them committed.

4. *The name ties the parts of mixed modes into one idea.*—
Every mixed mode consisting of many distinct simple ideas, it
seems reasonable to inquire, whence it has its unity, and how
such a precise multitude comes to make but one idea, since that
combination does not always exist together in nature ?   To which
I answer, It is plain it has its unity from an act of the mind
combining those several simple ideas together, and considering
them as one complex one, consisting of those parts ; and the mark
of this union, or that which is looked on generally to complete it,
is one name given to that combination.   For it is by their names
that men commonly regulate their account of their distinct
species of mixed modes, seldom allowing or considering any
number of simple ideas to make one complex one, but such collections as there be names for.   Thus, though the killing of an
old man be as fit in nature to be united into one complex idea
as the killing a man's father ; yet, there being no name standing
precisely for the one, as there is the name of "parricide" to
mark the other, it is not taken for a particular complex idea, nor
a distinct species of actions from that of killing a young man, or
any other man.

5. *The cause of making mixed modes.*—If we should inquire
a little farther, to see what it is that occasions men to make
several combinations of simple ideas into distinct and, as it were,
settled modes, and neglect others which, in the nature of things
themselves, have as much an aptness to be combined and make
distinct ideas, we shall find the reason of it to be the end of
language ; which being to mark or communicate men's thoughts
to one another with all the despatch that may be, they usually
make such collections of ideas into complex modes, and affix
names to them, as they have frequent use of it in their way of
living and conversation, leaving others which they have but
seldom an occasion to mention loose, and without names that tie
them together : they rather choosing to enumerate (when they
have need) such ideas as make them up, by the particular names
that stand for them, than to trouble their memories by multiplying
of complex ideas with names to them, which they shall seldom or
never have any occasion to make use of,

6. *Why words in one language have none answering in another.*
—This shows us how it comes to pass, that there are in every
language many particular words which cannot be rendered by
any one single word of another.   For the several fashions, customs, and manners of one nation, making several combinations
of ideas familiar and necessary in one, which another people have
had never any occasion to make, or perhaps so much as take

notice of, names come of course to be annexed to them, to avoid
long periphrases in things of daily conversation; and so they
become so many distinct complex ideas in their minds. Thus
ὀστρακισμὸς amongst the Greeks, and *proscriptio* amongst the
Romans, were words which other languages had no names that
exactly answered, because they stood for complex ideas which
were not in the minds of the men of other nations. Where there
was no such custom, there was no notion of any such actions;
no use of such combinations of ideas as were united, and, as it
were, tied together, by those terms: and therefore in other
countries there were no names for them.

7. *And languages change.*—Hence also we may see the reason
why languages constantly change, take up new and lay by old
terms. Because change of customs and opinions bringing with
it new combinations of ideas, which it is necessary frequently to
think on and talk about, new names, to avoid long descriptions,
are annexed to them, and so they become new species of complex
modes. What a number of different ideas are by this means
wrapped up in one short sound, and how much of our time and
breath is thereby saved, anyone will see who will but take the
pains to enumerate all the ideas that either " reprieve " or
" appeal " stand for; and instead of either of those names use
a periphrasis to make anyone understand their meaning.

8. *Mixed modes, where they exist.*—Though I shall have occasion to consider this more at large when I come to treat of words,
and their use; yet I could not avoid to take this much notice
here of the names of mixed modes, which, being fleeting and
transient combinations of simple ideas, which have but a short
existence anywhere but in the minds of men, and there, too,
have no longer any existence than whilst they are thought on,
have not so much anywhere the appearance of a constant and
lasting existence as in their names: which are therefore, in these
sort of ideas, very apt to be taken for the ideas themselves. For
if we should inquire where the idea of a triumph or apotheosis
exists, it is evident they could neither of them exist altogether
anywhere in the things themselves, being actions that required
time to their performance, and so could never all exist together;
and as to the minds of men, where the ideas of these actions
are supposed to be lodged, they have there, too, a very uncertain
existence; and therefore we are apt to annex them to the names
that excite them in us.

9. *How we get the ideas of mixed modes.*—There are therefore
three ways whereby we get the complex ideas of mixed modes.
(1.) By experience and observation of things themselves; thus
by seeing two men wrestle or fence, we get the idea of wrestling
or fencing. (2.) By invention, or voluntary putting together of
several simple ideas in our own minds: so he that first invented
printing, or etching, had an idea of it in his mind before it ever

existed. (8.) Which is the most usual way, by explaining the names of actions we never saw, or notions we cannot see; and by enumerating, and thereby, as it were, setting before our imaginations all those ideas which go to the making them up, and are the constituent parts of them. For, having by sensation and reflection stored our minds with simple ideas, and by use got the names that stand for them, we can by those names represent to another any complex idea we would have him conceive; so that it has in it no simple ideas but what he knows, and has with us the same name for. For all our complex ideas are ultimately resolvable into simple ideas, of which they are compounded, and originally made up, though perhaps their immediate ingredients, as I may so say, are also complex ideas. Thus the mixed mode which the word "lie" stands for, is made of these simple ideas: (1.) Articulate sounds. (2.) Certain ideas in the mind of the speaker. (8.) Those words the signs of those ideas. (4.) Those signs put together by affirmation or negation, otherwise than the ideas they stand for, are in the mind of the speaker. I think I need not go any farther in the analysis of that complex idea we call a "lie:" what I have said is enough to show that it is made up of simple ideas: and it could not be but an offensive tediousness to my reader, to trouble him with a more minute enumeration of every particular simple idea that goes to this complex one; which, from what has been said, he cannot but be able to make out to himself. The same may be done in all our complex ideas whatsoever; which, however compounded and decompounded, may at last be resolved into simple ideas, which are all the materials of knowledge or thought we have or can have. Nor shall we have reason to fear that the mind is hereby stinted to too scanty a number of ideas, if we consider what an inexhaustible stock of simple modes number and figure alone affords us. How far, then, mixed modes, which admit of the various combinations of different simple ideas and their infinite modes, are from being few and scanty, we may easily imagine. So that, before we have done, we shall see that nobody need be afraid he shall not have scope and compass enough for his thoughts to range in, though they be, as I pretend, confined only to simple ideas received from sensation or reflection, and their several combinations.

10. *Motion, thinking, and power have been most modified.*—It is worth our observing which of all our simple ideas have been most modified, and had most mixed modes made out of them, with names given to them; and those have been these three: thinking, and motion (which are the two ideas which comprehend in them all action), and power, from whence these actions are conceived to flow. These simple ideas, I say, of thinking, motion, and power, have been those which have been most modified, and out of whose modifications have been made most complex modes, with names

to them. For, action being the great business of mankind, and the whole matter about which all laws are conversant, it is no wonder that the several modes of thinking and motion should be taken notice of, the ideas of them observed and laid up in the memory, and have names assigned to them; without which, laws could be but ill made, or vice and disorder repressed. Nor could any communication be well had amongst men without such complex ideas, with names to them : and therefore men have settled names and supposed settled ideas in their minds of modes of actions distinguished by their causes, means, objects, ends, instruments, time, place, and other circumstances, and also of their powers fitted for those actions; *v. g.*, boldness is the power to speak or do what we intend before others, without fear or disorder; and the Greeks call the confidence of speaking by a peculiar name, παρρησία, which power or ability in man of doing anything, when it has been acquired by frequent doing the same thing, is that idea we name " habit;" when it is forward and ready upon every occasion to break into action, we call it " disposition." Thus testiness is a disposition or aptness to be angry.

To conclude : let us examine any modes of action; *v. g.*, consideration and assent, which are actions of the mind; running and speaking, which are actions of the body; revenge and murder, which are actions of both together; and we shall find them but so many collections of simple ideas, which together make up the complex ones signified by those names.

11. *Several words seeming to signify action, signify but the effect.*—Power being the source from whence all action proceeds, the substances wherein these powers are, when they exert this power into act, are called " causes;" and the substances which thereupon are produced, or the simple ideas which are introduced into any subject by the exerting of that power, are called " effects." The efficacy whereby the new substance or idea is produced, is called, in the subject exerting that power, "action;" but in the subject, wherein any simple idea is changed or produced, it is called "passion;" which efficacy however various, and the effects almost infinite, yet we can, I think, conceive it, in intellectual agents, to be nothing else but modes of thinking and willing; in corporeal agents, nothing else but modifications of motion. I say, I think we cannot conceive it to be any other but these two : for whatever sort of action besides these produces any effects, I confess myself to have no notion or idea of; and so it is quite remote from my thoughts, apprehensions, and knowledge; and as much in the dark to me as five other senses, or as the ideas of colours to a blind man : and therefore many words which seem to express some action, signify nothing of the action, or *modus operandi*, at all, but barely the effect, with some circumstances of the subject wrought on, or cause operating; *v. g.*, creation, annihilation, contain in them no idea of the action

or manner whereby they are produced, but barely of the cause, and the thing done. And when a countryman says the cold freezes water, though the word "freezing" seems to import some action, yet truly it signifies nothing but the effect; viz., that water, that was before fluid, is become hard and consistent; without containing any idea of the action whereby it is done.

12. *Mixed modes made also of other ideas.*—I think I shall not need to remark here, that though power and action make the greatest part of mixed modes, marked by names and familiar in the minds and mouths of men, yet other simple ideas, and their several combinations, are not excluded; much less, I think, will it be necessary for me to enumerate all the mixed modes which have been settled, with names to them. That would be to make a dictionary of the greatest part of the words made use of in divinity, ethics, law, and politics, and several other sciences. All that is requisite to my present design is, to show what sort of ideas those are which I called "mixed modes:" how the mind comes by them; and that they are compositions made up of simple ideas got from sensation and reflection; which, I suppose, I have done.

## CHAPTER XXIII.

### OF OUR COMPLEX IDEAS OF SUBSTANCES.

1. *Ideas of substances, how made.*—The mind being, as I have declared, furnished with a great number of the simple ideas conveyed in by the senses, as they are found in exterior things, or by reflection on its own operations, takes notice, also, that a certain number of these simple ideas go constantly together; which being presumed to belong to one thing, and words being suited to common apprehensions, and made use of for quick despatch, are called, so united in one subject, by one name; which, by inadvertency, we are apt afterward to talk of and consider as one simple idea, which indeed is a complication of many ideas together: because, as I have said, not imagining how these simple ideas can subsist by themselves, we accustom ourselves to suppose some *substratum* wherein they do subsist, and from which they do result; which therefore we call "substance."*

2. *Our idea of substance in general.*—So that if anyone will examine himself concerning his notion of pure substance in general, he will find he has no other idea of it at all, but only a supposition of he knows not what support of such qualities which are capable of producing simple ideas in us; which qualities are commonly called "accidents." If anyone should be asked, "What is the subject wherein colour or weight

* See Note A at the end of this chapter, p. 226.—EDIT.

inheres ?" he would have nothing to say but, "The solid extended parts." And if he were demanded, "What is it that solidity and extension inhere in?" he would not be in a much better case than the Indian before mentioned, who, saying that the world was supported by a great elephant, was asked, what the elephant rested on? to which his answer was, "A great tortoise:" but being again pressed to know what gave support to the broad-backed tortoise, replied,—something, he knew not what. And thus here, as in all other cases where we use words without having clear and distinct ideas, we talk like children; who, being questioned what such a thing is which they know not readily give this satisfactory answer,—that it is something; which in truth signifies no more, when so used, either by children or men, but that they know not what; and that the thing they pretend to know and talk of, is what they have no distinct idea of at all, and so are perfectly ignorant of it, and in the dark. The idea, then, we have, to which we give the general name "substance," being nothing but the supposed, but unknown, support of those qualities we find existing, which we imagine cannot subsist *sine re substante*, "without something to support them," we call that support *substantia;* which, according to the true import of the word, is, in plain English, "standing under," or "upholding."*

8. *Of the sorts of substances.*—An obscure and relative idea of substance in general being thus made, we come to have the ideas of particular sorts of substances, by collecting such combinations of simple ideas as are by experience and observation of men's senses taken notice of to exist together, and are therefore supposed to flow from the particular internal constitution or unknown essence of that substance. Thus we come to have the ideas of a man, horse, gold, water, &c., of which substances, whether anyone has any other clear idea, farther than of certain simple ideas co-existing together, I appeal to everyone's own experience. It is the ordinary qualities observable in iron or a diamond, put together, that make the true complex idea of those substances, which a smith or a jeweller commonly knows better than a philosopher; who, whatever substantial forms he may talk of, has no other idea of those substances than what is framed by a collection of those simple ideas which are to be found in them. Only we must take notice, that our complex ideas of substances, besides all these simple ideas they are made up of, have always the confused idea of something to which they belong and in which they subsist : and therefore, when we speak of any sort of substance we say it is a thing having such or such qualities; as, body is a thing that is extended, figured, and capable of motion; spirit, a thing capable of thinking; and so hardness, friability, and power to draw iron

* See Note B at the end of this chapter, p. 228.—EDIT.

we say, are qualities to be found in a loadstone. These and the like fashions of speaking, intimate that the substance is supposed always something, besides the extension, figure, solidity, motion, thinking, or other observable ideas, though we know not what it is.

4. *No clear idea of substance in general.*—Hence, when we talk or think of any particular sort of corporeal substances, as horse, stone, &c., though the idea we have of either of them be but the complication or collection of those several simple ideas of sensible qualities which we used to find united in the thing called "horse" or "stone;" yet because we cannot conceive how they should subsist alone, nor one in another, we suppose them existing in, and supported by, some common subject; which support we denote by the name "substance," though it be certain we have no clear or distinct idea of that thing we suppose a support.

5. *As clear an idea of spirit as body.*—The same happens concerning the operations of the mind; viz., thinking, reasoning, fearing, &c., which we concluding not to subsist of themselves, nor apprehending how they can belong to body, or be produced by it, we are apt to think these the actions of some other substance, which we call "spirit;" whereby yet it is evident, that having no other idea or notion of matter, but something wherein those many sensible qualities which affect our senses do subsist; by supposing a substance wherein thinking, knowing, doubting, and a power of moving, &c., do subsist; we have as clear a notion of the substance of spirit as we have of body; the one being supposed to be (without knowing what it is) the *substratum* to those simple ideas we have from without; and the other supposed (with a like ignorance of what it is) to be the *substratum* to those operations which we experiment in ourselves within. It is plain, then, that the idea of corporeal substance in matter is as remote from our conceptions and apprehensions as that of spiritual substance, or spirit; and therefore, from our not having any notion of the substance of spirit, we can no more conclude its non-existence than we can, for the same reason, deny the existence of body: it being as rational to affirm there is no body, because we have no clear and distinct idea of the substance of matter, as to say there is no spirit, because we have no clear and distinct idea of the substance of a spirit.

̄. *Of the sorts of substances.*—Whatever therefore be the secret and abstract nature of substance in general, all the ideas we have of particular, distinct sorts of substances, are nothing but several combinations of simple ideas co-existing in such, though unknown, cause of their union, as makes the whole subsist of itself. It is by such combinations of simple ideas, and nothing else, that we represent particular sorts of substances to ourselves; such are the ideas we have of their several species in our minds; and such only do we, by their specific names, signify to others; *v. g.,*

man, horse, sun, water, iron : upon hearing which words everyone, who understands the language, frames in his mind a combination of those several simple ideas which he has usually
observed or fancied to exist together under that denomination ;
all which he supposes to rest in, and be, as it were, adherent to,
that unknown common subject, which inheres not in anything
else ; though in the meantime it be manifest, and everyone
upon inquiry into his own thoughts will find, that he has no
other idea of any substance, *v. g.*, let it be gold, horse, iron, man,
vitriol, bread, but what he has barely of those sensible qualities
which he supposes to adhere, with a supposition of such a *substratum* as gives, as it were, a support to those qualities, or simple
ideas, which he has observed to exist united together.    Thus,
the idea of the sun, what is it but an aggregate of those several
simple ideas,—bright, hot, roundish, having a constant regular
motion, at a certain distance from us,—and perhaps some other ?
as he who thinks and discourses of the sun has been more or less
accurate in observing those sensible qualities, ideas, or properties
which are in that thing which he calls the " sun."

   7. *Power, a great part of our complex ideas of substances.*—For
he has the perfectest idea of any of the particular sorts of substances who has gathered and put together most of those simple
ideas which do exist in it, among which are to be reckoned its
active powers and passive capacities ; which, though not simple
ideas, yet in this respect, for brevity's sake, may conveniently
enough be reckoned amongst them.    Thus, the power of drawing
iron is one of the ideas of the complex one of that substance we
call a " loadstone," and a power to be so drawn is a part of the
complex one we call " iron ;" which powers pass for inherent
qualities in those subjects : because every subject being as apt,
by the powers we observe in it, to change some sensible qualities
in other subjects, as it is to produce in us those simple ideas
which we receive immediately from it, does, by those new
sensible qualities introduced into other subjects, discover to us
those powers which do thereby mediately affect our senses as
regularly as its sensible qualities do it immediately ; *v. g.*, we
immediately by our senses perceive in fire its heat and colour ;
which are, if rightly considered, nothing but powers in it to
produce those ideas in us : we also by our senses perceive the
colour and brittleness of charcoal, whereby we come by the
knowledge of another power in fire, which it has to change the
colour and consistency of wood.    By the former, fire immediately,
by the latter it mediately, discovers to us these several powers,
which therefore we look upon to be a part of the qualities of
fire, and so make them a part of the complex ideas of it.    For,
all those powers that we take cognizance of, terminating only in
the alteration of some sensible qualities in those subjects on
which they operate, and so making them exhibit to us new

sensible ideas; therefore it is that I have reckoned these powers amongst the simple ideas, which make the complex ones of the sorts of substances; though these powers, considered in themselves, are truly complex ideas. And in this looser sense I crave leave to be understood, when I name any of these potentialities amongst the simple ideas which we recollect in our minds when we think of particular substances. For the powers that are severally in them are necessary to be considered, if we will have true distinct notions of the several sorts of substances.

8. *And why.*—Nor are we to wonder that powers make a great part of our complex ideas of substances, since their secondary qualities are those which, in most of them, serve principally to distinguish substances one from another, and commonly make a considerable part of the complex idea of the several sorts of them. For, our senses failing us in the discovery of the bulk, texture, and figure of the minute parts of bodies, on which their real constitutions and differences depend, we are fain to make use of their secondary qualities, as the characteristical notes and marks whereby to frame ideas of them in our minds, and distinguish them one from another. All which secondary qualities, as has been shown, are nothing but bare powers. For the colour and taste of opium are, as well as its soporific or anodyne virtues, mere powers depending on its primary qualities, whereby it is fitted to produce different operations on different parts of our bodies.

9. *Three sorts of ideas make our complex ones of substances.*— The ideas that make our complex ones of corporeal substances are of these three sorts. First. The ideas of the primary qualities of things which are discovered by our senses, and are in them even when we perceive them not: such are the bulk, figure, number, situation, and motion of the parts of bodies, which are really in them, whether we take notice of them or no. Secondly. The sensible secondary qualities which, depending on these, are nothing but the powers those substances have to produce several ideas in us by our senses; which ideas are not in the things themselves otherwise than as anything is in its cause. Thirdly. The aptness we consider in any substance to give or receive such alterations of primary qualities as that the substance so altered should produce in us different ideas from what it did before; these are called "active and passive powers": all which powers, as far as we have any notice or notion of them, terminate only in sensible simple ideas. For, whatever alteration a loadstone has the power to make in the minute particles of iron, we should have no notion of any power it had at all to operate on iron, did not its sensible motion discover it; and I doubt not but there are a thousand changes that bodies we daily handle have a power to cause in one another, which we never suspect, because they never appear in sensible effects.

**10.** *Powers make a great part of our complex ideas of substances.*
—Powers therefore justly make a great part of our complex
ideas of substances. He that will examine his complex idea of
gold, will find several of its ideas that make it up to be only
powers : as the power of being melted, but of not spending itself
in the fire, of being dissolved in *aqua regia*, are ideas as necessary to make up our complex idea of gold, as its colour and
weight : which, if duly considered, are also nothing but different
powers. For, to speak truly, yellowness is not actually in gold ;
but is a power in gold to produce that idea in us by our eyes,
when placed in a due light : and the heat which we cannot leave
out of our idea of the sun, is no more really in the sun than the
white colour it introduces into wax. These are both equally
powers in the sun, operating, by the motion and figure of its
insensible parts, so on a man as to make him have the idea of
heat ; and so on wax as to make it capable to produce in a man
the idea of white.

**11.** *The now secondary qualities of bodies would disappear, if
we could discover the primary ones of their minute parts.*—Had
we senses acute enough to discern the minute particles of bodies,
and the real constitution on which their sensible qualities depend,
I doubt not but they would produce quite different ideas in us,
and that which is now the yellow colour of gold would then disappear, and instead of it we should see an admirable texture of
parts of a certain size and figure. This microscopes plainly discover to us; for, what to our naked eyes produces a certain
colour is, by thus augmenting the acuteness of our senses, discovered to be quite a different thing ; and the thus altering, as
it were, the proportion of the bulk of the minute parts of a
coloured object to our usual sight, produces different ideas from
what it did before. Thus sand or pounded glass, which is
opaque and white to the naked eye, is pellucid in a microscope ;
and a hair seen this way loses its former colour, and is in a
great measure pellucid, with a mixture of some bright sparkling
colours, such as appear from the refraction of diamonds and
other pellucid bodies. Blood to the naked eye appears all red ;
but by a good microscope, wherein its lesser parts appear, shows
only some few globules of red, swimming in a pellucid liquor ;
and how these red globules would appear, if glasses could be
found that yet could magnify them one thousand or ten thousand
times more, is uncertain.

**12.** *Our faculties of discovery suited to our state.*—The infinite
wise Contriver of us and all things about us hath fitted our
senses, faculties, and organs to the conveniences of life, and the
business we have to do here. We are able by our senses to know
and distinguish things, and to examine them so far as to
apply them to our uses, and several ways to accommodate the
exigencies of this life. We have insight enough into their admir-

able contrivances and wonderful effects to admire and magnify the wisdom, power, and goodness of their Author. Such a knowledge as this, which is suited to our present condition, we want not faculties to attain. But it appears not that God intended we should have a perfect, clear, and adequate knowledge of them; that perhaps is not in the comprehension of any finite being. We are furnished with faculties (dull and weak as they are) to discover enough in the creatures to lead us to the knowledge of the Creator, and the knowledge of our duty; and we are fitted well enough with abilities to provide for the conveniences of living: these are our business in the world. But were our senses altered, and made much quicker and acuter, the appearance and outward scheme of things would have quite another face to us; and, I am apt to think, would be inconsistent with our being, or at least well-being, in this part of the universe which we inhabit. He that considers how little our constitution is able to bear a remove into parts of this air not much higher than that we commonly breathe in, will have reason to be satisfied that, in this globe of earth allotted for our mansion, the all-wise Architect has suited our organs and the bodies that are to affect them one to another. If our sense of hearing were but a thousand times quicker than it is, how would a perpetual noise distract us! and we should, in the quietest retirement, be less able to sleep or meditate than in the middle of a sea-fight. Nay, if that most instructive of our senses, seeing, were in any man a thousand or a hundred thousand times more acute than it is now by the best microscope, things several millions of times less than the smallest object of his sight now would then be visible to his naked eyes, and so he would come nearer the discovery of the texture and motion of the minute parts of corporeal things, and in many of them probably get ideas of their internal constitutions: but then he would be in a quite different world from other people: nothing would appear the same to him and others: the visible ideas of everything would be different. So that I doubt whether he and the rest of men could discourse concerning the objects of sight, or have any communication with colours, their appearances being so wholly different. And perhaps such a quickness and tenderness of sight could not endure bright sunshine, or so much as open daylight: nor take in but a very small part of any object at once, and that too only at a very near distance. And if by the help of such microscopical eyes (if I may so call them), a man could penetrate farther than ordinary into the secret composition and radical texture of bodies, he would not make any great advantage by the change, if such an acute sight would not serve to conduct him to the market and exchange; if he could not see things he was to avoid at a convenient distance, nor distinguish things he had to do with by those sensible qualities others do. He that was sharp-sighted enough to see the configuration of the minute particles of the spring of a clock, and observe upon what peculiar structure and impulse its elastic motion depends, would no doubt discover something very admirable. But if eyes so framed could not view at once the hand, and the characters of the hour-plate, and thereby at a distance see what o'clock it was, their owner could not be much benefited by that acuteness; which, whilst it discovered the secret contrivance of the parts of the machine, made him lose its use.

13. *Conjecture about spirits.*—And here give me leave to propose an extravagant conjecture of mine, viz., that, since we have some reason (if there be any credit to be given to the report of things that our philosophy cannot account for) to imagine that spirits can assume to themselves bodies of different bulk, figure, and conformation of parts; whether one great advantage some of them have over us may not lie in this, that they can so frame and shape to themselves organs of sensation or perception as to suit them to their present design, and the circumstances of the object they would consider. For, how much would that man exceed all others in knowledge, who had but the faculty so to alter the structure of his eyes (that one sense), as to make it capable of all the several degrees of vision, which the assistance of glasses (casually at first lit on) has taught us to conceive! What wonders would he discover who could so fit his eyes to all sorts of objects, as to see when he pleased the figure and motion of the minute particles in the blood and other juices of animals, as distinctly as he does at other times the shape and motion of the animals themselves! But to us, in our present state, unalterable organs, so contrived as to discover the figure and motion of the minute parts of bodies whereon depend those sensible qualities we now observe in them, would perhaps be of no advantage. God has, no doubt, made them so as is best for us in our present condition. He hath fitted us for the neighbourhood of the bodies that surround us, and we have to do with; and though we cannot, by the faculties we have, attain to a perfect knowledge of things, yet they will serve us well enough for those ends above mentioned, which are our great concernment. I beg my reader's pardon for laying before him so wild a fancy concerning the ways of perception in beings above us; but how extravagant soever it be, I doubt whether we can imagine anything about the knowledge of angels but after this manner, some way or other, in proportion to what we find and observe in ourselves. And though we cannot but allow that the infinite power and wisdom of God may frame creatures with a thousand other faculties and ways of perceiving things without them than what we have, yet our thoughts can go no farther than our own, so impossible it is for us to enlarge our very guesses beyond the ideas received from our own sensation and reflection. The supposition, at least, that angels do sometimes assume bodies, needs not startle us, since

some of the most ancient and most learned Fathers of the church seemed to believe that they had bodies : and this is certain, that their state and way of existence is unknown to us.

14. *Complex ideas of substances.*—But to return to the matter in hand, the ideas we have of substances, and the ways we come by them; I say, Our specific ideas of substances are nothing else but a collection of a certain number of simple ideas, considered as united in one thing, These ideas of substances, though they are commonly called " simple apprehensions," and the names of them " simple terms ;" yet, in effect, are complex and compounded. Thus the idea which an Englishman signifies by the name " swan," is white colour, long neck, red beak, black legs, and whole feet, and all these of a certain size, with a power of swimming in the water, and making a certain kind of noise ; and perhaps to a man who has long observed those kind of birds, some other properties, which all terminate in sensible simple ideas, all united in one common subject.

15. *Idea of spiritual substances as clear as of bodily substances.*—Besides the complex ideas we have of material sensible substances, of which I have last spoken, by the simple ideas we have taken from those operations of our own minds, which we experiment daily in ourselves, as thinking, understanding, willing, knowing, and power of beginning motion, &c., co-existing in some substance, we are able to frame the complex idea of an immaterial spirit. And thus, by putting together the ideas of thinking, perceiving, liberty, and power of moving themselves and other things, we have as clear a perception and notion of immaterial substances as we have of material. For putting together the ideas of thinking and willing, or the power of moving or quieting corporeal motion, joined to substance, of which we have no distinct idea, we have the idea of an immaterial spirit ; and by putting together the ideas of coherent solid parts, and a power of being moved, joined with substance, of which, likewise we have no positive idea, we have the idea of matter. The one is as clear and distinct an idea as the other : the idea of thinking and moving a body being as clear and distinct ideas as the ideas of extension, solidity, and being moved. For our idea of substance is equally obscure, or none at all, in both ; it is but a supposed I-know-not-what, to support those ideas we call " accidents." It is for want of reflection that we are apt to think that our senses show us nothing but material things. Every act of sensation, when duly considered, gives us an equal view of both parts of nature, the corporeal and spiritual. For, whilst I know, by seeing or hearing, &c., that there is some corporeal being without me, the object of that sensation, I can more certainly know that there is some spiritual being within me that sees and hears. This I must be convinced cannot be the

action of bare insensible matter, nor even could be without an immaterial thinking being.

16. *No idea of abstract substance.*—By the complex idea of extended, figured, coloured, and all other sensible qualities which is all that we know of it, we are as far from the idea of the substance of body as if we knew nothing at all: nor, after all the acquaintance and familiarity which we imagine we have with matter, and the many qualities men assure themselves they perceive and know in bodies, will it, perhaps, upon examination be found, that they have any more or clearer primary ideas belonging to body than they have belonging to immaterial spirit.

17. *The cohesion of solid parts and impulse, the primary ideas of body.*—The primary ideas we have peculiar to body, as contra-distinguished to spirit, are the cohesion of solid, and consequently separable parts, and a power of communicating motion by impulse. These, I think, are the original ideas proper and peculiar to body; for figure is but the consequence of finite extension.

18. *Thinking and motivity, the primary ideas of spirit.*—The ideas we have belonging and peculiar to spirit are thinking, and will, or a power of putting body into motion by thought, and, which is consequent to it, liberty. For as body cannot but communicate its motion by impulse to another body, which it meets with at rest; so the mind can put bodies into motion, or forbear to do so, as it pleases. The ideas of existence, duration, and mobility are common to them both.

19. *Spirits capable of motion.*—There is no reason why it should be thought strange that I make mobility belong to spirit; for, having no other idea of motion but change of distance with other beings that are considered as at rest; and finding that spirits as well as bodies cannot operate but where they are, and that spirits do operate at several times in several places, I cannot but attribute change of place to all finite spirits;—for of the infinite Spirit I speak not here. For, my soul, being a real being, as well as my body, is certainly as capable of changing distance with any other body or being as body itself, and so is capable of motion. And if a mathematician can consider a certain distance or a change of that distance between two points, one may certainly conceive a distance and a change of distance between two spirits; and so conceive their motion, their approach or removal, one from another.

20. Everyone finds in himself, that his soul can think, will, and operate on his body, in the place where that is; but cannot operate on a body, or in a place, an hundred miles distant from it. Nobody can imagine, that his soul can think or move a body at Oxford, whilst he is at London; and cannot but know that, being united to his body, it constantly changes place all the

whole journey between Oxford and London, as the coach or
horse does that carries him; and I think may be said to be truly
all that while in motion : or, if that will not be allowed to afford
us a clear idea enough of its motion, its being separated from
the body in death, I think, will; for, to consider it as going out
of the body, or leaving it, and yet to have no idea of its motion,
seems to me impossible.

21. If it be said by anyone, that it cannot change place, because it hath none, for spirits are not in *loco*, but *ubi;* I suppose
that way of talking will not now be of much weight to many in
an age that is not much disposed to admire, or suffer themselves
to be deceived by, such unintelligible ways of speaking. But if
anyone thinks there is any sense in that distinction, and that it
is applicable to our present purpose, I desire him to put it into
intelligible English, and then from thence draw a reason to show
that immaterial spirits are not capable of motion. Indeed, motion
cannot be attributed to God, not because he is an immaterial,
but because he is an infinite, Spirit.

22. *Idea of soul and body compared.*—Let us compare, then,
our complex idea of an immaterial spirit with our complex idea
of body, and see whether there be any more obscurity in one
than in the other, and in which most. Our idea of body, as I
think, is an extended solid substance, capable of communicating
motion by impulse : and our idea of soul, as an immaterial spirit,
is of a substance that thinks, and has a power of exciting motion
in body, by will or thought. These, I think, are our complex
ideas of soul and body, as contra-distinguished; and now let us
examine which has most obscurity in it, and difficulty to be apprehended. I know that people, whose thoughts are immersed
in matter, and have so subjected their minds to their senses that
they seldom reflect on anything beyond them, are apt to say,
they cannot comprehend a thinking thing, which perhaps is
true : but I affirm, when they consider it well, they can no more
comprehend an extended thing.

23. *Cohesion of solid parts in body, as hard to be conceived
as thinking in a soul.*—If anyone say, he knows not what it is
thinks in him; he means, he knows not what the substance is of
that thinking thing: no more, say I, knows he what the substance is of that solid thing. Farther, if he says, he knows not
how he thinks; I answer, Neither knows he how he is extended;
how the solid parts of body are united or cohere together to
make extension. For though the pressure of the particles of air
may account for the cohesion of several parts of matter that are
grosser than the particles of air, and have pores less than the
corpuscles of air; yet the weight or pressure of the air will not
explain, nor can be a cause of, the coherence of the particles
of air themselves. And if the pressure of the ether, or any
subtiler matter than the air, may unite and hold fast together

the parts of a particle of air, as well as other bodies; yet it cannot make bonds for itself, and hold together the parts that make
up every the least corpuscle of that *materia subtilis*. So that that
hypothesis, how ingeniously soever explained, by showing that
the parts of sensible bodies are held together by the pressure of
other external insensible bodies, reaches not the parts of the
ether itself; and by how much the more evident it proves that
the parts of other bodies are held together by the external
pressure of the ether, and can have no other conceivable cause
of their cohesion and union, by so much the more it leaves us in
the dark concerning the cohesion of the parts of the corpuscles
of the ether itself; which we can neither conceive without
parts, they being bodies and divisible; nor yet how their parts
cohere, they wanting that cause of cohesion which is given of the
cohesion of the parts of all other bodies.

24. But, in truth, the pressure of any ambient fluid, how great
soever, can be no intelligible cause of the cohesion of the solid
parts of matter. For though such a pressure may hinder the
avulsion of two polished superficies one from another, in a line
perpendicular to them, as in the experiment of two polished
marbles; yet it can never, in the least, hinder the separation by
a motion, in a line parallel to those surfaces. Because the
ambient fluid, having a full liberty to succeed in each point of
space deserted by a lateral motion, resists such a motion of
bodies so joined, no more than it would resist the motion of that
body were it on all sides environed by that fluid, and touched no
other body: and therefore, if there were no other cause of cohesion, all parts of bodies must be easily separable by such a
lateral sliding motion. For, if the pressure of the ether be the
adequate cause of cohesion, wherever that cause operates not,
there can be no cohesion. And since it cannot operate against
such a lateral separation (as has been showed), therefore in
every imaginary plane, intersecting any mass of matter, there
could be no more cohesion than of two polished surfaces, which
will always, notwithstanding any imaginable pressure of a fluid,
easily slide one from another. So that perhaps, how clear an
idea soever we think we have of the extension of body, which
is nothing but the cohesion of solid parts, he that shall well consider it in his mind, may have reason to conclude, that it is as
easy for him to have a clear idea how the soul thinks, as how
body is extended. For since body is no farther nor otherwise
extended than by the union and cohesion of its solid parts, we
shall very ill comprehend the extension of body without understanding wherein consists the union and cohesion of its parts;
which seems to me as incomprehensible as the manner of
thinking, and how it is performed.

25. I allow it is usual for most people to wonder how anyone
should find a difficulty in what they think they every day

observe. "Do we not see," will they be ready to say, "the parts of bodies stick firmly together? Is there anything more common? And what doubt can there be made of it?" And the like I say concerning thinking, and voluntary motion: Do we not every moment experiment in it ourselves; and therefore can it be doubted? The matter of fact is clear, I confess; but when we would a little nearer look into it, and consider how it is done, there, I think, we are at a loss, both in the one and the other; and can as little understand how the parts of body cohere, as how we ourselves perceive or move. I would have anyone intelligibly explain to me, how the parts of gold or brass (that but now in fusion were as loose from one another as the particles of water, or the sands of an hour-glass) come in a few moments to be so united, and adhere so strongly one to another, that the utmost force of men's arms cannot separate them: a considering man will, I suppose, be here at a loss to satisfy his own or another man's understanding.

26. The little bodies that compose that fluid we call "water" are so extremely small, that I have never heard of anyone who by a microscope (and yet I have heard of some that have magnified to 10,000, nay to much above 100,000 times), pretended to perceive their distinct bulk, figure, or motion. And the particles of water are also so perfectly loose one from another, that the least force sensibly separates them; nay, if we consider their perpetual motion, we must allow them to have no cohesion one with another; and yet let but a sharp cold come, and they unite, they consolidate, these little atoms cohere, and are not, without great force, separable. He that could find the bonds that tie these heaps of loose little bodies together so firmly, he that could make known the cement that makes them stick so fast one to another, would discover a great and yet unknown secret: and yet, when that was done, would he be far enough from making the extension of body (which is the cohesion of its solid parts) intelligible, till he could show wherein consisted the union or consolidation of the parts of those bonds, or of that cement, or of the least particle of matter that exists. Whereby it appears, that this primary and supposed obvious quality of body will be found, when examined, to be as incomprehensible, as anything belonging to our minds, and a solid extended substance, as hard to be conceived as a thinking immaterial one, whatever difficulties some would raise against it.

27. For, to extend our thoughts a little farther, that pressure, which is brought to explain the cohesion of bodies, is as unintelligible as the cohesion itself. For, if matter be considered, as no doubt it is, finite, let anyone send his contemplation to the extremities of the universe, and there see what conceivable hoops, what bond, he can imagine, to hold this mass of matter in so close a pressure together, from whence steel has its firmness, and the

parts of a diamond their hardness and indissolubility. If matter be finite, it must have its extremes; and there must be something to hinder it from scattering asunder. If, to avoid this difficulty, anyone will throw himself into the supposition and abyss of infinite matter, let him consider what light he thereby brings to the cohesion of body; and whether he be ever the nearer making it intelligible, by resolving it into a supposition the most absurd and most incomprehensible of all other: so far is our extension of body (which is nothing but the cohesion of solid parts) from being clearer, or more distinct, when we would inquire into the nature, cause, or manner of it, than the idea of thinking.

28. *Communication of motion by impulse, or by thought, equally intelligible.*—Another idea we have of body, is the power of communication of motion by impulse; and of our souls, the power of exciting motion by thought. These ideas, the one of body, the other of our minds, every day's experience clearly furnishes us with : but if here again we inquire how this is done, we are equally in the dark. For in the communication of motion by impulse, wherein as much motion is lost to one body as is got to the other, which is the ordinariest case, we can have no other conception but of the passing of motion out of one body into another; which, I think, is as obscure and inconceivable, as how our minds move or stop our bodies by thought; which we every moment find they do. The increase of motion by impulse, which is observed or believed sometimes to happen, is yet harder to be understood. We have by daily experience clear evidence of motion produced both by impulse and by thought; but the manner how, hardly comes within our comprehension; we are equally at a loss in both. So that, however we consider motion, and its communication either from body or spirit, the idea which belongs to spirit is at least as clear as that which belongs to body. And if we consider the active power of moving, or, as I may call it, "motivity," it is much clearer in spirit than body, since two bodies, placed by one another at rest, will never afford us the idea of a power in the one to move the other, but by a borrowed motion : whereas the mind every day affords ideas of an active power of moving of bodies; and therefore it is worth our consideration, whether active power be not the proper attribute of spirits, and passive power of matter. Hence may be conjectured, that created spirits are not totally separate from matter; because they are both active and passive. Pure spirit, viz., God, is only active; pure matter is only passive; those beings that are both active and passive, we may judge to partake of both. But be that as it will, I think we have as many and as clear ideas belonging to spirit as we have belonging to body, the substance of each being equally unknown to us; and the idea of thinking in spirit, as clear as of extension in body : and the communication of motion by thought, which we attribute to spirit, is as evident

as that by impulse which we ascribe to body. Constant experience makes us sensible of both of these, though our narrow understandings can comprehend neither. For when the mind would look beyond those original ideas we have from sensation or reflection, and penetrate into their cause and manner of production, we find still it discovers nothing but its own short-sightedness.

29. To conclude: Sensation convinces us, that there are solid, extended substances; and reflection, that there are thinking ones: experience assures us of the existence of such beings; and that the one hath a power to move body by impulse, the other by thought; this we cannot doubt of. Experience, I say, every moment furnishes us with the clear ideas both of the one and the other. But beyond these ideas, as received from their proper sources, our faculties will not reach. If we would inquire farther into their nature, causes, and manner, we perceive not the nature of extension clearer than we do of thinking. If we would explain them any farther, one is as easy as the other; and there is no more difficulty to conceive how a substance we know not should by thought set body into motion, than how a substance we know not should by impulse set body into motion. So that we are no more able to discover wherein the ideas belonging to body consist, than those belonging to spirit. From whence it seems probable to me, that the simple ideas we receive from sensation and reflection are the boundaries of our thoughts; beyond which, the mind, whatever efforts it would make, is not able to advance one jot; nor can it make any discoveries, when it would pry into the nature and hidden causes of those ideas.

30. *Idea of body and spirit compared.*—So that, in short, the idea we have of spirit, compared with the idea we have of body stands thus: The substance of spirit is unknown to us; and so is the substance of body equally unknown to us: two primary qualities or properties of body, viz., solid coherent parts and impulse, we have distinct clear ideas of: so likewise we know and have distinct clear ideas of two primary qualities or properties of spirit, viz., thinking, and a power of action; *i.e.*, a power of beginning or stopping several thoughts or motions. We have also the ideas of several qualities inherent in bodies, and have the clear distinct ideas of them: which qualities are but the various modifications of the extension of cohering solid parts and their motion. We have likewise the ideas of several modes of thinking, viz., believing, doubting, intending, fearing, hoping; all which are but the several modes of thinking. We have also the ideas of willing, and moving the body consequent to it, and with the body itself too; for, as has been showed, spirit is capable of motion.

31. *The notion of spirit involves no more difficulty in it than that of body.*—Lastly. If this notion of immaterial spirit may have, perhaps, some difficulties in it not easy to be explained, we have

therefore no more reason to deny or doubt the existence of such
spirits, than we have to deny or doubt the existence of body because the notion of body is cumbered with some difficulties, very
hard and perhaps impossible to be explained or understood by us.
For I would fain have instanced anything in our notion of spirit
more perplexed, or nearer a contradiction, than the very notion
of body includes in it; the divisibility *in infinitum* of any finite
extension involving us, whether we grant or deny it, in consequences impossible to be explicated, or made in our apprehensions
consistent; consequences that carry greater difficulty and more
apparent absurdity, than anything can follow from the notion of
an immaterial knowing substance.

82. *We know nothing beyond our simple ideas.*—Which we are
not at all to wonder at, since we, having but some few superficial
ideas of things, discovered to us only by the senses from without,
or by the mind reflecting on what it experiments in itself within,
have no knowledge beyond that, much less of the internal constitution and true nature of things, being destitute of faculties
to attain it. And therefore experimenting and discovering in
ourselves knowledge and the power of voluntary motion, as certainly as we experiment or discover in things without us the
cohesion and separation of solid parts, which is the extension and
motion of bodies; we have as much reason to be satisfied with
our notion of immaterial spirit, as with our notion of body; and
the existence of the one as well as the other. For, it being no
more a contradiction that thinking should exist separate and
independent from solidity, than it is a contradiction that solidity
should exist separate and independent from thinking, they being
both but simple ideas, independent one from another; and having
as clear and distinct ideas in us of thinking as of solidity, I know
not why we may not as well allow a thinking thing without
solidity, *i.e.*, immaterial, to exist, as a solid thing without thinking, *i.e.*, matter, to exist; especially since it is no harder to conceive how thinking should exist without matter, than how matter
should think. For whensoever we would proceed beyond these
simple ideas we have from sensation and reflection, and dive
farther into the nature of things, we fall presently into darkness
and obscurity, perplexedness and difficulties; and can discover
nothing farther but our own blindness and ignorance. But
whichever of these complex ideas be clearest, that of body or
immaterial spirit, this is evident, that the simple ideas that make
them up are no other than what we have received from sensation
or reflection; and so is it of all our other ideas of substances,
even of God himself.

83. *Idea of God.*—For if we examine the idea we have of the
incomprehensible Supreme Being, we shall find, that we come by
it the same way; and that the complex ideas we have both of God
and separate spirits are made up of the simple ideas we receive

from reflection: *v. g.*, having, from what we experiment in ourselves, got the ideas of existence and duration, of knowledge and
power, of pleasure and happiness, and of several other qualities
and powers which it is better to have than to be without; when
we would frame an idea the most suitable we can to the Supreme
Being, we enlarge every one of these with our idea of infinity;
and so, putting them together, make our complex idea of God.
For, that the mind has such a power of enlarging some of its
ideas, received from sensation and reflection, has been already
showed.

34. If I find that I know some few things; and some of them,
or all, perhaps, imperfectly; I can frame an idea of knowing twice
as many, which I can double again as often as I can add to
number; and thus enlarge my idea of knowledge, by extending its
comprehension to all things existing or possible. The same also
I can do of knowing them more perfectly; *i.e.*, all their qualities,
powers, causes, consequences, and relations, &c., till all be perfectly known that is in them, or can any way relate to them;
and thus frame the idea of infinite or boundless knowledge. The
same may also be done of power, till we come to that we call
"infinite;" and also of the duration of existence without beginning or end; and so frame the idea of an eternal being. The
degrees of* extent, wherein we ascribe existence, power, wisdom,
and all other perfections (which we can have any ideas of), to
that Sovereign Being which we call "God," being all boundless
and infinite, we frame the best idea of him our minds are capable
of: all which is done, I say, by enlarging those simple ideas we
have taken from the operations of our own minds by reflection,
or by our senses from exterior things, to that vastness to which
infinity can extend them.

35. *Idea of God.*—For it is infinity which, joined to our ideas
of existence, power, knowledge, &c., makes that complex idea
whereby we represent to ourselves, the best we can, the Supreme
Being. For though in his own essence, which certainly we do
not know (not knowing the real essence of a pebble, or a fly, or
of our own selves), God be simple and uncompounded; yet, I
think, I may say we have no other idea of him but a complex one
of existence, knowledge, power, happiness, &c., infinite and
eternal: which are all distinct ideas, and some of them being
relative are again compounded of others; all which, being, as has
been shown, originally got from sensation and reflection, go to
make up the idea or notion we have of God.

36. *No ideas in our complex one of spirits, but those got from
sensation or reflection.*—This farther is to be observed, that there
is no idea we attribute to God, bating infinity, which is not also a
part of our complex idea of other spirits. Because, being capable

* This is the reading of the sixth; most other editions, including the fourth
(folio), of the Works, read " or."—EDIT

or no other simple ideas belonging to anything but body, but those which by reflection we receive from the operation of our own minds, we can attribute to spirits no other but what we receive from thence: and all the difference we can put between them in our contemplation of spirits, is only in the several extents and degrees of their knowledge, power, duration, happiness, &c. For that in our ideas, as well of spirits as of other things, we are restrained to those we receive from sensation and reflection, is evident from hence, that in our ideas of spirits, how much soever advanced in perfection beyond those of bodies, even to that of infinite, we cannot yet have any idea of the manner wherein they discover their thoughts one to another: though we must necessarily conclude that separate spirits, which are beings that have perfecter knowledge and greater happiness than we, must needs have also a perfecter way of communicating their thoughts than we have, who are fain to make use of corporeal signs and particular sounds, which are therefore of most general use, as being the best and quickest we are capable of. But of immediate communication having no experiment in ourselves, and consequently no notion of it at all, we have no idea how spirits which use not words can with quickness, or, much less, how spirits that have no bodies, can be masters of their own thoughts, and communicate or conceal them at pleasure, though we cannot but necessarily suppose they have such a power.

37. *Recapitulation.*—And thus we have seen what kind of ideas we have of substances of all kinds, wherein they consist, and how we come by them. From whence, I think, it is very evident,

First, That all our ideas of the several sorts of substances are nothing but collections of simple ideas, with a supposition of something to which they belong, and in which they subsist; though of this supposed something we have no clear distinct idea at all.

Secondly, That all the simple ideas that, thus united in one common substratum, make up our complex ideas of several sorts of substances, are no other but such as we have received from sensation or reflection. So that even in those which we think we are most intimately acquainted with, and come nearest the comprehension of our most enlarged conceptions, we cannot reach beyond those simple ideas. And even in those which seem most remote from all we have to do with, and do infinitely surpass anything we can perceive in ourselves by reflection, or discover by sensation in other things, we can attain to nothing but those simple ideas which we originally received from sensation or reflection; as is evident in the complex ideas we have of angels, and particularly of God himself.

Thirdly, That most of the simple ideas that make up our complex ideas of substances, when truly considered, are only powers, however we are apt to take them for positive qualities: *v. g.*, the greatest part of the ideas that make our complex idea of gold are yellowness, great weight, ductility, fusibility, and solubility in *aqua regia*, &c., all united together in an unknown substratum ; all which ideas are nothing 'else but so many relations to other substances, and are not really in the gold considered barely in itself, though they depend on those real and primary qualities of its internal constitution, whereby it has a fitness differently to operate and be operated on by several other substances.

---

### NOTE A.—Page 208.

THIS section, which was intended only to show how the individuals of distinct species of substances came to be looked upon as simple ideas, and so to have simple names, viz. from the supposed simple substratum or substance, which was looked upon as the thing itself in which inhere and from which resulted that complication of ideas by which it was represented to us, hath been mistaken for an account of the idea of substance in general ; and as such hath been reprehended in these words : "But how comes the general idea of substance to be framed in our minds ? Is this 'by abstracting and enlarging simple ideas ?' No : 'but it is by a complication of many simple ideas together ; because, not imagining how these simple ideas can subsist by themselves, we accustom ourselves to suppose some substratum wherein they do subsist, and from whence they do result ; which therefore we call *substance*.' And is this all, indeed, that is to be said for the being of substances, That we accustom ourselves to suppose a substratum ? Is that custom grounded upon true reason or not ? If not, then accidents or modes must subsist of themselves ; and these simple ideas need no tortoise to support them ; for figures and colours, &c., would do well enough of themselves, but for some fancies men have accustomed themselves to."

To which objection of the Bishop of Worcester our author answers thus :* "Herein your lordship seems to charge me with two faults : One, 'That I make the general idea of substance to be framed, not by abstracting and enlarging simple ideas, but by a complication of many simple ideas together;' the other, as if I had said, 'The being of substance had no other foundation but the fancies of men.'

"As to the first of these, I beg leave to remind your lordship, that I say in more places than one, and particularly book iii. chap. iii. section 6, and book i. chap. xi. sect. 9, where, *ex professo*, I treat of abstraction and general ideas, that they are all made by abstracting, and therefore could not be understood to mean, that *that* of substance was made any other way ; however my pen might have slipped, or the negligence of expression, where I might have something else than the general idea of substance in view, might make me seem to say so.

"That I was not speaking of the general idea of substance in the passage your lordship quotes, is manifest from the title of that chapter, which is, 'Of the complex ideas of substances.' And the first section

* In his First Letter to that Bishop, p. 27, &c.

of it, which your lordship cites for those words you have set down, stands thus :*

"In which words I do not observe any that deny the general idea of substance to be made by abstraction ; nor any that say, it is made by a complication of many simple ideas together.  But speaking in that place of the ideas of distinct substances, such as man, horse, gold, &c. I say they are made up of certain combinations of simple ideas ; which combinations are looked upon, each of them as one simple idea, though they are many ; and we call it by one name of *substance*, though made up of modes, from the custom of supposing a substratum, wherein that combination does subsist.  So that in this paragraph I only give an account of the idea of distinct substances, such as oak, elephant, iron, &c.; how, though they are made up of distinct complications of modes, yet they are looked on as one idea, called by one name, as making distinct sorts of substances.

"But that my notion of substance in general is quite different from these, and has no such combination of simple ideas in it, is evident from the immediate following words, where I say, 'The idea of pure substance in general, is only a supposition of we know not what support of such qualities as are capable of producing simple ideas in us.'†  And these I plainly distinguish all along, particularly where I say, 'Whatever therefore be the secret and abstract nature of substance in general, all the ideas we have of particular distinct substances are nothing but several combinations of simple ideas, co-existing in such, though unknown, cause of their union, as makes the whole subsist of itself.'

"The other thing laid to my charge is, as if I took the being of substance to be doubtful, or rendered it so by the imperfect and ill-grounded idea I have given of it.  To which I beg leave to say, that I ground not the being, but the idea, of substance on our accustoming ourselves to suppose some substratum ; for it is of the *idea* alone I speak there, and not of the *being* of substance.  And having everywhere affirmed and built upon it, That a man is a substance, I cannot be supposed to question or doubt of the being of substance, till I can question or doubt of my own being.  Farther, I say, 'Sensation convinces us, that there are solid, extended substances ; and reflection, that there are thinking ones.'‡  So that I think the being of substance is not shaken by what I have said ; and if the *idea* of it should be, yet (the being of things depending not on our ideas) the *being* of substance would not be at all shaken by my saying, we had but an obscure imperfect idea of it, and that that idea came from our accustoming ourselves to suppose some substratum ; or indeed, if I should say, we had no idea of substance at all.  For a great many things may be, and are granted to have a being, and be in nature, of which we have no ideas. For example : It cannot be doubted but there are distinct species of separate spirits, of which yet we have no distinct ideas at all ; it cannot be questioned but spirits have ways of communicating their thoughts, and yet we have no idea of it at all.

"The *being* then of substance being safe and secure, notwithstanding anything I have said, let us see whether the *idea* of it be not so too.

* The paragraph quoted is the first in p. 208.—Edit.
† Book ii. chap. xxiii. sect. 2.          ‡ Ibid. sect. 29.

Your lordship asks with concern, ' And is this all indeed that is to be said for the being' (if your lordship please let it be the 'idea') ' of substance, that we accustom ourselves to suppose a substratum? Is that custom grounded upon true reason or no?' I have said that it is grounded upon this, 'That we cannot conceive how simple ideas of sensible qualities should subsist alone; and therefore we suppose them to exist in, and to be supported by, some common subject; which support we denote by the name *substance.*'* Which I think is a true reason, because it is the same your lordship grounds the supposition of a substratum on in this very page; even on the repugnancy to our conceptions, that modes and accidents should subsist by themselves. So that I have the good luck here again to agree with your lordship, and consequently conclude I have your approbation in this, That the substratum to modes or accidents, which is our idea of substance in general, is founded in this—'that we cannot conceive how modes or accidents can subsist by themselves.'"

## NOTE B.—Page 209.

FROM this paragraph there hath been raised an objection by the Bishop of Worcester, as if our author's doctrine here concerning ideas had almost discarded substance out of the world; his words in this second paragraph being brought to prove, that he is "one of the gentlemen of this new way of reasoning, that have almost discarded substance out of the reasonable part of the world." To which our author replies :† "This, my lord, is an accusation which your lordship will pardon me, if I do not readily know what to plead to; because I do not understand what it is ' almost to discard substance out of the reasonable part of the world.' If your lordship means by it, that I deny or doubt that there is in the world any such thing as substance, that your lordship will acquit me of when your lordship looks again in this twenty-third chapter of the second book, which you have cited more than once, where you will find these words, sect. 4: ' When we talk or think of any particular sort of corporeal substances, as horse, stone, &c., though the idea we have of either of them be but the complication or collection of those several simple ideas of sensible qualities, which we use to find united in the thing called *horse* or *stone;* yet because we cannot conceive how they should subsist alone, nor one in another, we suppose them existing in, and supported by, some common subject, which support we denote by the name *substance;* though it be certain we have no clear or distinct idea of that thing we suppose a support.' And again, sect. 5: ' The same happens concerning the operations of the mind, viz. thinking, reasoning, fearing, &c., which we, considering not to subsist of themselves, nor apprehending how they can belong to body, or be produced by it, are apt to think these the actions of some other substance, which we call *spirit;* whereby yet it is evident, that having no other idea or notion of matter, but something wherein those many sensible qualities which affect our senses do subsist, by supposing a substance, wherein thinking, knowing, doubting, and a power of moving, &c., do subsist, we have as clear a notion of the nature or substance of spirit, as we have of body; though one

* Book ii. chap. xxiii. sect. 4.    † In his First Letter to that Bishop, p. 6, &c.

being supposed to be (without knowing what it is) the substratum to those simple ideas we have from without, and the other supposed (with a like ignorance of what it is) to be the substratum to those operations which we experiment in ourselves within.' And again, sect. 6 : ' Whatever therefore be the secret nature of substance in general, all the ideas we have of particular distinct substances are nothing but several combinations of simple ideas, co-existing in such, though unknown, cause of their union, as makes the whole subsist of itself.' And I farther say in the same section, ' that we suppose these combinations to rest in and to be adherent to that unknown, common subject, which inheres not in anything else. And [sect. 3] that ' our complex ideas of substances, besides all those ideas they are made up of, have always the confused idea of something to which they belong, and in which they subsist ; and therefore, when we speak of any sort of substance, we say it is a thing having such or such qualities ; as, body is a thing that is extended, figured, and capable of motion ; spirit a thing capable of thinking.

" ' These and the like fashions of speaking intimate, that the substance is supposed always something besides the extension, figure, solidity, motion, thinking, or other observable idea, though we know not what it is.'

" ' Our idea of body,' I say, ' is an extended, solid substance ; and our idea of our souls is of a substance that thinks.'* So that as long as there is any such thing as body or spirit in the world, I have done nothing towards the ' discarding substance out of the reasonable part of the world.' Nay, as long as there is any simple idea or sensible quality left, according to my way of arguing, substance cannot be discarded, because all simple ideas, all sensible qualities, carry with them a supposition of a substratum to exist in, and of a substance wherein they inhere ; and of this that whole chapter is so full, that I challenge anyone who reads it to think I have ' almost,' or one jot, ' discarded substance out of the reasonable part of the world.' And of this, *man, horse, sun, water, iron, diamond,* &c., which I have mentioned of distinct sorts of substances, will be my witnesses as long as any such thing remains in being ; of which I say, ' that the ideas of substances are such combinations of simple ideas, as are taken to represent distinct particular things, subsisting by themselves, in which the supposed or confused idea of substance is always the first and chief.'†

" If by ' almost discarding substance out of the reasonable part of the world,' your lordship means, that I have destroyed and almost discarded the true idea we have of it, by calling it a *substratum,* ' a supposition of we know not what support of such qualities as are capable of producing simple ideas in us,' an obscure relative idea ;'‡ ' that without knowing what it is, it is that which supports accidents ; so that of substance, we have no idea of what it is, but only a confused, obscure one of what it does :'§—I must confess this and the like I have said of our idea of substance ; and should be very glad to be convinced by your lordship, or anybody else, that I have spoken too meanly of it. He that would show me a more clear and distinct idea of substance, would do me a kindness I should thank him for. But

---

* Book ii. chap. xxiii. sect. 22.     † Ibid. chap. xii. sect. 6.
‡ Ibid. ii. chap. xxiii. sect. i.—iii.     § Ibid. chap. xiii. sect. 19.

this is the best I can hitherto find, either in my own thoughts or in the books of logicians; for their account or idea of it is, that it is *ens*, or *res per se subsistens et substans accidentibus;* which, in effect, is no more but that substance is a being or thing; or, in short, something they know not what, or of which they have no clearer idea than that it is something which supports accidents, or other simple ideas or modes, and is not supported itself as a mode or an accident. So that I do not see but Burgersdicius, Sanderson, and the whole tribe of logicians, must be reckoned with 'the gentlemen of this new way of reasoning, who have almost discarded substance out of the reasonable part of the world.'

"But supposing, my lord, that I, or these gentlemen, logicians of note, in the schools, should own, that we have a very imperfect, obscure, inadequate idea of substance; would it not be a little too hard to charge us with discarding substance out of the world? For what 'almost discarding,' and 'reasonable part of the world,' signifies, I must confess I do not clearly comprehend. But let 'almost,' and 'reasonable part,' signify here what they will, for I dare say your lordship meant something by them: would not your lordship think you were a little hardly dealt with, if for acknowledging yourself to have a very imperfect and inadequate idea of God, or of several other things which in this very treatise you confess our understandings come short in and cannot comprehend, you should be accused to be one of these gentlemen that have almost discarded God, or those other mysterious things, whereof you contend we have very imperfect and inadequate ideas, out of the reasonable world? For I suppose your lordship means by 'almost discarding out of the reasonable world,' something that is blamable, for it seems not to be inserted for a commendation; and yet I think he deserves no blame who owns the having imperfect, inadequate, obscure ideas, where he has no better. However, if it be inferred from thence, that either he almost excludes those things out of being, or out of rational discourse, if that be meant by 'the reasonable world;' for the first of these will not hold, because the being of things in the world depends not on our ideas; the latter indeed is true in some degree, but is no fault: for it is certain, that where we have imperfect, inadequate, confused, obscure ideas, we cannot discourse and reason about those things so well, fully, and clearly, as if we had perfect, adequate, clear, and distinct ideas."

Other objections are made against the following parts of this paragraph by that reverend prelate, viz. the repetition of the story of the Indian philosopher, and the talking like children about substance. To which our author replies:

"Your lordship, I must own, with great reason, takes notice that I paralleled more than once our idea of substance with the Indian philosopher's he-knew-not-what, which supported the tortoise, etc.

"This repetition is, I confess, a fault in exact writing; but I having acknowledged and excused it in these words in my Preface: 'I am not ignorant how little I herein consult my own reputation, when I knowingly let my Essay go with a fault so apt to disgust the most judicious, who are always the nicest readers:' and there farther add, that 'I did not publish my Essay for such great masters of knowledge as your lordship; but fitted it to men of my own size, to whom repetitions might be sometimes useful ;' it would not therefore have been besides your lordship's generosity (who were not intended to be provoked by this repetition) to have passed by such a fault as this, in one who pretends not beyond the lower rank of writers : but I see your lordship would have me exact and without any faults ; and I wish I could be so, the better to deserve your lordship's approbation.

" My saying that ' when we talk of substance, we talk like children who, being asked a question about something which they know not, readily give this satisfactory answer, that it is something,' your lordship seems mightily to lay to heart in these words that follow : ' If this be the truth of the case, we must still talk like children ; and I know not how it can be remedied. For if we cannot come at a rational idea of substance, we can have no principle of certainty to go upon in this debate.'

" If your lordship has any better and distincter idea of substance than mine is, which I have given an account of, your lordship is not at all concerned in what I have there said ; but those whose idea of substance, whether a rational or not rational idea, is like mine, something, he knows not what, must in that, with me, talk like children, when they speak of something, they know not what. For a philosopher that says, 'That which supports accidents is something, he knows not what ;' and a countryman that says, 'The foundation of the great church at Haarlem is supported by something, he knows not what ;' and a child that stands in the dark upon his mother's muff, and says he stands upon something, he knows not what ; in this respect talk all three alike. But if the countryman knows that the foundation of the church at Haarlem is supported by a rock, as the houses about Bristol are ; or by gravel, as the houses about London are ; or by wooden piles, as the houses in Amsterdam are ; it is plain, that then, having a clear and distinct idea of the thing that supports the church, he does not talk of this matter as a child ; nor will he of the support of accidents, when he has a clearer and more distinct idea of it than that it is barely something. But as long as we think like children in cases where our ideas are no clearer nor distincter than theirs, I agree with your lordship, that I know not how it can be remedied but that we must talk like them."

Farther, the bishop asks, Whether there be no difference between the bare being of a thing, and its subsistence by itself ? To which our author answers,* " Yes ; but what will that do to prove that, ' upon my principles, we can come to no certainty of reason that there is any such thing as substance ?' You seem by this question to conclude, that the idea of a thing that subsists by itself is a clear and distinct idea of substance ; but I beg leave to ask, Is the idea of the manner of subsistence of a thing the idea of the thing itself ? If it be not, we may have a clear and distinct idea of the manner, and yet have none but a very obscure and confused one of the thing. For example : I tell your lordship, that I know a thing that cannot subsist without a support, and I know another thing that does subsist without a support, and say no more of them ; can you, by having the clear and distinct ideas of having a support and not having a support, say that you have a clear and distinct idea of the thing that I know which has, and of the

* Mr. Locke's Third Letter, page 381.

thing that I know which has not, a support? If your lordship can, I beseech you to give me the clear and distinct idea of these, which I only call by the general name 'things,' that have or have not supports; for such there are, and such I shall give your lordship clear and distinct ideas of, when you shall please to call upon me for them; though I think your lordship will scarce find them by the general and confused idea of things, nor in the clearer and more distinct idea of having or not having a support.

"To show a blind man that he has no clear distinct idea of scarlet, I tell him that his notion of it *that it is a thing or being*, does not prove he has any clear or distinct idea of it; but barely that he takes it to be something, he knows not what. He replies, that he knows more than that, *v. g.* he knows that it subsists or inheres in another thing. 'And is there no difference,' says he, in your lordship's words, 'between the bare being of a thing, and its subsistence in another?' 'Yes,' say I to him; 'a great deal, they are very different ideas. But for all that, you have no clear and distinct idea of scarlet, not such an one as I have, who see and know it, and have another kind of idea of it besides that of inherence.'

"Your lordship has the idea of subsisting by itself, and therefore you conclude you have a clear and distinct idea of the thing that subsists by itself; which methinks is all one as if your countryman should say he hath an idea of a cedar of Lebanon, that it is a tree of a nature to need no prop to lean on for its support; therefore he has a clear and distinct idea of a cedar of Lebanon: which clear and distinct idea, when he comes to examine, is nothing but a general one of a tree with which his indetermined idea of a cedar is confounded. Just so is the idea of substance, which, however called clear and distinct, is confounded with the general indetermined idea of something. But suppose that the manner of subsisting by itself gives us a clear and distinct idea of substance, how does that prove 'that, upon my principles, we can come to no certainty of reason that there is any such thing as substance in the world?' which is the proposition to be proved."

---

## CHAPTER XXIV.

### OF COLLECTIVE IDEAS OF SUBSTANCES.

**1.** *One idea.*—Besides these complex ideas of several single substances, as of man, horse, gold, violet, apple, &c., the mind hath also "complex collective ideas" of substances; which I so call, because such ideas are made up of many particular substances considered together, as united into one idea, and which so joined are looked on as one; *v. g.*, the idea of such a collection of men as make an army, though consisting of a great number of distinct substances, is as much one idea as the idea of a man; and the great collective idea of all bodies whatsoever, signified by the name "world," is as much one idea as the idea of any the least particle of matter in it; it sufficing to the unity of any idea, that it be considered as one representation or picture, though made up of ever so many particulars.

2. *Made by the power of composing in the mind.*—These collective ideas of substances the mind makes by its power of composition, and uniting, severally, either simple or complex ideas into one, as it does by the same faculty make the complex ideas of particular substances, consisting of an aggregate of divers simple ideas united in one substance: and as the mind, by putting together the repeated ideas of unity, makes the collective mode or complex idea of any number, as a score, or a gross, &c., so by putting together several particular substances, it makes collective ideas of substances, as a troop, an army, a swarm, a city, a fleet: each of which everyone finds that he represents to his own mind by one idea, in one view; and so under that notion considers those several things as perfectly one, as one ship, or one atom. Nor is it harder to conceive how an army of ten thousand men should make one idea, than how a man should make one idea; it being as easy to the mind to unite into one the idea of a great number of men, and consider it as one, as it is to unite into one particular all the distinct ideas that make up the composition of a man, and consider them all together as one.

3. *All artificial things are collective ideas.*—Amongst such kind of collective ideas, are to be counted most part of artificial things, at least such of them as are made up of distinct substances: and in truth, if we consider all these collective ideas aright, as " army, constellation, universe," as they are united into so many single ideas, they are but the artificial draughts of the mind, bringing things very remote, and independent on one another, into one view, the better to contemplate and discourse of them, united into one conception, and signified by one name. For there are no things so remote, nor so contrary, which the mind cannot, by this art of composition, bring into one idea, as is visible in that signified by the name " universe."

---

## CHAPTER XXV.

### OF RELATION.

1. *Relation, what.*—Besides the ideas, whether simple or complex, that the mind has of things, as they are in themselves, there are others it gets from their comparison one with another. The understanding, in the consideration of anything, is not confined to that precise object: it can carry any idea, as it were, beyond itself, or, at least, look beyond it, to see how it stands in conformity to any other. When the mind so considers one thing, that it does, as it were, bring it to and set it by another, and

carry its view from one to the other: this is, as the words import, "relation" and "respect;" and the denominations given to positive things, intimating that respect, and serving as marks to lead the thoughts beyond the subject itself denominated to something distinct from it, are what we call "relatives;" and the things so brought together, "related." Thus, when the mind considers Caius as such a positive being, it takes nothing into that idea, but what really exists in Caius; *v. g.*, when I consider him as man, I have nothing in my mind but the complex idea of the species man. So likewise, when I say, "Caius is a white man," I have nothing but the bare consideration of man who hath that white colour. But when I give Caius the name "husband," I intimate some other person; and when I give him the name "whiter," I intimate some other thing: in both cases my thought is led to something beyond Caius, and there are two things brought into consideration. And since any idea, whether simple or complex, may be the occasion why the mind thus brings two things together, and as it were, takes a view of them at once, though still considered as distinct; therefore any of our ideas may be the foundation of relation. As in the above-mentioned instance, the contract and ceremony of marriage with Sempronia, is the occasion of the denomination or relation of husband; and the colour white, the occasion why he is said whiter than freestone.

2. *Relations without correlative terms, not easily perceived.* —These, and the like relations, expressed by relative terms, that have others answering them with a reciprocal intimation, as "father and son, bigger and less, cause and effect," are very obvious to everyone; and everybody, at first sight, perceives the relation. For "father and son, husband and wife," and such other correlative terms, seem so nearly to belong one to another, and, through custom, do so readily chime and answer one to another in people's memories, that, upon the naming of either of them, the thoughts are presently carried beyond the thing so named; and nobody overlooks or doubts of a relation where it is so plainly intimated. But where languages have failed to give correlative names, there the relation is not always so easily taken notice of. "Concubine" is, no doubt, a relative name as well as "wife:" but in languages where this and the like words have not a correlative term, there people are not so apt to take them to be so, as wanting that evident mark of relation which is between correlatives, which seem to explain one another, and not to be able to exist but together. Hence it is that many of those names which, duly considered, do include evident relations, have been called "external denominations." But all names, that are more than empty sounds, must signify some idea which is either in the thing to which the name is applied; and then it is positive, and is looked on as united to and existing in the thing

to which the denomination is given: or else it arises from the respect the mind finds in it to something distinct from it with which it considers it; and then it includes a relation.

3. *Some seemingly absolute terms contain relations.*—Another sort of relative terms there is, which are not looked on to be either relative or so much as external denominations; which yet, under the form and appearance of signifying something absolute in the subject, do conceal a tacit, though less observable relation. Such are the seemingly positive terms of "old, great, imperfect," &c., whereof I shall have occasion to speak more at large in the following chapters.

4. *Relation different from the things related.*—This farther may be observed, that the ideas of relation may be the same in men who have far different ideas of the things that are related, or that are thus compared: *v. g.,* those who have far different ideas of a man, may yet agree in the notion of a father: which is a notion superinduced to the substance, or man, and refers only to an act of that thing called "man," whereby he con- tributed to the generation of one of his own kind, let man be what it will.

5. *Change of relation may be without any change in the subject.* —The nature therefore of relation consists in the referring or comparing two things one to another; from which comparison one or both comes to be denominated. And if either of those things be removed or cease to be, the relation ceases, and the denomination consequent to it, though the other receive in itself no alteration at all: *v. g.,* Caius, whom I consider to-day as a father ceases to be so to-morrow, only by the death of his son, without any alteration made in himself. Nay, barely by the mind's changing the object, to which it compares anything, the same thing is capable of having contrary denominations at the same time: *v. g.,* Caius, compared to several persons, may truly be said to be older and younger, stronger and weaker, &c.

6. *Relation only betwixt two things.*—Whatsoever doth or can exist, or be considered as one thing, is positive; and so not only simple ideas and substances, but modes also, are positive beings; though the parts of which they consist are very often relative one to another; but the whole together considered as one thing, and producing in us the complex idea of one thing, which idea is in our minds as one picture, though an aggregate of divers parts and under one name, it is a positive or absolute thing or idea. Thus a triangle, though the parts thereof, compared one to another, be relative, yet the idea of the whole is a positive absolute idea. The same may be said of a family, a tune, &c., for there can be no relation but betwixt two things, considered as two things. There must always be in relation two ideas, or things, either in themselves really separate, or considered as distinct, and then a ground or occasion for their comparison.

**7.** *All things capable of relation.*—Concerning relation in general, these things may be considered.

First, That there is no one thing, whether simple idea, substance, mode, or relation, or name of either of them, which is not capable of almost an infinite number of considerations in reference to other things; and therefore this makes no small part of men's thoughts and words: *v. g.*, one single man may at once be concerned in and sustain all these following relations, and many more, viz., father, brother, son, grandfather, grandson, father-in-law, son-in-law, husband, friend, enemy, subject, general, judge, patron, client, professor, European, Englishman, islander, servant, master, possessor, captain, superior, inferior, bigger, less, older, younger, contemporary, like, unlike, &c., to an almost infinite number : he being capable of as many relations as there can be occasions of comparing him to other things, in any manner of agreement, disagreement, or respect whatsoever: for, as I said, relation is a way of comparing or considering two things together, and giving one or both of them some appellation from that comparison, and sometimes giving even the relation itself a name.

**8.** *The ideas of relations clearer often than of the subjects related.*—Secondly, This farther may be considered concerning relation, that though it be not contained in the real existence of things, but something extraneous and superinduced; yet the ideas which relative words stand for are often clearer and more distinct than of those substances to which they do belong. The notion we have of a father or brother is a great deal clearer and more distinct than that we have of a man: or, if you will, paternity is a thing whereof it is easier to have a clear idea than of humanity: and I can much easier conceive what a friend is than what God. Because the knowledge of one action, or one simple idea, is oftentimes sufficient to give the notion of a relation : but to the knowing of any substantial being, an accurate collection of sundry ideas is necessary. A man, if he compares two things together, can hardly be supposed not to know what it is wherein he compares them: so that when he compares any things together, he cannot but have a very clear idea of that relation. The ideas then of relations are capable at least of being more perfect and distinct in our minds than those of substances. Because it is commonly hard to know all the simple ideas which are really in any substance, but for the most part easy enough to know the simple ideas that make up any relation I think on, or have a name for: *v. g.*, comparing two men, in reference to one common parent, it is very easy to frame the ideas of brothers, without having yet the perfect idea of a man. For, significant relative words, as well as others, standing only for ideas; and those being all either simple, or made up of simple ones ; it suffices for the knowing the precise idea the relative term stands for, to have a clear conception of that which is the foundation of the relation

which may be done without having a perfect and clear idea of
the thing it is attributed to.  Thus having the notion that one
laid the egg out of which the other was hatched, I have a clear
idea of the relation of dam and chick between the two cassiowaries in St. James's Park ; though, perhaps, I have but a very
obscure and imperfect idea of those birds themselves.

9. *Relations all terminate in simple ideas.*—Thirdly, Though
there be a great number of considerations wherein things may
be compared one with another, and so a multitude of relations ;
yet they all terminate in, and are concerned about, those simple
ideas either of sensation or reflection, which I think to be the
whole materials of all our knowledge.  To clear this, I shall
show it in the most considerable relations that we have any
notion of ; and in some that seem to be the most remote from
sense or reflection : which yet will appear to have their ideas
from thence, and leave it past doubt, that the notions we have of
them are but certain simple ideas, and so originally derived from
sense or reflection.

10. *Terms leading the mind beyond the subject denominated
are relative.*—Fourthly, That relation being the considering of
one thing with another, which is extrinsical to it, it is evident
that all words that necessarily lead the mind to any other ideas
than are supposed really to exist in that thing to which the word
is applied, are relative words: *v. g.*, a man, black, merry, thought-
ful, thirsty, angry, extended; these and the like are all absolute,
because they neither signify nor intimate anything but what
does or is supposed really to exist in the man thus denominated :
but father, brother, king, husband, blacker, merrier, &c., are
words which, together with the thing they denominate, imply
also something else separate, and exterior to the existence of that
thing.

11. *Conclusion.*—Having laid down these premises concerning
relation in general, I shall now proceed to show in some instances,
how all the ideas we have of relation are made up, as the others
are, only of simple ideas; and that they all, how refined or remote
from sense soever they seem, terminate at last in simple ideas.
I shall begin with the most comprehensive relation, wherein all
things that do or can exist are concerned; and that is the relation
of cause and effect.  The idea whereof, how derived from the two
fountains of all our knowledge, sensation and reflection, I shall in
the next place consider.

## CHAPTER XXVI.

### OF CAUSE AND EFFECT AND OTHER RELATIONS.

**1.** *Whence their ideas got.*—In the notice that our senses take of the constant vicissitude of things, we cannot but observe that several particular both qualities and substances begin to exist; and that they receive this their existence from the due application and operation of some other being. From this observation we get our ideas of cause and effect. That which produces any simple or complex idea, we denote by the general name " cause;" and that which is produced, " effect." Thus finding that in that substance which we call " wax " fluidity, which is a simple idea that was not in it before, is constantly produced by the application of a certain degree of heat, we call the simple idea of heat, in relation to fluidity in wax, *the cause* of it, and fluidity *the effect.* So also finding that the substance, wood, which is a certain collection of simple ideas so called, by the application of fire is turned into another substance called " ashes," *i.e.*, another complex idea, consisting of a collection of simple ideas, quite different from that complex idea which we call " wood," we consider fire, in relation to ashes, as cause, and the ashes, as effect. So that whatever is considered by us to conduce or operate to the producing any particular simple idea, or collection of simple ideas, whether substance or mode, which did not before exist, hath thereby in our minds the relation of a cause, and so is denominated by us.

**2.** *Creation, generation, making, alteration.*—Having thus, from what our senses are able to discover in the operations of bodies on one another, got the notion of cause and effect, viz., that a cause is that which makes any other thing, either simple idea, substance, or mode, begin to be, and an effect is that which had its beginning from some other thing, the mind finds no great difficulty to distinguish the several originals of things into two sorts :—

First, When the thing is wholly made new, so that no part thereof did ever exist before; as when a new particle of matter doth begin to exist, *in rerum naturâ*, which had before no being: and this we call " creation."

Secondly, When a thing is made up of particles which did all of them before exist, but that very thing so constituted of pre-existing particles, which, considered all together, make up such a collection of simple ideas, had not any existence before as this man, this egg, rose, or cherry, &c. And this, when referred to a substance produced in the ordinary course of nature by an internal principle, but set on work by and received from some external agent or cause, and working by insensible ways which we perceive not, we call "generation." When the cause is extrinsical, and the effect produced by a sensible separation or juxtaposition of discernible parts, we call it "making;" and such are all artificial things. When any simple idea is produced which was not in that subject before, we call it "alteration." Thus a man is generated, a picture made, and either of them altered, when any new sensible quality or simple idea is produced in either of them, which was not there before; and the things thus made to exist, which were not there before, are effects; and those things which operated to the existence, causes. In which, and all other cases, we may observe, that the notion of cause and effect has its rise from ideas received by sensation or reflection: and that this relation, how comprehensive soever, terminates at last in them. For, to have the idea of cause and effect, it suffices to consider any simple idea or substance as beginning to exist by the operation of some other, without knowing the manner of that operation.

3. *Relations of time.*—Time and place are also the foundations of very large relations, and all finite beings at least are concerned in them. But having already shown in another place how we get these ideas, it may suffice here to intimate, that most of the denominations of things received from time are only relations: thus, when anyone says that "queen Elizabeth lived sixty-nine, and reigned forty-five years," these words import only the relation of that duration to some other, and means no more but this, that the duration of her existence was equal to sixty-nine, and the duration of her government to forty-five, annual revolutions of the sun; and so are all words answering *how long*. Again: "William the Conqueror invaded England about the year 1070," which means this,—that, taking the duration from our Saviour's time till now for one entire great length of time, it shows at what distance this invasion was from the two extremes: and so do all words of time, answering to the question *when*, which show only the distance of any point of time, from the period of a longer duration, from which we measure, and to which we thereby consider it as related.

4. There are yet, besides those, other words of time that ordinarily are thought to stand for positive ideas, which yet will, when considered, be found to be relative, such as are "young, old," &c., which include and intimate the relation anything has to a certain length of duration, whereof we have the idea in our minds. Thus having settled in our thoughts the idea of the ordinary duration of a man to be seventy years, when we say a man is young, we mean that his age is yet but a small part of that which usually men attain to; and when we denominate him "old," we mean that his duration is run out almost to the end of that which men do not usually exceed. And so it is but comparing the particular age or duration of this or that man to the

idea of that duration which we have in our minds, as ordinarily belonging to that sort of animals : which is plain in the application of these names to other things ; for a man is called " young " at twenty years, and " very young" at seven years, old : but yet a horse we call "old" at twenty, and a dog at seven, years ; because in each of these we compare their age to different ideas of duration, which are settled in our mind as belonging to these several sorts of animals, in the ordinary course of nature.  But the sun and stars, though they have outlasted several generations of men, we call not "old," because we do not know what period God hath set to that sort of beings : this term belonging properly to those things which we can observe, in the ordinary course of things, by a natural decay, to come to an end in a certain period of time : and so have in our minds, as it were, a standard, to which we can compare the several parts of their duration ; and by the relation they bear thereunto, call them young, or old ; which we cannot therefore do to a ruby or a diamond, things whose usual periods we know not.

5. *Relations of place and extension.*—The relation also that things have to one another in their places and distances, is very obvious to observe ; as "above, below, a mile distant from Charing-Cross, in England, and in London."  But as in duration, so in extension and bulk, there are some ideas that are relative, which we signify by names that are thought positive ; as " great " and " little " are truly relations.  For here also, having by observation settled in our mind the ideas of the bigness of several species of things from those we have been most accustomed to, we make them, as it were, the standards whereby to denominate the bulk of others.  Thus we call " a great apple," such a one as is bigger than the ordinary sort of those we have been used to : and " a little horse," such a one as comes not up to the size of that idea which we have in our minds to belong ordinarily to horses : and that will be a great horse to a Welshman, which is but a little one to a Fleming ; they two having, from the different breed of their countries, taken several-sized ideas to which they compare, and in relation to which they denominate, their " great " and their " little."

6. *Absolute terms often stand for relations.*—So likewise " weak " and " strong " are but relative denominations of power, compared to some ideas we have at that time of greater or less power.  Thus when we say " a weak man," we mean one that has not so much strength or power to move as usually men have, or usually those of his size have ; which is a comparing his strength to the idea we have of the usual strength of men, or men of such size.  The like when we say, "The creatures are all weak things ;" " weak," there, is but a relative term, signifying the disproportion there is in the power of God and the creatures.  And so abundance of words, in ordinary speech, stand only for relations,

(and perhaps the greatest part), which at first sight seem to have no such signification : *v. g.,* "The ship has necessary stores." "Necessary" and "stores," are both relative words ; one having a relation to the accomplishing the voyage intended, and the other to future use. All which relations, how they are confined to and terminate in ideas derived from sensation or reflection, is too obvious to need any explication.

<hr />

## CHAPTER XXVII.

### OF IDENTITY AND DIVERSITY.

**1.** *Wherein identity consists.*—Another occasion the mind often takes of comparing, is, the very being of things, when, considering anything as existing at any determined time and place, we compare it with itself existing at another time, and thereon form the ideas of identity and diversity. When we see anything to be in any place in any instant of time, we are sure (be it what it will) that it is that very thing, and not another, which at that same time exists in another place, how like and undistinguishable soever it may be in all other respects : and in this consists identity, when the ideas it is attributed to, vary not at all from what they were that moment wherein we consider their former existence, and to which we compare the present. For we never finding, nor conceiving it possible, that two things of the same kind should exist in the same place at the same time, we rightly conclude that whatever exists anywhere at any time, excludes all of the same kind, and is there itself alone. When therefore we demand whether anything be the same or no ? it refers always to something that existed such a time in such a place, which it was certain at that instant was the same with itself and no other : from whence it follows, that one thing cannot have two beginnings of existence, nor two things one beginning, it being impossible for two things of the same kind to be or exist in the same instant, in the very same place, or one and the same thing in different places. That therefore that had one beginning, is the same thing ; and that which had a different beginning in time and place from that, is not the same, but diverse. That which has made the difficulty about this relation, has been the little care and attention used in having precise notions of the things to which it is attributed.

**2.** *Identity of substances. Identity of modes.*—We have the ideas but of three sorts of substances : 1. God. 2. Finite intelligences. 3. Bodies. First. God is without beginning, eternal, unalterable, and everywhere ; and therefore concerning his identity, there can be no doubt. Secondly. Finite spirits having had each its determinate time and place of beginning to exist,

the relation to that time and place will always determine to each
of them its identity as long as it exists.   Thirdly.   The same will
hold of every particle of matter, to which no addition or subtraction of matter being made, it is the same.   For though these
three sorts of substances, as we term them, do not exclude one
another out of the same place: yet we cannot conceive but that
they must necessarily each of them exclude any of the same kind
out of the same place: or else the notions and names of "identity
and diversity" would be in vain, and there could be no such
distinction of substances, or anything else, one from another.
For example: Could two bodies be in the same place at the same
time, then those two parcels of matter must be one and the same,
take them great or little; nay, all bodies must be one and the
same.   For by the same reason that two particles of matter may
be in one place, all bodies may be in one place: which, when it
can be supposed, takes away the distinction of identity and
diversity, of one and more, and renders it ridiculous.   But, it
being a contradiction that two or more should be one, identity
and diversity are relations and ways of comparing well-founded,
and of use to the understanding.   All other things being but
modes or relations ultimately terminated in substances, the
identity and diversity of each particular existence of them too
will be by the same way determined: only as to things whose
existence is in succession, such as are the actions of finite beings,
v. g., motion and thought, both which consist in a continued
train of succession, concerning their diversity there can be no
question: because, each perishing the moment it begins, they
cannot exist in different times, or in different places, as permanent beings can at different times exist in distant places; and
therefore no motion or thought, considered as at different times,
can be the same, each part thereof having a different beginning
of existence.

8. *Principium individuationis.*—From what has been said, it
is easy to discover, what is so much inquired after, the *principium
individuationis;* and that, it is plain, is existence itself, which
determines a being of any sort to a particular time and place
incommunicable to two beings of the same kind.   This, though
it seems easier to conceive in simple substances or modes, yet,
when reflected on, is not more difficult in compounded ones,
if care be taken to what it is applied; v. g., let us suppose an
atom, i.e., a continued body under one immutable superficies,
existing in a determined time and place; it is evident, that, considered in any instant of its existence, it is, in that instant, the
same with itself.   For, being at that instant what it is and
nothing else, it is the same, and so must continue as long as it
existence is continued; for so long it will be the same and no
other.   In like manner, if two or more atoms be joined together
into the same mass, every one of those atoms will be the same,

by the foregoing rule: and whilst they exist united together, the mass, consisting of the same atoms, must be the same mass, or the same body, let the parts be ever so differently jumbled: but if one of these atoms be taken away, or one new one added, it is no longer the same mass, or the same body. In the state of living creatures, their identity depends not on a mass of the same particles, but on something else. For in them the variation of great parcels of matter alters not the identity; an oak, growing from a plant to a great tree, and then lopped, is still the same oak: and a colt, grown up to a horse, sometimes fat, sometimes lean, is all the while the same horse: though, in both these cases, there may be a manifest change of the parts; so that truly they are not either of them the same masses of matter, though there be truly one of them the same oak, and the other the same horse. The reason whereof is, that, in these two cases of a mass of matter and a living body, identity is not applied to the same thing.

4. *Identity of vegetables.*—We must therefore consider wherein an oak differs from a mass of matter; and that seems to me to be in this: That the one is only the cohesion of particles of matter anyhow united; the other such a disposition of them as constitutes the parts of an oak, and such an organization of those parts as is fit to receive and distribute nourishment, so as to continue and frame the wood, bark, and leaves, &c., of an oak, in which consists the vegetable life. That being then one plant which has such an organization of parts in one coherent body, partaking of one common life, it continues to be the same plant as long as it partakes of the same life, though that life be communicated to new particles of matter vitally united to the living plant in a like continued organization, conformable to that sort of plants. For this organization being at any one instant in any one collection of matter, is in that particular concrete distinguished from all other, and is that individual life which existing constantly from that moment both forwards and backwards, in the same continuity of insensibly succeeding parts united to the living body of the plant, it has that identity which makes the same plant, and all the parts of it parts of the same plant, during all the time that they exist united in that continued organization, which is fit to convey that common life to all the parts so united.

5. *Identity of animals.*—The case is not so much different in brutes, but that anyone may hence see what makes an animal, and continues it the same. Something we have like this in machines, and may serve to illustrate it. For example: what is a watch? It is plain it is nothing but a fit organization or construction of parts to a certain end, which, when a sufficient force is added to it, it is capable to attain. If we would suppose this machine one continued body, all whose organized parts were repaired, increased, or diminished, by a constant addition or

separation of insensible parts, with one common life, we should have something very much like the body of an animal, with this difference,—that in an animal the fitness of the organization, and the motion wherein life consists, begin together, the motion coming from within; but in machines, the force coming sensibly from without, is often away when the organ is in order, and well fitted to receive it.

6. *Identity of man.*—This also shows wherein the identity of the same man consists; viz., in nothing but a participation of the same continued life by constantly fleeting particles of matter, in succession vitally united to the same organized body. He that shall place the identity of man in anything else but, like that of other animals, in one fitly organized body, taken in any one instant, and from thence continued under one organization of life in several successively fleeting particles of matter united to it, will find it hard to make an embryo one of years, mad, and sober, the same man, by any supposition that will not make it possible for Seth, Ismael, Socrates, Pilate, St. Austin, and Cæsar Borgia, to be the same man. For if the identity of soul alone makes the same man, and there be nothing in the nature of matter why the same individual spirit may not be united to different bodies, it will be possible that those men living in distant ages, and of different tempers, may have been the same man : which way of speaking must be from a very strange use of the word "man," applied to an idea out of which body and shape is excluded: and that way of speaking would agree yet worse with the notions of those philosophers who allow of transmigration, and are of opinion that the souls of men may, for their miscarriages, be detruded into the bodies of beasts, as fit habitations, with organs suited to the satisfaction of their brutal inclinations. But yet, I think, nobody, could he be sure that the soul of Heliogabalus were in one of his hogs, would yet say that hog were a man or Heliogabalus.

7. *Identity suited to the idea.*—It is not therefore unity of substance that comprehends all sorts of identity, or will determine it in every case; but, to conceive and judge of it aright, we must consider what idea the word it is applied to stands for : it being one thing to be the same substance, another the same man, and a third the same person, if "person, man, and substance," are three names standing for three different ideas; for such as is the idea belonging to that name, such must be the identity : which, if it had been a little more carefully attended to, would possibly have prevented a great deal of that confusion which often occurs about this matter, with no small seeming difficulties, especially concerning personal identity, which therefore we shall in the next place a little consider.

8. *Same man.*—An animal is a living organized body; and consequently the same animal, as we have observed, is the same

continued life communicated to different particles of matter, as
they happen successively to be united to that organized living
body. And, whatever is talked of other definitions, ingenious
observation puts it past doubt, that the idea in our minds, of
which the sound "man," in our mouths is the sign, is nothing
else but of an animal of such a certain form: since I think I may
be confident, that whoever should see a creature of his own
shape and make, though it had no more reason all its life than a
cat or a parrot, would call him still a "man;" or whoever should
hear a cat or a parrot discourse, reason, and philosophize, would
call or think it nothing but a cat or a parrot; and say, the one
was a dull irrational man, and the other a very intelligent
rational parrot. A relation we have in an author of great note,
is sufficient to countenance the supposition of a rational parrot.
His words are,—

"I had a mind to know from prince Maurice's own mouth, the
account of a common, but much credited story, that I had heard
so often from many others of an old parrot he had in Brazil,
during his government there, that spoke, and asked and answered
common questions, like a reasonable creature; so that those of
his train there generally concluded it to be witchery or possession;
and one of his chaplains who lived long afterwards in Holland,
would never from that time endure a parrot, but said they all had
a devil in them. I had heard many particulars of this story, and
assevered by people hard to be discredited, which made me ask
prince Maurice what there was of it. He said, with his usual
plainness and dryness in talk, there was something true, but a
great deal false, of what had been reported. I desired to know of
him what there was of the first? He told me short and coldly,
that he had heard of such an old parrot when he came to Brazil;
and though he believed nothing of it, and it was a good way off,
yet he had so much curiosity as to send for it: that it was a very
great and a very old one; and when it came first into the room
where the prince was, with a great many Dutchmen about him, it
said presently, 'What a company of white men are here?' They
asked it what he thought that man was, pointing at the prince?
It answered, 'Some general or other.' When they brought it
close to him, he asked it, *D'où venez-vous?* It answered, *De
Marinnan.* The prince,—*A qui estes-vous?* The parrot,—*A un
Portugais.* Prince,—*Que fais-tu là?* Parrot,—*Je garde les poules.*
The prince laughed, and said, *Vous gardez les poules?* The
parrot answered, *Ouy, moy, et je sçay bien faire;* and made the
chuck four or five times that people use to make to chickens
when they call them.* I set down the words of this worthy

* "'Whence come ye?' It answered, 'From Marinnan.' The PRINCE,—'To
whom do you belong?' The PARROT,—'To a Portuguese.' PRINCE,—'What do
you there?' PARROT,—'I look after the chickens.' The PRINCE laughed, and said,
'You look after the chickens?' The PARROT answered, 'Yes, I, and I know well
enough how to do it.'"

dialogue in French, just as prince Maurice said them to me. I asked him in what language the parrot spoke? and he said, In Brazilian; I asked whether he understood Brazilian? He said, No: but he had taken care to have two interpreters by him, the one a Dutchman that spoke Brazilian, and the other a Brazilian that spoke Dutch; that he asked them separately and privately, and both of them agreed in telling him just the same thing that the parrot said. I could not but tell this odd story, because it is so much out of the way, and from the first hand, and what may pass for a good one; for I dare say this prince, at least, believed himself in all he told me, having ever passed for a very honest and pious man. I leave it to naturalists to reason, and to other men to believe, as they please upon it; however, it is not perhaps amiss to relieve or enliven a busy scene sometimes with such digressions, whether to the purpose or no."*

I have taken care that the reader should have the story at large in the author's own words, because he seems to me not to have thought it incredible; for it cannot be imagined that so able a man as he, who had sufficiency enough to warrant all the testimonies he gives of himself, should take so much pains, in a place where it had nothing to do, to pin so close—not only on a man whom he mentions as his friend, but on a prince, in whom he acknowledges very great honesty and piety—a story which, if he himself thought incredible, he could not but also think ridiculous. The prince, it is plain, who vouches this story, and our author, who relates it from him, both of them call this talker " a parrot;" and I ask anyone else, who thinks such a story fit to be told, whether if this parrot, and all of its kind, had always talked, as we have a prince's word for it, as this one did; whether, I say, they would not have passed for a race of rational animals; but yet whether for all that, they would have been allowed to be men, and not parrots? For I presume it is not the idea of a thinking or rational being alone that makes the idea of a man in most people's sense, but of a body, so and so shaped, joined to it; and if that be the idea of a man, the same successive body not shifted all at once must, as well as the same immaterial spirit, go to the making of the same man.

9. *Personal identity.*—This being premised, to find wherein personal identity consists, we must consider what " person " stands for; which, I think, is a thinking intelligent being, that has reason and reflection, and can consider itself as itself, the same thinking thing, in different times and places; which it does only by that consciousness which is inseparable from thinking, and it seems to me essential to it: it being impossible for anyone to perceive, without perceiving that he does perceive. When we see, hear, smell, taste, feel, meditate, or will anything, we know

* "Memoirs of what passed in Christendom, from 1672 to 1679," p. 57.

that we do so. Thus it is always as to our present sensations and perceptions : and by this everyone is to himself that which he calls " self ;" it not being considered, in this case, whether the same self be continued in the same or diverse substances. For since consciousness always accompanies thinking, and it is that that makes everyone to be what he calls " self," and thereby distinguishes himself from all other thinking things; in this alone consists personal identity, *i.e.*, the sameness of a rational being : and as far as this consciousness can be extended backwards to any past action or thought, so far reaches the identity of that person; it is the same self now it was then; and it is by the same self with this present one that now reflects on it, that that action was done.

10. *Consciousness makes personal identity.*—But it is farther inquired, whether it be the same identical substance ? This, few would think they had reason to doubt of, if these perceptions, with their consciousness, always remained present in the mind, whereby the same thinking thing would be always consciously present, and, as would be thought, evidently the same to itself. But that which seems to make the difficulty is this, that this consciousness being interrupted always by forgetfulness, there being no moment of our lives wherein we have the whole train of all our past actions before our eyes in one view; but even the best memories losing the sight of one part whilst they are viewing another; and we sometimes, and that the greatest part of our lives, not reflecting on our past selves, being intent on our present thoughts, and, in sound sleep, having no thoughts at all, or, at least, none with that consciousness which remarks our waking thoughts : I say, in all these cases, our consciousness being interrupted, and we losing the sight of our past selves, doubts are raised whether we are the same thinking thing, *i.e.*, the same substance, or no ? which, however reasonable or unreasonable, concerns not personal identity at all : the question being, what makes the same person ? and not, whether it be the same identical substance which always thinks in the same person? which in this case matters not at all; different substances, by the same consciousness (where they do partake in it), being united into one person, as well as different bodies by the same life are united into one animal, whose identity is preserved, in that change of substances, by the unity of one continued life. For it being the same consciousness that makes a man be himself to himself, personal identity depends on that only, whether it be annexed only to one individual substance, or can be continued in a succession of several substances. For as far as any intelligent being can repeat the idea of any past action with the same consciousness it had of it at first, and with the same consciousness it has of any present action; so far it is the same personal self. For it is by the consciousness it has of its present thoughts and actions that it

is self to itself now, and so will be the same self, as far as the same consciousness can extend to actions past or to come; and would be by distance of time, or change of substance, no more two persons than a man be two men, by wearing other clothes to-day than he did yesterday, with a long or short sleep between: the same consciousness uniting those distant actions into the same person, whatever substances contributed to their production.

11. *Personal identity in change of substances.*—That this is so, we have some kind of evidence in our very bodies, all whose particles—whilst vitally united to this same thinking conscious self, so that we feel when they are touched, and are affected by and conscious of good or harm that happens to them—are a part of ourselves; *i.e.*, of our thinking conscious self. Thus the limbs of his body is to every one a part of himself: he sympathises and is concerned for them. Cut off an hand and thereby separate it from that consciousness he had of its heat, cold, and other affections, and it is then no longer a part of that which is himself, any more than the remotest part of matter. Thus we see the substance, whereof personal self consisted at one time, may be varied at another, without the change of personal identity; there being no question about the same person, though the limbs, which but now were a part of it, be cut off.

12. *Whether in the change of thinking substances.*—But the question is, Whether, if the same substance which thinks be changed, it can be the same person, or remaining the same, it can be different persons?

And to this I answer, First, This can be no question at all to those who place thought in a purely material, animal constitution, void of an immaterial substance. For, whether their supposition be true or no, it is plain they conceive personal identity preserved in something else than identity of substance; as animal identity is preserved in identity of life, and not of substance. And therefore those who place thinking in an immaterial substance only, before they can come to deal with these men, must show why personal identity cannot be preserved in the change of immaterial substances, or variety of particular immaterial substances, as well as animal identity is preserved in the change of material substances, or variety of particular bodies: unless they will say, it is one immaterial spirit that makes the same life in brutes, as it is one immaterial spirit that makes the same person in men, which the Cartesians at least will not admit, for fear of making brutes thinking things too.

13. But next, as to the first part of the question, Whether, if the same thinking substance (supposing immaterial substances only to think) be changed, it can be the same person? I answer, That cannot be resolved but by those who know what kind of substances they are that do think, and whether the consciousness of past actions can be transferred from one thinking substance

to another.  I grant, were the same consciousness the same individual action, it could not; but it being but a present representation of a past action, why it may not be possible that *that*
may be represented to the mind to have been *which* really never
was, will remain to be shown.  And therefore how far the
consciousness of past actions is annexed to any individual agent,
so that another cannot possibly have it, will be hard for us to
determine, till we know what kind of action it is that cannot be
done without a reflex act of perception accompanying it, and
how performed by thinking substances who cannot think without
being conscious of it.  But that which we call "the same consciousness" not being the same individual act, why one
intellectual substance may not have represented to it as done by
itself what it never did, and was perhaps done by some other
agent; why, I say, such a representation may not possibly be
without reality of matter of fact, as well as several representations in dreams are, which yet, whilst dreaming, we take for true,
will be difficult to conclude from the nature of things.  And
that it never is so, will by us (till we have clearer views of the
nature of thinking substances) be best resolved into the goodness
of God, who, as far as the happiness or misery of any of his
sensible creatures is concerned in it, will not by a fatal error of
theirs transfer from one to another that consciousness which
draws reward or punishment with it.  How far this may be an
argument against those who would place thinking in a system of
fleeting animal spirits, I leave to be considered.  But yet, to
return to the question before us, it must be allowed, that if the
same consciousness (which, as has been shown, is quite a different
thing from the same numerical figure or motion in body) can be
transferred from one thinking substance to another, it will be
possible that two thinking substances may make but one person.
For the same consciousness being preserved, whether in the
same or different substances, the personal identity is preserved.

14. As to the second part of the question, Whether, the same
immaterial substance remaining, there may be two distinct persons?  Which question seems to me to be built on this, Whether
the same immaterial being, being conscious of the actions of
its past duration, may be wholly stripped of all the consciousness of its past existence, and lose it beyond the power of ever
retrieving again; and so, as it were, beginning a new account
from a new period, have a consciousness that cannot reach
beyond this new state?  All those who hold pre-existence are
evidently of this mind, since they allow the soul to have no remaining consciousness of what it did in that pre-existent state,
either wholly separate from body, or informing any other body;
and if they should not, it is plain experience would be against
them.  So that personal identity reaching no farther than consciousness reaches, a pre-existent spirit not having continued so

many ages in a state of silence, must needs make different persons. Suppose a Christian, Platonist, or Pythagorean, should, upon God's having ended all his works of creation the seventh day, think his soul hath existed ever since; and should imagine it has revolved in several human bodies, as I once met with one who was persuaded his had been the soul of Socrates: (how reasonably I will not dispute: this I know, that in the post he filled, which was no inconsiderable one, he passed for a very rational man; and the press has shown that he wanted not parts or learning:) would anyone say, that he, being not conscious of any of Socrates's actions or thoughts, could be the same person with Socrates? Let anyone reflect upon himself, and conclude, that he has in himself an immaterial spirit, which is that which thinks in him, and in the constant change of his body keeps him the same; and is that which he calls himself; let him also suppose it to be the same soul that was in Nestor or Thersites, at the siege of Troy, (for souls being, as far as we know anything of them, in their nature indifferent to any parcel of matter, the supposition has no apparent absurdity in it,) which it may have been as well as it is now the soul of any other man: but he now having no consciousness of any of the actions either of Nestor or Thersites, does or can he conceive himself the same person with either of them? Can he be concerned in either of their actions? attribute them to himself, or think them his own, more than the actions of any other man that ever existed? So that this consciousness not reaching to any of the actions of either of those men, he is no more one self with either of them, than if the soul or immaterial spirit that now informs him had been created and began to exist when it began to inform his present body, though it were ever so true that the same spirit that informed Nestor's or Thersites's body were numerically the same that now informs his. For this would no more make him the same person with Nestor, than if some of the particles of matter that were once a part of Nestor were now a part of this man; the same immaterial substance, without the same consciousness, no more making the same person by being united to anybody, than the same particle of matter, without consciousness, united to anybody, makes the same person. But let him once find himself conscious of any of the actions of Nestor, he then finds himself the same person with Nestor.

15. And thus we may be able, without any difficulty, to conceive the same person at the resurrection, though in a body not exactly in make or parts the same which he had here, the same consciousness going along with the soul that inhabits it. But yet the soul alone, in the change of bodies, would scarce to anyone, but to him that makes the soul the man, be enough to make the same man. For, should the soul of a prince, carrying with it the consciousness of the prince's past life, enter and inform the

body of a cobbler, as soon as deserted by his own soul, everyone sees he would be the same person with the prince, accountable only for the prince's actions : but who would say it was the same man? The body too goes to the making of the man, and would, I guess, to every body determine the man in this case, wherein the soul, with all its princely thoughts about it, would not make another man; but he would be the same cobbler to everyone besides himself. I know that, in the ordinary way of speaking, the same person and the same man stand for one and the same thing. And, indeed, everyone will always have a liberty to speak as he pleases, and to apply what articulate sounds to what ideas he think fit, and change them as often as he pleases. But yet, when we will inquire what makes the same spirit, man, or person, we must fix the ideas of spirit, man, or person in our minds; and having resolved with ourselves what we mean by them, it will not be hard to determine in either of them, or the like, when it is the same and when not.

16. *Consciousness makes the same person.*—But though the same immaterial substance or soul does not alone, wherever it be, and in whatsoever state, make the same man; yet it is plain, consciousness, as far as ever it can be extended, should it be to ages past, unites existences and actions, very remote in time, into the same person, as well as it does the existence and actions of the immediately preceding moment : so that whatever has the consciousness of present and past actions is the same person to whom they both belong. Had I the same consciousness that I saw the ark and Noah's flood, as that I saw an overflowing of the Thames last winter, or as that I write now, I could no more doubt that I who write this now, that saw the Thames overflowed last winter, and that viewed the flood at the general deluge, was the same self, place that self in what substance you please, than that I who write this am the same myself now whilst I write (whether I consist of all the same substance, material or immaterial, or no) that I was yesterday. For, as to this point of being the same self, it matters not whether this present self be made up of the same or other substances, I being as much concerned and as justly accountable for any action was done a thousand years since, appropriated to me now by this self-consciousness, as I am for what I did the last moment.

17. *Self depends on consciousness.*—Self is that conscious thinking thing (whatever substance made up of, whether spiritual or material, simple or compounded, it matters not) which is sensible or conscious of pleasure and pain, capable of happiness or misery, and so is concerned for itself, as far as that consciousness extends. Thus everyone finds, that whilst comprehended under that consciousness, the little finger is as much a part of itself as what is most so. Upon separation of this little finger, should this consciousness go along with the little finger, and leave the rest of

the body, it is evident the little finger would be the person, the same person; and self then would have nothing to do with the rest of the body. As in this case it is the consciousness that goes along with the substance, when one part is separate from another, which makes the same person, and constitutes this inseparable self, so it is in reference to substances remote in time. That with which the consciousness of this present thinking thing can join itself makes the same person, and is one self with it, and with nothing else; and so attributes to itself and owns all the actions of that thing as its own, as far as that consciousness reaches, and no farther; as everyone who reflects will perceive.

18. *Object of reward and punishment.*—In this personal identity is founded all the right and justice of reward and punishment; happiness and misery being that for which everyone is concerned for himself, not mattering what becomes of any substance not joined to or affected with that consciousness. For as it is evident in the instance I gave but now, if the consciousness went along with the little finger when it was cut off, that would be the same self which was concerned for the whole body yesterday, as making a part of itself, whose actions then it cannot but admit as its own now. Though, if the same body should still live, and immediately from the separation of the little finger have its own peculiar consciousness, whereof the little finger knew nothing, it would not at all be concerned for it, as a part of itself, or could own any of its actions, or have any of them imputed to him.

19. This may show us wherein personal identity consists, not in the identity of substance, but, as I have said, in the identity of consciousness; wherein if Socrates and the present mayor of Queenborough agree, they are the same person. If the same Socrates waking and sleeping do not partake of the same consciousness, Socrates waking and sleeping is not the same person; and to punish Socrates waking for what sleeping Socrates thought, and waking Socrates was never conscious of, would be no more of right than to punish one twin for what his brother-twin did, whereof he knew nothing, because their outsides were so like that they could not be distinguished; for such twins have been seen.

20. But yet possibly it will still be objected, "Suppose I wholly lose the memory of some parts of my life, beyond the possibility of retrieving them, so that perhaps I shall never be conscious of them again; yet am I not the same person that did those actions, had those thoughts, that I was once conscious of, though I have now forgot them?" To which I answer, That we must here take notice what the word "I" is applied to; which in this case is the man only. And the same man being presumed to be the same person, "I" is easily here supposed to stand also for the same person. But if it be possible for the same man to have distinct incommunicable consciousnesses at different times, it is

past doubt the same man would at different times make different persons; which, we see, is the sense of mankind in the solemnest declaration of their opinions, human laws not punishing the mad man for the sober man's actions, nor the sober man for what the mad man did, thereby making them two persons; which is somewhat explained by our way of speaking in English, when we say, "Such an one is not himself, or is beside himself;" in which phrases it is insinuated as if those who now or, at least, first used them, thought that self was changed, the self-same person was no longer in that man.

21. *Difference between identity of man and person.*—But yet it is hard to conceive that Socrates, the same individual man, should be two persons. To help us a little in this, we must consider what is meant by Socrates, or the same individual man.

First, It must be either the same individual, immaterial, thinking substance; in short, the same numerical soul, and nothing else.

Secondly, Or the same animal, without any regard to an immaterial soul.

Thirdly, Or the same immaterial spirit united to the same animal.

Now, take which of these suppositions you please, it is impossible to make personal identity to consist in anything but consciousness, or reach any farther than that does.

For by the first of them, it must be allowed possible that a man born of different women, and in distant times, may be the same man. A way of speaking which, whoever admits, must allow it possible for the same man to be two distinct persons, as any two that have lived in different ages, without the knowledge of one another's thoughts.

By the second and third, Socrates in this life and after it cannot be the same man any way but by the same consciousness; and so, making human identity to consist in the same thing wherein we place personal identity, there will be no difficulty to allow the same man to be the same person. But then they who place human identity in consciousness only, and not in something else, must consider how they will make the infant Socrates the same man with Socrates after the resurrection. But whatsoever to some men makes a man, and consequently the same individual man, wherein perhaps few are agreed, personal identity can by us be placed in nothing but consciousness (which is that alone which makes what we call "self"), without involving us in great absurdities.

22. "But is not a man drunk and sober the same person? Why else is he punished for the fact he commits when drunk, though he be never afterwards conscious of it?" Just as much the same person as a man that walks and does other things in

his sleep is the same person, and is answerable for any mischief he shall do in it. Human laws punish both with a justice suitable to their way of knowledge; because in these cases they cannot distinguish certainly what is real, what counterfeit; and so the ignorance in drunkenness or sleep is not admitted as a plea. For, though punishment be annexed to personality, and personality to consciousness, and the drunkard perhaps be not conscious of what he did; yet human judicatures justly punish him, because the fact is proved against him, but want of consciousness cannot be proved for him. But in the great day, wherein the secrets of all hearts shall be laid open, it may be reasonable to think, no one shall be made to answer for what he knows nothing of; but shall receive his doom, his conscience accusing or excusing.

23. *Consciousness alone makes self.*—Nothing but consciousness can unite remote existences into the same person; the identity of substance will not do it. For, whatever substance there is, however framed, without consciousness there is no person: and a carcass may be a person, as well as any sort of substance be so without consciousness.

Could we suppose two distinct incommunicable consciousnesses acting the same body, the one constantly by day, the other by night; and, on the other side, the same consciousness acting by intervals two distinct bodies: I ask, in the first case, whether the day and the night man would not be two as distinct persons as Socrates and Plato? and whether, in the second case, there would not be one person in two distinct bodies, as much as one man is the same in two distinct clothings? Nor is it at all material to say, that this same and this distinct consciousness, in the cases above mentioned, is owing to the same and distinct immaterial substances, bringing it with them to those bodies; which, whether true or no, alters not the case: since it is evident the personal identity would equally be determined by the consciousness, whether that consciousness were annexed to some individual immaterial substance or no. For, granting that the thinking substance in man must be necessarily supposed immaterial, it is evident that immaterial thinking thing may sometimes part with its past consciousness, and be restored to it again, as appears in the forgetfulness men often have of their past actions, and the mind many times recovers the memory of a past consciousness which it had lost for twenty years together. Make these intervals of memory and forgetfulness to take their turns regularly by day and night, and you have two persons with the same immaterial spirit, as much as in the former instance two persons with the same body. So that self is not determined by identity or diversity of substance, which it cannot be sure of, but only by identity of consciousness.

24. Indeed, it may conceive the substance whereof it is now made up to have existed formerly, united in the same conscious

being; but, consciousness removed, that substance is no more itself, or makes no more a part of it, than any other substance; as is evident in the instance we have already given of a limb cut off, of whose heat, or cold, or other affections, having no longer any consciousness, it is no more of a man's self than any other matter of the universe. In like manner it will be in reference to any immaterial substance, which is void of that consciousness whereby I am myself to myself: if there be any part of its existence which I cannot upon recollection join with that present consciousness whereby I am now myself, it is in that part of its existence no more myself than any other immaterial being. For, whatsoever any substance has thought or done, which I cannot recollect, and by my consciousness make my own thought and action, it will no more belong to me, whether a part of me thought or did it, than if it had been thought or done by any other immaterial being anywhere existing.

25. I agree, the more probable opinion is, that this consciousness is annexed to, and the affection of, one individual immaterial substance.

But let men, according to their diverse hypotheses, resolve of that as they please. This every intelligent being, sensible of happiness or misery, must grant, that there is something that is himself that he is concerned for, and would have happy; that this self has existed in a continued duration more than one instant, and therefore it is possible may exist, as it has done, months and years to come, without any certain bounds to be set to its duration; and may be the same self, by the same consciousness, continued on for the future. And thus, by this consciousness, he finds himself to be the same self which did such or such an action some years since, by which he comes to be happy or miserable now. In all which account of self, the same numerical substance is not considered as making the same self: but the same continued consciousness, in which several substances may have been united, and again separated from it, which whilst they continued in a vital union with that wherein this consciousness then resided, made a part of that same self. Thus any part of our bodies vitally united to that which is conscious in us, makes a part of ourselves: but upon separation from the vital union by which that consciousness is communicated, that which a moment since was part of ourselves is now no more so than a part of another man's self is a part of me, and it is not impossible but in a little time may become a real part of another person. And so we have the same numerical substance become a part of two different persons, and the same person preserved under the change of various substances. Could we suppose any spirit wholly stripped of all its memory or consciousness of past actions, as we find our minds always are of a great part of ours, and sometimes of them all, the union or separation of such a spiritual substance would make no variation of personal identity, any more than that of any particle of matter does. Any substance vitally united to the present thinking being, is a part of that very same self which now is: anything united to it by a consciousness of former actions, makes also a part of the same self, which is the same both then and now.

26. "*Person*," *a forensic term.*—"Person," as I take it, is the name for this self. Wherever a man finds what he calls "himself," there, I think, another may say is the same person. It is a forensic term appropriating actions and their merit; and so belongs only to intelligent agents capable of a law, and happiness and misery. This personality extends itself beyond present existence to what is past, only by consciousness; whereby it becomes concerned and accountable, owns and imputes to itself past action, just upon the same ground and for the same reason that it does the present. All which is founded in a concern for happiness, the unavoidable concomitant of consciousness; that which is conscious of pleasure and pain desiring that *that* self that is conscious should be happy. And therefore whatever past actions it cannot reconcile or appropriate to that present self by consciousness, it can be no more concerned in than if they had never been done: and to receive pleasure or pain, *i.e.*, reward or punishment, on the account of any such action, is all one as to be made happy or miserable in its first being without any demerit at all. For, supposing a man punished now for what he had done in another life, whereof he could be made to have no consciousness at all, what difference is there between that punishment and being created miserable? And therefore, conformable to this, the apostle tells us, that at the great day, when everyone shall "receive according to his doings, the secrets of all hearts shall be laid open." The sentence shall be justified by the consciousness all persons shall have that they themselves, in what bodies soever they appear, or what substances soever that consciousness adheres to, are the same that committed those actions, and deserve that punishment for them.

27. I am apt enough to think I have, in treating of this subject, made some suppositions that will look strange to some readers, and possibly they are so in themselves. But yet, I think, they are such as are pardonable in this ignorance we are in of the nature of that thinking thing that is in us, and which we look on as ourselves. Did we know what it was, or how it was tied to a certain system of fleeting animal spirits; or whether it could or could not perform its operations of thinking and memory out of a body organized as ours is; and whether it has pleased God that no one such spirit shall ever be united to any but one such body, upon the right constitution of whose organs its memory should depend, we might see the absurdity of some of those suppositions I have made. But taking, as we

ordinarily now do (in the dark concerning these matters), the soul of a man for an immaterial substance, independent from matter, and indifferent alike to it all, there can from the nature of things be no absurdity at all to suppose that the same soul may, at different times, be united to different bodies, and with them make up, for that time, one man: as well as we suppose a part of a sheep's body yesterday, should be a part of a man's body to-morrow, and in that union make a vital part of Melibæus himself, as well as it did of his ram.

28. *The difficulty from ill use of names.*—To conclude: Whatever substance begins to exist, it must, during its existence, necessarily be the same: whatever compositions of substances begin to exist, during the union of those substances, the concrete must be the same; whatsoever mode begins to exist, during its existence it is the same: and so if the composition be of distinct substances and different modes, the same rule holds. Whereby it will appear, that the difficulty or obscurity that has been about this matter rather rises from the names ill used, than from any obscurity in things themselves. For whatever makes the specific idea to which the name is applied, if that idea be steadily kept to, the distinction of any thing into the same and diverse will easily be conceived, and there can arise no doubt about it.

29. *Continued existence makes identity.*—For supposing a rational spirit be the idea of a man, it is easy to know what is the same man; viz., the same spirit, whether separate or in a body, will be the same man. Supposing a rational spirit vitally united to a body of a certain conformation of parts to make a man, whilst that rational spirit, with that vital conformation of parts, though continued in a fleeting successive body, remains, it will be the same man. But if to anyone the idea of a man be but the vital union of parts in a certain shape, as long as that vital union and shape remains, in a concrete no otherwise the same but by a continued succession of fleeting particles, it will be the same man. For, whatever be the composition whereof the complex idea is made, whenever existence makes it one particular thing under any denomination, the same existence, continued, preserves it the same individual under the same denomination.*

\* See note at the end of this chapter.—EDIT.

---

## NOTE.'

THE doctrine of identity and diversity contained in this chapter, the Bishop of Worcester pretends to be inconsistent with the doctrine of the Christian Faith, concerning the resurrection of the dead. His way of arguing from it is this: he says, "The reason of believing the resurrection of the same body, upon Mr. Locke's grounds, is from the idea of identity." To which our author answers:† "Give me leave, my

† In his Third Letter to the Bishop of Worcester, p. 165, &c.

lord, to say, that the reason of believing any article of the Christian
faith (such as your lordship is here speaking of), to me, and upon my
grounds, is its being a part of divine revelation.   Upon this ground I
believed it before I either writ that chapter of identity and diversity,
and before I ever thought of those propositions which your lordship
quotes out of that chapter ; and upon the same ground I believe it
still, and not from my idea of identity.   This saying of your lordship's
therefore, being a proposition neither self-evident, nor allowed by me
to be true, remains to be proved.   So that your foundation failing, all
your large superstructure built thereon comes to nothing.

   "But, my lord, before we go any farther, I crave leave humbly to
represent to your lordship, that I thought you undertook to make out
that my notion of ideas was inconsistent with the articles of the
Christian faith.   But that which your lordship instances in here is not,
that I yet know, an article of the Christian faith.   The resurrection of
the dead I acknowledge to be an article of the Christian faith ; but that
the resurrection of the same body, in your lordship's sense of 'the
same body,' is an article of the Christian faith, is what I confess I do
not yet know.

   "In the New Testament (wherein I think are contained all the
articles of the Christian faith) I find our Saviour and the apostles to
preach 'the resurrection of the dead' and 'the resurrection from the
dead' in many places ; but I do not remember any place where the
resurrection of the same body is so much as mentioned.   Nay, which
is very remarkable in the case, I do not remember, in any place of the
New Testament where the general resurrection at the last day is
spoken of, any such expression as 'the resurrection of the body,' much
less 'of the same body.'

   "I say, 'the general resurrection at the last day ;' because where
the resurrection of some particular persons presently upon our Saviour's
resurrection is mentioned, the words are, 'The graves were opened,
and many bodies of saints which slept arose, and came out of the
graves after his resurrection, and went into the holy city, and appeared
to many' (Matt. xxvii. 52, 53) ; of which peculiar way of speaking of
this resurrection, the passage itself gives a reason in these words,
'appeared to many ;' *i.e.*, those who slept appeared, so as to be known
to be risen.   But this could not be known, unless they brought with
them the evidences that they were those who had been dead ; whereof
there were these two proofs,—their graves were opened, and their
bodies not only gone out of them, but appeared to be the same to those
who had known them formerly alive, and knew them to be dead and
buried.   For if they had been those who had been dead so long that
all who knew them once alive were now gone, those to whom they
appeared might have known them to be men, but they could not have
known they were risen from the dead, because they never knew they
had been dead.   All that by their appearing they could have known
was, that they were so many living strangers, of whose resurrection
they knew nothing.   It was necessary therefore that they should come
in such bodies as might, in make and size, &c., appear to be the same
they had before, that they might be known to those of their acquaintance whom they appeared to.   And it is probable they were such as
were newly dead, whose bodies were not yet dissolved and dissipated ;

and therefore it is particularly said here (differently from what is said of the general resurrection), that their bodies arose, because they were the same that were then lying in their graves the moment before they arose.

"But your lordship endeavours to prove it must be the same body; and let us grant that your lordship, nay, and others, too, think you have proved it must be the same body; will you therefore say, that he holds what is inconsistent with an article of faith who, having never seen this your lordship's interpretation of the scripture, nor your reasons for the same body, in your sense of the 'same body;' or, if he has seen them, yet not understanding them, or, not perceiving the force of them, believes what the scripture proposes to him, viz., that at the last day the 'dead shall be raised,' without determining whether it shall be with the very same bodies or no?

"I know your lordship pretends not to erect your particular interpretations of scripture into articles of faith; and if you do not, he that believes the dead shall be raised, believes that article of faith which the scripture proposes; and cannot be accused of holding anything inconsistent with it, if it should happen that what he holds is inconsistent with another proposition, viz., that the dead shall be raised with the same bodies, in your lordship's sense; which I do not find proposed in holy writ as an article of faith.

"But your lordship argues 'it must be the same body;' which, as you explain 'same body,'* 'is not the same individual particles of matter which were united at the point of death,' nor the same particles of matter that the sinner had at the time of the commission of his sins; but that it must be the same material substance which was vitally united to the soul here; *i.e.*, as I understand it, the same individual particles of matter which were, some time or other during his life here, vitally united to his soul.

"Your first argument to prove that it must be the same body in this sense of 'the same body,' is taken from these words of our Saviour,† 'All that are in the graves shall hear his voice, and shall come forth.' (John v. 28, 29.) From whence your lordship argues, that these words, 'all that are in their graves,' relate to no other substance than what was united to the soul in life, because a different substance cannot be said to be in the graves and to come out of them; which words of your lordship's, if they prove anything, prove that the soul too is lodged in the grave, and raised out of it at the last day: for your lordship says, 'Can a different substance be said to be in their graves and come out of them?' So that, according to this interpretation of these words of our Saviour, no other substance being raised but what hears his voice; and no other substance hearing his voice but what, being called, comes out of the grave; and no other substance coming out of the grave but what was in the grave; anyone must conclude that the soul, unless it be in the grave, will make no part of the person that is raised, unless, as your lordship argues against me,‡ 'you can make it out that a substance which never was in the grave may come out of it,' or that the soul is no substance.

"But, setting aside the substance of the soul, another thing that will make anyone doubt whether this your interpretation of our Saviour's words be necessarily to be received as their true sense, is, that it will not be very easily reconciled to your saying you do not mean by the same body 'the same individual particles which were united at the point of death;'* and yet, by this interpretation of our Saviour's words, you can mean no other particles but such as were united at the point of death, because you mean no other substance but what comes out of the grave; and no substance, no particles come out, you say, but what were in the grave; and I think your lordship will not say, that the particles that were separate from the body by perspiration before the point of death were laid up in the grave.

"But your lordship, I find, has an answer to this,† viz. that 'by comparing this with other places, you find that the words [of our Saviour above quoted] are to be understood of the substance of the body to which the soul was united, and not to (I suppose your lordship writ 'of') 'those individual particles,' *i.e.*, those individual particles that are in the grave at the resurrection; for so they must be read to make your lordship's sense entire, and to the purpose of your answer here; and then methinks this last sense of our Saviour's words given by your lordship, wholly overturns the sense which you have given of them above, where from those words you press the belief of the resurrection of the same body, by this strong argument—that a substance could not, upon hearing the voice of Christ come out of the grave, which was never in the grave. There (as far as I can understand your words) your lordship argues that our Saviour's words must be understood of the particles in the grave, 'unless,' as your lordship says, 'one can make it out that a substance which never was in the grave may come out of it.' And here your lordship expressly says, that our Saviour's words are to be understood of the substance of that body to which the soul was [at any time] united, and not to those individual particles that are in the grave; which, put together, seems to me to say, that our Saviour's words are to be understood of those particles only that are in the grave, and not of those particles only which are in the grave, but of others also which have at any time been vitally united to the soul, but never were in the grave.

"The next text your lordship brings to make the resurrection of the same body in your sense, an article of faith, are these words of St. Paul: 'For we must all appear before the judgment-seat of Christ, that everyone may receive the things done in his body, according to that he hath done, whether it be good or bad.' (2 Cor. v. 10.) To which your lordship subjoins this question: 'Can these words be understood of any other material substance, but that body in which these things were done?'‡ Answer. A man may suspend his determining the meaning of the apostle to be, that a sinner shall suffer for his sins in the very same body wherein he committed them; because St. Paul does not say he shall have the very same body when he suffers that he had when he sinned. The apostle says, indeed, 'done in his body.' The body he had and did things in at five or fifteen, was no doubt his body as much as that which he did things in at fifty was his body, though his body were not the very same body at those different ages; and so will the body which he shall have after the resurrection be his body, though it be not the very same with that which he had at

* Page 34.   † Page 37.   ‡ Page 38.

five, or fifteen, or fifty. He that at threescore is broke on the wheel for a murder he committed at twenty, is punished for what he did in his body, though the body he has, *i.e.*, his body at threescore, be not the same, *i.e.*, made up of the same individual particles of matter that that body was which he had forty years before. When your lordship has resolved with yourself what that same immutable 'he' is, which at the last judgment shall receive the things done in his body, your lordship will easily see that the body he had when an embryo in the womb, when a child playing in coats, when a man marrying a wife, and when bed-rid dying of a consumption, and at last which he shall have after his resurrection, are each of them his body, though neither of them be the same body the one with the other.

"But, farther, to your lordship's question, 'Can these words be understood of any other material substance but that body in which these things were done?' I answer, These words of St. Paul may be understood of another material substance than that body in which these things were done; because your lordship teaches me, and gives me a strong reason, so to understand them. Your lordship says, that you 'do not say the same particles of matter which the sinner had at the very time of the commission of his sins shall be raised at the last day.'* And your lordship gives this reason for it: 'For then a long sinner must have a vast body, considering the continual spending of particles by perspiration.'† Now, my lord, if the apostle's words, as your lordship would argue, 'cannot be understood of any other material substance but that body in which these things were done,' and no body, upon the removal or change of some of the particles that at any time make it up, is the same material substance, or the same body; it will, I think, thence follow, that either the sinner must have all the same individual particles vitally united to his soul when he is raised, that he had vitally united to his soul when he sinned; or else St. Paul's words here cannot be understood to mean the same body in which the things were done: for if there were other particles of matter in the body wherein the thing was done than in that which is raised, that which is raised cannot be the same body in which they were done; unless, that alone which has just all the same individual particles when any action is done being the same body wherein it was done, that also which has not the same individual particles wherein that action was done can be the same body wherein it was done, which is in effect to make the same body sometimes to be the same, and sometimes not the same.

"Your lordship thinks it suffices to make the same body to have, not all, but no other particles of matter but such as were some time or other vitally united to the soul before: but such a body, made up of part of the particles some time or other vitally united to the soul, is no more the same body wherein the actions were done in the distant parts of the long sinner's life, than that is the same body in which a quarter, or half, or three quarters of the same particles that made it up are wanting. For example: a sinner has acted here in his body an hundred years; he is raised at the last day, but with what body? The same, says your lordship, that he acted in, because St. Paul says, he must 'receive the things done in his body.' What therefore must

* Page 84.  † Page 85.

his body at the resurrection consist of? Must it consist of all the
particles of matter that have ever been vitally united to his soul? for
they, in succession, have all of them made up his body wherein he did
these things. 'No,' says your lordship; 'that would make his body
too vast; it suffices to make the same body in which the things were
done that it consists of some of the particles, and no other but such
as were some time during his life vitally united to his soul.'* But,
according to this account, his body at the resurrection being, as your
lordship seems to limit it, near the same size it was in some part of
his life, it will be no more the same body in which the things were
done in the distant parts of his life, than that is the same body in
which half, or three quarters, or more of the individual matter that
then made it up, is now wanting. For example: let his body at fifty
years old consist of a million of parts; five hundred thousand at least
of those parts will be different from those which made up his body at
ten years and at an hundred. So that to take the numerical particles
that made up his body at fifty, or any other season of his life, or to
gather them promiscuously out of those which at different times have
successively been vitally united to his soul, they will no more make
the same body, which was his, wherein some of his actions were done,
than that is the same body which has but half the same particles; and
yet all your lordship's argument here for the same body is, because St.
Paul says it must be his body in which these things were done; which
it could not be, if any other substance were joined to it, i.e., if any
other particles of matter made up the body, which were not vitally
united to the soul when the action was done.

"Again: your lordship says, that you 'do not say the same individual particles' [shall make up the body at the resurrection] 'which
were united at the point of death; for there must be a great alteration
in them in a lingering disease, as if a fat man fall into a consumption;'†
because, it is likely, your lordship thinks these particles of a decrepit,
wasted, withered body would be too few, or unfit to make such a
plump, strong, vigorous, well-sized body, as it has pleased your lordship
to proportion out in your thoughts to men at the resurrection: and
therefore some small portion of the particles formerly united vitally to
that man's soul shall be re-assumed to make up his body to the bulk
your lordship judges convenient; but the greatest part of them shall
be left out to avoid the making his body more vast than your lordship
thinks will be fit, as appears by these your lordship's words immediately
following, viz., that you 'do not say the same particles the sinner had
at the very time of commission of his sins; for then a long sinner must
have a vast body.'‡

"But then, pray, my lord, what must an embryo do, who, dying
within a few hours after his body was vitally united to his soul, has no
particles of matter which were formerly vitally united to it, to make
up his body of that size and proportion which your lordship seems to
require in bodies at the resurrection? Or must we believe he shall
remain content with that small pittance of matter and that yet imperfect body to eternity, because it is an article of faith to believe the
resurrection of the very same body, i.e., made up of only such particles
as have been vitally united to the soul? For if it be so, as your lord-

* Page 35.          † Page 35.          ‡ Page 34.

ship says, that 'life is the result of the union of soul and body,'* it will follow, that the body of an embryo, dying in the womb, may be very little, not the thousandth part of any ordinary man. For since from the first conception and beginning of formation it has life, and 'life is the result of the union of the soul with the body;' an embryo that shall die either by the untimely death of the mother, or by any other accident presently after it has life, must, according to your lordship's doctrine, remain a man not an inch long to eternity; because there are not particles of matter formerly united to his soul to make him bigger, and no other can be made use of to that purpose; though what greater congruity the soul hath with any particles of matter which were once vitally united to it, but are now so no longer, than it hath with particles of matter which it was never united to, would be hard to determine, if that should be demanded.

"By these and not a few other the like consequences one may see what service they do to religion and the Christian doctrine, who raise questions and make articles of faith about the resurrection of the same body, where the scripture says nothing of the same body; or if it does, it is with no small reprimand to those who make such an inquiry. 'But some man will say, How are the dead raised up? and with what body do they come? Thou fool, that which thou sowest is not quickened, except it die: and that which thou sowest, thou sowest not that body that shall be, but bare grain, it may chance of wheat, or of some other grain : but God giveth it a body as it hath pleased him.' (1 Cor. xv. 35, &c.) Words, I should think, sufficient to deter us from determining anything for or against the same body's being raised at the last day. It suffices that all the dead shall be raised, and everyone appear and answer for the things done in this life, and receive according to the things he hath done in his body, whether good or bad. He that believes this, and has said nothing inconsistent herewith, I presume, may and must be acquitted from being guilty of anything inconsistent with the articles of the resurrection of the dead.

"But your lordship, to prove the resurrection of the same body to be an article of faith, farther asks, 'How could it be said, if any other substance be joined to the soul at the resurrection, as its body, that they were the things done in or by the body?'† Answer. Just as it may be said of a man at an hundred years old, that hath then another substance joined to his soul than he had at twenty, that the murder or drunkenness he was guilty of at twenty were things done in the body; how 'by the body' comes in here I do not see.

"Your lordship adds, 'and St. Paul's dispute about the manner of raising the body might soon have ended, if there were no necessity of the same body.' Answer. When I understand what argument there is in these words to prove the resurrection of the same body, without the mixture of one new atom of matter, I shall know what to say to it. In the meantime, this I understand, that St. Paul would have put as short an end to all disputes about this matter, if he had said, that there was a necessity of the same body, or that it should be the same body.

"The next text of scripture you bring for the same body is, 'If there be no resurrection of the dead, then is not Christ raised.' (1 Cor. xv. 16.) From which your lordship argues, 'It seems then other

* Page 43.                              † Page 58.

bodies are to be raised as his was.'* I grant, other dead as certainly
raised as Christ was; for else his resurrection would be of no use to
mankind. But I do not see how it follows that they shall be raised
with the same body, as Christ was raised with the same body, as your
lordship infers in these words annexed : 'And can there be any doubt,
whether his body was the same material substance which was united to
his soul before ?' I answer, None at all ; nor that it had just the same
undistinguished lineaments and marks, yea, and the same wounds, that
it had at the time of his death. If therefore your lordship will argue
from ' other bodies being raised as his was,' that they must keep proportion with his in sameness, then we must believe that every man
shall be raised with the same lineaments and other notes of distinction
he had at the time of his death, even with his wounds yet open, if he
had any, because our Saviour was so raised, which seems to me scarce
reconcilable with what your lordship says of a ' fat man falling into a
consumption,'† and dying.

"But whether it will consist or no with your lordship's meaning in
that place, this to me seems a consequence that will need to be better
proved, viz., that our bodies must be raised the same, just as our
Saviour's was, because St. Paul says, ' If there be no resurrection of
the dead, then is not Christ risen.' For it may be a good consequence,
' Christ is risen, and therefore there shall be a resurrection of the dead ;'
and yet this may not be a good consequence, ' Christ was raised with
the same body he had at his death, therefore all men shall be raised
with the same body they had at their death ;' contrary to what your
lordship says concerning ' a fat man dying of a consumption.' But the
case I think far different betwixt our Saviour and those to be raised
at the last day.

"1. His body ' saw not corruption ;' and therefore to give him
another body, new moulded, mixed with other particles which were not
contained in it as it lay in the grave whole and entire as it was laid
there, had been to destroy his body to frame him a new one without
any need. But why, with the remaining particles of a man's body long
since dissolved and mouldered into dust and atoms, (whereof possibly
a great part may have undergone variety of changes, and entered into
other concretions even in the bodies of other men,) other new particles
of matter mixed with them may not serve to make his body again, as
well as the mixture of new and different particles of matter with the
old did in the compass of his life make his body, I think no reason can
be given.

"This may serve to show why, though the materials of our Saviour's
body were not changed at his resurrection, yet it does not follow, but
that the body of a man dead and rotten in his grave, or burnt, may at
the last day have several new particles in it, and that without any
inconvenience ; since whatever matter is vitally united to his soul is
his body, as much as is that which was united to it when he was born,
or in any other part of his life.

"2. In the next place, the size, shape, figure, and lineaments of our
Saviour's body, even to his wounds into which doubting Thomas put
his fingers and his hands, were to be kept in the raised body of our
Saviour, the same they were at his death, to be a conviction to his

* Page 38.   † Page 84.

disciples to whom he showed himself, and who were to be witnesses
of his resurrection that their Master, the very same man, was crucified, dead, and buried, and raised again ; and therefore he was handled
by them, and ate before them, after he was risen, to give them in all
points full satisfaction, that it was really he, the same, and not another,
nor a spectre or apparition of him ; though I do not think your lordship will thence argue, that because others are to be raised as he was,
therefore it is necessary to believe that because he ate after his resurrection, others at the last day shall eat and drink after they are raised
from the dead ; which seems to me as good an argument as,—Because
his undissolved body was raised out of the grave just as it there lay
entire, without the mixture of any new particles ; therefore the corrupted and consumed bodies of the dead at the resurrection shall be
new framed only out of those scattered particles which were once
vitally united to their souls, without the least mixture of any one
single atom of new matter.  But at the last day, when all men are
raised, there will be no need to be assured of any one particular man's
resurrection.  It is enough that every one shall appear before the
judgment-seat of Christ, to receive according to what he had done in
his former life ; but in what sort of body he shall appear, or of what
particles made up, the scripture having said nothing but that it shall
be a spiritual body raised in incorruption, it is not for me to determine.
 "Your lordship asks, 'Were they [who saw our Saviour after his
resurrection] witnesses only of some material substance then united to
his soul ?'* In answer, I beg your lordship to consider, whether you
suppose our Saviour was to be known to be the same man (to the
witnesses that were to see him, and testify his resurrection) by his
soul, that could neither be seen nor known to be the same ; or by his
body, that could be seen and, by the discernible structure and marks
of it, be known to be the same ?  When your lordship has resolved
that, all that you say in that page will answer itself.  But because one
man cannot know another to be the same, but by the outward visible
lineaments and sensible marks he has been wont to be known and distinguished by ; will your lordship therefore argue, that the great Judge
at the last day, who gives to each man whom he raises his new body,
shall not be able to know who is who, unless he give to every one of
them a body just of the same figure, size, and features, and made
up of the very same individual particles he had in his former life ?
Whether such a way of arguing for the resurrection of the same body
to be an article of faith, contributes much to the strengthening the
credibility of the article of the resurrection of the dead, I shall leave
to the judgment of others.
 "Farther : for the proving the resurrection of the same body to be
an article of faith, your lordship says, 'But the apostle insists upon
the resurrection of Christ, not merely as an argument of the possibility of ours, but of the certainty of it ; because he arose as the first-
fruits : *Christ the first-fruits ; afterwards they that are Christ's at his
coming.*'† (1 Cor. xv. 20, 23.)  Answer. No doubt the resurrection of
Christ is a proof of the certainty of our resurrection.  But is it therefore a proof of the resurrection of the same body, consisting of the same
individual particles which concurred to the making up of our body here,

without the mixture of any one other particle of matter ? I confess I see no such consequence.

"But your lordship goes on : 'St. Paul was aware of the objections in men's minds about the resurrection of the same body ; and it is of great consequence, as to this article, to show upon what grounds he proceeds. *But some man will say, How are the dead raised up ? and with what body do they come ?* First, he shows, that the seminal parts of plants are wonderfully improved by the ordinary providence of God, in the manner of their vegetation.'* Answer. I do not perfectly understand what it is for 'The seminal parts of plants to be wonderfully improved by the ordinary providence of God, in the manner of their vegetation ;' or else perhaps I should better see how this here tends to the proof of the resurrection of the same body, in your lordship's sense.

"It continues, 'They sow bare grain of wheat, or of some other grain, but God giveth it a body as it hath pleased him, and to every seed his own body.' 'Here,' says your lordship, 'is an identity of the material substance supposed.'† It may be so. But to me a diversity 'of the material substance,' *i.e.*, of the component particles, is here supposed, or in direct words said. For the words of St. Paul, taken all together, run thus: 'That which thou sowest, thou sowest not that body which shall be, but bare grain,' (1 Cor. xv. 37,) and so on, as your lordship has set down the remainder of them. From which words of St. Paul the natural argument seems to me to stand thus: If the body that is put in the earth in sowing is not that body which shall be, then the body that is put in the grave is not that, *i.e.*, the same, body that shall be.

"But your lordship proves it to be the same body by these three Greek words of the text, τὸ ἴδιον σῶμα, which your lordship interprets thus : 'That proper body which belongs to it.'‡ Answer. Indeed by those Greek words, τὸ ἴδιον σῶμα, whether our translators have rightly rendered them 'his own body,' or your lordship more rightly, 'that proper body which belongs to it,' I formerly understood no more but this, that in the production of wheat and other grain from seed, God continued every species distinct, so that from grains of wheat sown, root, stalk, blade, ear, and grains of wheat were produced and not those of barley ; and so of the rest, which I took to be the meaning of, 'to every seed his own body. No, says your lordship, these words prove, that to every plant of wheat, and to every grain of wheat produced in it, is given the 'proper body that belongs to it,' which is the same body with the grain that was sown. Answer. This I confess I do not understand ; because I do not understand how one individual grain can be the same with twenty, fifty, or an hundred individual grains ; for such sometimes is the increase.

"But your lordship proves it. For, says your lordship, 'Every seed having that body in little, which is afterwards so much enlarged ; and in grain the seed is corrupted before its germination ; but it hath its proper organical parts, which make it the same body with that which it grows up to. For although grain be not divided into lobes, as other seeds are, yet it hath been found by the most accurate observations, that upon separating the membranes, these seminal parts are discerned

* Page 40.      † Ibid.      ‡ Ibid.

in them, which afterwards grow up to that body which we call corn.'*
In which words I crave leave to observe, that your lordship supposes
that a body may be enlarged by the addition of a hundred or a thousand times as much in bulk as its own matter, and yet continue the
same body ; which I confess I cannot understand.

"But in the next place, if that could be so, and that the plant, in its
full growth at harvest, increased by a thousand or a million of times
as much new matter added to it as it had when it lay in little concealed
in the grain that was sown, was the very same body ; yet I do not
think that your lordship will say, that every minute, insensible, and
inconceivably small grain of the hundred grains contained in that little
organized seminal plant, is every one of them the very same with that
grain which contains that whole little seminal plant and all those
invisible grains in it. For then it will follow, that one grain is the
same with an hundred, and an hundred distinct grains the same with
one ; which I shall be able to assent to, when I can conceive that all
the wheat in the world is but one grain.

"For, I beseech you, my lord, consider what it is St. Paul here
speaks of ; it is plain he speaks of that which is sown and dies, *i.e.*,
the grain that the husbandman takes out of his barn to sow in his
field. And of this grain, St. Paul says, that it is not 'that body that
shall be.' These two, viz. 'that which is sown,' and 'that body that
shall be,' are all the bodies that St. Paul here speaks of, to represent
the agreement or difference of men's bodies after the resurrection with
those they had before they died. Now, I crave leave to ask your
lordship, Which of these two is that little invisible seminal plant which
your lordship here speaks of? Does your lordship mean by it, the
grain that is sown ? But that is not what St. Paul speaks of : he could
not mean this embryonated little plant : for he could not denote it by
these words, 'that which thou sowest ;' for that he says must die ;
but this little embryonated plant, contained in the seed that is sown,
dies not. Or does your lordship mean by it, 'the body that shall be ?'
But neither by these words, 'the body that shall be,' can St. Paul be
supposed to denote this insensible little embryonated plant ; for that
is already in being contained in the seed that is sown, and therefore
could not be spoke of under the name of the 'body that shall be.'
And therefore, I confess, I cannot see of what use it is to your lordship to introduce here this third body, which St. Paul mentions not ;
and to make that the same or not the same with any other, when those
which St. Paul speaks of are, as I humbly conceive, these two visible
sensible bodies, the grain sown, and the corn grown up to ear ; with
neither of which this insensible, embryonated plant can be the same
body, unless an insensible body can be the same body with a sensible
body, and a little body can be the same body with one ten thousand
or an hundred thousand times as big as itself. So that yet I confess I
see not the resurrection of the same body proved from these words of
St. Paul to be an article of faith.

"Your lordship goes on : 'St. Paul indeed saith, that we sow not
that body that shall be ; but he speaks not of the identity, but the
perfection of it.'† Here my understanding fails me again : for I cannot
understand St. Paul to say, that the same identical sensible grain

of wheat, which was sown at seed-time, is the very same with every grain of wheat in the ear at harvest that sprang from it ; yet so I must understand it, to make it prove that the same sensible body that is laid in the grave shall be the very same with that which shall be raised at the resurrection. For I do not know of any seminal body in little, contained in the dead carcass of any man or woman, which, as your lordship says, in seeds, having its proper organical parts, 'shall afterwards be enlarged, and at the resurrection grow up into the same man.' For I never thought of any seed or seminal parts, either of plant or animal, 'so wonderfully improved by the providence of God,' whereby the same plant or animal should beget itself ; nor ever heard that it was by Divine Providence designed to produce the same individual, but for the producing of future and distinct individuals for the continuation of the same species.

"Your lordship's next words are, 'And although there be such a difference from the grain itself when it comes up to be perfect corn, with root, stalk, blade, and ear, that it may be said to outward appearance not to be the same body ; yet with regard to the seminal and organical parts, it is as much the same as a man grown up is the same with the embryo in the womb.'* Answer. It does not appear by any thing I can find in the text, that St. Paul here compared the body produced with the seminal and organical parts contained in the grain it sprang from, but with the whole sensible grain that was sown. Microscopes had not then discovered the little embryo plant in the seed ; and supposing it should have been revealed to St. Paul (though in the scripture we find little revelation of natural philosophy), yet an argument taken from a thing perfectly unknown to the Corinthians, whom he writ to, could be of no manner of use to them, nor serve at all either to instruct or convince them. But granting that those St. Paul writ to knew it as well as Mr. Lewenhooke, yet your lordship thereby proves not the raising of the same body ; your lordship says, 'It is as much the same' (I crave leave to add 'body'), 'as a man grown up is the same' ('same' what, I beseech your lordship ?) 'with the embryo in the womb.' For that the body of the embryo in the womb, and body of the man grown up, is the same body, I think no one will say ; unless he can persuade himself that a body that is not the hundredth part of another, is the same with that other ; which I think no one will do, till, having renounced this dangerous way by ideas of thinking and reasoning, he has learnt to say, that a part and the whole are the same.

"Your lordship goes on, 'And although many arguments may be used to prove that a man is not the same, because life, which depends upon the course of the blood, and the manner of respiration and nutrition, is so different in both states ; yet that man would be thought ridiculous that should seriously affirm, that it was not the same man.'† And your lordship says, 'I grant that the variation of great parcels of matter in plants alters not the identity, and that the organization of the parts in one coherent body, partaking of one common life, makes the identity of a plant.' Answer. My lord, I think the question is not about the same man, but the same body. For though I do say (somewhat differently from what your lordship sets down as my words

* Page 41.                         † Ibid

here), 'That that which has such an organization as is fit to receive
and distribute nourishment, so as to continue and frame the wood,
bark, and leaves, &c., of a plant, in which consists the vegetable life,
continues to be the same plant as long as it partakes of the same life,
though that life be communicated to new particles of matter, vitally
united to the living plant :'* yet I do not remember that I anywhere
say, that a plant, which was once no bigger than an oaten-straw, and
afterwards grows to be above a fathom about, is the same body, though
it be still the same plant.

"The well-known tree in Epping Forest, called the King's Oak,
which, from not weighing an ounce at first, grew to have many tons
of timber in it, was all along the same oak, the very same plant; but
nobody, I think, will say it was the same body when it weighed a ton,
as it was when it weighed but an ounce, unless he has a mind to
signalize himself by saying, that that is the same body which has a
thousand particles of different matter in it, for one particle that is
the same; which is no better than to say, that a thousand different
particles are but one and the same particle, and one and the same
particle is a thousand different particles; a thousand times a greater
absurdity than to say half is the whole, or the whole is the same with
the half; which will be improved ten thousand times yet farther, if
a man shall say (as your lordship seems to me to argue here), that
that great oak is the very same body with the acorn it sprang from,
because there was in that acorn an oak in little, which was afterwards
(as your lordship expresses it) so much enlarged, as to make that
mighty tree. For this embryo, if I may so call it, or oak in little,
being not the hundredth, or perhaps the thousandth, part of the
acorn, and the acorn being not the thousandth part of the grown
oak, it will be very extraordinary to prove the acorn and the grown
oak to be the same body by a way wherein it cannot be pretended
that above one particle of an hundred thousand, or a million, is the
same in the one body that it was in the other. From which way of
reasoning it will follow, that a nurse and her sucking-child have the
same body; and be past doubt, that a mother and her infant have the
same body. But this is a way of certainty found out to establish the
articles of faith, and to overturn the new method of certainty that your
lordship says I 'have started, which is apt to leave men's minds more
doubtful than before.'

"And now I desire your lordship to consider of what use it is to you
in the present case to quote out of my Essay these words, that 'partaking of one common life makes the identity of a plant,' since the
question is not about the identity of a plant, but about the identity of
a body; it being a very different thing to be the same plant, and to be
the same body. For that which makes the same plant does not make
the same body; the one being the partaking in the same continued
vegetable life, the other the consisting of the same numerical particles
of matter. And therefore your lordship's inference from my words
above quoted, in these which you subjoin, seems to me a very strange
one : viz., 'So that in things capable of any sort of life, the identity
is consistent with a continued succession of parts; and so the wheat,
grown up, is the same body with the grain that was sown.† For I

* Essay, book ii. chap. xxvii. sect. 4.          † Page 42.

believe if my words, from which you infer, 'and so the wheat grown up is the same body with the grain that was sown,' were put into a syllogism, this would hardly be brought to be the conclusion.

"But your lordship goes on with consequence upon consequence, though I have not eyes acute enough everywhere to see the connexion, till you bring it to the resurrection of the same body. The connexion of your lordship's words is as followeth: 'And thus the alteration of the parts of the body at the resurrection is consistent with its identity, if its organization and life be the same; and this is a real identity of the body, which depends not upon consciousness. From whence it follows, that, to make the same body, no more is required but restoring life to the organized parts of it.'* If the question were about raising the same plant, I do not say but there might be some appearance for making such an inference from my words as this, 'Whence it follows that, to make the same plant, no more is required but to restore life to the organized parts of it.' But this deduction, wherein, from those words of mine that speak only of the identity of a plant, your lordship infers there is no more required to make the same body than to make the same plant, being too subtle for me, I leave to my reader to find out.

"Your lordship goes on and says, that I 'grant likewise, that the identity of the same man consists in a participation of the same continued life, by constantly fleeting particles of matter in succession, vitally united to the same organized body.' Answer. I speak in these words of the identity of the same man: and your lordship thence roundly concludes, 'so that there is no difficulty of the sameness of the body.' But your lordship knows that I do not take these two sounds 'man' and 'body,' to stand for the same thing; nor the identity of the man to be the same with the identity of the body.

"But let us read out your lordship's words: 'So that there is no difficulty as to the sameness of the body, if life were continued; and if by divine power life be restored to that material substance which was before united by a re-union of the soul to it, there is no reason to deny the identity of the body: not from the consciousness of the soul, but from that light which is the result of the union of the soul and body.'†

"If I understand your lordship right, you, in these words, from the passages above quoted out of my book, argue, that from those words of mine it will follow, that it is or may be the same body that is raised at the resurrection. If so, my lord, your lordship has then proved, that my book is not inconsistent with, but conformable to, this article of the resurrection of the same body, which your lordship contends for, and will have to be an article of faith; for though I do by no means deny that the same bodies shall be raised at the last day, yet I see nothing your lordship has said to prove it to be an article of faith.

"But your lordship goes on with your proofs, and says, 'But St. Paul still supposes, that it must be that material substance to which the soul was before united. For, saith he, *It is sown in corruption, it is raised in incorruption: it is sown in dishonour, it is raised in glory: it is sown in weakness, it is raised in power: it is sown a natural body, it is raised a spiritual body.* Can such a material substance, which

* Page 41.    † Ibid.

was never united to the body, be said to be sown in corruption, and weakness, and dishonour? Either therefore he must speak of the same body, or his meaning cannot be comprehended.'* I answer, Can such a material substance which was never laid in the grave be said to be sown, &c.? For your lordship says, you 'do not say the same individual particles, which were united at the point of death, shall be raised at the last day ;'† and no other particles are laid in the grave but such as are united at the point of death; either therefore your lordship must speak of another body different from that which was sown, which shall be raised, or else your meaning, I think, cannot be comprehended.

"But whatever be your meaning, your lordship proves it to be St. Paul's meaning, 'that the same body shall be raised which was sown,' in these following words: 'For what does all this relate to a conscious principle?'‡ Answer, The scripture being express, that the same persons should be raised and appear before the judgment-seat of Christ, that everyone may receive according to what he had done in his body; it was very well suited to common apprehensions (which refined not about 'particles that had been vitally united to the soul'), to speak of the body which each one was to have after the resurrection, as he would be apt to speak of it himself. For it being his body both before and after the resurrection, everyone ordinarily speaks of his body as the same, though, in a strict and philosophical sense, as your lordship speaks, it be not the very same. Thus it is no impropriety of speech to say, 'This body of mine, which was formerly strong and plump, is now weak and wasted ;' though in such a sense as you are speaking in here, it be not the same body. Revelation declares nothing anywhere concerning the same body, in your lordship's sense of 'the same body,' which appears not to have been then thought of. The apostle directly proposes nothing for or against the same body, as necessary to be believed ; that which he is plain and direct in, is opposing and condemning such curious questions about the body, which could serve only to perplex, not to confirm what was material and necessary for them to believe, viz., a day of judgment and retribution to men in a future state ; and therefore it is no wonder that mentioning their bodies he should use a way of speaking suited to vulgar notions, from which it would be hard positively to conclude anything for the determining of this question (especially against expressions in the same discourse that plainly incline to the other side) in a matter which, as it appears, the apostle thought not necessary to determine, and the Spirit of God thought not fit to gratify anyone's curiosity in.

"But your lordship says, 'The apostle speaks plainly of that body which was once quickened, and afterwards falls to corruption, and is to be restored with more noble qualities.'§ I wish your lordship had quoted the words of St. Paul, wherein he speaks plainly of that numerical body that was once quickened : they would presently decide this question. But your lordship proves it by these following words of St. Paul : 'For this corruption must put on incorruption, and this mortal must put on immortality ;' to which your lordship adds, 'that you do not see how he could more expressly affirm the identity of this corruptible body, with that after the resurrection. How expressly it is affirmed by the apostle, shall be considered by and by. In the meantime it is past doubt, that your lordship best knows what you do or do not see. But this I will be bold to say, that if St. Paul had anywhere in this chapter (where there are so many occasions for it, if it had been necessary to have been believed) but said in express words, that the same bodies should be raised, everyone else who thinks of it, will see he had more expressly affirmed the identity of the bodies which men now have, with those they shall have after the resurrection.

"The remainder of your lordship's period is, 'And that without any respect to the principle of self-consciousness.'* Answer. These words, I doubt not, have some meaning, but I must own I know not what; either towards the proof of the resurrection of the same body, or to show that anything I have said concerning self-consciousness is inconsistent; for I do not remember that I have anywhere said, that the identity of body consisted in self-consciousness.

"From your preceding words, your lordship concludes thus: 'And so if the scripture be the sole foundation of our faith, this is an article of it.'† My lord, to make the conclusion unquestionable, I humbly conceive the words must run thus: 'And so if the scripture and your lordship's interpretation of it, be the sole foundation of our faith, the resurrection of the same body is an article of it.' For, with submission, your lordship has neither produced express words of scripture for it, nor so proved that to be the meaning of any of those words of scripture which you have produced for it, that a man who reads and sincerely endeavours to understand the scripture, cannot but find himself obliged to believe as expressly that the same bodies of the dead, in your lordship's sense, shall be raised, as that the dead shall be raised. And I crave leave to give your lordship this one reason for it: he who reads with attention this discourse of St. Paul, (1 Cor. xv.) where he discourses of the resurrection, will see, that he plainly distinguishes between the dead that shall be raised, and the bodies of the dead. For it is νεκροι, πάντες, οἱ, are the nominative cases to ἐγείρονται, ζωοποιηθήσονται, ἐγερθήσονται, all along and not σώματα, 'bodies;' (verses 15, 22, 23, 29, 32, 35, 52;) which one may with reason think would somewhere or other have been expressed, if all this had been said to propose it as an article of faith, that the very same bodies should be raised. The same manner of speaking the Spirit of God observes all through the New Testament, where it is said, 'raise the dead,' 'quicken' or 'make alive the dead,' 'the resurrection of the dead.' (Matt. xxii. 31; Mark xii. 26; John v. 21; Acts xxvi. 8; Rom. iv. 17; 2 Cor. i. 9; 1 Thess. iv. 14, 16.) Nay, these very words of our Saviour, urged by your lordship for the resurrection of the same body run thus: Πάντες οἱ ἐν τοῖς μνημείοις ἀκούσονται τῆς φωνῆς αὐτοῦ, καὶ ἐκπορεύσονται οἱ τὰ ἀγαθὰ ποιήσαντες εἰς ἀνάστασιν ζωῆς, οἱ δὲ τὰ φαῦλα πράξαντες εἰς ἀνάστασιν κρίσεως. (John v. 28, 29.) Would a well-meaning searcher of the scriptures be apt to think, that if the thing here intended by our Saviour were to teach, and propose it as an article of faith necessary to be believed by everyone, that the very same bodies of the dead should be raised; would not, I say, anyone be apt to think, that if our Saviour meant so, the words should have rather been, πάντα τὰ σώματα ἃ ἐν τοῖς μνημείοις, i.e., 'all the bodies that are in the graves,' rather than

* Page 44.                 † Ibid.

'all who are in the graves)' which must denote persons, and not, precisely bodies.

"Another evidence that St. Paul makes a distinction between the dead, and the bodies of the dead, so that the dead cannot be taken in this (1 Cor. xv.) to stand precisely for the bodies of the dead, are these words of the apostle: 'But some man will say, How are the dead raised? and with what bodies do they come?' (Verse 35.) Which words, 'dead' and 'they,' if supposed to stand precisely for the bodies of the dead, the question will run thus: 'How are the dead bodies raised? and with what bodies do the dead bodies come?' which seems to have no very agreeable sense.

"This therefore being so, that the Spirit of God keeps so expressly to this phrase or form of speaking in the New Testament, of 'raising,' 'quickening,' 'rising,' 'resurrection,' &c., 'of the dead,' where the resurrection at the last day is spoken of; and that the body is not mentioned but in answer to this question, 'With what bodies shall those dead who are raised come?' so that by 'the dead' cannot precisely be meant the dead bodies; I do not see but a good Christian, who reads the scripture with an intention to believe all that is there revealed to him concerning the resurrection, may acquit himself of his duty therein without entering into the inquiry whether the dead shall have the very same bodies or no. Which sort of inquiry the apostle, by the appellation he bestows here on him that makes it, seems not much to encourage. Nor, if he shall think himself bound to determine concerning the identity of the bodies of the dead raised at the last day, will he, by the remainder of St. Paul's answer, find the determination of the apostle to be much in favour of the very same body, unless the being told that the body sown is not that body that shall be; that the body raised is as different from that which was laid down, as the flesh of man is from the flesh of beasts, fishes, and birds; or as the sun, moon, and stars are different one from another; or as different as a corruptible, weak, natural, mortal body is from an incorruptible, powerful, spiritual, immortal body; and lastly, as different as a body that is flesh and blood is from a body that is not flesh and blood; for 'flesh and blood cannot,' says St. Paul in this very place, 'inherit the kingdom of God: (1 Cor. xv. 50:)—unless, I say, all this which is contained in St. Paul's words can be supposed to be the way to deliver this as an article of faith, which is required to be believed by everyone; viz., that the dead shall be raised with the very same bodies that they had before in this life; which article, proposed in these or the like plain and express words, could have left no room for doubt in the meanest capacities, nor for contest in the most perverse minds.

"Your lordship adds in the next words: 'And so it hath been always understood by the Christian church; viz., that the resurrection of the same body' (in your lordship's sense of 'same body') 'is an article of faith.'* Answer. What the Christian church has always understood, is beyond my knowledge. But for those who, coming short of your lordship's great learning, cannot gather their articles of faith from the understanding of all the whole Christian church ever since the preaching of the gospel, (who make the far greater part of Christians, I think I may say nine hundred ninety and nine of a thousand,)

* Page 44.

but are forced to have recourse to the scripture to find them there, I do not see that they will easily find there this proposed as an article of faith, that there shall be a resurrection of the same body; but that there shall be a resurrection of the dead, without explicitly determining that they shall be raised with bodies made up wholly of the same particles which were once vitally united to their souls in their former life, without the mixture of any one other particle of matter; which is that which your lordship means by 'the same body.'

"But supposing your lordship to have demonstrated this to be an article of faith (though I crave leave to own, that I do not see that all that your lordship has said here makes it so much as probable), what is all this to me? Yes, says your lordship in the following words:— my 'idea of personal identity is inconsistent with it; for it makes the same body which was here united to the soul not to be necessary to the doctrine of the resurrection: but any material substance united to the same principle of consciousness, makes the same body.'

"This is an argument of your lordship's which I am obliged to answer to. But is it not fit I should first understand it, before I answer it? Now, here I do not well know what it is to make a thing 'not to be necessary to the doctrine of the resurrection.' But to help myself out the best I can with a guess, I will conjecture (which, in disputing with learned men, is not very safe) your lordship's meaning is, that my idea of personal identity makes it not necessary that, for the raising the same person, the body should be the same.

"Your lordship's next word is 'but;' to which I am ready to reply, 'But' what? What does my idea of personal identity do? For something of that kind the adversative particle 'but' should, in the ordinary construction of our language, introduce, to make the proposition clear and intelligible; but here is no such thing. 'But' is one of your lordship's privileged particles, which I must not meddle with, for fear your lordship complain of me again as so 'severe a critic,' that, 'for the least ambiguity in any particle, fill up pages in my answer, to make my book look considerable for the bulk of it.' But since this proposition here, 'My idea of a personal identity makes the same body which was here united to the soul not necessary to the doctrine of the resurrection; but any material substance being united to the same principle of consciousness, makes the same body'—is brought to prove my idea of personal identity inconsistent with the article of the resurrection, I must make it out in some direct sense or other, that I may see whether it be both true and conclusive. I therefore venture to read it thus: 'My idea of personal identity makes the same body which was here united to the soul not to be necessary at the resurrection; but allows that any material substance being united to the same principle of consciousness, makes the same body: *ergo*, my idea of personal identity is inconsistent with the article of the resurrection of the same body.'

"If this be your lordship's sense in this passage, as I here have guessed it to be, or else I know not what it is, I answer,

"1. That 'my idea of personal identity' does not allow that 'any material substance being united to the same principle of consciousness, makes the same body.' I say no such thing in my book, nor any thing from whence it may be inferred ; and your lordship would have done me a favour to have set down the words where I say so, or those from which you infer so, and showed how it follows from anything I have said.

"2. Granting that it were a consequence from 'my idea of personal identity,' that 'any material substance being united to the same principle of consciousness makes the same body,' this would not prove that 'my idea of personal identity' was inconsistent with this proposition—that the same body shall be raised ; but on the contrary, affirms it : since if I affirm, as I do, that the same persons shall be raised, and it be a consequence of 'my idea of personal identity,' that 'any material substance being united to the same principle of consciousness makes the same body,' it follows, that if the same person be raised, the same body must be raised ; and so I have herein not only said nothing inconsistent with the resurrection of the same body, but have said more for it than your lordship.  For there can be nothing plainer than that in the scripture it is revealed, that the same persons shall be raised, and appear before the judgment-seat of Christ, to answer for what they have done in their bodies.  If therefore whatever matter be joined to the same principle of consciousness make the same body, it is demonstration that if the same persons are raised, they have the same bodies.

"How then your lordship makes this an inconsistency with the resurrection, is beyond my conception.  Yes, says your lordship, 'it is inconsistent with it ; for it makes the same body which was here united to the soul not to be necessary.'

"3. I answer, therefore, thirdly, that this is the first time I ever learnt that 'not necessary' was the same with 'inconsistent.'  I say, that a body made up of the same numerical parts of matter is not necessary to the making of the same person ; from whence it will indeed follow, that to the resurrection of the same person the same numerical particles of matter are not required.  What does your lordship infer from hence ?  To wit, this : Therefore he who thinks that the same particles of matter are not necessary to the making of the same person, cannot believe that the same persons shall be raised with bodies made of the very same particles of matter, if God should reveal that it shall be so, viz., that the same persons shall be raised with the same bodies they had before.  Which is all one as to say, that he who thought the blowing of rams' horns was not necessary in itself to the falling down of the walls of Jericho, could not believe that they should fall upon the blowing of rams' horns, when God had declared it should be so.

"Your lordship says my 'idea of personal identity is inconsistent with the article of the resurrection :' the reason you ground it on is this : because it makes not the same body necessary to the making of the same person.  Let us grant your lordship's consequence to be good : what will follow from it ?  No less than this : that your lordship's notion (for I dare not say your lordship has any so dangerous things as ideas) of 'personal identity is inconsistent with the article of the resurrection.'  The demonstration of it is thus : Your lordship says, 'It is not necessary that the body to be raised at the last day should consist of the same particles of matter which were united at the point of death ; for there must be a great alteration in them in a lingering disease, as if a fat man falls into a consumption : you do not say the same particles which the sinner had at the very time of commission of his sins ; for then a long sinner must have a vast body, considering the continual spending of particles by perspiration.[*] And again here your lordship says, you ' allow the notion of personal identity to belong to the same man under several changes of matter.'[†] From which words it is evident that your lordship supposes a person in this world may be continued and preserved the same in a body not consisting of the same individual particles of matter: and hence it demonstratively follows, that let your lordship's notion of personal identity be what it will, it makes the same body not to be necessary to the same person ; and therefore it is, by your lordship's rule, 'inconsistent with the article of the resurrection.' When your lordship shall think fit to clear your own notion of personal identity from this inconsistency with the article of the resurrection, I do not doubt but my idea of personal identity will be thereby cleared too. Till then all inconsistency with that article which your lordship has here charged on mine, will unavoidably fall upon your lordship's too.

"But, for the clearing of both, give me leave to say, my lord, that whatsoever is not necessary, does not thereby become inconsistent. It is not necessary to the same person, that his body should always consist of the same numerical particles: this is demonstration, because the particles of the bodies of the same persons in this life change every moment, and your lordship cannot deny it ; and yet this makes it not inconsistent with God's preserving, if he thinks fit, to the same persons bodies consisting of the same numerical particles always from the resurrection to eternity. And so likewise, though I say anything that supposes it not necessary that the same numerical particles which were vitally united to the soul in this life should be reunited to it at the resurrection, and constitute the body it shall then have ; yet it is not inconsistent with this, that God may, if he pleases, give to everyone a body consisting only of such particles as were before vitally united to his soul. And thus I think I have cleared my book from all that inconsistency which your lordship charges on it, and would persuade the world it has, with the article of the resurrection of the dead.

"Only before I leave it, I will set down the remainder of what your lordship says upon this head, that though I see not the coherence nor tendency of it, nor the force of any argument in it against me, yet that nothing may be omitted that your lordship has thought fit to entertain your reader with on this new point, nor anyone have reason to suspect that I have passed by any word of your lordship's (on this now-first-introduced subject), wherein he might find your lordship had proved what you had promised in your title-page. Your remaining words are these : 'The dispute is not how far personal identity in itself may consist in the very same material substance, for we allow the notion of personal identity to belong to the same man under several changes of matter ; but whether it doth not depend upon a vital union between the soul and body, and the life, which is consequent upon it ; and therefore in the resurrection the same material substance must be

[*] Pages 34, 35.      [†] Page 44.

re-united, or else it cannot be called a resurrection, but a renovation; *i.e.*, it may be a new life, but not a raising the body from the dead.'* I confess I do not see how what is here ushered in by the words 'and therefore,' is a consequence from the preceding words; but as to the propriety of the name, I think it will not be much questioned, that if the same man rise who was dead, it may very properly be called the 'resurrection of the dead,' which is the language of the scripture.

"I must not part with this article of the resurrection without returning my thanks to your lordship for making me take notice of a fault in my Essay.† When I writ that book, I took it for granted, as I doubt not but many others have done, that the scripture had mentioned in express terms the resurrection of the body. But upon the occasion your lordship has given me in your last Letter, to look a little more narrowly into what revelation has declared concerning the resurrection; and finding no such express words in the scripture as that the body shall rise or be raised, or the resurrection of the body, I shall in the next edition of it change these words of my book, 'The dead bodies of men shall rise,'‡ into these of the scripture, 'The dead shall rise.' Not that I question that the dead shall be raised with bodies; but in matters of revelation I think it not only safest, but our duty, as far as anyone delivers it for revelation, to keep close to the words of the scripture; unless he will assume to himself the authority of one inspired, or make himself wiser than the Holy Spirit himself. If I had spoke of the resurrection in precisely scripture terms, I had avoided giving your lordship the occasion of making here such a verbal reflection on my words: 'What! not if there be an idea of identity as to the body?' "§

* Page 44.    † Page 62.    ‡ Essay, book iv. chap. xviii. sect. 7.    § Page 68.

## CHAPTER XXVIII.

### OF OTHER RELATIONS.

**1.** *Proportional.*—Besides the before-mentioned occasions of time, place, and casualty of comparing, or referring things one to another, there are, as I have said, infinite others, some whereof I shall mention.

First, The first I shall name, is some one simple idea, which, being capable of parts or degrees, affords an occasion of comparing the subjects wherein it is to one another, in respect of that simple idea, *v. g.*, "whiter, sweeter, bigger, equal, more," &c. These relations, depending on the equality and excess of the same simple idea in several subjects, may be called, if one will, "proportional;" and that these are only conversant about those simple ideas received from sensation or reflection, is so evident that nothing need be said to evince it.

**2.** *Natural.*—Secondly, Another occasion of comparing things together, or considering one thing so as to include in that consideration some other thing, is the circumstances of their origin or beginning; which, being not afterwards to be altered, make the relations depending thereon as lasting as the subjects to which they belong; *v. g.*, father and son, brothers, cousin-germans, &c., which have their relations by one community of blood, wherein they partake in several degrees; countrymen, *i.e.*, those who were born in the same country or track of ground; and these I call "natural relations:" wherein we may observe, that mankind have fitted their notions and words to the use of common life, and not to the truth and extent of things. For it is certain that in reality the relation is the same betwixt the begetter and the begotten in the several races of other animals as well as men: but yet it is seldom said, "This bull is the grandfather of such a calf;" or that two pigeons are cousin-germans. It is very convenient, that by distinct names these relations should be observed and marked out in mankind, there being occasion, both in laws and other communications one with another, to mention and take notice of men under these relations: from whence also arise the obligations of several duties amongst men: whereas in brutes, men having very little or no cause to mind these relations, they have not thought fit to give them distinct and peculiar names. This, by the way, may give us some light into the different state and growth of languages; which, being suited only to the convenience of communication, are proportioned to the notions men have, and the commerce of thoughts familiar amongst them; and not to the reality or extent of things, nor to the various respects might be found among them, nor the different abstract considerations might be framed about them. Where they had no philosophical notions, there they had no terms to express them: and it is no wonder men should have framed no names for those things they found no occasion to discourse of. From whence it is easy to imagine why, as in some countries, they may not have so much as the name for a horse; and in others, where they are more careful of the pedigrees of their horses than of their own, that there they may have not only names for particular horses, but also of their several relations of kindred one to another.

8. *Instituted.*—Thirdly, Sometimes the foundation of considering things with reference to one another, is some act whereby anyone comes by a moral right, power, or obligation to do something. Thus a general is one that hath power to command an army; and an army under a general is a collection of armed men obliged to obey one man. A citizen or a burgher is one who has a right to certain privileges in this or that place. All this sort depending upon men's wills or agreement in society, I call "instituted," or "voluntary," and may be distinguished from the natural, in that they are, most if not all of them, some way or other alterable and separable from the persons to whom they have sometimes belonged, though neither of the substances so related be destroyed.

Now, though these are all reciprocal, as well as the rest, and contain in them a reference of two things one to the other; yet, because one of the two things often wants a relative name importing that reference, men usually take no notice of it, and the relation is commonly overlooked, *v. g.*, a patron and client are easily allowed to be relations : but a constable or dictator are not so readily, at first hearing, considered as such ; because there is no peculiar name for those who are under the command of a dictator or constable, expressing a relation to either of them ; though it be certain that either of them hath a certain power over some others; and so is so far related to them, as well as a patron is to his client, or general to his army.

4. *Moral.*—Fourthly, There is another sort of relation, which is the conformity or disagreement men's voluntary actions have to a rule to which they are referred, and by which they are judged of ; which, I think, may be called "moral relation," as being that which denominates our moral actions, and deserves well to be examined, there being no part of knowledge wherein we should be more careful to get determined ideas, and avoid, as much as may be, obscurity and confusion.  Human actions, when, with their various ends, objects, manners, and circumstances, they are framed into distinct complex ideas, are, as has been shown, so many mixed modes, a great part whereof have names affixed to them.  Thus, supposing gratitude to be a readiness to acknowledge and return kindness received; polygamy to be the having more wives than one at once : when we frame these notions thus in our minds, we have there so many determined ideas of mixed modes.  But this is not all that concerns our actions; it is not enough to have determined ideas of them, and to know what names belong to such and such combinations of ideas.  We have a farther and greater concernment; and that is, to know whether such actions so made up are morally good or bad.

5. *Moral good and evil.*—Good and evil, as hath been shown (book ii. chap. xx. sect. 2, and chap. xxi. sect. 42), are nothing but pleasure or pain, or that which occasions or procures pleasure or pain to us.  Moral good and evil, then, is only the conformity or disagreement of our voluntary actions to some law, whereby good and evil is drawn on us from the will and power of the law-maker; which good and evil, pleasure or pain, attending our observance or breach of the law, by the decree of the law-maker, is that we call "reward" and "punishment."

6. *Moral rules.*—Of these moral rules or laws, to which men generally refer, and by which they judge of the rectitude or pravity of their actions, there seem to me to be three sorts, with their three different enforcements, or rewards and punishments. For since it would be utterly in vain to suppose a rule set to the free actions of man, without annexing to it some enforcement of good and evil to determine his will, we must wherever we sup-

pose a law, suppose also some reward or punishment annexed to
that law.  It would be in vain for one intelligent being to set a
rule to the actions of another, if he had it not in his power to
reward the compliance with, and punish deviation from, his rule
by some good and evil that is not the natural product and consequence of the action itself.  For that, being a natural convenience or inconvenience, would operate of itself without a law.
This, if I mistake not, is the true nature of all law, properly
so called.

7. *Laws.*—The laws that men generally refer their actions to,
to judge of their rectitude or obliquity, seem to me to be these
three : (1) The divine law.  (2) The civil law.  (8) The law of
opinion or reputation, if I may so call it.  By the relation they
bear to the first of these, men judge whether their actions are
sins or duties; by the second, whether they be criminal or innocent; and by the third, whether they be virtues or vices.

8. *Divine law, the measure of sin and duty.*—First, the divine
law, whereby I mean the law which God has set to the actions of
men, whether promulgated to them by the light of nature, or the
voice of revelation.  That God has given a rule whereby men
should govern themselves, I think there is nobody so brutish as
to deny.  He has a right to do it; we are His creatures.  He
has goodness and wisdom to direct our actions to that which is
best; and He has power to enforce it by rewards and punishments, of infinite weight and duration, in another life; for
nobody can take us out of His hands.  This is the only true
touchstone of moral rectitude; and by comparing them to this
law it is that men judge of the most considerable moral good or
evil of their actions; that is, whether as duties or sins they are
like to procure them happiness or misery from the hands of the
Almighty.

9. *Civil law, the measure of crimes and innocence.*—Secondly,
The civil law, the rule set by the commonwealth to the actions
of those who belong to it, is another rule to which men refer
their actions, to judge whether they be criminal or no.  This
law nobody overlooks; the rewards and punishments that enforce it being ready at hand, and suitable to the power that
makes it; which is the force of the commonwealth, engaged to
protect the lives, liberties, and possessions of those who live
according to its laws, and has power to take away life, liberty, or
goods from him who disobeys; which is the punishment of
offences committed against this law.

10. *Philosophical law, the measure of virtue and vice.*—Thirdly,
The law of opinion or reputation.  "Virtue" and "vice" are
names pretended and supposed everywhere to stand for actions
in their own nature right or wrong : and as far as they really
are so applied, they so far are coincident with the divine law
above mentioned.  But yet, whatever is pretended, this is visible,

that these names, "virtue" and "vice," in the particular instances
of their application, through the several nations and societies of
men in the world, are constantly attributed only to such actions
as in each country and society are in reputation or discredit.
Nor is it to be thought strange, that men everywhere should
give the name of "virtue" to those actions which amongst them
are judged praiseworthy; and call that "vice," which they
account blameable; since otherwise they would condemn themselves, if they should think anything right, to which they allowed
not condemnation; anything wrong, which they let pass without
blame. Thus the measure of what is everywhere called and
esteemed "virtue" and "vice," is this approbation or dislike,
praise or blame, which, by a secret and tacit consent establishes
itself in the several societies, tribes, and clubs of men in the
world, whereby several actions come to find credit or disgrace
amongst them, according to the judgment, maxims, or fashions
of that place. For though men uniting into politic societies have
resigned up to the public the disposing of all their force, so
that they cannot employ it against any fellow-citizen any farther
than the law of the country directs; yet they retain still the
power of thinking well or ill, approving or disapproving, of the
actions of those whom they live amongst, and converse with; and
by this approbation and dislike, they establish amongst themselves what they will call "virtue" and "vice."

11. That this is the common measure of virtue and vice, will
appear to anyone who considers, that though that passes for vice
in one country which is counted a virtue, or at least not vice, in
another; yet everywhere virtue and praise, vice and blame, go
together. Virtue is everywhere that which is thought praiseworthy; and nothing else but that which has the allowance of
public esteem is called "virtue."* Virtue and praise are so
united, that they are called often by the same name. *Sunt sua
præmia laudi*, says Virgil; and so Cicero, *Nihil habet natura
præstantius quàm honestatem, quàm laudem, quàm dignitatem,
quàm decus;* which, he tells you, are all names for the same
thing. (*Tusc.* lib. 2.) This is the language of the heathen philosophers, who well understood wherein their notions of virtue
and vice consisted. And though, perhaps, by the different
temper, education, fashion, maxims, or interest of different sorts
of men, it fell out, that what was thought praiseworthy in one
place escaped not censure in another; and so in different societies
virtues and vices were changed: yet, as to the main, they for
the most part kept the same everywhere. For since nothing
can be more natural than to encourage with esteem and reputation that wherein everyone finds his advantage, and to blame
and discountenance the contrary, it is no wonder that esteem and
discredit, virtue and vice, should in a great measure everywhere

* See note at the end of this chapter.—EDIT.

correspond with the unchangeable rule of right and wrong which
the law of God hath established : there being nothing that so
directly and visibly secures and advances the general good of
mankind in this world, as obedience to the laws he has set them,
and nothing that breeds such mischiefs and confusion as the
neglect of them.  And therefore men, without renouncing all
sense and reason, and their own interest, which they are so constantly true to, could not generally mistake in placing their commendation and blame on that side that really deserved it not.
Nay, even those men whose practice was otherwise, failed not to
give their approbation right, few being depraved to that degree
as not to condemn, at least in others, the faults they themselves
were guilty of : whereby, even in the corruption of manners, the
true boundaries of the law of nature, which ought to be the rule
of virtue and vice, were pretty well preserved.  So that even
the exhortations of inspired teachers have not feared to appeal
to common repute : " Whatsoever is lovely, whatsoever is of
good report, if there be any virtue, if there be any praise," &c.
(Phil. iv. 8).

12. *Its enforcements, commendation, and discredit.*—If anyone
shall imagine that I have forgot my own notion of a law, when I
make the law whereby men judge of virtue and vice to be nothing
else but the consent of private men who have not authority
enough to make a law; especially wanting that which is so
necessary and essential to a law, a power to enforce it : I think
I may say, that he who imagines commendation and disgrace not
to be strong motives on men to accommodate themselves to the
opinions and rules of those with whom they converse, seems
little skilled in the nature or history of mankind : the greatest
part whereof he shall find to govern themselves chiefly, if not
solely, by this law of fashion; and, so they do that which keeps
them in reputation with their company, little regard the laws of
God or the magistrate.  The penalties that attend the breach of
God's laws, some, nay, perhaps most, men seldom seriously reflect
on ; and amongst those that do, many, whilst they break the
law, entertain thoughts of future reconciliation, and making
their peace for such breaches : and as to the punishments due
from the laws of the commonwealth, they frequently flatter themselves with the hope of impunity.  But no man escapes the
punishment of their censure and dislike who offends against the
fashion and opinion of the company he keeps, and would recommend himself to.  Nor is there one of ten thousand who is stiff
and insensible enough to bear up under the constant dislike and
condemnation of his own club.  He must be of a strange and
unusual constitution who can content himself to live in constant
disgrace and disrepute with his own particular society.  Solitude
many men have sought, and been reconciled to : but nobody that
has the least thought or sense of a man about him, can live in

society under the constant dislike and ill opinion of his familiars, and those he converses with. This is a burden too heavy for human sufferance: and he must be made up of irreconcilable contradictions, who can take pleasure in company, and yet be insensible of contempt and disgrace from his companions.

13. *These three laws the rules of moral good and evil.*—These three, then, First, The law of God, Secondly, The law of politic societies, Thirdly, The law of fashion, or private censure—are those to which men variously compare their actions: and it is by their conformity to one of these laws that they take their measures, when they would judge of their moral rectitude, and denominate their actions good or bad.

14. *Morality is the relation of actions to these rules.*— Whether the rule to which, as to a touchstone, we bring our voluntary actions to examine them by, and try their goodness, and accordingly to name them; which is, as it were, the mark of the value we set upon them: whether, I say, we take that rule from the fashion of the country, or the will of a law-maker, the mind is easily able to observe the relation any action hath to it, and to judge whether the action agrees or disagrees with the rule; and so hath a notion of moral goodness or evil, which is either conformity or not conformity of any action to that rule: and therefore is often called "moral rectitude." This rule being nothing but a collection of several simple ideas, the conformity thereto is but so ordering the action that the simple ideas belonging to it may correspond to those which the law requires. And thus we see how moral beings and notions are founded on, and terminated in, these simple ideas we have received from sensation or reflection. For example, let us consider the complex idea we signify by the word "murder;" and when we have taken it asunder, and examined all the particulars, we shall find them to amount to a collection of simple ideas derived from reflection or sensation, viz., First, From reflection on the operations of our own minds, we have the ideas of willing, considering, purposing beforehand malice, or wishing ill to another; and also of life, or perception, and self-motion. Secondly, From sensation, we have the collection of those simple sensible ideas which are to be found in a man, and of some action whereby we put an end to perception and motion in the man; all which simple ideas are comprehended in the word "murder." This collection of simple ideas being found by me to agree or disagree with the esteem of the country I have been bred in, and to be held by most men there worthy praise or blame, I call the action "virtuous" or "vicious": if I have the will of a supreme, invisible law-maker for my rule, then, as I suppose the action commanded or forbidden by God, I call it "good" or "evil," "sin" or "duty": and if I compare it to the civil law, the rule made by the legislative power of the country, I call it "lawful" or "unlawful," a "crime" or "no

crime." So that whencesoever we take the rule of moral actions,
or by what standard soever we frame in our minds the ideas of
virtues or vices, they consist only and are made up of collections
of simple ideas which we originally received from sense or reflection, and their rectitude or obliquity consists in the agreement or
disagreement with those patterns prescribed by some law.

15. To conceive rightly of moral actions, we must take notice
of them under this twofold consideration. First, As they are in
themselves each made up of such a collection of simple ideas.
Thus "drunkenness" or "lying" signify such or such a collection of simple ideas, which I call "mixed modes:" and in this
sense they are as much positive absolute ideas, as the drinking
of a horse, or speaking of a parrot. Secondly, Our actions are
considered as good, bad, or indifferent; and in this respect they
are relative, it being their conformity to, or disagreement with,
some rule that makes them to be regular or irregular, good or bad:
and so, as far as they are compared with a rule, and thereupon
denominated, they come under "relation." Thus the challenging
and fighting with a man, as it is a certain positive mode, or particular sort of action, by particular ideas distinguished from all
others, is called "duelling:" which, when considered in relation
to the law of God, will deserve the name "sin;" to the law of
fashion, in some countries, "valour and virtue;" and to the
municipal laws of some governments, "a capital crime." In this
case, when the positive mode has one name, and another name
as it stands in relation to the law, the distinction may as easily
be observed as it is in substances, where one name, *v. g.*, "man,"
is used to signify the thing, another, *v. g.*, "father," to signify
the relation.

16. *The denominations of actions often mislead us.*—But
because very frequently the positive idea of the action, and its
moral relation are comprehended together under one name, and
the same word made use of to express both the mode or action,
and its moral rectitude or obliquity, therefore the relation itself
is less taken notice of; and there is often no distinction made
between the positive idea of the action, and the reference it has to
a rule. By which confusion of these two distinct considerations
under one term, those who yield too easily to the impressions of
sounds, and are forward to take names for things, are often misled
in their judgment of actions. Thus the taking from another
what is his, without his knowledge or allowance, is properly
called "stealing:" but that name being commonly understood
to signify also the moral pravity of the action, and to denote its
contrariety to the law, men are apt to condemn whatever they
hear called "stealing" as an ill action, disagreeing with the rule
of right. And yet the private taking away his sword from a
madman, to prevent his doing mischief, though it be properly
denominated "stealing," as the name of such a mixed mode, yet

when compared to the law of God, and considered in its relation to that supreme rule, it is no sin or transgression, though the name " stealing " ordinarily carries such an intimation with it.

17. *Relations innumerable.*—And thus much for the relation of human actions to a law, which therefore I call "moral relations."

It would make a volume to go over all sorts of relations : it is therefore not to be expected that I should here mention them all. It suffices to our present purpose to show by these what the ideas are we have of this comprehensive consideration called " relation :" which is so various, and the occasions of it so many, (as many as there can be of comparing things one to another,) that it is not very easy to reduce it to rules, or under just heads. Those I have mentioned, I think, are some of the most consider-able, and such as may serve to let us see from whence we get our ideas of relations, and wherein they are founded. But before I quit this argument, from what has been said, give me leave to observe.

18. *All relations terminate in simple ideas.*—First, That it is evident that all relation terminates in, and is ultimately founded on, those simple ideas we have got from sensation or reflection : so that all that we have in our thoughts ourselves, (if we think of anything, or have any meaning), or would signify to others, when we use words standing for relations, is nothing but some simple ideas, or collections of simple ideas, compared one with another. This is so manifest in that sort called " proportional," that nothing can be more. For when a man says, " Honey is sweeter than wax," it is plain that his thoughts in this relation terminate in this simple idea, " sweetness," which is equally true of all the rest ; though, where they are compounded or decompounded, the simple ideas they are made up of are perhaps seldom taken notice of. *V. g.* when the word " father " is mentioned : First, There is meant that particular species, or collective idea, signified by the word " man :" Secondly, Those sensible simple ideas signified by the word " generation :" and, Thirdly, The effects of it, and all the simple ideas signified by the word " child." So the word "friend," being taken for a man who loves, and is ready to do good to, another, has all these following ideas to the making of it up. First, All the simple ideas comprehended in the word " man " or " intelligent being." Secondly, The idea of " love." Thirdly, The idea of " readiness " or " disposition." Fourthly, The idea of " action," which is any kind of thought or motion. Fifthly, The idea of " good," which signifies anything that may advance his happiness ; and terminates at last, if examined, in particular simple ideas, of which the word " good " in general signifies any-one, but, if removed from all simple ideas quite, it signifies nothing at all. And thus also all moral words terminate at last, though perhaps more remotely, in a collection of simple ideas : the immediate signification of relative words being very often

other supposed known relations; which, if traced one to another, still end in simple ideas.

19. *We have ordinarily as clear (or clearer) a notion of the relation, as of its foundation.*—Secondly, That in relations, we have for the most part, if not always, as clear a notion of the relation, as we have of those simple ideas wherein it is founded : agreement or disagreement, whereon relation depends, being things whereof we have commonly as clear ideas as of any other whatsoever ; it being but the distinguishing simple ideas or their degrees one from another, without which we could have no distinct knowledge at all.   For if I have a clear idea of sweetness, light, or extension, I have, too, of equal, or more, or less, of each of these : if I know what it is for one man to be born of a woman, viz., Sempronia, I know what it is for another man to be born of the same woman, Sempronia ; and so have as clear a notion of brothers as of births, and perhaps clearer. For if I believed that Sempronia digged Titus out of the parsley-bed (as they use to tell children), and thereby became his mother ; and that afterwards in the same manner, she digged Caius out of the parsley-bed ; I had as clear a notion of the relation of brothers between them, as if I had all the skill of a midwife ; the notion that the same woman contributed, as mother, equally to their births (though I were ignorant or mistaken, in the manner of it), being that on which I grounded the relation ; and that they agreed in that circumstance of birth, let it be what it will.   The comparing them, then, in their descent from the same person, without knowing the particular circumstances of that descent, is enough to found my notion of their having or not having the relation of brothers. But though the ideas of particular relations are capable of being as clear and distinct in the minds of those who will duly consider them as those of mixed modes, and more determinate than those of substances ; yet the names belonging to relation are often of as doubtful and uncertain signification, as those of substances or mixed modes ; and much more than those of simple ideas. Because relative words being the marks of this comparison, which is made only by men's thoughts, and is an idea only in men's minds, men frequently apply them to different comparisons of things according to their own imaginations, which do not always correspond with those of others using the same names.

20. *The notion of the relation is the same, whether the rule any action is compared to, be true or false.*—Thirdly, That in these I call " moral relations," I have a true notion of relation, by comparing the action with the rule, whether the rule be true or false. For, if I measure anything by a yard, I know whether the thing I measure be longer or shorter than that supposed yard, though, perhaps, the yard I measure by be not exactly the standard ; which, indeed, is another inquiry.   For though the rule be erroneous, and I mistaken in it, yet the agreement or disagree-

ment observable in that which I compare with it makes me perceive the relation. Though measuring by a wrong rule, I shall thereby be brought to judge amiss of its moral rectitude, because I have tried it by that which is not the true rule; but I am not mistaken in the relation which that action bears to that rule I compare it to, which is agreement or disagreement.

## NOTE.—Page 281.

Our author, in his preface to the fourth edition, taking notice how apt men have been to mistake him, added what here follows : "Of this the ingenious author of the 'Discourse concerning the Nature of Man' has given me a late instance, to mention no other. For the civility of his expressions and the candour that belongs to his order forbid me to think that he would have closed his preface with an insinuation, as if, in what I had said, book ii. chap. xxviii., concerning the third rule which men refer their actions to, I went about to make virtue vice and vice virtue, unless he had mistaken my meaning ; which he could not have done, if he had but given himself the trouble to consider what the argument was I was then upon, and what was the chief design of that chapter, plainly enough set down in the fourth section and those following. For I was there not laying down moral rules, but showing the original and nature of moral ideas, and enumerating the rules men make use of in moral relations, whether those rules were true or false ; and, pursuant thereunto, I tell what has everywhere that denomination which, in the language of that place, answers to virtue and vice in ours, which alters not the nature of things, though men generally do judge of and denominate their actions according to the esteem and fashion of the place or sect they are of.

"If he had been at the pains to reflect on what I had said, book i. chap. iii. sect. 18, and in this present chapter, sect. 13—15 and 20, he would have known what I think of the eternal and unalterable nature of right and wrong, and what I call virtue and vice ; and if he had observed that in the place he quotes I only report as matter of fact what others call virtue and vice, he would not have found it liable to any great exception. For I think I am not much out in saying, that one of the rules made use of in the world for a ground or measure of a moral relation is that esteem and reputation which several sorts of actions find variously in the several societies of men, according to which they are there called 'virtues' or 'vices:' and whatever authority the learned Mr. Lowde places in his 'Old English Dictionary,' I dare say it nowhere tells him (if I should appeal to it) that the same action is not in credit called and counted a virtue in one place, which, being in disrepute, passes for and under the name of 'vice' in another. The taking notice that men bestow the names of 'virtue' and 'vice' according to this rule of reputation, is all I have done or can be laid to my charge to have done towards the making vice virtue and virtue vice. But the good man does well, and as becomes his calling, to be watchful in such points, and to take the alarm even at expressions which, standing alone by themselves, might sound ill and be suspected.

"It is to this zeal, allowable in his function, that I forgive his citing, as he does, these words of mine in sect. 11 of this chapter : 'The exhortations of inspired teachers have not feared to appeal to common repute, *Whatsoever things are lovely, whatsoever things are of good report, if there be any virtue, if there be any praise,* &c. (Phil. iv. 8),' without taking notice of those immediately preceding, which introduce them and run thus : ' Whereby in the corruption of manners the true boundaries of the law of nature, which ought to be the rule of virtue and vice, were pretty well preserved, so that even the exhortations of inspired teachers,' &c.; by which words, and the rest of that section, it is plain that I brought that passage of St. Paul not to prove that the general measure of what men call ' virtue' and ' vice' throughout the world, was the reputation and fashion of each particular society within itself ; but to show that though it were so, yet, for reasons I there give, men, in that way of denominating their actions, did not for the most part, much vary from the law of nature, which is that standing and unalterable rule by which they ought to judge of the moral rectitude and pravity of their actions, and accordingly denominate them 'virtues' or ' vices.'   Had Mr. Lowde considered this, he would have found it little to his purpose to have quoted that passage in a sense I used it not ; and would, I imagine, have spared the explication he subjoins to it, as not very necessary.   But I hope this second edition will give him satisfaction in the point, and that this matter is now so expressed as to show him there was no cause of scruple.

"Though I am forced to differ from him in those apprehensions he has expressed in the latter end of his preface, concerning what I had said about virtue and vice, yet we are better agreed than he thinks, in what he says in his third chapter, p. 78, concerning natural inscription and innate notions.   I shall not deny him the privilege he claims, p. 52, to state the question as he pleases, especially when he states it so as to leave nothing in it contrary to what I have said ; for according to him, innate notions being conditional things, depending upon the concurrence of several other circumstances, in order to the soul's exerting them, all that he says for innate, imprinted, impressed notions (for of innate ideas he says nothing at all), amounts at last only to this, that there are certain propositions which, though the soul from the beginning, or when a man is born, does not know, yet by assistance from the outward senses, and the help of some previous cultivation, it may afterwards come certainly to know the truth of ; which is no more than what I have affirmed in my first book.   For I suppose, by the soul's exerting them, he means its beginning to know them, or else the soul's exerting of notions will be to me a very unintelligible expression ; and I think at best is a very unfit one in this case, it misleading men's thoughts by an insinuation, as if these notions were in the mind before the soul exerts them, *i.e.*, before they are known ; whereas truly before they are known there is nothing of them in the mind but a capacity to know them, when the concurrence of those circumstances, which this ingenious author thinks necessary, in order to the soul's exerting them, brings them into our knowledge.

"P. 52, I find him express it thus : 'These natural notions are not so imprinted upon the soul as that they naturally and necessarily exert themselves (even in children and idiots) without any assistance

from the outward senses, or without the help of some previous cultivation.' Here he says, they exert themselves, as, p. 78, that the soul
exerts them. When he has explained to himself or others what he
means by the soul's exerting innate notions, or their exerting themselves, and what that previous cultivation and circumstances in order
to their being exerted are, he will, I suppose, find there is so little of
controversy between him and me in the point, bating that he calls that
'exerting of notions,' which I, in a more vulgar style, call 'knowing,'
that I have reason to think he brought in my name upon this occasion
only out of the pleasure he has to speak civilly of me, which I must
gratefully acknowledge he has done everywhere he mentions me, not
without conferring on me, as some others have done, a title I have no
right to."

## CHAPTER XXIX.

### OF CLEAR AND OBSCURE, DISTINCT AND CONFUSED IDEAS.

1. *Ideas, some clear and distinct, others obscure and confused.*
—Having shown the original of our ideas, and taken a view of
their several sorts; considered the difference between the simple
and the complex, and observed how the complex ones are divided
into those of modes, substances, and relations; all which, I think,
is necessary to be done by anyone who would acquaint himself
thoroughly with the progress of the mind in its apprehension and
knowledge of things; it will, perhaps, be thought I have dwelt
long enough upon the examination of ideas. I must, nevertheless, crave leave to offer some few other considerations concerning them. The first is, that some are clear, and others
obscure; some distinct, and others confused.

2. *"Clear" and "obscure" explained by sight.*—The perception of the mind being most aptly explained by words relating to
the sight, we shall best understand what is meant by "clear" and
"obscure" in our ideas, by reflecting on what we call "clear"
and "obscure" in the objects of sight. Light being that which
discovers to us visible objects, we give the name of "obscure" to
that which is not placed in a light sufficient to discover minutely
to us the figure and colours which are observable in it, and
which in a better light would be discernible. In like manner
our simple ideas are clear, when they are such as the objects
themselves, from whence they were taken, did or might, in a
well-ordered sensation or perception, present them. Whilst the
memory retains them thus, and can produce them to the mind
whenever it has occasion to consider them, they are clear ideas.
So far as they either want anything of that original exactness,
or have lost any of their first freshness, and are, as it were, faded
or tarnished by time, so far are they obscure. Complex ideas, as
they are made up of simple ones, so they are clear when the

deas that go to their composition are clear; and the number and order of those simple ideas, that are the ingredients of any complex one, is determinate and certain.

3. *Causes of obscurity.*—The cause of obscurity in simple ideas seems to be either dull organs, or very slight and transient impressions made by the objects, or else a weakness in the memory, not able to retain them as received. For to return again to visible objects, to help us to apprehend this matter: if the organs or faculties of perception, like wax over-hardened with cold, will not receive the impression of the seal, from the usual impulse wont to imprint it; or, like wax of a temper too soft, will not hold it well when well imprinted; or else supposing the wax of a temper fit, but the seal not applied with a sufficient force to make a clear impression: in any of these cases, the print left by the seal will be obscure. This, I suppose, needs no application to make it plainer.

4. *Distinct and confused, what.*—As a clear idea is that whereof the mind has such a full and evident perception as it does receive from an outward object operating duly on a well-disposed organ, so a distinct idea is that wherein the mind perceives a difference from all other, and a confused idea is such an one as is not sufficiently distinguishable from another from which it ought to be different.

5. *Objection.*—"If no idea be confused but such as is not sufficiently distinguishable from another from which it should be different, it will be hard," may anyone say, "to find anywhere a confused idea. For, let any idea be as it will, it can be no other but such as the mind perceives it to be; and that very perception sufficiently distinguishes it from all other ideas, which cannot be other, *i.e.*, different, without being perceived to be so. No idea, therefore, can be undistinguishable from another from which it ought to be different, unless you would have it different from itself: for from all other it is evidently different."

6. *Confusion of ideas is in reference to their names.*—To remove this difficulty, and to help us to conceive aright what it is that makes the confusion ideas are at any time chargeable with, we must consider that things ranked under distinct names are supposed different enough to be distinguished, that so each sort, by its peculiar name, may be marked, and discoursed of apart upon any occasion: and there is nothing more evident than that the greatest part of different names are supposed to stand for different things. Now, every idea a man has being visibly what it is, and distinct from all other ideas but itself, that which makes it confused is, when it is such that it may as well be called by another name as that which it is expressed by, the difference which keeps the things (to be ranked under those two different names) distinct, and makes some of them belong rather to the one, and some of them to the other, of those names, being left

out; and so the distinction, which was intended to be kept up by those different names, is quite lost.

*7. Defaults which make confusion.*—The defaults which usually occasion this confusion, I think, are chiefly these following:—

*First, Complex ideas made up of too few simple ones.*—First, When any complex idea (for it is complex ideas that are most liable to confusion) is made up of too small a number of simple ideas, and such only as are common to other things, whereby the differences that make it deserve a different name are left out. Thus he that has an idea made up of barely the simple ones of a beast with spots, has but a confused idea of a leopard, it not being thereby sufficiently distinguished from a lynx, and several other sorts of beasts that are spotted. So that such an idea, though it hath the peculiar name "leopard," is not distinguishable from those designed by the names "lynx," or "panther," and may as well come under the name "lynx" as "leopard." How much the custom of defining of words by general terms contributes to make the ideas we would express by them confused and undetermined, I leave others to consider. This is evident, that confused ideas are such as render the use of words uncertain, and take away the benefit of distinct names. When the ideas for which we use different terms have not a difference answerable to their distinct names, and so cannot be distinguished by them, there it is that they are truly confused.

8. *Secondly, Or its simple ones jumbled disorderly together.* —Secondly, Another default which makes our ideas confused is, when though the particulars that made up any idea are in number enough, yet they are so jumbled together that it is not easily discernible whether it more belongs to the name that is given it than to any other. There is nothing properer to make us conceive this confusion than a sort of pictures usually shown, as surprising pieces of art, wherein the colours, as they are laid by the pencil on the table itself, mark out very odd and unusual figures, and have no discernible order in their position. This draught, thus made up of parts wherein no symmetry nor order appears, is, in itself, no more a confused thing than the picture of a cloudy sky, wherein though there be as little order of colours or figures to be found, yet nobody thinks it is a confused picture. What is it then that makes it to be thought confused, since the want of symmetry does not? as it is plain it does not; for another draught made barely in imitation of this could not be called confused. I answer, That which makes it to be thought confused is, the applying it to some name to which it does no more discernibly belong than to some other. *V. g.*, when it is said to be the picture of a man, or Cæsar, then anyone with reason counts it confused: because it is not discernible, in that state, to belong more to the name "man," or "Cæsar," than to the name "baboon," or "Pompey," which are supposed to stand for different ideas from

those signified by "man," or "Cæsar." But when a cylindrical mirror, placed right, hath reduced those irregular lines on the table into their due order and proportion, then the confusion ceases, and the eye presently sees that it is a man, or Cæsar; *i.e.*, that it belongs to those names, and that it is sufficiently distinguishable from a baboon, or Pompey; *i.e.*, from the ideas signified by those names. Just thus it is with our ideas, which are, as it were, the pictures of things. No one of these mental draughts, however the parts are put together, can be called confused, (for they are plainly discernible as they are,) till it be ranked under some ordinary name, to which it cannot be discerned to belong, any more than it does to some other name of an allowed different signification.

9. *Thirdly, Or are mutable and determined.*—Thirdly, A third defect that frequently gives the name of "confused," to our ideas is, when any one of them is uncertain and undetermined. Thus we may observe men who, not forbearing to use the ordinary words of their language till they have learned their precise signification, change the idea they make this or that term stand for, almost as often as they use it. He that does this, out of uncertainty of what he should leave out or put into his idea of " church," or "idolatry," every time he thinks of either, and holds not steady to any one precise combination of ideas that makes it up, is said to have a confused idea of idolatry or the church : though this be still for the same reason that the former, viz., because a mutable idea (if we will allow it to be one idea) cannot belong to one name rather than another, and so loses the distinction that distinct names are designed for.

10. *Confusion without reference to names hardly conceivable.*— By what has been said, we may observe how much names, as supposed steady signs of things, and by their difference to stand for and keep things distinct that in themselves are different, are the occasion of denominating ideas distinct or confused, by a secret and unobserved reference the mind makes of its ideas to such names. This, perhaps, will be fuller understood after what I say of words, in the third book, has been read and considered. But without taking notice of such a reference of ideas to distinct names, as the signs of distinct things, it will be hard to say what a confused idea is. And therefore when a man designs by any name, a sort of things, or any one particular thing, distinct from all others, the complex idea he annexes to that name is the more distinct, the more particular the ideas are, and the greater and more determinate the number and order of them is whereof it is made up. For the more it has of these, the more has it still of the perceivable differences whereby it is kept separate and distinct from all ideas belonging to other names, even those that approach nearest to it, and thereby all confusion with them is avoided.

**11.** *Confusion concerns always two ideas.*—Confusion, making it a difficulty to separate two things that should be separated, concerns always two ideas; and those most which most approach one another. Whenever therefore we suspect any idea to be confused, we must examine what other it is in danger to be confounded with, or which it cannot easily be separated from; and that will always be found an idea belonging to another name, and so should be a different thing, from which yet it is not sufficiently distinct; being either the same with it, or making a part of it, or, at least, as properly called by that name as the other it is ranked under; and so keeps not that difference from that other idea, which the different names import.

**12.** *Causes of confusion.*—This, I think, is the confusion proper to ideas, which still carries with it a secret reference to names. At least, if there be any other confusion of ideas this is that which most of all disorders men's thoughts and discourses: ideas, as ranked under names, being those that for the most part men reason of within themselves, and always those which they commune about with others. And therefore where there are supposed two different ideas, marked by two different names, which are not as distinguishable as the sounds that stand for them, there never fails to be confusion; and where any ideas are distinct, as the ideas of those two sounds they are marked by, there can be between them no confusion. The way to prevent it is to collect and unite into one complex idea, as precisely as is possible, all those ingredients whereby it is differenced from others; and to them so united in a determinate number and order, apply steadily the same name. But this neither accommodating men's ease or vanity, or serving any design but that of naked truth, which is not always the thing aimed at, such exactness is rather to be wished than hoped for. And since the loose application of names to undetermined, variable, and almost no ideas serves both to cover our own ignorance, as well as to perplex and confound others, which goes for learning and superiority in knowledge, it is no wonder that most men should use it themselves whilst they complain of it in others. Though, I think, no small part of the confusion to be found in the notions of men might, by care and ingenuity, be avoided; yet I am far from concluding it everywhere wilful. Some ideas are so complex, and made up of so many parts, that the memory does not easily retain the very same precise combination of simple ideas under one name; much less are we able constantly to divine for what precise complex idea such a name stands in another man's use of it. From the first of these follows confusion in a man's own reasonings and opinions within himself; from the latter frequent confusion in discoursing and arguing with others. But having more at large treated of words, their defects and abuses, in the following book, I shall here say no more of it.

**13.** *Complex ideas may be distinct in one part and confused in another.*—Our complex ideas being made up of collections (and so variety) of simple ones, may accordingly be very clear and distinct in one part, and very obscure and confused in another. In a man who speaks of a chiliaedron, or a body of a thousand sides, the idea of the figure may be very confused, though that of the number be very distinct: so that he being able to discourse and demonstrate concerning that part of his complex idea which depends upon the number of a thousand, he is apt to think he has a distinct idea of a chiliaedron; though it be plain he has no precise idea of its figure, so as to distinguish it by that from one that has but nine hundred and ninety-nine sides; the not observing whereof, causes no small error in men's thoughts, and confusion in their discourses.

**14.** *This, if not heeded, causes confusion in our arguings.*—He that thinks he has a distinct idea of the figure of a chiliaedron, let him for trial's sake take another parcel of the same uniform matter, viz., gold or wax, of an equal bulk, and make it into a figure of nine hundred and ninety-nine sides: he will, I doubt not, be able to distinguish these two ideas one from another, by the number of sides; and reason and argue distinctly about them, whilst he keeps his thoughts and reasoning to that part only of these ideas which is contained in their numbers; as that the sides of the one could be divided into two equal numbers; and of the other, not, &c. But when he goes about to distinguish them by their figure, he will there be presently at a loss, and not be able, I think, to frame in his mind two ideas, one of them distinct from the other, by the bare figure of these two pieces of gold; as he could, if the same parcel of gold were made one into a cube, the other a figure of five sides. In which incomplete ideas, we are very apt to impose on ourselves, and wrangle with others, especially where they have particular and familiar names. For being satisfied in that part of the idea which we have clear, and the name which is familiar to us being applied to the whole, containing that part also which is imperfect and obscure, we are apt to use it for that confused part, and draw deductions from it in the obscure part of its signification, as confidently as we do from the other.

**15.** *Instance in eternity.*—Having frequently in our mouths the name "eternity," we are apt to think we have a positive comprehensive idea of it; which is as much as to say, that there is no part of that duration which is not clearly contained in our idea. It is true, that he that thinks so may have a clear idea of duration; he may also have a very clear idea of a very great length of duration; he may also have a clear idea of the comparison of that great one with still a greater: but it not being possible for him to include in his idea of any duration, let it be as great as it will, the whole extent together of a duration where he supposes no end, that part of his idea, which is still beyond the bounds of that large duration he represents to his own thoughts, is very obscure and undetermined. And hence it is that in disputes and reasonings concerning eternity, or any other infinite, we are apt to blunder and involve ourselves in manifest absurdities.

16. *Divisibility of matter.*—In matter, we have no clear ideas of the smallness of parts much beyond the smallest that occur to any of our senses; and therefore when we talk of the divisibility of matter *in infinitum*, though we have clear ideas of division and divisibility, and have also clear ideas of parts made out of a whole by division: yet we have but very obscure and confused ideas of corpuscles, or minute bodies, so to be divided, when by former divisions they are reduced to a smallness much exceeding the perception of any of our senses; and so all that we have clear and distinct ideas of, is of what division in general or abstractly is, and the relation of *totum* and *pars* : but of the bulk of the body, to be thus infinitely divided after certain progressions, I think we have no clear nor distinct idea at all. For I ask anyone, whether taking the smallest atom of dust he ever saw, he has any distinct idea (bating still the number, which concerns not extension) betwixt the 100,000th and the 1,000,000th part of it? Or if he thinks he can refine his ideas to that degree without losing sight of them, let him add ten cyphers to each of those numbers. Such a degree of smallness is not unreasonable to be supposed, since a division carried on so far brings it no nearer the end of infinite division than the first division into two halves does. I must confess, for my part, I have no clear distinct ideas of the different bulk or extension of those bodies, having but a very obscure one of either of them. So that, I think, when we talk of division of bodies *in infinitum*, our idea of their distinct bulks, which is the subject and foundation of division, comes, after a little progression, to be confounded, and almost lost in obscurity. For that idea which is to represent only bigness, must be very obscure and confused, which we cannot distinguish from one ten times as big but only by number; so that we have clear, distinct ideas, we may say, of ten and one, but no distinct ideas of two such extensions. It is plain from hence, that when we talk of infinite divisibility of body or extension, our distinct and clear ideas are only of numbers : but the clear, distinct ideas of extension, after some progress of division, are quite lost; and of such minute parts we have no distinct ideas at all; but it returns, as all our ideas of infinite do, at last to that of number always to be added: but thereby never amounts to any distinct idea of actual, infinite parts. We have, it is true, a clear idea of division, as often as we will think of it; but thereby we have no more a clear idea of infinite parts in matter, than we have a clear idea of an infinite number, by being able still to add new numbers to any assigned number we have: endless divisibility giving us no more a clear

and distinct idea of actually infinite parts, than endless addibility (if I may so speak) gives us a clear and distinct idea of an actually infinite number; they both being only in a power still of increasing the number, be it already as great as it will. So that of what remains to be added (wherein consists the infinity), we have but an obscure, imperfect, and confused idea; from or about which we can argue or reason with no certainty or clearness, no more than we can in arithmetic, about a number of which we have no such distinct idea as we have of 4 or 100; but only this relative obscure one, that, compared to any other, it is still bigger: and we have no more a clear, positive idea of it, when we say or conceive it is bigger or more than 400,000,000, than if we should say it is bigger than 40 or 4; 400,000,000 having no nearer a proportion to the end of addition or number, than 4. For he that adds only 4 to 4, and so proceeds, shall as soon come to the end of all addition, as he that adds 400,000,000 to 400,000,000. And so likewise in eternity, he that has an idea of but four years, has as much a positive complete idea of eternity, as he that has one of 400,000,000 of years; for what remains of eternity beyond either of these two numbers of years, is as clear to the one as the other; *i.e.*, neither of them has any clear, positive idea of it at all. For he that adds only 4 years to 4, and so on, shall as soon reach eternity, as he that adds 400,000,000 of years, and so on; or, if he please, doubles the increase as often as he will; the remaining abyss being still as far beyond the end of all these progressions, as it is from the length of a day or an hour. For nothing finite bears any proportion to infinite; and therefore our ideas, which are all finite, cannot bear any. Thus it is also in our idea of extension, when we increase it by addition, as well as when we diminish it by division, and would enlarge our thoughts to infinite space. After a few doublings of those ideas of extension, which are the largest we are accustomed to have, we lose the clear distinct idea of that space: it becomes a confusedly great one, with a surplus of still greater; about which when we would argue or reason, we shall always find ourselves at a loss: confused ideas in our arguings and deductions from that part of them which is confused always leading us into confusion.

## CHAPTER XXX.

### OF REAL AND FANTASTICAL IDEAS.

1. *Real ideas are conformable to their archetypes.*—Besides what we have already mentioned concerning ideas, other considerations belong to them, in reference to things from whence they are taken, or which they may be supposed to represent; and thus, I think, they may come under a threefold distinction; and are,

First, Either real or fantastical.

Secondly, Adequate or inadequate.

Thirdly, True or false.

First, By "real ideas," I mean such as have a foundation in nature; such as have a conformity with the real being and existence of things, or with their archetypes. "Fantastical or chimerical," I call such as have no foundation in nature, nor have any conformity with that reality of being to which they are tacitly referred as to their archetypes. If we examine the several sorts of ideas before mentioned, we shall find, that,

2. *Simple ideas all real.*—First, Our simple ideas are all real, all agree to the reality of things. Not that they are all of them the images or representations of what does exist; the contrary whereof, in all but the primary qualities of bodies, hath been already showed. But though whiteness and coldness are no more in snow than pain is; yet those ideas of whiteness and coldness, pain, &c., being in us the effects of powers in things without us, ordained by our Maker to produce in us such sensations, they are real ideas in us, whereby we distinguish the qualities that are really in things themselves. For these several appearances being designed to be the marks whereby we are to know and distinguish things which we have to do with, our ideas do as well serve us to that purpose, and are as real distinguishing characters, whether they be only constant effects or else exact resemblances of something in the things themselves: the reality lying in that steady correspondence they have with the distinct constitutions of real beings. But whether they answer to those constitutions, as to causes or patterns, it matters not; it suffices that they are constantly produced by them. And thus our simple ideas are all real and true, because they answer and agree to those powers of things which produce them in our minds, that being all that is requisite to make them real, and not fictions at pleasure. For in simple ideas (as has been shown), the mind is wholly confined to the operation of things upon it, and can make to itself no simple idea, more than what it has received.

3. *Complex ideas are voluntary combinations.*—Though the mind be wholly passive in respect of its simple ideas, yet, I think, we may say, it is not so in respect of its complex ideas: for, those being combinations of simple ideas put together, and united under one general name, it is plain that the mind of man uses some kind of liberty in forming those complex ideas: how else comes it to pass, that one man's idea of gold or justice is different from another's, but because he has put in or left out of his some simple idea which the other has not? The question then is, Which of these are real, and which barely imaginary, combinations? What collections agree to the reality of things, and what not? And to this, I say, that,

**4. *Mixed modes made of consistent ideas are real.*—**Secondly,
Mixed modes and relations having no other reality but what
they have in the minds of men, there is nothing more required
to those kinds of ideas to make them real but that they be so
framed that there be a possibility of existing conformable to
them.  These ideas, being themselves archetypes, cannot differ
from their archetypes, and so cannot be chimerical, unless anyone will jumble together in them inconsistent ideas.  Indeed, as
any of them have the names of a known language assigned to
them, by which he that has them in his mind would signify
them to others, so bare possibility of existing is not enough ;
they must have a conformity to the ordinary signification of the
name that is given them, that they may not be thought fantastical : as if a man would give the name of "justice" to that idea
which common use calls "liberality."  But this fantasticalness
relates more to propriety of speech, than reality of ideas.  For
a man to be undisturbed in danger, sedately to consider what
is fittest to be done, and to execute it steadily, is a mixed mode
or a complex idea of an action which may exist.  But to be
undisturbed in danger, without using one's reason or industry,
is what is also possible to be ; and so is as real an idea as the
other.  Though the first of these, having the name "courage"
given to it, may, in respect of that name, be a right or a wrong
idea : but the other, whilst it has not a common received name
of any known language assigned to it, is not capable of any
deformity,* being made with no reference to anything but
itself.

**5. *Ideas of substances are real when they agree with the exist-
ence of things.*—**Thirdly, Our complex ideas of substances, being
made all of them in reference to things existing without us, and
intended to be representations of substances as they really are,
are no farther real than as they are such combinations of simple
ideas as are really united, and co-exist in things without us.
On the contrary, those are fantastical which are made up of
such collections of simple ideas as were really never united,
never were found together in any substance ; *v. g.*, a rational
creature, consisting of a horse's head, joined to a body of human
shape, or such as the centaurs are described : or, a body yellow,
very malleable, fusible, and fixed, but lighter than common
water : or, an uniform, unorganized body, consisting as to sense,
all of similar parts, with perception and voluntary motion joined
to it.  Whether such substances as these can possibly exist or
no, it is probable we do not know : but be that as it will, these
ideas of substances being made conformable to no pattern existing that we know, and consisting of such collections of ideas as
no substance ever showed us united together, they ought to pass

* In more modern language, *difformity ;* in opposition to *conformity* and *conformable* in the early part of the paragraph.—EDIT.

with us for barely imaginary; but much more are those complex ideas so, which contain in them any inconsistency or contradiction of their parts.

---

## CHAPTER XXXI.

### OF ADEQUATE AND INADEQUATE IDEAS.

**1.** *Adequate ideas are such as perfectly represent their archetypes.* — Of our real ideas, some are adequate, and some are inadequate. Those I call "adequate" which perfectly represent those archetypes which the mind supposes them taken from; which it intends them to stand for, and to which it refers them. Inadequate ideas are such which are but a partial or incomplete representation of those archetypes to which they are referred. Upon which account it is plain,

**2.** *Simple ideas all adequate.*—First, That all our simple ideas are adequate. Because being nothing but the effects of certain powers in things, fitted and ordained by God to produce such sensations in us, they cannot but be correspondent and adequate to those powers: and we are sure they agree to the reality of things. For if sugar produce in us the ideas which we call "whiteness," and "sweetness," we are sure there is a power in sugar to produce those ideas in our minds, or else they could not have been produced by it. And so each sensation answering the power that operates on any of our senses, the idea so produced is a real idea (and not a fiction of the mind, which has no power to produce any simple idea), and cannot but be adequate, since it ought only to answer that power: and so all simple ideas are adequate. It is true, the things producing in us these simple ideas are but few of them denominated by us, as if they were only the causes of them; but as if those ideas were real beings in them. For though fire be called "painful to the touch," whereby is signified the power of producing in us the idea of pain; yet it is denominated also "light," and "hot;" as if light and heat were really something in the fire more than a power to excite these ideas in us; and therefore are called qualities in or of the fire. But these being nothing, in truth, but powers to excite such ideas in us, I must in that sense be understood when I speak of secondary qualities, as being in things; or of their ideas, as being in the objects that excite them in us: such ways of speaking, though accommodated to the vulgar notions, without which one cannot be well understood, yet truly signify nothing but those powers which are in things to excite certain sensations or ideas in us; since, wore there no fit organs to receive the impressions fire makes on the sight and touch, nor a mind joined to those organs to receive the ideas of light and

heat, by those impressions from the fire or the sun, there would
yet be no more light or heat in the world than there would be
pain if there were no sensible creature to feel it, though the sun
should continue just as it is now, and Mount Ætna flame higher
than ever it did. Solidity, and extension, and the termination
of it, figure, with motion and rest, whereof we have the ideas,
would be really in the world as they are, whether there were any
sensible being to perceive them or no; and therefore those we
have reason to look on as the real modifications of matter, and
such as are the exciting causes of all our various sensations from
bodies. But this being an inquiry not belonging to this place, I
shall enter no farther into it, but proceed to show what complex
ideas are adequate, and what not.

3. *Modes are all adequate.*—Secondly, Our complex ideas of
modes, being voluntary collections of simple ideas which the
mind puts together, without reference to any real archetypes or
standing patterns existing anywhere, are and cannot but be
adequate ideas. Because they, not being intended for copies of
things really existing, but for archetypes made by the mind to
rank and denominate things by, cannot want any thing; they
having each of them that combination of ideas, and thereby that
perfection, which the mind intended they should: so that the
mind acquiesces in them, and can find nothing wanting. Thus
by having the idea of a figure with three sides meeting at three
angles, I have a complete idea, wherein I require nothing else to
make it perfect. That the mind is satisfied with the perfection
of this its idea, is plain in that it does not conceive that any
understanding hath or can have a more complete or perfect idea
of that thing it signifies by the word "triangle," supposing it to
exist, than itself has in that complex idea of three sides and three
angles; in which is contained all that is or can be essential to it,
or necessary to complete it, wherever or however it exists. But
in our ideas of substances it is otherwise. For, there, desiring
to copy things as they really do exist, and to represent to ourselves that constitution on which all their properties depend, we
perceive our ideas attain not that perfection we intend: we find
they still want something we should be glad were in them; and
so are all inadequate. But mixed modes and relations, being
archetypes without patterns, and so having nothing to represent
but themselves, cannot but be adequate, every thing being so to
itself. He that at first put together the idea of danger perceived,
absence of disorder from fear, sedate consideration of what was
justly to be done, and executing of that without disturbance or
being deterred by the danger of it, had certainly in his mind that
complex idea made up of that combination; and intending it to
be nothing else but what it is, nor to have in it any other simple
ideas but what it hath, it could not also but be an adequate idea.
and, laying this up in his memory, with the name "courage"

annexed to it, to signify it to others, and denominate from thence any action he should observe to agree with it, had thereby a standard to measure and denominate actions by, as they agreed to it. This idea thus made, and laid up for a pattern, must necessarily be adequate, being referred to nothing else but itself, nor made by any other original but the good-liking and will of him that first made this combination.

4. *Modes in reference to settled names may be inadequate.*— Indeed, another, coming after, and in conversation learning from him the word " courage " may make an idea, to which he gives that name " courage ", different from what the first author applied it to, and has in his mind when he uses it. And in this case, if he designs that his idea in thinking should be conformable to the other's idea, as the name he uses in speaking is conformable in sound to his from whom he learned it, his idea may be very wrong and inadequate. Because in this case, making the other man's idea the pattern of his idea in thinking, as the other man's word or sound is the pattern of his in speaking, his idea is so far defective and inadequate, as it is distant from the archetype and pattern he refers it to, and intends to express and signify by the name he uses for it; which name he would have to be a sign of the other man's idea (to which, in its proper use, it is primarily annexed), and of his own as agreeing to it; to which if his own does not exactly correspond, it is faulty and inadequate.

5. Therefore these complex ideas of modes, when they are referred by the mind, and intended to correspond, to the ideas in the mind of some other intelligent being, expressed by the names we apply to them, they may be very deficient, wrong, and inadequate; because they agree not to that which the mind designs to be their archetype and pattern; in which respect only an idea of modes can be wrong, imperfect, or inadequate. And on this account, our ideas of mixed modes are the most liable to be faulty of any other; but this refers more to proper speaking, than knowing right.

6. *Ideas of substances, as referred to real essences, not adequate.*—Thirdly, What ideas we have of substances, I have above showed. Now, those ideas have in the mind a double reference. (1.) Sometimes they are referred to a supposed real essence of each species of things. (2.) Sometimes they are only designed to be pictures and representations in the mind of things that do exist by ideas of those qualities that are discoverable in them. In both which ways, these copies of those originals and archetypes are imperfect and inadequate.

First, It is usual for men to make the names of substances stand for things, as supposed to have certain real essences, whereby they are of this or that species : and names standing for nothing but the ideas that are in men's minds, they must consequently refer their ideas to such real essences as to their archetypes. That men (especially such as have been bred up in the learning taught in this part of the world), do suppose certain specific essences of substances, which each individual, in its several kinds, is made conformable to and partakes of, is so far from needing proof, that it will be thought strange if anyone should do otherwise. And thus they ordinarily apply the specific names they rank particular substances under, to things, as distinguished by such specific real essences. Who is there almost who would not take it amiss if it should be doubted whether he called himself " man" with any other meaning than as having the real essence of a man ? And yet if you demand what those real essences are, it is plain men are ignorant, and know them not. From whence it follows, that the ideas they have in their minds, being referred to real essences, as to archetypes which are unknown, must be so far from being adequate, that they cannot be supposed to be any representation of them at all. The complex ideas we have of substances are, as it has been shown, certain collections of simple ideas that have been observed or supposed constantly to exist together. But such a complex idea cannot be the real essence of any substance ; for then the properties we discover in that body would depend on that complex idea, and be deducible from it, and their necessary connexion with it be known ; as all properties of a triangle depend on, and, as far as they are discoverable, are deducible from, the complex idea of three lines, including a space. But it is plain, that in our complex ideas of substances are not contained such ideas on which all the other qualities that are to be found in them do depend. The common idea men have of iron, is a body of a certain colour, weight, and hardness; and a property that they look on as belonging to it is malleableness. But yet this property has no necessary connection with that complex idea, or any part of it: and there is no more reason to think that malleableness depends on that colour, weight, and hardness, than that that colour or that weight depends on its malleableness. And yet, though we know nothing of these real essences, there is nothing more ordinary than that men should attribute the sorts of things to such essences. The particular parcel of matter which makes the ring I have on my finger, is forwardly, by most men, supposed to have a real essence, whereby it is gold; and from whence those qualities flow which I find in it, viz., its peculiar colour, weight, hardness, fusibility, fixedness, and change of colour, upon a slight touch of mercury, &c. This essence, from which all these properties flow, when I inquire into it, and search after it, I plainly perceive I cannot discover: the farthest I can go is only to presume, that, it being nothing but body, its real essence or internal constitution, on which these qualities depend, can be nothing but the figure, size, and connection of its solid parts ; of neither of which having any distinct perception at all, I can have no idea of its essence, which is the cause that it has that particular shining yellowness, a greater weight than anything I know of the same bulk, and a fitness to have its colour changed by the touch of quicksilver. If anyone will say that the real essence and internal constitution, on which these properties depend, is not the figure, size, and arrangement or connexion of its solid parts, but something else, called its "particular form;" I am farther from having any idea of its real essence than I was before; for I have an idea of figure, size, and situation of solid parts in general, though I have none of the particular figure, size, or putting together of parts, whereby the qualities above-mentioned are produced; which qualities I find in that particular parcel of matter that is on my finger, and not in another parcel of matter with which I cut the pen I write with. But when I am told that something besides the figure, size, and posture of the solid parts of that body is its essence, something called "substantial form:" of that, I confess, I have no idea at all, but only of the sound, "form;" which is far enough from an idea of its real essence or constitution. The like ignorance as I have of the real essence of this particular substance, I have also of the real essence of all other natural ones : of which essences, I confess, I have no distinct ideas at all; and I am apt to suppose others, when they examine their own knowledge, will find in themselves, in this one point, the same sort of ignorance.

7. Now then, when men apply to this particular parcel of matter on my finger a general name already in use, and denominate it "gold," do they not ordinarily or are they not understood to give it that name as belonging to particular species of bodies, having a real internal essence ; by having of which essence, this particular substance comes to be of that species, and to be called by that name ? If it be so, as it is plain it is, the name, by which things are marked as having that essence, must be referred primarily to that essence ; and consequently the idea to which that name is given must be referred also to that essence, and be intended to represent it. Which essence, since they who so use the names know not, their ideas of substances must be all inadequate in that respect, as not containing in them that real essence which the mind intends they should.

8. *Ideas of substances, as collections of their qualities, are all inadequate.*—Secondly, Those who, neglecting that useless supposition of unknown real essences whereby they are distinguished, endeavour to copy the substances that exist in the world by putting together the ideas of those sensible qualities which are found co-existing in them, though they come much nearer a likeness of them, than those who imagine they-know-not-what real specific essences; yet they arrive not at perfectly adequate ideas of those substances they would thus copy into their minds; nor do those copies exactly and fully contain all that is to be found in

their archetypes. Because those qualities and powers of substances, whereof we make their complex ideas, are so many and
various that no man's complex idea contains them all. That our
complex ideas of substances do not contain in them all the simple
ideas that are united in the things themselves, is evident, in that
men do rarely put into their complex idea of any substance all
the simple ideas they do know to exist in it. Because endeavouring to make the signification of their specific names as clear
and as little cumbersome as they can, they make their specific
ideas of the sorts of substances, for the most part, of a few of
those simple ideas which are to be found in them : but these
having no original precedency or right to be put in and make
the specific idea, more than others that are left out, it is plain
that, both these ways, our ideas of substances are deficient and
inadequate. These simple ideas, whereof we make our complex
ones of substances, are all of them (bating only the figure and
bulk of some sorts) powers ; which being relations to other substances, we can never be sure that we know all the powers that
are in any one body, till we have tried what changes it is fitted
to give to, or receive from, other substances in their several
ways of application : which being impossible to be tried upon
any one body, much less upon all, it is impossible we should have
adequate ideas of any substance made up of a collection of all its
properties.

9. Whosoever first lit on a parcel of that sort of substance we
denote by the word " gold," could not rationally take the bulk
and figure he observed in that lump to depend on its real essence
or internal constitution. Therefore those never went into his
idea of that species of body ; but its peculiar colour, perhaps, and
weight, were the first he abstracted from it to make the complex
idea of that species : which both are but powers; the one to
affect our eyes after such a manner, and to produce in us that
idea we call " yellow;" and the other to force upwards any other
body of equal bulk, they being put into a pair of equal scales one
against another. Another perhaps added to these, the ideas of
fusibility and fixedness, two other passive powers in relation to
the operation of fire upon it; another, its ductility and solubility
in *aqua regia*, two other powers relating to the operation of other
bodies in changing its outward figure or separation of it into
insensible parts. These, or part of these put together, usually
make the complex idea in men's minds of that sort of body we
call " gold."

10. But no one who hath considered the properties of bodies
in general, or this sort in particular, can doubt that this, called
" gold," has infinite other properties not contained in that complex idea. Some who have examined this species more accurately
could, I believe, enumerate ten times as many properties in gold,
all of them as inseparable from its internal constitution, as its

colour or weight: and it is probable if anyone who knew all the, properties that are by divers men known of this metal, there would an hundred times as many ideas go to the complex idea of gold, as any one man yet has in his; and yet, perhaps, that not be the thousandth part of what is to be discovered in it: the changes which that one body is apt to receive and make in other bodies, upon due application, exceeding far, not only what we know, but what we are apt to imagine. Which will not appear so much a paradox to anyone who will but consider how far men are yet from knowing all the properties of that one (no very compound) figure, a triangle; though it be no small number that are already by mathematicians discovered of it.

11. *Ideas of substances, as collections of their qualities, are all inadequate.*—So that all our complex ideas of substances are imperfect and inadequate. Which would be so also in mathematical figures, if we were to have our complex ideas of them only by collecting their properties in reference to other figures. How uncertain and imperfect would our ideas be of an ellipsis, if we had no other idea of it but some few of its properties! Whereas, having in our plain idea the whole essence of that figure, we from thence discover those properties, and demonstratively see how they flow and are inseparable from it.

12. *Simple ideas ἔκτυπα, and adequate.*—Thus the mind has three sorts of abstract ideas, or nominal essences:

First, Simple ideas which are ἔκτυπα, or "copies;" but yet certainly adequate. Because being intended to express nothing but the power in things to produce in the mind such a sensation, that sensation, when it is produced, cannot but be the effect of that power. So the paper I write on, having the power, in the light (I speak according to the common notion of light), to produce in me the sensation which I call "white," it cannot but be the effect of such a power in something without the mind, since the mind has not the power to·produce any such idea in itself; and being meant for nothing else but the effect of such a power, that simple idea is real and adequate: the sensation of "white" in my mind being the effect of that power which is in the paper to produce it, is perfectly adequate to that power; or else that power would produce a different idea.

13. *Ideas of substances are ἔκτυπα, inadequate.* Secondly, The complex ideas of substances are *ectypes* or "copies," too; but not perfect ones, not adequate; which is very evident to the mind, in that it plainly perceives that whatever collection of simple ideas it makes of any substance that exists, it cannot be sure that it exactly answers all that are in that substance: since, not having tried all the operations of all other substances upon it, and found all the alterations it would receive from or cause in other substances, it cannot have an exact adequate collection of all its active and passive capacities; and so not have an adequate

complex idea of the powers of any substance existing and its relations, which is that sort of complex idea of substances we have. And after all, if we could have, and actually had, in our complex idea, an exact collection of all the secondary qualities or powers of any substance, we should not yet thereby have an idea of the essence of that thing. For since the powers or qualities that are observable by us are not the real essence of that substance, but depend on it, and flow from it, any collection whatsoever of these qualities cannot be the real essence of that thing. Whereby it is plain that our ideas of substances are not adequate; are not what the mind intends them to be. Besides, a man has no idea of substance in general, nor knows what substance is in itself.

14. *Ideas of modes and relations are archetypes, and cannot but be adequate.*—Thirdly, Complex ideas of modes and relations are originals and archetypes; are not copies, nor made after the pattern of any real existence, to which the mind intends them to be conformable, and exactly to answer. These being such collections of simple ideas that the mind itself puts together, and such collections that each of them contains in it precisely all that the mind intends it should, they are archetypes and essences of modes that may exist; and so are designed only for and belong only to such modes as, when they do exist, have an exact conformity with those complex ideas. The ideas thereof of modes and relations cannot but be adequate.

## CHAPTER XXXII.

### OF TRUE AND FALSE IDEAS.

1. *Truth and falsehood properly belong to propositions.*— Though truth and falsehood belong, in propriety of speech, only to propositions, yet ideas are oftentimes termed "true or false" (as what words are there that are not used with great latitude, and with some deviation from their strict and proper significations?) though I think, that when ideas themselves are termed "true or false," there is still some secret or tacit proposition which is the foundation of that denomination: as we shall see, if we examine the particular occasions wherein they come to be called "true or false." In all which we shall find some kind of affirmation or negation, which is the reason of that denomination. For our ideas being nothing but bare appearances or perceptions in our minds, cannot properly and simply in themselves be said to be true or false, no more than a single name of anything can be said to be true or false.

2. *Metaphysical truth contains a tacit proposition.*—Indeed, both ideas and words may be said to be true in a metaphysical

sense of the word "truth," as all other things that any way exist are said to be true; *i.e.*, really to be such as they exist. Though in things called "true," even in that sense, there is, perhaps, a secret reference to our ideas, looked upon as the standards of that truth, which amounts to a mental proposition, though it be usually not taken notice of.

3. *No idea, as an appearance in the mind, true or false.*—But it is not in that metaphysical sense of truth which we inquire here, when we examine whether our ideas are capable of being true or false; but in the more ordinary acceptation of those words, and so, I say, that the ideas in our minds being only so many perceptions or appearances there, none of them are false; the idea of a centaur having no more falsehood in it, when it appears in our minds, than the name "centaur" has falsehood in it, when it is pronounced by our mouths, or written on paper. For, truth or falsehood lying always in some affirmation or negation, mental or verbal, our ideas are not capable, any of them, of being false, till the mind passes some judgment on them; that is, affirms or denies something of them.

4. *Ideas referred to anything may be true or false.*—Whenever the mind refers any of its ideas to anything extraneous to them, they are then capable to be called true or false. Because the mind in such a reference makes a tacit supposition of their conformity to that thing; which supposition, as it happens to be true or false, so the ideas themselves come to be denominated. The most usual cases wherein this happens are these following:

5. *Other men's ideas, real existence, and supposed real essences, are what men usually refer ideas to.*—First, When the mind supposes any idea it has conformable to that in other men's minds, called by the same common name; *v. g.*, when the mind intends or judges its ideas of justice, temperance, religion, to be the same with what other men give those names to.

Secondly, When the mind supposes any idea it has in itself to be conformable to some real existence. Thus the two ideas of a man and a centaur, supposed to be the ideas of real substances, are the one true and the other false; the one having a conformity to what has really existed, the other not.

Thirdly, When the mind refers any of its ideas to that real constitution and essence of anything, whereon all its properties depend: and thus the greatest part, if not all our ideas of substances, are false.

6. *The cause of such references.*—These suppositions the mind is very apt tacitly to make concerning its own ideas. But yet, if we will examine it, we shall find it is chiefly, if not only, concerning its abstract complex ideas. For the natural tendency of the mind being towards knowledge, and finding that, if it should proceed by and dwell upon only particular things, its progress would be very slow, and its work endless: therefore to

shorten its way to knowledge, and make each perception the more comprehensive, the first thing it does, as the foundation of the easier enlarging its knowledge, either by contemplation of the things themselves that it would know, or conference with others about them, is to bind them into bundles, and rank them so into sorts, that what knowledge it gets of any of them, it may thereby with assurance extend to all of that sort; and so advance by larger steps in that which is its great business, knowledge. This, as I have elsewhere showed, is the reason why we collect things under comprehensive ideas, with names annexed to them, into *genera* and *species, i.e.,* into " kinds " and " sorts."

7. If therefore we will warily attend to the motions of the mind, and observe that course it usually takes in its way to knowledge, we shall, I think, find that the mind, having got any idea which it thinks it may have use of, either in contemplation or discourse, the first thing it does is to abstract it, and then get a name to it; and so lay it up in its storehouse, the memory, as containing the essence of a sort of things of which that name is always to be the mark. Hence it is, that we may often observe, that when anyone sees a new thing of a kind that he knows not, he presently asks what it is, meaning by that inquiry nothing but the name; as if the name carried with it the knowledge of the species, of the essence of it, whereof it is indeed used as the mark, and is generally supposed annexed to it.

8. *The cause of such references.*—But this abstract idea being something in the mind between the thing that exists, and the name that is given to it, it is in our ideas that both the rightness of our knowledge, and the propriety or intelligibleness of our speaking, consists. And hence it is that men are so forward to suppose that the abstract ideas they have in their minds, are such as agree to the things existing without them, to which they are referred; and are the same also to which the names they give them do, by the use and propriety of that language, belong. For, without this double conformity of their ideas, they find they should both think amiss of things in themselves, and talk of them unintelligibly to others.

9. *Simple ideas may be false in reference to others of the same name, but are least liable to be so.*—First, then, I say, that when the truth of our ideas is judged of by the conformity they have to the ideas which other men have and commonly signify by the same name, they may be any of them false. But yet simple ideas are least of all liable to be so mistaken : because a man by his senses, and every day's observation, may easily satisfy himself what the simple ideas are which their several names that are in common use stand for, they being but few in number, and such as, if he doubts or mistakes in, he may easily rectify by the objects they are to be found in. Therefore it is seldom that anyone mistakes in his names of simple ideas, or applies the name

" red " to the idea of " green," or the name " sweet " to the idea
" bitter :" much less are men apt to confound the names of ideas
belonging to different senses, and call a colour by the name of a
taste, &c., whereby it is evident, that the simple ideas they call
by any name are commonly the same that others have and mean
when they use the same names.

10. *Ideas of mixed modes most liable to be false in this sense.*—
Complex ideas are much more liable to be false in this respect;
and the complex ideas of mixed modes much more than those of
substances: because in substances (especially those which the
common and unborrowed names of any language are applied to)
some remarkable sensible qualities, serving ordinarily to distinguish one sort from another, easily preserve those who take any
care in the use of their words from applying them to sorts of
substances to which they do not at all belong. But in mixed
modes we are much more uncertain, it being not so easy to determine of several actions whether they are to be called " justice "
or " cruelty," "liberality " or " prodigality." And so, in referring our ideas to those of other men called by the same names,
ours may be false; and the idea in our minds, which we express
by the word " justice," may, perhaps, be that which ought to
have another name.

11. *Or at least to be thought false.*—But whether or no our
ideas of mixed modes are more liable than any sort to be different
from those of other men, which are marked by the same names;
this at least is certain, that this sort of falsehood is much more
familiarly attributed to our ideas of mixed modes than to any
other. When a man is thought to have a false idea of justice, or
gratitude, or glory, it is for no other reason but that his agrees
not with the ideas which each of those names are the signs of in
other men.

12. The reason whereof seems to me to be this: That the
abstract ideas of mixed modes, being men's voluntary combinations of such a precise collection of simple ideas, and so the
essence of each species being made by men alone, whereof we
have no other sensible standard existing anywhere but the name
itself, or the definition of that name; we having nothing else
to refer these our ideas of mixed modes to, as a standard to
which we could conform them, but the ideas of those who are
thought to use those names in their most proper significations;
rnd, so as our ideas conform or differ from *them*, they pass for
true or false. And thus much concerning the truth and falsehood of our ideas, in reference to their names.

13. Secondly, as to the truth and falsehood of our ideas, in
reference to the real existence of things. When that is made
the standard of their truth, none of them can be termed false
but only our complex ideas of substances.

**14. *First, Simple ideas in this sense not false, and why.*—**First, Our simple ideas being barely such perceptions as God has fitted us to receive, and given power to external objects to produce in us by established laws and ways, suitable to his wisdom and goodness, though incomprehensible to us; their truth consists in nothing else but in such appearances as are produced in us, and must be suitable to those powers he has placed in external objects, or else they could not be produced in us: and thus answering those powers, they are, what they should be, true ideas. Nor do they become liable to any imputation of falsehood, if the mind (as in most men I believe it does) judges these ideas to be in the things themselves. For God, in his wisdom, having set them as marks of distinction in things, whereby we may be able to discern one thing from another, and so choose any of them for our uses as we have occasion, it alters not the nature of our simple idea, whether we think that the idea of blue be in the violet itself or in our mind only; and only the power of producing it by the texture of its parts, reflecting the particles of light after a certain manner, to be in the violet itself. For that texture in the object, by a regular and constant operation, producing the same idea of blue in us, it serves us to distinguish, by our eyes, that from any other thing, whether that distinguishing mark as it is really in the violet be only a peculiar texture of parts, or else that very colour the idea whereof (which is in us) is the exact resemblance. And it is equally from that appearance to be denominated " blue," whether it be that real colour, or only a peculiar texture in it, that causes in us that idea : since the name " blue " notes properly nothing but that mark of distinction that is in a violet discernible only by our eyes, whatever it consists in, that being beyond our capacities distinctly to know, and, perhaps, would be of less use to us, if we had faculties to discern.

**15. *Though one man's idea of blue should be different from another's.*—**Neither would it carry any imputation of falsehood to our simple ideas, if, by the different structure of our organs, it were so ordered that the same object should produce in several men's minds different ideas at the same time; *v. g.*, if the idea that a violet produced in one man's mind by his eyes were the same that a marigold produced in another man's, and *vice versâ.* For since this could never be known; because one man's mind could not pass into another man's body, to perceive what appearances were produced by those organs; neither the ideas hereby nor the names would be at all confounded, or any falsehood be in either. For, all things that had the texture of a violet producing constantly the idea which he called " blue;" and those which had the texture of a marigold producing constantly the idea which he as constantly called " yellow;" whatever those appearances were in his mind, he would be able as regularly to distinguish things for his use by those appearances, and understand and signify those distinctions, marked by the names " blue " and " yellow," as if the appearances, or ideas in his mind, received from those two flowers, were exactly the same with the ideas in other men's minds. I am nevertheless very apt to think, that the sensible ideas produced by any object in different men's minds are most commonly very near and undiscernibly alike. For which opinion, I think, there might be many reasons offered: but that being besides my present business, I shall not trouble my reader with them; but only mind him, that the contrary supposition, if it could be proved, is of little use either for the improvement of our knowledge or conveniency of life; and so we need not trouble ourselves to examine it.

16. *First, Simple ideas in this sense not false, and why.*— From what has been said concerning our simple ideas, I think it evident, that our simple ideas can none of them be false in respect of things existing without us. For, the truth of these appearances, or perceptions in our minds, consisting, as has been said, only in their being answerable to the powers in external objects to produce by our senses such appearances in us, and each of them being in the mind such as it is, suitable to the power that produced it, and which alone it represents, it cannot, upon that account, or as referred to such a pattern, be false. Blue or yellow, bitter or sweet, can never be false ideas, these perceptions in the mind are just such as they are there, answering the powers appointed by God to produce them; and so are truly what they are, and are intended to be. Indeed, the names may be misapplied; but that in this respect makes no falsehood in the ideas: as if a man ignorant in the English tongue should call purple " scarlet."

17. *Secondly, Modes not false.*—Secondly, Neither can our complex ideas of modes, in reference to the essence of anything really existing, be false. Because whatever complex idea I have of any mode, it hath no reference to any pattern existing, and made by nature: it is not supposed to contain in it any other ideas than what it hath, nor to represent anything but such a complication of ideas as it does. Thus when I have the idea of such an action of a man who forbears to afford himself such meat, drink, and clothing, and other conveniences of life as his riches and estate will be sufficient to supply and his station requires, I have no false idea; but such an one as represents an action, either as I find or imagine it; and so is capable of neither truth nor falsehood. But when I give the name " frugality " or virtue to this action, then it may be called a false idea, if thereby it be supposed to agree with that idea to which, in propriety of speech, the name of " frugality " doth belong, or to be conformable to that law which is the standard of virtue and vice.

18. *Thirdly, Ideas of substances when false.*—Thirdly, Our

complex ideas of substances, being all referred to patterns in things themselves, may be false. That they are all false when looked upon as the representations of the unknown essences of things, is so evident that there needs nothing to be said of it. I shall therefore pass over that chimerical supposition, and consider them as collections of simple ideas in the mind, taken from combinations of simple ideas existing together constantly in things, of which patterns they are the supposed copies: and in this reference of them to the existence of things, they are false ideas: (1) When they put together simple ideas, which in the real existence of things have no union; as when to the shape and size that exist together in a horse, is joined in the same complex idea the power of barking like a dog; which three ideas, however put together into one in the mind, were never united in nature; and this therefore may be called a false idea of a horse. (2.) Ideas of substances are in this respect also false, when, from any collection of simple ideas that do always exist together, there is separated by a direct negation, any other simple idea which is constantly joined with them. Thus, if to extension, solidity, fusibility, the peculiar weightiness, and yellow colour of gold, anyone join in his thoughts the negation of a greater degree of fixedness than is in lead or copper, he may be said to have a false complex idea, as well as when he joins to those other simple ones the idea of perfect, absolute fixedness. For either way, the complex idea of gold, being made up of such simple ones as have no union in nature, may be termed false. But if he leave out of this his complex idea that of fixedness quite, without either actually joining to or separating of it from the rest in his mind, it is, I think, to be looked on as an inadequate and imperfect idea, rather than a false one; since, though it contains not all the simple ideas that are united in nature, yet it puts none together but what do really exist together.

19. *Truth or falsehood always supposes affirmation or negation.*—Though, in compliance with the ordinary way of speaking, I have showed in what sense and upon what ground our ideas may be sometimes called true or false; yet if we will look a little nearer into the matter, in all cases where any idea is called true or false, it is from some judgment that the mind makes, or is supposed to make, that is true or false. For, truth or falsehood being never without some affirmation or negation, express or tacit, it is not to be found but where signs are joined or separated, according to the agreement or disagreement of the things they stand for. The signs we chiefly use are either ideas or words wherewith we make either mental or verbal propositions. Truth lies in so joining or separating these representatives as the things they stand for do in themselves agree or disagree; and falsehood in the contrary, as shall be more fully showed hereafter.

20. *Ideas in themselves neither true nor false.*—Any idea, then,

# TRUE AND FALSE IDEAS

which we have in our minds, whether conformable or not to the existence of things, or to any ideas in the minds of other men, cannot properly for this alone be called false. For these representations, if they have nothing in them but what is really existing in things without, cannot be thought false, being exact representations of something: nor yet if they have anything in them differing from the reality of things, can they properly be said to be false representations or ideas of things they do not represent. But the mistake and falsehood is,

21. *But are false, First, When judged agreeable to another man's idea without being so.*—First, When the mind having any idea, it judges and concludes it the same that is in other men's minds, signified by the same name; or that it is conformable to the ordinary, received signification or definition of that word, when indeed it is not: which is the most usual mistake in mixed modes, though other ideas also are liable to it.

22. *Secondly, When judged to agree to real existence, when they do not.*—Secondly, When it having a complex idea made up of such a collection of simple ones as nature never puts together, it judges it to agree to a species of creatures really existing; as when it joins the weight of tin to the colour, fusibility, and fixedness of gold.

23. *Thirdly, When judged adequate, without being so.*— Thirdly, When in its complex idea it has united a certain number of simple ideas that do really exist together in some sorts of creatures, but has also left out others as much inseparable, it judges this to be a perfect complete idea of a sort of things which really it is not; *v. g.,* having joined the ideas of substance, yellow, malleable, most heavy, and fusible, it takes that complex idea to be the complete idea of gold, when yet its peculiar fixedness and solubility in *aqua regia* are as inseparable from those other ideas or qualities of that body as they are one from another.

24. *Fourthly, When judged to represent the real essence.*— Fourthly, The mistake is yet greater when I judge that this complex idea contains in it the real essence of any body existing, when at least it contains but some few of those properties which flow from its real essence and constitution. I say, only some few of those properties; for, those properties consisting mostly in the active and passive powers it has in reference to other things, all that are vulgarly known of any one body, and of which the complex idea of that kind of things is usually made, are but a very few in comparison of what a man, that has several ways tried and examined it, knows of that one sort of things; and all that the most expert man knows are but few in comparison of what are really in that body, and depend on its internal or essential constitution. The essence of a triangle lies in a very little compass, consists in a very few ideas; three lines, including a space, make up that essence: but the properties that flow from this

essence are more than can be easily known or enumerated. So I imagine it is in substances: their real essences lie in a little compass; though the properties flowing from that internal constitution are endless.

25. *Ideas, when false.*—To conclude: a man having no notion of anything without him but by the idea he has of it in his mind (which idea he has a power to call by what name he pleases), he may, indeed, make an idea neither answering the reality of things, nor agreeing to the ideas commonly signified by other people's words; but cannot make a wrong or false idea of a thing which is no otherwise known to him but by the idea he has of it; *v. g.*, when I frame an idea of the legs, arms, and body of a man, and join to this a horse's head and neck, I do not make a false idea of anything; because it represents nothing without me. But when I call it a "man" or "Tartar," and imagine it either to represent some real being without me, or to be the same idea that others call by the same name; in either of these cases I may err. And upon this account it is that it comes to be termed a "false idea;" though, indeed, the falsehood lies not in the idea, but in that tacit mental proposition, wherein a conformity and resemblance is attributed to it which it has not. But yet, if, having framed such an idea in my mind, without thinking either that existence, or the name "man" or "Tartar," belongs to it, I will call it "man" or "Tartar," I may be justly thought fantastical in the naming, but not erroneous in my judgment, nor the idea any way false.

26. *More properly to be called "right" or "wrong."*—Upon the whole matter, I think, that our ideas, as they are considered by the mind, either in reference to the proper signification of their names, or in reference to the reality of things, may very fitly be called "right" or "wrong" ideas, according as they agree or disagree to those patterns to which they are referred. But if anyone had rather call them "true" or "false," it is fit he use a liberty which everyone has to call things by those names he thinks best; though, in propriety of speech, 'truth" or "falsehood" will, I think, scarce agree to them, but as they, some way or other, virtually contain in them some mental proposition. The ideas that are in a man's mind, simply considered, cannot be wrong, unless complex ones, wherein inconsistent parts are jumbled together. All other ideas are in themselves right; and the knowledge about them, right and true knowledge: but when we come to refer them to anything, as to their patterns and archetypes, then they are capable of being wrong, as far as they disagree with such archetypes.

## CHAPTER XXXIII.

### OF THE ASSOCIATION OF IDEAS.

**1.** *Something unreasonable in most men.*—There is scarce anyone that does not observe something that seems odd to him, and is in itself really extravagant, in the opinions, reasonings, and actions of other men. The least flaw of this kind, if at all different from his own, everyone is quick-sighted enough to espy in another, and will by the authority of reason forwardly condemn, though he be guilty of much greater unreasonableness in his own tenets and conduct, which he never perceives, and will very hardly, if at all, be convinced of.

**2.** *Not wholly from self-love.*—This proceeds not wholly from self-love, though that has often a great hand in it. Men of fair minds, and not given up to the overweening of self-flattery, are frequently guilty of it; and in many cases one with amazement hears the arguings, and is astonished at the obstinacy, of a worthy man who yields not to the evidence of reason, though laid before him as clear as daylight.

**3.** *Nor from education.*—This sort of unreasonableness is usually imputed to education and prejudice, and for the most part truly enough, though that reaches not the bottom of the disease, nor shows distinctly enough whence it rises or wherein it lies. Education is often rightly assigned for the cause, and prejudice is a good general name for the thing itself; but yet, I think, he ought to look a little farther who would trace this sort of madness to the root it springs from, and so explain it as to show whence this flaw has its original in very sober and rational minds, and wherein it consists.

**4.** *A degree of madness.*—I shall be pardoned for calling it by so harsh a name as "madness," when it is considered, that opposition to reason deserves that name, and is really madness; and there is scarce a man so free from it but that if he should always, on all occasions, argue or do as in some cases he constantly does, would not be thought fitter for Bedlam than civil conversation. I do not here mean when he is under the power of an unruly passion, but in the steady calm course of his life. That which will yet more apologize for this harsh name, and ungrateful imputation on the greatest part of mankind, is, that inquiring a little by-the-by into the nature of madness (book ii. chap. xi. sect. 13), I found it to spring from the very same root, and to depend on the very same cause, we are here speaking of. This consideration of the thing itself, at a time when I thought not the least on the subject which I am now treating of, suggested it to me. And if this be a weakness to which all men are so liable, if this be a taint which so universally infects mankind, the greater care should be taken to lay it open under its due name, thereby to excite the greater care in its prevention and cure.

5. *From a wrong connexion of ideas.*—Some of our ideas have a natural correspondence and connexion one with another; it is the office and excellency of our reason to trace these, and hold them together in that union and correspondence which is founded in their peculiar beings. Besides this, there is another connexion of ideas wholly owing to chance or custom: ideas that in themselves are not at all of kin, come to be so united in some men's minds that it is very hard to separate them; they always keep in company, and the one no sooner at any time comes into the understanding, but its associate appears with it; and if they are more than two which are thus united, the whole gang, always inseparable, show themselves together.

6. *This connexion, how made.*—This strong combination of ideas, not allied by nature, the mind makes in itself either voluntarily or by chance; and hence it comes in different men to be very different, according to their different inclinations, educations, interests, &c. Custom settles habits of thinking in the understanding, as well as of determining in the will, and of motions in the body; all which seem to be but trains of motion in the animal spirits, which, once set a-going, continue in the same steps they have been used to, which, by often treading, are worn into a smooth path, and the motion in it becomes easy, and as it were natural. As far as we can comprehend thinking, thus ideas seem to be produced in our minds; or if they are not, this may serve to explain their following one another in an habitual train, when once they are put into that track, as well as it does to explain such motions of the body. A musician used to any tune will find, that, let it but once begin in his head, the ideas of the several notes of it will follow one another orderly in his understanding, without any care or attention, as regularly as his fingers move orderly over the keys of the organ to play out the tune he has begun, though his unattentive thoughts be else-where a-wandering. Whether the natural cause of these ideas, as well as of that regular dancing of his fingers, be the motion of his animal spirits, I will not determine, how probable soever by this instance it appears to be so: but this may help us a little to conceive of intellectual habits, and of the tying together of ideas.

7. *Some antipathies an effect of it.*—That there are such associations of them made by custom in the minds of most men I think nobody will question who has well considered himself or others; and to this, perhaps, might be justly attributed most of the sympathies and antipathies observable in men, which work as strongly, and produce as regular effects, as if they were natural, and are therefore called so, though they at first had no other

original but the accidental connexion of two ideas; which either the strength of the first impression or future indulgence so united, that they always afterwards kept company together in that man's mind, as if they were but one idea. I say, "most of the antipathies," I do not say "all;" for some of them are truly natural, depend upon our original constitution, and are born with us; but a great part of those which are counted natural, would have been known to be from unheeded though perhaps early impressions or wanton fancies at first, which would have been acknowledged the original of them if they had been warily observed. A grown person, surfeiting with honey, no sooner hears the name of it but his fancy immediately carries sickness and qualms to his stomach, and he cannot bear the very idea of it; other ideas of dislike, and sickness and vomiting, presently accompany it, and he is disturbed; but he knows from whence to date this weakness, and can tell how he got this indisposition. Had this happened to him by an overdose of honey when a child, all the same effects would have followed, but the cause would have been mistaken, and the antipathy counted natural.

8. I mention this not out of any great necessity there is, in this present argument, to distinguish nicely between natural and acquired antipathies; but I take notice of it for another purpose, viz., that those who have children, or the charge of their education, would think it worth their while diligently to watch and carefully to prevent the undue connexion of ideas in the minds of young people. This is the time most susceptible of lasting impressions; and though those relating to the health of the body are by discreet people minded and fenced against, yet I am apt to doubt that those which relate more peculiarly to the mind, and terminate in the understanding or passions, have been much less heeded than the thing deserves; nay, those relating purely to the understanding have, as I suspect, been by most men wholly overlooked.

9. *A great cause of errors.*—This wrong connexion in our minds of ideas, in themselves loose and independent one of another, has such an influence, and is of so great force, to set us awry in our actions, as well moral as natural, passions, reasonings, and notions themselves, that perhaps there is not any one thing that deserves more to be looked after.

10. *Instances.*—The ideas of goblins and sprights have really no more to do with darkness than light; yet let but a foolish maid inculcate these often on the mind of a child, and raise them there together, possibly he shall never be able to separate them again so long as he lives; but darkness shall ever afterwards bring with it those frightful ideas, and they shall be so joined that he can no more bear the one than the other.

11. A man receives a sensible injury from another, thinks on the man and that action over and over, and, by ruminating on

them strongly or much in his mind, so cements those two ideas
together, that he makes them almost one; never thinks on the
man, but the pain and displeasure he suffered comes into his mind
with it, so that he scarce distinguishes them, but has as much an
aversion for the one as the other. Thus hatreds are often begotten from slight and almost innocent occasions, and quarrels
propagated and continued in the world.

12. A man has suffered pain or sickness in any place, he saw
his friend die in such a room; though these have in nature
nothing to do with one another, yet when the idea of the place
occurs to his mind, it brings (the impression being once made)
that of the pain and displeasure with it; he confounds them in
his mind, and can as little bear the one as the other.

13. *Why time cures some disorders in the mind which reason
cannot.*—When this combination is settled, and whilst it lasts,
it is not in the power of reason to help us, and relieve us from
the effects of it. Ideas in our minds, when they are there, will
operate according to their natures and circumstances: and here
we see the cause why time cures certain affections, which reason,
though in the right and allowed to be so, has not power over,
nor is able against them to prevail with those who are apt to
hearken to it in other cases. The death of a child, that was the
daily delight of his mother's eyes and joy of her soul, rends from
her heart the whole comfort of her life, and gives her all the
torment imaginable: use the consolations of reason in this case,
and you were as good preach ease to one on the rack, and hope
to allay, by rational discourses, the pain of his joints tearing
asunder. Till time has by disuse separated the sense of that
enjoyment, and its loss, from the idea of the child returning to
her memory, all representations, though ever so reasonable, are
in vain; and therefore some in whom the union between these
ideas is never dissolved, spend their lives in mourning, and carry
an incurable sorrow to their graves.

14. *Farther instances of the effects of the association of ideas.*
—A friend of mine knew one perfectly cured of madness by a
very harsh and offensive operation. The gentleman, who was thus
recovered, with great sense of gratitude and acknowledment
owned the cure all his life after, as the greatest obligation he
could have received; but whatever gratitude and reason suggested to him, he could never bear the sight of the operator:
that image brought back with it the idea of that agony which he
suffered from his hands, which was too mighty and intolerable
for him to endure.

15. Many children, imputing the pain they endured at school
to their books they were corrected for, so join these ideas
together that a book becomes their aversion, and they are never
reconciled to the study and use of them all their lives after;
and thus reading becomes a torment to them, which otherwise

possibly they might have made the great pleasure of their lives. There are rooms convenient enough that some men cannot study in, and fashions of vessels which, though never so clean and commodious, they cannot drink out of, and that by reason of some accidental ideas which are annexed to them, and make them offensive; and who is there that hath not observed some man to flag at the appearance or in the company of some certain person not otherwise superior to him, but because having once on some occasion got the ascendant, the idea of authority and distance goes along with that of the person, and he that has been thus subjected is not able to separate them.

16. Instances of these kinds are so plentiful everywhere, that if I add one more, it is only for the pleasant oddness of it. It is of a young gentleman, who having learnt to dance, and that to great perfection, there happened to stand an old trunk in the room where he learnt. The idea of this remarkable piece of household stuff had so mixed itself with the turns and steps of all his dances, that though in that chamber he could dance excellently well, yet it was only whilst that trunk was there, nor could he perform well in any other place, unless that or some such other trunk had its due position in the room. If this story shall be suspected to be dressed up with some comical circumstances a little beyond precise nature, I answer for myself, that I had it some years since from a very sober and worthy man, upon his own knowledge, as I report it; and I dare say there are very few inquisitive persons, who read this, who have not met with accounts, if not examples, of this nature, that may parallel, or at least justify, this.

17. *Its influence on intellectual habits.*—Intellectual habits and defects this way contracted, are not less frequent and powerful, though less observed. Let the ideas of "being" and "matter" be strongly joined either by education or much thought; whilst these are still combined in the mind, what notions, what reasonings, will there be about separate spirits! Let custom from the very childhood have joined figure and shape to the idea of God, and what absurdities will that mind be liable to about the Deity!

Let the idea of infallibility be inseparably joined to any person, and these two constantly together possess the mind, and then one body in two places at once shall, unexamined, be swallowed for a certain truth, by an implicit faith, whenever that imagined infallible person dictates and demands assent without inquiry.

18. *Observable in different sects.*—Some such wrong and unnatural combinations of ideas will be found to establish the irreconcilable opposition between different sects of philosophy and religion; for we cannot imagine every one of their followers to impose wilfully on himself, and knowingly refuse truth offered by plain reason. Interest, though it does a great deal in the

case, yet cannot be thought to work whole societies of men to so universal a perverseness, as that every one of them to a man should knowingly maintain falsehood: some at least must be allowed to do what all pretend to, *i.e.*, to pursue truth sincerely; and therefore there must be something that blinds their understandings, and makes them not see the falsehood of what they embrace for real truth. That which thus captivates their reasons, and leads men of sincerity blindfold from common-sense, will, when examined, be found to be what we are speaking of: some independent ideas, of no alliance to one another, are, by education, custom, and the constant din of their party, so coupled in their minds that they always appear there together, and they can no more separate them in their thoughts, than if they were but one idea, and they operate as if they were so. This gives sense to jargon, demonstration to absurdities, and consistency to nonsense, and is the foundation of the greatest (I had almost said of all the) errors in the world: or, if it does not reach so far, it is at least the most dangerous one, since, so far as it obtains, it hinders men from seeing and examining. When two things, in themselves disjoined, appear to the sight constantly united; if the eye sees these things riveted which are loose, where will you begin to rectify the mistakes that follow in two ideas, that they have been accustomed so to join in their minds as to substitute one for the other, and, as I am apt to think, often without perceiving it themselves? This, whilst they are under the deceit of it, makes them uncapable of conviction, and they applaud themselves as zealous champions for truth, when indeed they are contending for error; and the confusion of two different ideas, which a customary connection of them in their minds hath to them made in effect but one, fills their heads with false views, and their reasonings with false consequences.

19. *Conclusion.*—Having thus given an account of the original sorts and extent of our ideas, with several other considerations about these (I know not whether I may say) instruments, or materials, of our knowledge: the method I at first proposed to myself, would now require that I should immediately proceed to show what use the understanding makes of them, and what knowledge we have by them. This was that which, in the first general view I had of this subject, was all that I thought I should have to do: but upon a nearer approach, I find that there is so close a connection between ideas and words, and our abstract ideas and general words have so constant a relation one to another, that it is impossible to speak clearly and distinctly of our knowledge, which all consists in propositions, without considering first the nature, use, and signification of language; which therefore must be the business of the next book.

# BOOK III.

## CHAPTER I.

### OF WORDS OR LANGUAGE IN GENERAL.

1. *Man fitted to form articulate sounds.*—God, having designed man for a sociable creature, made him not only with an inclination and under a necessity to have fellowship with those of his own kind, but furnished him also with language, which was to be the great instrument and common tie of society. Man therefore had by nature his organs so fashioned as to be fit to frame articulate sounds, which we call " words." But this was not enough to produce language; for parrots and several other birds will be taught to make articulate sounds distinct enough, which yet by no means are capable of language.

2. *To make them signs of ideas.*—Besides articulate sounds, therefore, it was farther necessary that he should be able to use these sounds as signs of internal conceptions, and to make them stand as marks for the ideas within his own mind; whereby they might be made known to others, and the thoughts of men's minds be conveyed from one to another.

3. *To make general signs.*—But neither was this sufficient to make words so useful as they ought to be. It is not enough for the perfection of language that sounds can be made signs of ideas, unless those signs can be so made use of as to comprehend several particular things: for the multiplication of words would have perplexed their use, had every particular thing need of a distinct name to be signified by. To remedy this inconvenience, language had yet a farther improvement in the use of general terms, whereby one word was made to mark a multitude of particular existences: which advantageous use of sounds was obtained only by the difference of the ideas they were made signs of: those names becoming general which are made to stand for general ideas, and those remaining particular where the ideas they are used for are particular.

4. Besides these names which stand for ideas, there be other words which men make use of, not to signify any idea, but the want or absence of some ideas simple or complex, or all ideas together; such as are *nihil* in Latin, and in English "ignorance" and "barrenness." All which negative or privative words cannot be said properly to belong to or signify no ideas; for then they would be perfectly insignificant sounds; but they relate to positive ideas, and signify their absence.

5. *Words ultimately derived from such as signify sensible ideas.* —It may also lead us a little towards the original of all our notions

and knowledge, if we remark how great a dependence our words have on common sensible ideas; and how those which are made use of to stand for actions and notions quite removed from sense, have their rise from thence, and from obvious sensible ideas are transferred to more abstruse significations, and made to stand for ideas that come not under the cognizance of our senses: *v. g.*, to "imagine, apprehend, comprehend, adhere, conceive, instil, disgust, disturbance, tranquillity," &c., are all words taken from the operations of sensible things, and applied to certain modes of thinking. Spirit, in its primary signification, is "breath;" angel, a "messenger:" and I doubt not but, if we could trace them to their sources, we should find, in all languages, the names which stand for things that fall not under our senses to have had their first rise from sensible ideas. By which we may give some kind of guess what kind of notions they were, and whence derived, which filled their minds who were the first beginners of languages; and how nature, even in the naming of things, unawares suggested to men the originals and principles of all their knowledge: whilst to give names, that might make known to others any operations they felt in themselves, or any other ideas that came not under their senses, they were fain to borrow words from ordinary known ideas of sensation, by that means to make others the more easily to conceive those operations they experimented in themselves, which made no outward sensible appearances; and then, when they had got known and agreed names to signify those internal operations of their own minds, they were sufficiently furnished to make known by words all their other ideas, since they could consist of nothing but either of outward sensible perceptions, or of the inward operations of their minds about them; we having, as has been proved, no ideas at all but what originally come either from sensible objects without, or what we feel within ourselves from the inward workings of our own spirits, of which we are conscious to ourselves within.

6. *Distribution.*—But, to understand better the use and force of language as subservient to instruction and knowledge, it will be convenient to consider,

First, To what it is that names, in the use of language, are immediately applied.

Secondly, Since all (except proper) names are general, and so stand not particularly for this or that single thing, but for sorts and ranks of things, it will be necessary to consider, in the next place, what the sorts and kinds, or, if you rather like the Latin names, what the *species* and *genera* of things are, wherein they consist, and how they come to be made. These being (as they ought) well looked into, we shall the better come to find the right use of words, the natural advantages and defects of language, and the remedies that ought to be used to avoid the inconveniences of obscurity or uncertainty in the signification of words; without which it is impossible to discourse with any clearness or order concerning knowledge: which being conversant about propositions, and those most commonly universal ones, has greater connection with words than perhaps is suspected.

These considerations, therefore, shall be the matter of the following chapters.

---

## CHAPTER II.

### OF THE SIGNIFICATION OF WORDS.

1. *Words are sensible signs necessary for communication.*—Man, though he have great variety of thoughts, and such from which others as well as himself might receive profit and delight, yet they are all within his own breast, invisible, and hidden from others, nor can of themselves be made appear. The comfort and advantage of society not being to be had without communication of thoughts, it was necessary that man should find out some external sensible signs, whereby those invisible ideas which his thoughts are made up of might be made known to others. For this purpose nothing was so fit, either for plenty or quickness, as those articulate sounds which, with so much ease and variety, he found himself able to make. Thus we may conceive how words, which were by nature so well adapted to that purpose, came to be made use of by men as the signs of their ideas; not by any natural connexion that there is between particular articulate sounds and certain ideas, for then there would be but one language amongst all men; but by a voluntary imposition, whereby such a word is made arbitrarily the mark of such an idea. The use, then, of words is to be sensible marks of ideas, and the ideas they stand for are their proper and immediate signification.

2. *Words are the sensible signs of his ideas who uses them.*—The use men have of these marks being either to record their own thoughts for the assistance of their own memory, or, as it were, to bring out their ideas, and lay them before the view of others: words in their primary or immediate signification stand for nothing but the ideas in the mind of him that uses them, how imperfectly soever or carelessly those ideas are collected from the things which they are supposed to represent. When a man speaks to another, it is that he may be understood; and the end of speech is, that those sounds, as marks, may make known his ideas to the hearer. That, then, which words are the marks of are the ideas of the speaker: nor can any one apply them, as marks, immediately to any thing else but the ideas that he himself hath. For, this would be to make them signs of his own conceptions, and yet apply them to other ideas; which would be

to make them signs and not signs of his ideas at the same time;
and so, in effect to have no signification at all. Words being
voluntary signs, they cannot be voluntary signs imposed by him
on things he knows not. That would be to make them signs of
nothing, sounds without signification. //A man cannot make his
words the signs either of qualities in things, or of conceptions in
the mind of another, whereof he has none in his own. Till he
has some ideas of his own, he cannot suppose them to correspond
with the conceptions of another man, nor can he use any signs
for them: for thus they would be the signs of he knows not what,
which is in truth to be the signs of nothing. But when he
represents to himself other men's ideas by some of his own, if he
consent to give them the same names that other men do, it is
still to his own ideas; to ideas that he has, and not to ideas that
he has not.

3./ This is so necessary in the use of language, that in this
respect, the knowing and the ignorant, the learned and unlearned,
use the words they speak (with any meaning) all alike. They, in
every man's mouth, stand for the ideas he has, and which he
would express by them./ A child having taken notice of nothing
in the metal he hears called "gold," but the bright shining yellow
colour, he applies the word "gold" only to his own idea of that
colour, and nothing else; and therefore calls the same colour in
a peacock's tail, "gold." Another, that hath better observed,
adds to shining yellow great weight: and then the sound "gold,"
when he uses it, stands for a complex idea of a shining yellow
and very weighty substance. Another adds to those qualities
fusibility: and then the word "gold" to him signifies a body,
bright, yellow, fusible, and very heavy. Another adds malleability. Each of these uses equally the word "gold," when they
have occasion to express the idea which they have applied it
to: but it is evident that each can apply it only to his own idea;
nor can he make it stand as a sign of such a complex idea as he
has not.

4. *Words often secretly referred.*—But though words, as they
are used by men, can properly and immediately signify nothing
but the ideas that are in the mind of the speaker, yet they in
their thoughts give them a secret reference to two other things.

*First, To the ideas in other men's minds.*—First, They suppose
their words to be marks of the ideas in the minds also of other
men, with whom they communicate: for else they should talk in
vain, and could not be understood, if the sounds they applied to
one idea were such as by the hearer were applied to another,
which is to speak two languages. But in this men stand not
usually to examine whether the idea they and those they discourse with have in their minds be the same: but think it enough
that they use the word, as they imagine, in the common acceptation of that language; in which they suppose, that the idea they

make it a sign of is precisely the same to which the understanding men of that country apply that name.

5. *Secondly, To the reality of things.*—Secondly, Because men would not be thought to talk barely of their own imaginations, but of things as really they are; therefore they often suppose their words to stand also for the reality of things. But this relating more particularly to substances and their names, as perhaps the former does to simple ideas and modes, we shall speak of these two different ways of applying words more at large when we come to treat of the names of mixed modes and substances in particular: though give me leave here to say, that it is a perverting the use of words, and brings unavoidable obscurity and confusion into their signification, whenever we make them stand for any thing but those ideas we have in our own minds.

6. *Words by use readily excite ideas.*—Concerning words also it is farther to be considered: First, That they being immediately the signs of men's ideas, and by that means, the instruments whereby men communicate their conceptions, and express to one another those thoughts and imaginations they have within their own breasts, there comes, by constant use, to be such a connexion between certain sounds and the ideas they stand for, that the names heard almost as readily excite certain ideas, as if the objects themselves which are apt to produce them did actually affect the senses. Which is manifestly so in all obvious sensible qualities, and in all substances that frequently and familiarly occur to us.

7. *Words often used without signification.*—Secondly, That though the proper and immediate signification of words are ideas in the mind of the speaker, yet because, by familiar use from our cradles, we come to learn certain articulate sounds very perfectly, and have them readily on our tongues, and always at hand in our memories, but yet are not always careful to examine or settle their significations perfectly; it often happens that men, even when they would apply themselves to an attentive consideration, do set their thoughts more on words than things. Nay, because words are many of them learned before the ideas are known for which they stand; therefore some, not only children, but men, speak several words no otherwise than parrots do, only because they have learned them, and have been accustomed to those sounds. But so far as words are of use and signification, so far is there is a constant connexion between the sound and the idea, and a designation that the one stand for the other: without which application of them they are nothing but so much insignificant noise.

8. *Their signification perfectly arbitrary.*—Words, by long and familiar use, as has been said, come to excite in men certain ideas so constantly and readily, that they are apt to suppose a natural connexion between them. But that they signify only

men's peculiar ideas, and that by a perfectly arbitrary imposition, is evident in that they often fail to excite in others (even that use the same language) the same ideas we take them to be the signs of: and every man has so inviolable a liberty to make words stand for what ideas he pleases, that no one hath the power to make others have the same ideas in their minds that he has, when they use the same words that he does. And therefore the great Augustus himself, in the possession of that power which ruled the world, acknowledged he could not make a new Latin word: which was as much as to say, that he could not arbitrarily appoint what idea any sound should be a sign of in the mouths and common language of his subjects. It is true, common use, by a tacit consent, appropriates certain sounds to certain ideas in all languages, which so far limits the signification of that sound, that unless a man applies it to the same idea, he does not speak properly: and let me add, that unless a man's words excite the same ideas in the hearer, which he makes them stand for in speaking, he does not speak intelligibly. But whatever be the consequence of any man's using of words differently, either from their general meaning, or the particular sense of the person to whom he addresses them, this is certain, their signification, in his use of them, is limited to his ideas, and they can be signs of nothing else.

## CHAPTER III.

### OF GENERAL TERMS.

**1. *The greatest part of words general.*—**All things that exist being particulars, it may perhaps be thought reasonable that words, which ought to be conformed to things, should be so too, I mean in their signification: but yet we find the quite contrary. The far greatest part of words, that make all languages, are general terms: which has not been the effect of neglect or chance, but of reason and necessity.

**2. *For every particular thing to have a name is impossible.*—**First, It is impossible that every particular thing should have a distinct peculiar name. For the signification and use of words depending on that connexion which the mind makes between its ideas and the sounds it uses as signs of them, it is necessary, in the application of names to things, that the mind should have distinct ideas of the things, and retain also the particular name that belongs to every one, with its peculiar appropriation to that idea. But it is beyond the power of human capacity to frame and retain distinct ideas of all the particular things we meet with: every bird and beast men saw, every tree and plant that affected the senses, could not find a place in the most capacious understanding. If it be looked on as an instance of a prodigious memory, that some generals have been able to call every soldier in their army by his proper name, we may easily find a reason why men have never attempted to give names to each sheep in their flock, or crow that flies over their heads; much less to call every leaf of plants or grain of sand that came in their way by a peculiar name.

3. *And useless.*—Secondly, If it were possible, it would yet be useless, because it would not serve to the chief end of language. Men would in vain heap up names of particular things, that would not serve them to communicate their thoughts. Men learn names, and use them in talk with others, only that they may be understood: which is then only done when, by use or consent, the sound I make by the organs of speech excites, in another man's mind who hears it, the idea I apply it to in mine when I speak it. This cannot be done by names applied to particular things, whereof I alone having the ideas in my mind, the names of them could not be significant or intelligible to another who was not acquainted with all those very particular things which had fallen under my notice.

4. Thirdly, But yet granting this also feasible (which I think is not), yet a distinct name for every particular thing would not be of any great use for the improvement of knowledge: which, though founded in particular things, enlarges itself by general views; to which things reduced into sorts under general names, are properly subservient. These, with the names belonging to them, come within some compass, and do not multiply every moment beyond what either the mind can contain, or use requires. And therefore in these, men have for the most part stopped: but yet not so as to hinder themselves from distinguishing particular things by appropriated names, where convenience demands it. And therefore in their own species, which they have most to do with, and wherein they have often occasion to mention particular persons, they make use of proper names; and there distinct individuals have distinct denominations.

5. *What things have proper names.*—Besides persons, countries also, cities, rivers, mountains, and other the like distinctions of place, have usually found peculiar names, and that for the same reason; they being such as men have often an occasion to mark particularly. and, as it were, set before others in their discourses with them. And I doubt not but if we had reason to mention particular horses as often as we have to mention particular men, we should have proper names for the one as familiar as for the other; and Bucephalus would be a word as much in use as Alexander. And therefore we see that amongst jockeys, horses have their proper names to be known and distinguished by, as commonly as their servants; because amongst them there is often occasion to mention this or that particular horse when he is out of sight.

**6.** *How general words are made.*—The next thing to be considered is, how general words come to be made. For, since all things that exist are only particulars, how come we by general terms, or where find we those general natures they are supposed to stand for? Words become general by being made the signs of general ideas: and ideas become general by separating from them the circumstances of time, and place, and any other ideas that may determine them to this or that particular existence. By this way of abstraction they are made capable of representing more individuals than one; each of which, having in it a conformity to that abstract idea, is (as we call it) of that sort.

**7.** But, to deduce this a little more distinctly, it will not perhaps be amiss to trace our notions and names from their beginning, and observe by what degrees we proceed, and by what steps we enlarge our ideas from our first infancy. There is nothing more evident than that the ideas of the persons children converse with (to instance in them alone), are, like the persons themselves, only particular. The ideas of the nurse and the mother are well framed in their minds; and, like pictures of them there, represent only those individuals. The names they first gave to them are confined to these individuals; and the names of "nurse" and "mamma" the child uses, determine themselves to those persons. Afterwards, when time and a larger acquaintance has made them observe that there are a great many other things in the world, that, in some common agreements of shape and several other qualities, resemble their father and mother, and those persons they have been used to, they frame an idea which they find those many particulars do partake in; and to that they give, with others, the name "man," for example. And thus they come to have a general name, and a general idea. Wherein they make nothing new, but only leave out of the complex idea they had of Peter and James, Mary and Jane, that which is peculiar to each, and retain only what is common to them all.

**8.** By the same way that they come by the general name and idea of "man," they easily advance to more general names and notions. For, observing that several things that differ from their idea of "man," and cannot therefore be comprehended under that name, have yet certain qualities wherein they agree with man, by retaining only those qualities, and uniting them into one idea, they have again another and a more general idea; to which having given a name, they make a term of a more comprehensive extension: which new idea is made, not by any new addition, but only, as before, by leaving out the shape and some other properties signified by the name "man," and retaining only a body, with life, sense, and spontaneous motion, comprehended under the name "animal."

**9.** *General natures are nothing but abstract ideas.*—That this is the way whereby men first formed general ideas, and general names to them, I think, is so evident, that there needs no other proof of it but the considering of a man's self or others, and the ordinary proceedings of their minds in knowledge : and he that thinks general natures or notions are anything else but such abstract and partial ideas of more complex ones, taken at first from particular existences, will, I fear, be at a loss where to find them. For, let any one reflect, and then tell me wherein does his idea of "man" differ from that of "Peter" and "Paul," or his idea of "horse" from that of "Bucephalus," but in the leaving out something that is peculiar to each individual, and retaining so much of those particular complex ideas of several particular existences as they are found to agree in ? Of the complex ideas signified by the names "man" and "horse," leaving out but those particulars wherein they differ, and retaining only those wherein they agree, and of those making a new distinct complex idea, and giving the name "animal" to it, one has a more general term, that comprehends with man, several other creatures. Leave out of the idea of "animal" sense and spontaneous motion, and the remaining complex idea, made up of the remaining simple ones of "body, life, and nourishment," becomes a more general one under the more comprehensive term, *vivens.* And, not to dwell longer upon this particular so evident in itself, by the same way the mind proceeds to "body," "substance," and at last to "being," "thing," and such universal terms, which stand for any of our ideas whatsoever. To conclude: this whole mystery of *genera* and *species*, which make such a noise in the schools, and are, with justice, so little regarded out of them, is nothing else but abstract ideas, more or less comprehensive, with names annexed to them. In all which, this is constant and invariable, that every more general term stands for such an idea as is but a part of any of those contained under it.

**10.** *Why the genus is ordinarily made use of in definitions.*—This may show us the reason why, in the defining of words, which is nothing but declaring their signification, we make use of the genus, or next general word that comprehends it. Which is not out of necessity, but only to save the labour of enumerating the several simple ideas which the next general word or genus stands for ; or perhaps sometimes the shame of not being able to do it. But though defining by *genus* and *differentia* (I crave leave to use these terms of art, though originally Latin, since they most properly suit those notions they are applied to), I say, though defining by the genus be the shortest way, yet, I think, it may be doubted whether it be the best. This I am sure, it is not the only, and so not absolutely necessary. For, definition being nothing but making another understand by words what idea the term defined stands for, a definition is best made by

enumerating those simple ideas that are combined in the signification of the term defined : and if instead of such an enumeration
men have accustomed themselves to use the next general term, it
has not been out of necessity or for greater clearness, but for
quickness and despatch sake. For, I think, that to one who
desired to know what idea the word "man" stood for; if it should
be said, that man was a solid extended substance, having life,
sense, spontaneous motion, and the faculty of reasoning, I doubt
not but the meaning of the term "man" would be as well understood, and the idea it stands for be at least as clearly made
known, as when it is defined to be a "rational animal;" which,
by the several definitions of "animal," *vivens* and *corpus*, resolves
itself into those enumerated ideas. I have, in explaining the
term "man," followed here the ordinary definition of the schools :
which, though, perhaps, not the most exact, yet serves well
enough to my present purpose. And one may in this instance,
see what gave occasion to the rule that a definition must consist
of *genus* and *differentia :* and it suffices to show us the little
necessity there is of such a rule, or advantage in the strict
observing of it. For definitions, as has been said, being only the
explaining of one word by several others, so that the meaning or
idea it stands for may be certainly known; languages are not
always so made according to the rules of logic, that every term
can have its signification exactly and clearly expressed by two
others. Experience sufficiently satisfies us to the contrary : or
else those who have made this rule have done ill, that they have
given us so few definitions conformable to it. But of definitions
more in the next chapter.

11. *General and universal are creatures of the understanding.*—
To return to general words : it is plain, by what has been said,
that general and universal belong not to the real existence of
things; but are the inventions and creatures of the understanding, made by it for its own use, and concern only signs, whether
words or ideas. Words are general, as has been said, when used
for signs of general ideas, and so are applicable indifferently to
many particular things; and ideas are general when they are
set up as the representatives of many particular things : but
universality belongs not to things themselves, which are all of
them particular in their existence, even those words and ideas
which in their signification are general. When therefore we
quit particulars, the generals that rest are only creatures of our
own making, their general nature being nothing but the capacity
they are put into by the understanding of signifying or representing many particulars. For the signification they have is
nothing but a relation that by the mind of man is added
to them.*

12. *Abstract ideas are the essences of the* genera *and* species.--

* See note at the end of this chapter, p. 336.—EDIT.

The next thing therefore to be considered, is, what kind of signification it is that general words have. For as it is evident that they do not signify barely one particular thing, for then they would not be general terms, but proper names; so on the other side it is as evident they do not signify a plurality; for "man" and "men" would then signify the same, and the distinction of "numbers" (as grammarians call them) would be superfluous and useless. That then which general words signify, is a sort of things; and each of them does that by being a sign of an abstract idea in the mind; to which idea as things existing are found to agree, so they come to be ranked under that name; or, which is all one, be of that sort. Whereby it is evident, that the essences of the sorts, or (if the Latin word pleases better) *species* of things, are nothing else but these abstract ideas. For the having the essence of any species, being that which makes any thing to be of that species, and the conformity to the idea to which the name is annexed being that which gives a right to that name, the having the essence, and the having that conformity, must needs be the same thing: since to be of any species, and to have a right to the name of that species, is all one. As, for example: to be a man or of the species man, and to have right to the name "man," is the same thing. Again: to be a man, or of the species man, and have the essence of a man, is the same thing. Now, since nothing can be a man, or have a right to the name "man" but what has a conformity to the abstract idea the name "man' stands for; nor any thing be a man, or have a right to the species man, but what has the essence of that species; it follows, that the abstract idea for which the name stands, and the essence of the species, is one and the same. From whence it is easy to observe, that the essences of the sorts of things, and consequently the sorting of this, is the workmanship of the understanding that abstracts and makes those general ideas.

13. *They are the workmanship of the understanding, but have their foundation in the similitude of things.*—I would not here be thought to forget, much less to deny, that nature, in the production of things, makes several of them alike: there is nothing more obvious, especially in the races of animals, and all things propagated by seed. But yet, I think, we may say, the sorting of them under names is the workmanship of the understanding, taking occasion, from the similitude it observes amongst them, to make abstract general ideas, and set them up in the mind with names annexed to them, as patterns or forms; for in that sense the word "form" has a very proper signification, to which as particular things existing are found to agree, so they come to be of that species, have that denomination, or are put into that *classis*. For, when we say, "This is a man, that a horse; this justice, that cruelty; this a watch, that a jack;" what do we else but rank things under different specific names, as agreeing to those abstract ideas

of which we have made those names the signs? And what are
the essences of those species set out and marked by names, but
those abstract ideas in the mind; which are, as it were, the bonds
between particular things that exist, and the names they are to
be ranked under? And when general names have any connexion
with particular beings, these abstract ideas are the medium that
unites them: so that the essences of species, as distinguished and
denominated by us, neither are nor can be anything but those
precise abstract ideas we have in our minds. And therefore the
supposed real essences of substances, if different from our abstract
ideas, cannot be the essences of the species we rank things into.
For two species may be one as rationally as two different essences
be the essences of one species; and I demand, what are the
alterations may or may not be in a horse or lead, without making
either of them to be of another species? In determining the
species of things by our abstract ideas, this is easy to resolve.
But if any one will regulate himself herein by supposed real
essences, he will, I suppose, be at a loss: and he will never be
able to know when anything precisely ceases to be of the species
of a horse or lead.

14. *Each distinct abstract idea is a distinct essence.*—Nor will
any one wonder that I say, these essences, or abstract ideas (which
are the measures of name, and the boundaries of species), are the
workmanship of the understanding, who considers that at least
the complex ones are often, in several men, different collections
of simple ideas: and therefore that is covetousness to one man,
which is not so to another. Nay, even in substances, where their
abstract ideas seem to be taken from the things themselves, they
are not constantly the same; no, not in that species which is
most familiar to us, and with which we have the most intimate
acquaintance: it having been more than once doubted, whether
the fœtus born of a woman were a man, even so far as that it hath
been debated whether it were or were not to be nourished and
baptized: which could not be if the abstract idea or essence to
which the name "man" belonged were of nature's making, and
were not the uncertain and various collection of simple ideas,
which the understanding puts together, and then, abstracting it,
affixed a name to it. So. that in truth every distinct abstract
idea is a distinct essence: and the names that stand for such
distinct ideas, are the names of things essentially different. Thus,
a circle is as essentially different from an oval as a sheep from a
goat, and rain is as essentially different from snow as water from
earth; that abstract idea which is the essence of one, being impossible to be communicated to the other. And thus any two
abstract ideas, that in any part vary one from another, with two
distinct names annexed to them, constitute two distinct sorts, or,
if you please, *species*, as essentially different as any two the most
remote or opposite in the world.

**15.** *Real and nominal essence.*—But since the essences of things are thought, by some (and not without reason), to be wholly unknown; it may not be amiss to consider the several significations of the word "essence."

First, Essence may be taken for the being of any thing, whereby it is what it is. And thus the real internal (but generally in substances unknown) constitution of things, whereon their discoverable qualities depend, may be called their "essence." This is the proper original signification of the word, as is evident from the formation of it; *essentia*, in its primary notation, signifying properly "being." And in this sense it is still used when we speak of the essence of particular things without giving them any name.

Secondly, The learning and disputes of the schools having been much busied about *genus* and *species*, the word "essence" has almost lost its primary signification; and, instead of the real constitution of things, has been almost wholly applied to the artificial constitution of *genus* and *species*. It is true there is ordinarily supposed a real constitution of the sorts of things: and it is past doubt there must be some real constitution, on which any collection of simple ideas co-existing must depend. But it being evident that things are ranked under names into sorts or species only as they agree to certain abstract ideas to which we have annexed those names, the essence of each genus or sort comes to be nothing but that abstract idea, which the general or "sortal" (if I may have leave so to call it from "sort," as I do "general" from *genus*) name stands for. And this we shall find to be that which the word "essence" imports in its most familiar use. These two sorts of essences, I suppose, may not unfitly be termed, the one the "real," the other the "nominal," essence.

**16.** *Constant connexion between the name and nominal essence.*— Between the nominal essence and the name there is so near a connexion, that the name of any sort of things cannot be attributed to any particular being but what has this essence, whereby it answers that abstract idea whereof that name is the sign.

**17.** *Supposition that species are distinguished by their real essences, useless.*—Concerning the real essences of corporeal substances (to mention those only), there are, if I mistake not, two opinions. The one is of those who, using the word "essence" for they know not what, suppose a certain number of those essences, according to which all natural things are made, and wherein they do exactly every one of them partake, and so become of this or that species. The other and more rational opinion is of those who look on all natural things to have a real but unknown constitution of their insensible parts, from which flow those sensible qualities which serve us to distinguish them one from another, according as we have occasion to rank them into sorts under common denominations. The former of these opinions, which supposes these essences as a certain number of forms or moulds wherein all natural things that exist are cast and do equally partake, has, I imagine, very much perplexed the knowledge of natural things. The frequent productions of monsters, in all the species of animals, and of changelings, and other strange issues of human birth, carry with them difficulties not possible to consist with this hypothesis; since it is as impossible that two things, partaking exactly of the same real essence, should have different properties, as that two figures partaking of the same real essence of a circle, should have different properties. But were there no other reason against it, yet the supposition of essences that cannot be known, and the making them nevertheless to be that which distinguishes the species of things, is so wholly useless and unserviceable to any part of our knowledge, that that alone were sufficient to make us lay it by, and content ourselves with such essences of the sorts or species of things as come within the reach of our knowledge: which, when seriously considered, will be found, as I have said, to be nothing else but those abstract complex ideas to which we have annexed distinct general names.

18. *Real and nominal essence the same in simple ideas and modes different in substances.*—Essences being thus distinguished into nominal and real, we may further observe, that in the species of simple ideas and modes, they are always the same: but in substances, always quite different. Thus a figure including a space between three lines, is the real as well as nominal essence of a triangle; it being not only the abstract idea to which the general name is annexed, but the very *essentia*, or " being," of the thing itself, that foundation from which all its properties flow, and to which they are all inseparably annexed. But it is far otherwise concerning that parcel of matter which makes the ring on my finger, wherein these two essences are apparently different. For it is the real constitution of its insensible parts, on which depend all those properties of colour, weight, fusibility, fixedness, &c., which makes it to be gold, or gives it a right to that name, which is therefore its nominal essence; since nothing can be called "gold" but what has a conformity of qualities to that abstract complex idea, to which that name is annexed. But this distinction of essences, belonging particularly to substances, we shall, when we come to consider their names, have an occasion to treat of more fully.

19. *Essences ingenerable and incorruptible.*—That such abstract ideas with names to them, as we have been speaking of, are essences, may farther appear by what we are told concerning essences; viz., that they are all ingenerable and incorruptible. Which cannot be true of the real constitutions of things, which begin and perish with them. All things that exist, besides their Author, are all liable to change; especially those things we are

acquainted with, and have ranked into bands, under distinct
names or ensigns. Thus that which was grass to-day, is to-
morrow the flesh of a sheep; and, within few days after, becomes
part of a man; in all which and the like changes, it is evident
their real essence, *i. e.*, that constitution whereon the properties
of these several things depended, is destroyed, and perishes with
them. But essences being taken for ideas established in the
mind, with names annexed to them, they are supposed to remain
steadily the same, whatever mutations the particular substances
are liable to. For whatever becomes of Alexander and Bucephalus, the ideas to which "man" and "horse" are annexed,
are supposed nevertheless to remain in the same; and so the
essences of those species are preserved whole and undestroyed,
whatever changes happen to any or all of the individuals of those
species. By this means the essence of a species rests safe and
entire, without the existence of so much as one individual of
that kind. For were there now no circle existing any where in
the world (as, perhaps, that figure exists not any where exactly
marked out), yet the idea annexed to that name would not cease
to be what it is; nor cease to be as a pattern, to determine
which of the particular figures we meet with, have, or have not,
a right to the name "circle," and so to show which of them, by
having that essence, was of that species. And though there
neither were nor had been in nature such a beast as an unicorn,
nor such a fish as a mermaid; yet, supposing those names to
stand for complex abstract ideas, that contained no inconsistency
in them, the essence of a mermaid is as intelligible as that of a
man; and the idea of an unicorn, as certain, steady, and permanent as that of a horse. From what has been said, it is evident,
that the doctrine of the immutability of essences proves them to
be only abstract ideas, and is founded on the relation established
between them, and certain sounds as signs of them; and will
always be true, as long as the same name can have the same
signification.

20. *Recapitulation.*—To conclude: This is that which in short
I would say, viz., that all the great business of *genera* and
*species*, and their essences, amounts to no more but this—that
men making abstract ideas, and settling them in their minds,
with names annexed to them, do thereby enable themselves to
consider things, and discourse of them, as it were, in bundles,
for the easier and readier improvement and communication of
their knowledge; which would advance but slowly, were their
words and thoughts confined only to particulars.

## NOTE.—Page 330.

AGAINST this the bishop of Worcester objects, and our author answers* as followeth : "However," saith the bishop, "the abstracted ideas are the work of the mind, yet they are not mere creatures of the mind ; as appears by an instance produced of the essence of the sun being in one single individual : in which case it is granted, that the idea may be so abstracted that more suns might agree in it, and it is as much a sort as if there were as many suns as there are stars. So that here we have a real essence subsisting in one individual, but capable of being multiplied into more, and the same essence remaining. But in this one sun there is a real essence, and not a mere nominal or abstracted essence : but suppose there were more suns, would not each of them have the real essence of the sun ? For, what is it makes the second sun, but having the same real essence with the first ? If it were but a nominal essence, then the second would have nothing but the name."

"This, as I understand it," replies Mr. Locke, "is to prove, that the abstract general essence of any sort of things, or things of the same denomination, *v. g.,* of man or marigold, hath a real being out of the understanding, which, I confess, I am not able to conceive. Your lordship's proof here brought out of my Essay concerning the sun, I humbly conceive, will not reach it : because what is said there does not at all concern the real but nominal essence ; as is evident from hence, that the idea I speak of there is a complex idea : but we have no complex idea of the internal constitution or real essence of the sun. Besides, I say expressly, that our distinguishing substances into species by names is not at all founded on their real essences. So that the sun being one of these substances, I cannot, in the place quoted by your lordship, be supposed to mean by ' essence of the sun,' the real essence of the sun, unless I had so expressed. But all this argument will be at an end, when your lordship shall have explained what you mean by these words, ' true sun.' In my sense of them, any thing will be a true sun to which the name ' sun ' may be truly and properly applied ; and to that substance or thing the name ' sun ' may be truly and properly applied, which has united in it that combination of sensible qualities by which any thing else that is called ' sun ' is distinguished from other substances, *i. e.,* by the nominal essence ; and thus our sun is denominated and distinguished from a fixed star, not by a real essence that we do not know (for if we did, it is possible we should find the real essence or constitution of one of the fixed stars to be the same with that of our sun), but by a complex idea of sensible qualities co-existing, which, wherever they are found, ' make a true sun.' And thus I crave leave to answer your lordship's question : ' For what is it makes the second sun to be a true sun, but having the same real essence with the first ? If it were but a nominal essence, then the second would have nothing but the name.'

"I humbly conceive, if it had the ' nominal essence,' it would have something besides ' the name,' viz., that nominal essence which is sufficient to denominate it truly ' a sun,' or to make it be ' a true sun,'

* In his first Letter, p. 189, &c.

though we know nothing of that real essence whereon that nominal one depends. Your lordship will then argue, that that 'real essence' is in the 'second sun,' and 'makes the second sun.' I grant it, when the 'second sun' comes to exist so as to be perceived by us to have all the ideas contained in our complex idea, *i. e.*, in our 'nominal essence' of a 'sun.' For should it be true (as is now believed by astronomers) that the real essence of the sun were in any of the fixed stars, yet such a star could not for that be by us called 'a sun,' whilst it answers not our complex idea, or nominal essence of a sun. But how far that will prove, that the essences of things, as they are knowable by us, have a reality in them distinct from that of abstract ideas in the mind, which are merely creatures of the mind, I do not see; and we shall farther inquire in considering your lordship's following words: 'Therefore,' say you, 'there must be a real essence in every individual of the same kind.' Yes, and I beg leave of your lordship to say, of a different kind too. For that alone is it which makes it to be what it is.

"That every individual substance has a real, internal, individual constitution, *i. e.*, a real essence, that makes it to be what it is, I readily grant. Upon this your lordship says, 'Peter, James, and John are all true and real men.' Answer. Without doubt, supposing them to be men, they are 'true and real men,' *i. e.*, supposing the name of that species belongs to them. And so three bobaques are all true and real bobaques, supposing the name of that species of animals belongs to them.

"For I beseech your lordship to consider, whether, in your way of arguing, by naming them Peter, James, and John, names familiar to us as appropriated to individuals of the species man, your lordship does not first suppose them men, and then very safely ask, whether they be not all 'true and real men?' But if I should ask your lordship, whether Wewena, Chuckery, and Cousheda were true and real men or no? your lordship would not be able to tell me until, I having pointed out to your lordship the individuals called by those names, your lordship, by examining whether they had in them those sensible qualities which your lordship has combined into that complex idea to which you give the specific name 'man,' determined them all or some of them to be of the species which you call 'man,' and so to be 'true and real men:' which when your lordship has determined, it is plain you did it by that which is only the nominal essence, as not knowing the real one. But your lordship farther asks, 'What is it makes Peter, James, and John real men? Is it the attributing the general name to them? No, certainly; but that the true and real essence of a man is in every one of them.'

"If, when your lordship asks, 'What makes them men?' your lordship used the word 'making' in the proper sense for the efficient cause, and in that sense it were true, that the essence of a man, *i. e.*, the specific essence of that species made a man, it would undoubtedly follow that this specific essence had a reality beyond that of being only a general, abstract idea in the mind. But when it is said, that it is 'the true and real essence of a man in every one of them that makes Peter, James, and John true and real men,' the true and real meaning of these words is no more but that the essence of that species, *i. e.*, the properties answering the complex, abstract idea to which the specific name is given, being found in them, that makes them be properly and truly called men, or is the reason why they are called men. Your lordship adds, 'And we must be as certain of this, as we are that they are men.'

" How, I beseech your lordship, are we certain that they are men, but only by our senses finding those properties in them which answers the abstract, complex idea which is in our minds of the specific idea, to which we have annexed the specific name man ?' This I take to be the true meaning of what your lordship says in the next words, viz., ' They take their denomination of being men from that common nature or essence which is in them ; ' and I am apt to think these words will not hold true in any other sense.

" Your lordship's fourth inference begins thus : ' That the general idea is not made from the simple ideas by the mere act of the mind abstracting from circumstances, but from reason and consideration of the nature of things.'

" I thought, my lord, ' that reason and consideration ' had been ' acts of the mind, mere acts of the mind,' when any thing was done by them. Your lordship gives a reason for it, viz., ' For when we see several individuals that have the same powers and properties, we thence infer, that there must be something common to all, which makes them of one kind.'

" I grant the inference to be true ; but must beg leave to deny that this proves, that the general idea the name is annexed to is not made by the mind. I have said (and it agrees with what your lordship here says), that ' the mind, in making its complex ideas of substances, only follows nature, and puts no ideas together which are not supposed to have an union in nature : nobody joins the voice of a sheep with the shape of an horse, nor the colour of lead with the weight and fixedness of gold, to be the complex ideas of any real substances, unless he has a mind to fill his head with chimeras, and his discourse with unintelligible words. Men, observing certain qualities always joined and existing together, therein copied nature, and of ideas so united made their complex ones of substances,' &c.* Which is very little different from what your lordship here says, that it is from our observation of individuals that we come to infer that ' there is something common to them all.' But I do not see how it will thence follow, that the general or specific idea is not made by the mere act of the mind. No, says your lordship, 'there is something common to them all, which makes them of one kind ; and if the difference of kinds be real, that which makes them all of one kind must not be a nominal but real essence.'

" This may be some objection to the name of 'nominal essence ;' but is, as I humbly conceive, none to the thing designed by it. There is an internal constitution of things, on which their properties depend. This your lordship and I are agreed of, and this we call the ' real essence.' There are also certain complex ideas, or combinations of these properties in men's minds, to which they commonly annex specific names, or names of sorts or kinds of things. This, I believe, your lordship does not deny. These complex ideas, for want of a better name, I have called ' nominal essences :' how properly, I will

* Book iii. chap. vi. sect. 28, 29

not dispute. But if any one will help me to a better name for them, I am ready to receive it : till then I must, to express myself, use this. Now, my lord, body, life, and the power of reasoning being not the real essence of a man, as I believe your lordship will agree, will your lordship say, that they are not enough to make the thing wherein they are found, of the kind called 'man,' and not of the kind called ' baboon,' because the difference of these kinds is real ? If this be not real enough to make the thing of one kind and not of another, I do not see how *animal rationale* can be enough really to distinguish a man from an horse ; for that is but the nominal, not real, essence of that kind designed by the name 'man.' And yet, I suppose, every one thinks it real enough to make a real difference between that and other kinds. And if nothing will serve the turn to *make* things of one kind and not of another (which as I have showed, signifies no more but ranking of them under different specific names) but their real, unknown constitutions, which are the real essences we are speaking of, I fear it would be a long while before we should have really different kinds of substances, or distinct names for them, unless we could distinguish them by these differences, of which we have no distinct conceptions. For I think it would not be readily answered me, if I should demand, wherein lies the real difference in the internal constitution of a stag from that of a buck, which are each of them very well known to be of one kind, and not of the other ; and nobody questions but that the kinds whereof each of them is, are really different.

"Your lordship farther says, 'And this difference doth not depend upon the complex ideas of substances, whereby men arbitrarily join modes together in their minds.' I confess, my lord, I know not what to say to this, because I do not know what these ' complex ideas of substances ' are ' whereby men arbitrarily join modes together in their minds.' But I am apt to think there is a mistake in the matter, by the words that follow, which are these : 'For, let them mistake in their complication of ideas, either in leaving out or putting in what doth not belong to them ; and let their ideas be what they please ; the real essence of a man, and a horse, and a tree, are just what they were.'

"The mistake I spoke of, I humbly suppose, is this : That things are here taken to be distinguished by their real essences ; when, by the very way of speaking of them, it is clear that they are already distinguished by their nominal essences, and are so taken to be. For what, I beseech your lordship, does your lordship mean when you say, 'The real essence of a man, and a horse, and a tree,' but that there are such kinds already set out by the signification of these names, 'man, horse, tree?' And what, I beseech your lordship, is the signification of each of these specific names but the complex idea it stands for ? And that complex idea is the nominal essence, and nothing else. So that, taking ' man,' as your lordship does here, to stand for a kind or sort of individuals, all which agree in that common, complex idea, which that specific name stands for, it is certain that the real essence of all the individuals, comprehended under the specific name ' man,' in your use of it, would be just the same, let others leave out or put into their complex idea of ' man ' what they please ; because the real essence on which that unaltered complex idea, *i. e.*, those properties depend, must necessarily be concluded to be the same.

" For I take it for granted, that in using the name 'man' in this place, your lordship uses it for that complex idea which is in your lordship's mind of that species. So that your lordship, by putting it for, or substituting it in the place of, that complex idea where you say the real essence of it is just as it was, or the very same it was, does suppose the idea it stands for to be steadily* the same.   For if I change the signification of the word ' man,' whereby it may not comprehend just the same individuals which in your lordship's sense it does, but shut out some of those that to your lordship are men in your signification of the word ' man,' or take in others to which your lordship does not allow the name 'man ;' I do not think you will say, that the real essence of man, in both these senses, is the same ; and yet your lordship seems to say so when you say, ' Let men mistake in the complication of their ideas, either in leaving out or putting in what does not belong to them ; and let their ideas be what they please ; the real essence of the individuals comprehended under the names annexed to these ideas will be the same :' for so, I humbly conceive, it must be put, to make out what your lordship aims at.     For as your lordship puts it by the name of ' man,' or any other specific name, your lordship seems to me to suppose that that name stands for, and not for, the same idea, at the same time.

" For example, my lord, let your lordship's idea, to which you annex the sign ' man,' be a rational animal ; let another man's idea be a rational animal of such a shape ; let a third man's idea be of an animal of such a size and shape, leaving out rationality ; let a fourth's be an animal with a body of such a shape, and an immaterial substance, with a power of reasoning ; let a fifth leave out of his idea an immaterial substance : it is plain every one of these will call his a ' man,' as well as your lordship ; and yet it is as plain that ' man,' as standing for all these distinct, complex ideas, cannot be supposed to have the same internal constitution, *i. e.*, the same real essence. The truth is, every distinct, abstract idea, with a name to it, makes a real, distinct kind, whatever the real essence (which we know not of any of them) be.

" And therefore I grant it true what your lordship says in the next words : 'And let the nominal essences differ never so much, the real, common essences or nature of the several kinds are not at all altered by them :' *i. e.*, That our thoughts or ideas cannot alter the real constitutions that are in things that exist, there is nothing more certain. But yet it is true, that the change of ideas to which we annex them, can and does alter the signification of their names, and thereby alter the kinds which by these names we rank and sort them into.   Your lordship farther adds, ' And these real essences are unchangeable,' *i. e.*, the internal constitutions ' are unchangeable.'   Of what, I beseech your lordship, are the 'internal constitutions unchangeable?'   Not of any thing that exists, but of God alone ; for they may be changed all as easily by that hand that made them, as the internal frame of a watch.   What, then, is it that is unchangeable?   The internal constitution or real essence of a species ;  which, in plain English, is no more but this : Whilst the same specific name, *v. g.*, of 'man, horse, or tree,' is annexed to or made the sign of the same abstract, complex idea under which I rank several individuals, it is impossible but the real constitution on

* This is the reading of the fourth edition in folio ; those in octavo have *ideally.*—EDIT.

wnich that unaltered, complex idea or nominal essence depends, must be the same : *i. e.,* in other words : Where we find all the same proper· ties, we have reason to conclude there is the same real, internal con· stitution from which those properties flow.

"But your lordship proves the real essences to be unchangeable, because God makes them, in these following words : 'For however there may happen some variety in individuals by particular accidents, yet the essences of men, and horses, and trees, remain always the same ; because they do not depend on the ideas of men, but on the will of the Creator, who hath made several sorts of beings.'

"It is true, the real constitutions or essences of particular things existing, 'do not depend on the ideas of men, but on the will of the Creator ;' but their being ranked into sorts, under such and such names, does depend, and wholly depend, on the ideas of men."

----

# CHAPTER IV.

## OF THE NAMES OF SIMPLE IDEAS.

1. *Names of simple ideas, modes, and substances, have each something peculiar.*—Though all words, as I have shown, signify nothing immediately but the ideas in the mind of the speaker, yet, upon a nearer survey, we shall find that the names of simple ideas, mixed modes (under which I comprise relations too), and natural substances, have each of them something peculiar, and different from the other. For example :—

2. *First, Names of simple ideas and substances intimate real existence.*—First, The names of simple ideas and substances, with the abstract ideas in the mind which they immediately signify, intimate also some real existence, from which was derived their original pattern. But the names of mixed modes terminate in the idea that is in the mind, and lead not the thoughts any far- ther, as we shall see more at large in the following chapter.

3. *Secondly, Names of simple ideas and modes signify always both real and nominal essence.*—Secondly, The names of simple ideas and modes signify always the real as well as nominal essence of their species. But the names of natural substances signify rarely, if ever, any thing but barely the nominal essences of those species, as we shall show in the chapter that treats of the names of substances in particular.

4. *Thirdly, Names of simple ideas undefinable.*—Thirdly, The names of simple ideas are not capable of any definitions ; the names of all complex ideas are. It has not, that I know, hither- to been taken notice of by any body, what words are, and what are not, capable of being defined : the want whereof is (as I am apt to think) not seldom the occasion of great wrangling and obscurity in men's discourses, whilst some demand definitions of terms that cannot be defined ; and others think they ought to

rest satisfied in an explication made by a more general word and its restriction (or, to speak in terms of art, by a genus and difference), when even after such definition made according to rule, those who hear it have often no more a clear conception of the meaning of the word than they had before. This, at least, I think, that the showing what words are, and what are not, capable of definitions, and wherein consists a good definition, is not wholly besides our present purpose; and perhaps will afford so much light to the nature of these signs and our ideas, as to deserve a more particular consideration.

5. *If all were definable, it would be a process* in infinitum.—I will not here trouble myself to prove that all terms are not definable, from that progress, *in infinitum*, which it will visibly lead us into if we should allow that all names could be defined. For if the terms of one definition were still to be defined by another, where at last should we stop? But I shall, from the nature of our ideas, and the signification of our words, show why some names can, and others cannot, be defined, and which they are.

6. *What a definition is.*—I think it is agreed, that a definition is nothing else but "the showing the meaning of one word by several other not synonymous terms." The meaning of words being only the ideas they are made to stand for by him that uses them, the meaning of any term is then showed, or the word is defined, when by other words the idea it is made the sign of and annexed to in the mind of the speaker is, as it were, represented or set before the view of another; and thus its signification ascertained. This is the only use and end of definitions; and therefore the only measure of what is or is not a good definition.

7. *Simple ideas, why undefinable.*—This being premised, I say, that "the names of simple ideas," and those only, "are capable of being defined." The reason whereof is this, that the several terms of a definition signifying several ideas, they can all together by no means represent an idea which has no composition at all: and therefore a definition (which is properly nothing but the showing the meaning of one word by several others not signifying each the same thing) can in the names of simple ideas have no place.

8. *Instances: motion.*—The not observing this difference in our ideas and their names, has produced that eminent trifling in the schools, which is so easy to be observed in the definitions they give us of some few of these simple ideas. For, as to the greatest part of them, even those masters of definitions were fain to leave them untouched, merely by the impossibility they found in it. What more exquisite jargon could the wit of man invent than this definition?—"The act of a being in power, as far forth as in power;" which would puzzle any rational man, to whom it was not already known by its famous absurdity, to guess what word it could ever be supposed to be the explication of. If

Tully, asking a Dutchman what *beweeginge* was, should have received this explication in his own language, that it was *actus entis in potentiâ quatenus in potentiâ;* I ask whether any one can imagine he could thereby have understood what the word *beweeginge* signified, or have guessed what idea a Dutchman ordinarily had in his mind, and would signify to another, when he used that sound ?

9. Nor have the modern philosophers, who have endeavoured to throw off the jargon of the schools and speak intelligibly, much better succeeded in defining simple ideas, whether by explaining their causes, or any otherwise. The atomists, who define motion to be "a passage from one place to another :" what do they more than put one synonymous word for another ? For what is "passage" other than motion ? And if they were asked what "passage" was, how would they better define it than by "motion ?" For is it not at least as proper and significant to say, "Passage is a motion from one place to another," as to say, "Motion is a passage ?" &c. This is to translate, and not to define, when we change two words of the same signification one for another; which, when one is better understood than the other, may serve to discover what idea the unknown stands for; but it is very far from a definition, unless we will say, every English word in the dictionary is the definition of the Latin word it answers, and that "motion" is a definition of *motus.* Nor will the successive application of the parts of the superficies of one body to those of another, which the Cartesians give us, prove a much better definition of motion, when well examined.

10. *Light.*—"The act of perspicuous, as far forth as perspicuous," is another peripatetic definition of a simple idea; which, though not more absurd than the former of motion, yet betrays its uselessness and insignificancy more plainly, because experience will easily convince any one that it cannot make the meaning of the word "light" (which it pretends to define) at all understood by a blind man : but the definition of motion appears not at first sight so useless, because it escapes this way of trial. For, this simple idea entering by the touch as well as sight, it is impossible to show an example of any one, who has no other way to get the idea of motion but barely by the definition of that name. Those who tell us, that light is a great number of little globules striking briskly on the bottom of the eye, speak more intelligibly than the schools : but yet these words, ever so well understood, would make the idea the word "light" stands for, no more known to a man that understands it not before, than if one should tell him that light was nothing but a company of little tennis-balls, which fairies all day long struck with rackets against some men's foreheads, whilst they passed by others. For, granting this explication of the thing to be true; yet the idea of the cause of light, if we had it ever so exact,

would no more give us the idea of light itself as it is such a particular perception in us, than the idea of the figure and motion
of a sharp piece of steel would give us the idea of that pain
which it is able to cause in us. For the cause of any sensation,
and the sensation itself, in all the simple ideas of one sense, are
two ideas; and two ideas so different and distant one from
another, that no two can be more so. And therefore should Des
Cartes's globules strike ever so long on the *retina* of a man who
was blind by a *gutta serena*, he would thereby never have any
idea of light, or anything approaching to it, though he understood what little globules were, and what striking on another
body was, ever so well. And therefore the Cartesians very well
distinguish between that light which is the cause of that sensation in us, and the idea which is produced in us by it, and is that
which is properly light.

11. *Simple ideas, why undefinable, farther explained.*—Simple
ideas, as has been shown, are only to be got by those impressions
objects themselves make on our minds by the proper inlets appointed to each sort. If they are not received this way, all the
words in the world made use of to explain or define any of their
names, will never be able to produce in us the idea it stands for.
For words, being sounds, can produce in us no other simple ideas
than of those very sounds; nor excite any in us but by that
voluntary connexion which is known to be between them and
those simple ideas which common use has made them signs of.
He that thinks otherwise, let him try if any words can give him
the taste of a pine-apple, and make him have the true idea of
the relish of that celebrated delicious fruit. So far as he is told
it has a resemblance with any tastes whereof he has the ideas
already in his memory, imprinted there by sensible objects not
strangers to his palate, so far may he approach that resemblance
in his mind. But this is not giving us that idea by a definition,
but exciting in us other simple ideas by their known names;
which will be still very different from the true taste of that fruit
itself. In light and colours, and all other simple ideas, it is the
same thing: for the signification of sounds is not natural, but
only imposed and arbitrary. And no definition of "light," or
"redness," is more fitted or able to produce either of those ideas
in us, than the sound "light" or "red" by itself. For to hope
to produce an idea of light or colour by a sound, however formed,
is to expect that sounds should be visible, or colours audible;
and to make the ears do the office of all the other senses. Which
is all one as to say, that we might taste, smell, and see by the
ears: a sort of philosophy worthy only of Sancho Pança, who
had the faculty to see Dulcinea by hearsay. And therefore he
that has not before received into his mind, by the proper inlet,
the simple idea which any word stands for, can never come to
know the signification of that word by any other words or

sounds whatsoever, put together according to any rules of definition. The only way is by applying to his senses the proper
object; and so producing that idea in him for which he has
learned the name already. A studious blind man, who had
mightily beat his head about visible objects, and made use of the
explication of his books and friends to understand those names
of light and colours which often came in his way, bragged one
day, that he now understood what "scarlet" signified. Upon
which his friend demanding, what scarlet was? the blind man
answered, It was like the sound of a trumpet. Just such an understanding of the name of any other simple idea will he have
who hopes to get it only from a definition, or other words made
use of to explain it.

12. *The contrary showed in complex ideas by instances of a
statue and rainbow.*—The case is quite otherwise in complex
ideas, which consisting of several simple ones, it is in the power
of words, standing for the several ideas that make that composition, to imprint complex ideas in the mind which were never
there before, and so make their names be understood. In such
collections of ideas passing under one name, definition, or the
teaching the signification of one word by several others, has
place, and may make us understand the names of things which
never came within the reach of our senses, and frame ideas suitable to those in other men's minds, when they use those names:
provided that none of the terms of the definition stand for any
such simple ideas which he to whom the explication is made has
never yet had in his thought. Thus the word "statue" may be
explained to a blind man by other words, when "picture"
cannot; his senses having given him the idea of figure, but not
of colours, which therefore words cannot excite in him. This
gained the prize to the painter against the statuary: each of
which contending for the excellency of his art, and the statuary
bragging that his was to be preferred because it reached farther,
and even those who had lost their eyes could yet perceive the
excellency of it: the painter agreed to refer himself to the
judgment of a blind man; who being brought where there was
a statue made by the one and a picture drawn by the other, he
was first led to the statue, in which he traced with his hands all
the lineaments of the face and body, and with great admiration
applauded the skill of the workman; but being led to the picture,
and having his hands laid upon it, was told, that now he touched
the head, and then the forehead, eyes, nose, &c., as his hand
moved over the parts of the picture on the cloth without finding
any the least distinction: whereupon he cried out, that certainly
that must needs be a very admirable and divine piece of workmanship which could represent to them all those parts where he
could neither feel nor perceive any thing.

13. He that should use the word "rainbow" to one who knew

all those colours, but yet had never seen that phenomenon, would, by enumerating the figure, largeness, position, and order of the colours, so well define that word that it might be perfectly understood. But yet that definition, how exact and perfect soever, would never make a blind man understand it; because several of the simple ideas that make that complex one being such as he never received by sensation and experience, no words are able to excite them in his mind.

14. *The names of complex ideas, when to be made intelligible by words.*—Simple ideas, as has been showed, can only be got by experience from those objects which are proper to produce in us those perceptions. When by this means we have our minds stored with them, and know the names for them, then we are in a condition to define, and by definition to understand, the names of complex ideas that are made up of them. But when any term stands for a simple idea that a man has never yet had in his mind, it is impossible, by any words, to make known its meaning to him. When any term stands for an idea a man is acquainted with, but is ignorant that that term is the sign of it, there another name, of the same idea which he has been accustomed to, may make him understand its meaning. But in no case whatsoever is any name of any simple idea capable of a definition.

15. *Fourthly, Names of simple ideas least doubtful.*—Fourthly, But though the names of simple ideas have not the help of definition to determine their signification, yet that hinders not but that they are generally less doubtful and uncertain than those of mixed modes and substances; because they standing only for one simple perception, men, for the most part, easily and perfectly agree in their signification, and there is little room for mistake and wrangling about their meaning. He that knows once that "whiteness" is the name of that colour he has observed in snow or milk, will not be apt to misapply that word as long as he retains that idea; which, when he has quite lost, he is not apt to mistake the meaning of it, but perceives he understands it not. There is neither a multiplicity of simple ideas to be put together, which makes the doubtfulness in the names of mixed modes; nor a supposed, but an unknown, real essence, with properties depending thereon, the precise number whereof are also unknown, which makes the difficulty in the names of substances. But, on the contrary, in simple ideas the whole signification of the name is known at once, and consists not of parts, whereof more or less being put in, the idea may be varied, and so the signification of its name be obscure or uncertain.

16. *Fifthly, Simple ideas have few ascents* in lineâ prædicamentali.—Fifthly, this farther may be observed concerning simple ideas and their names, that they have but few ascents *in lineâ prædicamentali* (as they call it), from the lowest species to the *summum genus*. The reason whereof is, that the lowest

species being but one simple idea, nothing can be left out of it, that so, the difference being taken away, it may agree with some other thing in one idea common to them both; which, having one name, is the genus of the other two: *v. g.*, there is nothing can be left out of the idea of white and red to make them agree in one common appearance, and so have one general name; as rationality being left out of the complex idea of man, makes it agree with brute, in the more general idea and name of "animal." And therefore, when, to avoid unpleasant enumerations, men would comprehend both white and red, and several other such simple ideas, under one general name; they have been fain to do it by a word which denotes only the way they get into the mind. For when white, red, and yellow are all comprehended under the genus or name " colour," it signifies no more but such ideas as are produced in the mind only by the sight, and have entrance only through the eyes. And when they would frame yet a more general term, to comprehend both colours and sounds, and the like simple ideas, they do it by a word that signifies all such as come into the mind only by one sense : and so the general term "quality," in its ordinary acceptation, comprehends colours, sounds, tastes, smells, and tangible qualities, with distinction from extension, number, motion, pleasure, and pain, which make impressions on the mind, and introduce their ideas by more senses than one.

17. *Sixthly, Names of simple ideas stand for ideas not at all arbitrary.*—Sixthly, The names of simple ideas, substances, and mixed modes, have also this difference, that those of mixed modes stand for ideas perfectly arbitrary: those of substances are not perfectly so, but refer to a pattern, though with some latitude : and those of simple ideas are perfectly taken from the existence of things, and are not arbitrary at all. Which what difference it makes in the significations of their names, we shall see in the following chapters.

The names of simple modes differ little from those of simple ideas.

## CHAPTER V.

### OF THE NAMES OF MIXED MODES AND RELATIONS.

1. *They stand for abstract ideas, as other general names.*—The names of mixed modes being general, they stand, as has been shown, for sorts or species of things, each of which has its peculiar essence. The essences of these species also, as has been showed, are nothing but the abstract ideas in the mind, to which the name is annexed. Thus far the names and essences of mixed modes have nothing but what is common to them with other

ideas: but if we take a little nearer survey of them, we shall find that they have something peculiar, which, perhaps, may deserve our attention.

2. *First, The ideas they stand for are made by the understanding.*—The first particularity I shall observe in them is, that the abstract ideas, or, if you please, the essences of the several species of mixed modes, are made by the understanding: wherein they differ from those of simple ideas; in which sort the mind has no power to make any one, but only receives such as are presented to it by the real existence of things operating upon it.

3. *Secondly, Made arbitrarily, and without patterns.*—In the next place, these essences of the species of mixed modes are not only made by the mind, but made very arbitrarily, made without patterns, or reference to any real existence; wherein they differ from those of substances, which carry with them the supposition of some real being from which they are taken, and to which they are conformable. But in its complex ideas of mixed modes, the mind takes a liberty not to follow the existence of things exactly. It unites and retains certain collections as so many distinct specific ideas; whilst others, that as often occur in nature, and are as plainly suggested by outward things, pass neglected without particular names or specifications. Nor does the mind, in these of mixed modes, as in the complex ideas of substances, examine them by the real existence of things, or verify them by patterns containing such peculiar compositions in nature. To know whether his idea of adultery or incest be right, will a man seek it any where amongst things existing? Or is it true because any one has been witness to such an action? No: but it suffices here that men have put together such a collection into one complex idea that makes the archetype and specific idea, whether ever any such action were committed *in rerum naturâ,* or no.

4. *How this is done.*—To understand this aright, we must consider wherein this making of these complex ideas consists: and that is not in the making any new idea, but putting together those which the mind had before. Wherein the mind does these three things: First, It chooses a certain number. Secondly, It gives them connexion, and makes them into one idea. Thirdly, It ties them together by a name. If we examine how the mind proceeds in these, and what liberty it takes in them, we shall easily observe how these essences of the species of mixed modes are the workmanship of the mind, and consequently, that the species themselves are of men's making.

5. *Evidently arbitrary, in that the idea is often before the existence.*—Nobody can doubt but that these ideas of mixed modes are made by a voluntary collection of ideas put together in the mind, independent from any original patterns in nature, who will but reflect that this sort of complex ideas may be made, abstracted,

and have names given them, and so a species be constituted,
before any one individual of that species ever existed.  Who can
doubt but the ideas of sacrilege or adultery might be framed in
the mind of men, and have names given them, and so these
species of mixed modes be constituted, before either of them was
ever committed ; and might be as well discoursed of and reasoned
about, and as certain truths discovered of them, whilst yet they
had no being but in the understanding, as well as now that they
have but too frequently a real existence?  Whereby it is plain
how much the sorts of mixed modes are the creatures of the
understanding, where they have a being as subservient to all the
ends of real truth and knowledge as when they really exist: and
we cannot doubt but law-makers have often made laws about
species of actions which were only the creatures of their own
understandings ; beings that had no other existence but in their
own minds.  And, I think, nobody can deny but that the resurrection was a species of mixed modes in the mind before it really
existed.

6. *Instances : murder, incest, stabbing.*—To see how arbitrarily
these essences of mixed modes are made by the mind, we need but
take a view of almost any of them.  A little looking into them
will satisfy us, that it is the mind that combines several scattered
independent ideas into one complex one; and, by the common
name it gives them, makes them the essence of a certain species,
without regulating itself by any connexion they have in nature.
For what greater connexion in nature has the idea of a man,
than the idea of a sheep, with killing, that this is made a particular species of action, signified by the word "murder" and
the other not?  Or what union is there in nature between the
idea of the relation of a father, with killing, than that of a son
or neighbour ; that those are combined into one complex idea,
and thereby made the essence of the distinct species "parricide,"
whilst the other makes no distinct species at all?  But though
they have made killing a man's father or mother a distinct species
from killing his son or daughter, yet, in some other cases, son and
daughter are taken in too, as well as father and mother; and
they are all equally comprehended in the same species, as in that
of "incest."  Thus the mind in mixed modes arbitrarily unites
into complex ideas such as it finds convenient, whilst others, that
have altogether as much union in nature, are left loose, and
never combined into one idea, because they have no need of one
name.  It is evident, then, that the mind, by its free choice, gives
a connexion to a certain number of ideas, which in nature have
no more union with one another than others that it leaves out :
why else is the part of the weapon the beginning of the wound
is made with, taken notice of to make the distinct species called
"stabbing," and the figure and matter of the weapon left out?
I do not say, this is done without reason, as we shall see more

by and by; but this I say, that it is done by the free choice of
the mind, pursuing its own ends; and that therefore these species
of mixed modes are the workmanship of the understanding: and
there is nothing more evident than that, for the most part, in
the framing these ideas, the mind searches not its patterns in
nature, nor refers the ideas it makes to the real existence of
things; but puts such together as may best serve its own purposes, without tying itself to a precise imitation of any thing
that really exists.

7. *But still subservient to the end of language.*—But though
these complex ideas, or essences of mixed modes, depend on the
mind, and are made by it with great liberty; yet they are not
made at random, and jumbled together without any reason at all.
Though these complex ideas be not always copied from nature,
yet they are always suited to the end for which abstract ideas are
made: and though they be combinations made of ideas, that are
loose enough, and have as little union in themselves, as several
other, to which the mind never gives a connexion that combines
them into one idea: yet, they are always made for the convenience
of communication, which is the chief end of language. The use
of language is by short sounds, to signify with ease and despatch
general conceptions; wherein not only abundance of particulars
may be contained, but also a great variety of independent ideas
collected into one complex one. In the making therefore of the
species of mixed modes, men have had regard only to such combinations as they had occasion to mention one to another. Those
they have combined into distinct complex ideas, and given names
to; whilst others that in nature have as near a union, are left
loose and unregarded. For, to go no farther than human actions
themselves: if they would make distinct abstract ideas of all the
varieties might be observed in them, the number must be infinite,
and the memory confounded with the plenty, as well as overcharged to little purpose. It suffices that men make and name
so many complex ideas of these mixed modes, as they find they
have occasion to have names for in the ordinary occurrence of
their affairs. If they join to the idea of killing, the idea of
father or mother, and so make a distinct species from killing a
man's son or neighbour, it is because of the different heinousness
of the crime, and the distinct punishment is due to the murder-
ing a man's father and mother, different from what ought to be
inflicted on the murder of a son or neighbour; and therefore they
find it necessary to mention it by a distinct name, which is the
end of making that distinct combination. But though the ideas
of mother and daughter are so differently treated, in reference
to the idea of killing, that the one is joined with it to make a
distinct abstract idea with a name, and so a distinct species, and
the other not; yet in respect of carnal knowledge, they are both
taken in under incest; and that still for the same convenience of

expressing under one name, and reckoning of one species, such unclean mixtures as have a peculiar turpitude beyond others; and this to avoid circumlocutions and tedious descriptions.

8. *Whereof the intranslatable words of divers languages are a proof.*—A moderate skill in different languages will easily satisfy one of the truth of this; it being so obvious to observe great store of words in one language, which have not any that answer them in another: which plainly shows, that those of one country, by their customs and manner of life, have found occasion to make several complex ideas, and give names to them, which others never collected into specific ideas. This could not have happened, if these species were the steady workmanship of nature; and not collections made and abstracted by the mind, in order to naming, and for the convenience of communication. The terms of our law, which are not empty sounds, will hardly find words that answer them in the Spanish or Italian, no scanty languages; much less, I think, could any one translate them into the Caribbee or Westoe tongues: and the *versura* of the Romans, or *corban* of the Jews, have no words in other languages to answer them: the reason whereof is plain from what has been said. Nay, if we will look a little more nearly into this matter, and exactly compare different languages, we shall find, that though they have words which, in translations and dictionaries, are supposed to answer one another; yet there is scarce one of ten, amongst the names of complex ideas, especially of mixed modes, that stands for the same precise idea which the word does that in dictionaries it is rendered by. There are no ideas more common, and less compounded, than the measures of time, extension, and weight, and the Latin names, *hora, pes, libra,* are, without difficulty, rendered by the English names, "hour," "foot," and "pound:" but yet there is nothing more evident, than that the ideas a Roman annexed to these Latin names were very far different from those which an Englishman expresses by those English ones. And, if either of these should make use of the measures that those of the other language designed by their names, he would be quite out in his account. These are too sensible proofs to be doubted; and we shall find this much more so in the names of more abstract and compounded ideas; such as are the greatest part of those which make up moral discourses: whose names when men come curiously to compare with those they are translated into in other languages, they will find very few of them exactly to correspond in the whole extent of their significations.

9. *This shows species to be made for communication.*—The reason why I take so particular notice of this, is, that we may not be mistaken about *genera* and *species,* and their essences, as if they were things regularly and constantly made by nature, and had a real existence in things; when they appear, upon a more wary survey, to be nothing else but an artifice of the understanding,

for the easier signifying such collections of ideas as it should often have occasion to communicate by one general term; under which, divers particulars as far forth as they agreed to that abstract idea, might be comprehended. And if the doubtful signification of the word "species" may make it sound harsh to some that I say, that "the species of mixed modes are made by the understanding:" yet, I think, it can by nobody be denied, that it is the mind makes those abstract complex ideas to which specific names are given. And if it be true, as it is, that the mind makes the patterns for sorting and naming of things, I leave it to be considered who makes the boundaries of the sort or species; since with me "species" and "sort" have no other difference than that of a Latin and English idiom.

10. *In mixed modes it is the name that ties the combination together, and makes it a species.*—The near relation that there is between species, essences, and their general name, at least in mixed modes, will farther appear when we consider, that it is the name that seems to preserve those essences, and give them their lasting duration. For the connexion between the loose parts of those complex ideas being made by the mind, this union, which has no particular foundation in nature, would cease again, were there not something that did, as it were, hold it together, and keep the parts from scattering. Though, therefore, it be the mind that makes the collection, it is the name which is, as it were, the knot that ties them fast together. What a vast variety of different ideas does the word *triumphus* hold together, and deliver to us as one species! Had this name been never made, or quite lost, we might, no doubt, have had descriptions of what passed in that solemnity; but yet, I think, that which holds those different parts together in the unity of one complex idea, is that very word annexed to it: without which the several parts of that would no more be thought to make one thing than any other show, which, having never been made but once, had never been united into one complex idea under one denomination. How much, therefore, in mixed modes, the unity necessary to any essence depends on the mind, and how much the continuation and fixing of that unity depends on the name in common use annexed to it, I leave to be considered by those who look upon essences and species as real established things in nature.

11. Suitable to this, we find that men, speaking of mixed modes, seldom imagine or take any other for species of them, but such as are set out by name: because they being of man's making only in order to naming, no such species are taken notice of, or supposed to be, unless a name be joined to it, as the sign of man's having combined into one idea several loose ones; and by that name giving a lasting union to the parts, which would otherwise cease to have any, as soon as the mind laid by that abstract idea, and ceased actually to think on it. But when

a name is once annexed to it, wherein the parts of that complex idea have a settled and permanent union; then is the essence, as it were, established, and the species looked on as complete. For to what purpose should the memory charge itself with such compositions, unless it were by abstraction to make them general? And to what purpose make them general, unless it were that they might have general names for the convenience of discourse and communication? Thus we see that killing a man with a sword, or a hatchet, are looked on as no distinct species of action: but if the point of the sword first enter the body, it passes for a distinct species, where it has a distinct name, as in England, in whose language it is called "stabbing:" but in another country, where it has not happened to be specified under a peculiar name, it passes not for a distinct species. But in the species of corporeal substances, though it be the mind that makes the nominal essence: yet since those ideas, which are combined in it, are supposed to have an union in nature, whether the mind joins them or no, therefore those are looked on as distinct species, without any operation of the mind either abstracting or giving a name to that complex idea.

12. *For the originals of mixed modes we look no farther than the mind, which also shows them to be the workmanship of the understanding.*—Conformable also to what has been said concerning the essences of the species of mixed modes, that they are the creatures of the understanding rather than the works of nature: conformable, I say, to this, we find that their names lead our thoughts to the mind, and no farther. When we speak of justice or gratitude, we frame to ourselves no imagination of any thing existing, which we would conceive; but our thoughts terminate in the abstract ideas of those virtues, and look no farther; as they do, when we speak of a horse or iron, whose specific ideas we consider not as barely in the mind, but as in things themselves, which afford the original patterns of those ideas. But in mixed modes, at least the most considerable parts of them, which are moral beings, we consider the original patterns as being in the mind; and to those we refer for the distinguishing of particular beings under names. And hence I think it is, that these essences of the species of mixed modes are by a more particular name called "notions;" as by a peculiar right appertaining to the understanding.

13. *Their being made by the understanding without patterns, shows the reason why they are so compounded.*—Hence likewise we may learn, why the complex ideas of mixed modes are commonly more compounded and decompounded than those of natural substances. Because they being the workmanship of the understanding pursuing only its own ends, and the conveniency of expressing in short those ideas it would make known to another, does with great liberty unite often into one abstract idea things

that in their nature have no coherence, and so under one term bundle together a great variety of compounded and decompounded ideas. Thus the name of "procession," what a great mixture of independent ideas of persons, habits, tapers, orders, motions, sounds, does it contain in that complex one which the mind of man has arbitrarily put together to express by that one name! Whereas the complex ideas of the sorts of substances are usually made up of only a small number of simple ones; and in the species of animals, these two, viz., shape and voice, commonly make the whole nominal essence.

14. *Names of mixed modes stand always for their real essences.* —Another thing we may observe from what has been said, is that the names of mixed modes always signify (when they have any determined signification) the real essences of their species. For, these abstract ideas being the workmanship of the mind, and not referred to the real existence of things, there is no supposition of any thing more signified by that name but barely that complex idea the mind itself has formed, which is all it would have expressed by it: and is that on which all the properties of the species depend, and from which alone they all flow: and so in these the real and nominal essence is the same; which of what concernment it is to the certain knowledge of general truth, we shall see hereafter.

15. *Why their names are usually got before their ideas.*—This also may show us the reason, why for the most part the names of mixed modes are got before the ideas they stand for are perfectly known. Because, there being no species of these ordinarily taken notice of but what have names, and those species, or rather their essences, being abstract complex ideas made arbitrarily by the mind, it is convenient, if not necessary, to know the names before one endeavour to frame these complex ideas, unless a man will fill his head with a company of abstract complex ideas, which others having no names for, he has nothing to do with but to lay by and forget again. I confess that, in the beginning of languages, it was necessary to have the idea before one gave it the name: and so it is still where, making a new complex idea, one also, by giving it a new name, makes a new word. But this concerns not languages made, which have generally pretty well provided for ideas which men have frequent occasion to have and communicate: and in such, I ask, whether it be not the ordinary method, that children learn the names of mixed modes before they have their ideas? What one of a thousand ever frames the abstract idea of glory and ambition before he has heard the names of them? In simple ideas and substances, I grant, it is otherwise; which being such ideas as have a real existence and union in nature, the ideas or names are got one before the other, as it happens.

16. *Reason of my being so large on this subject.*—What has been

said here of mixed modes is with very little difference applicable also to relations ; which, since every man himself may observe, I may spare myself the pains to enlarge on : especially since what I have here said concerning words in this third book, will possibly be thought by some to be much more than what so slight a subject required. I allow, it might be brought into a narrower compass : but I was willing to stay my reader on an argument that appears to me new, and a little out of the way (I am sure it is one I thought not of when I began to write), that by searching it to the bottom, and turning it on every side, some part or other might meet with every one's thoughts, and give occasion to the most averse or negligent to reflect on a general miscarriage ; which, though of great consequence, is little taken notice of. When it is considered what a pudder is made about essences, and how much all sorts of knowledge, discourse, and conversation are pestered and disordered by the careless and confused use and application of words, it will, perhaps, be thought worth while thoroughly to lay it open. And I shall be pardoned if I have dwelt long on an argument which I think therefore needs to be inculcated; because the faults men are usually guilty of in this kind are not only the greatest hindrances of true knowledge, but are so well thought of as to pass for it. Men would often see what a small pittance of reason and truth, or possibly none at all, is mixed with those huffing opinions they are swelled with, if they would but look beyond fashionable sounds, and observe what ideas are or are not comprehended under those words with which they are so armed at all points, and with which they so confidently lay about them. I shall imagine I have done some service to truth, peace, and learning, if, by any enlargement on this subject, I can make men reflect on their own use of language ; and give them reason to suspect, that since it is frequent for others, it may also be possible for them to have sometimes very good and approved words in their mouths and writings, with very uncertain, little, or no signification ; and therefore it is not unreasonable for them to be wary herein themselves, and not to be unwilling to have them examined by others. With this design, therefore, I shall go on with what I have farther to say concerning this matter.

## CHAPTER VI.

### OF THE NAMES OF SUBSTANCES.

**1.** *The common names of substances stand for sorts.*—The common names of substances, as well as other general terms, stand for sorts : which is nothing else but the being made signs of such complex ideas, wherein several particular substances do or might agree, by virtue of which they are capable of being comprehended in one common conception, and be signified by one name. I say, "do or might agree:" for though there be but one sun existing in the world, yet the idea of it being abstracted, so that more substances (if there were several) might each agree in it; it is as much a sort as if there were as many suns as there are stars. They want not their reasons who think there are, and that each fixed star would answer the idea the name "sun" stands for, to one who were placed in a due distance; which, by the way, may show us how much the sorts, or if you please, *genera* and *species*, of things (for those Latin terms signify to me no more than the English word "sort") depend on such collections of ideas as men have made, and not on the real nature of things: since it is not impossible but that, in propriety of speech, that might be a sun to one which is a star to another.

2. *The essence of each sort is the abstract idea.*—The measure and boundary of each sort or species whereby it is constituted that particular sort and distinguished from others, is that we call its "essence," which is nothing but that abstract idea to which that name is annexed: so that every thing contained in that idea is essential to that sort. This, though it be all the essence of natural substances that we know, or by which we distinguish them into sorts; yet I call it by a peculiar name, the "nominal essence," to distinguish it from that real constitution of substances upon which depends this nominal essence, and all the properties of that sort; which therefore, as has been said, may be called the "real essence:" *v. g.*, the nominal essence of gold is that complex idea the word "gold" stands for, let it be, for instance, a body yellow, of a certain weight, malleable, fusible, and fixed. But the real essence is the constitution of the insensible parts of that body, on which those qualities and all the other properties of gold depend. How far these two are different, though they are both called "essence," is obvious, at first sight to discover.

3. *The nominal and real essence different.*—For though, perhaps, voluntary motion, with sense and reason, joined to a body of a certain shape, be the complex idea to which I and others annex the name "man," and so be the nominal essence of the species so called: yet nobody will say that that complex idea is the real essence and source of all those operations which are to be found in any individual of that sort. The foundation of all those qualities which are the ingredients of our complex idea, is something quite different: and had we such a knowledge of that constitution of man from which his faculties of moving, sensation, and reasoning, and other powers flow, and on which his so regular shape depends, as it is possible angels have, and it is certain his Maker has, we should have a quite other idea of his essence than what now is contained in our definition of that species, be it what

it will: and our idea of any individual man would be as far different from what it now is, as is his who knows all the springs and wheels, and other contrivances within, of the famous clock at Strasburg, from that which a gazing countryman has of it, who barely sees the motion of the hand, and hears the clock strike, and observes only some of the outward appearances.

4. *Nothing essential to individuals.*—That "essence," in the ordinary use of the word, relates to sorts, and that it is considered in particular beings no farther than they are ranked into sorts, appears from hence: that take but away the abstract ideas by which we sort individuals, and rank them under common names, and then the thought of anything essential to any of them instantly vanishes: we have no notion of the one without the other; which plainly shows their relation. It is necessary for me to be as I am: God and nature has made me so: but there is nothing I have is essential to me. An accident or disease may very much alter my colour or shape; a fever or fall may take away my reason or memory, or both; and an apoplexy leave neither sense nor understanding, no, nor life. Other creatures of my shape may be made with more and better, or fewer and worse, faculties than I have: and others may have reason and sense in a shape and body very different from mine. None of these are essential to the one or the other, or to any individual whatsoever, till the mind refers it to some sort or species of things; and then presently, according to the abstract idea of that sort, something is found essential. Let any one examine his own thoughts, and he will find, that as soon as he supposes or speaks of essential, the consideration of some species, or the complex idea, signified by some general name, comes into his mind: and it is in reference to that, that this or that quality is said to be essential. So that if it be asked, whether it be essential to me, or any other particular corporeal being to have reason? I say, No; no more than it is essential to this white thing I write on to have words in it. But if that particular being be to be counted of the sort "man," and to have the name "man" given it, then reason is essential to it, supposing reason to be a part of the complex idea the name "man" stands for: as it is essential to this thing I write on to contain words, if I will give it the name "treatise," and rank it under that species. So that "essential" and "not essential" relate only to our abstract ideas, and the names annexed to them; which amounts to no more but this, that whatever particular thing has not in it those qualities which are contained in the abstract idea which any general term stands for, cannot be ranked under that species, nor be called by that name, since that abstract idea is the very essence of that species.

5. Thus, if the idea of body, with some people, be bare extension or space, then solidity is not essential to body: if others make the idea to which they give the name "body," to be soli-

dity and extension, then solidity is essential to body. That therefore, and that alone, is considered as essential which makes a part of the complex idea the name of a sort stands for, without which no particular thing can be reckoned of that sort, nor be entitled to that name. Should there be found a parcel of matter that had all the other qualities that are in iron, but wanted obedience to the loadstone, and would neither be drawn by it, nor receive direction from it; would any one question whether it wanted any thing essential? It would be absurd to ask, whether a thing really existing wanted any thing essential to it? Or could it be demanded, whether this made an essential or specific difference or no? since we have no other measure of essential or species but our abstract ideas. And to talk of specific differences in nature, without reference to general ideas and names, is to talk unintelligibly. For, I would ask any one, What is sufficient to make an essential difference in nature between any two particular beings, without any regard had to some abstract idea, which is looked upon as the essence and standard of a species? All such patterns and standards being quite laid aside, particular beings, considered barely in themselves, will be found to have all their qualities equally essential; and every thing in each individual will be essential to it, or, which is more, nothing at all. For though it may be reasonable to ask, whether obeying the magnet be essential to iron? yet, I think, it is very improper and insignificant to ask, whether it be essential to the particular parcel of matter I cut my pen with? without considering it under the name "iron," or as being of a certain species. And if, as has been said, our abstract ideas which have names annexed to them, are the boundaries of species, nothing can be essential but what is contained in those ideas.

6. It is true I have often mentioned a real essence, distinct in substances from those abstract ideas of them, which I call their "nominal essence." By this "real essence," I mean that real constitution of any thing which is the foundation of all those properties that are combined in, and are constantly found to co-exist with, the nominal essence; that particular constitution which every thing has within itself, without any relation to any thing without it. But essence, even in this sense, relates to a sort, and supposes a species: for, being that real constitution on which the properties depend, it necessarily supposes a sort of things, properties belonging only to species, and not to individuals; v. g., supposing the nominal essence of gold to be body of such a peculiar colour and weight, with malleability and fusibility, the real essence is that constitution of the parts of matter on which these qualities and their union depend; and is also the foundation of its solubility in *aqua regia*, and other properties accompanying that complex idea. Here are essences and properties, but all upon supposition of a sort, or general abstract idea, which is

considered as immutable; but there is no individual parcel of matter to which any of these qualities are so annexed as to be essential to it or inseparable from it. That which is essential belongs to it as a condition, whereby it is of this or that sort: but take away the consideration of its being ranked under the name of some abstract idea, and then there is nothing necessary to it, nothing inseparable from it. Indeed, as to the real essences of substances, we only suppose their being, without precisely knowing what they are: but that which annexes them still to the species is the nominal essence, of which they are the supposed foundation and cause.

7. *The nominal essence bounds the species.*—The next thing to be considered is, by which of those essences it is that substances are determined into sorts or species; and that, it is evident, is by the nominal essence. For it is that alone that the name, which is the mark of the sort, signifies. It is impossible therefore that any thing should determine the sorts of things which we rank under general names, but that idea which that name is designed as a mark for; which is that, as has been shown, which we call the "nominal essence." Why do we say, "This is a horse, and that a mule; this is an animal, that an herb?" How comes any particular thing to be of this or that sort, but because it has that nominal essence, or, which is all one, agrees to that abstract idea that name is annexed to? And I desire any one but to reflect on his own thoughts when he hears or speaks any of those or other names of substances, to know what sort of essences they stand for.

8. And that the species of things to us are nothing but the ranking them under distinct names, according to the complex ideas in us, and not according to precise, distinct, real essences in them, is plain from hence, that we find many of the individuals that are ranked into one sort, called by one common name, and so received as being of one species, have yet qualities depending on their real constitutions, as far different one from another as from others from which they are accounted to differ specifically. This, as it is easy to be observed by all who have to do with natural bodies, so chymists especially are often, by sad experience, convinced of it, when they, sometimes in vain, seek for the same qualities in one parcel of sulphur, antimony, or vitriol, which they have found in others. For though they are bodies of the same species, having the same nominal essence, under the same name; yet do they often, upon severe ways of examination, betray qualities so different one from another as to frustrate the expectation and labour of very wary chymists. But if things were distinguished into species according to their real essences, it would be as impossible to find different properties in any two individual substances of the same species, as it is to find different properties in two circles or two equilateral triangles. That is properly the essence to us which determines every particular to this or that *classis;*

or, which is the same thing, to this or that general name : and
what can that be else but that abstract idea to which that name
is annexed ? and so has, in truth, a reference, not so much to the
being of particular things as to their general denominations.

9. *Not the real essence, which we know not.*—Nor, indeed, can
we rank and sort things, and consequently (which is the end of
sorting) denominate them, by their real essences, because we
know them not. Our faculties carry us no farther towards the
knowledge and distinction of substances than a collection of those
sensible ideas which we observe in them; which, however made
with the greatest diligence and exactness we are capable of, yet
is more remote from the true internal constitution from which
those qualities flow than, as I said, a countryman's idea is from
the inward contrivance of that famous clock at Strasburg, whereof
he only sees the outward figure and motions. There is not so
contemptible a plant or animal that does not confound the most
enlarged understanding. Though the familiar use of things
about us take off our wonder, yet it cures not our ignorance.
When we come to examine the stones we tread on, or the iron
we daily handle, we presently find we know not their make, and
can give no reason of the different qualities we find in them. It
is evident the internal constitution, whereon their properties
depend, is unknown to us. For, to go no farther than the
grossest and most obvious we can imagine amongst them, what
is that texture of parts, that real essence, that makes lead and
antimony fusible; wood and stones not ? What makes lead and
iron malleable; antimony and stones not? And yet how
infinitely these come short of the fine contrivances and unconceivable real essences of plants or animals, every one knows.
The workmanship of the all-wise and powerful God, in the great
fabric of the universe and every part thereof, farther exceeds the
capacity and comprehension of the most inquisitive and intelligent man, than the best contrivance of the most ingenious man
doth the conceptions of the most ignorant of rational creatures.
Therefore we in vain pretend to range things into sorts, and dispose them into certain classes, under names, by their real essences,
that are so far from our discovery or comprehension. A blind
man may as soon sort things by their colours, and he that has
lost his smell as well distinguish a lily and a rose by their odours,
as by those internal constitutions which he knows not. He that
thinks he can distinguish sheep and goats by their real essences
that are known to him, may be pleased to try his skill in those
species called *cassiowary* and *querechinchio ;* and, by their internal
real essences, determine the boundaries of those species, without
knowing the complex idea of sensible qualities that each of those
names stands for, in the countries where those animals are to
be found.

10. *Not substantial forms, which we know less.*—Those therefore

who have been taught, that the several species of substances had
their distinct, internal, substantial forms, and that it was those
forms which made the distinction of substances into their true
*species* and *genera*, were led yet farther out of the way by having
their minds set upon fruitless inquiries after substantial forms
wholly unintelligible, and whereof we have scarce so much as
any obscure or confused conception in general.

11. *That the nominal essence is that whereby we distinguish
species, farther evident from spirits.*—That our ranking and
distinguishing natural substances into species, consists in the
nominal essences the mind makes, and not in the real essences to
be found in the things themselves, is farther evident from our
ideas of spirits. For, the mind getting, only by reflecting on its
own operations, those simple ideas which it attributes to spirits,
it hath or can have no other notion of spirit but by attributing
all those operations it finds in itself to a sort of beings, without
consideration of matter. And even the most advanced notion we
have of God, is but attributing the same simple ideas which we
have got from reflection on what we find in ourselves, and which
we conceive to have more perfection in them than would be in
their absence ; attributing, I say, those simple ideas to Him in
an unlimited degree. Thus, having got, from reflecting on ourselves, the idea of existence, knowledge, power, and pleasure,
each of which we find it better to have than to want; and the
more we have of each the better; joining all these together,
with infinity to each of them, we have the complex idea of an
eternal, omniscient, omnipotent, infinitely wise and happy being.
And though we are told that there are different species of angels,
yet we know not how to frame distinct, specific ideas of them :
not out of any conceit that the existence of more species than
one of spirits is impossible, but because, having no more simple
ideas (nor being able to frame more) applicable to such beings,
but only those few taken from ourselves, and from the actions of
our own minds in thinking, and being delighted, and moving
several parts of our bodies, we can no otherwise distinguish in
our conceptions the several species of spirits one from another,
but by attributing those operations and powers we find in ourselves to them in a higher or lower degree; and so have no very
distinct, specific ideas of spirits, except only of God, to whom we
attribute both duration and all those other ideas with infinity,
to the other spirits with limitation. Nor, as I humbly conceive,
do we, between God and them in our ideas, put any difference by
any number of simple ideas which we have of one, and not of
the other, but only that of infinity. All the particular ideas of
existence, knowledge, will, power, and motion, &c., being ideas
derived from the operations of our minds, we attribute all of
them to all sorts of spirits, with the difference only of degrees,
to the utmost we can imagine, even infinity, when we would

frame as well as we can, an idea of the First Being; who yet, it is certain, is infinitely more remote in the real excellency of his nature from the highest and perfectest of all created beings than the greatest man, nay, purest seraphim, is from the most contemptible part of matter; and consequently must infinitely exceed what our narrow understandings can conceive of him.

12. *Whereof there are probably numberless species.*—It is not impossible to conceive, nor repugnant to reason, that there may be many species of spirits as much separated and diversified one from another by distinct properties whereof we have no ideas, as the species of sensible things are distinguished one from another by qualities which we know and observe in them. That there should be more species of intelligent creatures above us than there are of sensible and material below us, is probable to me from hence, that in all the visible corporeal world, we see no chasms, or gaps. All quite down from us the descent is by easy steps, and a continued series of things, that in each remove differ very little one from the other. There are fishes that have wings, and are not strangers to the airy region: and there are some birds that are inhabitants of the water, whose blood is cold as fishes', and their flesh so like in taste that the scrupulous are allowed them on fish days. There are animals so near of kin both to birds and beasts, that they are in the middle between both; amphibious animals link the terrestrial and aquatic together; seals live at land and at sea, and porpoises have the warm blood and entrails of a hog, not to mention what is confidently reported of mermaids or sea-men. There are some brutes that seem to have as much knowledge and reason as some that are called men: and the animal and vegetable kingdoms are so nearly joined, that if you will take the lowest of one and the highest of the other, there will scarce be perceived any great difference between them; and so on till we come to the lowest and the most inorganical parts of matter, we shall find every where that the several species are linked together, and differ but in almost insensible degrees. And when we consider the infinite power and wisdom of the Maker, we have reason to think that it is suitable to the magnificent harmony of the universe, and the great design and infinite goodness of the Architect, that the species of creatures should also, by gentle degrees, ascend upward from us towards his infinite perfection, as we see they gradually descend from us downwards: which if it be probable, we have reason then to be persuaded that there are far more species of creatures above us than there are beneath; we being in degrees of perfection much more remote from the infinite being of God, than we are from the lowest state of being, and that which approaches nearest to nothing. And yet of all those distinct species, for the reasons above said, we have no clear distinct ideas.

**13.** *The nominal essence that of the species, proved from water and ice.*—But, to return to the species of corporeal substances: If I should ask any one whether ice and water were two distinct species of things, I doubt not but I should be answered in the affirmative : and it cannot be denied but he that says they are two distinct species, is in the right. But if an Englishman, bred in Jamaica, who perhaps had never seen or heard of ice, coming into England in the winter, find the water he put in his basin at night in a great part frozen in the morning; and, not knowing any peculiar name it had, should call it " hardened water: " I ask, whether this would be a new species to him, different from water ? And I think it would be answered here, It would not be to him a new species, no more than congealed jelly when it is cold is a distinct species from the same jelly fluid and warm ; or than liquid gold in the furnace is a distinct species from hard gold in the hands of a workman. And if this be so, it is plain that our distinct species are nothing but distinct complex ideas, with distinct names annexed to them. It is true, every substance that exists has its peculiar constitution, whereon depend those sensible qualities and powers we observe in it ; but the ranking of things into species, which is nothing but sorting them under several titles, is done by us according to the ideas that we have of them: which though sufficient to distinguish them by names, so that we may be able to discourse of them when we have them not present before us ; yet if we suppose it to be done by their real internal constitutions, and that things existing are distinguished by nature into species by real essences, according as we distinguish them into species by names, we shall be liable to great mistakes.

**14.** *Difficulties against a certain number of real essences.*—To distinguish substantial beings into species, according to the usual supposition, that there are certain precise essences or forms of things whereby all the individuals existing are by nature distinguished into species, these things are necessary :

**15.** First, To be assured that nature, in the production of things, always designs them to partake of certain regulated, established essences, which are to be the models of all things to be produced. This, in that crude sense it is usually proposed, would need some better explication before it can fully be assented to.

**16.** Secondly, It would be necessary to know whether nature always attains that essence it designs in the production of things. The irregular and monstrous births that in divers sorts of animals have been observed, will always give us reason to doubt of one or both of these.

**17.** Thirdly, It ought to be determined whether those we call " monsters " be really a distinct species according to the scholastic notion of the word " species; " since it is certain that every thing that exists has its particular constitution : and yet we find, that some of these monstrous productions have few or none of those qualities which are supposed to result from and accompany the essence of that species from whence they derive their originals, and to which by their descent they seem to belong.

18. *Our nominal essences of substances, not perfect collections of properties.*—Fourthly, The real essences of those things which we distinguish into species, and as so distinguished we name, ought to be known ; *i. e.*, we ought to have ideas of them. But since we are ignorant in these four points, the supposed real essences of things stand us not instead for the distinguishing substances into species.

19. Fifthly, The only imaginable help in this case would be, that having framed perfect complex ideas of the properties of things, flowing from their different real essences, we should thereby distinguish them into species. But neither can this be done: for, being ignorant of the real essence itself, it is impossible to know all those properties that flow from it, and are so annexed to it that, any one of them being away, we may certainly conclude that that essence is not there, and so the thing is not of that species. We can never know what are the precise number of properties depending on the real essence of gold; any one of which failing, the real essence of gold, and consequently gold, would not be there, unless we knew the real essence of gold itself, and by that determined that species. By the word "gold" here, I must be understood to design a particular piece of matter, *v. g.*, the last guinea that was coined. For if it should stand here in its ordinary signification for that complex idea which I or any one else calls "gold," *i. e.*, for the nominal essence of gold, it would be jargon: so hard is it to show the various meaning and imperfection of words, when we have nothing else but words to do it by.

20. By all which it is clear, that our distinguishing substances into species by names, is not at all founded on their real essences ; nor can we pretend to arrange and determine them exactly into species according to internal essential differences.

21. *But such a collection as our name stands for.*—But since, as has been remarked, we have need of general words, though we know not the real essences of things; all we can do is to collect such a number of simple ideas as by examination we find to be united together in things existing, and thereof to make one complex idea. Which, though it be not the real essence of any substance that exists, is yet the specific essence to which our name belongs, and is convertible with it; by which we may at least try the truth of these nominal essences. For example: there be that say, that the essence of body is extension; if it be so, we can never mistake in putting the essence of any thing for the thing itself. Let us, then, in discourse put extension for

body ; and when we would say that body moves, let us say that extension moves, and see how it will look. He that should say, that one extension by impulse moves another extension, would, by the bare expression, sufficiently show the absurdity of such a notion. The "essence" of any thing in respect of us, is the whole complex idea comprehended and marked by that name ; and in substances, besides the several distinct simple ideas that make them up, the confused one of substance, or of an unknown support and cause of their union, is always a part : and therefore the essence of body is not bare extension, but an extended solid thing ; and so to say, "An extended solid thing moves or impels another," is all one, and as intelligible, as to say, "Body moves or impels." Likewise to say that "a rational animal is capable of conversation," is all one as to say, "a man." But no one will say, that rationality is capable of conversation, because it makes not the whole essence to which we give the name "man."

22. *Our abstract ideas are to us the measures of species : instance in that of man.*—There are creatures in the world that have shapes like ours, but are hairy, and want language and reason. There are naturals amongst us that have perfectly our shape, but want reason, and some of them language too. There are creatures, as it is said (*sit fides penes authorem*, but there appears no contradiction that there should be such), that with language, and reason, and a shape in other things agreeing with ours, have hairy tails ; others where the males have no beards, and others where the females have. If it be asked, whether these be all men or no, all of human species ? it is plain, the question refers only to the nominal essence ; for those of them to whom the definition of the word "man," or the complex idea signified by that name, agrees, are men, and the other not. But if the inquiry be made concerning the supposed real essence, and whether the internal constitution and frame of these several creatures be specifically different, it is wholly impossible for us to answer, no part of that going into our specific idea ; only we have reason to think that where the faculties or outward frame so much differs, the internal constitution is not exactly the same. But what difference in the internal real constitution makes a specific difference, it is in vain to inquire, whilst our measures of species be, as they are, only our abstract ideas which we know ; and not that internal constitution, which makes no part of them. Shall the difference of hair only on the skin be a mark of a different internal, specific constitution between a changeling and a drill, when they agree in shape, and want of reason and speech ? and shall not the want of reason and speech be a sign to us of different real constitutions and species between a changeling and a reasonable man ? And so of the rest, if we pretend that the distinction of species or sorts is fixedly established by the real frame and secret constitutions of things.

**23.** *Species not distinguished by generation.*—Nor let any one say, that the power of propagation in animals by the mixture of male and female, and in plants by seeds, keep the supposed real species distinct and entire. For, granting this to be true, it would help us in the distinction of the species of things no farther than the tribes of animals and vegetables. What must we do for the rest? But in those too it is not sufficient: for if history lie not, women have conceived by drills; and what real species by that measure such a production will be in nature, will be a new question; and we have reason to think this not impossible. since mules and jumarts, the one from the mixture of an ass and a mare, the other from the mixture of a bull and a mare, are so frequent in the world. I once saw a creature that was the issue of a cat and a rat, and had the plain marks of both about it; wherein nature appeared to have followed the pattern of neither sort alone, but to have jumbled them both together. To which, he that shall add the monstrous productions that are so frequently to be met with in nature, will find it hard, even in the race of animals, to determine by the pedigree of what species every animal's issue is; and be at a loss about the real essence, which he thinks certainly conveyed by generation, and has alone a right to the specific name. But, farther: if the species of animals and plants are to be distinguished only by propagation, must I go to the Indies to see the sire and dam of the one, and the plant from which the seed was gathered that produced the other, to know whether this be a tiger, or that tea?

**24.** *Not by substantial forms.*—Upon the whole matter it is evident, that it is their own collections of sensible qualities that men make the essences of their several sorts of substances; and that their real internal structures are not considered by the greatest part of men in the sorting them. Much less were any substantial forms ever thought on by any, but those who have in this one part of the world learned the language of the schools: and yet those ignorant men who pretend not any insight into the real essences, nor trouble themselves about substantial forms, but are content with knowing things one from another by their sensible qualities, are often better acquainted with their differences, can more nicely distinguish them from their uses, and better know what they may expect from each, than those learned, quick-sighted men who look so deep into them, and talk so confidently of something more hidden and essential.

**25.** *The specific essences are made by the mind.*—But supposing that the real essences of substances were discoverable by those that would severely apply themselves to that inquiry; yet we could not reasonably think, that the ranking of things under general names was regulated by those internal real constitutions, or anything else but their obvious appearances; since languages, in all countries, have been established long before sciences. So

that they have not been philosophers or logicians, or such who
have troubled themselves about forms and essences, that have
made the general names that are in use amongst the several
nations of men: but those more or less comprehensive terms
have for the most part, in all languages, received their birth and
signification from ignorant and illiterate people, who sorted and
denominated things by those sensible qualities they found in
them; thereby to signify them, when absent, to others, whether
they had an occasion to mention a sort or particular thing.

26. *Therefore very various and uncertain.*—Since, then, it is
evident that we sort and name substances by their nominal, and
not by their real, essences, the next thing to be considered is,
how and by whom these essences come to be made. As to the
latter, it is evident they are made by the mind, and not by nature:
for were they nature's workmanship, they could not be so various
and different in several men, as experience tells us they are. For
if we will examine it, we shall not find the nominal essence of any
one species of substances in all men the same; no, not of that
which of all others we are the most intimately acquainted with.
It could not possibly be, that the abstract idea to which the name
"man" is given should be different in several men, if it were of
nature's making; and that to one it should be *animal rationale*,
and to another *animal implume, bipes, latis unguibus*. He that
annexes the name "man" to a complex idea, made up of sense
and spontaneous motion, joined to a body of such a shape, has
thereby one essence of the species man: and he that, upon farther
examination, adds rationality, as another essence of the species
he calls "man:" by which means the same individual will be a
true man to the one, which is not so to the other. I think, there
is scarce any one who will allow this upright figure, so well known,
to be the essential difference of the species man; and yet how
far men determine of the sorts of animals rather by their shape
than descent, is very visible; since it has been more than once
debated whether several human *fœtus* should be preserved, or
received to baptism or no, only because of the difference of their
outward configuration from the ordinary make of children,
without knowing whether they were not as capable of reason as
infants cast in another mould: some whereof, though of an
approved shape, are never capable of as much appearance of
reason, all their lives, as is to be found in an ape or an elephant;
and never give any signs of being acted by a rational soul.
Whereby it is evident, that the outward figure, which only was
found wanting, and not the faculty of reason, which nobody could
know would be wanting in its due season, was made essential to
the human species. The learned divine and lawyer must, on
such occasions, renounce his sacred definition of *animal rationale*,
and substitute some other essence of the human species. Monsieur Menage furnishes us with an example worth the taking

notice of on this occasion. "When the abbot of St. Martin,"
says he, "was born, he had so little of the figure of a man that it
bespake him rather a monster. It was for some time under
deliberation whether he should be baptized or no. However, he
was baptized and declared a man, provisionally [till time should
show what he would prove.] Nature had moulded him so un-
towardly, that he was called all his life *the abbot Malotru*, i. e.,
'ill-shaped.' He was of Caen."—*Menagiana*, ²⁷⁸/₄₅₀. This child, we
see, was very near being excluded out of the species of man
barely by his shape. He escaped very narrowly as he was; and
it is certain a figure a little more oddly turned had cast him, and
he had been executed as a thing not to be allowed to pass for a
man. And yet there can be no reason given, why, if the lineaments of his face had been a little altered, a rational soul could
not have been lodged in him, why a visage somewhat longer, or
a nose flatter, or a wider mouth could not have consisted, as
well as the rest of his ill figure, with such a soul, such parts, as
made him, disfigured as he was, capable to be a dignitary in the
church.

27. Wherein then, would I gladly know, consist the precise
and unmovable boundaries of that species? It is plain, if we
examine, there is no such thing made by nature, and established
by her amongst men. The real essence of that or any other sort
of substances, it is evident, we know not; and therefore are so
undetermined in our nominal essences which we make ourselves,
that if several men were to be asked concerning some oddly-
shaped *fœtus* as soon as born, whether it were a man or no, it is
past doubt one should meet with different answers. Which
could not happen if the nominal essences, whereby we limit and
distinguish the species of substances, were not made by man
with some liberty; but were exactly copied from precise boundaries set by nature, whereby it distinguished all substances
into certain species. Who would undertake to resolve what
species that monster was of which is mentioned by Licetus, (lib.
i. cap. iii.) with a man's head and hog's body? or those other,
which to the bodies of men had the heads of beasts, as dogs,
horses, &c.? If any of these creatures had lived, and could have
spoke, it would have increased the difficulty. Had the upper
part to the middle been of human shape, and all below swine; had
it been murder to destroy it? Or must the bishop have been consulted, whether it were man enough to be admitted to the font
or no? as I have been told it happened in France some years
since, in somewhat a like case. So uncertain are the boundaries
of species of animals to us, who have no other measures than the
complex ideas of our own collecting: and so far are we from
certainly knowing what a man is; though, perhaps, it will be
judged great ignorance to make any doubt about it. And yet,
I think I may say, that the certain boundaries of that species are

so far from being determined, and the precise number of simple ideas which make the nominal essence so far from being settled and perfectly known, that very material doubts may still arise about it: and, I imagine, none of the definitions of the word "man" which we yet have, nor descriptions of that sort of animal, are so perfect and exact as to satisfy a considerate, inquisitive person; much less to obtain a general consent, and to be that which men would every where stick by in the decision of cases, and determining of life and death, baptism or no baptism, in productions that might happen.

28. *But not so arbitrary as mixed modes.*—But though these nominal essences of substances are made by the mind, they are not yet made so arbitrarily as those of mixed modes. To the making of any nominal essence, it is necessary, First, that the ideas whereof it consists, have such an union as to make but one idea, how compounded soever. Secondly, That the particular ideas so united be exactly the same, neither more nor less. For if two abstract complex ideas differ either in number or sorts of their component parts, they make two different, and not one and the same essence. In the first of these, the mind, in making its complex ideas of substances, only follows nature: and puts none together, which are not supposed to have an union in nature. Nobody joins the voice of a sheep with the shape of a horse, nor the colour of lead with the weight and fixedness of gold, to be the complex ideas of any real substances; unless he has a mind to fill his head with chimeras, and his discourse with unintelligible words. Men, observing certain qualities always joined and existing together, therein copied nature; and of ideas so united made their complex ones of substances. For though men may make what complex ideas they please, and give what names to them they will; yet, if they will be understood when they speak of things really existing, they must, in some degree, conform their ideas to the things they would speak of: or else men's language will be like that of Babel; and every man's words, being intelligible only to himself, would no longer serve to conversation and the ordinary affairs of life, if the ideas they stand for be not some way answering the common appearances and agreement of substances as they really exist.

29. *Though very imperfect.*—Secondly, Though the mind of man, in making its complex ideas of substances, never puts any together that do not really, or are not supposed to, co-exist; and so it truly borrows that union from nature; yet the number it combines depends upon the various care, industry, or fancy of him that makes it. Men generally content themselves with some few sensible obvious qualities; and often, if not always, leave out others as material, and as firmly united as those that they take. Of sensible substances there are two sorts; one of organized bodies, which are propagated by seed; and in these the shape is

that which to us is the leading quality, and most characteristical part, that determines the species: and therefore in vegetables and animals an extended solid substance of such a certain figure usually serves the turn.  For, however some men seem to prize their definition of *animal rationale*, yet should there a creature be found that had language and reason, but partook not of the usual shape of man, I believe it would hardly pass for a man, how much soever it were *animal rationale*.  And if Balaam's ass had, all his life, discoursed as rationally as he did once with his master, I doubt yet whether any one would have thought him worthy the name "man," or allowed him to be of the same species with himself.  As in vegetables and animals it is the shape, so in most other bodies not propagated by seed it is the colour we most fix on, and are most led by.  Thus where we find the colour of gold, we are apt to imagine all the other qualities comprehended in our complex idea to be there also: and we commonly take these two obvious qualities, viz., shape and colour, for so presumptive ideas of several species, that in a good picture we readily say, "This is a lion, and that a rose; this is a gold, and that a silver goblet," only by the different figures and colours represented to the eye by the pencil.

30. *Which yet serve for common converse.*—But though this serves well enough for gross and confused conceptions and unaccurate ways of talking and thinking; yet men are far enough from having agreed on the precise number of simple ideas or qualities belonging to any sort of things signified by its name. Nor is it a wonder, since it requires much time, pains, and skill, strict inquiry, and long examination, to find out what and how many those simple ideas are, which are constantly and inseparably united in nature, and are always to be found together in the same subject.  Most men, wanting either time, inclination, or industry enough for this, even to some tolerable degree, content themselves with some few obvious and outward appearances of things, thereby readily to distinguish and sort them for the common affairs of life: and so, without farther examination, give them names, or take up the names already in use.  Which, though in common conversation they pass well enough for the signs of some few obvious qualities co-existing, are yet far enough from comprehending, in a settled signification, a precise number of simple ideas; much less all those which are united in nature.  He that shall consider, after so much stir about *genus* and *species*, and such a deal of talk of specific differences, how few words we have yet settled definitions of, may with reason imagine, that those forms which there hath been so much noise made about are only chimeras; which give us no light into the specific natures of things.  And he that shall consider how far the names of substances are from having significations wherein all who use them do agree, will have reason to conclude, that

though the nominal essences of substances are all supposed to be copied from nature, yet they are all, or most of them, very imperfect; since the composition of those complex ideas is, in several men, very different: and therefore that these boundaries of species are as men, and not as nature makes them, if at least there are in nature any such prefixed bounds. It is true, that many particular substances are so made by nature, that they have agreement and likeness one with another, and so afford a foundation of being ranked into sorts. But the sorting of things by us, or the making of determinate species, being in order to naming and comprehending them under general terms, I cannot see how it can be properly said that nature sets the boundaries of the species of things: or, if it be so, our boundaries of species are not exactly conformable to those in nature. For we, having need of general names for present use, stay not for a perfect discovery of all those qualities which would best show us their most material differences and agreements; but we ourselves divide them, by certain obvious appearances, into species, that we may the easier, under general names, communicate our thoughts about them. For, having no other knowledge of any substance, but of the simple ideas that are united to it, and observing several particular things to agree with others in several of those simple ideas, we make that collection our specific idea, and give it a general name; that in recording our own thoughts, and in our discourse with others, we may in one short word design all the individuals that agree in that complex idea, without enumerating the simple ideas that make it up; and so not waste our time and breath in tedious descriptions: which we see they are fain to do, who would discourse of any new sort of things they have not yet a name for.

31. *Essences of species under the same name very different.*—But, however these species of substances pass well enough in ordinary conversation, it is plain that this complex idea, wherein they observe several individuals to agree, is by different men made very differently; by some more and others less accurately. In some, this complex idea contains a greater and in others a smaller number of qualities, and so is apparently such as the mind makes it. The yellow shining colour makes gold to children; others add weight, malleableness, and fusibility; and others, yet other qualities which they find joined with that yellow colour, as constantly as its weight and fusibility: for in all these and the like qualities, one has as good a right to be put into the complex idea of that substance wherein they are all joined, as another. And therefore different men, leaving out or putting in several simple ideas which others do not, according to their various examination, skill, or observation of that subject, have different essences of gold; which must therefore be of their own and not of nature's making.

**32.** *The more general our ideas are, the more incomplete and partial they are.*—If the number of simple ideas that make the nominal essence of the lowest species or first sorting of individuals, depends on the mind of man variously collecting them, it is much more evident that they do so in the more comprehensive *classes*, which by the masters of logic are called *genera*. These are complex ideas designedly imperfect: and it is visible at first sight that several of those qualities that are to be found in the things themselves, are purposely left out of generical ideas. For as the mind, to make general ideas comprehending several particulars, leaves out those of time, and place, and such other that make them incommunicable to more than one individual; so, to make other yet more general ideas that may comprehend different sorts, it leaves out those qualities that distinguish them, and puts into its new collection only such ideas as are common to several sorts. The same convenience that made men express several parcels of yellow matter coming from Guinea and Peru under one name, sets them also upon making of one name that may comprehend both gold, and silver, and some other bodies of different sorts. This is done by leaving out those qualities which are peculiar to each sort; and retaining a complex idea made up of those that are common to them all. To which the name "metal" being annexed, there is a genus constituted; the essence whereof being that abstract idea, containing only malleableness and fusibility, with certain degrees of weight and fixedness, wherein some bodies of several kinds agree, leaves out the colour, and other qualities peculiar to gold and silver, and the other sorts comprehended under the name "metal." Whereby it is plain that men follow not exactly the patterns set them by nature, when they make their general ideas of substances; since there is no body to be found which has barely malleableness and fusibility in it, without other qualities as inseparable as those. But men, in making their general ideas, seeking more the convenience of language and quick despatch by short and comprehensive signs, than the true and precise nature of things as they exist, have, in the framing their abstract ideas, chiefly pursued that end, which was, to be furnished with store of general and variously comprehensive names. So that in this whole business of *genera* and *species*, the genus, or more comprehensive, is but a partial conception of what it is in the species, and the species but a partial idea of what is to be found in each individual. If, therefore, any one will think that a man, and a horse, and an animal, and a plant, &c., are distinguished by real essences made by nature, he must think nature to be very liberal of these real essences, making one for body, another for an animal, and another for a horse, and all these essences liberally bestowed upon Bucephalus. But if we would rightly consider what is done in all these *genera* and *species*, or sorts, we should find that there is no new thing made, but only more or less comprehensive signs whereby we may be enabled to express, in a few syllables, great numbers of particular things, as they agree in more or less general conceptions which we have framed to that purpose. In all which we may observe, that the more general term is always the name of a less complex idea; and that each genius is but a partial conception of the species comprehended under it. So that, if these abstract general ideas be thought to be complete, it can only be in respect of a certain established relation between them and certain names which are made use of to signify them; and not in respect of any thing existing, as made by nature.

33. *This all accommodated to the end of speech.*—This is adjusted to the true end of speech, which is, to be the easiest and shortest way of communicating our notions. For thus he that would make and discourse of things as they agreed in the complex idea of extension and solidity, needed but use the word "body," to denote all such. He that to these would join others, signified by the words "life," "sense," and "spontaneous motion," needed but use the word "animal," to signify all which partook of those ideas : and he that had made a complex idea of a body, with life, sense, and motion, with the faculty of reasoning, and a certain shape joined to it, needed but use the short monosyllable "man," to express all particulars that correspond to that complex idea. This is the proper business of *genus* and *species;* and this men do, without any consideration of real essences or substantial forms, which come not within the reach of our knowledge when we think of those things; nor within the signification of our words when we discourse with others.

34. *Instance in cassiowaries.*—Were I to talk with any one of a sort of birds I lately saw in St. James's Park, about three or four feet high, with a covering of something between feathers and hair, of a dark brown colour, without wings, but in the place thereof two or three little branches, coming down like sprigs of Spanish broom; long great legs, with feet only of three claws, and without a tail; I must make this description of it, and so may make others understand me. But when I am told that the name of it is "cassiowary," I may then use that word to stand in discourse for all my complex idea mentioned in that description; though by that word, which is now become a specific name, I know no more of the real essence or constitution of that sort of animals than I did before, and knew probably as much of the nature of that species of birds before I learned the name, as many Englishmen do of "swans" or "herons," which are specific names, very well known of sorts of birds common in England.

35. *Men determine the sorts: instance, gold.*—From what has been said, it is evident that men make sorts of things. For, it being different essences alone that make different species, it is plain that they who make those abstract ideas which are the

nominal essences, do thereby make the species, or sort. Should there be a body found having all the other qualities of gold except malleableness, it would, no doubt, be made a question whether it were gold or no; *i. e.*, whether it were of that species. This could be determined only by that abstract idea to which every one annexed the name "gold:" so that it would be true gold to him, and belong to that species, who included not malleableness in his nominal essence signified by the sound "gold;" and, on the other side, it would not be true gold, or of that species to him who included malleableness in his specific idea. And who, I pray, is it that makes these diverse species even under one and the same name, but men that make two different abstract ideas, consisting not exactly of the same collection of qualities? Nor is it a mere supposition to imagine, that a body may exist wherein the other obvious qualities of gold may be without malleableness; since it is certain that gold itself will be sometimes so "eager" (as artists call it), that it will as little endure the hammer as glass itself. What we have said of the putting in, or leaving malleableness out of, the complex idea the name "gold" is by any one annexed to, may be said of its peculiar weight, fixedness, and several other the like qualities: for, whatsoever is left out or put in, it is still the complex idea to which that name is annexed that makes the species: and, as any particular parcel of matter answers that idea, so the name of the sort belongs truly to it, and it is of that species. And thus any thing is true gold, perfect metal. All which determination of the species, it is plain, depends on the understanding of man making this or that complex idea.

36. *Nature makes the similitude.*—This, then, in short, is the case: nature makes many particular things which do agree one with another in many sensible qualities, and probably, too, in their internal frame and constitution; but it is not this real essence that distinguishes them into species; it is men, who taking occasion from the qualities they find united in them, and wherein they observe often several individuals to agree, range them into sorts in order to their naming, for the convenience of comprehensive signs; under which, individuals, according to their conformity to this or that abstract idea, come to be ranked as under ensigns; so that this is of the blue, that the red, regiment; this is a man, that a drill: and in this, I think, consists the whole business of *genus* and *species*.

37. *And continues it in the races of things.*—I do not deny but nature, in the constant production of particular beings, makes them not always new and various, but very much alike and of kin one to another; but I think it nevertheless true, that the boundaries of the species, whereby men sort them, are made by men; since the essences of the species, distinguished by different names, are, as has been proved, of man's making, and seldom

adequate to the internal nature of the things they are taken from. So that we may truly say, such a manner of sorting of things is the workmanship of men.

38. *Each abstract idea is an essence.*—One thing I doubt not but will seem very strange in this doctrine; which is, that, from what has been said, it will follow that each abstract idea, with a name to it, makes a distinct species. But who can help it, if truth will have it so? For so it must remain till somebody can show us the species of things, limited and distinguished by something else; and let us see that general terms signify not our abstract ideas, but something different from them. I would fain know why a shock and a hound are not as distinct species as a spaniel and an elephant. We have no other idea of the different essence of an elephant and a spaniel, than we have of the different essence of a shock and a hound; all the essential difference whereby we know and distinguish them one from another, consisting only in the different collection of simple ideas to which we have given those different names.

39. *Genera and* species *are in order to naming.*—How much the making of *species* and *genera* is in order to general names, and how much general names are necessary, if not to the being, yet at least to the completing, of a species, and making it pass for such, will appear, besides what has been said above concerning ice and water, in a very familiar example. A silent and a striking watch are but one species to those who have but one name for them: but he that has the name "watch" for one, and "clock" for the other, and distinct complex ideas to which those names belong, to him they are different species. It will be said, perhaps, that the inward contrivance and constitution is different between these two, which the watchmaker has a clear idea of. And yet, it is plain, they are but one species to him when he has but one name for them. For what is sufficient in the inward contrivance to make a new species? There are some watches that are made with four wheels, others with five: is this a specific difference to the workman? Some have strings and physies,* and others none; some have the balance loose, and others regulated by a spiral spring, and others by hogs' bristles: are any or all of these enough to make a specific difference to the workman that knows each of these, and several other different contrivances, in the internal constitutions of watches? It is certain each of these hath a real difference from the rest; but whether it be an essential, a specific difference or no, relates only to the complex idea to which the name "watch" is given: as long as they all agree in the idea which that name stands for, and that name does not, as a generical name, comprehend different species under it, they are not essentially nor specifically different. But if any one will make minuter divisions from differences that he knows

* Supposed by Dr. Johnson to be *fusees.*—EDIT

in the internal frame of watches, and to such precise complex ideas give names that shall prevail, they will then be new species to them who have those ideas with names to them, and can, by those differences, distinguish watches into these several sorts; and then "watch" will be a generical name. But yet they would be no distinct species to men ignorant of clock-work and the inward contrivances of watches, who had no other idea but the outward shape and bulk, with the marking of the hours by the hand. For to them all those other names would be but synonymous terms for the same idea, and signify no more nor no other thing but a "watch." Just thus I think it is in natural things. Nobody will doubt that the wheels or springs (if I may so say) within, are different in a rational man and a changeling, no more than that there is a difference in the frame between a drill and a changeling. But whether one or both these differences be essential or specifical, is only to be known to us by their agreement or disagreement with the complex idea that the name "man" stands for: for by that alone can it be determined whether one, or both, or neither, of those be a man or no.

40. *Species of artificial things less confused than natural.*—From what has been before said, we may see the reason why, in the species of artificial things, there is generally less confusion and uncertainty than in natural. Because an artificial thing being a production of man, which the artificer designed, and therefore well knows the idea of, the name of it is supposed to stand for no other idea, nor to import any other essence, than what is certainly to be known and easy enough to be apprehended. For the idea or essence of the several sorts of artificial things, consisting, for the most part, in nothing but the determinate figure of sensible parts; and sometimes motion depending thereon, which the artificer fashions in matter, such as he finds for his turn; it is not beyond the reach of our faculties to attain a certain idea thereof; and so settle the signification of the names whereby the species of artificial things are distinguished, with less doubt, obscurity, and equivocation than we can in things natural, whose differences and operations depend upon contrivances beyond the reach of our discoveries.

41. *Artificial things of distinct species.*—I must be excused here, if I think artificial things are of distinct species as well as natural: since I find they are as plainly and orderly ranked into sorts, by different abstract ideas with general names annexed to them, as distinct one from another as those of natural substances. For why should we not think a watch and pistol as distinct species one from another as a horse and a dog, they being expressed in our minds by distinct ideas, and to others by distinct appellations?

42. *Substances alone have proper names.*—This is farther to be observed concerning substances, that they alone, of all our

several sorts of ideas, have particular or proper names, whereby one only particular thing is signified. Because, in simple ideas, modes, and relations, it seldom happens that men have occasion to mention often this or that particular when it is absent. Besides, the greatest part of mixed modes being actions which perish in their birth, are not capable of a lasting duration, as substances which are the actors; and wherein the simple ideas, that make up the complex ideas designed by the name, have a lasting union.

43. *Difficulty to treat of words with words.*—I must beg pardon of my reader for having dwelt so long upon this subject, and perhaps with some obscurity. But I desire it may be considered how difficult it is to lead another by words into the thoughts of things, stripped of those specifical differences we give them: which things if I name not, I say nothing; and if I do name them, I thereby rank them into some sort or other, and suggest to the mind the usual abstract idea of that species, and so cross my purpose. For, to talk of a man, and to lay by, at the same time, the ordinary signification of the name "man," which is our complex idea usually annexed to it, and bid the reader consider man as he is in himself, and as he is really distinguished from others in his internal constitution or real essence, that is, by something he knows not what, looks like trifling: and yet thus one must do who would speak of the supposed real essences and species of things as thought to be made by nature, if it be but only to make it understood that there is no such thing signified by the general names which substances are called by. But because it is difficult by known familiar names to do this, give me leave to endeavour, by an example, to make the different consideration the mind has of specific names and ideas a little more clear, and to show how the complex ideas of modes are referred sometimes to archetypes in the minds of other intelligent beings—or, which is the same, to the signification annexed by others to their received names—and sometimes to no archetypes at all. Give me leave also to show how the mind always refers its ideas. of substances either to the substances themselves, or to the signification of their names, as to the archetypes; and also to make plain the nature of species, or sorting of things, as apprehended and made use of by us: and of the essences belonging to those species, which is, perhaps, of more moment to discover the extent and certainty of our knowledge than we at first imagine.

44. *Instances of mixed modes in* kinneah *and* niouph.—Let us suppose Adam in the state of a grown man, with a good understanding, but in a strange country, with all things new and unknown about him; and no other faculties to attain the knowledge of them but what one of this age has now. He observes Lamech more melancholy than usual, and imagines it

to be from a suspicion he has of his wife Adah, (whom he most ardently loved,) that she has too much kindness for another man.  Adam discourses these his thoughts to Eve, and desires her to take care that Adah commit not folly: and in these discourses with Eve, he makes use of these two new words, *kinneah* and *niouph*.  In time Adam's mistake appears, for he finds Lamech's trouble proceeded from having killed a man: but yet the two names, *kinneah* and *niouph*, the one standing for suspicion in a husband of his wife's disloyalty to him, and the other for the act of committing disloyalty, lost not their distinct significations.  It is plain, then, that here were two distinct complex ideas of mixed modes, with names to them, two distinct species of actions essentially different; I ask, Wherein consisted the essences of these two distinct species of actions?  And it is plain it consisted in a precise combination of simple ideas, different in one from the other.  I ask whether the complex idea in Adam's mind, which he called *kinneah*, were adequate or no?  And it is plain it was; for, it being a combination of simple ideas, which he, without any regard to any archetype, without respect to any thing as a pattern, voluntarily put together, abstracted, and gave the name *kinneah* to, to express in short to others by that one sound all the simple ideas contained and united in that complex one, it must necessarily follow that it was an adequate idea.  His own choice having made that combination, it had all in it he intended it should, and so could not but be perfect, could not but be adequate, it being referred to no other archetype which it was supposed to represent.

45.  These words, *kinneah* and *niouph*, by degrees grew into common use, and then the case was somewhat altered.  Adam's children had the same faculties, and thereby the same power that he had, to make what complex ideas of mixed modes they pleased in their own minds; to abstract them, and make what sounds they pleased the signs of them: but the use of names being to make our ideas within us known to others, that cannot be done but when the same sign stands for the same idea in two who would communicate their thoughts and discourse together.  Those therefore of Adam's children that found these two words, *kinneah* and *niouph*, in familiar use, could not take them for insignificant sounds; but must needs conclude they stood for something, for certain ideas, abstract ideas, they being general names, which abstract ideas were the essences of the species distinguished by those names.  If, therefore, they would use these words as names of species already established and agreed on, they were obliged to conform the ideas in their minds signified by these names, to the ideas that they stood for in other men's minds, as to their patterns and archetypes; and then, indeed, their ideas of these complex modes were liable to be inadequate, as being very apt (especially those that consisted

of combinations of many simple ideas) not to be exactly conformable to the ideas in other men's minds, using the same names; though for this there be usually a remedy at hand, which is, to ask the meaning of any word we understand not of him that uses it: it being as impossible to know certainly what the words "jealousy" and "adultery" (which I think answer קִנְאָה and נִאוּף) stand for in another man's mind with whom I would discourse about them; as it was impossible in the beginning of language to know what *kinneah* and *niouph* stood for in another man's mind without explication, they being voluntary signs in every one.

46. *Instance of substances in* zahab.—Let us now also consider, after the same manner, the names of substances in their first application. One of Adam's children, roving in the mountains, lights on a glittering substance which pleases his eye; home he carries it to Adam, who, upon consideration of it, finds it to be hard, to have a bright yellow colour, and an exceeding great weight. These, perhaps, at first, are all the qualities he takes notice of in it, and, abstracting this complex idea, consisting of a substance having that peculiar bright yellowness, and a weight very great in proportion to its bulk, he gives it the name *zahab*, to denominate and mark all substances that have these sensible qualities in them. It is evident now that, in this case, Adam acts quite differently from what he did before in forming those ideas of mixed modes, to which he gave the name *kinneah* and *niouph*. For there he put ideas together only by his own imagination, not taken from the existence of any thing: and to them he gave names to denominate all things that should happen to agree to those his abstract ideas, without considering whether any such thing did exist or no; the standard there was of his own making. But in the forming his idea of this new substance he takes the quite contrary course; here he has a standard made by nature; and therefore being to represent that to himself, by the idea he has of it, even when it is absent, he puts in no simple idea into his complex one but what he has the perception of from the thing itself. He takes care that his idea be conformable to this archetype, and intends the name should stand for an idea so conformable.

47. This piece of matter, thus denominated *zahab* by Adam, being quite different from any he had seen before, nobody, I think, will deny to be a distinct species, and to have its peculiar essence; and that the name *zahab* is the mark of the species, and a name belonging to all things partaking in that essence. But here it is plain, the essence Adam made the name *zahab* stand for was nothing but a body hard, shining, yellow, and very heavy. But the inquisitive mind of man, not content with the knowledge of these, as I may say, superficial qualities, puts Adam upon farther examination of this matter. He therefore

knocks and beats it with flints to see what was discoverable in the inside: he finds it yield to blows, but not easily separate into pieces: he finds it will bend without breaking. Is not now ductility to be added to his former idea, and make part of the essence of the species that name *zahab* stands for? Further trials discover fusibility and fixedness. Are not they also, by the same reason that any of the others were, to be put into the complex idea signified by the name *zahab?* If not, what reason will there be shown more for the one than the other? If these must, then all the other properties which any farther trials shall discover in this matter ought, by the same reason, to make a part of the ingredients of the complex idea which the name *zahab* stands for, and so be the essence of the species marked by that name. Which properties, because they are endless, it is plain that the idea made after this fashion by this archetype will be always inadequate.

48. *Their ideas imperfect, and therefore various.*—But this is not all: it would also follow that the names of substances would not only have, (as in truth they have,) but would also be supposed to have different significations, as used by different men, which would very much cumber the use of language. For if every distinct quality that were discovered in any matter by any one, were supposed to make a necessary part of the complex idea signified by the common name given it, it must follow that men must suppose the same word to signify different things in different men: since they cannot doubt but different men may have discovered several qualities in substances of the same denomination, which others know nothing of.

49. *Therefore, to fix their species, a real essence is supposed.*—To avoid this, therefore, they have supposed a real essence belonging to every species from which these properties all flow, and would have their names of the species stand for that. But they not having any idea of that real essence in substances, and their words signifying nothing but the ideas they have, that which is done by this attempt is only to put the name or sound in the place and stead of the thing having that real essence, without knowing what the real essence is; and this is that which men do when they speak of species of things, as supposing them made by nature and distinguished by real essences.

50. *Which supposition is of no use.*—For let us consider, when we affirm that all gold is fixed, either it means that fixedness is a part of the definition, part of the nominal essence the word "gold" stands for; and so this affirmation, "All gold is fixed," contains nothing but the signification of the term "gold." Or else it means that fixedness, not being a part of the definition of the word "gold," is a property of that substance itself: in which case it is plain that the word "gold" stands in the place of a substance, having the real essence of a species of things made by

nature. In which way of substitution it has so confused and uncertain a signification, that though this proposition, "Gold is fixed," be in that sense an affirmation of something real; yet it is a truth will always fail us in its particular application, and so is of no real use nor certainty. For let it be never so true that all gold, *i.e.*, all that has the real essence of gold, is fixed, what serves this for, whilst we know not in this sense what is or is not gold? For if we know not the real essence of gold, it is impossible we should know what parcel of matter has that essence, and so whether it be true gold or no.

51. *Conclusion.* To conclude: what liberty Adam had at first to make any complex ideas of mixed modes by no other pattern but by his own thoughts, the same have all men ever since had. And the same necessity of conforming his ideas of substances to things without him, as to archetypes made by nature, that Adam was under, if he would not wilfully impose upon himself, the same are all men ever since under too. The same liberty also that Adam had of affixing any new name to any idea, the same has any one still (especially the beginners of languages, if we can imagine any such), but only with this difference, that in places where men in society have already established a language amongst them, the significations of words are very warily and sparingly to be altered. Because, men being furnished already with names for their ideas, and common use having appropriated known names to certain ideas, an affected misapplication of them cannot but be very ridiculous. He that hath new notions will, perhaps, venture sometimes on the coining new terms to express them; but men think it a boldness, and it is uncertain whether common use will ever make them pass for current. But, in communication with others, it is necessary that we conform the ideas we make the vulgar words of any language stand for to their known proper significations (which I have explained at large already), or else to make known that new signification we apply them to.

---

# CHAPTER VII.

### OF PARTICLES.

1. *Particles connect parts or whole sentences together.*—Besides words, which are names of ideas in the mind, there are a great many others that are made use of to signify the connection that the mind gives to ideas or propositions, one with another. The mind, in communicating its thoughts to others, does not only need signs of the ideas it has then before it, but others also, to show or intimate some particular action of its own, at that time relating to those ideas. This it does several ways; as, "is," and

" is not," are the general marks of the mind affirming or denying. But besides affirmation, or negation, without which there is in words no truth or falsehood, the mind does, in declaring its sentiments to others, connect, not only the parts of propositions, but whole sentences one to another, with their several relations and dependencies, to make a coherent discourse.

2. *In them consists the art of well speaking.*—The words whereby it signifies what connection it gives to the several affirmations and negations that it unites in one continued reasoning or narration, are generally called "particles:" and it is in the right use of these that more particularly consists the clearness and beauty of a good style. To think well, it is not enough that a man has ideas clear and distinct in his thoughts, nor that he observes the agreement or disagreement of some of them; but he must think in train, and observe the dependence of his thoughts and reasonings one upon another; and to express well such methodical and rational thoughts, he must have words to show what connection, restriction, distinction, opposition, emphasis, &c., he gives to each respective part of his discourse. To mistake in any of these is to puzzle, instead of informing, his hearer: and therefore it is, that those words which are not truly by themselves the names of any ideas, are of such constant and indispensable use in language, and do much contribute to men's well expressing themselves.

3. *They show what relation the mind gives to its own thoughts.*— This part of grammar has been, perhaps, as much neglected as some others over-diligently cultivated. It is easy for men to write, one after another, of cases and genders, moods and tenses, gerunds and supines: in these and the like, there has been great diligence used; and particles themselves, in some languages, have been, with great show of exactness, ranked into their several orders. But though "prepositions" and "conjunctions," &c., are names well known in grammar, and the particles contained under them carefully ranked into their distinct sub-divisions; yet he who would show the right use of particles, and what significancy and force they have, must take a little more pains, enter into his own thoughts, and observe nicely the several postures of his mind in discoursing.

4. Neither is it enough, for the explaining of these words, to render them, as is usual in dictionaries, by words of another tongue which come nearest to their signification: for what is meant by them is commonly as hard to be understood in one as another language. They are all marks of some action or intimation of the mind; and therefore, to understand them rightly, the several views, postures, stands, turns, limitations, and exceptions, and several other thoughts of the mind, for which we have either none or very deficient names, are diligently to be studied. Of these there are a great variety, much exceeding the number of

particles that most languages have to express them by; and therefore it is not to be wondered that most of these particles have diverse and sometimes almost opposite significations. In the Hebrew tongue, there is a particle consisting but of one single letter, of which there are reckoned up, as I remember, seventy, I am sure above fifty, several significations.

5. *Instance in "but."*—"But" is a particle, none more familiar in our language: and he that says it is a discretive conjunction, and that it answers *sed* in Latin, or *mais* in French, thinks he has sufficiently explained it. But it seems to me to intimate several relations the mind gives to the several propositions or parts of them, which it joins by this monosyllable.

First. "But, to say no more:" here it intimates a stop of the mind in the course it was going, before it came to the end of it.

Secondly. "I saw but two plants:" here it shows that the mind limits the sense to what is expressed, with a negation of all other.

Thirdly. "You pray; but it is not that God would bring you to the true religion."

Fourthly. "But that he would confirm you in your own." The first of these "buts" intimates a supposition in the mind of something otherwise than it should be; the latter shows that the mind makes a direct opposition between that and what goes before it.

Fifthly. "All animals have sense; but a dog is an animal:" here it signifies little more but that the latter proposition is joined to the former, as the minor of a syllogism.

6. *This matter but lightly touched here.*—To these, I doubt not, might be added a great many other significations of this particle, if it were my business to examine it in its full latitude, and consider it in all the places it is to be found: which if one should do, I doubt whether in all those manners it is made use of, it would deserve the title of "discretive," which grammarians give to it. But I intend not here a full explication of this sort of signs. The instances I have given in this one may give occasion to reflect upon their use and force in language, and lead us into the contemplation of several actions of our minds in discoursing, which it has found a way to intimate to others by these particles, some whereof constantly, and others in certain constructions, have the sense of a whole sentence contained in them.

## CHAPTER VIII.

### OF ABSTRACT AND CONCRETE TERMS.

1. *Abstract terms not predicable one of another, and why.*—Tne ordinary words of language, and our common use of them, would have given us light into the nature of our ideas, if they had been but considered with attention. The mind, as has been shown, has a power to abstract its ideas, and so they become essences, general essences, whereby the sorts of things are distinguished. Now each abstract idea being distinct, so that of any two the one can never be the other, the mind will, by its intuitive knowledge, perceive their difference; and therefore in propositions no two whole ideas can ever be affirmed one of another. This we see in the common use of language, which permits not any two abstract words, or names of abstract ideas, to be affirmed one of another. For, how near of kin soever they may seem to be, and how certain soever it is that man is an animal, or rational, or white, yet every one, at first hearing, perceives the falsehood of these propositions; "Humanity is animality," or "rationality," or "whiteness:" and this is as evident as any of the most allowed maxims. All our affirmations, then, are only inconcrete, which is the affirming not one abstract idea to be another, but one abstract idea to be joined to another; which abstract ideas, in substances, may be of any sort; in all the rest, are little else but of relations; and in substances the most frequent are of powers. *V. g.*, "A man is white," signifies that the thing that has the essence of a man has also in it the essence of whiteness, which is nothing but the power to produce the idea of whiteness in one whose eyes can discover ordinary objects; or, "A man is rational," signifies that the same thing that hath the essence of a man hath also in it the essence of rationality, *i. e.*, a power of reasoning.

2. *They shew the difference of our ideas.*—This distinction of names shows us also the difference of our ideas: for if we observe them, we shall find that our simple ideas have all abstract as well as concrete names: the one whereof is (to speak the language of grammarians) a substantive, the other an adjective; as, "whiteness, white, sweetness, sweet." The like also holds in our ideas of modes and relations, as, "justice, just, equality, equal;" only with this difference, that some of the concrete names of relations, amongst men chiefly, are substantives, as *paternitas, pater;* whereof it were easy to render a reason. But as to our ideas of substances, we have very few or no abstract names at all. For though the Schools have introduced *animalitas, humanitas, corporeitas,* and some others;

yet they hold no proportion with that infinite number of names of substances to which they never were ridiculous enough to attempt the coining of abstract ones: and those few that the schools forged, and put into the mouths of their scholars, could never yet get admittance into common use, or obtain the licence of public approbation.    Which seems to me at least to intimate the confession of all mankind, that they have no ideas of the real essences of substances, since they have not names for such ideas : which no doubt they would have had, had not their consciousness to themselves of their ignorance of them kept them from so idle an attempt.    And therefore though they had ideas enough to distinguish gold from a stone, and metal from wood ; yet they but timorously ventured on such terms as *aurietas* and *saxietas*, *metalleitas* and *ligneitas*, or the like name, which should pretend to signify the real essences of those substances whereof they knew they had no ideas.    And, indeed, it was only the doctrine of substantial forms, and the confidence of mistaken pretenders to a knowledge that they had not, which first coined and then introduced *animalitas*, and *humanitas*, and the like; which yet went very little farther than their own schools, and could never get to be current amongst understanding men. Indeed, *humanitas* was a word familiar amongst the Romans, but in a far different sense; and stood not for the abstract essence of any substance, but was the abstract name of a mode, and its concrete *humanus*, not *homo*.

## CHAPTER IX.

### OF THE IMPERFECTION OF WORDS.

1. *Words are used for recording and communicating our thoughts.* —From what has been said in the foregoing chapters, it is easy to perceive what imperfection there is in language, and how the very nature of words makes it almost unavoidable for many of them to be doubtful and uncertain in their significations.    To examine the perfection or imperfection of words, it is necessary first to consider their use and end : for as they are more or less fitted to attain that, so they are more or less perfect.    We have, in the former part of this discourse, often, upon occasion, mentioned a double use of words.

First, One for the recording of our own thoughts.

Secondly, The other for the communicating of our thoughts to others.

2. *Any words will serve for recording.*—As to the first of these, for the recording our own thoughts for the help of our own memories, whereby, as it were, we talk to ourselves, any words will serve the turn.    For, since sounds are voluntary and indif-

ferent signs of any ideas, a man may use what words he pleases
to signify his own ideas to himself: and there will be no imperfection in them, if he constantly use the same sign for the
same idea: for then he cannot fail of having his meaning understood, wherein consists the right use and perfection of language.

3. *Communication by words civil or philosophical.*—Secondly,
As to communication of words, that too has a double use.

I. Civil.

II. Philosophical.

First, By their civil use, I mean such a communication of
thoughts and ideas by words as may serve for the upholding
common conversation and commerce about the ordinary affairs
and conveniences of civil life, in the societies of men one amongst
another.

Secondly, By the philosophical use of words, I mean such an
use of them as may serve to convey the precise notions of things,
and to express, in general propositions, certain and undoubted
truths which the mind may rest upon and be satisfied with, in its
search after true knowledge. These two uses are very distinct;
and a great deal less exactness will serve in the one than in the
other, as we shall see in what follows.

4. *The imperfection of words is the doubtfulness of their signification.*—The chief end of language in communication being to be
understood, words serve not well for that end, neither in civil
nor philosophical discourse, when any word does not excite in
the hearer the same idea which it stands for in the mind of the
speaker. Now since sounds have no natural connexion with our
ideas, but have all their signification from the arbitrary imposition of men, the doubtfulness and uncertainty of their signification,
which is the imperfection we here are speaking of, has its cause
more in the ideas they stand for, than in any incapacity there is
in one sound more than in another to signify any idea: for in
that regard, they are all equally perfect.

That then which makes doubtfulness and uncertainty in the
signification of some more than other words, is the difference of
ideas they stand for.

5. *Causes of their imperfection.*—Words having naturally no
signification, the idea which each stands for must be learned and
retained by those who would exchange thoughts and hold intelligible discourse with others, in any language. But this is hardest
to be done, where,

First, The ideas they stand for are very complex, and made up
of a great number of ideas put together.

Secondly, Where the ideas they stand for have no certain connexion in nature; and so no settled standard any where in nature
existing to rectify and adjust them by.

Thirdly, where the signification of the word is referred to a
standard, which standard is not easy to be known.

Fourthly, Where the signification of the word, and the real essence of the thing, are not exactly the same.

These are difficulties that attend the signification of several words that are intelligible. Those which are not intelligible at all, such as names standing for any simple ideas, which another has not organs or faculties to attain; as the names of colours to a blind man, or sounds to a deaf man; need not here be mentioned.

In all these cases we shall find an imperfection in words: which I shall more at large explain, in their particular application to our several sorts of ideas: for if we examine them, we shall find, that the names of mixed modes are most liable to doubtfulness and imperfection for the two first of these reasons: and the names of substances chiefly for the two latter.

6. *The names of mixed modes doubtful.*—First, The names of mixed modes are many of them liable to great uncertainty and obscurity in their signification.

*First, Because the ideas they stand for are so complex.*—I. Because of that great composition these complex ideas are often made up of. To make words serviceable to the end of communication, it is necessary (as has been said) that they excite in the hearer exactly the same idea they stand for in the mind of the speaker. Without this, men fill one another's heads with noise and sounds; but convey not thereby their thoughts, and lay not before one another their ideas, which is the end of discourse and language. But when a word stands for a very complex idea, that is compounded and decompounded, it is not easy for men to form and retain that idea so exactly, as to make the name in common use stand for the same precise idea without any the least variation. Hence it comes to pass, that men's names, of very compound ideas, such as for the most part are moral words, have seldom, in two different men, the same precise signification; since one man's complex idea seldom agrees with another's, and often differs from his own, from that which he had yesterday or will have to-morrow.

7. *Secondly, Because they have no standards.*—II. Because the names of mixed modes, for the most part, want standards in nature, whereby men may rectify and adjust their significations; therefore they are very various and doubtful. They are assemblages of ideas put together at the pleasure of the mind, pursuing its own ends of discourse, and suited to its own notions, whereby it designs not to copy anything really existing, but to denominate and rank things, as they come to agree with those archetypes or forms it has made. He that first brought the word " sham," " wheedle," or " banter " in use, put together, as he thought fit, those ideas he made it stand for: and as it is with any new names of modes that are now brought into any language, so was it with the old ones when, they were first made use of. Names there-

fore, that stand for collections of ideas which the mind makes at pleasure, must needs be of doubtful signification when such collections are nowhere to be found constantly united in nature, nor any patterns to be shown whereby men may adjust them. What the word "murder" or "sacrilege," &c., signifies, can never be known from things themselves. There be many of the parts of those complex ideas which are not visible in the action itself: the intention of the mind, or the relation of holy things, which make a part of murder or sacrilege, have no necessary connexion with the outward and visible action of him that commits either: and the pulling the trigger of the gun, with which the murder is committed, and is all the action that perhaps is visible, has no natural connexion with those other ideas that make up the complex one, named "murder." They have their union and combination only from the understanding which unites them under one name: but, uniting them without any rule or pattern, it cannot be but that the signification of the name that stands for such voluntary collections should be often various in the minds of different men, who have scarce any standing rule to regulate themselves and their notions by any such arbitrary ideas.

8. *Propriety not a sufficient remedy.*—It is true, common use, that is, the rule of propriety, may be supposed here to afford some aid to settle the signification of language; and it cannot be denied but that in some measure it does. Common use regulates the meaning of words pretty well for common conversation; but nobody having an authority to establish the precise signification of words, nor determine to what ideas any one shall annex them, common use is not sufficient to adjust them to philosophical discourses; there being scarce any name, of any very complex idea (to say nothing of others), which in common use has not a great latitude, and which, keeping within the bounds of propriety, may not be made the sign of far different ideas. Besides, the rule and measure of propriety itself being nowhere established, it is often matter of dispute whether this or that way of using a word be propriety of speech or no. From all which it is evident, that the names of such kind of very complex ideas are naturally liable to this imperfection, to be of doubtful and uncertain signification; and, even in men that have a mind to understand one another, do not always stand for the same idea in speaker and hearer. Though the names "glory" and "gratitude" be the same in every man's mouth through a whole country, yet the complex collective idea, which every one thinks on or intends by that name, is apparently very different in men using the same language.

9. *The way of learning these names contributes also to their doubtfulness.*—The way also wherein the names of mixed modes are ordinarily learned, does not a little contribute to the doubtfulness of their signification. For if we will observe how children learn languages, we shall find, that, to make them understand

what the names of simple ideas or substances stand for, people ordinarily show them the thing whereof they would have them have the idea; and then repeat to them the name that stands for it, as, "white, sweet, milk, sugar, cat, dog." But as for mixed modes, especially the most material of them, moral words, the sounds are usually learned first; and then, to know what complex ideas they stand for, they are either beholden to the explication of others, or (which happens for the most part) are left to their own observation and industry; which being little laid out in the search of the true and precise meaning of names, these moral words are, in most men's mouths, little more than bare sounds; or, when they have any, it is for the most part but a very loose and undetermined, and consequently obscure and confused, signification. And even those themselves, who have with more attention, settled their notions, do yet hardly avoid the inconvenience to have them stand for complex ideas, different from those which other, even intelligent and studious, men make them the signs of. Where shall one find any either controversial debate or familiar discourse concerning "honour, faith, grace, religion, church," &c., wherein it is not easy to observe the different notions men have of them; which is nothing but this, that they are not agreed in the signification of those words; nor have in their minds the same complex ideas which they make them stand for; and so all the contests that follow thereupon are only about the meaning of a sound. And hence we see that, in the interpretation of laws, whether divine or human, there is no end; comments beget comments, and explications make new matter for explications: and of limiting, distinguishing, varying the signification of these moral words, there is no end. These ideas of men's making are, by men still having the same power, multiplied *in infinitum*. Many a man, who was pretty well satisfied of the meaning of a text of scripture, or clause in the code, at first reading, has, by consulting commentators, quite lost the sense of it, and by those elucidations given rise or increase to his doubts, and drawn obscurity upon the place. I say not this, that I think commentaries needless; but to show how uncertain the names of mixed modes naturally are, even in the mouths of those who had both the intention and the faculty of speaking as clearly as language was capable to express their thoughts.

10. *Hence unavoidable obscurity in ancient authors.*—What obscurity this has unavoidably brought upon the writings of men who have lived in remote ages and different countries, it will be needless to take notice; since the numerous volumes of learned men, employing their thoughts that way, are proofs more than enough to show what attention, study, sagacity, and reasoning are required to find out the true meaning of ancient authors. But, there being no writings we have any great concernment to be very solicitous about the meaning of, but those that contain

either truths we are required to believe or laws we are to obey, and draw inconveniences on us when we mistake or transgress, we may be less anxious about the sense of other authors; who writing but their own opinions, we are under no greater necessity to know them than they to know ours. Our good or evil depending not on their decrees, we may safely be ignorant of their notions: and therefore in the reading of them, if they do not use their words with a due clearness and perspicuity, we may lay them aside, and, without any injury done them, resolve thus with ourselves,

*Si non vis intelligi, debes negligi.*

11. *Names of substances of doubtful signification.*—If the signification of the names of mixed modes are uncertain because there be no real standards existing in nature to which those ideas are referred and by which they may be adjusted, the names of substances are of a doubtful signification for a contrary reason, viz., because the ideas they stand for are supposed conformable to the reality of things, and are referred to standards made by nature. In our ideas of substances we have not the liberty, as in mixed modes, to frame what combinations we think fit to be the characteristical notes to rank and denominate things by. In these we must follow nature, suit our complex ideas to real existences, and regulate the signification of their names by the things themselves, if we will have our names to be the signs of them, and stand for them. Here, it is true, we have patterns to follow; but patterns that will make the signification of their names very uncertain: for, names must be of a very unsteady and various meaning, if the ideas they stand for be referred to standards without us, that either cannot be known at all, or can be known but imperfectly and uncertainly.

12. *Names of substances referred, First, to real essences that cannot be known.*—The names of substances have, as has been showed, a double reference in their ordinary use.

First, Sometimes they are made to stand for, and so their signification is supposed to agree to, the real constitution of things, from which all their properties flow, and in which they all centre. But this real constitution, or (as it is apt to be called) essence, being utterly unknown to us, any sound that is put to stand for it must be very uncertain in its application; and it will be impossible to know what things are or ought to be called "an horse," or "antimony," when those words are put for real essences that we have no ideas of at all. And therefore, in this supposition, the names of substances being referred to standards that cannot be known, their significations can never be adjusted and established by those standards.

13. *Secondly, To co-existing qualities which are known but imperfectly.*—Secondly, The simple ideas that are found to co-exist

in substances being that which their names immediately signify, these, as united in the several sorts of things, are the proper standards to which their names are referred, and by which their significations may best be rectified. But neither will these archetypes so well serve to this purpose, as to leave these names without very various and uncertain significations. Because these simple ideas that co-exist, and are united in the same subject, being very numerous, and having all an equal right to go into the complex specific idea, which the specific name is to stand for, men, though they propose to themselves the very same subject to consider, yet frame very different ideas about it: and so the name they use for it unavoidably comes to have, in several men, very different significations. The simple qualities which make up the complex ideas being most of them powers, in relation to changes which they are apt to make in or receive from other bodies, are almost infinite. He that shall but observe what a great variety of alterations any one of the baser metals is apt to receive from the different application only of fire, and how much a greater number of changes any of them will receive in the hands of a chymist by the application of other bodies, will not think it strange that I count the properties of any sort of bodies not easy to be collected and completely known by the ways of inquiry which our faculties are capable of. They being therefore at least so many that no man can know the precise and definite number, they are differently discovered by different men, according to their various skill, attention, and ways of handling; who therefore cannot choose but have different ideas of the same substance, and therefore make the signification of its common name very various and uncertain. For the complex ideas of substances being made up of such simple ones as are supposed to co-exist in nature, every one has a right to put into his complex idea those qualities he has found to be united together. For though in the substance, gold, one satisfies himself with colour and weight, yet another thinks solubility in *aqua regia* as necessary to be joined with that colour in his idea of gold, as any one does its fusibility; solubility in *aqua regia* being a quality as constantly joined with its colour and weight, as fusibility or any other: others put in its ductility, or fixedness, &c., as they have been taught by tradition or experience. Who of all these has established the right signification of the word "gold?" or who shall be the judge to determine? Each has his standard in nature which he appeals to, and with reason thinks he has the same right to put into his complex idea signified by the word "gold," those qualities which upon trial he has found united; as another, who has not so well examined, has to leave them out; or a third, who has made other trials, has to put in others. For, the union in nature of these qualities being the true ground of their union in one complex idea, who can say one of them has more reason to be put in or

left out than another?   From whence it will always unavoidably
follow, that the complex ideas of substances, in men using the
same name for them, will be very various ; and so the significations of those names very uncertain.

14. Besides, there is scarce any particular thing existing,
which, in some of its simple ideas, does not communicate with a
greater, and in others with a less, number of particular beings :
who shall determine in this case, which are those that are to
make up the precise collection that is to be signified by the
specific name ; or can with any just authority prescribe which
obvious or common qualities are to be left out, or which more
secret or more particular are to be put into the signification of
the name of any substance?   All which together seldom or
never fail to produce that various and doubtful signification in
the names of substances, which causes such uncertainty, disputes,
or mistakes, when we come to a philosophical use of them.

15. *With this imperfection, they may serve for civil, but not well
for philosophical, use.*—It is true, as to civil and common conversation, the general names of substances, regulated in their ordinary signification by some obvious qualities, (as by the shape
and figure in things of known seminal propagation, and in other
substances for the most part by colour, joined with some other
sensible qualities,) do well enough to design the things men
would be understood to speak of : and so they usually conceive
well enough the substances meant by the word "gold" or
"apple," to distinguish the one from the other.   But in philosophical inquiries and debates, where general truths are to be
established, and consequences drawn from positions laid down,
there the precise signification of the names of substances will be
found not only not to be well established, but also very hard to
be so.   For example : He that shall make malleableness, or a
certain degree of fixedness, a part of his complex idea of gold,
may make propositions concerning gold, and draw consequences
from them, that will truly and clearly follow from gold taken in
such a signification : but yet such as another man can never be
forced to admit, nor be convinced of their truth, who makes not
malleableness, or the same degree of fixedness, part of that complex idea that the name "gold," in his use of it, stands for.

16. *Instance, liquor.*—This is a natural and almost unavoidable
imperfection in almost all the names of substances, in all languages whatsoever, which men will easily find when, once
passing from confused or loose notions, they come to more strict
and close inquiries.   For then they will be convinced how
doubtful and obscure those words are in their signification,
which in ordinary use appeared very clear and determined.   I
was once in a meeting of very learned and ingenious physicians,
where by chance there arose a question, Whether any liquor
passed through the filaments of the nerves?   The debate having

been managed a good while, by variety of arguments on both sides, I (who had been used to suspect that the greatest part of disputes were more about the signification of words, than a real difference in the conception of things) desired, that before they went any farther on in this dispute, they would first examine and establish amongst them what the word "liquor" signified. They at first were a little surprised at the proposal; and had they been persons less ingenious, they might perhaps have taken it for a very frivolous or extravagant one: since there was no one there that thought not himself to understand very perfectly what the word "liquor" stood for; which I think, too, none of the most perplexed names of substances. However, they were pleased to comply with my motion; and, upon examination, found that the signification of that word was not so settled and certain as they had all imagined; but that each of them made it a sign of a different complex idea. This made them perceive that the main of their dispute was about the signification of that term; and that they differed very little in their opinions concerning some fluid and subtile matter passing through the conduits of the nerves, though it was not so easy to agree whether it was to be called "liquor" or no; a thing which when each considered, he thought it not worth the contending about.*

17. *Instance, gold.*—How much this is the case in the greatest part of disputes that men are engaged so hotly in, I shall, perhaps, have an occasion in another place to take notice. Let us only here consider a little more exactly the fore-mentioned instance of the word "gold," and we shall see how hard it is precisely to determine its signification. I think all agree to make it stand for a body of a certain yellow shining colour; which being the idea to which children have annexed that name, the shining yellow part of a peacock's tail is properly to them gold. Others finding fusibility joined with that yellow colour in certain parcels of matter, make of that combination a complex idea to which they give the name "gold" to denote a sort of substances; and so exclude from being gold all such yellow shining bodies as by fire will be reduced to ashes; and admit to be of that species, or to be comprehended under that name "gold," only such substances as having that shining yellow colour will by fire be reduced to fusion, and not to ashes. Another by the same reason adds the weight, which, being a quality as straitly joined with that colour as its fusibility, he thinks has the same reason to be joined in its idea, and to be signified by its name: and therefore the other, made up of body of such a colour, and fusibility, to be imperfect; and so on of all the rest: wherein no one can show a reason why some of the inseparable qualities, that are always united in nature, should be put into the nominal

* The fourth folio edition and others have this reading: "A thing which, when considered, they thought it not worth the contending about."—EDIT.

essence, and others left out: or why the word " gold," signifying that sort of body the ring on his finger is made of, should determine that sort rather by its colour, weight, and fusibility, than by its colour, weight, and solubility in *aqua regia*: since the dissolving it by that liquor is as inseparable from it as the fusion by fire; and they are both of them nothing but the relation which that substance has to two other bodies, which have a power to operate differently upon it. For by what right is it that fusibility comes to be a part of the essence signified by the word " gold," and solubility but a property of it? Or why is its colour part of the essence, and its malleableness but a property? That which I mean is this, that these being all but properties, depending on its real constitution, and nothing but powers either active or passive in reference to other bodies, no one has authority to determine the signification of the word " gold " (as referred to such a body existing in nature) more to one collection of ideas to be found in that body than to another: whereby the signification of that name must unavoidably be very uncertain: since, as has been said, several people observe *several* properties in the same substance; and, I think I may say, nobody *all*. And therefore we have but very imperfect descriptions of things, and words have very uncertain significations.

18. *The names of simple ideas the least doubtful.*—From what has been said it is easy to observe, what has been before remarked, viz., that the names of simple ideas are, of all others, the least liable to mistakes, and that for these reasons: First, Because the ideas they stand for, being each but one single perception, are much easier got and more clearly retained than the more complex ones; and therefore are not liable to the uncertainty which usually attends those compounded ones of substances and mixed modes, in which the precise number of simple ideas that make them up are not easily agreed, and so readily kept in the mind. And, Secondly, Because they are never referred to any other essence but barely that perception they immediately signify: which reference is that which renders the significations of the names of substances naturally so perplexed, and gives occasion to so many disputes. Men that do not perversely use their words, or on purpose set themselves to cavil, seldom mistake, in any language which they are acquainted with, the use and signification of the names of simple ideas: white and sweet, yellow and bitter, carry a very obvious meaning with them, which every one precisely comprehends, or easily perceives he is ignorant of, and seeks to be informed. But what precise collection of simple ideas modesty or frugality stand for in another's use, is not so certainly known. And, however we are apt to think we well enough know what is meant by " gold " or " iron;" yet the precise complex idea others make them the signs of is not so certain: and I believe it is very

seldom that in speaker and hearer they stand for exactly the same collection. Which must needs produce mistakes and disputes, when they are made use of in discourses wherein men have to do with universal propositions, and would settle in their minds universal truths, and consider the consequences that follow from them.

19. *And next to them, simple modes.*—By the same rule, the names of simple modes are, next to those of simple ideas, least liable to doubt and uncertainty, especially those of figure and number, of which men have so clear and distinct ideas. Whoever, that had a mind to understand them, mistook the ordinary meaning of "seven," or a "triangle?" And in general the least compounded ideas in every kind have the least dubious names.

20. *The most doubtful are the names of very compounded mixed modes and substances.*—Mixed modes therefore, that are made up but of a few and obvious simple ideas, have usually names of no very uncertain signification. But the names of mixed modes, which comprehend a great number of simple ideas, are commonly of a very doubtful and undetermined meaning, as has been shown. The names of substances, being annexed to ideas that are neither the real essences nor exact representations of the patterns they are referred to, are liable yet to greater imperfection and uncertainty, especially when we come to a philosophical use of them.

21. *Why this imperfection charged upon words.*—The great disorder that happens in our names of substances proceeding for the most part from our want of knowledge and inability to penetrate into their real constitutions, it may probably be wondered why I charge this as an imperfection rather upon our words than understandings. This exception has so much appearance of justice, that I think myself obliged to give a reason why I have followed this method. I must confess, then, that when I first began this discourse of the understanding, and a good while after, I had not the least thought that any consideration of words was at all necessary to it. But when, having passed over the original and composition of our ideas, I began to examine the extent and certainty of our knowledge, I found it had so near a connexion with words, that unless their force and manner of signification were first well observed, there could be very little said clearly and pertinently concerning knowledge: which, being conversant about truth, had constantly to do with propositions. And though it terminated in things, yet it was for the most part so much by the intervention of words, that they seemed scarce separable from our general knowledge. At least, they interpose themselves so much between our understandings and the truth which it would contemplate and apprehend, that, like the medium through which visible objects pass, their security and disorder does not seldom cast a mist before our

eyes, and impose upon our understandings. If we consider, in the fallacies men put upon themselves as well as others, and the mistakes in men's disputes and notions, how great a part is owing to words and their uncertain or mistaken significations, we shall have reason to think this no small obstacle in the way to knowledge; which I conclude we are the more carefully to be warned of, because it has been so far from being taken notice of as an inconvenience, that the arts of improving it have been made the business of men's study, and obtained the reputation of learning and subtilty, as we shall see in the following chapter. But I am apt to imagine that, were the imperfections of language, as the instrument of knowledge, more thoroughly weighed, a great many of the controversies that make such a noise in the world would of themselves cease; and the way to knowledge, and perhaps peace too, lie a great deal opener than it does.

22. *This should teach us moderation in imposing our own sense of old authors.*—Sure I am, that the signification of words, in all languages, depending very much on the thoughts, notions, and ideas of him that uses them, must unavoidably be of great uncertainty to men of the same language and country. This is so evident in the Greek authors, that he that shall peruse their writings will find, in almost every one of them, a distinct language, though the same words. But when to this natural difficulty in every country there shall be added different countries and remote ages, wherein the speakers and writers had very different notions, tempers, customs, ornaments and figures of speech, &c., every one of which influenced the signification of their words then, though to us now they are lost and unknown, it would become us to be charitable one to another in our interpretations or misunderstanding of those ancient writings; which, though of great concernment to be understood, are liable to the unavoidable difficulties of speech, which (if we except the names of simple ideas, and some very obvious things) is not capable, without a constant defining the terms, of conveying the sense and intention of the speaker without any manner of doubt and uncertainty to the hearer. And in discourses of religion, law, and morality, as they are matters of the highest concernment, so there will be the greatest difficulty.

23. The volumes of interpreters and commentators on the Old and New Testament are but too manifest proofs of this. Though everything said in the text be infallibly true, yet the reader may be, nay, cannot choose but be, very fallible in the understanding of it. Nor is it to be wondered that the will of God, when clothed in words, should be liable to that doubt and uncertainty which unavoidably attends that sort of conveyance, when even his Son, whilst clothed in flesh, was subject to all the frailties and inconveniences of human nature, sin excepted. And we ought to magnify his goodness, that he hath spread before all

the world such legible characters of his works and providence, and given all mankind so sufficient a light of reason, that they to whom this written word never came, could not (whenever they set themselves to search) either doubt of the being of a God, or of the obedience due to him. Since, then, the precepts of natural religion are plain, and very intelligible to all mankind, and seldom come to be controverted; and other revealed truths, which are conveyed to us by books and languages, are liable to the common and natural obscurities and difficulties incident to words: methinks it would become us to be more careful and diligent in observing the former, and less magisterial, positive, and imperious in imposing our own sense and interpretations of the latter.

## CHAPTER X.

### OF THE ABUSE OF WORDS.

**1.** *Abuse of words.*—Besides the imperfection that is naturally in language, and the obscurity and confusion that is so hard to be avoided in the use of words, there are several wilful faults and neglects which men are guilty of in this way of communication, whereby they render these signs less clear and distinct in their signification than naturally they need to be.

**2.** *First, Words without any, or without clear, ideas.*—First, In this kind, the first and most palpable abuse is, the using of words without clear and distinct ideas; or, which is worse, signs without any thing signified. Of these there are two sorts :—

**I.** One may observe, in all languages, certain words that, if they be examined, will be found, in their first original and their appropriated use, not to stand for any clear and distinct ideas. These, for the most part, the several sects of philosophy and religion have introduced. For their authors or promoters, either affecting something singular, and out of the way of common apprehensions, or to support some strange opinions, or cover some weakness of their hypothesis, seldom fail to coin new words, and such as, when they come to be examined, may justly be called " insignificant terms." For, having either had no determinate collection of ideas annexed to them when they were first invented, or at least such as, if well examined, will be found inconsistent, it is no wonder if afterwards, in the vulgar use of the same party, they remain empty sounds with little or no signification, amongst those who think it enough to have them often in their mouths, as the distinguishing characters of their church or school, without much troubling their heads to examine what are the precise ideas they stand for. I shall not need here to heap up instances; every one's reading and conversation will sufficiently furnish him : or if he wants to be better stored, the great mint-masters of these kind of terms, I mean the schoolmen and metaphysicians (under which, I think, the disputing natural and moral philosophers of these latter ages may be comprehended), have wherewithal abundantly to content him.

3. II. Others there be who extend this abuse yet farther, who take so little care to lay by words which, in their primary notation, have scarce any clear and distinct ideas which they are annexed to, that, by an unpardonable negligence, they familiarly use words which the propriety of language has affixed to very important ideas, without any distinct meaning at all. " Wisdom, glory, grace," &c., are words frequent enough in every man's mouth; but if a great many of those who use them should be asked what they mean by them, they would be at a stand, and not know what to answer: a plain proof that, though they have learned those sounds, and have them ready at their tongues' end, yet there are no determined ideas laid up in their minds, which are to be expressed to others by them.

4. *Occasioned by learning names before the ideas they belong to.* —Men having been accustomed from their cradles to learn words which are easily got and retained, before they knew or had framed the complex ideas to which they were annexed, or which were to be found in the things they were thought to stand for, they usually continue to do so all their lives; and, without taking the pains necessary to settle in their minds determined ideas, they use their words for such unsteady and confused notions as they have, contenting themselves with the same words other people use; as if their very sound necessarily carried with it constantly the same meaning. This though men make a shift with in the ordinary occurrences of life, where they find it necessary to be understood, and therefore they make signs till they are so; yet this insignificancy in their words, when they come to reason concerning either their tenets or interest, manifestly fills their discourse with abundance of empty, unintelligible noise and jargon, especially in moral matters where the words for the most part, standing for arbitrary and numerous collections of ideas, not regularly and permanently united in nature, their bare sounds are often only thought on, or at least very obscure and uncertain notions annexed to them. Men take the words they find in use amongst their neighbours; and that they may not seem ignorant what they stand for, use them confidently, without much troubling their heads about a certain fixed meaning; whereby, besides the ease of it, they obtain this advantage, that as in such discourses they seldom are in the right, so they are as seldom to be convinced that they are in the wrong; it being all one to go about to draw those men out of their mistakes who have no settled notions, as to dispossess a vagrant of his habitation, who has no settled abode. This I guess to be so; and every one may observe in himself and others whether it be or no.

**5.** *Secondly, Unsteady application of them.*—Secondly, Another great abuse of words is, inconsistency in the use of them. It is hard to find a discourse written of any subject, especially of controversy, wherein one shall not observe, if he read with attention, the same words (and those commonly the most material in the discourse, and upon which the argument turns) used sometimes for one collection of simple ideas, and sometimes for another which is a perfect abuse of language. Words being intended for signs of my ideas, to make them known to others, not by any natural signification, but by a voluntary imposition, it is plain cheat and abuse when I make them stand sometimes for one thing and sometimes for another: the wilful doing whereof can be imputed to nothing but great folly or greater dishonesty. And a man, in his accounts with another, may, with as much fairness, make the characters of numbers, stand sometimes for one and sometimes for another collection of units, (*v. g.*, this character **3** stands sometimes for three, sometimes for four, and sometimes for eight), as in his discourse or reasoning, make the same words stand for different collections of simple ideas. If men should do so in their reckonings, I wonder who would have to do with them! One who would speak thus in the affairs and business of the world, and call eight sometimes seven, and sometimes nine, as best served his advantage, would presently have clapped upon him one of the two names men constantly are disgusted with. And yet in arguings and learned contests the same sort of proceeding passes commonly for wit and learning: but to me it appears a greater dishonesty than the misplacings of counters in the casting up a debt; and the cheat the greater by how much truth is of greater concernment and value than money.

**6.** *Thirdly, Affected obscurity by wrong application.*—Another abuse of language is an affected obscurity, by either applying old words to new and unusual significations, or introducing new and ambiguous terms without defining either: or else putting them so together as may confound their ordinary meaning. Though the peripatetic philosophy has been most eminent in this way, yet other sects have not been wholly clear of it. There is scarce any of them that are not cumbered with some difficulties (such is the imperfection of human knowledge), which they have been fain to cover with obscurity of terms and to confound the signification of words, which, like a mist before people's eyes, might hinder their weak parts from being discovered. That "body" and "extension," in common use, stand for two distinct ideas, is plain to any one that will but reflect a little. For, were their signification precisely the same, it would be proper and as intelligible to say "the body of an extension," as "the extension of a body;" and yet there are those who find it necessary to confound their signification. To this abuse, and the mischiefs of confounding the signification of words, logic and the liberal sciences, as they have been handled in the Schools, have given reputation; and the admired art of disputing hath added much to the natural imperfection of languages, whilst it has been made use of and fitted to perplex the signification of words more than to discover the knowledge and truth of things: and that he will look into that sort of learned writings, will find the words there much more obscure, uncertain, and undetermined in their meaning than they are in ordinary conversation.

7. *Logic and dispute has much contributed to this.*—This is unavoidably to be so, where men's parts and learning are estimated by their skill in disputing. And if reputation and reward shall attend these conquests, which depend mostly on the fineness and niceties of words, it is no wonder if the wit of men so employed should perplex, involve, and subtilize the significations of sounds, so as never to want something to say in opposing or defending any question; the victory being adjudged not to him who had truth on his side, but the last word in the dispute.

8. *Calling it "subtilty."*—This, though a very useless skill, and that which I think the direct opposite to the ways of knowledge, hath yet passed hitherto under the laudable and esteemed names of "subtilty" and "acuteness;" and has had the applause of the Schools, and encouragement of one part of the learned men of the world. And no wonder since the philosophers of old (the disputing and wrangling philosophers I mean, such as Lucian wittily and with reason taxes), and the Schoolmen since, aiming at glory and esteem for their great and universal knowledge, easier a great deal to be pretended to than really acquired, found this a good expedient to cover their ignorance with a curious and inexplicable web of perplexed words, and procure to themselves the admiration of others by unintelligible terms, the apter to produce wonder because they could not be understood: whilst it appears in all history that these profound doctors were no wiser nor more useful than their neighbours, and brought but small advantage to human life, or the societies wherein they lived: unless the coining of new words, where they produced no new things to apply them to, or the perplexing or obscuring the signification of old ones, and so bringing all things into question and dispute, were a thing profitable to the life of man, or worthy commendation and reward.

9. *This learning very little benefits society.*—For, notwithstanding these learned disputants, these all knowing doctors, it was to the unscholastic statesman that the governments of the world owed their peace, defence, and liberties; and from the illiterate and contemned mechanic (a name of disgrace) that they received the improvements of useful arts. Nevertheless, this artificial ignorance and learned gibberish prevailed mightily in these last ages, by the interest and artifice of those who found no easier way to that pitch of authority and dominion they have attained,

than by amusing the men of business and ignorant with hard words, or employing the ingenious and idle in intricate disputes about unintelligible terms, and holding them perpetually entangled in that endless labyrinth. Besides, there is no such way to gain admittance, or give defence to strange and absurd doctrines, as to guard them round about with legions of obscure, doubtful, and undefined words; which yet make these retreats more like the dens of robbers, or holes of foxes, than the fortresses of fair warriors : which if it be hard to get them out of, it is not for the strength that is in them, but the briers and thorns, and the obscurity of the thickets they are beset with. For, untruth being unacceptable to the mind of man, there is no other defence left for absurdity but obscurity.

10. *But destroys the instruments of knowledge and communication.* —Thus learned ignorance, and this art of keeping even inquisitive men from true knowledge, hath been propagated in the world, and hath much perplexed whilst it pretended to inform the understanding. For we see that other well-meaning and wise men, whose education and parts had not acquired that acuteness, could intelligibly express themselves to one another, and in its plain use make a benefit of language. But though unlearned men well enough understood the words "white" and "black," &c., and had constant notions of the ideas signified by those words; yet there were philosophers found who had learning and subtilty enough to prove that snow was black; *i. e.*, to prove that white was black. Whereby they had the advantage to destroy the instruments and means of discourse, conversation, instruction, and society; whilst, with great art and subtilty, they did no more but perplex and confound the signification of words, and thereby render language less useful than the real defects of it had made it; a gift which the illiterate had not attained to.

11. *As useful as to confound the sound of the letters.*—These learned men did equally instruct men's understandings and profit their lives, as he who should alter the signification of known characters, and, by a subtile device of learning, far surpassing the capacity of the illiterate, dull, and vulgar, should, in his writing, show, that he could put A for B, and D for E, &c., to the no small admiration and benefit of his reader; it being as senseless to put "black," which is a word agreed on to stand for one sensible idea, to put it, I say, for another or the contrary idea, *i. e.*, to call snow "black," as to put this mark, A, which is a character agreed on to stand for one modification of sound made by a certain motion of the organs of speech, for B, which is agreed on to stand for another modification of sound made by another certain motion of the organs of speech.

12. *This art has perplexed religion and justice.*—Nor hath this mischief stopped in logical niceties or curious empty speculations:

it hath invaded the great concernments of human life and society, obscured and perplexed the material truths of law and divinity, brought confusion, disorder, and uncertainty into the affairs of mankind, and, if not destroyed, yet in great measure rendered useless, those two great rules, religion and justice. What have the greatest part of the comments and disputes upon the laws of God and man served for, but to make the meaning more doubtful, and perplex the sense? What has been the effect of those multiplied curious distinctions and acute niceties, but obscurity and uncertainty, leaving the words more unintelligible, and the reader more at a loss? How else comes it to pass that princes, speaking or writing to their servants, in their ordinary commands, are easily understood? speaking to their people, in their laws, are not so? And, as I remarked before, doth it not often happen that a man of an ordinary capacity very well understands a text or a law that he reads, till he consults an expositor, or goes to counsel; who, by that time he hath done explaining them, makes the words signify either nothing at all, or what he pleases?

13. *And ought not to pass for learning.*—Whether any by-interests of these professions have occasioned this, I will not here examine; but I leave it to be considered, whether it would not be well for mankind, whose concernment it is to know things as they are and to do what they ought, and not to spend their lives in talking about them, or tossing words to and fro: whether it would not be well, I say, that the use of words were made plain and direct; and that language, which was given us for the improvement of knowledge and bond of society, should not be employed to darken truth, and unsettle people's rights; to raise mists, and render unintelligible both morality and religion; or that at least, if this will happen, it should not be thought learning or knowledge to do so.

14. *Fourthly, Taking them for things.*—Fourthly, Another great abuse of words is the taking them for things. This, though it, in some degree, concerns all names in general, yet more particularly affects those of substances. To this abuse those men are most subject who confine their thoughts to any one system, and give themselves up into a firm belief of the perfection of any received hypothesis: whereby they come to be persuaded, that the terms of that sect are so suited to the nature of things that they perfectly correspond with their real existence. Who is there that has been bred up in the peripatetic philosophy, who does not think the ten names, under which are ranked the ten predicaments, to be exactly conformable to the nature of things? Who is there of that school that is not persuaded, that "substantial forms," "vegetative souls," "abhorrence of a vacuum," "intentional species," &c., are something real? These words men have learned from their very entrance upon knowledge, and have

found their masters and systems lay great stress upon them: and therefore they cannot quit the opinion that they are conformable to nature, and are the representations of something that really exists. The Platonists have their "soul of the world," and the Epicureans their "endeavour towards motion" in their "atoms when at rest." There is scarce any sect in philosophy has not a distinct set of terms that others understand not. But yet this gibberish, which, in the weakness of human understanding, serves so well to palliate men's ignorance and cover their errors, comes by familiar use amongst those of the same tribe to seem the most important part of language, and of all other the terms the most significant: and should aërial and ethereal vehicles come once, by the prevalency of that doctrine, to be generally received any where, no doubt those terms would make impressions on men's minds, so as to establish them in the persuasion of the reality of such things, as much as peripatetic forms and intentional species have heretofore done.

15. *Instance in matter.*—How much names taken for things are apt to mislead the understanding, the attentive reading of philosophical writers would abundantly discover; and that, perhaps, in words little suspected of any such misuse. I shall instance in one only, and that a very familiar one. How many intricate disputes have there been about matter, as if there were some such thing really in nature distinct from body; as it is evident the word "matter" stands for an idea distinct from the idea of body! For, if the idea these two terms stood for were precisely the same, they might indifferently in all places be put one for another. But we see, that though it be proper to say, "There is one matter of all bodies," one cannot say, "There is one body of all matters: " we familiarly say, "One body is bigger than another;" but it sounds harsh (and I think is never used) to say, "One matter is bigger than another:" Whence comes this then? Viz., from hence, that though matter and body be not really distinct, but wherever there is the one there is the other; yet "matter" and "body" stand for two different conceptions, whereof the one is incomplete, and but a part of the other. For, "body" stands for a solid, extended, figured substance, whereof "matter" is but a partial and more confused conception, it seeming to me to be used for the substance and solidity of body, without taking in its extension and figure: and therefore it is that, speaking of matter, we speak of it always as one, because, in truth, it expressly contains nothing but the idea of a solid substance, which is every where the same, every where uniform. This being our idea of matter, we no more conceive or speak of different matters in the world, than we do of different solidities; though we both conceive and speak of different bodies, because extension and figure are capable of variation. But since solidity cannot exist without extension

and figure, the taking "matter" to be the name of something really existing under that precision, has no doubt produced those obscure and unintelligible discourses and disputes which have filled the heads and books of philosophers concerning *materia prima;* which imperfection or abuse, how far it may concern a great many other general terms, I leave to be considered. This, I think, I may at least say, that we should have a great many fewer disputes in the world, if words were taken for what they are, the signs of our ideas only, and not for things themselves. For when we argue about "matter," or any the like term, we truly argue only about the idea we express by that sound whether that precise idea agree to any thing really existing in nature or no. And if men would tell what ideas they make their words stand for, there could not be half that obscurity or wrangling in the search or support of truth that there is.

16. *This makes errors lasting.*—But whatever inconvenience follows from this mistake of words, this I am sure, that by constant and familiar use they charm men into notions far remote from the truth of things. It would be a hard matter to persuade any one that the words which his father or schoolmaster, the parson of the parish, or such a reverend doctor used, signified nothing that really existed in nature: which perhaps is none of the least causes that men are so hardly drawn to quit their mistakes, even in opinions purely philosophical, and where they have no other interest but truth. For the words they have a long time been used to remaining firm in their minds, it is no wonder that the wrong notions annexed to them should not be removed.

17. *Fifthly, Setting them for what they cannot signify.*—Fifthly, Another abuse of words is the setting them in the place of things which they do or can by no means signify. We may observe, that, in the general names of substances, whereof the nominal essences are only known to us when we put them into propositions, and affirm or deny any thing about them, we do most commonly tacitly suppose or intend they should stand for the real essence of a certain sort of substances. For when a man says, "Gold is malleable," he means and would insinuate something more than this, that what I call "gold" is malleable, (though truly it amounts to no more,) but would have this understood, viz., that gold, *i. e.*, what has the real essence of gold, is malleable; which amounts to thus much, that malleableness depends on, and is inseparable from, the real essence of gold. But a man, not knowing wherein that real essence consists, the connexion in his mind of malleableness is not truly with an essence he knows not, but only with the sound "gold" he puts for it. Thus when we say, that *animal rationale* is, and *animal implume, bipes, latis unguibus* is not, a good definition of a man; it is plain we suppose the name "man" in this case to

stand for the real essence of a species, and would signify that "a
rational animal" better described that real essence than "a two-
legged animal with broad nails, and without feathers." For
else, why might not Plato as properly make the word ἄνθρωπος,
or "man," stand for his complex idea, made up of the ideas of a
body distinguished from others by a certain shape, and other
outward appearances, as Aristotle make the complex idea, to
which he gave the name ἄνθρωπος, or "man," of body and the
faculty of reasoning joined together; unless the name ἄνθρωπος, or
"man," were supposed to stand for something else than what it
signifies; and to be put in the place of some other thing than
the idea a man professes he would express by it?

18. *V. g., Putting them for the real essences of substances.*—It is
true, the names of substances would be much more useful, and
propositions made in them much more certain, were the real
essences of substances the ideas in our minds which those words
signified. And it is for want of those real essences that our
words convey so little knowledge or certainty in our discourses
about them: and therefore the mind, to remove that imperfection as much as it can, makes them, by a secret supposition, to
stand for a thing having that real essence, as if thereby it made
some nearer approaches to it. For though the word "man" or
"gold" signify nothing truly but a complex idea of properties
united together in one sort of substances: yet there is scarce
any body, in the use of these words, but often supposes each of
those names to stand for a thing having the real essence on which
those properties depend. Which is so far from diminishing the
imperfection of our words, that by a plain abuse it adds to it,
when we would make them stand for something which, not
being in our complex idea, the name we use can no ways be
the sign of.

19. *Hence we think every change of our idea in substances, not to
change the species.*—This shows us the reason why, in mixed modes,
any of the ideas that make the composition of the complex one
being left out or changed, it is allowed to be another thing, *i. e.*,
to be of another species, as is plain in chance-medley, man-
slaughter, murder, parricide, &c. The reason whereof is, because
the complex idea, signified by that name, is the real as well as
nominal essence; and there is no secret reference of that name
to any other essence but that. But in substances it is not so.
For, though in that called "gold" one puts into his complex idea
what another leaves out, and *vice versâ*; yet men do not usually
think that therefore the species is changed: because they secretly
in their minds refer that name, and suppose it annexed, to a real
immutable essence of a thing existing, on which those properties
depend. He that adds to his complex idea of gold that of fixedness or solubility in *aqua regia*, which he put not in it before, is
not thought to have changed the species; but only to have a

more perfect idea by adding another simple idea, which is always, in fact, joined with those other of which his former complex idea consisted. But this reference of the name to a thing whereof we have not the idea, is so far from helping at all, that it only serves the more to involve us in difficulties. For, by this tacit reference to the real essence of that species of bodies, the word "gold" (which, by standing for a more or less perfect collection of simple ideas, serves to design that sort of body well enough in civil discourse) comes to have no signification at all, being put for somewhat whereof we have no idea at all, and so can signify nothing at all when the body itself is away. For, however it may be thought all one; yet, if well considered, it will be found a quite different thing to argue about "gold" in name, and about a parcel of the body itself, *v.g.*, a piece of leaf-gold laid before us: though in discourse we are fain to substitute the name for the thing.

20. *The cause of the abuse, a supposition of nature's working always regularly.*—That which, I think, very much disposes men to substitute their names for the real essences of species, is the supposition before mentioned, that nature works regularly in the production of things, and sets the boundaries to each of those species by giving exactly the same real internal constitution to each individual, which we rank under one general name. Whereas any one who observes their different qualities can hardly doubt, that many of the individuals called by the same name are, in their internal constitution, as different one from another, as several of those which are ranked under different specific names. This supposition, however, that the same precise internal constitution goes always with the same specific name, makes men forward to take those names for the representatives of those real essences, though indeed they signify nothing but the complex ideas they have in their minds when they use them. So that, if I may so say, signifying one thing, and being supposed for or put in the place of another, they cannot but in such a kind of use cause a great deal of uncertainty in men's discourses; especially in those who have thoroughly imbibed the doctrine of substantial forms, whereby they firmly imagine the several species of things to be determined and distinguished.

21. *This abuse contains two false suppositions.*—But, however preposterous and absurd it be to make our names stand for ideas we have not, or (which is all one) essences that we know not, it being in effect to make our words the signs of nothing; yet it is evident to any one, who reflects ever so little on the use men make of their words, that there is nothing more familiar. When a man asks whether this or that thing he sees, let it be a drill or a monstrous foetus, be a man or no; it is evident the question is not, whether that particular thing agree to his complex idea expressed by the name "man," but whether it has in it the real

essence of a species of things which he supposes his name "man" to stand for. In which way of using the names of substances there are these false suppositions contained:—

First, That there are certain precise essences according to which nature makes all particular things, and by which they are distinguished into species. That every thing as a real constitution whereby it is what it is, and on which its sensible qualities depend, is past doubt: but I think it has been proved that this makes not the distinction of species as we rank them, nor the boundaries of their names.

Secondly, This tacitly also insinuates as if we had ideas of these proposed essences. For to what purpose else is it to inquire, whether this or that thing have the real essence of the species man, if we did not suppose that there were such a specific essence known? Which yet is utterly false: and therefore such application of names, as would make them stand for ideas which we have not, must needs cause great disorder in discourses and reasonings about them, and be a great inconvenience in our communication by words.

22. *Sixthly, A supposition that words have a certain and evident signification.*—Sixthly, There remains yet another more general, though perhaps less observed, abuse of words; and that is, that men having by a long and familiar use annexed to them certain ideas, they are apt to imagine so near and necessary a connexion between the names and the signification they use them in, that they forwardly suppose one cannot but understand what their meaning is, and therefore one ought to acquiesce in the words delivered; as if it were past doubt that, in the use of those common received sounds, the speaker and hearer had necessarily the same precise ideas. Whence, presuming that when they have in discourse used any term, they have thereby, as it were, set before others the very thing they talk of; and so likewise taking the words of others as naturally standing for just what they themselves have been accustomed to apply them to; they never trouble themselves to explain their own or understand clearly others' meaning. From whence commonly proceeds noise and wrangling, without improvement or information; whilst men take words to be the constant, regular marks of agreed notions, which, in truth, are no more but the voluntary and unsteady signs of their own ideas. And yet men think it strange if, in discourse or (where it is often absolutely necessary) in dispute, one sometimes asks the meaning of their terms; though the arguings one may every day observe in conversation make it evident that there are few names of complex ideas which any two men use for the same just precise collection. It is hard to name a word which will not be a clear instance of this; "life" is a term, none more familiar. Any one almost would take it for an affront to be asked what he meant by it. And yet if it comes in question whether a plant,

that lies ready formed in the seed, have life; whether the embryo in an egg before incubation, or a man in a swoon without sense or motion, be alive or no; it is easy to perceive, that a clear, distinct, settled idea does not always accompany the use of so known a word as that of "life" is. Some gross and confused conceptions men indeed ordinarily have, to which they apply the common words of their language; and such a loose use of their words serves them well enough in their ordinary discourses or affairs. But this is not sufficient for philosophical inquiries. Knowledge and reasoning require precise determinate ideas. And though men will not be so inportunately dull as not to understand what others say, without demanding an explication of their terms, nor so troublesomely critical as to correct others in the use of the words they receive from them; yet where truth and knowledge are concerned in the case, I know not what fault it can be to desire the explication of words whose sense seems dubious; or why a man should be ashamed to own his ignorance in what sense another man uses his words, since he has no other way of certainly knowing it but by being informed. This abuse of taking words upon trust has no where spread so far, nor with so ill effects, as amongst men of letters. The multiplication and obstinacy of disputes which has so laid waste the intellectual world, is owing to nothing more than this ill use of words. For, though it be generally believed that there is great diversity of opinions in the volumes and variety of controversies the world is distracted with, yet the most I can find that the contending learned men of different parties do in their arguings one with another, is, that they speak different languages. For I am apt to imagine, that when any of them, quitting terms, think upon things, and know what they think, they think all the same: though perhaps what they would have, be different.

23. *The ends of language: First: To convey our ideas.* — To conclude this consideration of the imperfection and abuse of language: The ends of language, in our discourse with others, being chiefly these three; First, To make known one man's thoughts or ideas to another: Secondly, To do it with as much ease and quickness as is possible: and, Thirdly, Thereby to convey the knowledge of things. Language is either abused or deficient when it fails of any of these three.

*First*, Words fail in the first of these ends, and lay not open one man's ideas to another's view: First, When men have names in their mouths without any determined ideas in their minds whereof they are the signs: or Secondly, When they apply the common received names of any language to ideas, to which the common use of that language does not apply them: or, Thirdly, When they apply them very unsteadily, making them stand now for one and by and by for another idea.

**24.** *Secondly, To do it with quickness.*—Secondly, Men fail of conveying their thoughts with all the quickness and ease that may be, when they have complex ideas without having distinct names for them. This is sometimes the fault of the language itself, which has not in it a sound yet applied to such a signification: and sometimes the fault of the man, who has not yet learned the name for that idea he would show another.

**25.** *Thirdly, Therewith to convey the knowledge of things.*—Thirdly, There is no knowledge of things conveyed by men's words, when their ideas agree not to the reality of things. Though it be a defect that it has its original in our ideas, which are not so conformable to the nature of things as attention, study, and application might make them; yet it fails not to extend itself to our words, too, when we use them as signs of real beings which yet never had any reality or existence.

**26.** *How men's words fail in all these.*—First, He that hath words of any language without distinct ideas in his mind to which he applies them, does, so far as he uses them in discourse, only make a noise without any sense or signification; and, how learned soever he may seem by the use of hard words, or learned terms, is not much more advanced thereby in knowledge, than he would be in learning who had nothing in his study but the bare titles of books, without possessing the contents of them. For all such words, however put into discourse according to the right construction of grammatical rules, or the harmony of well-turned periods, do yet amount to nothing but bare sounds, and nothing else.

**27.** Secondly, He that has complex ideas without particular names for them, would be in no better a case than a bookseller who had in his warehouse volumes that lay there unbound, and without titles, which he could therefore make known to others only by showing the loose sheets, and communicate them only by tale. This man is hindered in his discourse for want of words to communicate his complex ideas, which he is therefore forced to make known by an enumeration of the simple ones that compose them; and so is fain often to use twenty words to express what another man signifies in one.

**28.** Thirdly, He that puts not constantly the same sign for the same idea, but uses the same words sometimes in one and sometimes in another signification, ought to pass in the schools and conversation for as fair a man as *he* does in the market and exchange *who* sells several things under the same name.

**29.** Fourthly, He that applies the words of any language to ideas different from those to which the common use of that country applies them, however his own understanding may be filled with truth and light, will not by such words be able to convey much of it to others without defining his terms. For, however the sounds are such as are familiarly known and easily

enter the ears of those who are accustomed to them, yet, standing
for other ideas than those they usually are annexed to, and are
wont to excite in the minds of the hearers, they cannot make
known the thoughts of him who thus uses them.

30. Fifthly, He that hath imagined to himself substances such
as never have been, and filled his head with ideas which have not
any correspondence with the real nature of things, to which yet
he gives settled and defined names, may fill his discourse, and
perhaps another man's head, with the fantastical imaginations
of his own brain, but will be very far from advancing thereby
one jot in real and true knowledge.

31. He that hath names without ideas, wants meaning in his
words, and speaks only empty sounds. He that hath complex
ideas without names for them, wants liberty and despatch in his
expressions, and is necessitated to use periphrases. He that uses
his words loosely and unsteadily will either be not minded or not
understood. He that applies his names to ideas different from
their common use, wants propriety in his language, and speaks
gibberish. And he that hath ideas of substances disagreeing
with the real existences of things, so far wants the materials of
true knowledge in his understanding, and hath, instead thereof,
chimeras.

32. *How in substances.*—In our notions concerning substances
we are liable to all the former inconveniences: *v. g.*, (1.) He
that uses the word "tarantula," without having any imagination
or idea of what it stands for, pronounces a good word: but so
long means nothing at all by it. (2.) He that in a new-dis-
covered country shall see several sorts of animals and vegetables
unknown to him before, may have as true ideas of them as of a
horse or a stag; but can speak of them only by a description,
till he shall either take the names the natives call them by, or
give them names himself. (3.) He that uses the word "body"
sometimes for pure extension, and sometimes for extension and
solidity together, will talk very fallaciously. (4.) He that gives
the name "horse" to that idea which common usage calls
"mule," talks improperly, and will not be understood. (5.) He
that thinks the name "centaur" stands for some real being,
imposes on himself, and mistakes words for things.

33. *How in modes and relations.*—In modes and relations generally, we are liable only to the four first of these inconveniences,
viz., (1.) I may have in my memory the names of modes, as
"gratitude" or "charity," and yet not have any precise ideas
annexed in my thoughts to those names. (2.) I may have ideas,
and not know the names that belong to them: *v. g.*, I may have
the idea of a man's drinking till his colour and humour be altered,
till his tongue trips, and his eyes look red, and his feet fail him,
and yet not know that it is to be called "drunkenness." (3.) I
may have the ideas of virtues or vices, and names also, but apply

them amiss; *v. g.*, when I apply the name "frugality" to that idea which others call and signify by this sound, "covetousness." (4.) I may use any of those names with inconstancy. (5.) But in modes and relations, I cannot have ideas disagreeing to the exist-ence of things: for, modes being complex ideas made by the mind at pleasure, and relation being but my way of considering or comparing two things together, and so also an idea of my own making, these ideas can scarce be found to disagree with any thing existing; since they are not in the mind as the copies of things regularly made by nature, nor as properties inseparably flowing from the internal constitution or essence of any substance; but, as it were, patterns lodged in my memory, with names annexed to them to denominate actions and relations by, as they come to exist. But the mistake is commonly in my giving a wrong name to my conceptions; and so using words in a different sense from other people, I am not understood but am thought to have wrong ideas of them, when I give wrong names to them. Only if I put in my ideas of mixed modes or relations any incon-sistent ideas together, I fill my head also with chimeras; since such ideas, if well examined, cannot so much as exist in the mind, much less any real being be ever denominated from them.

34. *Seventhly, Figurative speech also an abuse of language.*—Since wit and fancy finds easier entertainment in the world than dry truth and real knowledge, figurative speeches and allusion in language will hardly be admitted as an imperfection or abuse of it. I confess, in discourses where we seek rather pleasure and delight, than information and improvement, such ornaments as are borrowed from them can scarce pass for faults. But yet, if we would speak of things as they are, we must allow that all the art of rhetoric, besides order and clearness, all the artificial and figurative application of words eloquence hath invented, are for nothing else but to insinuate wrong ideas, move the passions, and thereby mislead the judgment; and so indeed are perfect cheats: and therefore, however laudable or allowable oratory may render them in harangues and popular addresses, they are certainly, in all discourses that pretend to inform or instruct, wholly to be avoided; and, where truth and knowledge are concerned, cannot but be thought a great fault either of the language or person that makes use of them. What and how various they are, will be superfluous here to take notice; the books of rhetoric which abound in the world will instruct those who want to be informed. Only I cannot but observe how little the preservation and im-provement of truth and knowledge is the care and concern of mankind; since the arts of fallacy are endowed and preferred. It is evident how much men love to deceive and be deceived, since rhetoric, that powerful instrument of error and deceit, has its established professors, is publicly taught, and has always been had in great reputation; and I doubt not but it will be thought

great boldness, if not brutality, in me to have said thus much
against it. Eloquence, like the fair sex, has too prevailing
beauties in it to suffer itself ever to be spoken against. And it
is in vain to find fault with those arts of deceiving wherein men
find pleasure to be deceived.

## CHAPTER XI.

### OF THE REMEDIES OF THE FOREGOING IMPERFECTIONS AND ABUSES.

1. *They are worth seeking.*—The natural and improved imperfections of languages we have seen above at large; and speech
being the great bond that holds society togethe, and the common
conduit whereby the improvements of knowledge are conveyed
from one man and one generation to another; it would well
deserve our most serious thoughts to consider what remedies are
to be found for these inconveniences above mentioned.

2. *Are not easy.*—I am not so vain to think that any one can
pretend to attempt the perfect reforming the languages of the
world, no, not so much as of his own country, without rendering
himself ridiculous. To require that men should use their words
constantly in the same sense, and for none but determined and
uniform ideas, would be to think that all men should have the
same notions, and should talk of nothing but what they have
clear and distinct ideas of. Which is not to be expected by any
one, who hath not vanity enough to imagine he can prevail with
men to be very knowing or very silent. And he must be very
little skilled in the world who thinks that a voluble tongue shall
accompany only a good understanding; or that men's talking
much or little shall hold proportion only to their knowledge.

3. *But yet necessary to philosophy.*—But though the market
and exchange must be left to their own ways of talking, and
gossipings not be robbed of their ancient privilege; though the
Schools and men of argument would perhaps take it amiss to
have any thing offered to abate the length or lessen the number
of their disputes; yet, methinks, those who pretend seriously to
search after or maintain truth, should think themselves obliged
to study how they might deliver themselves without obscurity,
doubtfulness, or equivocation, to which men's words are naturally liable, if care be not taken.

4. *Misuse of words the cause of great errors.*—For he that shall
well consider the errors and obscurity, the mistakes and confusion, that are spread in the world by an ill use of words, will
find some reason to doubt whether language, as it has been employed, has contributed more to the improvement or hinderance
of knowledge amongst mankind. How many are there, that,

when they would think on things, fix their thoughts only on words, especially when they would apply their minds to moral matters ? And who then can wonder, if the result of such contemplations and reasonings, about little more than sounds, whilst the ideas they annexed to them are very confused, or very unsteady, or perhaps none at all; who can wonder, I say, that such thoughts and reasonings end in nothing but obscurity and mistake, without any clear judgment or knowledge ?

5. *Obstinacy.*—This inconvenience, in an ill use of words, men suffer in their own private meditations: but much more manifest are the disorders which follow from it in conversation, discourse, and arguings with others. For, language being the great conduit whereby men convey their discoveries, reasonings, and knowledge, from one to another, he that makes an ill use of it, though he does not corrupt the fountains of knowledge which are in things themselves, yet he does, as much as in him lies, break or stop the pipes, whereby it is distributed to the public use and advantage of mankind. He that uses words without any clear and steady meaning, what does he but lead himself and others into errors ? And he that designedly does it, ought to be looked on as an enemy to truth and knowledge. And yet who can wonder, that all the sciences and part. of knowledge have been so overcharged with obscure and equivocal terms and insignificant and doubtful expressions, capable to make the most attentive or quick-sighted very little or not at all the more knowing or orthodox; since subtilty, in those who make profession to teach or defend truth, hath passed so much for a virtue ? a virtue indeed which consisting, for the most part, in nothing but the fallacious and illusory use of obscure or deceitful terms, is only fit to make men more conceited in their ignorance, and obstinate in their errors.

6. *And wrangling.*—Let us look into the books of controversy, of any kind, there we shall see that the effect of obscure, unsteady, or equivocal terms, is nothing but noise and wrangling about sounds, without convincing or bettering a man's understanding. For, if the idea be not agreed on betwixt the speaker and hearer for which the words stand, the argument is not about things, but names. As often as such a word whose signification is not ascertained betwixt them comes in use, their understandings have no other object wherein they agree but barely the sound; the things that they think on at that time, as expressed by that word, being quite different.

7. *Instance bat, and bird.*—Whether a bat be a bird or not, is not a question; whether a bat be another thing than indeed it is, or have other qualities than indeed it has; for that would be extremely absurd to doubt of: but the question is, (1.) Either between those that acknowledged themselves to have but imperfect ideas of one or both of those sorts of things, for which these names are supposed to stand; and then it is a real inquiry concerning the

nature of a bird or a bat, to make their yet imperfect ideas of it more complete, by examining whether all the simple ideas to which, combined together, they both give the name "bird" be all to be found in a bat: but this is a question only of inquirers (not disputers), who neither affirm nor deny, but examine. Or, (2.) It is a question between disputants; whereof the one affirms, and the other denies, that a bat is a bird. And then the question is barely about the signification of one or both these words; in that, they not having both the same complex ideas to which they give these two names, one holds and the other denies that these two names may be affirmed one of another. Where they agree in the signification of these two names, it were impossible they should dispute about them. For they would presently and clearly see (were that adjusted between them) whether all the simple ideas of the more general name "bird" were found in the complex idea of a bat or no; and so there could be no doubt, whether a bat were a bird or no. And here I desire it may be considered, and carefully examined, whether the greatest part of the disputes in the world are not merely verbal and about the signification of words; and whether if the terms they are made in were defined, and reduced in their signification (as they must be where they signify any thing) to determined collections of the simple ideas they do or should stand for, those disputes would not end of themselves and immediately vanish. I leave it then to be considered what the learning of disputation is, and how well they are employed for the advantage of themselves or others whose business is only the vain ostentation of sounds; *i.e.*, those who spend their lives in disputes and controversies. When I shall see any of those combatants strip all his terms of ambiguity and obscurity, (which every one may do in the words he uses himself,) I shall think him a champion for knowledge, truth, and peace, and not the slave of vain-glory, ambition, or a party.

8. To remedy the defects of speech before mentioned to some degree, and to prevent the inconveniences that follow from them, I imagine the observation of these following rules may be of use, till somebody better able shall judge it worth his while to think more maturely on this matter, and oblige the world with his thoughts on it.

*First remedy : To use no word without an idea.*—First, A man should take care to use no word without a signification, no name without an idea for which he makes it stand. This rule will not seem altogether needless to any one who shall take the pains to recollect how often he has met with such words as "instinct," "sympathy," and "antipathy," &c., in the discourse of others, so made use of as he might easily conclude, that those that used them had no ideas in their minds to which they applied them; but spoke them only as sounds, which usually served instead of reasons on the like occasions. Not but that these words and the like have very proper significations in which they may be used; but there being no natural connexion between any words and any ideas, these and any other may be learned by rote, and pronounced or writ by men, who have no ideas in their minds to which they have annexed them, and for which they make them stand; which is necessary they should, if men would speak intelligibly even to themselves alone.

9. *Secondly, To have distinct ideas annexed to them in modes.*— Secondly, It is not enough a man uses his words as signs of some ideas: those ideas he annexes them to, if they be simple, must be clear and distinct; if complex, must be determinate; *i. e.*, the precise collection of simple ideas settled in the mind, with that sound annexed to it as the sign of that precise determined collection, and no other. This is very necessary in names of modes, and especially moral words; which, having no settled objects in nature from whence their ideas are taken as from their original, are apt to be very confused. "Justice" is a word in every man's mouth, but most commonly with a very undetermined, loose signification: which will always be so unless a man has in his mind a distinct comprehension of the component parts that complex idea consists of: and if it be decompounded, must be able to resolve it still on till he at last comes to the simple ideas that make it up: and unless this be done, a man makes an ill use of the word, let it be "justice" for example, or any other. I do not say, a man needs stand to recollect, and make this analysis at large, every time the word "justice" comes in his way: but this, at least, is necessary, that he have so examined the signification of that name, and settled the idea of all its parts in his mind, that he can do it when he pleases. If one who makes this complex idea of justice to be such a treatment of the person or goods of another as is according to law, hath not a clear and distinct idea what law is, which makes a part of his complex idea of justice, it is plain his idea of justice itself will be confused and imperfect. This exactness will, perhaps, be judged very troublesome; and therefore most men will think they may be excused from settling the complex ideas of mixed modes so precisely in their minds. But yet I must say, till this be done it must not be wondered that they have a great deal of obscurity and confusion in their own minds, and a great deal of wrangling in their discourses with others.

10. *And conformable in substances.*—In the names of substances, for a right use of them something more is required than barely determined ideas. In these the names must also be conformable to things as they exist: but of this, I shall have occasion to speak more at large by and by. This exactness is absolutely necessary in inquiries after philosophical knowledge, and in controversies about truth. And though it would be well, too, if it extended itself to common conversation and the ordinary affairs of life;

yet, I think, that is scarce to be expected. Vulgar notions suit
vulgar discourses: and both, though confused enough, yet serve
pretty well the market and the wake. Merchants and lovers,
cooks and tailors, have words wherewithal to despatch their
ordinary affairs; and so, I think, might philosophers and disputants too, if they had a mind to understand, and to be clearly
understood.

11. *Thirdly, Propriety.*—Thirdly, It is not enough that men
have ideas, determined ideas, for which they make these signs
stand; but they must also take care to apply their words, as near
as may be, to such ideas as common use has annexed them to.
For, words, especially of languages already framed, being no man's
private possession, but the common measure of commerce and
communication, it is not for any one, at pleasure, to change the
stamp they are current in, nor alter the ideas they are affixed to;
or at least when there is a necessity to do so, he is bound to give
notice of it. Men's intentions in speaking are, or at least should
be, to be understood; which cannot be without frequent expla-
nations, demands, and other the like incommodious interruptions,
where men do not follow common use. Propriety of speech is
that which gives our thoughts entrance into other men's minds
with the greatest ease and advantage; and therefore deserves
some part of our care and study, especially in the names of moral
words. The proper signification and use of terms is best to be
learned from those who in their writings and discourses appear
to have had the clearest notions, and applied to them their
terms with the exactest choice and fitness. This way of using a
man's words according to the propriety of the language, though
it have not always the good fortune to be understood, yet most
commonly leaves the blame of it on him who is so unskilful in
the language he speaks as not to understand it, when made use
of as it ought to be.

12. *Fourthly, To make known their meaning.*—Fourthly, But
because common use has not so visibly annexed any signification
to words, as to make men know always certainly what they
precisely stand for; and because men in the improvement of
their knowledge come to have ideas different from the vulgar
and ordinary received ones, for which they must either make
new words (which men seldom venture to do, for fear of being
thought guilty of affectation or novelty), or else must use old
ones in a new signification; therefore after the observation of the
foregoing rules, it is sometimes necessary for the ascertaining
the signification of words, to declare their meaning; where either
common use has left it uncertain and loose (as it has in most
names of very complex ideas), or where the term, being very
material in the discourse, and that upon which it chiefly turns,
is liable to any doubtfulness or mistake.

**13.** *And that three ways.*—As the ideas men's words stand for are of different sorts, so the way of making known the ideas they stand for, when there is occasion, is also different. For though defining be thought the proper way to make known the proper signification of words; yet there are some words that will not be defined, as there be others whose precise meaning cannot be made known but by definition; and perhaps a third, which partake somewhat of both the other, as we shall see in the names of simple ideas, modes, and substances.

**14.** *First, In simple ideas, by synonymous terms or showing.*— First, When a man makes use of the name of any simple idea, which he perceives is not understood, or is in danger to be mistaken, he is obliged, by the laws of ingenuity and the end of speech, to declare his meaning, and make known what idea he makes it stand for. This, as has been shown, cannot be done by definition; and therefore when a synonymous word fails to do it, there is but one of these ways left. (First,) Sometimes the naming the subject, wherein that simple idea is to be found, will make its name be understood by those who are acquainted with that subject, and know it by that name. So to make a countryman understand what *feuille-morte* colour signifies, it may suffice to tell him, it is the colour of withered leaves falling in autumn. (Secondly,) But the only sure way of making known the signification of the name of any simple idea, is, by presenting to his senses that subject which may produce it in his mind, and make him actually have the idea that word stands for.

**15.** *Secondly, In mixed modes, by definition.*—Secondly, Mixed modes, especially those belonging to morality, being most of them such combinations of ideas as the mind puts together of its own choice, and whereof there are not always standing patterns to be found existing, the signification of their names cannot be made known as those of simple ideas, by any showing; but, in recompense thereof, may be perfectly and exactly defined. For, they being combinations of several ideas that the mind of man has arbitrarily put together without reference to any archetypes, men may, if they please, exactly know the ideas that go to each composition, and so both use these words in a certain and undoubted signification, and perfectly declare, where there is occasion, what they stand for. This, if well considered, would lay great blame on those who make not their discourses about moral things very clear and distinct. For since the precise signification of the names of mixed modes, or, which is all one, the real essence of each species, is to be known, they being not of nature's but man's making, it is a great negligence and perverseness to discourse of moral things with uncertainty and obscurity; which is more pardonable in treating of natural substances, where doubtful terms are hardly to be avoided for a quite contrary reason, as we shall see by and by.

**16.** *Morality capable of demonstration.*—Upon this ground it is that I am bold to think, that morality is capable of demonstration, as well as mathematics; since the precise real essence of the things moral words stand for may be perfectly known; and so the congruity or incongruity of the things themselves be certainly discovered, in which consists perfect knowledge. Nor let any one object, that the names of substances are often to be made use of in morality, as well as those of modes, from which will arise obscurity. For as to substances, when concerned in moral discourses, their divers natures are not so much inquired into as supposed; *v. g.*, when we say that "man is subject to law," we mean nothing by "man" but a corporeal, rational creature: what the real essence or other qualities of that creature are in this case, is no way considered. And therefore, whether a child or changeling be a man in a physical sense, may amongst the naturalists be as disputable as it will, it concerns not at all "the moral man," as I may call him, which is this immoveable, unchangeable idea, a corporeal, rational being. For, were there a monkey or any other creature to be found, that had the use of reason to such a degree as to be able to understand general signs, and to deduce consequences about general ideas, he would no doubt be subject to law, and, in that sense, be a man, how much soever he differed in shape from others of that name. The names of substances, if they be used in them as they should, can no more disturb moral than they do mathematical discourses: where, if the mathematician speaks of a cube or globe of gold, or any other body, he has his clear settled idea, which varies not, though it may, by mistake, be applied to a particular body to which it belongs not.

**17.** *Definitions can make moral discourses clear.*—This I have here mentioned by the by, to show of what consequence it is for men, in their names of mixed modes, and consequently in all their moral discourses, to define their words when there is occasion: since thereby moral knowledge may be brought to so great clearness and certainty. And it must be great want of ingenuity (to say no worse of it) to refuse to do it: since a definition is the only way whereby the precise meaning of moral words can be known; and yet a way whereby their meaning may be known certainly, and without leaving any room for any contest about it. And therefore the negligence or perverseness of mankind cannot be excused, if their discourses in morality be not much more clear than those in natural philosophy: since they are about ideas in the mind, which are none of them false or disproportionate; they having no external beings for the archetypes which they are referred to, and must correspond with. It is far easier for men to frame in their minds an idea which shall be the standard to which they will give the name "justice," with which pattern, so made, all actions that agree shall pass under that denomination; than, having seen Aristides, to frame an idea that shall in all things be exactly like him, who is as he is, let men make what idea they please of him. For the one, they need but know the combination of ideas that are put together within in their own minds; for the other, they must inquire into the whole nature and abstruse, hidden constitution, and various qualities of a thing existing without them.

18. *And is the only way.* — Another reason that makes the defining of mixed modes so necessary, especially of moral words, is what I mentioned a little before, viz., that it is the only way whereby the signification of the most of them can be known with certainty. For the ideas they stand for, being for the most part such whose component parts nowhere exist together, but scattered and mingled with others, it is the mind alone that collects them and gives them the union of one idea: and it is only by words, enumerating the several simple ideas which the mind has united, that we can make known to others what their names stand for; the assistance of the senses in this case not helping us by the proposal of sensible objects, to show the ideas which our names of this kind stand for, as it does often in the names of sensible simple ideas, and also to some degree in those of substances.

19. *Thirdly, In substance, by showing and defining.*—Thirdly, For the explaining the signification of the names of substances as they stand for the ideas we have of their distinct species, both the fore-mentioned ways, viz., of showing and defining, are requisite in many cases to be made use of. For there being ordinarily in each sort some leading qualities, to which we suppose the other ideas which make up our complex idea of that species annexed, we forwardly give the specific name to that thing wherein that characteristical mark is found, which we take to be the most distinguishing idea of that species. These leading or characteristical (as I may so call them) ideas, in the sorts of animals and vegetables, is (as has been before remarked, chap. vi. sect. 29, and chap. ix. sect. 15) mostly figure, and in inanimate bodies colour, and in some both together. Now,

20. *Ideas of the leading qualities of substances are best got by showing.*—These leading sensible qualities are those which make the chief ingredients of our specific ideas, and consequently the most observable and invariable part in the definitions of our specific names, as attributed to sorts of substances coming under our knowledge. For though the sound "man," in its own nature, be as apt to signify a complex idea made up of animality and rationality united in the same subject, as to signify any other combination; yet used as a mark to stand for a sort of creatures we count of our own kind, perhaps the outward shape is as necessary to be taken into our complex idea signified by the word "man," as any other we find in it: and therefore why

Plato's *animal implume, bipes, latis unguibus*, should not be as good a definition of the name "man," standing for that sort of creatures, will not be easy to show; for it is the shape, as the leading quality, that seems more to determine that species than a faculty of reasoning, which appears not at first, and in some never. And if this be not allowed to be so, I do not know how they can be excused from murder who kill monstrous births (as we call them), because of an unordinary shape, without knowing whether they have a rational soul or no; which can be no more discerned in a well-formed than ill-shaped infant as soon as born. And who is it has informed us, that a rational soul can inhabit no tenement, unless it has just such a sort of frontispiece, or can join itself to and inform no sort of body but one that is just of such an outward structure?

21. Now these leading qualities are best made known by showing, and can hardly be made known otherwise. For, the shape of a horse or cassiowary will be but rudely and imperfectly imprinted on the mind by words: the sight of the animals doth it a thousand times better. And the idea of the particular colour of gold is not to be got by any description of it, but only by the frequent exercise of the eyes about it; as is evident in those who are used to this metal, who will frequently distinguish true from counterfeit, pure from adulterate, by the sight; where others (who have as good eyes, but yet by use have not got the precise nice idea of that peculiar yellow) shall not perceive any difference. The like may be said of those other simple ideas, peculiar in their kind to any substance; for which precise ideas there are no peculiar names. The particular ringing sound there is in gold, distinct from the sound of other bodies, has no particular name annexed to it, no more than the particular yellow that belongs to that metal.

22. *The ideas of their powers best by definition.*—But because many of the simple ideas that make up our specific ideas of substances, are powers which lie not obvious to our senses in the things as they ordinarily appear: therefore, in the signification of our names or substances, some part of the signification will be better made known by enumerating those simple ideas, than in showing the substance itself. For he that, to the yellow shining colour of gold got by sight, shall, from my enumerating them, have the ideas of great ductility, fusibility, fixedness, and solubility in *aqua regia*, will have a perfecter idea of gold than he can have by seeing a piece of gold, and thereby imprinting in his mind only its obvious qualities. But if the formal constitution of this shining, heavy, ductile thing (from whence all these its properties flow) lay open to our senses, as the formal constitution or essence of a triangle does, the signification of the word "gold" might as easily be ascertained as that of "triangle."

23. *A reflection on the knowledge of spirits.*—Hence we may

take notice how much the foundation of all our knowledge of corporeal things lies in our senses. For how spirits, separate from bodies (whose knowledge and ideas of these things are certainly much more perfect than ours,) know them, we have no notion, no idea at all. The whole extent of our knowledge or imagination reaches not beyond our own ideas, limited to our ways of perception: though yet it be not to be doubted that spirits of a higher rank than those immersed in flesh may have as clear ideas of the radical constitution of substances as we have of a triangle, and so perceive how all their properties and operations flow from thence: but the manner how they come by that knowledge exceeds our conceptions.

24. *Ideas also of substances must be conformable to things.*—But though definitions will serve to explain the names of substances as they stand for our ideas, yet they leave them not without great imperfection as they stand for things. For, our names of substances being not put barely for our ideas, but being made use of ultimately to represent things, and so are put in their place, their signification must agree with the truth of things, as well as with men's ideas. And therefore in substances we are not always to rest in the ordinary complex idea commonly received as the signification of that word, but must go a little farther, and inquire into the nature and properties of the things themselves, and thereby perfect, as much as we can, our ideas of their distinct species; or else learn them from such as are used to that sort of things, and are experienced in them. For since it is intended their names should stand for such collections of simple ideas as do really exist in things themselves, as well as for the complex idea in other men's minds, which in their ordinary acceptation they stand for: therefore to define their names right, natural history is to be inquired into; and their properties are, with care and examination, to be found out. For it is not enough, for the avoiding inconveniences in discourses and arguings about natural bodies and substantial things, to have learned, from the propriety of the language, the common but confused or very imperfect idea to which each word is applied, and to keep them to that idea in our use of them: but we must, by acquainting ourselves with the history of that sort of things, rectify and settle our complex idea belonging to each specific name; and in discourse with others (if we find them mistake us) we ought to tell what the complex idea is that we make such a name stand for. This is the more necessary to be done by all those who search after knowledge and philosophical verity, in that children being taught words whilst they have but imperfect notions of things, apply them at random and without much thinking, and seldom frame determined ideas to be signified by them. Which custom (it being easy, and serving well enough for the ordinary affairs of life and conversation) they are apt to continue when

they are men: and so begin at the wrong end, learning words
first and perfectly, but make the notions to which they apply
those words afterwards very overtly.    By this means it come to
pass, that men speaking the proper language of their country,
*i. e.*, according to grammar-rules of that language, do yet speak
very improperly of things themselves ; and, by their arguing one
with another, make but small progress in the discoveries of useful truths, and the knowledge of things, as they are to be found
in themselves, and not in our imaginations ; and it matters not
much, for the improvement of our knowledge, how they are
called.

25. *Not easy to be made so.*—It were therefore to be wished
that men versed in physical inquiries, and acquainted with the
several sorts of natural bodies, would set down those simple ideas
wherein they observe the individuals of each sort constantly to
agree.    This would remedy a great deal of that confusion which
comes from several persons applying the same name to a collection of a smaller or greater number of sensible qualities, proportionably as they have been more or less acquainted with or
accurate in examining the qualities of any sort of things which
come under one denomination.    But a dictionary of this sort containing, as it were, a natural history, requires too many hands, as
well as too much time, cost, pains, and sagacity, ever to be hoped
for ; and till that be done, we must content ourselves with such
definitions of the names of substances as explain the sense men
use them in.    And it would be well, where there is occasion, if
they would afford us so much.    This yet is not usually done ;
but men talk to one another, and dispute in words whose meaning is not agreed between them, out of a mistake that the
significations of common words are certainly established, and
the precise ideas they stand for perfectly known ; and that
it is a shame to be ignorant of them.    Both which suppositions are false : no names of complex ideas having so settled,
determined significations, that they are constantly used for
the same precise ideas.    Nor is it a shame for a man not to
have a certain knowledge of any thing but by the necessary
ways of attaining it ; and so it is no discredit not to know
what precise idea any sound stands for in another man's mind,
without he declare it to me by some other way than barely
using that sound, there being no other way without such a
declaration, certainly to know it.    Indeed, the necessity of communication by language brings men to 'an agreement in the
signification of common words, within some tolerable latitude,
that may serve for ordinary conversation : and so a man cannot
be supposed wholly ignorant of the ideas which are annexed to
words by common use, in a language familiar to him.    But common use, being but a very uncertain rule, which reduces itself
at last to the ideas of particular men, proves often but a very

variable standard. But though such a dictionary as I have above mentioned will require too much time, cost, and pains to be hoped for in this age, yet, methinks, it is not unreasonable to propose, that words standing for things which are known and distinguished by their outward shapes, should be expressed by little draughts and prints made of them. A vocabulary made after this fashion would, perhaps, with more ease and in less time, teach the true signification of many terms, especially in languages of remote countries or ages, and settle truer ideas in men's minds of several things, whereof we read the names in ancient authors, than all the large and laborious comments of learned critics. Naturalists that treat of plants and animals, have found the benefit of this way: and he that has had occasion to consult them, will have reason to confess that he has a clearer idea of *apium* or *ibex* from a little print of that herb or beast, than he could have from a long definition of the names of either of them. And so no doubt he would have of *strigil* and *sistrum*, if, instead of "a curry-comb" and "cymbal," which are the English names dictionaries render them by, he could see stamped in the margin small pictures of these instruments, as they were in use amongst the ancients. *Toga, tunica, pallium*, are words easily translated by "gown," "coat," and "cloak:" but we have thereby no more true ideas of the fashion of those habits amongst the Romans, than we have of the faces of the tailors who made them. Such things as these, which the eye distinguishes by their shapes, would be best let into the mind by draughts made of them, and more determine the signification of such words than any other words set for them, or made use of to define them. But this only by the by.

26. *Fifthly, By constancy in their signification.*—Fifthly, If men will not be at the pains to declare the meaning of their words, and definitions of their terms are not to be had; yet this is the least can be expected, that, in all discourses wherein one man pretends to instruct or convince another, he should use the same word constantly in the same sense. If this were done (which nobody can refuse without great disingenuity), many of the books extant might be spared; many of the controversies in dispute would be at an end; several of those great volumes, swollen with ambiguous words now used in one sense and by and by in another, would shrink into a very narrow compass; and many of the philosophers' (to mention no other) as well as poets' works might be contained in a nut-shell.

27. *When the variation is to be explained.*—But, after all, the provision of words is so scanty in respect of that infinite variety of thoughts, that men wanting terms to suit their precise notion, will, notwithstanding their utmost caution, be forced often to use the same word in somewhat different senses. And though in the continuation of a discourse, or the pursuit of an argument,

there be hardly room to digress into a particular definition, as often as a man varies the signification of any term; yet the import of the discourse will, for the most part, if there be no designed fallacy, sufficiently lead candid and intelligent readers into the true meaning of it: but where that is not sufficient to guide the reader, there it concerns the writer to explain his meaning, and show in what sense he there uses that term.

---

# BOOK IV.

## CHAPTER I.

### OF KNOWLEDGE IN GENERAL.

1. *Our knowledge conversant about our ideas.*—Since the mind, in all its thoughts and reasonings, hath no other immediate object but its own ideas, which it alone does or can contemplate, it is evident that our knowledge is only conversant about them.

2. *Knowledge is the perception of the agreement or disagreement of two ideas.*—Knowledge then seems to me to be nothing but the perception of the connection and agreement, or disagreement and repugnancy, of any of our ideas. In this alone it consists. Where this perception is, there is knowledge; and where it is not, there, though we may fancy, guess, or believe, yet we always come short of knowledge. For, when we know that white is not black, what do we else but perceive that these two ideas do not agree? When we possess ourselves with the utmost security of the demonstration that the three angles of a triangle are equal to two right ones, what do we more but perceive, that equality to two right ones does necessarily agree to, and is inseparable from, the three angles of a triangle?*

3. *This agreement fourfold.*—But, to understand a little more distinctly, wherein this agreement or disagreement consists, I think we may reduce it all to these four sorts: (1.) Identity, or diversity. (2.) Relation. (3.) Co-existence, or necessary connection. (4.) Real existence.

4. *First, Of identity or diversity.*—First, As to the first sort of agreement or disagreement, viz., identity or diversity. It is the first act of the mind, when it has any sentiments or ideas at all, to perceive its ideas, and, so far as it perceives them, to know each what it is, and thereby also to perceive their difference, and that one is not another. This is so absolutely necessary, that without it there could be no knowledge, no reasoning, no imagination, no distinct thoughts at all. By this the mind clearly and infallibly perceives each idea to agree with itself, and to be what it is; and all distinct ideas to disagree, *i. e.*, the one not to be the

* See note at the end of this chapter, p. 428.—EDIT.

other : and this it does without pains, labour, or deduction, but at first view, by its natural power of perception and distinction. And though men of art have reduced this into those general rules, "What is, is;" and, "It is impossible for the same thing to be and not to be," for ready application in all cases wherein there may be occasion to reflect on it; yet it is certain that the first exercise of this faculty is about particular ideas. A man infallibly knows, as soon as ever he has them in his mind, that the ideas he calls "white" and "round" are the very ideas they are, and that they are not other ideas which he calls "red" or "square." Nor can any maxim or proposition in the world make him know it clearer or surer than he did before, and without any such general rule. This, then, is the first agreement or disagreement which the mind perceives in its ideas, which it always perceives at first sight; and if there ever happen any doubt about it, it will always be found to be about the names, and not the ideas themselves, whose identity and diversity will always be perceived as soon and as clearly as the ideas themselves are, nor can it possibly be otherwise.

5. *Secondly, Relative.*—Secondly, The next sort of agreement or disagreement the mind perceives in any of its ideas may, I think, be called "relative," and is nothing but the perception of the relation between any two ideas, of what kind soever, whether substances, modes, or any other. For, since all distinct ideas must eternally be known not to be the same, and so be universally and constantly denied one of another: there could be no room for any positive knowledge at all, if we could not perceive any relation between our ideas, and find out the agreement or disagreement they have one with another, in several ways the mind takes of comparing them.

6. *Thirdly, Of co-existence.*—Thirdly, The third sort of agreement or disagreement to be found in our ideas, which the perception of the mind is employed about, is co-existence, or non-co-existence in the same subject; and this belongs particularly to substances. Thus when we pronounce concerning "gold" that it is fixed, our knowledge of this truth amounts to no more but this, that fixedness, or a power to remain in the fire unconsumed, is an idea that always accompanies and is joined with that particular sort of yellowness, weight, fusibility, malleableness and solubility in *aqua regia*, which make our complex idea, signified by the word "gold."

7. *Fourthly, Of real existence.*—Fourthly, The fourth and last sort is that of actual real existence agreeing to any idea. Within these four sorts of agreement or disagreement is, I suppose, contained all the knowledge we have or are capable of; for, all the inquiries that we can make concerning any of our ideas, all that we know or can affirm concerning any of them, is, that it is or is not the same with some other; that it does or does not always

co-exist with some other idea in the same subject; that it has
this or that relation to some other idea; or that it has a real
existence without the mind. Thus, "Blue is not yellow," is of
identity. "Two triangles upon equal bases between two parallels
are equal," is of relation. "Iron is susceptible of magnetical impressions," is of co-existence. "God is," is of real existence.
Though identity and co-existence are truly nothing but relations,
yet they are so peculiar ways of agreement or disagreement of
our ideas, that they deserve well to be considered as distinct
heads, and not under relation in general; since they are so
different grounds of affirmation and negation, as will easily
appear to any one who will but reflect on what is said in several
places of this Essay. I should now proceed to examine the
several degrees of our knowledge, but that it is necessary first to
consider the different acceptations of the word "knowledge."

8. *Knowledge actual or habitual.*—There are several ways
wherein the mind is possessed of truth, each of which is called
"knowledge."

First, There is "actual knowledge," which is the present view
the mind has of the agreement or disagreement of any of its ideas,
or of the relation they have one to another.

Secondly, A man is said to know any proposition which having been once laid before his thoughts, he evidently perceived
the agreement or disagreement of the ideas whereof it consists;
and so lodged it in his memory, that whenever that proposition
comes again to be reflected on, he, without doubt or hesitation, embraces the right side, assents to and is certain of the truth of it.
This, I think, one may call "habitual knowledge;" and thus a
man may be said to know all those truths which are lodged in
his memory by a foregoing clear and full perception, whereof the
mind is assured past doubt as often as it has occasion to reflect
on them. For, our finite understandings being able to think
clearly and distinctly but on one thing at once, if men had no
knowledge of any more than what they actually thought on, they
would all be very ignorant; and he that knew most would know
but one truth, that being all he was able to think on at one
time.

9. *Habitual knowledge twofold.*—Of habitual knowledge there
are also, vulgarly speaking, two degrees:—

First, The one is of such truths laid up in the memory as,
whenever they occur to the mind, it actually perceives the relation is between those ideas. And this is in all those truths
whereof we have an intuitive knowledge, where the ideas themselves, by an immediate view, discover their agreement or disagreement one with another.

Secondly, The other is of such truths, whereof the mind having
been convinced, it retains the memory of the conviction without
the proofs. Thus a man that remembers certainly that he once

perceived the demonstration that the three angles of a triangle are
equal to two right ones, is certain that he knows it, because he
cannot doubt of the truth of it. In his adherence to a truth
where the demonstration by which it was at first known is forgot,
though a man may be thought rather to believe his memory than
really to know, and this way of entertaining a truth seemed
formerly to me like something between opinion and knowledge, a
sort of assurance which exceeds bare belief, for that relies on the
testimony of another; yet, upon a due examination, I find it
comes not short of perfect certainty, and is, in effect, true knowledge. That which is apt to mislead our first thoughts into a
mistake in this matter is, that the agreement or disagreement of
the ideas in this case is not perceived, as it was at first, by an
actual view of all the intermediate ideas whereby the agreement
or disagreement of those in the proposition was at first perceived;
but by other intermediate ideas, that show the agreement or
disagreement of the ideas contained in the proposition whose
certainty we remember. For example: in this proposition, that
"the three angles of a triangle are equal to two right ones," one
who has seen and clearly perceived the demonstration of this
truth, knows it to be true, when that demonstration has gone
out of his mind, so that at present it is not actually in view, and
possibly cannot be recollected: but he knows it in a different
way from what he did before. The agreement of the two ideas
joined in that proposition is perceived; but it is by the intervention of other ideas than those which at first produced that perception. He remembers, *i. e.*, he knows (for remembrance is but
the reviving of some past knowledge) that he was once certain
of the truth of this proposition, that "the three angles of a triangle are equal to two right ones." The immutability of the
same relations between the same immutable things is now the
idea that shows him, that if the three angles of a triangle were
once equal to two right ones, they will always be equal to two
right ones. And hence he comes to be certain, that what was
once true in the case is always true; what ideas once agreed will
always agree: and, consequently, what he once knew to be true
he will always know to be true, as long as he can remember that
he once knew it. Upon this ground it is that particular demonstrations in mathematics afford general knowledge. If, then, the
perception that the same ideas will eternally have the same
habitudes and relations be not a sufficient ground of knowledge,
there could be no knowledge of general propositions in mathematics; for no mathematical demonstration would be any other
than particular: and when a man had demonstrated any proposition concerning one triangle or circle, his knowledge would
not reach beyond that particular diagram. If he would extend
it farther, he must renew his demonstration in another instance,
before he could know it to be true in another like triangle, and

so on; by which means one could never come to the knowledge of any general propositions. Nobody, I think, can deny that Mr. Newton certainly knows any proposition that he now at any time reads in his book to be true, though he has not in actual view that admirable chain of intermediate ideas whereby he at first discovered it to be true. Such a memory as that, able to retain such a train of particulars, may be well thought beyond the reach of human faculties : when the very discovery, perception, and laying together that wonderful connexion of ideas is found to surpass most readers' comprehension. But yet it is evident the author himself knows the proposition to be true, remembering he once saw the connexion of those ideas, as certainly as he knows such a man wounded another, remembering that he saw him run him through. But because the memory is not always so clear as actual perception, and does in all men more or less decay in length of time, this, amongst other differences, is one which shows that demonstrative knowledge is much more imperfect than intuitive, as we shall see in the following chapter.

## NOTE.—Page 424.

The placing of certainty, as Mr. Locke does, in the perception of the agreement or disagreement of our ideas, the bishop of Worcester suspects may be of dangerous consequence to that article of faith which he has endeavoured to defend ; to which Mr. Locke answers :[*] " Since your Lordship hath not, as I remember, shown, or gone about to show, how this proposition, viz., 'that certainty consists in the perception of the agreement or disagreement of two ideas,' is opposite or inconsistent with 'that article of faith which your lordship has endeavoured to defend,' it is plain it is but your lordship's fear that it may ' be of dangerous consequence to it ;' which, as I humbly conceive, is no proof that it is in any way inconsistent with that article.

"Nobody, I think, can blame your lordship, or any one else, for being concerned for any article of the Christian faith ; but if that concern (as it may, and as we know it has done) makes any one apprehend danger where no danger is, are we therefore to give up and condemn any proposition because any one, though of the first rank and magnitude, fears ' it may be of dangerous consequence ' to any truth of religion, without showing that it is so ?  If such fears be the measures whereby to judge of truth and falsehood, the affirming that there are antipodes would be still a heresy ; and the doctrine of the motion of the earth must be rejected, as overthrowing the truth of the scripture ; for of that ' dangerous consequence ' it has been apprehended to be by many learned and pious divines, out of their great concern for religion. And yet, notwithstanding those great apprehensions ' of what dangerous consequence it might be,' it is now universally received by learned men as an undoubted truth, and writ for by some whose belief of the scripture is not at all questioned, and

[*] In his Second Letter to the Bishop of Worcester, p. 83, &c.

particularly very lately by a divine of the church of England, with great strength of reason, in his wonderfully ingenious 'New Theory of the Earth.'

"The reason your lordship gives of your fears, that 'it may be of such dangerous consequence to that article of faith which your lordship endeavours to defend,' though it occurs in more places than one; is only this: viz., that 'it is made use of by ill men to do mischief;' *i. e.*, to oppose 'that article of faith which your lordship has endeavoured to defend.' But, my lord, if it be a reason to lay by any thing as bad because it is or may be used to an ill purpose, I know not what will be innocent enough to be kept. Arms, which were made for our defence, are sometimes made use of to do 'mischief;' and yet they are not thought of 'dangerous consequence' for all that. Nobody lays by his sword and pistols, or thinks them of such 'dangerous consequence' as to be neglected or thrown away, because robbers and the worst of men sometimes make use of them to take away honest men's lives or goods: and the reason is, because they were designed and will serve to preserve them. And who knows but this may be the present case? If your lordship thinks that placing of certainty in the perception of the agreement or disagreement of ideas be to be rejected as false, because you apprehend 'it may be of dangerous consequence to that article of faith;' on the other side, perhaps, others with me may think it a defence against error, and so (as being of good use) to be received and adhered to.

"I would not, my lord, be hereby thought to set up my own or any one's judgment against your lordship's. But I have said this only to show, while the argument lies for or against the truth of any proposition barely in an imagination that it may be of consequence to the supporting or overthrowing of any remote truth, it will be impossible that way to determine of the truth or falsehood of that proposition. For imagination will be set up against imagination, and the stronger probably will be against your lordship; the strongest imaginations being usually in the weakest heads. The only way, in this case, to put it past doubt, is to show the inconsistency of the two propositions, and then it will be seen that one overthrows the other, the true the false one.

"Your lordship says, indeed, this is a 'new method of certainty.' I will not say so myself, for fear of deserving a second reproof from your lordship, for being too forward to assume to myself the 'honour of being an original.' But this, I think, gives me occasion, and will excuse me from being thought impertinent, if I ask your lordship, whether there be any other or older 'method of certainty,' and what it is? For if there be no other nor older than this, either this was always the 'method of certainty,' and so mine is no 'new' one, or else the world is obliged to me for this 'new' one, after having been so long in the want of so necessary a thing as a 'method of certainty.' If there be an older, I am sure your lordship cannot but know it; your condemning mine as 'new,' as well as your thorough insight into antiquity, cannot but satisfy every body that you do. And therefore, to set the world right in a thing of that great concernment, and to overthrow mine, and thereby prevent the 'dangerous consequence' there is in my having unseasonably started it, will not, I humbly conceive, misbecome your lordship's care of 'that article you have endeavoured to defend,' nor the good-will you bear to truth in general. For I will be answerable for myself that I shall, and I think I may be for all others that they all will, give off the placing of certainty in the perception of the agreement or disagreement of ideas, if your lordship will be pleased to show that it lies in anything else.

"But truly, not to ascribe to myself an invention of what has been as old as knowledge is in the world, I must own I am not guilty of what your lordship is pleased to call 'starting new methods of certainty.' Knowledge, ever since there has been any in the world, has consisted in one particular action of the mind; and so, I conceive, will continue to do to the end of it: and to start new methods of knowledge or certainty, (for they are to me the same thing,) i. e., to find out and propose new methods of attaining knowledge, either with more ease and quickness, or in things yet unknown, is what I think nobody could blame: but this is not that which your lordship here means by 'new methods of certainty.' Your lordship, I think, means by it, the placing of certainty in something wherein either it does not consist, or else wherein it was not placed before now, if this were to be called a 'new method of certainty.' As to the latter of these, I shall know whether I am guilty or no when your lordship will do me the favour to tell me wherein it was placed before: which your lordship knows I professed myself ignorant of when I writ my book, and so I am still. But if 'starting of new methods of certainty' be the placing of certainty in something wherein it does not consist, whether I have done that or no, I must appeal to the experience of mankind.

"There are several actions of men's minds that they are conscious to themselves of performing, as willing, believing, knowing, &c., which they have so particular a sense of, that they can distinguish them one from another; or else they could not say when they willed, when they believed, and when they knew any thing. But though these actions were different enough from one another not to be confounded by those who spoke of them, yet nobody that I had met with had in their writings particularly set down wherein the act of knowing precisely consisted.

"To this reflection upon the actions of my own mind, the subject of my Essay concerning Human Understanding naturally led me; wherein if I have done any thing 'new,' it has been to describe to others, more particularly than had been done before, what it is their minds do when they perform that action which they call 'knowing;' and if, upon examination, they observe I have given a true account of that action of their minds in all the parts of it, I suppose it will be in vain to dispute against what they find and feel in themselves. And if I have not told them right, and exactly what they find and feel in themselves when their minds perform the act of knowing, what I have said will be all in vain; men will not be persuaded against their senses. Knowledge is an internal perception of their minds; and if, when they reflect on it, they find it is not what I have said it is, my groundless conceit will not be hearkened to, but be exploded by every body, and die of itself; and nobody need to be at any pains to drive it out of the world. So impossible is it to find out or start 'new methods of certainty,' or to have them received, if any one places it in any thing but in that wherein it really consists ; much less can any one be in danger to be misled into error by any such 'new,' and to every one visibly senseless, project. Can it be supposed that any one could start a new method of seeing, and persuade men thereby that they do not see what they do see? Is it to be feared that any one can cast such a mist over their eyes, that they should not know when they see, and so be led out of their way by it?

"Knowledge, I find in myself, and I conceive in others, consists in the perception of the agreement or disagreement of the immediate objects of the mind in thinking, which I call 'ideas;' but whether it does so in others, or no, must be determined by their own experience reflecting upon the action of their mind in knowing ; for that I cannot alter, nor I think they themselves. But whether they will call those immediate objects of their minds in thinking 'ideas' or no, is perfectly in their own choice. If they dislike that name, they may call them 'notions,' or 'conceptions,' or how they please ; it matters not, if they use them so as to avoid obscurity and confusion. If they are constantly used in the same and a known sense, every one has the liberty to please himself in his terms; there lies neither truth, nor error, nor science in that ; though those that take them for things, and not for what they are—bare arbitrary signs of our ideas—make a great deal ado often about them ; as if some great matter lay in the use of this or that sound. All that I know or can imagine of difference about them is, that those words are always best whose significations are best known in the sense they are used, and so are least apt to breed confusion.

"My lord, your lordship has been pleased to find fault with my use of the new term 'ideas,' without telling me a better name for the immediate objects of the mind in thinking. Your lordship has also been pleased to find fault with my definition of knowledge without doing me the favour to give me a better : for it is only about my definition of knowledge, that all this stir concerning certainty is made. For with me to know, and to be certain, is the same thing ; what I know, that I am certain of ; and what I am certain of, that I know. What reaches to knowledge, I think may be called 'certainty;' and what comes short of certainty, I think cannot be called knowledge; as your lordship could not but observe in the 18th section of chap. iv. of my fourth book, which you have quoted.

"My definition of knowledge, in the beginning of the fourth book of my 'Essay,' stands thus : 'Knowledge seems to me to be nothing but the perception of the connexion and agreement, or disagreement and repugnancy, of any of our ideas.' This definition your lordship dislikes, and apprehends 'it may be of dangerous consequence as to that article of Christian faith which your lordship has endeavoured to defend.' For this there is a very easy remedy ; it is but for your lordship to set aside this definition of knowledge by giving us a better, and this danger is over. But your lordship seems rather to have a controversy with my book for having it in it, and to put me upon the defence of it ; for which I must acknowledge myself obliged to your lordship for affording me so much of your time, and for allowing me the honour of conversing so much with one so far above me in all respects.

" Your lordship says, ' It may be of dangerous consequence to that article of Christian faith which you have endeavoured to defend.' Though the laws of disputing allow bare denial as a sufficient answer to sayings without any offer of a proof, yet, my lord, to show how willing I am to give your lordship all satisfaction in what you apprehend may be of ' dangerous consequence' in my book as to that article, I shall not stand still sullenly, and put your lordship upon the difficulty of showing wherein that danger lies ; but shall, on the other side, endeavour to show your lordship that that definition of mine, whether true or false, right or wrong, can be of no ' dangerous consequence to that article of faith.' The reason which I shall offer for it is this : Because it can be of no consequence to it at all.

" That which your lordship is afraid it may be dangerous to, is an ' article of faith ;' that which your lordship labours and is concerned for, is the ' certainty of faith.' Now, my lord, I humbly conceive the ' certainty of faith,' if your lordship thinks fit to call it so, has nothing to do with the certainty of knowledge. And to talk of the ' certainty of faith,' seems all one to me as to talk of the knowledge of believing —a way of speaking not easy to me to understand.

" Place knowledge in what you will, start what ' new methods of certainty' you please, ' that are apt to leave men's minds more doubtful than before,' place certainty on such grounds as will leave little or no knowledge in the world ; (for these are the arguments your lordship uses against my definition of knowledge ;) this shakes not at all, nor in the least concerns the assurance of faith ; that is quite distinct from it, neither stands nor falls with knowledge.

" Faith stands by itself, and upon grounds of its own ; nor can be removed from them, and placed on those of knowledge. Their grounds are so far from being the same, or having any thing common, that when it is brought to certainty, faith is destroyed ; it is knowledge then, and faith no longer.

" With what assurance soever of believing I assent to any ' article of faith,' so that I steadfastly venture my all upon it, it is still but believing. Bring it to certainty, and it ceases to be faith. I believe that Jesus Christ was crucified, dead, and buried, rose again the third day from the dead, and ascended into heaven : let now such methods of knowledge or certainty ' be started, as leave men's minds more doubtful than before :' let the grounds of knowledge be resolved into what any one pleases, it touches not my faith ; the foundation of that stands as sure as before, and cannot be at all shaken by it : and one may as well say, that anything that weakens the sight, or casts a mist before the eyes, endangers the hearing, as that any thing which alters the nature of knowledge (if that could be done) should be of ' dangerous consequence to an article of faith.'

" Whether then I am or I am not mistaken, in the placing certainty in the perception of the agreement or disagreement of ideas ; whether this account of knowledge be true or false, enlarges or straitens the bounds of it more than it should ; faith still stands upon its own basis, which is not at all altered by it : and every article of that has just the same unmoved foundation, and the very same credibility, that it had before. So that, my lord, whatever I have said about certainty, and how much soever I may be out in it, if I am mistaken, your lordship has no reason to apprehend any 'danger' to any 'article of faith' from thence; every one of them stands upon the same bottom it did before, out of the reach of what belongs to knowledge and certainty. And thus much of my 'way of certainty by ideas;' which I hope will satisfy your lordship how far it is from being 'dangerous to any article of the Christian faith' whatsoever."

---

## CHAPTER II.

### OF THE DEGREES OF OUR KNOWLEDGE.

1. *Intuitive.*—All our knowledge consisting, as I have said, in the view the mind has of its own ideas, which is the utmost light and greatest certainty we, with our faculties and in our way of knowledge, are capable of, it may not be amiss to consider a little the degrees of its evidence. The different clearness of our knowledge seems to me to lie in the different way of perception the mind has of the agreement or disagreement of any of its ideas. For if we will reflect on our own ways of thinking, we shall find that sometimes the mind perceives the agreement or disagreement of two ideas immediately by themselves, without the intervention of any other: and this, I think, we may call "intuitive knowledge." For in this the mind is at no pains of proving or examining, but perceives the truth, as the eye doth light, only by being directed towards it. Thus the mind perceives that white is not black, that a circle is not a triangle, that three are more than two, and equal to one and two. Such kind of truths the mind perceives at the first sight of the ideas together, by bare intuition, without the intervention of any other idea; and this kind of knowledge is the clearest and most certain that human frailty is capable of. This part of knowledge is irresistible, and, like bright sunshine, forces itself immediately to be perceived as soon as ever the mind turns its view that way; and leaves no room for hesitation, doubt, or examination, but the mind is presently filled with the clear light of it. It is on this intuition that depends all the certainty and evidence of all our knowledge, which certainty every one finds to be so great that he cannot imagine, and therefore not require, a greater: for a man cannot conceive himself capable of a greater certainty, than to know that any idea in his mind is such as he perceives it to be; and that two ideas, wherein he perceives a difference, are different, and not precisely the same. He that demands a greater certainty than this demands he knows not what, and shows only that he has a mind to be a sceptic without being able to be so. Certainty depends so wholly on this intuition, that in the next degree of knowledge, which I call "demonstrative," this intuition is necessary in all the connexions of the inter-

mediate ideas, without which we cannot attain knowledge and certainty.

2. *Demonstrative.*—The next degree of knowledge is, where the mind perceives the agreement or disagreement of any ideas, but not immediately. Though wherever the mind perceives the agreement or disagreement of any of its ideas, there be certain knowledge; yet it does not always happen that the mind sees that agreement or disagreement which there is between them, even where it is discoverable; and in that case remains in ignorance, and at most gets no farther than a probable conjecture. The reason why the mind cannot always perceive presently the agreement or disagreement of two ideas, is, because those ideas concerning whose agreement or disagreement the inquiry is made, cannot by the mind be so put together as to show it. In this case then, when the mind cannot so bring its ideas together as, by their immediate comparison and, as it were, juxtaposition or application one to another, to perceive their agreement or disagreement, it is fain, by the intervention of other ideas (one or more, as it happens), to discover the agreement or disagreement which it searches; and this is that which we call "reasoning." Thus the mind, being willing to know the agreement or disagreement in bigness between the three angles of a triangle and two right ones, cannot, by an immediate view and comparing them, do it: because the three angles of a triangle cannot be brought at once, and be compared with any one or two angles; and so of this the mind has no immediate, no intuitive knowledge. In this case the mind is fain to find out some other angles, to which the three angles of a triangle have an equality; and finding those equal to two right ones, comes to know their equality to two right ones.

3. *Depends on proofs.*—Those intervening ideas which serve to show the agreement of any two others, are called " proofs;" and where the agreement or disagreement is by this means plainly and clearly perceived, it is called "demonstration," it being shown to the understanding, and the mind made to see that it is so. A quickness in the mind to find out these intermediate ideas (that shall discover the agreement or disagreement of any other), and to apply them right, is, I suppose, that which is called "sagacity."

4. *But not so easy.*—This knowledge by intervening proofs, though it be certain, yet the evidence of it is not altogether so clear and bright, nor the assent so ready, as in intuitive knowledge. For though in demonstration the mind does at last perceive the agreement or disagreement of the ideas it considers, yet it is not without pains and attention : there must be more than one transient view to find it. A steady application and pursuit is required to this discovery : and there must be a progression by steps and degrees before the mind can in this way

arrive at certainty, and come to perceive the agreement or repugnancy between two ideas that need proofs and the use of reason to show it.

5. *Not without precedent doubt.*—Another difference between intuitive and demonstrative knowledge, is, that though in the latter all doubt be removed, when by the intervention of the intermediate ideas the agreement or disagreement is perceived; yet before the demonstration there was a doubt; which in intuitive knowledge cannot happen to the mind that has its faculty of perception left to a degree capable of distinct ideas, no more than it can be a doubt to the eye (that can distinctly see white and black), whether this ink and this paper be all of a colour. If there be sight in the eyes, it will at first glimpse, without hesitation, perceive the words printed on this paper, different from the colour of the paper: and so, if the mind have the faculty of distinct perception, it will perceive the agreement or disagreement of those ideas that produce intuitive knowledge. If the eyes have lost the faculty of seeing, or the mind of perceiving, we in vain inquire after the quickness of sight in one, or clearness of perception in the other.

6. *Not so clear.*—It is true, the perception produced by demonstration is also very clear; yet it is often with a great abatement of that evident lustre and full assurance that always accompany that which I call "intuitive;" like a face reflected by several mirrors one to another, where, as long as it retains the similitude and agreement with the object, it produces a knowledge; but it is still in every successive reflection with a lessening of that perfect clearness and distinctness which is in the first, till at last, after many removes, it has a great mixture of dimness, and is not at first sight so knowable, especially to weak eyes. Thus it is with knowledge made out by a long train of proofs.

7. *Each step must have intuitive evidence.*—Now, in every step reason makes in demonstrative knowledge, there is an intuitive knowledge of that agreement or disagreement it seeks with the next intermediate idea, which it uses as a proof: for if it were not so, that yet would need a proof; since without the perception of such agreement or disagreement there is no knowledge produced. If it be perceived by itself, it is intuitive knowledge: if it cannot be perceived by itself, there is need of some intervening idea, as a common measure, to show their agreement or disagreement. By which it is plain, that every step in reasoning that produces knowledge has intuitive certainty; which when the mind perceives, there is no more required but to remember it, to make the agreement or disagreement of the ideas, concerning which we inquire, visible and certain. So that to make any thing a demonstration, it is necessary to perceive the immediate agreement of the intervening ideas, whereby the agreement or disagreement of the two ideas under examination (whereof the

one is always the first, and the other the last in the account) is found. This intuitive perception of the agreement or disagreement of the intermediate ideas, in each step and progression of the demonstration, must also be carried exactly in the mind, and a man must be sure that no part is left out: which, because in long deductions, and the use of many proofs, the memory does not always so readily and exactly retain; therefore it comes to pass, that this is more imperfect than intuitive knowledge, and men embrace often falsehood for demonstrations.

8. *Hence the mistake*, ex præcognitis et præconcessis.—The necessity of this intuitive knowledge, in each step of scientifical or demonstrative reasoning, gave occasion, I imagine, to that mistaken axiom, that all reasoning was *ex præcognitis et præconcessis;* which, how far it is mistaken, I shall have occasion to show more at large where I come to consider propositions, and particularly those propositions which are called "maxims;" and to show that it is by a mistake that they are supposed to be the foundations of all our knowledge and reasonings.

9. *Demonstration not limited to quantity.*—It has been generally taken for granted, that mathematics alone are capable of demonstrative certainty: but to have such an agreement or disagreement as may intuitively be perceived being, as I imagine, not the privilege of the ideas of number, extension, and figure alone, it may possibly be the want of due method and application in us, and not of sufficient evidence in things, that demonstration has been thought to have so little to do in other parts of knowledge, and been scarce so much as aimed at by any but mathematicians. For, whatever ideas we have wherein the mind can perceive the immediate agreement or disagreement that is between them, there the mind is capable of intuitive knowledge; and where it can perceive the agreement or disagreement of any two ideas, by an intuitive perception of the agreement or disagreement they have with any intermediate ideas, there the mind is capable of demonstration, which is not limited to ideas of extension, figure, number, and their modes.

10. *Why it has been so thought.*—The reason why it has been generally sought for and supposed to be only in those, I imagine, has been not only the general usefulness of those sciences, but because, in comparing their equality or excess, the modes of numbers have every the least difference very clear and perceivable: and though in extension every the least excess is not so perceptible, yet the mind has found out ways to examine and discover demonstratively the just equality of two angles, or extensions, or figures; and both these, *i. e.*, numbers and figures, can be set down by visible and lasting marks, wherein the ideas under consideration are perfectly determined; which for the most part they are not, where they are marked only by names and words.

11. But in other simple ideas, whose modes and· differences are made and counted by degrees, and not quantity, we have not so nice and accurate a distinction of their differences as to perceive or find ways to measure their just equality or the least differences. For, those other simple ideas being appearances or sensations produced in us by the size, figure, number, and motion of minute corpuscles singly insensible, their different degrees also depend upon the variation of some or all of those causes; which, since it cannot be observed by us in particles of matter whereof each is too subtile to be perceived, it is impossible for us to have any exact measures of the different degrees of these simple ideas. For, supposing the sensation or idea we name "whiteness," be produced in us by a certain number of globules, which, having a verticity about their own centres, strike upon the *retina* of the eye with a certain degree of rotation, as well as progressive swiftness; it will hence easily follow, that the more the superficial parts of any body are so ordered as to reflect the greater number of globules of light, and to give them that proper rotation which is fit to produce this sensation of white in us, the more white will that body appear that from an equal space sends to the *retina* the greater number of such corpuscles with that peculiar sort of motion. I do not say, that the nature of light consists in very small round globules, nor of whiteness in such a texture of parts as gives a certain rotation to those globules when it reflects them; for I am not now treating physically of light or colours : but this, I think, I may say, that I cannot (and I would be glad any one would make intelligible that he did) conceive how bodies without us can any ways affect our senses, but by the immediate contact of the sensible bodies themselves, as in tasting and feeling, or the impulse of some insensible particles coming from them, as in seeing, hearing, and smelling; by the different impulse of which parts, caused by their different size, figure, and motion, the variety of sensations is produced in us.

12. Whether then they be globules or no; or whether they have a verticity about their own centres that produces the idea of whiteness in us; this is certain, that the more particles of light are reflected from a body, fitted to give them that peculiar motion which produces the sensation of whiteness in us, and possibly, too, the quicker that peculiar motion is, the whiter does the body appear from which the greater number are reflected, as is evident in the same piece of paper put in the sunbeams, in the shade, and in a dark hole; in each of which it will produce in us the idea of whiteness in far different degrees.

13. Not knowing therefore what number of particles, nor what motion of them, is fit to produce any precise degree of whiteness, we cannot demonstrate the certain equality of any two degrees of whiteness; because we have no certain standard to measure them by, nor means to distinguish every the least real difference;

the only help we have being from our senses, which in this point
fail us. But where the difference is so great as to produce in the
mind clearly distinct ideas, whose differences can be perfectly
retained, there these ideas of colours, as we see in different
kinds, as blue and red, are as capable of demonstration as ideas
of number and extension. What I have here said of whiteness
and colours, I think, holds true in all secondary qualities and
their modes.

14. *Sensitive knowledge of particular existence.*—These two, viz.,
intuition and demonstration, are the degrees of our knowledge;
whatever comes short of one of these, with what assurance
soever embraced, is but faith or opinion, but not knowledge, at
least in all general truths. There is, indeed, another perception
of the mind employed about the particular existence of finite
beings without us; which, going beyond bare probability, and
yet not reaching perfectly to either of the foregoing degrees of
certainty, passes under the name of "knowledge." There can
be nothing more certain, than that the idea we receive from
an external object is in our minds; this is intuitive knowledge.
But whether there be any thing more than barely that idea in
our minds, whether we can thence certainly infer the existence
of any thing without us which corresponds to that idea, is that
whereof some men think there may be a question made; because
men may have such ideas in their minds when no such thing
exists, no such object affects their senses. But yet here, I think,
we are provided with an evidence that puts us past doubting;
for I ask any one, whether he be not invincibly conscious to
himself of a different perception when he looks on the sun by
day, and thinks on it by night; when he actually tastes wormwood, or smells a rose, or only thinks on that savour or odour?
We as plainly find the difference there is between any idea
revived in our minds by our own memory, and actually coming
into our minds by our senses, as we do between any two distinct
ideas. If any one say, "A dream may do the same thing, and
all these ideas may be produced in us without any external
objects;" he may please to dream that I make him this answer:
(1.) That it is no great matter whether I remove his scruple or
no: where all is but dream, reasoning and arguments are of no
use, truth and knowledge nothing. (2.) That I believe he will
allow a very manifest difference between dreaming of being in
the fire, and being actually in it. But yet if he be resolved to
appear so sceptical as to maintain, that what I call "being
actually in the fire" is nothing but a dream; and that we cannot
thereby certainly know that any such thing as fire actually
exists without us; I answer, that we certainly finding that
pleasure or pain follows upon the application of certain objects
to us, whose existence we perceive, or dream that we perceive,
by our senses: this certainty is as great as our happiness or

misery, beyond which we have no concernment to ki ow or to be.
So that, I think, we may add to the two former sorts of knowledge this also, of the existence of particular external objects by
that perception and consciousness we have of the actual entrance
of ideas from them, and allow these three degrees of knowledge,
viz., intuitive, demonstrative, and sensitive: in each of which
there are different degrees and ways of evidence and certainty.

15. *Knowledge not always clear, where the ideas are so.*—But
since our knowledge is founded on and employed about our
ideas only, will it not follow from thence that it is conformable
to our ideas; and that where our ideas are clear and distinct,
or obscure and confused, our knowledge will be so too ? To which
I answer, No ; for our knowledge consisting in the perception
of the agreement or disagreement of any two ideas, its clearness
or obscurity consists in the clearness or obscurity of that perception, and not in the clearness or obscurity of the ideas themselves;
*v. g.*, a man that has as clear ideas of the angles of a triangle,
and of equality to two right ones, as any mathematician in the
world, may yet have but a very obscure perception of their
agreement, and so have but a very obscure knowledge of it.
But ideas which by reason of their obscurity or otherwise are
confused, cannot produce any clear or distinct knowledge ;
because as far as any ideas are confused, so far the mind cannot
perceive clearly whether they agree or disagree. Or, to express
the same thing in a way less apt to be misunderstood, he that
hath not determined the ideas to the words he uses cannot make
propositions of them, of whose truth he can be certain.

---

## CHAPTER III.

### OF THE EXTENT OF HUMAN KNOWLEDGE.

1. KNOWLEDGE, as has been said, lying in the perception of the
agreement or disagreement of any of our ideas, it follows from
hence, that,

*First, No farther than we have ideas.*—First, We can have knowledge no farther than we have ideas.

2. *Secondly, No farther than we can perceive their agreement or
disagreement.*—Secondly, That we can have no knowledge farther
than we can have perception of that agreement or disagreement:
which perception being, (1.) Either by intuition, or the immediate
comparing any two ideas; or, (2.) by reason, examining the
agreement or disagreement of two ideas by the intervention of
some others ; or, (3.) By sensation, perceiving the existence of
particular things ; hence it also follows,

3. *Thirdly, Intuitive knowledge extends itself not to all the relations of all our ideas.*—Thirdly, that we cannot have an intuitive

knowledge that shall extend itself to all our ideas, and all that we would know about them; because we cannot examine and perceive all the relations they have one to another by juxtaposition, or an immediate comparison one with another. Thus having the ideas of an obtuse and an acute-angled triangle, both drawn from equal bases, and between parallels, I can by intuitive knowledge perceive the one not to be the other; but cannot that way know whether they be equal or no; because their agreement or disagreement in equality can never be perceived by an immediate comparing them; the difference of figure makes their parts uncapable of an exact immediate application; and therefore there is need of some intervening qualities to measure them by, which is demonstration or rational knowledge.

4. *Fourthly, Nor demonstrative knowledge.*—Fourthly, It follows also, from what is above observed, that our rational knowledge cannot reach to the whole extent of our ideas: because between two different ideas we would examine, we cannot always find such mediums as we can connect one to another with an intuitive knowledge, in all the parts of the deduction; and wherever that fails, we come short of knowledge and demonstration.

5. *Fifthly, Sensitive knowledge narrower than either.*—Fifthly, Sensitive knowledge, reaching no farther than the existence of things actually present to our senses, is yet much narrower than either of the former.

6. *Sixthly, Our knowledge therefore narrower than our ideas.*—From all which it is evident, that the extent of our knowledge comes not only short of the reality of things, but even of the extent of our own ideas. Though our knowledge be limited to our ideas, and cannot exceed them either in extent or perfection: and though these be very narrow bounds in respect of the extent of all being, and far short of what we may justly imagine to be in some even created understandings not tied down to the dull and narrow information is to be received from some few and not very acute ways of perception, such as are our senses; yet it would be well with us if our knowledge were but as large as our ideas, and there were not many doubts and inquiries concerning the ideas we have, whereof we are not, nor I believe ever shall be in this world, resolved. Nevertheless, I do not question but that human knowledge, under the present circumstances of our beings and constitutions, may be carried much farther than it hitherto has been, if men would sincerely, and with freedom of mind, employ all that industry and labour of thought in improving the means of discovering truth which they do for the colouring or support of falsehood, to maintain a system, interest, or party they are once engaged in. But yet, after all, I think I may, without injury to human perfection, be confident that our knowledge would never reach to all we might desire to know concerning those ideas we have; nor be able to surmount all the difficulties,

and resolve all the questions, might arise concerning any of them. We have the ideas of a square, a circle, and equality: and yet, perhaps, shall never be able to find a circle equal to a square, and certainly know that it is so. We have the ideas of matter and thinking, but possibly shall never be able to know whether any mere material being thinks or no;* it being impossible for us, by the contemplation of our own ideas without revelation, to discover whether Omnipotency has not given to some systems of matter, fitly disposed, a power to perceive and think, or else joined and fixed to matter, so disposed, a thinking immaterial substance: it being, in respect of our notions, not much more remote from our comprehension to conceive that God can, if he pleases, superadd to matter a faculty of thinking, than that he should superadd to it another substance with a faculty of thinking; since we know not wherein thinking consists, nor to what sort of substances the Almighty has been pleased to give that power which cannot be in any created being but merely by the good pleasure and bounty of the Creator. For I see no contradiction in it, that the first eternal thinking Being should, if he pleased, give to certain systems of created senseless matter, put together as he thinks fit, some degrees of sense, perception, and thought: though, as I think I have proved (lib. iv. chap. x.), it is no less than a contradiction to suppose matter (which is evidently in its own nature void of sense and thought) should be that eternal first thinking being. What certainty of knowledge can any one have that some perceptions, such as, *v. g.*, pleasure and pain, should not be in some bodies themselves, after a certain manner modified and moved, as well as that they should be in an immaterial substance upon the motion of the parts of body? body, as far as we can conceive, being able only to strike and affect body; and motion, according to the utmost reach of our ideas, being able to produce nothing but motion: so that when we allow it to produce pleasure or pain, or the idea of a colour or sound, we are fain to quit our reason, go beyond our ideas, and attribute it wholly to the good pleasure of our Maker. For, since we must allow he has annexed effects to motion, which we can no way conceive motion able to produce, what reason have we to conclude that he could not order them as well to be produced in a subject we cannot conceive capable of them, as well as in a subject we cannot conceive the motion of matter can any way operate upon? I say not this that I would any way lessen the belief of the soul's immateriality: I am not here speaking of probability, but knowledge: and I think, not only that it becomes the modesty of philosophy not to pronounce magisterially, where we want that evidence that can produce knowledge; but also, that it is of use to us to discern how far our knowledge does reach; for the state we are at present in, not being that of

* See Note at the end of this chapter, p. 458.—EDIT.

vision, we must, in many things, content ourselves with faith and probability : and in the present question about the immateriality of the soul, if our faculties cannot arrive at demonstrative certainty, we need not think it strange. All the great ends of morality and religion are well enough secured, without philosophical proofs of the soul's immateriality; since it is evident that he who made us at first begin to subsist here sensible intelligent beings, and for several years continued us in such a state, can and will restore us to the like state of sensibility in another world, and make us capable there to receive the retribution he has designed to men according to their doings in this life. And therefore it is not of such mighty necessity to determine one way or the other, as some, over zealous for or against the immateriality of the soul, have been forward to make the world believe : who either, on the one side, indulging too much their thoughts immersed altogether in matter, can allow no existence to what is not material : or who, on the other side, finding not cogitation within the natural powers of matter, examined over and over again by the utmost intension of mind, have the confidence to conclude that Omnipotency itself cannot give perception and thought to a substance which has the modification of solidity. He that considers how hardly sensation is, in our thoughts, reconcileable to extended matter, or existence to any thing that hath no extension at all, will confess that he is very far from certainly knowing what his soul is. It is a point which seems to me to be put out of the reach of our knowledge : and he who will give himself leave to consider freely, and look into the dark and intricate part of each hypothesis, will scarce find his reason able to determine him fixedly for or against the soul's materiality; since on which side soever he views it, either as an unextended substance, or as a thinking extended matter, the difficulty to conceive either will, whilst either alone is in his thoughts, still drive him to the contrary side : an unfair way which some men take with themselves ; who, because of the unconceivableness of something they find in one, throw themselves violently into the contrary hypothesis, though altogether as unintelligible to an unbiassed understanding. This serves not only to show the weakness and the scantiness of our knowledge, but the insignificant triumph of such sort of arguments which, drawn from our own views, may satisfy us that we can find no certainty on one side of the question; but do not at all thereby help us to truth by running into the opposite opinion, which on examination will be found clogged with equal difficulties. For what safety, what advantage to any one is it, for the avoiding the seeming absurdities, and, to him, insurmountable rubs he meets with in one opinion, to take refuge in the contrary, which is built on something altogether as inexplicable, and as far remote from his comprehension ? It is past controversy, that we have in us something that thinks; our very doubts about what it is confirm the certainty of its being, though we must content ourselves in the ignorance of what kind of being it is: and it is as vain to go about to be sceptical in this, as it is unreasonable in most other cases to be positive against the being of any thing, because we cannot comprehend its nature. For I would fain know, what substance exists that has not something in it which manifestly baffles our understandings. Other spirits, who see and know the nature and inward constitution of things, how much must they exceed us in knowledge? To which if we add larger comprehension, which enables them at one glance to see the connexion and agreement of very many ideas, and readily supplies to them the intermediate proofs, which we, by single and slow steps, and long poring in the dark, hardly at last find out, and are often ready to forget one before we have hunted out another, we may guess at some part of the happiness of superior ranks of spirits, who have a quicker and more penetrating sight, as well as a larger field of knowledge. But, to return to the argument in hand: our knowledge, I say, is not only limited to the paucity and imperfections of the ideas we have, and which we employ it about, but even comes short of that too: but how far it reaches, let us now inquire.

7. *How far our knowledge reaches.*—The affirmations or negations we make concerning the ideas we have, may, as I have before intimated in general, be reduced to these four sorts, viz., identity, co-existence, relation, and real existence. I shall examine how far our knowledge extends in each of these:—

8. *First. Our knowledge of identity and diversity, as far as our ideas.*—First, As to identity and diversity, in this way of the agreement or disagreement of ideas, our intuitive knowledge is as far extended as our ideas themselves; and there can be no idea in the mind which does not presently, by an intuitive knowledge, perceive to be what it is, and to be different from any other.

9. *Secondly. Of co-existence, a very little way.*—Secondly, As to the second sort, which is the agreement or disagreement of our ideas in co-existence, in this our knowledge is very short, though in this consists the greatest and most material part of our knowledge concerning substances. For our ideas of the species of substances being, as I have showed, nothing but certain collections of simple ideas united in one subject, and so co-existing together;—*v. g.*, our idea of "flame" is a body hot, luminous, and moving upward; of "gold," a body heavy to a certain degree, yellow, malleable, and fusible. These, or some such complex ideas as these in men's minds, do these two names of the different substances, "flame" and "gold," stand for. When we would know any thing farther concerning these, or any other sort of substances, what do we inquire but what other qualities or powers

these substances have or have not? which is nothing else but to know what other simple ideas do or do not co-exist with those that make up that complex idea.

10. *Because the connexion between most simple ideas is unknown.* —This, how weighty and considerable a part soever of human science, is yet very narrow, and scarce any at all. The reason whereof is, that the simple ideas whereof our complex ideas of substances are made up are, for the most part, such as carry with them, in their own nature, no visible necessary connexion or inconsistency with any other simple ideas, whose co-existence with them we would inform ourselves about.

11. *Especially of secondary qualities.*—The ideas that our complex ones of substances are made up of, and about which our knowledge concerning substances is most employed, are those of their secondary qualities; which depending all (as has been shown) upon the primary qualities of their minute and insensible parts, or, if not upon them, upon something yet more remote from our comprehension, it is impossible we should know which have a necessary union or inconsistency one with another: for, not knowing the root they spring from, not knowing what size, figure, and texture of parts they are on which depend and from which result those qualities which make our complex idea of gold, it is impossible we should know what other qualities result from or are incompatible with the same constitution of the insensible parts of gold; and so, consequently, must always co-exist with that complex idea we have of it, or else are inconsistent with it.

12. *Because all connexion between any secondary and primary qualities is undiscoverable.*—Besides this ignorance of the primary qualities of the insensible parts of bodies, on which depend all their secondary qualities, there is yet another and more incurable part of ignorance, which sets us more remote from a certain knowledge of the co-existence or in-co-existence (if I may so say) of different ideas in the same subject; and that is, that there is no discoverable connexion between any secondary quality and those primary qualities that it depends on.

13. That the size, figure, and motion of one body should cause a change in the size, figure, and motion of another body, is not beyond our conception. The separation of the parts of one body upon the intrusion of another, and the change from rest to motion upon impulse; these, and the like, seem to us to have some connexion one with another. And if we know these primary qualities of bodies, we might have reason to hope we might be able to know a great deal more of these operations of them one upon another: but our minds not being able to discover any connexion betwixt these primary qualities of bodies, and the sensations that are produced in us by them, we can never be able to establish certain and undoubted rules of the consequence or co-existence of any secondary qualities, though we could discover the size,

figure, or motion of those invisible parts which immediately produce them. We are so far from knowing what figure, size, or motion of parts produce a yellow colour, a sweet taste, or a sharp sound, that we can by no means conceive how any size, figure, or motion of any particles can possibly produce in us the idea of any colour, taste, or sound whatsoever; there is no conceivable connexion betwixt the one and the other.

14. In vain therefore shall we endeavour to discover by our ideas (the only true way of certain and universal knowledge) what other ideas are to be found constantly joined with that of our complex idea of any substance: since we neither know the real constitution of the minute parts on which their qualities do depend; nor, did we know them, could we discover any necessary connexion between them and any of the secondary qualities; which is necessary to be done before we can certainly know their necessary co-existence. So that, let our complex idea of any species of substances be what it will, we can hardly, from the simple ideas contained in it, certainly determine the necessary co-existence of any other quality whatsoever. Our knowledge in all these inquiries reaches very little farther than our experience. Indeed some few of the primary qualities have a necessary dependence and visible connexion one with another, as figure necessarily supposes extension, receiving or communicating motion by impulse supposes solidity. But though these and perhaps some others of our ideas have, yet there are so few of them that have, a visible connexion one with another, that we can by intuition or demonstration discover the co-existence of very few of the qualities are to be found united in substances: and we are left only to the assistance of our senses to make known to us what qualities they contain. For, of all the qualities that are co-existent in any subject, without this dependence and evident connexion of their ideas one with another, we cannot know certainly any two to co-exist any farther than experience, by our senses, informs us. Thus though we see the yellow colour, and upon trial find the weight, malleableness, fusibility, and fixedness that are united in a piece of gold; yet, because no one of these ideas has any evident dependence or necessary connexion with the other, we cannot certainly know that where any four of these are the fifth will be there also, how highly probable soever it may be: because the highest probability amounts not to certainty; without which there can be no true knowledge. For this co-existence can be no farther known than it is perceived: and it cannot be perceived but either in particular subjects by the observation of our senses, or in general by the necessary connexion of the ideas themselves.

15. *Of repugnancy to co-existence, larger.*—As to incompatibility or repugnancy to co-existence, we may know that any subject can have of each sort of primary qualities but one particular at

once; *v. g.*, each particular extension, figure, number of parts, motion, excludes all other of each kind. The like also is certain of all sensible ideas peculiar to each sense; for whatever of each kind is present in any subject, excludes all other of that sort; *v. g.*, no one subject can have two smells or two colours at the same time. To this, perhaps, will be said, "Has not an *opal* or the infusion of *lignum nephriticum* two colours at the same time?" To which I answer, that these bodies, to eyes differently placed, may at the same time afford different colours: but I take liberty also to say, that to eyes differently placed it is different parts of the object that reflect the particles of light: and therefore it is not the same part of the object, and so not the very same subject, which at the same time appears both yellow and azure. For it is as impossible that the very same particle of any body should at the same time differently modify or reflect the rays of light, as that it should have two different figures and textures at the same time.

16. *Of the co-existence of powers, a very little way.*—But as to the power of substances to change the sensible qualities of other bodies, which makes a great part of our inquiries about them, and is no inconsiderable branch of our knowledge; I doubt, as to these, whether our knowledge reaches much farther than our experience; or whether we can come to the discovery of most of these powers, and be certain that they are in any subject, by the connexion with any of those ideas which to us make its essence. Because the active and passive powers of bodies, and their ways of operating, consisting in a texture and motion of parts which we cannot by any means come to discover, it is but in very few cases we can be able to perceive their dependence on or repugnance to any of those ideas which make our complex one of that sort of things. I have here instanced in the corpuscularian hypothesis, as that which is thought to go farthest in an intelligible explication of the qualities of bodies; and I fear the weakness of human understanding is scarce able to substitute another, which will afford us a fuller and clearer discovery of the necessary connexion and co-existence of the powers which are to be observed united in several sorts of them. This at least is certain, that whichever hypothesis be clearest and truest (for of that it is not my business to determine), our knowledge concerning corporeal substances will be very little advanced by any of them, till we are made to see what qualities and powers of bodies have a necessary connexion or repugnancy one with another: which, in the present state of philosophy, I think, we know but to a very small degree: and I doubt whether, with those faculties we have, we shall ever be able to carry our general knowledge (I say not particular experience) in this part much farther. Experience is that which in this part we must depend on. And it were to be wished that it were more improved. We find the advantages

some men's generous pains have this way brought to the stock of natural knowledge. And if others, especially the philosophers by fire, who pretend to it, had been so wary in their observations and sincere in their reports as those who call themselves philosophers ought to have been, our acquaintance with the bodies here about us, and our insight into their powers and operations, had been yet much greater.

17. *Of spirits yet narrower.*—If we are at a loss in respect of the powers and operations of bodies, I think it is easy to conclude we are much more in the dark in reference to spirits, whereof we naturally have no ideas but what we draw from that of our own, by reflecting on the operations of our own souls within us, as far as they can come within our observation. But how inconsiderable a rank the spirits that inhabit our bodies hold amongst those various, and possibly innumerable, kinds of nobler beings; and how far short they come of the endowments and perfections of cherubims and seraphims, and infinite sorts of spirits above us, is what by a transient hint, in another place, I have offered to my reader's consideration.

18. *Thirdly, Of other relations, it is not easy to say how far.*—As to the third sort of our knowledge, viz., the agreement or disagreement of any of our ideas in any other relation: this, as it is the largest field of our knowledge, so it is hard to determine how far it may extend: because the advances that are made in this part of knowledge depending on our sagacity in finding intermediate ideas that may show the relations and habitudes of ideas, whose co-existence is not considered, it is a hard matter to tell when we are at an end of such discoveries, and when reason has all the helps it is capable of for the finding of proofs, or examining the agreement or disagreement of remote ideas. They that are ignorant of algebra, cannot imagine the wonders in this kind are to be done by it: and what farther improvements and helps, advantageous to other parts of knowledge, the sagacious mind of man may yet find out, it is not easy to determine. This at least I believe, that the ideas of quantity are not those alone that are capable of demonstration and knowledge; and that other, and perhaps more useful, parts of contemplation would afford us certainty, if vices, passions, and domineering interest did not oppose or menace such endeavours.

*Morality capable of demonstration.*—The idea of a Supreme Being, infinite in power, goodness, and wisdom, whose workmanship we are, and on whom we depend; and the idea of ourselves, as understanding, rational beings, being such as are clear in us, would, I suppose, if duly considered and pursued, afford such foundations of our duty and rules of action as might place morality amongst the sciences capable of demonstration: wherein I doubt not, but from self-evident propositions, by necessary consequences, as incontestable as those in mathematics, the measures of right and wrong might be made out, to any one that will apply himself with the same indifferency and attention to the one as he does to the other of these sciences. The relation of other modes may certainly be perceived, as well as those of number and extension: and I cannot see why they should not also be capable of demonstration, if due methods were thought on to examine or pursue their agreement or disagreement. "Where there is no property, there is no injustice," is a proposition as certain as any demonstration in Euclid: for, the idea of property being a right to anything, and the idea to which the name "injustice" is given being the invasion or violation of that right; it is evident that these ideas being thus established, and these names annexed to them, I can as certainly know this proposition to be true as that a triangle has three angles equal to two right ones. Again: "No government allows absolute liberty:" the idea of government being the establishment of society upon certain rules or laws, which require conformity to them; and the idea of absolute liberty being for any one to do whatever he pleases: I am as capable of being certain of the truth of this proposition as of any in the mathematics.

19. *Two things have made moral ideas thought uncapable of demonstration: their complexedness, and want of sensible representation.*—That which, in this respect, has given the advantage to the ideas of quantity, and made them thought more capable of certainty and demonstration, is,

First, That they can be set down and represented by sensible marks, which have a greater and nearer correspondence with them than any words or sounds whatsoever. Diagrams drawn on paper are copies of the ideas in the mind, and not liable to the uncertainty that words carry in their signification. An angle, circle, or square, drawn in lines, lies open to the view, and cannot be mistaken: it remains unchangeable, and may at leisure be considered and examined, and the demonstration be revised, and all the parts of it may be gone over more than once, without any danger of the least change in the ideas. This cannot be thus done in moral ideas: we have no sensible marks that resemble them, whereby we can set them down: we have nothing but words to express them by; which though, when written, they remain the same, yet the ideas they stand for may change in the same man; and it is very seldom that they are not different in different persons.

Secondly, Another thing that makes the greater difficulty in ethics is, that moral ideas are commonly more complex than those of the figures ordinarily considered in mathematics. From whence these two inconveniences follow: First, that their names are of more uncertain signification; the precise collection of simple ideas they stand for not being so easily agreed on, and so the sign that is used for them in communication always and in thinking often, does not steadily carry with it the same idea. Upon which the same disorder, confusion, and error follows as would if a man, going to demonstrate something of an heptagon, should, in the diagram he took to do it, leave out one of the angles, or by oversight make the figure with one angle more than the name ordinarily imported, or he intended it should when at first he thought of his demonstration. This often happens, and is hardly avoidable in very complex moral ideas, where, the same name being retained, one angle, *i. e.*, one simple idea, is left out or put in in the complex one (still called by the same name) more at one time than another. Secondly, From the complexedness of these moral ideas there follows another inconvenience, viz., that the mind cannot easily retain those precise combinations so exactly and perfectly as is necessary in the examination of the habitudes and correspondencies, agreements or disagreements, of several of them one with another; especially where it is to be judged of by long deductions, and the intervention of several other complex ideas, to show the agreement or disagreement of two remote ones.

The great help against this which mathematicians find in diagrams and figures, which remain unalterable in their draughts, is very apparent; and the memory would often have great difficulty otherwise to retain them so exactly, whilst the mind went over the parts of them, step by step, to examine their several correspondencies. And though, in casting up a long sum, either in addition, multiplication, or division, every part be only a progression of the mind taking a view of its own ideas and considering their agreement or disagreement, and the resolution of the question be nothing but the result of the whole, made up of such particulars whereof the mind has a clear perception; yet without setting down the several parts by marks whose precise significations are known, and by marks that last and remain in view when the memory had let them go, it would be almost impossible to carry so many different ideas in mind, without confounding or letting slip some parts of the reckoning, and thereby making all our reasonings about it useless. In which case, the ciphers or marks help not the mind at all to perceive the agreement of any two or more numbers, their equalities or proportions : *that* the mind has only by intuition of its own ideas of the numbers themselves. But the numerical characters are helps to the memory to record and retain the several ideas about which the demonstration is made, whereby a man may know how far his intuitive knowledge in surveying several of the particulars has proceeded; that so he may, without confusion, go on to what is yet unknown, and, at last, have in one view before him the result of all his perceptions and reasonings.

᾽20. *Remedies of those difficulties.*—One part of these disadvantages in moral ideas, which has made them be thought not capable

of demonstration, may in a good measure be remedied by definitions, setting down that collection of simple ideas which every
term shall stand for, and then using the terms steadily and constantly for that precise collection. And what methods algebra,
or something of that kind, may hereafter suggest, to remove the
other difficulties, is not easy to foretell. Confident I am, that if
men would in the same method, and with the same indifferency,
search after moral as they do mathematical truths, they would
find them to have a stronger connexion one with another, and a
more necessary consequence from our clear and distinct ideas,
and to come nearer perfect demonstration, than is commonly
imagined. But much of this is not to be expected, whilst the
desire of esteem, riches, or power makes men espouse the well-
endowed opinions in fashion, and then seek arguments either to
make good their beauty, or varnish over and cover their
deformity: nothing being so beautiful to the eye as truth *is* to
the mind, nothing so deformed and irreconcileable to the understanding as a lie. For, though many a man can with satisfaction
enough own a no-very-handsome wife in his bosom, yet who is
bold enough openly to avow that he has espoused a falsehood,
and received into his breast so ugly a thing as a lie? Whilst
the parties of men cram their tenets down all men's throats
whom they can get into their power, without permitting them to
examine their truth or falsehood; and will not let truth have
fair play in the world, nor men the liberty to search after it;
what improvements can be expected of this kind? what greater
light can be hoped for in the moral sciences? The subject part
of mankind, in most places, might, instead thereof, with Egyptian
bondage, expect Egyptian darkness, were not the candle of the
Lord set up by himself in men's minds, which it is impossible for
the breath or power of man wholly to extinguish.

21. *Fourthly, Of real existence. We have an* INTUITIVE *knowledge of our own,* DEMONSTRATIVE *of God's,* SENSITIVE *of some few
other things'.*—As to the fourth sort of our knowledge, viz., of the
real actual existence of things, we have an intuitive knowledge
of our own existence; a demonstrative knowledge of the existence
of a God; of the existence of anything else, we have no other
but a sensitive knowledge, which extends not beyond the objects
present to our senses.

22. *Our ignorance great.*—Our knowledge being so narrow, as
I have showed, it will, perhaps, give us some light into the present
state of our minds, if we look a little into the dark side, and take
a view of our ignorance: which, being infinitely larger than our
knowledge, may serve much to the quieting of disputes and
improvement of useful knowledge, if, discovering how far we have
clear and distinct ideas, we confine our thoughts within the contemplation of those things that are within the reach of our
understandings, and launch not out into that abyss of darkness

(where we have not eyes to see, nor faculties to perceive any thing), out of a presumption that nothing is beyond our comprehension. But to be satisfied of the folly of such a conceit, we need not go far. He that knows any thing, knows this in the first place, that he need not seek long for instances of his ignorance. The meanest and most obvious things that come in our way have dark sides, that the quickest sight cannot penetrate into. The clearest and most enlarged understandings of thinking men find themselves puzzled and at a loss in every particle of matter. We shall the less wonder to find it so when we consider the causes of our ignorance, which, from what has been said, I suppose, will be found to be chiefly these three:

FIRST, Want of ideas.

SECONDLY, Want of a discoverable connexion between the ideas we have.

THIRDLY, Want of tracing and examining our ideas.

23. *First, One cause of it, want of ideas, either such as we have no conception of.*—FIRST, There are some things, and those not a few, that we are ignorant of for want of ideas.

First, All the simple ideas we have are confined (as I have shown) to those we receive from corporeal objects by sensation, and from the operations of our own minds as the objects of reflection. But how much these few and narrow inlets are disproportionate to the vast whole extent of all beings, will not be hard to persuade those who are not so foolish as to think their span the measure of all things. What other simple ideas it is possible the creatures in other parts of the universe may have by the assistance of senses and faculties more or perfecter than we have, or different from ours, it is not for us to determine; but to say or think there are no such because we conceive nothing of them, is no better an argument than if a blind man should be positive in it, that there was no such thing as sight and colours because he had no manner of idea of any such thing, nor could by any means frame to himself any notions about seeing. The ignorance and darkness that is in us no more hinders nor confines the knowledge that is in others, than the blindness of a mole is an argument against the quick-sightedness of an eagle. He that will consider the infinite power, wisdom, and goodness of the Creator of all things, will find reason to think it was not all laid out upon so inconsiderable, mean, and impotent a creature as he will find man to be, who, in all probability, is one of the lowest of all intellectual beings. What faculties therefore other species of creatures have to penetrate into the nature and inmost constitutions of things, what ideas they may receive of them far different from ours, we know not. This we know and certainl; find, that we want several other views of them besides those we have, to make discoveries of them more perfect. And we may be convinced that the ideas we can attain to by our faculties are very disproportionate to things themselves, when a positive, clear, distinct one of substance itself, which is the foundation of all the rest, is concealed from us. But want of ideas of this kind, being a part as well as cause of our ignorance, cannot be described. Only this, I think, I may confidently say of it, that the intellectual and sensible world are in this perfectly alike—that that part which we see of either of them holds no proportion with what we see not; and whatsoever we can reach with our eyes or our thoughts of either of them, is but a point, almost nothing, in comparison of the rest.

24. *Or want of such ideas as particularly we have not, because of their remoteness.*—Secondly, Another great cause of ignorance is the want of ideas we are capable of. As the want of ideas which our faculties are not able to give us shuts us wholly from those views of things which it is reasonable to think other beings, perfecter than we, have, of which we know nothing; so the want of ideas I now speak of keeps us in ignorance of things we conceive capable of being known to us. Bulk, figure, and motion, we have ideas of. But though we are not without ideas of these primary qualities of bodies in general, yet not knowing what is the particular bulk, figure, and motion of the greatest part of the bodies of the universe, we are ignorant of the several powers, efficacies, and ways of operation, whereby the effects which we daily see are produced. These are hid from us in some things by being too remote; and, in others, by being too minute. When we consider the vast distance of the known and visible parts of the world, and the reasons we have to think that what lies within our ken is but a small part of the immense universe, we shall then discover a huge abyss of ignorance. What are the particular fabrics of the great masses of matter which make up the whole stupendous frame of corporeal beings, how far they are extended, what is their motion, and how continued or communicated, and what influence they have one upon another, are contemplations that, at first glimpse, our thoughts lose themselves in. If we narrow our contemplation, and confine our thoughts to this little canton, I mean this system of our sun, and the grosser masses of matter that visibly move about it, what several sorts of vegetables, animals, and intellectual corporeal beings, infinitely different from those of our little spot of earth, may there probably be in the other planets, to the knowledge of which, even of their outward figures and parts, we can no way attain whilst we are confined to this earth, there being no natural means, either by sensation or reflection, to convey their certain ideas into our minds! They are out of the reach of those inlets of all our knowledge; and what sorts of furniture and inhabitants those mansions contain in them, we cannot so much as guess, much less have clear and distinct ideas of them.

25. *Or because of their minuteness.*—If à great, nay, far the

greatest part of the several ranks of bodies in the universe escape our notice by their remoteness, there are others that are no less concealed from us by their minuteness. These insensible corpuscles being the active parts of matter and the great instruments of nature, on which depend not only all their secondary qualities, but also most of their natural operations, our want of precise distinct ideas of their primary qualities keeps us in an incurable ignorance of what we desire to know about them. I doubt not but if we could discover the figure, size, texture, and motion of the minute constituent parts of any two bodies, we should know without trial several of their operations one upon another, as we do now the properties of a square or a triangle. Did we know the mechanical affections of the particles of rhubarb, hemlock, opium, and a man, as a watchmaker does those of a watch, whereby it performs its operations, and of a file, which, by rubbing on them, will alter the figure of any of the wheels, we should be able to tell beforehand that rhubarb will purge, hemlock kill, and opium make a man sleep, as well as a watchmaker can, that a little piece of paper laid on the balance will keep the watch from going till it be removed; or that some small part of it being rubbed by a file, the machine would quite lose its motion, and the watch go no more. The dissolving of silver in *aqua fortis*, and gold in *aqua regia*, and not *vice versâ*, would be then perhaps no more difficult to know, than it is to a smith to understand why the turning of one key will open a lock, and not the turning of another. But whilst we are destitute of senses acute enough to discover the minute particles of bodies, and to give us ideas of their mechanical affections, we must be content to be ignorant of their properties and ways of operation; nor can we be assured about them any farther than some few trials we make are able to reach. But whether they will succeed again another time, we cannot be certain. This hinders our certain knowledge of universal truths concerning natural bodies, and our reason carries us herein very little beyond particular matter of fact.

26. *Hence no science of bodies.*—And therefore I am apt to doubt, that how far soever human industry may advance useful and experimental philosophy in physical things, scientifical will still be out of our reach; because we want perfect and adequate ideas of those very bodies which are nearest to us, and most under our command. Those which we have ranked into classes under names, and we think ourselves best acquainted with, we have but very imperfect and incomplete ideas of. Distinct ideas of the several sorts of bodies that fall under the examination of our senses perhaps we may have; but adequate ideas, I suspect, we have not of any one amongst them. And though the former of these will serve us for common use and discourse; yet whilst we want the latter, we are not capable of scientifical knowledge, nor shall ever be able to discover general instructive, unques-

tionable truths concerning them. Certainty and demonstration are things we must not, in these matters, pretend to. By the colour, figure, taste, and smell, and other sensible qualities, we have as clear and distinct ideas of sage and hemlock, as we have of a circle and a triangle; but having no ideas of the particular primary qualities of the minute parts of either of these plants, nor of other bodies which we would apply them to, we cannot tell what effects they will produce; nor when we see those effects can we so much as guess, much less know, their manner of production. Thus, having no ideas of the particular mechanical affections of the minute parts of bodies that are within our view and reach, we are ignorant of their constitutions, powers, and operations; and of bodies more remote we are yet more ignorant, not knowing so much as their very outward shapes, or the sensible and grosser parts of their constitutions.

27. *Much less of spirits.*—This, at first sight, will show us how disproportionate our knowledge is to the whole extent even of material beings; to which if we add the consideration of that infinite number of spirits that may be, and probably are, which are yet more remote from our knowledge, whereof we have no cognizance, nor can frame to ourselves any distinct ideas of their several ranks and sorts, we shall find this cause of ignorance conceal from us, in an impenetrable obscurity, almost the whole intellectual world; a greater, certainly, and more beautiful world than the material. For, bating some very few, and those, if I may so call them, "superficial," ideas of spirit, which by reflection we get of our own, and from thence the best we can collect of the Father of all spirits, the eternal independent author of them and us and all things, we have no certain information so much as of the existence of other spirits but by revelation. Angels of all sorts are naturally beyond our discovery; and all those intelligences whereof it is likely there are more orders than of corporeal substances, are things whereof our natural faculties give us no certain account at all. That there are minds and thinking beings in other men, as well as himself, every man has a reason, from their words and actions, to be satisfied; and the knowledge of his own mind cannot suffer a man that considers to be ignorant that there is a God. But that there are degrees of spiritual beings between us and the great God, who is there that by his own search and ability can come to know? Much less have we distinct ideas of their different natures, conditions, states, powers, and several constitutions, wherein they agree or differ from one another and from us. And therefore, in what concerns their different species and properties, we are under an absolute ignorance.

28. *Secondly, Want of a discoverable connexion between ideas we have.*—Secondly, What a small part of the substantial beings

that are in the universe the want of ideas leaves open to our knowledge, we have seen. In the next place, another cause of ignorance of no less moment is a want of a discoverable connexion between those ideas which we have. For wherever we want that, we are utterly uncapable of universal and certain knowledge; and are, as in the former case, left only to observation and experiment; which how narrow and confined it is, how far from general knowledge, we need not be told. I shall give some few instances of this cause of our ignorance, and so leave it. It is evident that the bulk, figure, and motion of several bodies about us, produce in us several sensations, as of colours, sounds, taste, smell, pleasure, and pain, &c. These mechanical affections of bodies having no affinity at all with those ideas they produce in us, (there being no conceivable connexion between any impulse of any sort of body, and any perception of a colour or smell which we find in our minds,) we can have no distinct knowledge of such operations beyond our experience; and can reason no otherwise about them than as effects produced by the appointment of an infinitely wise Agent which perfectly surpass our comprehensions. As the ideas of sensible secondary qualities which we have in our minds, can by us be no way deduced from bodily causes, nor any correspondence or connexion be found between them and those primary qualities which experience shows us produce them in us; so, on the other side, the operation of our minds upon our bodies is as unconceivable. How any thought should produce a motion in body, is as remote from the nature of our ideas, as how any body should produce any thought in the mind. That it is so, if experience did not convince us, the consideration of the things themselves would never be able in the least to discover to us. These and the like, though they have a constant and regular connexion in the ordinary course of things; yet that connexion being not discoverable in the ideas themselves, which appearing to have no necessary dependence one on another, we can attribute their connexion to nothing else but the arbitrary determination of that all-wise Agent who has made them to be, and to operate as they do, in a way wholly above our weak understandings to conceive.

29. *Instances.*—In some of our ideas there are certain relations, habitudes, and connexions so visibly included in the nature of the ideas themselves, that we cannot conceive them separable from them by any power whatsoever. And in these only we are capable of certain and universal knowledge. Thus the idea of a right-lined triangle necessarily carries with it an equality of its angles to two right ones. Nor can we conceive this relation, this connexion of these two ideas, to be possibly mutable, or to depend on any arbitrary power, which of choice made it thus, or could make it otherwise. But the coherence

and continuity of the parts of matter, the production of sensa.. tion in us of colours and sounds, &c., by impulse and motion, nay the original rules and communication of motion, being such wherein we can discover no natural connexion with any ideas we have, we cannot but ascribe them to the arbitrary will and good pleasure of the wise Architect. I need not, I think, here mention the resurrection of the dead, the future state of this globe of earth, and such other things which are by every one acknowledged to depend wholly on the determination of a free agent. The things that, as far as our observation reaches, we constantly find to proceed regularly, we may conclude do act by a law set them; but yet by a law that we know not; whereby, though causes work steadily, and effects constantly flow from them, yet their connexions and dependences being not discoverable in our ideas, we can have but an experimental knowledge of them. From all which it is easy to perceive what a darkness we are involved in, how little it is of being, and the things that are, that we are capable to know. And therefore we shall do no injury to our knowledge when we modestly think with ourselves, that we are so far from being able to comprehend the whole nature of the universe and all the things contained in it, that we are not capable of a philosophical knowledge of the bodies that are about us, and make a part of us: concerning their secondary qualities, powers, and operations, we can have no universal certainty. Several effects come every day within the notice of our senses, of which we have so far sensitive knowledge; but the causes, manner, and certainty of their production, for the two foregoing reasons, we must be content to be ignorant of. In these we can go no farther than particular experience informs us of matter of fact, and by analogy to guess what effects the like bodies are, upon other trials, like to produce. But as to a perfect science of natural bodies (not to mention spiritual beings), we are, I think, so far from being capable of any such thing, that I conclude it lost labour to seek after it.

30. *Thirdly, Want of tracing our ideas.*—Thirdly, Where we have adequate ideas, and where there is a certain and discoverable connexion between them, yet we are often ignorant for want of tracing those ideas which we have or may have; and for want of finding out those intermediate ideas which may show us what habitude of agreement or disagreement they have one with another. And thus many are ignorant of mathematical truths, not out of any imperfection of their faculties, or uncertainty in the things themselves; but for want of application in acquiring, examining, and by due ways comparing those ideas. That which has most contributed to hinder the due tracing of our ideas, and finding out their relations and agreements or disagreements one with another has been, I suppose, the ill use of words. It is impossible that men should ever truly seek, or certainly discover,

the agreement or disagreement of ideas themselves, whilst their thoughts flutter about, or stick only in sounds of doubtful and uncertain significations. Mathematicians, abstracting their thoughts from names, and accustoming themselves to set before their minds the ideas themselves that they would consider, and not sounds instead of them, have avoided thereby a great part of that perplexity, puddering, and confusion, which has so much hindered men's progress in other parts of knowledge. For whilst they stick in words of undetermined and uncertain signification, they are unable to distinguish true from false, certain from probable, consistent from inconsistent, in their own opinions. This having been the fate or misfortune of a great part of the men of letters, the increase brought into the stock of real knowledge has been very little in proportion to the schools, disputes, and writings, the world has been filled with; whilst students, being lost in the great wood of words, knew not whereabout they were, how far their discoveries were advanced, or what was wanting in their own or the general stock of knowledge. Had men, in the discoveries of the material, done as they have in those of the intellectual, world, involved all in the obscurity of uncertain and doubtful ways of talking, volumes writ of navigation and voyages, theories and stories of zones and tides multiplied and disputed, nay, ships built and fleets set out, would never have taught us the way beyond the line; and the antipodes would be still as much unknown as when it was declared heresy to hold there were any. But having spoken sufficiently of words, and the ill or careless use that is commonly made of them, I shall not say any thing more of it here.

31. *Extent in respect of universality.*—Hitherto we have examined the extent of our knowledge in respect of the several sorts of beings that are. There is another extent of it in respect of universality which will also deserve to be considered: and in this regard our knowledge follows the nature of our ideas. If the ideas are abstract, whose agreement or disagreement we perceive, our knowledge is universal. For what is known of such general ideas will be true of every particular thing in whom that essence, *i. e.*, that abstract idea, is to be found: and what is once known of such ideas will be perpetually and for ever true. So that, as to all general knowledge, we must search and find it only in our own minds, and it is only the examining of our own ideas that furnisheth us with that. Truths belonging to essences of things (that is, to abstract ideas) are eternal, and are to be found out by the contemplation only of those essences, as the existence of things is to be known only from experience. But having more to say of this in the chapters where I shall speak of general and real knowledge, this may here suffice as to the universality of our knowledge in general.

## NOTE.—Page 441.

AGAINST that assertion of Mr. Locke, "That possibly we shall never be able to know whether any material beings think or not," &c., the Bishop of Worcester argues thus : " If this be true, then, for all that we can know by our ideas of matter and thinking, matter may have a power of thinking ; and if this hold, then it is impossible to prove a spiritual substance in us from the idea of thinking : for how can we be assured by our ideas, that God hath not given such a power of thinking to matter so disposed as our bodies are? especially since it is said, 'that in respect of our notions, it is not much more remote from our comprehension to conceive, that God can, if he pleases, superadd to our idea of matter a faculty of thinking, than that he should superadd to it another substance with a faculty of thinking.' * Whoever asserts this, can never prove a spiritual substance in us from a faculty of thinking, because he cannot know from the idea of matter and thinking, that matter so disposed cannot think ; and he cannot be certain that God hath not framed the matter of our bodies so as to be capable of it."

To which Mr. Locke answers thus :† " Here your lordship argues, that, upon my principles, 'it cannot be proved that there is a spiritual substance in us.' To which give me leave, with submission, to say, that I think it may be proved from my principles, and I think I have done it ; and the proof in my book stands thus : First, We experiment in ourselves thinking. The idea of this action or mode of thinking is inconsistent with the idea of self-subsistence, and therefore has a necessary connexion with a support or subject of inhesion : the idea of that support is what we call 'substance ;' and so from thinking experimented in us, we have a proof of a thinking substance in us, which in my sense is a spirit. Against this your lordship will argue, that by what I have said of the possibility that God may, if he pleases, superadd to matter a faculty of thinking, it can never be proved that there is a spiritual substance in us, because upon that supposition it is possible it may be a material substance that thinks in us. I grant it ; but add, that the general idea of substance being the same every where, the modification of thinking, or the power of thinking joined to it, makes it a spirit, without considering what other modifications it has, as whether it has the modification of solidity or no. As on the other side, substance, that has the modification of solidity, is matter, whether it has the modification of thinking or no. And therefore if your lordship means by a 'spiritual,' an immaterial substance, I grant I have not proved, nor upon my principles can it be proved (your lordship meaning, as I think you do, demonstratively proved), that there is an immaterial substance in us that thinks. Though I presume, what I have said about the supposition of a system of matter‡ thinking (which there demonstrates that God is immaterial) will prove it in the highest degree probable, that the thinking substance in us is immaterial. But your lordship thinks not probability enough ; and by

* Essay of Human Understanding, book iv. chap. iii. sect. 6.
† In his First Letter to the Bishop of Worcester, pp. 64, 65, &c.
‡ Essay of Human Understanding, book iv. chap. x. sect. 16.

charging the want of demonstration upon my principles, that the
thinking thing in us is immaterial, your lordship seems to conclude it
demonstrable from principles of philosophy. That demonstration I
should with joy receive from your lordship or any one. For though
all the great ends of morality and religion are well enough secured
without it, as I have shown,* yet it would be a great advance of our
knowledge in nature and philosophy.

"To what I have said in my book, to show that all the great ends
of religion and morality are secured barely by the immortality of the
soul, without a necessary supposition that the soul is immaterial, I
crave leave to add, that immortality may and shall be annexed to
that which, in its own nature, is neither immaterial nor immortal, as
the apostle expressly declares in these words : 'For this corruptible
must put on incorruption, and this mortal must put on immortality.'
(1 Cor. xv. 53.)

"Perhaps my using the word 'spirit' for a thinking substance, without excluding materiality out of it, will be thought too great a liberty,
and such as deserves censure, because I leave immateriality out of the
idea I make it a sign of. I really own, that words should be sparingly
ventured on in a sense wholly new ; and nothing but absolute necessity
can excuse the boldness of using any term in a sense whereof we can
produce no example. But, in the present case, I think I have great
authorities to justify me. The soul is agreed, on all hands, to be that
in us which thinks ; and he that will look into the first book of Cicero's
Tusculan Questions, and into the sixth book of Virgil's Æneids, will
find that these two great men, who, of all the Romans, best understood
philosophy, thought, or at least did not deny, the soul to be a subtile
matter, which might come under the name of *aura*, or *ignis*, or *æther*,
and this soul they both of them called *spiritus*, in the notion of which,
it is plain, they included only thought and active motion, without the
total exclusion of matter. Whether they thought right in this, I do
not say ; that is not the question : but whether they spoke properly,
when they called an active, thinking, subtile substance, out of which
they excluded only gross and palpable matter, *spiritus*, 'spirit,' I
think that nobody will deny, that if any among the Romans can be
allowed to speak properly, Tully and Virgil are the two who may most
securely be depended on for it ; and one of them, speaking of the soul,
says, *Dum spiritus hos regit artus ;* and the other *Vita continetur corpore
et spiritu*, where, it is plain, by *corpus* he means (as generally every
where) only gross matter that may be felt and handled, as appears by
these words, *Si cor, aut sanguis, aut cerebrum est animus, certè quoniam
est corpus, interibit cum reliquo corpore; si anima est, fortè dissipabitur;
si ignis, extinguetur.* (*Tusc. Quæst.* lib. i. cap. 11.) Here Cicero opposes
*corpus* to *ignis* and *anima*, i. e., *aura*, or 'breath.' And the foundation
of that his distinction of the soul, from that which he calls *corpus*, or
'body,' he gives a little lower in these words : *Tanta ejus tenuitas ut
fugiat aciem.* (*Ibid.* cap. 22.) Nor was it the Heathen world alone that
had this notion of spirit ; the most enlightened of all the ancient
people of God, Solomon himself, speaks after the same manner : 'That
which befalleth the sons of men, befalleth beasts ; even one thing
befalleth them : as the one dieth, so dieth the other ; yea, they have

* Book iv. chap. iii. sect. 6,

all one spirit.' (Eccles. iii. 19.) So I translate the Hebrew word רוּחַ here, for so I find it translated the very next verse but one : 'Who knoweth the spirit of a man that goeth upward, and the spirit of a beast that goeth down to the earth ?' (verse 21) in which places it is plain that Solomon applies the word רוּחַ, and our translators of him the word 'spirit,' to a substance, out of which immateriality was not wholly excluded, unless 'the spirit of a beast that goeth downwards to the earth' be immaterial. Nor did the way of speaking in our Saviour's time vary from this. St. Luke tells us (chap. xxiv. 37), that when our Saviour, after his resurrection, stood in the midst of them, 'they were affrighted, and supposed that they had seen' πνεῦμα, the Greek word which always answers 'spirit' in English, and so the translators of the Bible render it here, 'they supposed that they had seen a spirit.' But our Saviour says to them, 'Behold my hands and my feet, that it is I myself : handle me and see ; for a spirit hath not flesh and bones, as you see me have.' (Verse 39.) Which words of our Saviour put the same distinction between 'body' and 'spirit' that Cicero did in the place above cited, viz., that the one was a gross com-pages that could be felt and handled, and the other such as Virgil describes the ghost or soul of Anchises :—

> *Ter conatus ibi collo dare brachia circum,*
> *Ter frustra comprensa manus effugit imago,*
> *Par levibus ventis volucrique simillima somno.*

"I would not be thought hereby to say, that 'spirit' never does signify a purely immaterial substance. In that sense the scripture, I take it, speaks, when it says, 'God is a spirit ;' and in that sense I have used it ; and in that sense I have proved from my principles, that there is a spiritual substance ; and am certain that there is a spiritual immaterial substance, which is, I humbly conceive, a direct answer to your lordship's question in the beginning of this argument, viz., 'How we come to be certain that there are spiritual substances, supposing this principle to be true,' that the simple ideas by sensation and reflec-tion are the sole matter and foundation of all reasoning ? But this hinders not but that if God, that infinite, omnipotent, and perfectly immaterial Spirit, should please to give to a system of very subtile matter, sense and motion, it might, with propriety of speech, be called 'spirit,' though materiality were not excluded out of its complex idea. Your lordship proceeds : 'It is said indeed elsewhere, *that it is repug-nant to the idea of senseless matter, that it should put into itself sense, per-ception, and knowledge.*\* But this does not reach the present case ; which is, not what matter can do of itself, but what matter prepared by an omnipotent hand can do. And what certainty can we have that he hath not done it ? We can have none from the ideas ; for those are given up in this case ; and consequently, we can have no certainty upon these principles, whether we have any spiritual substance within us or not.'

"Your lordship, in this paragraph, proves that, from what I say, 'we can have no certainty whether we have any spiritual substance in us or not.' If by 'spiritual substance' your lordship means an immaterial substance in us, as you speak, page 246, I grant what your

---

\* Essay on the Human Understanding, book iv. chap. x.

lordship says is true, that it cannot, upon 'these principles,' be demonstrated. But I must crave leave to say, at the same time, that, upon 'these principles,' it can be proved to the highest degree of probability. If by 'spiritual substance' your lordship means a thinking substance, I must dissent from your lordship, and say, that we can have a certainty, upon my principles, that there is a spiritual substance in us. In short, my lord, upon my principles, *i. e.*, from the idea of thinking, we can have a certainty that there is a thinking substance in us; from hence we have a certainty that there is an eternal thinking Substance. This thinking Substance which has been from eternity, I have proved to be immaterial. This eternal, immaterial, thinking Substance has put into us a thinking substance, which, whether it be a material or immaterial substance, cannot be infallibly demonstrated from our ideas; though from them it may be proved, that it is to the highest degree probable that it is immaterial."

Again : the Bishop of Worcester undertakes to prove from Mr. Locke's principles, that we may be certain "that the first eternal thinking Being, or omnipotent Spirit, cannot, if he would, give to certain systems of created sensible matter, put together as he sees fit, some degrees of sense, perception, and thought."

To which Mr. Locke has made the following answer in his Third Letter, pp. 396, 397, &c. :—

"Your first argument I take to be this, that, according to me, the knowledge we have being by our ideas, and our idea of matter in general being a solid substance, and our idea of body a solid extended figured substance; if I admit matter to be capable of thinking, I confound the idea of matter with the idea of a spirit : to which I answer, No; no more than I confound the idea of matter with the idea of a horse, when I say, that matter in general is a solid extended substance; and that a horse is a material animal, or an extended solid substance with sense and spontaneous motion.

"The idea of matter is an extended solid substance; wherever there is such a substance, there is matter, and the essence of matter, whatever other qualities not contained in that essence it shall please God to superadd to it. For example : God creates an extended solid substance without the superadding any thing else to it, and so we may consider it at rest : to some parts of it he superadds motion, but it has still the essence of matter; other parts of it he frames into plants, with all the excellences of vegetation, life, and beauty, which are to be found in a rose or a peach-tree, &c., above the essence of matter in general, but it is still but matter; to other parts he adds sense and spontaneous motion, and those other properties that are to be found in an elephant. Hitherto it is not doubted but the power of God may go, and that the properties of a rose, a peach, or an elephant, superadded to matter, change not the properties of matter; but matter is in these things matter still. But if one venture to go one step farther and say, 'God may give to matter thought, reason, and volition, as well as sense and spontaneous motion,' there are men ready presently to limit the power of the omnipotent Creator, and tell us, 'He cannot do it, because it destroys the essence, or changes the essential properties of matter.' To make good which assertion, they have no more to say, but that 'thought and reason are not included in the essence of matter.' I grant it; but whatever excellency, not contained in its essence, be superadded to matter, it does not destroy the essence of matter, if it leaves it an extended solid substance; wherever that is, there is the essence of matter; and if every thing of greater perfection, superadded to such a substance, destroys the essence of matter, what will become of the essence of matter in a plant, or an animal, whose properties far exceed those of a mere extended solid substance?

"But it is further urged, 'that we cannot conceive how matter can think.' I grant it; but to argue from thence, that God therefore cannot give to matter a faculty of thinking, is to say, God's omnipotency is limited to a narrow compass, because man's understanding is so, and brings down God's infinite power to the size of our capacities. If God can give no power to any parts of matter but what men can account for from the essence of matter in general; if all such qualities and properties must destroy the essence or change the essential properties of matter, which are to our conceptions above it, and we cannot conceive to be the natural consequence of that essence; it is plain that the essence of matter is destroyed, and its essential properties changed, in most of the sensible parts of this our system; for it is visible that all the planets have revolutions about certain remote centres, which I would have any one explain, or make conceivable, by the bare essence or natural power depending on the essence of matter in general without something added to that essence, which we cannot conceive; for, the moving of matter in a crooked line, or the attraction of matter by matter, is all that can be said in the case, either of which it is above our reach to derive from the essence of matter or body in general, though one of these two must unavoidably be allowed to be superadded in this instance to the essence of matter in general. The omnipotent Creator advised not with us in the making of the world, and his ways are not the less excellent because they are past our finding out.

"In the next place, the vegetable part of the creation is not doubted to be wholly material; and yet he that will look into it, will observe excellences and operations in this part of matter, which he will not find contained in the essence of matter in general, nor be able to conceive how they can be produced by it. And will he therefore say, that 'the essence of matter is destroyed in them,' because they have properties and operations not contained in the essential properties of matter as matter, nor explicable by the essence of matter in general?

"Let us advance one step farther, and we shall, in the animal world, meet with yet greater perfections and properties no ways explicable by the essence of matter in general. If the omnipotent Creator had not superadded to the earth, which produced the irrational animals, qualities far surpassing those of the dull dead earth out of which they were made, life, sense, and spontaneous motion, nobler qualities than were before in it, it had still remained rude, senseless matter; and if to the individuals of each species he had not superadded a power of propagation, the species had perished with those individuals; but by these essences or properties of each species, superadded to the matter which they were made of, the essences or properties of matter in general were not destroyed or changed, any more than any thing that was in the individuals before was destroyed or changed by the power of generation, superadded to them by the first benediction of the Almighty.

"In all such cases, the superinducement of greater perfections and nobler qualities destroys nothing of the essence or perfections that were there before, unless there can be showed a manifest repugnancy between them ; but all the proof offered for that is only, that ' we cannot conceive how matter, without such superadded perfections, can produce such effects ;' which is, in truth, no more than to say, ' Matter in general, or every part of matter, as matter, has them not ;' but is no reason to prove, that God, if he pleases, cannot superadd them to some parts of matter ; unless it can be proved to be a contradiction, that God should give to some parts of matter qualities and perfections which matter in general has not, though we cannot conceive how matter is invested with them, or how it operates by virtue of those new endowments. Nor is it to be wondered that we cannot, whilst we limit all its operations to those qualities it had before, and would explain them by the known properties of matter in general without any such superinduced perfections. For if this be a right rule of reasoning, to deny a thing to be, because we cannot conceive the manner how it comes to be, I shall desire them who use it to stick to this rule, and see what work it will make both in divinity, as well as philosophy, and whether they can advance any thing more in favour of scepticism.

"For, to keep within the present subject of the power of thinking and self-motion, bestowed by Omnipotent Power on some parts of matter : the objection to this is, ' I cannot conceive how matter should think.' What is the consequence ? *Ergo*, God cannot give it a power to think. Let this stand for a good reason, and then proceed in other cases by the same. You cannot conceive how matter can attract matter at any distance, much less at the distance of 1,000,000 miles ; *ergo*, God cannot give it such a power. You cannot conceive how matter should feel, or move itself, or affect an immaterial being, or be moved by it ; *ergo*, God cannot give it such powers ; which is in effect to deny gravity and the revolutions of the planets about the sun, to make brutes mere machines without sense or spontaneous motion, and to allow man neither sense nor voluntary motion.

"Let us apply this rule one degree farther. You cannot conceive how an extended solid substance should think ; therefore, God cannot make it think. Can you conceive how your own soul, or any substance, thinks ? You find, indeed, that you do think, and so do I ; but I want to be told how the action of thinking is performed. This, I confess, is beyond my conception ; and I would be glad any one who conceives it would explain it to me. God, I find, has given me this faculty ; and since I cannot but be convinced of his power in this instance, which though I every moment experiment in myself, yet I cannot conceive the manner of, what would it be less than an insolent absurdity to deny his power in other like cases, only for this reason, Because I cannot conceive the manner how ?

"To explain this matter a little farther : God has created a substance ; let it be, for example, a solid extended substance. Is God bound to give it, besides being, a power of action ? That, I think, nobody will say   He therefore may leave it in a state of inactivity and it will be never the less a substance ; for action is not necessary to the being of any substance that God does create. God has likewise created and made to exist, *de novo*, an immaterial substance, which will not lose its being of a substance, though God should bestow on it nothing more but this bare being, without giving it any activity at all. Here are now two distinct substances, the one material, the other immaterial, both in a state of perfect inactivity. Now, I ask, what power God can give to one of these substances (supposing them to retain the same distinct natures that they had as substances in their state of inactivity), which he cannot give to the other ? In that state, it is plain neither of them thinks ; for thinking being an action, it cannot be denied that God can put an end to any action of any created substance, without annihilating of the substance whereof it is an action ; and if it be so, he can also create or give existence to such a substance, without giving that substance any action at all. By the same reason it is plain, that neither of them can move itself. Now, I would ask why Omnipotency cannot give to either of these substances, which are equally in a state of perfect inactivity, the same power that it can give to the other ? Let it be, for example, that of spontaneous or self-motion, which is a power that it is supposed God can give to an unsolid substance, but denied that he can give to a solid substance.

" If it be asked why they limit the omnipotency of God, in reference to the one rather than the other of these substances ? all that can be said to it is, that they cannot conceive how the solid substance should ever be able to move itself. And as little, say I, are they able to conceive how a created unsolid substance should move itself. ' But there may be something in an immaterial substance that you do not know.' I grant it, and in a material one too. For example : gravitation of matter towards matter, and in the several proportions observable, inevitably shows that there is something in matter that we do not understand, unless we can conceive self-motion in matter, or an inexplicable and inconceivable attraction in matter, at immense and almost incomprehensible distances. It must therefore be confessed, that there is something in solid as well as unsolid substances that we do not understand. But this we know, that they may each of them have their distinct beings, without any activity superadded to them, unless you will deny that God can take from any being its power of acting, which it is probable will be thought too presumptuous for any one to do ; and I say, it is as hard to conceive self-motion in a created immaterial as in a material being, consider it how you will : and therefore this is no reason to deny Omnipotency to be able to give a power of self-motion to a material substance, if he pleases, as well as to an immaterial, since neither of them can have it from themselves, nor can we conceive how it can be in either of them.

" The same is visible in the other operation of thinking : both these substances may be made and exist without thought ; neither of them has or can have the power of thinking from itself : God may give it to either of them, according to the good pleasure of his omnipotency ; and in whichever of them it is, it is equally beyond our capacity to conceive how either of those substances thinks. But for that reason to deny that God, who had power enough to give them both a being out of nothing, can by the same omnipotency give them what other powers and perfections he pleases, has no better a foundation than to deny his power of creation, because we cannot conceive how it is performed ; and there at last this way of reasoning must terminate.

"That Omnipotency cannot make a substance to be solid and not solid at the same time, I think, with due reverence, we may say ; but that a solid substance may not have qualities, perfections, and powers which have no natural or visibly necessary connection with solidity and extension, is too much for us, who 'are but of yesterday, and know nothing,' to be positive in. If God cannot join things together by connections inconceivable to us, we must deny even the consistency and being of matter itself ; since every particle of it, having some bulk, has its parts connected by ways inconceivable to us. So that all the difficulties that are raised against the thinking of matter, from our ignorance or narrow conceptions, stand not at all in the way of the power of God, if he pleases to ordain it so ; nor proves anything against his having actually endued some particles of matter, so disposed as he thinks fit, with a faculty of thinking, till it can be shown that it contains a contradiction to suppose it.

"Though to me sensation be comprehended under thinking in general, yet in the foregoing discourse I have spoke of sense in brutes as distinct from thinking ; because your lordship, as I remember, speaks of sense in brutes. But here I take liberty to observe, that if your lordship allows brutes to have sensation, it will follow, either that God can and doth give to some parcels of matter a power of perception and thinking, or that all animals have immaterial, and consequently, according to your lordship, immortal, souls as well as men ; and to say that fleas and mites, &c., have immortal souls as well as men, will possibly be looked on as going a great way to serve an hypothesis.

"I have been pretty large in making this matter plain, that they who are so forward to bestow hard censures or names on the opinions of those who differ from them, may consider whether sometimes they are not more due to their own : and that they may be persuaded a little to temper that heat, which, supposing the truth in their current opinions, gives them, as they think, a right to lay what imputations they please on those who would fairly examine the grounds they stand upon. For, talking with a supposition and insinuations that truth and knowledge, nay, and religion too, stands and falls with their systems, is at best but an imperious way of begging the question, and assuming to themselves, under the pretence of zeal for the cause of God, a title to infallibility. It is very becoming that men's zeal for truth should go as far as their proofs, but not go for proofs themselves. He that attacks received opinions with any thing but fair arguments, may, I own, be justly suspected not to mean well, nor to be led by the love of truth ; but the same may be said of him too who so defends them. An error is not the better for being common, nor truth the worse for having lain neglected : and if it were put to the vote any where in the world, I doubt, as things are managed, whether truth would have the majority, at least whilst the authority of men, and not the examination of things, must be its measure. The imputation of scepticism and those broad insinuations, to render what I have writ suspected, so frequent as if that were the great business of all this pains you have been at about me, has made me say thus much, my lord, rather as my sense of the way to establish truth in its full force and beauty, than that I think the world will need to have any thing said to it to make it distinguish between your lordship's and my design in writing; which therefore I securely leave to the judgment of the reader and return to the argument in hand.

"What I have above said, I take to be a full answer to all that your lordship would infer from my idea of matter, of liberty, and of identity, and from the power of abstracting. You ask,* 'How can my idea of liberty agree with the idea that bodies can operate only by motion and impulse?' Answer. By the omnipotency of God, who can make all things agree that involve not a contradiction. It is true, I say,† that 'bodies operate by impulse and nothing else.' And so I thought when I writ it, and can yet conceive no other way of their operation. But I am since convinced by the judicious Mr. Newton's incomparable book, that it is too bold a presumption to limit God's power in this point by my narrow conceptions. The gravitation of matter towards matter by ways unconceivable to me, is not only a demonstration that God can, if he pleases, put into bodies powers and ways of operation, above what can be derived from our idea of body, or can be explained by what we know of matter, but also an unquestionable and every-where visible instance that he has done so. And therefore, in the next edition of my book, I shall take care to have that passage rectified.

"As to self-consciousness, your lordship asks,‡ 'What is there like self-consciousness in matter?' Nothing at all in matter as matter. But that God cannot bestow on some parcels of matter a power of thinking, and with it self-consciousness, will never be proved by ask-ing,§ 'How is it possible to apprehend that mere body should perceive that it doth perceive?' The weakness of our apprehension I grant in the case: I confess, as much as you please, that we cannot conceive how a solid, no, nor how an unsolid, created substance thinks; but this weakness of our apprehensions reaches not the power of God, whose weakness is stronger than any thing in men.

"Your argument from abstraction we have in this question,‖ 'If it be in the power of matter to think, how comes it to be so impossible for such organised bodies as the brutes have to enlarge their ideas by abstraction?' Answer. This seems to suppose, that I place thinking within the natural power of matter. If that be your meaning, my lord, I neither say nor suppose that all matter has naturally in it a faculty of thinking, but the direct contrary. But if you mean that certain parcels of matter, ordered by the Divine Power as seems fit to him, may be made capable of receiving from his omnipotency the faculty of thinking; that indeed I say, and, that being granted, the answer to your question is easy, since, if Omnipotency can give thought to any solid substance, it is not hard to conceive that God may give that faculty in an higher or lower degree as it pleases him, who knows what disposition of the subject is suited to such a particular way or degree of thinking.

"Another argument to prove that God cannot endue any parcel of matter with the faculty of thinking, is taken from those words of

* First Answer, page 73.    † Essay, book ii. chap. viii. sect. 11.
‡ First Answer, p. 74.    § Ibid.    ‖ Ibid., p. 76.

mine,* where I show by what connexion of ideas we may come to
know that God is an immaterial substance. They are these: 'The
idea of an eternal, actual, knowing Being, with the idea of immateriality,
by the intervention of the idea of matter, and of its actual division,
divisibility, and want of perception,' &c. From whence your lordship
thus argues :† 'Here the want of perception is owned to be so
essential to matter, that God is therefore concluded to be immaterial.'
Answer. Perception and knowledge in that one eternal Being, where
it has its source, it is visible, must be essentially inseparable from it ;
therefore the actual want of perception in so great part of the particular
parcels of matter, is a demonstration that the first Being, from whom
perception and knowledge is inseparable, is not matter. How far this
makes the want of perception an essential property of matter, I will
not dispute ; it suffices that it shows that perception is not an essential
property of matter ; and therefore matter cannot be that eternal original being to which perception and knowledge is essential. Matter,
I say, naturally is without perception : '*Ergo*,' says your lordship,
'want of perception is an essential property of matter, and God does
not change the essential properties of things, their nature remaining.'
From whence you infer, that God cannot bestow on any parcel of
matter (the nature of matter remaining) a faculty of thinking. If the
rules of logic since my days be not changed, I may safely deny this
consequence. For an argument that runs thus, 'God does not, *ergo*
he cannot,' I was taught when I came first to the university, would not
hold. For I never said God did ; but that 'I see no contradiction in
it, that he should, if he pleased, give to some systems of senseless
matter a faculty of thinking;'‡ and I know nobody, before Des
Cartes, that ever pretended to show that there was any contradiction
in it. So that, at worst, my not being able to see in matter any such
incapacity as makes it impossible for Omnipotency to bestow on it a
faculty of thinking, makes me opposite only to the Cartesians. For,
as far as I have seen or heard, the Fathers of the Christian church
never pretended to demonstrate that matter was incapable to receive
a power of sensation, perception, and thinking, from the hand of the
omnipotent Creator. Let us therefore, if you please, suppose the form
of your argumentation right, and that your lordship means, 'God
cannot;' and then, if your argument be good, it proves that God
could not give to Balaam's ass a power to speak to his master as he
did : for the want of rational discourse being natural to that species, it
is but for your lordship to call it an 'essential property,' and then God
cannot change the essential properties of things, their nature remaining : whereby it is proved that God cannot, with all his omnipotency,
give to an ass a power to speak as Balaam's did.

"You say,§ my lord, you 'do not set bounds to God's omnipotency ;
for he may, if he please, change a body into an immaterial substance,'
*i. e.*, take away from a substance the solidity which it had before, and
which made it matter, and then give it a faculty of thinking which it
had not before, and which makes it a spirit, the same substance remaining. For if the same substance remains not, body is not changed
into an immaterial substance, but the solid substance and all belonging

* First Letter, p. 139.   † First Answer, p. 77.
‡ Book iv. chap. iii. sect. 6.   § First Answer, p. 78.

to it is annihilated, and an immaterial substance created ; which is not a change of one thing into another, but the destroying of one, and making another *de novo*. In this change therefore of a body or material substance into an immaterial, let us observe these distinct considerations :—

"First, You say, 'God may, if he pleases, take away from a solid substance solidity, which is that which makes it a material substance or body ; and may make it an immaterial substance,' *i. e.*, a substance without solidity. But this privation of one quality gives it not another ; the bare taking away a lower or less noble quality does not give it an higher or nobler ; that must be the gift of God. For the bare privation of one and a meaner quality cannot be the position of an higher and better ; unless any one will say, that cogitation, or the power of thinking, results from the nature of substance itself ; which if it do, then wherever there is substance there must be cogitation, or a power of thinking. Here then, upon your lordship's own principles, is an immaterial substance without the faculty of thinking.

"In the next place, you will not deny but God may give to this substance, thus deprived of solidity, a faculty of thinking ; for you suppose it made capable of that by being made immaterial, whereby you allow that the same numerical substance may be sometimes wholly incogitative, or without a power of thinking, and at other times perfectly cogitative, or endued with a power of thinking.

"Farther : you will not deny but God can give it solidity, and make it material again. For I conclude it will not be denied, that God can make it again what it was before. Now I crave leave to ask your lordship, why God, having given to this substance the faculty of thinking after solidity was taken from it, cannot restore to it solidity again without taking away the faculty of thinking ? When you have resolved this, my lord, you will have proved it impossible for God's omnipotence to give to a solid substance a faculty of thinking ; but, till then, not having proved it impossible, and yet denying that God can do it, is to deny that he can do what is in itself possible ; which, as I humbly conceive, is visibly to set bounds to God's omnipotency, though you say here,* you 'do not set bounds to God's omnipotency.'

"If I should imitate your lordship's way of writing, I should not omit to bring in Epicurus here, and take notice that this was his way : *Deum verbis ponere, re tollere :* and then add, that 'I am certain you do not think he promoted the great ends of religion and morality.' For it is with such candid and kind insinuations as these, that you bring in both Hobbes† and Spinoza‡ into your discourse here about God's being able, if he please, to give to some parcels of matter, ordered as he thinks fit, a faculty of thinking ; neither of those authors having, as appears by any passages you bring out of them, said any thing to this question ; nor having, as it seems, any other business here, but by their names skilfully to give that character to my book with which you would recommend it to the world.

"I pretend not to inquire what measure of zeal, nor for what, guides your lordship's pen in such a way of writing as yours has all along been with me : only I cannot but consider what reputation it would give to the writings of the fathers of the church, if they should think truth required or religion allowed them to imitate such patterns. But, God be thanked, there be those amongst them who do not admire such ways of managing the cause of truth or religion : they being sensible, that if every one who believes or can pretend he has truth on his side is thereby authorized, without proof, to insinuate whatever may serve to prejudice men's minds against the other side, there will be great ravage made on charity and practice, without any gain to truth or knowledge ; and that the liberties frequently taken by disputants to do so, may have been the cause that the world in all ages has received so much harm and so little advantage from controversies in religion.

" These are the arguments which your lordship has brought to confute one saying in my book, by other passages in it, which therefore, being all but *argumenta ad hominem*, if they did prove what they do not, are of no other use than to gain a victory over me : a thing, methinks, so much beneath your lordship, that it does not deserve one of your pages. The question is, whether God can, if he pleases, bestow on any parcel of matter, ordered as he thinks fit, a faculty of perception and thinking. You say,* you 'look upon a mistake herein to be of dangerous consequence, as to the great ends of religion and morality.' If this be so, my lord, I think one may well wonder why your lordship has brought no arguments to establish the truth itself, which you look on to be of such dangerous consequence to be mistaken in ; but have spent so many pages only in a personal matter, in endeavouring to show that I had inconsistencies in my book, which if any such thing had been showed, the question would be still as far from being decided and the danger of mistaking about it as little prevented, as if nothing of all this had been said. If therefore your lordship's care of the great ends of religion and morality have made you think it necessary to clear this question, the world has reason to conclude there is little to be said against that proposition which is to be found in my book, concerning the possibility that some parcels of matter might be so ordered by Omnipotence as to be endued with a faculty of thinking, if God so pleased, since your lordship's concern for the promoting the great ends of religion and morality, has not enabled you to produce one argument against a proposition that you think of so dangerous consequence to them.

" And here I crave leave to observe, that, though in your title-page you promised to prove that my notion of ideas is inconsistent with itself (which if it were, it could hardly be proved to be inconsistent with any thing else), and with the articles of the Christian faith ; yet your attempts all along have been to prove me in some passages of my book inconsistent with myself, without having shown any proposition in my book inconsistent with any article of the Christian faith.

" I think your lordship has indeed made use of one argument of your own ; but it is such an one that I confess I do not see how it is apt much to promote religion, especially the Christian religion, founded on revelation. I shall set down your lordship's words, that they may be considered. You say,† that you are 'of opinion, that the great ends of religion and morality are best secured by the proofs of the immortality of the soul from its nature and properties, and which you think proves it immaterial.' Your lordship ' does not question whether

God can give immortality to a material substance;' but you say, 'it takes off very much from the evidence of immortality, if it depend wholly upon God's giving that which of its own nature it is not capable of,' &c.   So likewise you say,* 'If a man cannot be certain but that matter may think' (as I affirm), 'then what becomes of the soul's immateriality' (and consequently immortality) 'from its operations?' But for all this, say I, his assurance of faith remains on its own basis. Now you appeal to any man of sense, 'whether the finding the uncertainty of his own principles which he went upon in point of reason, doth not weaken the credibility of these fundamental articles, when they are considered purely as matters of faith ?   For, before there was a natural credibility in them on the account of reason ; but, by going on wrong grounds of certainty, all that is lost, and, instead of being certain, he is more doubtful than ever.   And if the evidence of faith falls so much short of that of reason, it must needs have less effect upon men's minds when the subserviency of reason is taken away, as it must be when the grounds of certainty by reason are vanished.   Is it at all probable, that he who finds reason deceive him in such fundamental points, should have his faith stand firm and unmovable on the account of revelation ?   For, in matters of revelation, there must be some antecedent principles supposed before we can believe any thing on the account of it.'

"More to the same purpose we have some pages farther, where, from some of my words, your lordship says,† 'you cannot but observe, that we have no certainty, upon my grounds, that self-consciousness depends upon an individual immaterial substance ; and, consequently, that a material substance may, according to my principles, have self-consciousness in it; at least, that I am not certain of the contrary.' Whereupon your lordship bids me consider, 'whether this doth not a little affect the whole article of the resurrection.'   What does all this tend to, but to make the world believe that I have lessened the credibility of the immortality of the soul and the resurrection, by saying, that though it be most highly probable that the soul is immaterial, yet upon my principles it cannot be demonstrated ; because it is not impossible to God's omnipotency, if he pleases, to bestow upon some parcels of matter, disposed as he sees fit, a faculty of thinking?

"This your accusation of my lessening the credibility of these articles of faith is founded on this, that the article of the immortality of the soul abates of its credibility, if it be allowed that its immateriality (which is the supposed proof from reason and philosophy of its immortality) cannot be demonstrated from natural reason : which argument of your lordship's bottoms, as I humbly conceive, on this, that divine revelation abates of its credibility in all those articles it proposes, proportionably as human reason fails to support the testimony of God.   And all that your lordship in those passages has said, when examined, will, I suppose, be found to import thus much, viz., Does God propose any thing to mankind to be believed ?   It is very fit and credible to be believed, if reason can demonstrate it to be true. But if human reason comes short in the case, and cannot make it out, its credibility is thereby lessened ; which is in effect to say, that the veracity of God is not a firm and sure foundation of faith to rely upon,

* Second Answer, page 28.          . † Ibid., page 35.

without the concurrent testimony of reason ; *i. e.*, with reverence be it spoken, God is not to be believed on his own word, unless what he reveals be in itself credible, and might be believed without him.

" If this be a way to promote religion, the Christian religion, in all its articles, I am not sorry that it is not a way to be found in any of my writings ; for I imagine any thing like this would (and I should think deserved to) have other titles than bare ' scepticism ' bestowed upon it, and would have raised no small outcry against any one who is not to be supposed to be in the right in all that he says, and so may securely say what he pleases. Such as I, the *profanum vulgus*, who take too much upon us, if we would examine, have nothing to do but to hearken and believe, though what be said should subvert the very foundations of the Christian faith.

" What I have above observed, is so visibly contained in your lord-ship's argument, that when I met with it in your Answer to my First Letter, it seemed so strange from a man of your lordship's character, and in a dispute in defence of the doctrine of the Trinity, that I could hardly persuade myself but it was a slip of your pen ; but when I found it in your Second Letter* made use of again, and seriously enlarged as an argument of weight to be insisted upon, I was convinced that it was a principle that you heartily embraced, how little favour-able soever it was to the articles of the Christian religion, and particularly those which you undertook to defend.

" I desire my reader to peruse the passages as they stand in your Letters themselves, and see whether what you say in them does not amount to this, that a revelation from God is more or less credible, according as it has a stronger or weaker confirmation from human reason. For,

" 1. Your lordship says, you ' do not question whether God can give immortality to a material substance ; ' but you say ' it takes off very much from the evidence of immortality, if it depends wholly upon God's giving that which of its own nature it is not capable of.'†

" To which I reply, any one's not being able to demonstrate the soul to be immaterial, takes off not very much, nor at all, from the evidence of its immortality, if God has revealed that it shall be immortal ; because the veracity of God is a demonstration of the truth of what he has revealed, and the want of another demonstration of a proposi-tion that is demonstratively true takes not off from the evidence of it. For where there is a clear demonstration, there is as much evidence as any truth can have that is not self-evident. God has revealed that the souls of men shall live for ever. ' But,' says your lordship, ' from this evidence it takes off very much, if it depends wholly upon God's giving that which, of its own nature, it is not capable of ; ' *i. e.*, the revelation and testimony of God loses much of its evidence, if this depends wholly upon the good pleasure of God, and cannot be demon-stratively made out by natural reason, that the soul is immaterial, and consequently in its own nature immortal. For that is all that here is or can be meant by these words, ' which of its own nature it is not capable of,' to make them to the purpose. For the whole of your lordship's discourse here is to prove that the soul cannot be material, because then the evidence of its being immortal would be very much

* Second Answer, pages 28, 29.          † First Answer, page 55.

lessened. Which is to say, that it is not as credible upon divine reve-lation, that a material substance should be immortal, as an immaterial; or, which is all one, that God is not equally to be believed, when he declares that a material substance shall be immortal, as when he declares that an immaterial shall be so, because the immortality of a material substance cannot be demonstrated from natural reason.

"Let us try this rule of your lordship's a little farther. God hath revealed that the bodies men shall have after the resurrection, as well as their souls, shall live to eternity. Does your lordship believe the eternal life of the one of these more than of the other, because you think you can prove it of one of them by natural reason, and of the other not? Or can any one who admits of divine revelation in the case, doubt of one of them more than the other? or think this propo-sition less credible, 'The bodies of men, after the resurrection, shall live for ever?' than this, that 'the souls of men shall, after the resur-rection, live for ever?' For that he must do, if he thinks either of them is less credible than the other. If this be so, reason is to be consulted how far God is to be believed, and the credit of divine testi-mony must receive its force from the evidence of reason; which is evidently to take away the credibility of divine revelation in all super-natural truths, wherein the evidence of reason fails. And how much such a principle as this tends to the support of the doctrine of the Trinity, or the promoting the Christian religion, I shall leave it to your lordship to consider.

"I am not so well read in Hobbes or Spinoza, as to be able to say what were their opinions in this matter. But possibly there be those who will think your lordship's authority of more use to them in the case, than those justly decried names; and be glad to find your lord-ship a patron of the oracles of reason, so little to the advantage of the oracles of divine revelation. This at least, I think, may be subjoined to the words at the bottom of the next page,* that 'those who have gone about to lessen the credibility of the articles of faith, which evidently they do who say, they are less credible because they cannot be made out demonstratively by natural reason, have not been thought to secure several of the articles of the Christian faith, especially those of the Trinity, incarnation, and resurrection of the body;' which are those upon the account of which I am brought by your lordship into this dispute.

"I shall not trouble the reader with your lordship's endeavours, in the following words, to prove that if the soul be not an immaterial substance, it can be nothing but life; your very first words visibly confuting all that you allege to that purpose. They are, 'If the soul be a material substance, it is really nothing but life;'† which is to say, that if the soul be really a substance, it is not really a substance, but 'really nothing' else but an affection of a substance; for the life, whether of a material or immaterial substance, is not the substance itself, but an affection of it.

"2. You say,‡ 'Although we think the separate state of the soul after death is sufficiently revealed in the scripture, yet it creates a great difficulty in understanding it, if the soul be nothing but life, or a material substance, which must be dissolved when life is ended. For

* First Answer, page 65.    † Ibid., page 55.    ‡ Ibid., page 57.

if the soul be a material substance, it must be made up as others are
of the cohesion of solid and separate parts, how minute and invisible
soever they be. And what is it which should keep them together
when life is gone? So that it is no easy matter to give an account
how the soul should be capable of immortality, unless it be an immaterial substance; and then we know, the solution and texture of bodies
cannot reach the soul, being of a different nature.'

"Let it be as hard a matter as it will to give an account what it is
that should keep the parts of a material soul together, after it is separated from the body; yet it will be always as easy to give an account
of it, as to 'give an account what it is which shall keep together a
material and immaterial substance.' And yet the difficulty that there
is to 'give an account of that,' I hope does not, with your lordship,
'weaken the credibility' of the inseparable union of soul and body to
eternity: and I persuade myself that 'the men of sense,' to whom your
lordship appeals in the case, do not find their belief of the 'fundamental point' much 'weakened' by that difficulty. I thought heretofore (and, by your lordship's permission, would think so still) that the
union of parts of matter one with another is as much in the hands of
God as the union of a material and immaterial substance; and that
it does not 'take off very much,' or at all 'from the evidence of
immortality,' which depends on that union, that 'it is no easy matter
to give an account what it is that should keep them together:' though
its 'depending wholly upon the gift and good pleasure of God,' where
the manner 'creates great difficulty in the understanding,' and our
reason cannot discover in the nature of things how it is, be that which,
your lordship so positively says, 'lessens the credibility of the fundamental articles of the resurrection and immortality.'

"But, my lord, to remove this objection a little, and to show of how
small force it is even with yourself, give me leave to presume, that
your lordship as firmly believes the immortality of the body after the
resurrection, as any other article of faith: if so, then it being 'no easy
matter to give an account what it is that shall keep together' the
parts of a material soul, to one that believes it is material, can no
more 'weaken the credibility' of its immortality, than the like difficulty 'weakens the credibility' of the immortality of the body. For
when your lordship shall find it 'an easy matter to give an account'
what it is, besides the good pleasure of God, 'which shall keep
together' the parts of our material bodies to eternity, or even soul
and body; I doubt not but any one who shall think the soul material,
will also find it as 'easy to give an account' what it is that shall
keep those parts of matter also together to eternity.

"Were it not that the warmth of controversy is apt to make men
so far forget as to take up those principles themselves (when they will
serve their turn) which they have highly condemned in others, I
should wonder to find your lordship to argue, that because it is a difficulty to 'understand what should keep together the minute parts of a
material soul when life is gone; and because it is not an easy matter
to give an account how the soul should be capable of immortality,
unless it be an immaterial substance;' therefore it is not so credible
as if it 'were easy to give an account' by natural reason, how it could
be. For to this it is that all this your discourse tends, as is evident

by what is already set down out of page 55 ; and will be more fully
made out by what your lordship says in other places, though there
needs no such proofs, since it would all be nothing against me in any
other sense.

"I thought your lordship had in other places asserted and insisted
on this truth, that no part of divine revelation was the less to be
believed, because the thing itself 'created great difficulty in the
understanding,' and the manner of it was hard to be explained, 'and
it was no easy matter to give an account' how it was. This, as I take
it, your lordship condemned in others as a very unreasonable principle, and such as would subvert all the articles of the Christian
religion that were mere matters of faith, as I think it will : and is it
possible, that you should make use of it here yourself, against the
article of 'life and immortality,' that Christ has brought to light
through the gospel, and neither was nor could be made out by natural
reason without revelation ? But you will say, you speak only of the
soul ; and your words are, that 'it is no easy matter to give an
account how the soul should be capable of immortality, unless it be an
immaterial substance.' I grant it ; but crave leave to say, that there
is not any one of those difficulties that are or can be raised about the
manner how a material soul can be immortal, which do not as well
reach the immortality of the body.

"But if it were not so, I am sure this principle of your lordship's
would reach other articles of faith, wherein our natural reason finds
it not so easy to give an account how those mysteries are : and which
therefore, according to your principles, must be less credible than
other articles that 'create less difficulty to the understanding.' For
your lordship says, that 'you appeal to any man of sense,* whether
to a man who thought by his principles he could demonstrate the immortality of the soul, the 'finding the uncertainty of those principles
he went upon in point of reason,' *i. e.*, the finding he could not
certainly prove it by natural reason, 'doth not weaken the credibility
of that fundamental article, when it is considered purely as a matter
of faith ?' Which, in effect, I humbly conceive, amounts to this, that
a proposition divinely revealed, that cannot be proved by natural
reason, is less credible than one that can : which seems to me to come
very little short of this, with due reverence be it spoken, that God is
less to be believed when he affirms a proposition that cannot be proved
by natural reason, than when he proposes what can be proved by it.
The direct contrary to which is my opinion, though you endeavour
to make it good, by these following words, 'If the evidence of faith
falls so much short of that of reason, it must needs have less effect
upon men's minds when the subserviency of reason is taken away ; as
it must be when the grounds of certainty by reason are vanished. Is
it at all probable that he who finds his reason deceive him in such
fundamental points, should have his faith stand firm and unmovable
on the account of revelation ?'† Than which I think there are
hardly plainer words to be found out to declare that the credibility of
God's testimony depends on the natural evidence or probability of the
things we receive from revelation, and rises and falls with it ; and
that the truths of God, or the articles of mere faith, lose so much of

their 'credibility,' as they want proof from reason : which, if true, revelation may come to have no 'credibility' at all. For if, in this present case, the credibility of this proposition, 'The souls of men shall live for ever,' revealed in scripture, be lessened by confessing it cannot be demonstratively proved from reason, though it be asserted to be most highly probable ; must not, by the same rule, its credibility dwindle away to nothing, if natural reason should not be able to make it out to be so much as probable, or should place the probability from natural principles on the other side ? For if mere want of demonstration 'lessens the credibility' of any proposition divinely revealed, must not want of probability or contrary probability from natural reason quite take away its credibility ? Here at last it must end, if in any one case the veracity of God, and the credibility of the truths we receive from him by revelation, be subjected to the verdicts of human reason, and be allowed to receive any accession or diminution from other proofs, or want of other proofs, of its certainty or probability.

"If this be your lordship's way to promote religion or defend its articles, I know not what argument the greatest enemies of it could use more effectual for the subversion of those you have undertaken to defend ; this being to resolve all revelation perfectly and purely into natural reason, to bound its credibility by that, and leave no room for faith in other things than what can be accounted for by natural reason without revelation.

"Your lordship insists much upon it,* as if I had contradicted what I had said in my Essay,† by saying, 'that upon my principles it cannot be demonstratively proved that it is an immaterial substance in us that thinks, however probable it be.' He that will be at the pains to read that chapter of mine, and consider it, will find that my business there was to show that it was no harder to conceive an immaterial than a material substance ; and that from the ideas of thought, and a power of moving of matter, which we experienced in ourselves, (ideas originally not belonging to matter as matter,) there was no more difficulty to conclude there was an immaterial substance in us, than that we had material parts. These ideas of thinking, and power of moving of matter, I in another place showed did demonstratively lead us to the certain knowledge of the existence of an immaterial thinking being, in whom we have the idea of spirit in the strictest sense ; in which sense I also applied it to the soul, in that twenty-third chapter of my Essay ; the easily conceivable possibility, nay, great probability, that the thinking substance in us is immaterial, giving me sufficient ground for it. In which sense I shall think I may safely attribute it to the thinking substance in us, till your lordship shall have better proved from my words that it is impossible it should be immaterial. For I only say that it is possible, *i. e.*, involves no contradiction, that God, the omnipotent immaterial Spirit, should, if he pleases, give to some parcels of matter, disposed as he thinks fit, a power of thinking and moving : which parcels of matter so endued with a power of thinking and motion might properly be called 'spirits,' in contradistinction to unthinking matter. In all which, I presume, there is no manner of contradiction.

"I justified my use of the word 'spirit' in that sense from the

* First Answer, pages 48—54.   † Book ii. chap. xxiii.

authorities of Cicero and Virgil, applying the Latin word *spiritus*, from whence 'spirit' is derived, to the soul as a thinking thing, without excluding materiality out of it.   To which your lordship replies, that 'Cicero, in his Tusculan Questions, supposes the soul not to be a finer sort of body, but of a different nature from the body ; that he calls the body the prison of the soul ; and says, that a wise man's business is to draw off his soul from his body.'*   And then your lordship concludes, as is usual, with a question,—'Is it possible now to think so great a man looked on the soul but as a modification of the body, which must be at an end with life ?'  Answer.  No ; it is impossible that a man of so good sense as Tully, when he uses the word *corpus* or 'body' for the gross and visible parts of a man, which he acknowledges to be mortal, should look on the soul to be a modification of that body, in a discourse wherein he was endeavouring to persuade another that it was immortal.   It is to be acknowledged that truly great men, such as he was, are not wont so manifestly to contradict themselves.   He had therefore no thought concerning the modification of the body of man in the case : he was not such a trifler as to examine whether the modification of the body of a man was immortal, when that body itself was mortal : and therefore that which he reports as Dicæarchus's opinion, he dismisses in the beginning without any more ado.  (Cap. xi.)  But Cicero's was a direct, plain, and sensible inquiry, viz., What the soul was ? to see whether from thence he could discover its immortality.   But in all that discourse in his first book of Tusculan Questions, where he lays out so much of his reading and reason, there is not one syllable showing the least thought that the soul was an immaterial substance, but many things directly to the contrary.

"Indeed, 1. He shuts out the body taken, in the sense he uses *corpus* all along,† for the sensible organical parts of a man ; and is positive that is not the soul : and 'body' in this sense, taken for the human body, he calls 'the prison of the soul ;' and says a wise man, instancing in Socrates and Cato, is glad of a fair opportunity to get out of it.   But he nowhere says any such thing of matter : he calls not matter in general the prison of the soul, nor talks a word of being separate from it.

"2. He concludes that the soul is not, like other things here below, made up of a composition of the elements.  (Cap. xxvii.)

"3. He excludes the two gross elements, earth and water, from being the soul.  (Cap. xxvi.)

"So far he is clear and positive ; but beyond this he is uncertain ; beyond this he could not get.   For in some places he speaks doubtfully, whether the soul be not air or fire.  *Anima sit animus ignisve nescio.*  (Cap. xxv.)  And therefore he agrees with Panætius, that, if it be at all elementary, it is, as he calls it, *inflammata anima*, 'inflamed air ;' and for this he gives several reasons.  (Cap. xviii. xix.)  And though he thinks it to be of a peculiar nature of its own, yet he is so far from thinking it immaterial, that he says, (cap. xix.), that, 'admitting it to be of an aërial or igneous nature, would not be inconsistent with any thing he had said.'

"That which he seems most inclined to, is, that the soul was not at all elementary, but was of the same substance with the heavens ; which Aristotle, to distinguish from the four elements and the changeable bodies here below, which he supposed made up of them, called *quinta essentia.* That this was Tully's opinion is plain from these words, *Ergo, animus qui, ut ego dico, divinus est, ut Euripides audet dicere Deus ; et quidem si Deus aut anima aut ignis est, idem est animus hominis. Nam ut illa natura cœlestis et terrâ vacat et humore, sic utriusque harum rerum humanus animus est expers. Sin autem est quinta quædam natura ab Aristotele inducta, primum hæc et deorum est et animorum. Hanc nos sententiam secuti, his ipsis verbis in Consolatione hæc expressimus.* (Cap. xxvi.) And then he goes on (cap. xxvii.), to repeat those his own words, which your lordship has quoted out of him, wherein he had affirmed, in his treatise *De Consolatione,* the soul not to have its original from the earth, or to be mixed or made of any thing earthly ; but had said, *Singularis est igitur quædam natura et vis animi sejuncta ab his usitatis notisque naturis :* whereby, he tells us, he meant nothing but Aristotle's *quinta essentia;* which being unmixed, being that of which the gods and souls consisted, he calls it *divinum cœleste,* and concludes it eternal, it being, as he speaks, *sejuncta ab omni mortali concretione.* From which it is clear, that, in all his inquiry about the substance of the soul, his thoughts went not beyond the four elements, or Aristotle's *quinta essentia,* to look for it. In all which there is nothing of immateriality, but quite the contrary.

"He was willing to believe (as good and wise men have always been) that the soul was immortal ; but for that, it is plain he never thought of its immateriality, but as the eastern people do, who believe the soul to be immortal, but have nevertheless no thought, no conception of its immateriality. It is remarkable what a very considerable and judicious author says in the case. 'No opinion,' says he, 'has been so universally received as that of the immortality of the soul ; but its immateriality is a truth, the knowledge whereof has not spread so far. And indeed it is extremely difficult to let into the mind of a Siamite the idea of a pure spirit. This the missionaries, who have been longest among them, are positive in. All the Pagans of the east do truly believe, that there remains something of a man after his death, which subsists independently and separately from his body. But they give extension and figure to that which remains, and attribute to it all the same members, all the same substances, both solid and liquid, which our bodies are composed of. They only suppose that the souls are of a matter subtile enough to escape being seen or handled. Such were the shades and the manes of the Greeks and the Romans. And it is by these figures of the souls, answerable to those of the bodies, that Virgil supposed Æneas knew Palinurus, Dido, and Anchises, in the other world.'*

"This gentleman was not a man that travelled into those parts for his pleasure, and to have the opportunity to tell strange stories, collected by chance, when he returned : but one chosen on purpose (and he seems well chosen for the purpose) to inquire into the singularities of Siam. And he has so well acquitted himself of the commission, which his Epistle Dedicatory tells us he had, to inform himself exactly of what was most remarkable there, that had we but an account of

* LOUBERE, *Du Royaume de Siam,* tom. i. cap. xix. sect. 4.

other countries of the east as he has given us of this kingdom which he was an envoy to, we should be much better acquainted than we are with the manners, notions, and religions, of that part of the world, inhabited by civilized nations, who want neither good sense nor acuteness of reason, though not cast into the mould of the logic and philosophy of our schools.

"But, to return to Cicero: It is plain, that, in his inquiries about the soul, his thoughts went not at all beyond matter. This the expressions that drop from him in several places of this book evidently show. For example: 'That the souls of excellent men and women ascended into heaven; of others, that they remained here on earth.' (Cap. xii.) 'That the soul is hot and warms the body: that at its leaving the body it penetrates and divides and breaks through our thick, cloudy, moist air: that it stops in the region of fire, and ascends no farther, the equality of warmth and weight making that its proper place, where it is nourished and sustained with the same things wherewith the stars are nourished and sustained: and that by the convenience of its neighbourhood it shall there have a clearer view and fuller knowledge of the heavenly bodies.' (Cap. xix.) 'That the soul also from this height shall have a pleasant and fairer prospect of the globe of the earth, the disposition of whose parts will then lie before it in one view.' (Cap. xx.) 'That it is hard to determine what confirmation, size, and place, the soul has in the body: that it is too subtile to be seen: that it is in the human body as in a house or a vessel, or a receptacle.' (Cap. xxii.) All which are expressions that sufficiently evidence, that he who used them had not in his mind separated materiality from the idea of the soul.

"It may perhaps be replied, that a great part of this which we find in cap. xix. is said upon the principles of those who would have the soul to be *anima inflammata*, 'inflamed air.' I grant it. But it is also to be observed, that in this nineteenth and the two following chapters, he does not only not deny, but even admits, that so material a thing as inflamed air may think.

"The truth of the case, in short, is this: Cicero was willing to believe the soul immortal; but when he sought in the nature of the soul itself something to establish this his belief into a certainty of it, he found himself at a loss. He confessed he knew not what the soul was; but the not knowing what it was, he argues, (cap. ii.) was no reason to conclude it was not. And thereupon he proceeds to the repetition of what he had said in his sixth book *De Repub.* concerning the soul. The argument which, borrowed from Plato, he there makes use of, if it have any force in it, not only proves the soul to be immortal, but more than, I think, your lordship will allow to be true: for it proves it to be eternal, and without beginning as without end, *Neque nata certe est, et æterna est,* says he.

"Indeed, from the faculties of the soul he concludes right, 'that it is of divine original:' but as to the substance of the soul, he, at the end of this discourse concerning its faculties, (cap. xxv.) as well as at the beginning of it, (cap. xxii.) is not ashamed to own his ignorance of what it is: *Anima sit animus, ignisve, nescio; nec me pudet, ut istos, fateri nescire quod nesciam. Illud, si ulla alia de re obscurâ affirmare possum, sive anima sive ignis sit animus, eum jurarem esse divinum.* (Cap xxv.) So that all the certainty he could attain to about the soul, was, that he was confident there was something divine in it, *i. e.*, there were faculties in the soul that could not result from the nature of matter, but must have their original from a divine power ; but yet those quali- ties, as divine as they were, he acknowledged might be placed in breath or fire, which I think your lordship will not deny to be material substances. So that all those divine qualities, which he so much and justly extols in the soul, led him not, as appears, so much as to any the least thought of immateriality. This is demonstration, that he built them not upon an exclusion of materiality out of the soul ; for he avowedly professes he does not know but breath or fire might be this thinking thing in us : and in all his considerations about the sub- stance of the soul itself, he stuck in air or fire, or Aristotle's *quinta essentia ;* for beyond those it is evident he went not.

" But with all his proofs out of Plato, to whose authority he defers so much, with all the arguments his vast reading and great parts could furnish him with for the immortality of the soul, he was so little satisfied, so far from being certain, so far from any thought that he had or could prove it, that he over and over again professes his ignorance and doubt of it. In the beginning he enumerates the several opinions of the philosophers, which he had well studied, about it : and then full of uncertainty says, *Harum sententiarum quæ vera sit, Deus aliquis viderit ; quæ veri simillima, magna quæstio.* (Cap. xi.) And towards the latter end, having gone them all over again, and one after another examined them, he professes himself still at a loss, not knowing on which to pitch, nor what to determine. *Mentis acies,* says he, *seipsam intuens nonnunquam hebescit, ob eamque causam contem- plandi diligentiam omittimus. Itaque dubitans, circumspectans, hæsitans, multa adversa revertens, tanquam in rate in mari immenso, nostra vehitur oratio.* (Cap. xxx.) And, to conclude this argument : When the person he introduces as discoursing with him, tells him he is resolved to keep firm to the belief of immortality, Tully answers, *Laudo id quidem, etsi nihil animis oportet confidere ; movemur enim sæpe aliquo acute concluso, labamus, mutamusque sententiam clarioribus etiam in rebus ; in his est enim aliqua obscuritas.* (Cap. lxxxii.)

" So unmovable is that truth delivered by the Spirit of truth, that though the light of nature gave some obscure glimmering, some uncertain hopes of a future state, yet human reason could attain to no clearness, no certainty about it, but that it was Jesus Christ alone who had ' brought life and immortality to light through the gospel.' (2 Tim. i. 10.) Though we are now told, that to own the inability of natural reason to bring 'immortality to light,' or, which passes for the same, to own principles upon which the immateriality of the soul (and, as it is urged, consequently its immortality) cannot be demonstratively proved, does lessen the belief of this article of revelation, which Jesus Christ alone has brought to light, and which consequently the scrip- ture assures us is established and made certain only by revelation. This would not perhaps have seemed strange from those who are justly complained of for slighting the revelation of the gospel, and therefore would not be much regarded if they should contradict so plain a text of scripture in favour of their all-sufficient reason : but what use the promoters of scepticism and infidelity, in an age so much

suspected by your lordship, may make of what comes from one of
your great authority and learning, may deserve your consideration.

" And thus, my lord, I hope I have satisfied you concerning Cicero's
opinion about the soul in his first book of Tusculan Questions ; which,
though I easily believe, as your lordship says, ' you are no stranger to,
yet I humbly conceive you have not shown (and upon a careful
perusal of that treatise again, I think I may boldly say, you cannot
show) one word in it that expresses any thing like a notion in Tully
of the soul's immateriality, or its being an immaterial substance.

"From what you bring out of Virgil, your lordship concludes, ' that
he no more than Cicero does me any kindness in this matter, being
both assertors of the soul's immortality.'* My lord, were not the
question of the soul's immateriality, according to custom, changed
here into that of its immortality, which I am no less an assertor of
than either of them, Cicero and Virgil do me all the kindness I
desired of them in this matter ; and that was to show that they attributed the word *spiritus* to the soul of man, without any thought of its
immateriality ; and this the verses you yourself bring out of Virgil,—

> *Et cum frigida mors animæ seduxerit artus,*
> *Omnibus umbra locis adero, dabis improbe, pœnas,†*

confirm, as well as those I quoted out of his sixth book ; and, for this
Monsieur de la Loubere shall be my witness in the words above set
down out of him ; where he shows, that there be those amongst the
Heathens of our days, as well as Virgil and others amongst the ancient
Greeks and Romans, who thought the souls or ghosts of men departed
did not die with the body, without thinking them to be perfectly immaterial ; the latter being much more incomprehensible to them than
the former.

" Your lordship's answer‡ concerning what is said, Eccles. xiii.,
turns wholly upon Solomon's taking the soul to be immortal, which
was not what I questioned : all that I quoted that place for, was to
show, that ' spirit ' in English might properly be applied to the soul,
without any notion of its immateriality, as רוח was by Solomon ;
which, whether he thought the souls of men to be immaterial, does
little appear in that passage where he speaks of the souls of men and
beasts together, as he does.  But, farther, what I contended for is
evident from that place, in that the word 'spirit' is there applied, by
our translators, to the souls of beasts, which your lordship, I think,
does not rank amongst the immaterial, and consequently immortal,
spirits, though they have sense and spontaneous motion.

" But you say, ' If the soul be not of itself a free thinking substance,
you do not see what foundation there is in nature for a day of judgment.'§ Answer.  Though the heathen world did not of old, nor do
to this day, ' see a foundation in nature for a day of judgment ;' yet
in revelation, if that will satisfy your lordship, every one may ' see a
foundation for a day of judgment, because God has positively declared
it ;' though God has not by that revelation taught us what the substance of the soul is ; nor has anywhere said 'that the soul of itself is
a free agent.'  Whatsoever any created substance is, it is not of itself,

but is by the good pleasure of its Creator : whatever degrees of perfection it has, it has from the bountiful hand of its Maker. For, it is true in a natural as well as a spiritual sense what St. Paul says, 'Not that we are sufficient of ourselves to think any thing as of ourselves, but our sufficiency is of God.' (2 Cor. iii. 5.)

"But your lordship, as I guess by your following words, would argue that a material substance cannot be a free agent ; whereby I suppose you only mean, that you cannot see or conceive how a solid substance should begin, stop, or change its own motion. To which give me leave to answer : That when you can make it conceivable how any created, finite, dependent substance can move itself, or alter or stop its own motion, which it must to be a free agent, I suppose you will find it no harder for God to bestow this power on a solid than an unsolid created substance. Tully, in the place above quoted,* could not conceive this power to be in any thing but what was from eternity : *Cum pateat igitur æternum id esse quod seipsum moveat, quis est qui hanc naturam animis esse tributam neget ?* But though you cannot see how any created substance, solid or not solid, can be a free agent ; (pardon me, my lord, if I put in both, until your lordship please to explain it of either, and show the manner how either of them can, of itself, move itself or any thing else ;) yet I do not think you will so far deny men to be free agents, from the difficulty there is to see how they are free agents, as to doubt whether there be foundation enough for a day of judgment.

"It is not for me to judge how far your lordship's speculations reach : but finding in myself nothing to be truer than what the wise Solomon tells me, 'As thou knowest not what is the way of the spirit, nor how the bones do grow in the womb of her that is with child ; even so thou knowest not the works of God who maketh all things,' (Eccles. xi. 5 ;) I gratefully receive and rejoice in the light of revelation, which sets me at rest in many things, the manner whereof my poor reason can by no means make out to me. Omnipotency, I know, can do any thing that contains in it no contradiction ; so that I readily believe whatever God has declared, though my reason find difficulties in it which it cannot master. As in the present case, God having revealed that there shall be a day of judgment, I think *that* foundation enough to conclude men are free enough to be made answerable for their actions, and to receive according to what they have done ; though how man is a free agent, surpass my explication or comprehension.

"In answer to the place I brought out of St. Luke, (chap. xxiv. 39,) your lordship asks, 'Whether from these words of our Saviour it follows, that a spirit is only an appearance ?' † I answer : No, nor do I know who drew such an inference from them : but it follows, that in apparitions there is something that appears, and that which appears is not wholly immaterial ; and yet this was properly called πνεῦμα, and was often looked upon by those who called it πνεῦμα, in Greek, and now call it 'spirit' in English, to be the ghost or soul of one departed : which I humbly conceive justifies my use of the word 'spirit' for a thinking voluntary agent, whether material or immaterial.

"Your lordship says,‡ 'That I grant that it cannot upon these principles be demonstrated, that the spiritual substance in us is imma-terial:' from whence you conclude, 'that then my grounds of certainty from ideas are plainly given up.' This being a way of arguing that you often make use of, I have often had occasion to consider it, and cannot, after all, see the force of this argument. I acknowledge that this or that proposition cannot upon my principles be demonstrated; *ergo*, I grant this proposition to be false, 'That certainty consists in the perception of the agreement or disagreement of ideas.' For that is my ground of certainty; and till that be given up, my grounds of certainty are not given up."

## CHAPTER IV.

### OF THE REALITY OF HUMAN KNOWLEDGE.

1. *Objection. Knowledge placed in ideas may be all bare vision.* —I doubt not but my reader by this time may be apt to think that I have been all this while only building a castle in the air; and be ready to say to me, "To what purpose all this stir? 'Knowledge,' say you, 'is only the perception of the agreement or disagreement of our own ideas;' but who knows what those ideas may be? Is there any thing so extravagant as the imagi-nations of men's brains? Where is the head that has no chimeras in it? Or if there be a sober and a wise man, what difference will there be, by your rules, between his knowledge, and that of the most extravagant fancy in the world? They both have their ideas, and perceive their agreement and disagreement one with another. If there be any difference between them, the advantage will be on the warm-headed man's side, as having the more ideas, and the more lively. And so, by your rules, he will be the more knowing. If it be true, that all knowledge lies only in the perception of the agreement or disagreement of our own ideas, the visions of an enthusiast, and the reasonings of a sober man, will be equally certain. It is no matter how things are: so a man observe but the agreement of his own imaginations, and talk conformably, it is all truth, all certainty. Such castles in the air will be as strongholds of truth as the demonstrations of Euclid. That an harpy is not a centaur, is by this way as certain knowledge, and as much a truth, as that a square is not a circle.

"But of what use is all this fine knowledge of men's own imaginations to a man that inquires after the reality of things? It matters not what men's fancies are, it is the knowledge of things that is only to be prized: it is this alone gives a value to our reasonings, and preference to one man's knowledge over another's, that it is of things as they really are, and not of dreams and fancies."

2. *Answer. Not so where ideas agree with things.*—To which I

answer, That if our knowledge of our ideas terminate in them, and reach no farther, where there is something farther intended, our most serious thoughts will be of little more use than the reveries of a crazy brain; and the truths built thereon of no more weight than the discourses of a man who sees things clearly in a dream, and with great assurance utters them. But I hope before I have done to make it evident that this way of certainty, by the knowledge of our own ideas, goes a little farther than bare imagination; and I believe it will appear, that all the certainty of general truths a man has lies in nothing else.

3. It is evident the mind knows not things immediately, but only by the intervention of the ideas it has of them. Our knowledge therefore is real only so far as there is a conformity between our ideas and the reality of things. But what shall be here the criterion? How shall the mind, when it perceives nothing but its own ideas, know that they agree with things themselves? This, though it seems not to want difficulty, yet I think there be two sorts of ideas that we may be assured agree with things.

4. *As, First, all simple ideas do.*—First, The first are simple ideas, which since the mind, as has been showed, can by no means make to itself, must necessarily be the product of things operating on the mind in a natural way, and producing therein those perceptions which by the wisdom and will of our Maker they are ordained and adapted to. From whence it follows, that simple ideas are not fictions of our fancies, but the natural and regular productions of things without us really operating upon us; and so carry with them all the conformity which is intended, or which our state requires; for they represent to us things under those appearances which they are fitted to produce in us, whereby we are enabled to distinguish the sorts of particular substances, to discern the states they are in, and so to take them for our necessities, and apply them to our uses. Thus the idea of whiteness or bitterness, as it is in the mind, exactly answering that power which is in any body to produce it there, has all the real conformity it can or ought to have with things without us. And this conformity between our simple ideas and the existence of things is sufficient for real knowledge.

5. *Secondly, All complex ideas except of substances.*—Secondly, All our complex ideas except those of substances being archetypes of the mind's own making, not intended to be the copies of any thing, nor referred to the existence of any thing, as to their originals, cannot want any conformity necessary to real knowledge. For that which is not designed to represent any thing but itself, can never be capable of a wrong representation, nor mislead us from the true apprehension of any thing by its dislikeness to it; and such, excepting those of substances, are all

our complex ideas: which, as I have showed in another place, are combinations of ideas which the mind by its free choice puts together without considering any connexion they have in nature. And hence it is, that in all these sorts the ideas themselves are considered as the archetypes, and things no otherwise regarded but as they are conformable to them. So that we cannot but be infallibly certain, that all the knowledge we attain concerning these ideas is real, and reaches things themselves; because in all our thoughts, reasonings, and discourses of this kind, we intend things no farther than as they are conformable to our ideas. So that in these we cannot miss of a certain and undoubted reality.

6. *Hence the reality of mathematical knowledge.*—I doubt not but it will be easily granted that the knowledge we have of mathematical truths, is not only certain but real knowledge; and not the bare empty vision of vain, insignificant chimeras of the brain: and yet, if we will consider, we shall find that it is only of our own ideas. The mathematician considers the truth and properties belonging to a rectangle or circle, only as they are in idea in his own mind. For it is possible he never found either of them existing mathematically, *i. e.*, precisely true, in his life. But yet the knowledge he has of any truths or properties belonging to a circle, or any other mathematical figure, are never the less true and certain even of real things existing: because real things are no farther concerned, nor intended to be meant by any such propositions, than as things really agree to those archetypes in his mind. Is it true of the idea of a triangle, that its three angles are equal to two right ones? It is true also of a triangle wherever it really exists. Whatever other figure exists that is not exactly answerable to that idea of a triangle in his mind, is not at all concerned in that proposition. And therefore he is certain all his knowledge concerning such ideas is real knowledge: because, intending things no farther than they agree with those his ideas, he is sure what he knows concerning those figures when they have barely an ideal existence in his mind, will hold true of them also when they have a real existence in matter; his consideration being barely of those figures, which are the same wherever or however they exist.

7. *And of moral.*—And hence it follows that moral knowledge is as capable of real certainty as mathematics. For, certainty being but the perception of the agreement or disagreement of our ideas, and demonstration nothing but the perception of such agreement by the intervention of other ideas or mediums, our moral ideas as well as mathematical being archetypes themselves, and so adequate and complete ideas, all the agreement or disagreement which we shall find in them will produce real knowledge, as well as in mathematical figures.

**8.** *Existence not required to make it real.*—For the attaining of knowledge and certainty, it is requisite that we have determined ideas: and to make our knowledge real, it is requisite that the ideas answer their archetypes. Nor let it be wondered that I place the certainty of our knowledge in the consideration of our ideas with so little care and regard (as it may seem) to the real existence of things: since most of those discourses which take up the thoughts and engage the disputes of those who pretend to make it their business to inquire after truth and certainty, will, I presume, upon examination, be found to be general propositions and notions in which existence is not at all concerned. All the discourses of the mathematicians about the squaring of a circle, conic sections, or any other part of mathematics, concern not the existence of any of those figures: but their demonstrations, which depend on their ideas, are the same, whether there be any square or circle existing in the world, or no. In the same manner, the truth and certainty of moral discourses abstracts from the lives of men, and the existence of those virtues in the world whereof they treat: nor are Tully's Offices less true because there is nobody in the world that exactly practises his rules, and lives up to that pattern of a virtuous man which he has given us, and which existed nowhere when he writ but in idea. If it be true in speculation, *i. e.*, in idea, that murder deserves death, it will also be true in reality of any action that exists conformable to that idea of murder. As for other actions, the truth of that proposition concerns them not. And thus it is of all other species of things which have no other essences but those ideas which are in the minds of men.

**9.** *Nor will it be less true or certain because moral ideas are of our own making and naming.*—But it will here be said, that "if moral knowledge be placed in the contemplation of our own moral ideas, and those, as other modes, be of our own making, what strange notions will there be of justice and temperance! What confusion of virtues and vices, if every one may make what ideas of them he pleases!" No confusion nor disorder in the things themselves, nor the reasonings about them; no more than (in mathematics) there would be a disturbance in the demonstration, or a change in the properties of figures and their relations one to another, if a man should make a triangle with four corners, or a *trapezium* with four right angles: that is, in plain English, change the names of the figures, and call that by one name which mathematicians called ordinarily by another. For, let a man make to himself the idea of a figure with three angles, whereof one is a right one, and call it, if he please, *equilaterum* or *trapezium*, or anything else, the properties of and demonstrations about that idea will be the same as if he called it a "rectangular triangle." I confess, the change of the name by the impropriety of speech will at first disturb him who knows not what idea it stands for: but as soon as the figure is drawn, the consequences and demonstration are plain and clear. Just the same is it in moral knowledge; let a man have the idea of taking from others, without their consent, what their honest industry has possessed them of, and call this "justice," if he please. He that takes the name here without the idea put to it, will be mistaken by joining another idea of his own to that name: but strip the idea of that name, or take it such as it is in the speaker's mind, and the same things will agree to it as if you called it "injustice." Indeed, wrong names in moral discourses breed usually more disorder, because they are not so easily rectified as in mathematics, where the figure once drawn and seen makes the name useless and of no force. For what need of a sign when the thing signified is present and in view? But in moral names that cannot be so easily and shortly done, because of the many decompositions that go to the making up the complex ideas of those modes. But yet, for all this, miscalling of any of those ideas contrary to the usual significa-tion of the words of that language, hinders not but that we may have certain and demonstrative knowledge of their several agreements and disagreements, if we will carefully, as in mathe-matics, keep to the same precise ideas, and trace them in their several relations one to another without being led away by their names. If we but separate the idea under consideration from the sign that stands for it, our knowledge goes equally on in the discovery of real truth and certainty, whatever sounds we make use of.

10. *Misnaming disturbs not the certainty of the knowledge.*—One thing more we are to take notice of, that where God, or any other law-maker, hath defined any moral names, there they have made the essence of that species to which that name belongs; and there it is not safe to apply or use them otherwise: but in other cases it is bare impropriety of speech to apply them con-trary to the common usage of the country. But yet even this too disturbs not the certainty of that knowledge, which is still to be had by a due contemplation and comparing of those even nick-named ideas.

11. *Ideas of substances have their archetypes without us.*—Thirdly, There is another sort of complex ideas, which being referred to archetypes without us may differ from them, and so our knowledge about them may come short of being real. Such are our ideas of substances, which consisting of a collection of simple ideas, supposed taken from the works of nature, may yet vary from them, by having more or different ideas united in them that are to be found united in the things themselves: from whence it comes to pass, that they may and often do fail of being exactly conformable to things themselves.

12. *So far as they agree with those, so far our knowledge con-*

*cerning them is real.*—I say, then, that to have ideas of substances which, by being conformable to things, may afford us real knowledge, it is not enough, as in modes, to put together such ideas as have no inconsistence, though they did never before so exist; *v. g.*, the ideas of sacrilege or perjury, &c., were as real and true ideas before as after the existence of any such fact. But our ideas of substances, being supposed copies, and referred to archetypes without us, must still be taken from something that does or has existed; they must not consist of ideas put together at the pleasure of our thoughts without any real pattern they were taken from, though we can perceive no inconsistence in such a combination. The reason whereof is, because we, knowing not what real constitution it is of substances whereon our simple ideas depend, and which really is the cause of the strict union of some of them one with another, and the exclusion of others; there are very few of them that we can be sure are or are not inconsistent in nature, any farther than experience and sensible observation reach. Herein therefore is founded the reality of our knowledge concerning substances, that all our complex ideas of them must be such, and such only, as are made up of such simple ones as have been discovered to co-exist in nature. And our ideas, being thus true, though not perhaps very exact copies, are yet the subjects of real (as far as we have any) knowledge of them : which, as has been already showed, will not be found to reach very far; but so far as it does, it will still be real knowledge. Whatever ideas we have, the agreement we find they have with others will still be knowledge. If those ideas be abstract, it will be general knowledge. But to make it real concerning substances, the ideas must be taken from the real existence of things. Whatever simple ideas have been found to co-exist in any substance, these we may with confidence join together again, and so make abstract ideas of substances. For whatever have once had an union in nature, may be united again.

13. *In our inquiries about substances we must consider ideas, and not confine our thoughts to names or species supposed set out by names.*—This if we rightly consider, and confine not our thoughts and abstract ideas to names, as if there were or could be no other sorts of things than what known names had already determined, and, as it were, set out, we should think of things with greater freedom and less confusion than perhaps we do. It would possibly be thought a bold paradox, if not a very dangerous falsehood, if I should say, that some changelings who have lived forty years together without any appearance of reason, are something between a man and a beast : which prejudice is founded upon nothing else but a false supposition, that these two names, "man" and "beast," stand for distinct species so set out by real essences, that there can come no other species between them;

whereas if we will abstract from those names, and the supposition of such specific essences made by nature, wherein all things of the same denominations did exactly and equally partake; if we would not fancy that there were a certain number of these essences wherein all things, as in moulds, were cast and formed; we should find that the idea of the shape, motion, and life of a man without reason is as much a distinct idea, and makes as much a distinct sort of things, from man and beast, as the idea of the shape of an ass with reason would be different from either that of man or beast, and be a species of an animal between or distinct from both.

14. *Objection against a changeling being something between a man and a beast, answered.*—Here every body will be ready to ask, "If changelings may be supposed something between man and beast, pray what are they?" I answer, "Changelings," which is as good a word to signify something different from the signification of "man" or "beast," as the names "man" and "beast" are to have significations different one from the other. This, well considered, would resolve this matter, and show my meaning without any more ado. But I am not so unacquainted with the zeal of some men, which enables them to spin consequences, and to see religion threatened whenever any one ventures to quit their forms of speaking, as not to foresee what names such a proposition as this is like to be charged with: and without doubt it will be asked, "If changelings are something between man and beast, what will become of them in the other world?" To which I answer, First, It concerns me not to know or inquire. To their own Master they stand or fall. It will make their state neither better nor worse, whether we determine any thing of it or no. They are in the hands of a faithful Creator and a bountiful Father, who disposes not of his creatures according to our narrow thoughts or opinions, nor distinguishes them according to names and species of our contrivance. And we that know so little of this present world we are in, may I think, content ourselves without being peremptory in defining the different states which creatures shall come into when they go off this stage. It may suffice us that He hath made known to all those who are capable of instruction, discourse, and reasoning, that they shall come to an account, and receive according to what they have done in this body.

15. But, Secondly, I answer, The force of these men's question (viz., "Will you deprive changelings of a future state?") is founded on one of two suppositions, which are both false. The first is, that all things that have the outward shape and appearance of a man must necessarily be designed to an immortal future being after this life. Or, secondly, that whatever is of human birth must be so. Take away these imaginations, and such questions will be groundless and ridiculous. I desire, then,

those who think there is no more but an accidental difference between themselves and changelings, the essence in both being exactly the same, to consider whether they can imagine immortality annexed to any outward shape of the body; the very proposing it is, I suppose, enough to make them disown it. No one yet that ever I heard of, how much soever immersed in matter, allowed that excellency to any figure of the gross sensible outward parts, as to affirm eternal life due to it, or a necessary consequence of it; or that any mass of matter should, after its dissolution here, be again restored hereafter to an everlasting state of sense, perception, and knowledge, only because it was moulded into this or that figure, and had such a particular frame of its visible parts. Such an opinion as this, placing immortality in a certain superficial figure, turns out of doors all consideration of soul or spirit; upon whose account alone some corporeal beings have hitherto been concluded immortal, and others, not. This is to attribute more to the outside than inside of things; to place the excellency of a man more in the external shape of his body than internal perfections of his soul: which is but little better than to annex the great and inestimable advantage of immortality and life everlasting, which he has above other material beings, to annex it, I say, to the cut of his beard, or the fashion of his coat. For, this or that outward make of our bodies no more carries with it the hopes of an eternal duration, than the fashion of a man's suit gives him reasonable grounds to imagine it will never wear out, or that it will make him immortal. It will perhaps be said, that nobody thinks that the shape makes any thing immortal, but it is the shape is the sign of a rational soul within, which is immortal. I wonder who made it the sign of any such thing: for barely saying it will not make it so. It would require some proofs to persuade one of it. No figure that I know speaks any such language. For it may as rationally be concluded, that the dead body of a man, wherein there is to be found no more appearance or action of life than there is in a statue, has yet nevertheless a living soul in it, because of its shape; as that there is a rational soul in a changeling, because he has the outside of a rational creature, when his actions carry far less marks of reason with them in the whole course of his life than what are to be found in many a beast.

16. *Monsters.*—"But it is the issue of rational parents, and must therefore be concluded to have a rational soul." I know not by what logic you must so conclude. I am sure this is a conclusion that men no where allow of. For, if they did, they would not make bold, as every where they do, to destroy ill-formed and mis-shaped productions. "Ay, but these are monsters." Let them be so; what will your drivelling, unintelligent, intractable changeling be? Shall a defect in the body make a monster; a defect in the mind (the far more noble and,

in the common phrase, the far more essential part) not? Shall the want of a nose or a neck make a monster, and put such issue out of the rank of men; the want of reason and understanding not? This is to bring all back again to what was exploded just now: this is to place all in the shape, and to take the measure of a man only by his outside. To show that, according to the ordinary way of reasoning in this matter, people do lay the whole stress on the figure, and resolve the whole essence of the species of man (as they make it) into the outward shape, how unreasonable soever it be, and how much soever they disown it, we need but trace their thoughts and practice a little farther, and then it will plainly appear. The well-shaped changeling is a man, has a rational soul, though it appear not: "This is past doubt," say you. Make the ears a little longer and more pointed, and the nose a little flatter, than ordinary, and then you begin to boggle: make the face yet narrower, flatter, and longer, and then you are at a stand: add still more and more of the likeness of a brute to it, and let the head be perfectly that of some other animal, then presently it is a monster; and it is demonstration with you that it hath no rational soul, and must be destroyed. Where now, I ask, will be the just measure of the utmost bounds of that shape that carries with it a rational soul? For, since there have been human fœtuses produced, half beast and half man; and others three parts one, and one part the other; and so it is possible they may be in all the variety of approaches to the one or the other shape, and may have several degrees of mixture of the likeness of a man or a brute; I would gladly know what are those precise lineaments which, according to this hypothesis, are or are not capable of a rational soul to be joined to them? What sort of outside is the certain sign that there is or is not such an inhabitant within? For, till that be done, we talk at random of man; and shall always, I fear, do so as long as we give ourselves up to certain sounds, and the imaginations of settled and fixed species in nature, we know not what. But, after all, I desire it may be considered that those who think they have answered the difficulty by telling us that a mis-shaped *fœtus* is a monster, run into the same fault they are arguing against, by constituting a species between man and beast. For what else, I pray, is their monster in the case (if the word "monster" signifies any thing at all), but something neither man nor beast, but partaking somewhat of either? And just so is the changeling before mentioned. So necessary is it to quit the common notion of species and essences, if we will truly look into the nature of things, and examine them by what our faculties can discover in them as they exist, and not by groundless fancies that have been taken up about them.

17. *Words and species.*—I have mentioned this here, because I think we cannot be too cautious that words and species, in the

ordinary notions which we have been used to of them, impose not on us. For, I am apt to think, therein lies one great obstacle to our clear and distinct knowledge, especially in reference to substances; and from thence has rose a great part of the difficulties about truth and certainty. Would we accustom ourselves to separate our contemplations and reasonings from words, we might, in a great measure, remedy this inconvenience within our own thoughts: but yet it would still disturb us in our discourse with others, as long as we retain the opinion, that species and their essences were any thing else but our abstract ideas, (such as they are,) with names annexed to them to be the signs of them.

18. *Recapitulation.*—Wherever we perceive the agreement or disagreement of any of our ideas, there is certain knowledge: and wherever we are sure those ideas agree with the reality of things, there is certain real knowledge. Of which agreement of our ideas with the reality of things having here given the marks, I think I have shown wherein it is that certainty, real certainty, consists. Which, whatever it was to others, was, I confess, to me heretofore one of those *desiderata* which I found great want of.

---

## CHAPTER V.

### OF TRUTH IN GENERAL.

1. *What truth is.*—" What is truth?" was an inquiry many ages since; and it being that which all mankind either do or pretend to search after, it cannot but be worth our while carefully to examine wherein it consists; and so acquaint ourselves with the nature of it, as to observe how the mind distinguishes it from falsehood.

2. *A right joining or separating of signs; i.e., ideas or words.*— Truth then seems to me, in the proper import of the word, to signify nothing but the joining or separating of signs, as the things signified by them do agree or disagree one with another. The joining or separating of signs here meant, is what by another name we call "proposition." So that truth properly belongs only to propositions: whereof there are two sorts, viz., mental and verbal; as there are two sorts of signs commonly made use of, viz., ideas and words.

3. *Which make mental or verbal propositions.*—To form a clear notion of truth, it is very necessary to consider truth of thought, and truth of words, distinctly one from another: but yet it is very difficult to treat of them asunder; because it is unavoidable, in treating of mental propositions, to make use of words; and then the instances given of mental propositions cease imme-

diately to be barely mental, and become verbal. For, a mental proposition being nothing but a bare consideration of the ideas as they are in our minds stripped of names, they lose the nature of purely mental propositions as soon as. they are put into words.

4. *Mental propositions are very hard to be treated of.*—And that which makes it yet harder to treat of mental and verbal propositions separately, is, that most men, if not all, in their thinking and reasonings within themselves, make use of words instead of ideas, at least when the subject of their meditation contains in it complex ideas. Which is a great evidence of the imperfection and uncertainty of our ideas of that kind, and may, if attentively made use of, serve for a mark to show us what are those things we have clear and perfect established ideas of, and what not. For, if we will curiously observe the way our mind takes in thinking and reasoning, we shall find, I suppose, that when we make any propositions within our own thoughts about white or black, sweet or bitter, a triangle or a circle, we can and often do frame in our minds the ideas themselves without reflecting on the names. But when we would consider or make propositions about the more complex ideas, as of a man, vitriol, fortitude, glory, we usually put the name for the idea : because, the ideas these names stand for being for the most part imperfect, confused, and undetermined, we reflect on the names themselves, because they are more clear, certain, and distinct, and readier occur to our thoughts, than the pure ideas : and so we make use of these words instead of the ideas themselves, even when we would meditate and reason within ourselves, and make tacit mental propositions. In substances, as has been already noted, this is occasioned by the imperfection of our ideas : we making the name stand for the real essence, of which we have no idea at all. In modes, it is occasioned by the great number of simple ideas that go to the making them up. For, many of them being compounded, the name occurs much easier than the complex idea itself, which requires time and attention to be recollected and exactly represented to the mind even in those men who have formerly been at the pains to do it; and is utterly impossible to be done by those who, though they have ready in their memory the greatest part of the common words of their language, yet perhaps never troubled themselves in all their lives to consider what precise ideas the most of them stood for. Some confused or obscure notions have served their turns; and many who talk very much of religion and conscience, of church and faith, of power and right, of obstructions and humours, melancholy and choler, would perhaps have little left in their thoughts and meditations if one should desire them to think only of the things themselves, and lay by those words with which they so often confound others, and not seldom themselves also.

5. *Being nothing but the joining or separating ideas without*

*words.*—But to return to the consideration of truth. We must, I say, observe two sorts of propositions that we are capable of, making,

First, Mental, wherein the ideas in our understandings are, without the use of words, put together or separated by the mind perceiving or judging of their agreement or disagreement.

Secondly, Verbal propositions, which are words, the signs of our ideas, put together or separated in affirmative or negative sentences. By which way of affirming or denying, these signs, made by sounds, are as it were put together or separated one from another. So that proposition consists in joining or separating signs, and truth consists in the putting together or separating these signs, according as the things which they stand for agree or disagree.

6. *When mental propositions contain real truth, and when verbal.* —Every one's experience will satisfy him that the mind, either by perceiving or supposing the agreement or disagreement of any of its ideas, does tacitly within itself put them into a kind of proposition affirmative or negative, which I have endeavoured to express by the terms "putting together" and "separating." But this action of the mind, which is so familiar to every thinking and reasoning man, is easier to be conceived by reflecting on what passes in us when we affirm or deny, than to be explained by words. When a man has in his mind the idea of two lines, viz., the side and diagonal of a square, whereof the diagonal is an inch long, he may have the idea also of the division of that line into a certain number of equal parts; *v. g.*, into five, ten, an hundred, a thousand, or any other number; and may have the idea of that inch-line being divisible or not divisible into such equal parts as a certain number of them will be equal to the side-line. Now, whenever he perceives, believes, or supposes such a kind of divisibility to agree or disagree to his idea of that line, he as it were joins or separates those two ideas, viz., the idea of that line, and the idea of that kind of divisibility, and so makes a mental proposition which is true or false, according as such a kind of divisibility, a divisibility into such aliquot parts, does really agree to that line or no. When ideas are so put together or separated in the mind, as they or the things they stand for do agree or not, that is, as I may call it "mental truth." But truth of words is something more, and that is the affirming or denying of words one of another, as the ideas they stand for agree or disagree: and this again is twofold; either purely verbal and trifling, which I shall speak of (chap. x.) or real and instructive, which is the object of that real knowledge which we have spoken of already.

7. *Objection against verbal truth, that thus it may all be chimerical.*—But here again will be apt to occur the same doubt about truth, that did about knowledge: and it will be objected, that

"if truth be nothing but the joining or separating of words in propositions, as the ideas they stand for agree or disagree in men's minds, the knowledge of truth is not so valuable a thing as it is taken to be, nor worth the pains and time men employ to the search of it: since, by this account, it amounts to no more than the conformity of words to the chimeras of men's brains. Who knows not what odd notions many men's heads are filled with, and what strange ideas all men's brains are capable of? But if we rest here we know the truth of nothing by this rule, but of the visionary world in our own imaginations; nor have other truth, but what as much concerns harpies and centaurs as men and horses. For those and the like may be ideas in our heads, and have their agreement and disagreement there, as well as the ideas of real beings, and so have as true propositions made about them. And it will be altogether as true a proposition to say, 'All centaurs are animals,' as that 'all men are animals;' and the certainty of one as great as the other. For in both the propositions the words are put together according to the agreement of the ideas in our minds: and the agreement of the idea of 'animal' with that of 'centaur,' is as clear and visible to the mind as the agreement of the idea of 'animal' with that of 'man;' and so these two propositions are equally true, equally certain. But of what use is all such truth to us?"

8. *Answered. Real truth is about ideas agreeing to things.*—Though what has been said in the foregoing chapter to distinguish real from imaginary knowledge might suffice here, in answer to this doubt, to distinguish real truth from chimerical, or (if you please) barely nominal, they depending both on the same foundation; yet it may not be amiss here again to consider, that though our words signify nothing but our ideas, yet being designed by them to signify things, the truth they contain, when put into propositions, will be only verbal when they stand for ideas in the mind that have not an agreement with the reality of things. And therefore truth, as well as knowledge, may well come under the distinction of " verbal " and " real; " that being only verbal truth wherein terms are joined according to the agreement or disagreement of the ideas they stand for, without regarding whether our ideas are such as really have or are capable of having an existence in nature. But then it is they contain real truth when these signs are joined as our ideas agree; and when our ideas are such as we know are capable of having an existence in nature: which in substances we cannot know but by knowing that such have existed.

9. *Falsehood is the joining of names otherwise than their ideas agree.*—Truth is the marking down in words the agreement or disagreement of ideas as it is. Falsehood is the marking down in words the agreement or disagreement of ideas otherwise than it is. And so far as these ideas thus marked by sounds agree to

their archetypes, so far only is the truth real. The knowledge of this truth consists in knowing what ideas the words stand for, and the perception of the agreement or disagreement of those ideas, according as it is marked by those words.

10. *General propositions to be treated of more at large.*—But because words are looked on as the great conduits of truth and knowledge, and that, in conveying and receiving of truth, and commonly in reasoning about it, we make use of words and propositions, I shall more at large inquire wherein the certainty of real truths, contained in propositions, consists, and where it is to be had; and endeavour to show in what sort of universal propositions we are capable of being certain of their real truth or falsehood.

I shall begin with general propositions, as those which most employ our thoughts and exercise our contemplation. General truths are most looked after by the mind, as those that most enlarge our knowledge; and by their comprehensiveness, satisfying us at once of many particulars, enlarge our view and shorten our way to knowledge.

11. *Moral and metaphysical truth.*—Besides truth taken in the strict sense before mentioned, there are other sorts of truths; as, (1.) Moral truth, which is speaking things according to the persuasion of our own minds, though the proposition we speak agree not to the reality of things. (2.) Metaphysical truth, which is nothing but the real existence of things conformable to the ideas to which we have annexed their names. This, though it seems to consist in the very beings of things, yet when considered a little nearly will appear to include a tacit proposition, whereby the mind joins that particular thing to the idea it had before settled with a name to it. But these considerations of truth, either having been before taken notice of, or not being much to our present purpose, it may suffice here only to have mentioned them.

## CHAPTER VI.

### OF UNIVERSAL PROPOSITIONS, THEIR TRUTH AND CERTAINTY.

1. *Treating of words necessary to knowledge.*—Though the examining and judging of ideas by themselves, their names being quite laid aside, be the best and surest way to clear and distinct knowledge; yet, through the prevailing custom of using sounds for ideas, I think it is very seldom practised. Every one may observe how common it is for names to be made use of instead of the ideas themselves, even when men think and reason within their own breasts; especially if the ideas be very complex, and made up of a great collection of simple ones. This makes the consideration of words and propositions so necessary a part of

the treatise of knowledge, that it is very hard to speak intelligibly of the one without explaining the other.

2. *General truths hardly to be understood but in verbal propositions.*—All the knowledge we have being only of particular or general truths, it is evident that whatever may be done in the former of these, the latter, which is that which with reason is most sought after, can never be well made known, and is very seldom apprehended, but as conceived and expressed in words. It is not therefore out of our way, in the examination of our knowledge, to inquire into the truth and certainty of universal propositions.

3. *Certainty twofold, of truth and of knowledge.*—But that we may not be misled in this case by that which is the danger every where, I mean by the doubtfulness of terms, it is fit to observe that certainty is twofold; certainty of truth, and certainty of knowledge. Certainty of truth is, when words are so put together in propositions as exactly to express the agreement or disagreement of the ideas they stand for, as really it is. Certainty of knowledge is, to perceive the agreement or disagreement of ideas, as expressed in any proposition. This we usually call "knowing," or "being certain of the truth of any proposition."

4. *No proposition can be known to be true, where the essence of each species mentioned is not known.*—Now, because we cannot be certain of the truth of any general proposition unless we know the precise bounds and extent of the species its terms stand for, it is necessary we should know the essence of each species, which is that which constitutes and bounds it. This, in all simple ideas and modes, is not hard to do. For in these the real and nominal essence being the same, or, which is all one, the abstract idea, which the general term stands for, being the sole essence and boundary that is or can be supposed of the species, there can be no doubt how far the species extends, or what things are comprehended under each term: which it is evident are all that have an exact conformity with the idea it stands for, and no other. But in substances, wherein a real essence distinct from the nominal is supposed to constitute, determine, and bound the species, the extent of the general word is very uncertain: because not knowing this real essence, we cannot know what is or is not of that species, and consequently what may or may not with certainty be affirmed of it. And thus speaking of a man, or gold, or any other species of natural substances, as supposed constituted by a precise real essence which nature regularly imparts to every individual of that kind, whereby it is made to be of that species, we cannot be certain of the truth of any affirmation or negation made of it. For man, or gold, taken in this sense and used for species of things constituted by real essences, different from the complex idea in the mind of the speaker, stand for we know not what: and the extent of these species with such boundaries are

so unknown and undetermined, that it is impossible with any certainty to affirm that all men are rational, or that all gold is yellow. But where the nominal essence is kept to as the boundary of each species, and men extend the application of any general term no farther than to the particular things in which the complex idea it stands for is to be found, there they are in no danger to mistake the bounds of each species, nor can be in doubt, on this account, whether any propositions be true or no. I have chose to explain this uncertainty of propositions in this scholastic way, and have made use of the terms of "essences" and "species," on purpose to show the absurdity and inconvenience there is to think of them as of any other sort of realities, than barely abstract ideas with names to them. To suppose that the species of things are any thing but the sorting of them under general names, according as they agree to several abstract ideas, of which we make those names the signs, is to confound truth, and introduce uncertainty into all general propositions that can be made about them. Though therefore these things might, to people not possessed with scholastic learning, be perhaps treated of in a better and clearer way; yet those wrong notions of essences or species, having got root in most people's minds who have received any tincture from the learning which has prevailed in this part of the world, are to be discovered and removed to make way for that use of words which should convey certainty with it.

5. *This more particularly concerns substances.*—The names of substances, then, whenever made to stand for species which are supposed to be constituted by real essences which we know not, are not capable to convey certainty to the understanding: of the truth of general propositions made up of such terms we cannot be sure. The reason whereof is plain. For, how can we be sure that this or that quality is in gold, when we know not what is or is not gold? since in this way of speaking nothing is gold but what partakes of an essence, which we not knowing cannot know where it is or is not, and so cannot be sure that any parcel of matter in the world is or is not in this sense gold; being incurably ignorant whether it has or has not that which makes any thing to be called "gold," *i. e.*, that real essence of gold whereof we have no idea at all: this being as impossible for us to know, as it is for a blind man to tell in what flower the colour of a pansy is or is not to be found, whilst he has no idea of the colour of a pansy at all. Or if we could (which is impossible) certainly know where a real essence which we know not, is, *v. g.*, in what parcels of matter the real essence of gold is, yet could we not be sure that this or that quality could with truth be affirmed of gold: since it is impossible for us to know that this or that quality or idea has a necessary connexion with a real essence, of which we have no idea at all, whatever species that supposed real essence may be imagined to constitute.

6. *The truth of few universal propositions concerning substances is to be known.*—On the other side, the names of substances, when made use of, as they should be, for the ideas men have in their minds, though they carry a clear and determined signification with them, will not yet serve us to make many universal propositions, of whose truth we can be certain. Not because in this use of them we are uncertain what things are signified by them, but because the complex ideas they stand for are such combinations of simple ones as carry not with them any discoverable connexion or repugnancy but with a very few other ideas.

7. *Because co-existence of ideas in few cases is to be known.*—The complex ideas that our names of the species of substances properly stand for, are collections of such qualities as have been observed to co-exist in an unknown substratum which we call "substance;" but what other qualities necessarily co-exist with such combinations, we cannot certainly know, unless we can discover their natural dependence; which in their primary qualities we can go but a very little way in; and in all their secondary qualities we can discover no connexion at all, for the reasons mentioned, (chap. iii.) viz., (1.) Because we know not the real constitutions of substances, on which each secondary quality particularly depends. (2.) Did we know that it would serve us only for experimental (not universal) knowledge; and reach with certainty no farther than that bare instance; because our understandings can discover no conceivable connexion between any secondary quality, and any modification whatsoever of any of the primary ones. And therefore there are very few general propositions to be made concerning substances which can carry with them undoubted certainty.

8. *Instance in gold.*—"All gold is fixed," is a proposition whose truth we cannot be certain of, how universally soever it be believed. For if, according to the useless imagination of the schools, any one supposes the term "gold" to stand for a species of things set out by nature by a real essence belonging to it, it is evident he knows not what particular substances are of that species; and so cannot, with certainty, affirm any thing universally of gold. But if he makes gold stand for a species, determined by its nominal essence, let the nominal essence, for example, be the complex idea of a body, of a certain yellow colour, malleable, fusible, and heavier than any other known; in this proper use of the word "gold," there is no difficulty to know what is or is not gold. But yet no other quality can with certainty be universally affirmed or denied of gold, but what hath a discoverable connexion or inconsistency with that nominal essence. Fixedness, for example, having no necessary connexion that we can discover with the colour, weight, or any other simple idea of our complex one, or with the whole combination together; it is

impossible that we should certainly know the truth of this proposition, that "all gold is fixed."

9. As there is no discoverable connexion between fixedness and the colour, weight, and other simple ideas of that nominal essence of gold ; so, if we make our complex idea of gold "a body yellow, fusible, ductile, weighty, and fixed," we shall be at the same uncertainty concerning solubility in *aqua regia;* and for the same reason: since we can never, from consideration of the ideas themselves, with certainty affirm or deny of a body, whose complex idea is made up of yellow, very weighty, ductile, fusible, and fixed, that it is soluble in *aqua regia :* and so on of the rest of its qualities. I would gladly meet with one general affirmation, concerning any quality of gold, that any one can certainly know is true. It will, no doubt, be presently objected, " Is not this an universal certain proposition, ' All gold is malleable ? ' " To which I answer, It is a very certain proposition, if malleableness be a part of the complex idea the word " gold" stands for. But then here is nothing affirmed of gold, but that that sound stands for an idea in which malleableness is contained : and such a sort of truth and certainty as this it is to say, "A centaur is four-footed." But if malleableness makes not a part of the specific essence the name " gold" stands for, it is plain, "All gold is malleable," is not a certain proposition ; because, let the complex idea of gold be made up of which soever of its other qualities you please, malleableness will not appear to depend on that complex idea, nor follow from any simple one contained in it: the connexion that malleableness has (if it has any) with those other qualities being only by the intervention of the real constitution of its insensible parts, which since we know not, it is impossible we should perceive that connexion, unless we could discover that which ties them together.

10. *As far as any such co-existence can be known, so far universal propositions may be certain. But this will go but a little way, because*—The more, indeed, of these co-existing qualities we unite into one complex idea, under one name, the more precise and determinate we make the signification of that word ; but yet never make it thereby more capable of universal certainty in respect of other qualities not contained in our complex idea ; since we perceive not their connexion or dependence one on another, being ignorant both of that real constitution in which they are all founded, and also how they flow from it. For the chief part of our knowledge concerning substances is not, as in other things, barely of the relation of two ideas that may exist separately ; but, is of the necessary connexion and co-existence of several distinct ideas in the same subject, or of their repugnances so to co-exist. Could we begin at the other end, and discover what it was wherein that colour consisted, what made a

body lighter or heavier, what texture of parts made it malleable, fusible, and fixed, and fit to be dissolved in this sort of liquor, and not in another; if (I say) we had such an idea as this of bodies, and could perceive wherein all sensible qualities originally consist, and how they are produced, we might frame such abstract ideas of them as would furnish us with matter of more general knowledge, and enable us to make universal propositions that should carry general truth and certainty with them. But whilst our complex ideas of the sorts of substances are so remote from that internal real constitution on which their sensible qualities depend, and are made up of nothing but an imperfect collection of those apparent qualities our senses can discover, there can be very few general propositions concerning substances, of whose real truth we can be certainly assured; since there are but few simple ideas of whose connexion and necessary co-existence we can have certain and undoubted knowledge. I imagine, amongst all the secondary qualities of substances and the powers relating to them, there cannot any two be named whose necessary co-existence, or repugnance to co-exist, can certainly be known, unless in those of the same sense, which necessarily exclude one another, as I have elsewhere showed. No one, I think, by the colour that is in any body, can certainly know what smell, taste, sound, or tangible qualities it has, nor what alterations it is capable to make or receive on or from other bodies. The same may be said of the sound or taste, &c. Our specific names of substances standing for any collections of such ideas, it is not to be wondered that we can with them make very few general propositions of undoubted real certainty. But yet so far as any complex idea of any sort of substances contains in it any simple idea whose necessary co-existence with any other may be discovered, so far universal propositions may with certainty be made concerning it: *v. g.*, could any one discover a necessary connexion between malleableness and the colour or weight of gold, or any other part of the complex idea signified by that name, he might make a certain universal proposition concerning gold in this respect; and the real truth of this proposition, that " all gold is malleable," would be as certain as of this, " The three angles of all right-lined triangles are equal to two right ones."

11. *The qualities which make our complex ideas of substances, depend mostly on external, remote, and unperceived causes.*—Had we such ideas of substances as to know what real constitutions produce those sensible qualities we find in them, and how those qualities flowed from thence, we could, by the specific ideas of their real essences in our own minds, more certainly find out their properties, and discover what qualities they had or had not, than we can now by our senses: and to know the properties of gold, it would be no more necessary that gold should exist, and

that we should make experiments upon it, than it is necessary for the knowing the properties of a triangle, that a triangle should exist in any matter: the idea in our minds would serve for the one as well as the other. But we are so far from being admitted into the secrets of nature, that we scarce so much as ever approach the first entrance towards them. For, we are wont to consider the substances we meet with, each of them as an entire thing by itself, having all its qualities in itself, and independent of other things; overlooking for the most part the operations of those invisible fluids they are encompassed with; and upon whose motions and operations depend the greatest part of those qualities which are taken notice of in them, and are made by us the inherent marks of distinction whereby we know and denominate them. Put a piece of gold any where by itself, separate from the reach and influence of all other bodies, it will immediately lose all its colour and weight, and perhaps malleableness too: which, for aught I know, would be changed into a perfect friability. Water, in which to us fluidity is an essential quality, left to itself, would cease to be fluid. But if inanimate bodies owe so much of their present state to other bodies without them, that they would not be what they appear to us were those bodies that environ them removed, it is yet more so in vegetables, which are nourished, grow, and produce leaves, flowers, and seeds, in a constant succession. And if we look a little nearer into the state of animals, we shall find that their dependence, as to life, motion, and the most considerable qualities to be observed in them, is so wholly on extrinsical causes and qualities of other bodies that make no part of them, that they cannot subsist a moment without them: though yet those bodies on which they depend are little taken notice of, and make no part of the complex ideas we frame of those animals. Take the air but a minute from the greatest part of living creatures, and they presently lose sense, life, and motion. This the necessity of breathing has forced into our knowledge. But how many other extrinsical, and possibly very remote, bodies do the springs of those admirable machines depend on, which are not vulgarly observed, or so much as thought on; and how many are there which the severest inquiry can never discover! The inhabitants of this spot of the universe, though removed so many millions of miles from the sun, yet depend so much on the duly tempered motion of particles coming from or agitated by it, that were this earth removed but a small part of that distance out of its present situation, and placed a little farther or nearer that source of heat, it is more than probable that the greatest part of the animals in it would immediately perish: since we find them so often destroyed by an excess or defect of the sun's warmth, which an accidental position in some parts of this our little globe exposes them to. The qualities observed in a loadstone must needs have their source far beyond the confines of that body; and the ravage made often on several sorts of animals by invisible causes, the certain death (as we are told) of some of them by barely passing the line, or, as it is certain of others, by being removed into a neighbouring country, evidently show that the concurrence and operation of several bodies, with which they are seldom thought to have any thing to do, is absolutely necessary to make them be what they appear to us, and to preserve those qualities by which we know and distinguish them. We are then quite out of the way when we think that things contain within themselves the qualities that appear to us in them: and we in vain search for that constitution within the body of a fly or an elephant, upon which depend those qualities and powers we observe in them. For which perhaps, to understand them aright, we ought to look not only beyond this our earth and atmosphere, but even beyond the sun or remotest star our eyes have yet discovered. For, how much the being and operation of particular substances in this our globe depend on causes utterly beyond our view, is impossible for us to determine. We see and perceive some of the motions and grosser operations of things here about us; but whence the streams come that keep all these curious machines in motion and repair, how conveyed and modified, is beyond our notice and apprehension; and the great parts and wheels, as I may so say, of this stupendous structure of the universe, may, for aught we know, have such a connexion and dependence in their influences and operations one upon another, that perhaps things in this our mansion would put on quite another face, and cease to be what they are, if some one of the stars or great bodies incomprehensibly remote from us should cease to be or move as it does. This is certain, things, however absolute and entire they seem in themselves, are but retainers to other parts of nature for that which they are most taken notice of by us. Their observable qualities, actions, and powers are owing to something without them; and there is not so complete and perfect a part that we know of nature which does not owe the being it has, and the excellences of it, to its neighbours; and we must not confine our thoughts within the surface of any body, but look a great deal farther, to comprehend perfectly those qualities that are in it.

12. If this be so, it is not to be wondered that we have very imperfect ideas of substances; and that the real essences on which depend their properties and operations are unknown to us. We cannot discover so much as that size, figure, and texture of their minute and active parts which is really in them; much less the different motions and impulses made in and upon them by bodies from without, upon which depends, and by which is formed, the greatest and most remarkable part of those qualities we observe in them, and of which our complex ideas of them are

made up. This consideration alone is enough to put an end to
all our hopes of ever having the ideas of their real essences;
which whilst we want, the nominal essences we make use of
instead of them will be able to furnish us but very sparingly
with any general knowledge or universal propositions capable of
real certainty.

13. *Judgment may reach farther, but that is not knowledge.*—We
are not therefore to wonder if certainty be to be found in very
few general propositions made concerning substances; our knowledge of their qualities and properties go very seldom farther
than our senses reach and inform us.   Possibly inquisitive and
observing men may, by strength of judgment, penetrate farther;
and on probabilities taken from wary observations, and hints
well laid together, often guess right at what experience has not
yet discovered to them.   But this is but guessing still; it
amounts only to opinion, and has not that certainty which is
requisite to knowledge.   For all general knowledge lies only in
our own thoughts, and consists barely in the contemplation of
our own abstract ideas.   Wherever we perceive any agreement
or disagreement amongst them, there we have general knowledge;
and, by putting the names of those ideas together accordingly in
propositions, can with certainty pronounce general truths.   But,
because the abstract ideas of substances for which their specific
names stand whenever they have any distinct and determinate
signification, have a discoverable connexion or inconsistency with
but a very few other ideas, the certainty of universal propositions concerning substances is very narrow and scanty in that
part, which is our principal inquiry concerning them; and there
is scarce any of the names of substances, let the idea it is applied
to be what it will, of which we can generally and with certainty
pronounce that it has or has not this or that other quality
belonging to it, and constantly co-existing or inconsistent with
that idea wherever it is to be found.

14. *What is requisite for our knowledge of substances.*—Before
we can have any tolerable knowledge of this kind, we must,
First, know what changes the primary qualities of one body do
regularly produce in the primary qualities of another, and how.
Secondly, We must know what primary qualities of any body
produce certain sensations or ideas in us.   This is in truth no
less than to know all the effects of matter under its divers modifications of bulk, figure, cohesion of parts, motion, and rest;
which, I think, every body will allow, is utterly impossible to be
known by us without revelation.   Nor, if it were revealed to us
what sort of figure, bulk, and motion of corpuscles, would produce
in us the sensation of a yellow colour, and what sort of figure,
bulk, and texture of parts in the superficies of any body were fit
to give such corpuscles their due motion to produce that colour;
would that be enough to make universal propositions with cer-

tainty concerning the several sorts of them, unless we had
faculties acute enough to perceive the precise bulk, figure,
texture, and motion of bodies in those minute parts by which
they operate on our senses, that so we might by those frame our
abstract ideas of them.    I have mentioned here only corporeal
substances, whose operations seem to lie more level to our understandings : for as to the operations of spirits, both their thinking
and moving of bodies, we, at first sight, find ourselves at a loss ;
though perhaps when we have applied our thoughts a little
nearer to the consideration of bodies and their operations, and
examined how far our notions even in these reach, with any
clearness, beyond sensible matter of fact, we shall be found to
confess, that even in these, too, our discoveries amount to very
little beyond perfect ignorance and incapacity.

15. *Whilst our ideas of substances contain not their real constitutions, we can make but few general certain propositions concerning
them.*—This is evident : the abstract complex ideas of substances
for which their general names stand, not comprehending their
real constitutions, can afford us but very little universal certainty.
Because our ideas of them are not made up of that on which
those qualities we observe in them and would inform ourselves
about do depend, or with which they have any certain connexion.
*V. g.*, Let the idea to which we give the name "man" be, as it
commonly is, "a body of the ordinary shape, with sense, voluntary motion and reason joined to it."    This being the abstract
idea, and consequently the essence, of our species man, we can
make but very few general certain propositions concerning
"man" standing for such an idea : because, not knowing the
real constitution on which sensation, power of motion, and
reasoning, with that peculiar shape, depend, and whereby they
are united together in the same subject, there are very few
other qualities with which we can perceive them to have a
necessary connexion : and therefore we cannot with certainty
affirm, that all men sleep by intervals, that no man can be
nourished by wood or stones, that all men will be poisoned by
hemlock ; because these ideas have no connexion or repugnancy
with this our nominal essence of man, with this abstract idea
that name stands for.    We must in these and the like appeal to
trial in particular subjects, which can reach but a little way.
We must content ourselves with probability in the rest ; but can
have no general certainty whilst our specific idea of man contains not that real constitution which is the root wherein all his
inseparable qualities are united, and from whence they flow.
Whilst our idea the word "man" stands for, is only an imperfect
collection of some sensible qualities and powers in him, there is
no discernible connexion or repugnance between our specific idea
and the operation of either the parts of hemlock or stones upon
his constitution.    There are animals that safely eat hemlock,

and others that are nourished by wood and stones: but as long as we want ideas of those real constitutions of different sorts of animals whereon these and the like qualities and powers depend, we must not hope to reach certainty in universal propositions concerning them. Those few ideas only which have a discernible connexion with our nominal essence, or any part of it, can afford us such propositions. But these are so few and of so little moment, that we may justly look on our certain general knowledge of substances as almost none at all.

16. *Wherein lies the general certainty of propositions.*—To conclude: general propositions, of what kind soever, are then only capable of certainty, when the terms used in them stand for such ideas whose agreement or disagreement as there expressed, is capable to be discovered by us. And we are then certain of their truth or falsehood, when we perceive the ideas the terms stand for to agree or not agree, according as they are affirmed or denied one of another. Whence we may take notice, that general certainty is never to be found but in our ideas. Whenever we go to seek it elsewhere in experiment or observations without us, our knowledge goes not beyond particulars. It is the contemplation of our own abstract ideas that alone is able to afford us general knowledge.

---

# CHAPTER VII.

## OF MAXIMS.

1. *They are self-evident.*—There are a sort of propositions which under the name of "maxims and axioms," have passed for principles of science: and, because they are self-evident, have been supposed innate, although nobody (that I know) ever went about to show the reason and foundation of their clearness or cogency. It may, however, be worth while to inquire into the reason of their evidence, and see whether it be peculiar to them alone, and also examine how far they influence and govern our other knowledge.

2. *Wherein that self-evidence consists.*—Knowledge, as has been shown, consists in the perception of the agreement or disagreement of ideas: now where that agreement or disagreement is perceived immediately by itself, without the intervention or help of any other, there our knowledge is self-evident. This will appear to be so to any one who will but consider any of those propositions which, without any proof, he assents to at first sight; for in all of them he will find that the reason of his assent is from that agreement or disagreement which the mind, by an immediate comparing them, finds in those ideas, answering the affirmation or negation in the proposition.

**3.** *Self-evidence not peculiar to received axioms.*—This being so, in the next place let us consider whether this self-evidence be peculiar only to those propositions which commonly pass under the name of "maxims," and have the dignity of axioms allowed them. And here it is plain, that several other truths, not allowed to be axioms, partake equally with them in this self-evidence. This we shall see, if we go over these several sorts of agreement or disagreement of ideas which I have above mentioned, viz., identity, relation, co-existence, and real existence; which will discover to us, that not only those few propositions which have had the credit of maxims are self-evident, but a great many, even almost an infinite number, of other propositions are such.

**4.** *First, As to identity and diversity, all propositions are equally self-evident.*—For, First, the immediate perception of the agreement or disagreement of identity being founded in the mind's having distinct ideas, this affords us as many self-evident propositions as we have distinct ideas. Every one that has any knowledge at all has, as the foundation of it, various and distinct ideas: and it is the first act of the mind (without which it can never be capable of any knowledge) to know every one of its ideas by itself, and distinguish it from others. Every one finds in himself, that he knows the ideas he has; that he knows also when any one is in his understanding, and what it is; and that when more than one are there, he knows them distinctly and unconfusedly one from another. Which always being so (it being impossible but that he should perceive what he perceives), he can never be in doubt, when any idea is in his mind, that it is there, and is that idea it is; and that two distinct ideas, when they are in his mind, are there, and are not one and the same idea. So that all such affirmations and negations are made without any possibility of doubt, uncertainty, or hesitation, and must necessarily be assented to as soon as understood; that is, as soon as we have in our minds determined ideas which the terms in the propositions stand for. And therefore wherever the mind with attention considers any proposition so as to perceive the two ideas signified by the terms, and affirmed or denied one of the other, to be the same or different, it is presently and infallibly certain of the truth of such a proposition: and this equally whether these propositions be in terms standing for more general ideas, or such as are less so; *v. g.*, whether the general idea of being be affirmed of itself, as in this proposition, "Whatsoever is, is;" or a more particular idea be affirmed of itself, as, "A man is a man," or, "Whatsoever is white, is white:" or whether the idea of being in general be denied of not being, which is the only (if I may so call it) idea different from it, as in this other proposition, "It is impossible for the same thing to be and not to be;" or any idea of any particular being be denied of another different from it, as, "A man is not a horse; red is not blue." The difference of the ideas as soon as the terms are understood makes the truth of the proposition presently visible, and that with an equal certainty and easiness in the less as well as the more general propositions; and all for the same reason, viz., because the mind perceives, in any ideas that it has, the same idea to be the same with itself; and two different ideas to be different and not the same. And this it is equally certain of, whether these ideas be more or less general, abstract, and comprehensive. It is not therefore alone to these two general propositions—"Whatsoever is, is;" and, "It is impossible for the same thing to be, and not to be,"—that this self-evidence belongs by any peculiar right. The perception of being or not being belongs no more to these vague ideas, signified by the terms "whatsoever" and "thing," than it does to any other ideas. These two general maxims, amounting to no more, in short, but this, that "the same is the same," and "same is not different," are truths known in more particular instances, as well as in these general maxims, and known also in particular instances, before these general maxims are ever thought on, and draw all their force from the discernment of the mind employed about particular ideas. There is nothing more visible than that the mind, without the help of any proof or reflection on either of these general propositions, perceives so clearly, and knows so certainly, that the idea of white is the idea of white, and not the idea of blue, and that the idea of white when it is in the mind, is there, and is not absent, that the consideration of these axioms can add nothing to the evidence or certainty of its knowledge. Just so it is (as every one may experiment in himself) in all the ideas a man has in his mind: he knows each to be itself, and not to be another, and to be in his mind, and not away, when it is there, with a certainty that cannot be greater: and therefore the truth of no general proposition can be known with a greater certainty, nor add any thing to this. So that in respect of identity, our intuitive knowledge reaches as far as our ideas. And we are capable of making as many self-evident propositions as we have names for distinct ideas. And I appeal to every one's own mind, whether this proposition, "A circle is a circle," be not as self-evident a proposition as that consisting of more general terms, "Whatsoever is, is:" and again, whether this proposition, "Blue is not red," be not a proposition that the mind can no more doubt of as soon as it understands the words, than it does of that axiom, "It is impossible for the same thing to be, and not to be." And so of all the like.

5. *Secondly, In co-existence we have few self-evident propositions.* —Secondly, As to co-existence, or such necessary connexion between two ideas, that, in the subject where one of them·is

supposed, there the other must necessarily be also; of such
agreement or disagreement as this the mind has an immediate
perception but in very few of them; and therefore in this sort
we have but very little intuitive knowledge. Nor are there to
be found very many propositions that are self-evident, though
some there are; *v. g.*, the idea of filling a place equal to the
contents of its superficies, being annexed to our idea of body, I
think it is a self-evident proposition, that "two bodies cannot
be in the same place."

6. *Thirdly, In other relations we may have.*—Thirdly, As to the
relations of modes, mathematicians have framed many axioms
concerning that one relation of equality: As, "Equals taken from
equals, the remainder will be equals;" which with the rest of
that kind, however they are received for maxims by the mathematicians, and are unquestionable truths; yet I think that any
one who considers them will not find that they have a clearer
self-evidence than these, that "one and one are equal to two;"
that "if you take from the five fingers of one hand two, and from
the five fingers of the other hand two, the remaining numbers
will be equal." These and a thousand other such propositions
may be found in numbers which, at the very first hearing, force
the assent, and carry with them an equal, if not a greater clearness than those mathematical axioms.

7. *Fourthly, Concerning real existence we have none.*—Fourthly,
As to real existence, since that has no connexion with any other
of our ideas but that of ourselves and of a first being, we have
in that concerning the real existence of all other beings not so
much as demonstrative, much less a self-evident, knowledge;
and therefore concerning those there are no maxims.

8. *These axioms do not much influence our other knowledge.*—
In the next place let us consider what influence these received
maxims have upon the other parts of our knowledge. The rules
established in the schools, that all reasonings are *ex præcognitis
et præconcessis*, seem to lay the foundation of all other knowledge in these maxims, and to suppose them to be *præcognita;*
whereby I think are meant these two things: First, That these
axioms are those truths that are first known to the mind; and,
Secondly, that upon them the other parts of our knowledge
depend.

9. *Because they are not the truths we first knew.*—First, That
they are not the truths first known to the mind is evident to
experience, as we have shown in another place. (Book i. chap.
ii.) Who perceives not, that a child certainly knows that a
stranger is not its mother, that its sucking-bottle is not the rod,
long before he knows that it is impossible for the same thing to
be, and not to be? And how many truths are there about
numbers which it is obvious to observe that the mind is perfectly
acquainted with, and fully convinced of, before it ever thought on

these general maxims to which mathematicians in their arguings do sometimes refer them! Whereof the reason is very plain: for, that which makes the mind assent to such propositions being nothing else but the perception it has of the agreement or disagreement of its ideas, according as it finds them affirmed or denied one of another in words it understands, and every idea being known to be what it is, and every two distinct ideas being known not to be the same, it must necessarily follow, that such self-evident truths must be first known which consist of ideas that are first in the mind; and the ideas first in the mind, it is evident, are those of particular things, from whence, by slow degrees, the understanding proceeds to some few general ones; which, being taken from the ordinary and familiar objects of sense, are settled in the mind with general names to them. Thus particular ideas are first received and distinguished, and so knowledge got about them; and next to them the less general or specific, which are next to particular: for, abstract ideas are not so obvious or easy to children or the yet unexercised mind, as particular ones. If they seem so to grown men, it is only because by constant and familiar use they are made so: for when we nicely reflect upon them, we shall find that general ideas are fictions and contrivances of the mind, that carry difficulty with them, and do not so easily offer themselves as we are apt to imagine. For example: Does it not require some pains and skill to form the general idea of a triangle? (which is yet none of the most abstract, comprehensive, and difficult;) for it must be neither oblique, nor rectangle, neither equilateral, equicrural, nor scalenon; but all and none of these at once. In effect, it is something imperfect, that cannot exist; an idea wherein some parts of several different and inconsistent ideas are put together. It is true, the mind in this imperfect state has need of such ideas, and makes all the haste to them it can, for the conveniency of communication and enlargement of knowledge; to both which it is naturally very much inclined. But yet one has reason to suspect such ideas are marks of our imperfection; at least this is enough to show that the most abstract and general ideas are not those that the mind is first and most easily acquainted with, nor such as its earliest knowledge is conversant about.

10. *Because on them the other parts of our knowledge do not depend.*—Secondly, From what has been said, it plainly follows that these magnified maxims are not the principles and foundations of all our other knowledge. For, if there be a great many other truths which have as much self-evidence as they, and a great many that we know before them, it is impossible they should be the principles from which we deduce all other truths. Is it impossible to know that one and two are equal to three, but by virtue of this or some such axiom, viz., "The whole is equal to

all its parts taken together?"   Many a one knows that one and two are equal to three, without having heard or thought on that or any other axiom by which it might be proved; and knows it as certainly as any other man knows that "the whole is equal to all its parts," or any other maxim; and all from the same reason of self-evidence, the quality of those ideas being as visible and certain to him without that or any other axiom as with it, it needing no proof to make it perceived.   Nor after the knowledge that the whole is equal to all its parts, does he know that one and two are equal to three better or more certainly than he did before.   For, if there be any odds in those ideas, the whole and parts are more obscure, or at least more difficult to be settled in the mind, than those of one, two, and three.   And indeed I think I may ask these men, who will needs have all knowledge besides those general principles themselves to depend on general, innate, and self-evident principles, "What principle is requisite to prove that one and one are two, that two and two are four, that three times two are six?" which being known without any proof, do evince that either all knowledge does not depend on certain *præcognita*, or general maxims, called "principles," or else that these are principles; and if these are to be counted principles, a great part of numeration will be so.   To which if we add all the self-evident propositions which may be made about all our distinct ideas, principles will be almost infinite, at least innumerable, which men arrive to the knowledge of at different ages; and a great many of these innate principles they never come to know all their lives.   But whether they come in view of the mind earlier or later, this is true of them, that they are all known by their native evidence, are wholly independent, receive no light nor are capable of any proof one from another, much less the more particular from the more general, or the more simple from the more compounded; the more simple and less abstract being the most familiar, and the easier and earlier apprehended.   But whichever be the clearest ideas, the evidence and certainty of all such propositions is in this, that a man sees the same idea to be the same idea, and infallibly perceives two different ideas to be different ideas.   For, when a man has in his understanding the ideas of one and of two, the idea of yellow and the idea of blue, he cannot but certainly know that the idea of one is the idea of one, and not the idea of two, and that the idea of yellow is the idea of yellow, and not the idea of blue.   For, a man cannot confound the ideas in his mind which he has distinct; that would be to have them confused and distinct at the same time, which is a contradiction; and to have none distinct, is to have no use of our faculties, to have no knowledge at all.   And therefore what idea soever is affirmed of itself, or whatsoever two entire distinct ideas are denied one of another, the mind cannot but assent to such a proposition as infallibly true as soon as it understands the terms, without hesitation or need of proof, or regarding those made in more general terms, and called "maxims."

11. *What use these general maxims have.*—What shall we then say? Are these general maxims of no use? By no means; though perhaps their use is not that which it is commonly taken to be. But since doubting in the least of what hath been by some men ascribed to these maxims may be apt to be cried out against, as overturning the foundations of all the sciences, it may be worth while to consider them with respect to other parts of our knowledge, and examine more particularly to what purposes they serve, and to what not.

(1.) It is evident, from what has been already said, that they are of no use to prove or confirm less general self-evident propositions.

(2.) It is as plain that they are not, nor have been, the foundations whereon any science hath been built. There is, I know, a great deal of talk, propagated from scholastic men, of sciences and the maxims on which they are built: but it has been my ill luck never to meet with any such sciences; much less any one built upon these two maxims, "What is, is;" and, "It is impossible for the same thing to be and not to be." And I would be glad to be shown where any such science, erected upon these or any other general axioms, is to be found; and should be obliged to any one who would lay before me the frame and system of any science so built on these or any such like maxims, that could not be shown to stand as firm without any consideration of them. I ask, whether these general maxims have not the same use in the study of divinity, and in theological questions, that they have in the other sciences? They serve here, too, to silence wranglers, and put an end to dispute. But I think that nobody will therefore say, that the Christian religion is built on these maxims, or that the knowledge we have of it is derived from these principles. It is from revelation we have received it, and without revelation these maxims had never been able to help us to it. When we find out an idea, by whose intervention we discover the connexion of two others, this is a revelation from God to us by the voice of reason. For we then come to know a truth that we did not know before. When God declares any truth to us, this is a revelation to us by the voice of his Spirit, and we are advanced in our knowledge. But in neither of these do we receive our light or knowledge from maxims. But in the one, the things themselves afford it, and we see the truth in them by perceiving their agreement or disagreement; in the other, God himself affords it immediately to us, and we see the truth of what he says in his unerring veracity.

(3.) They are not of use to help men forward in the advancement of sciences, or new discoveries of yet unknown truths. Mr. Newton, in his never-enough-to-be-admired book, has demonstrated several propositions which are so many new truths, before unknown to the world, and are farther advanced in mathematical knowledge: but for the discovery of these, it was not the general maxims "What is, is," or "The whole is bigger than a part," or the like, that helped him. These were not the clues that led him into the discovery of the truth and certainty of those propositions. Nor was it by them that he got the knowledge of those demonstrations; but by finding out intermediate ideas, that showed the agreement or disagreement of the ideas, as expressed in the propositions he demonstrated.   This is the great exercise and improvement of human understanding in the enlarging of knowledge, and advancing the sciences; wherein they are far enough from receiving any help from the contemplation of these or the like magnified maxims.  Would those who have this traditional admiration of these propositions, that they think no step can be made in knowledge without the support of an axiom, no stone laid in the building of the sciences without a general maxim, but distinguish between the method of acquiring knowledge, and of communicating; between the method of raising any science, and that of teaching it to others as far as it is advanced; 'they would see that those general maxims were not the foundations on which the first discoverers raised their admirable structures, nor the keys that unlocked and opened those secrets of knowledge. Though afterwards, when schools were erected, and sciences had their professors to teach what others had found out, they often made use of maxims, *i. e.*, laid down certain propositions which were self-evident, or to be received for true, which, being settled in the minds of their scholars as unquestionable verities, they on occasion made use of to convince them of truths in particular instances, that were not so familiar to their minds as those general axioms which had before been inculcated to them, and carefully settled in their minds.   Though these particular instances, when well reflected on, are no less self-evident to the understanding, than the general maxims brought to confirm them: and it was in those particular instances that the first discoverer found the truth, without the help of the general maxims : and so may any one else do, who with attention considers them.

To come therefore to the use that is made of maxims.

(1.) They are of use, as has been observed, in the ordinary methods of teaching sciences as far as they are advanced: but of little or none in advancing them farther.

(2.) They are of use in disputes, for the silencing of obstinate wranglers, and bringing those contests to some conclusion. Whether a need of them to that end came not in, in the manner following, I crave leave to inquire.  The schools, having made disputation the touchstone of men's abilities, and the criterion of knowledge, adjudged victory to him that kept the field; and he that had the last word was concluded to have the better of the argument, if not of the cause. But because by this means there was like to be no decision between skilful combatants, whilst one never failed of a *medius terminus* to prove any proposition, and the other could as constantly, without or with a distinction, deny the major or minor; to prevent, as much as could be, the running out of disputes into an endless chain of syllogisms, certain general propositions, most of them indeed self-evident, were introduced into the Schools; which being such as all men allowed and agreed in, were looked on as general measures of truth, and served instead of principles (where the disputants had not laid down any other between them), beyond which there was no going, and which must not be receded from by either side. And thus these maxims getting the name of "principles," beyond which men in dispute could not retreat, were by mistake taken to be the originals and sources from whence all knowledge began, and the foundations whereon the sciences were built; because, when in their disputes they came to any of these, they stopped there, and went no farther—the matter was determined. But how much this is a mistake hath been already shown.

This method of the Schools, which have been thought the fountains of knowledge, introduced, as I suppose, the like use of these maxims into a great part of conversation out of the Schools, to stop the mouths of cavillers, whom any one is excused from arguing any longer with, when they deny these general self-evident principles received by all reasonable men who have once thought of them; but yet their use herein is but to put an end to wrangling. They, in truth, when urged in such cases, teach nothing; that is already done by the intermediate ideas made use of in the debate, whose connexion may be seen without the help of those maxims, and so the truth known before the maxim is produced, and the argument brought to a first principle. Men would give off a wrong argument before it came to that, if in their disputes they proposed to themselves the finding and embracing of truth, and not a contest for victory. And thus maxims have their use to put a stop to their perverseness, whose ingenuity should have yielded sooner. But the method of the Schools having allowed and encouraged men to oppose and resist evident truths till they are baffled, *i. e.*, till they are reduced to contradict themselves or some established principle, it is no wonder that they should not, in civil conversation, be ashamed of that which in the Schools is counted a virtue and a glory, viz., obstinately to maintain that side of the question they have chosen, whether true or false to the last extremity, even after conviction: a strange way to attain truth and knowledge; and that which I think the rational part of mankind, not corrupted by education, could scarce believe should ever be admitted amongst the lovers of truth, and students of religion or nature; or introduced into the seminaries of those who are to propagate the truths of religion or philosophy amongst the ignorant and unconvinced. How much such a way of learning is likely to turn young men's minds from the sincere search and love of truth, nay, and to make them doubt whether there is any such thing, or at least worth adhering to, I shall not now inquire. This I think, that, bating those places which brought the peripatetic philosophy into their Schools, where it continued many ages, without teaching the world any thing but the art of wrangling, these maxims were nowhere thought the foundations on which the sciences were built, nor the great helps to the advancement of knowledge.

As to these general maxims, therefore, they are, as I have said of great use in disputes, to stop the mouths of wranglers; but not of much use to the discovery of unknown truths, or to help the mind forward in its search after knowledge: for who ever began to build his knowledge on this general proposition, "What is, is;" or, "It is impossible for the same thing to be and not to be:" and from either of these, as from a principle of science deduced a system of useful knowledge? Wrong opinions often involving contradictions, one of these maxims, as a touchstone may serve well to show whither they lead. But yet, however fit to lay open the absurdity or mistake of a man's reasoning or opinion, they are of very little use for enlightening the understanding: and it will not be found that the mind receives much help from them in its progress in knowledge; which would be neither less, nor less certain, were these two general propositions never thought on. It is true, as I have said, they sometimes serve in argumentation to stop a wrangler's mouth, by showing the absurdity of what he saith, and by exposing him to the shame of contradicting what all the world knows, and he himself cannot but own, to be true. But it is one thing to show a man that he is in an error, and another to put him in possession of truth; and I would fain know what truths these two propositions are able to teach, and by their influence make us know, which we did not know before, or could not know without them. Let us reason from them as well as we can, they are only about identical predications; and influence, if any at all, none but such. Each particular proposition concerning identity or diversity, is as clearly and certainly known in itself, if attended to, as either of these general ones; only these general ones, as serving in all cases, are therefore more inculcated and insisted on. As to other less general maxims, many of them are no more than bare verbal propositions, and teach us nothing but the respect and import of names one to another. "The whole is equal to all its parts;" what real truth, I beseech you, does it teach us? What more is contained in that maxim, than what the signification of the word *totum*, or the "whole," does of itself import? And he that knows that the word "whole" stands for what is made up of all its parts, knows very little less than that the whole is equal to all

its parts. And upon the same ground I think that this proposition, "A hill is higher than a valley," and several the like,
may also pass for maxims. But yet masters of mathematics,
when they would, as teachers of what they know, initiate others
in that science, do not without reason place this and some other
such maxims at the entrance of their systems; that their scholars,
having in the beginning perfectly acquainted their thoughts with
these propositions made in such general terms, may be used to
make such reflections, and have these more general propositions
as formed rules and sayings, ready to apply to all particular cases.
Not that if they be equally weighed, they are more clear and
evident than the particular instances they are brought to confirm; but that being more familiar to the mind, the very naming
them is enough to satisfy the understanding. But this, I say, is
more from our custom of using them, and the establishment they
have got in our minds by our often thinking of them, than from
the different evidence of the things. But before custom has
settled methods of thinking and reasoning in our minds, I am
apt to imagine, it is quite otherwise; and that the child, when a
part of his apple is taken away, knows it better in that particular
instance, than by this general proposition, "The whole is equal
to all its parts;" and that if one of these have need to be confirmed to him by the other, the general has more need to be let
into his mind by the particular, than the particular by the
general. For in particulars our knowledge begins, and so spreads
itself by degrees to generals; though afterwards the mind takes
the quite contrary course, and, having drawn its knowledge into
as general propositions as it can, makes those familiar to its
thoughts, and accustoms itself to have recourse to them, as to
the standards of truth and falsehood. By which familiar use of
them as rules to measure the truth of other propositions, it comes
in time to be thought, that more particular propositions have
their truth and evidence from their conformity to these more
general ones, which in discourse and argumentation are so frequently urged and constantly admitted. And this I think to be
the reason why, amongst so many self-evident propositions, the
most general only have had the title of "maxims."

12. *Maxims, if care be not taken in the use of words, may prove
contradictions.*—One thing farther, I think, it may not be amiss to
observe concerning these general maxims; that they are so far
from improving or establishing our minds in true knowledge,
that if our notions be wrong, loose, or unsteady, and we resign
up our thoughts to the sound of words, rather than fix them on
settled determined ideas of things; I say, these general maxims
will serve to confirm us in mistakes; and in such a way of use
of words which is most common, will serve to prove contradictions. *V. g.*, he that with Des Cartes shall frame in his mind an
idea of what he calls "body" to be nothing but extension, may

easily demonstrate that there is no vacuum, *i. e.*, no space void of body, by this maxim, "What is, is:" for, the idea to which he annexes the name "body" being bare extension, his knowledge that space cannot be without body is certain: for he knows his own idea of extension clearly and distinctly, and knows that it is what it is, and not another idea, though it be called by these three names, "extension, body, space." Which three words, standing for one and the same idea, may, no doubt, with the same evidence and certainty be affirmed one of another, as each of itself; and it is as certain, that whilst I use them all to stand for one and the same idea, this predication is as true and identical in its signification, "that space is body," as this predication is true and identical, "that body is body," both in signification and sound.

13. *Instance in vacuum.*—But if another shall come and make to himself another idea, different from Des Cartes's of the thing, which yet, with Des Cartes, he calls by the same name "body," and make his idea, which he expresses by the word "body," to be of a thing that hath both extension and solidity together, he will as easily demonstrate that there may be a vacuum or space without a body, as Des Cartes demonstrated the contrary. Because the idea to which he gives the name "space" being barely the simple one of extension; and the idea to which he gives the name "body" being the complex idea of extension and resistibility or solidity together in the same subject; these two ideas are not exactly one and the same, but in the understanding as distinct as the ideas of one and two, white and black, or as of corporeity and humanity, if I may use those barbarous terms: and therefore the predication of them in our minds or in words standing for them, is not identical, but the negation of them one of another; viz., this proposition, "Extension or space is not body," is as true and evidently certain as this maxim, "It is impossible for the same thing to be and not to be," can make any proposition.

14. *They prove not the existence of things without us.*—But yet, though both these propositions (as you see) may be equally demonstrated, viz., that there may be a vacuum, and that there cannot be a vacuum, by these two certain principles, viz., "What is, is," and, "The same thing cannot be and not be;" yet neither of these principles will serve to prove to us, that any or what bodies do exist: for that, we are left to our senses to discover to us as far as they can. Those universal and self-evident principles, being only our constant, clear, and distinct knowledge of our own ideas more general or comprehensive, can assure us of nothing that passes without the mind; their certainty is founded only upon the knowledge we have of each idea by itself, and of its distinction from others; about which we cannot be mistaken whilst they are in our minds, though we may be, and often are

mistaken, when we retain the names without the ideas, or use them confusedly sometimes for one and sometimes for another idea. In which cases, the force of these axioms, reaching only to the sound and not the signification of the word, serves only to lead us into confusion, mistake, and error. It is to show men, that these maxims, however cried up for the great guards to truth, will not secure them from error in a careless, loose use of their words, that I have made this remark. In all that is here suggested concerning their little use for the improvement of knowledge, or dangerous use in undetermined ideas, I have been far enough from saying or intending they should be laid aside, as some have been too forward to charge me. I affirm them to be truths, self-evident truths; and so cannot be laid aside. As far as their influence will reach, it is in vain to endeavour, nor would I attempt to abridge it. But yet without any injury to truth or knowledge, I may have reason to think their use is not answerable to the great stress which seems to be laid on them, and I may warn men not to make an ill use of them for the confirming themselves in errors.

15. *Their application dangerous about complex ideas.*—But let them be of what use they will in verbal propositions, they cannot discover or prove to us the least knowledge of the nature of substances, as they are found and exist without us, any farther than grounded on experience. And though the consequence of these two propositions, called "principles," be very clear, and their use not dangerous or hurtful in the probation of such things wherein there is no need at all of them for proof, but such as are clear by themselves without them, viz., where our ideas are determined, and known by the names that stand for them: yet when these principles, viz., "What is, is," and, "It is impossible for the same thing to be and not to be," are made use of in the probation of propositions wherein are words standing for complex ideas, *v. g.*, "man, horse, gold, virtue;" there they are of infinite danger, and most commonly make men receive and retain falsehood for manifest truth, and uncertainty for demonstration: upon which follows error, obstinacy, and all the mischiefs that can happen from wrong reasoning. The reason whereof is not that these principles are less true or of less force in proving propositions made of terms standing for complex ideas, than where the propositions are about simple ideas; but because men mistake generally, thinking that where the same terms are preserved, the propositions are about the same things, though the ideas they stand for are in truth different. Therefore these maxims are made use of to support those which in sound and appearance are contradictory propositions; as is clear in the demonstrations above mentioned about a vacuum. So that whilst men take words for things, as usually they do, these maxims may and do

commonly serve to prove contradictory propositions: as shall yet
be farther made manifest.

16. *Instance in man.*—For instance: Let "man" be that concerning which you would by these first principles demonstrate
any thing, and we shall see that so far as demonstration is by
these principles it is only verbal, and gives us no certain,
universal, true proposition, or knowledge of any being existing
without us. First, A child having framed the idea of a man, it
is probable that his idea is just like that picture which the
painter makes of the visible appearances joined together; and
such a complication of ideas together in his understanding makes
up the single complex idea which he calls "man;" whereof
white or flesh-colour in England being one, the child can demonstrate to you that a negro is not a man, because white colour was
one of the constant simple ideas of the complex idea he calls
"man:" and therefore he can demonstrate by the principle, "It
is impossible for the same thing to be and not to be," that "a
negro is not a man;" the foundation of his certainty being not
that universal proposition which, perhaps, he never heard nor
thought of, but the clear, distinct, perception he hath of his own
simple ideas of black and white, which he cannot be persuaded
to take, nor can ever mistake one for another, whether he knows
that maxim or no. And to this child, or any one who hath such
an idea which he calls "man," can you never demonstrate that
a man hath a soul, because his idea of man includes no such
notion or idea in it: and therefore to him the principle of "what
is, is," proves not this matter; but it depends upon collection
and observation, by which he is to make his complex idea called
"man."

17. Secondly, Another, that hath gone farther in framing and
collecting the idea he calls "man," and to the outward shape
adds laughter and rational discourse, may demonstrate that
infants and changelings are no men by this maxim, "It is
impossible for the same thing to be and not to be:" and I have
discoursed with very rational men who have actually denied that
they are men.

18. Thirdly, Perhaps another makes up the complex idea
which he calls "man" only out of the ideas of body in general,
and the powers of language and reason, and leaves out the
shape wholly. This man is able to demonstrate that a man may
have no hands, but be *quadrupes*, neither of those being included
in his idea of man; and in whatever body or shape be found
speech and reason joined, that was a man: because, having a
clear knowledge of such a complex idea, it is certain that "what
is, is."

19. *Little use of these maxims in proofs where we have clear and
distinct ideas.*—So that, if rightly considered, I think we may
say, that where our ideas are determined in our minds, and have

annexed to them by us known and steady names under those settled determinations, there is little need or no use at all of these maxims to prove the agreement or disagreement of any of them. He that cannot discern the truth or falsehood of such propositions, without the help of these and the like maxims, will not be helped by these maxims to do it: since he cannot be supposed to know the truth of these maxims themselves without proof, if he cannot know the truth of others without proof, which are as self-evident as these. Upon this ground it is that intuitive knowledge neither requires nor admits any proof, one part of it more than another. He that will suppose it does, takes away the foundation of all knowledge and certainty: and he that needs any proof to make him certain, and give his assent to this proposition, that "two are equal to two," will also have need of a proof to make him admit that "what is, is." He that needs a probation to convince him that two are not three, that white is not black, that a triangle is not a circle, &c., or any other two determined distinct ideas are not one and the same, will need also a demonstration to convince him that "it is impossible for the same thing to be and not to be."

20. *Their use dangerous where our ideas are confused.*—And as these maxims are of little use where we have determined ideas, so they are, as I have showed, of dangerous use where our ideas are not determined; and where we use words that are not annexed to determined ideas, but such as are of a loose and wandering signification, sometimes standing for one and sometimes for another idea; from which follows mistake and error, which these maxims (brought as proofs to establish propositions wherein the terms stand for undetermined ideas) do by their authority confirm and rivet.

---

# CHAPTER VIII.

## OF TRIFLING PROPOSITIONS.

1. *Some propositions bring no increase to our knowledge.*— Whether the maxims treated of in the foregoing chapter be of that use to real knowledge as is generally supposed, I leave to be considered. This, I think, may confidently be affirmed, that there are universal propositions which, though they be certainly true, yet they add no light to our understandings, bring no increase to our knowledge. Such are,

2. *As, First, identical propositions.*—First, All purely identical propositions. These obviously and at first blush appear to contain no instruction in them: for when we affirm the said term of itself, whether it be barely verbal, or whether it contains any clear and real idea, it shows us nothing but what we must

certainly know before, whether such a proposition be either made by or proposed to us. Indeed, that most general one, "What is, is," may serve sometimes to show a man the absurdity he is guilty of, when by circumlocution or equivocal terms he would, in particular instances, deny the same thing of itself; because nobody will so openly bid defiance to common sense as to affirm visible and direct contradictions in plain words; or if he does, a man is excused if he breaks off any farther discourse with him. But yet, I think, I may say, that neither that received maxim, nor any other identical proposition, teaches us anything: and though in such kind of propositions this great and magnified maxim, boasted to be the foundation of demonstration, may be and often is made use of to confirm them; yet all it proves amounts to no more than this, that the same word may with great certainty be affirmed of itself, without any doubt of the truth of any such proposition; and let me add also, without any real knowledge.

3. For at this rate, any very ignorant person who can but make a proposition, and knows what he means when he says "Ay," or "No," may make a million of propositions of whose truths he may be infallibly certain, and yet not know one thing in the world thereby; v. g., "What is a soul, is a soul;" or, "A soul is a soul;" "A spirit is a spirit;" "A fetiche is a fetiche," &c., these all being equivalent to this proposition, viz., "What is, is;" i. e., "What hath existence, hath existence;" or, "Who hath a soul, hath a soul." What is this more than trifling with words? It is but like a monkey shifting his oyster from one hand to the other; and had he had but words, might no doubt have said, "Oyster in right hand is subject, and oyster in left hand is predicate;" and so might have made a self-evident proposition of oyster, i. e., "Oyster is oyster;" and yet with all this not have been one whit the wiser or more knowing: and that way of handling the matter would, much at one, have satisfied the monkey's hunger or a man's understanding; and they two would have improved in knowledge and bulk together. I know there are some who, because identical propositions are self-evident, show a great concern for them, and think they do great service to philosophy by crying them up, as if in them was contained all knowledge, and the understanding were led into all truth by them only. I grant as forwardly as any one, that they are all true and self-evident. I grant, farther, that the foundation of all our knowledge lies in the faculty we have of perceiving the same idea to be the same, and of discerning it from those that are different, as I have shown in the foregoing chapter. But how that vindicates the making use of identical propositions for the improvement of knowledge from the imputation of trifling, I do not see. Let any one repeat as often as he pleases, that "the will is the will," or lay what stress on it he thinks fit; of what

use is this, and an infinite the like propositions, for the enlarging
our knowledge? Let a man abound as much as the plenty of
words which he has will permit him in such propositions as
these: "A law is a law, and obligation is obligation;" "Right
is right, and wrong is wrong;" will these and the like ever help
him to an acquaintance with ethics? or instruct him or others in
the knowledge of morality? Those who know not, nor perhaps
ever will know, what is right and what is wrong, nor the measures
of them, can with as much assurance make and infallibly know
the truth of these and all such propositions, as he that is best
instructed in morality can do. But what advance do such propositions give in the knowledge of any thing necessary or useful
for their conduct?

He would be thought to do little less than trifle, who, for the
enlightening the understanding in any part of knowledge, should
be busy with identical propositions, and insist on such maxims
as these: "Substance is substance, and body is body;" "A
vacuum is a vacuum, and a vortex is a vortex;" "A centaur is
a centaur, and a chimera is a chimera," &c. For these and all
such are equally true, equally certain, and equally self-evident.
But yet they cannot but be counted trifling, when made use of as
principles of instruction, and stress laid on them as helps to
knowledge; since they teach nothing but what every one, who
is capable of discourse, knows without being told, viz., that the
same term is the same term, and the same idea the same idea.
And upon this account it was that I formerly did and do still
think, the offering and inculcating such propositions, in order to
give the understanding any new light or inlet into the knowledge
of things, no better than trifling.

Instruction lies in something very different; and he that would
enlarge his own or another's mind to truths he does not yet know,
must find out intermediate ideas, and then lay them in such order
one by another, that the understanding may see the agreement
or disagreement of those in question. Propositions that do this
are instructive: but they are far from such as affirm the same
term of itself; which is no way to advance one's self or others in
any sort of knowledge. It no more helps to that, than it would
help any one in his learning to read to have such propositions as
these inculcated to him, "An A is an A, and a B is a B;" which
a man may know as well as any schoolmaster, and yet never be
able to read a word as long as he lives. Nor do these or any
such identical propositions help him one jot forwards in the skill
of reading, let him make what use of them he can.

If those who blame my calling them "trifling propositions"
had but read, and been at the pains to understand, what I had
above writ in very plain English, they could not but have seen
that by "identical propositions" I mean only such wherein the
same term, importing the same idea, is affirmed of itself: which

I take to be the proper signification of "identical propositions;" and concerning all such, I think I may continue safely to say, that to propose them as instructive is no better than trifling. For no one who has the use of reason can miss them, where it is necessary they should be taken notice of: nor doubt of their truth, when he does take notice of them.

But if men will call propositions "identical" wherein the same term is affirmed of itself, whether they speak more properly than I, others must judge: this is certain, all that they say of propositions that are not "identical" in my sense, concerns not me, nor what I have said; all that I have said relating to those propositions wherein the same term is affirmed of itself. And I would fain see an instance wherein any such can be made use of to the advantage and improvement of any one's knowledge. Instances of other kinds, whatever use may be made of them, concern not me, as not being such as I call "identical."

4. *Secondly, When a part of any complex idea is predicated of the whole.*—Secondly, Another sort of trifling propositions is, when a part of the complex idea is predicated of the name of the whole; a part of the definition, of the word defined. Such are all propositions wherein the *genus* is predicated of the *species;* or more comprehensive, of less comprehensive terms: for, what information, what knowledge, carries this proposition in it, viz., "Lead is a metal," to a man who knows the complex idea the name "lead" stands for? all the simple ideas that go to the complex one signified by the term "metal," being nothing but what he before comprehended, and signified by the name "lead." Indeed, to a man that knows the signification of the word "metal," and not of the word "lead," it is a shorter way to explain the signification of the word "lead" by saying, "It is a metal," which at once expresses several of its simple ideas, than to enumerate them one by one, telling him, "It is a body very heavy, fusible, and malleable."

5. *As part of the definition of the term defined.*—A like trifling it is to predicate any other part of the definition of the term defined; or to affirm any one of the simple ideas of a complex one, of the name of the whole complex idea, as, "All gold is fusible." For, fusibility being one of the simple ideas that goes to the making up the complex one the sound "gold" stands for, what can it be but playing with sounds to affirm that of the name of "gold" which is comprehended in its received signification? It would be thought little better than ridiculous to affirm gravely as a truth of moment, that "gold is yellow;" and I see not how it is any jot more material to say, "It is fusible," unless that quality be left out of the complex idea of which the sound "gold" is the mark in ordinary speech. What instruction can it carry with it, to tell one that which he hath been told already, or he is supposed to know before? For I am sup-

posed to know the signification of the word another uses to me, or else he is to tell me. And if I know that the name "gold" stands for this complex idea of body, yellow, heavy, fusible, malleable, it will not much instruct me to put it solemnly afterwards in a proposition, and gravely say, "All gold is fusible." Such propositions can only serve to show the disingenuity of one who will go from the definition of his own terms, by reminding him sometimes of it; but carry no knowledge with them but of the signification of words, however certain they be.

6. *Instance, man and palfrey.*—"Every man is an animal or living body," is as certain a proposition as can be; but no more conducing to the knowledge of things than to say, "A palfrey is an ambling horse, or a neighing, ambling animal;" both being only about the signification of words, and make me know but this, that body, sense, and motion, or power of sensation and moving, are three of those ideas that I always comprehend and signify by the word "man;" and where they are not to be found together, the name "man" belongs not to that thing: and so of the other, that body, sense, and a certain way of going, with a certain kind of voice, are some of those ideas which I always comprehend and signify by the word "palfrey:" and when they are not to be found together, the name "palfrey" belongs not to that thing. It is just the same, and to the same purpose, when any term standing for any one or more of the simple ideas that altogether make up that complex idea which is called "a man," is affirmed of the term "man;" *v. g.*, suppose a Roman signified by the word *homo*, all these distinct ideas united in one subject, *corporeitas, sensibilitas, potentia se movendi, rationalitas, risibilitas;* he might, no doubt, with great certainty universally affirm one, more, or all of these together of the word *homo*, but did no more than say, that the word *homo*, in his country, comprehended in its signification all these ideas. Much like a romance-knight, who, by the word "palfrey" signified these ideas, "body of a certain figure, four-legged, with sense, motion, ambling, neighing, white, used to have a woman on his back," might with the same certainty universally affirm also any or all of these of the word "palfrey:" but did thereby teach no more but that the word "palfrey," in his or romance language, stood for all these, and was not to be applied to any thing where any of these was wanting. But he that shall tell me, that "in whatever thing sense, motion, reason, and laughter were united, that thing had actually a notion of God, or would be cast into a sleep by opium," made indeed an instructive proposition; because neither "having the notion of God," nor "being cast into sleep by opium," being contained in the idea signified by the word "man," we are by such propositions taught something more than barely what the word "man" stands for: and therefore the knowledge contained in it is more than verbal.

**7. *For this teaches but the signification of words.*—**Before a man makes any proposition, he is supposed to understand the terms he uses in it, or else he talks like a parrot, only making a noise by imitation, and framing certain sounds which he has learned of others; but not as a rational creature, using them for signs of ideas which he has in his mind. The hearer also is supposed to understand the terms as the speaker uses them, or else he talks jargon, and makes an unintelligible noise. And therefore he trifles with words who makes such a proposition, which when it is made contains no more than one of the terms does, and which a man was supposed to know before; *v. g.*, "A triangle hath three sides," or, "Saffron is yellow." And this is no farther tolerable than where a man goes to explain his terms to one who is supposed or declares himself not to understand him: and then it teaches only the signification of that word, and the use of that sign.

**8. *But no real knowledge.*—**We can know then the truth of two sorts of propositions with perfect certainty; the one is, of those trifling propositions which have a certainty in them, but it is only a verbal certainty, but not instructive. And, secondly, we can know the truth, and so may be certain in propositions which affirm something of another, which is a necessary consequence of its precise complex idea, but not contained in it: as that "the external angle of all triangles is bigger than either of the opposite internal angles;" which relation of the outward angle to either of the opposite internal angles, making no part of the complex idea signified by the name "triangle," this is a real truth, and conveys with it instructive real knowledge.

**9. *General propositions concerning substances are often trifling.*** —We having little or no knowledge of what combinations there be of simple ideas existing together in substances but by our senses, we cannot make any universal certain propositions concerning them any farther than our nominal essences lead us; which being to a very few and inconsiderable truths, in respect of those which depend on their real constitutions, the general propositions that are made about substances, if they are certain, are, for the most part, but trifling; and if they are instructive, are uncertain, and such as we can have no knowledge of their real truth, how much soever constant observation and analogy may assist our judgments in guessing. Hence it comes to pass, that one may often meet with very clear and coherent discourses that amount yet to nothing. For, it is plain, that names of substantial beings, as well as others, as far as they have relative significations affixed to them, may, with great truth, be joined negatively and affirmatively in propositions, as their relative definitions make them fit to be so joined; and propositions consisting of such terms may, with the same clearness, be deduced one from another, as those that convey the most real truths;

and all this without any knowledge of the nature or reality of things existing without us. By this method one may make demonstrations and undoubted propositions in words, and yet thereby advance not one jot in the knowledge of the truth of things; *v. g.*, he that having learned these following words with their ordinary, mutually relative acceptations annexed to them, *v. g.*, "substance, man, animal, form, soul, vegetative, sensitive, rational," may make several undoubted propositions about the soul, without knowing at all what the soul really is; and of this sort a man may find an infinite number of propositions, reasonings, and conclusions, in books of metaphysics, school divinity, and some sort of natural philosophy; and after all know as little of God, spirits, or bodies, as he did before he set out.

10. *And why.*—He that hath liberty to define, *i. e.*, determine the signification of his names of substances, (as certainly every one does in effect who makes them stand for his own ideas,) and makes their significations at a venture, taking them from his own or other men's fancies, and not from an examination or inquiry into the nature of things themselves, may, with little trouble, demonstrate them one of another, according to those several respects and mutual relations he has given them one to another; wherein, however things agree or disagree in their own nature, he needs mind nothing but his own notions, with the names he hath bestowed upon them: but thereby no more increases his own knowledge than he does his riches who, taking a bag of counters, calls one in a certain place "a pound;" another in another place "a shilling;" and a third in a third place "a penny;" and so proceeding, may undoubtedly reckon right and cast up a great sum, according to his counters so placed, and standing for more or less as he pleases, without being one jot the richer, or without even knowing how much a pound, shilling, or penny is, but only that one is contained in the other twenty times, and contains the other twelve: which a man may also do in the signification of words, by making them in respect of one another more or less or equally comprehensive.

11. *Thirdly, Using words variously is trifling with them.*— Though yet concerning most words used in discourses, especially argumentative and controversial, there is this more to be complained of, which is the worst sort of trifling, and which sets us yet farther from the certainty of knowledge we hope to attain by them, or find in them, viz., that most writers are so far from instructing us in the nature and knowledge of things, that they use their words loosely and uncertainly, and do not, by using them constantly and steadily in the same significations, make plain and clear deductions of words one from another, and make their discourses coherent and clear, (how little soever it were instructive;) which were not difficult to do, did they not find it convenient to shelter their ignorance or obstinacy under the

obscurity and perplexedness of their terms: to which, perhaps, inadvertency and ill custom do in many men much contribute.

12. *Marks of verbal propositions.*—To conclude, barely verbal propositions may be known by these following marks:—

*First, Predication in abstract.*—First, All propositions wherein two abstract terms are affirmed one of another, are barely about the signification of sounds. For, since no abstract idea can be the same with any other but itself, when its abstract name is affirmed of any other term, it can signify no more but this, that it may or ought to be called by that name; or that these two names signify the same idea. Thus should any one say that "parsimony is frugality," that "gratitude is justice," that this or that action is or is not temperance; however specious these and the like propositions may at first sight seem, yet when we come to press them, and examine nicely what they contain, we shall find that it all amounts to nothing but the signification of those terms.

13. *Secondly, A part of the definition predicated of any term.*—Secondly, All propositions wherein a part of the complex idea which any term stands for is predicated of that term, are only verbal; *v. g.*, to say that "gold is a metal" or "heavy." And thus all propositions wherein more comprehensive words, called *genera*, are affirmed of subordinate, or less comprehensive, called *species* or individuals, are barely verbal.

When by these two rules we have examined the propositions that make up the discourses we ordinarily meet with, both in and out of books, we shall perhaps find that a greater part of them than is usually suspected are purely about the signification of words, and contain nothing in them but the use and application of these signs.

This, I think, I may lay down for an infallible rule, that wherever the distinct idea any word stands for is not known and considered, and something not contained in the idea is not affirmed or denied of it, there our thoughts stick wholly in sounds, and are able to attain no real truth or falsehood. This perhaps, if well heeded, might save us a great deal of useless amusement and dispute; and very much shorten our trouble and wandering in the search of real and true knowledge.

## CHAPTER IX.

### OF OUR KNOWLEDGE OF EXISTENCE.

1. *General certain propositions concern not existence.*—Hitherto we have only considered the essences of things, which, being only abstract ideas, and thereby removed in our thoughts from particular existence, (that being the proper operation of the

mind in abstraction, to consider an idea under no other existence but what it has in the understanding,) give us no knowledge of real existence at all. Where, by the way, we may take notice, that universal propositions, of whose truth or falsehood we can have certain knowledge, concern not existence; and farther, that all particular affirmations or negations that would not be certain if they were made general, are only concerning existence; they declaring only the accidental union or separation of ideas in things existing, which in their abstract natures have no known necessary union or repugnancy.

2. *A threefold knowledge of existence.*—But leaving the nature of propositions, and different ways of predication, to be considered more at large in another place, let us proceed now to inquire concerning our knowledge of the existence of things, and how we come by it. I say then, that we have the knowledge of our own existence by intuition; of the existence of God by demonstration; and of other things by sensation.

3. *Our knowledge of our own existence is intuitive.*—As for our own existence, we perceive it so plainly and so certainly that it neither needs nor is capable of any proof. For nothing can be more evident to us than our own existence. I think, I reason, I feel pleasure and pain: can any of these be more evident to me than my own existence? If I doubt of all other things, that very doubt makes me perceive my own existence, and will not suffer me to doubt of that. For, if I know I feel pain, it is evident I have as certain perception of my own existence, as of the existence of the pain I feel: or if I know I doubt, I have as certain perception of the existence of the thing doubting, as of that thought which I call "doubt." Experience, then, convinces us that we have an intuitive knowledge of our own existence, and an internal infallible perception that we are. In every act of sensation, reasoning, or thinking, we are conscious to ourselves of our own being; and, in this matter, come not short of the highest degree of certainty.

## CHAPTER X.

### OF OUR KNOWLEDGE OF THE EXISTENCE OF A GOD.

1. *We are capable of knowing certainly that there is a God.*— Though God has given us no innate ideas of himself; though he has stamped no original characters on our minds, wherein we may read his being; yet, having furnished us with those faculties our minds are endowed with, he hath not left himself without witness; since we have sense, perception, and reason, and cannot want a clear proof of him as long as we carry ourselves about us. Nor can we justly complain of our ignorance in this great point,

since he has so plentifully provided us with the means to discover and know him, so far as is necessary to the end of our being, and the great concernment of our happiness. But though this be the most obvious truth that reason discovers, and though its evidence be (if I mistake not) equal to mathematical certainty; yet it requires thought and attention, and the mind must apply itself to a regular deduction of it from some part of our intuitive knowledge, or else we shall be as uncertain and ignorant of this as of other propositions which are in themselves capable of clear demonstration. To show, therefore, that we are capable of knowing, *i. e.*, being certain, that there is a God, and how we may come by this certainty, I think we need go no farther than ourselves, and that undoubted knowledge we have of our own existence.

2. *Man knows that he himself is.*—I think it is beyond question, that man has a clear perception of his own being; he knows certainly that he exists, and that he is something. He that can doubt whether he be any thing or no, I speak not to; no more than I would argue with pure nothing, or endeavour to convince nonentity that it were something. If any one pretends to be so sceptical as to deny his own existence (for really to doubt of it is manifestly impossible), let him, for me, enjoy his beloved happiness of being nothing, until hunger or some other pain convince him of the contrary. This, then, I think I may take for a truth, which every one's certain knowledge assures him of beyond the liberty of doubting, viz., that he is something that actually exists.

3. *He knows also that nothing cannot produce a being, therefore something eternal.*—In the next place, man knows by an intuitive certainty that bare nothing can no more produce any real being, than it can be equal to two right angles. If a man knows not that nonentity, or the absence of all being, cannot be equal to two right angles, it is impossible he should know any demonstration in Euclid. If therefore we know there is some real being, and that nonentity cannot produce any real being, it is an evident demonstration, that from eternity there has been something; since what was not from eternity had a beginning; and what had a beginning must be produced by something else.

4. *That Eternal Being must be most powerful.*—Next, it is evident, that what had its being and beginning from another, must also have all that which is in and belongs to its being from another too. All the powers it has, must be owing to and received from the same source. This eternal source, then, of all being, must also be the source and original of all power; and so this Eternal Being must be also the most powerful.

5. *And most knowing.*—Again: a man finds in himself perception and knowledge. We have then got one step farther; and we are certain now that there is not only some being, but some knowing, intelligent being in the world.

There was a time, then, when there was no knowing being, and when knowledge began to be; or else there has been also a knowing Being from eternity. If it be said, "There was a time when no being had any knowledge, when that Eternal Being was void of all understanding;" I reply, that then it was impossible there should ever have been any knowledge; it being as impossible that things wholly void of knowledge, and operating blindly and without any perception, should produce a knowing being, as it is impossible that a triangle should make itself three angles bigger than two right ones. For it is as repugnant to the idea of senseless matter that it should put into itself sense, perception, and knowledge, as it is repugnant to the idea of a triangle that it should put into itself greater angles than two right ones.

6. *And therefore God.*—Thus from the consideration of ourselves, and what we infallibly find in our own constitutions, our reason leads us to the knowledge of this certain and evident truth, that there is an eternal, most powerful, and most knowing Being; which whether any one will please to call "God," it matters not. The thing is evident; and from this idea, duly considered, will easily be deduced all those other attributes which we ought to ascribe to this Eternal Being. If, nevertheless, any one should be found so senselessly arrogant as to suppose man alone knowing and wise, but yet the product of mere ignorance and chance; and that all the rest of the universe acted only by that blind hap-hazard; I shall leave with him that very rational and emphatical rebuke of Tully, lib. ii. *De Leg.*, to be considered at his leisure: "What can be more sillily arrogant and misbecoming than for a man to think that he has a mind and understanding in him, but yet in all the universe beside there is no such thing? or that those things which, with the utmost stretch of his reason, he can scarce comprehend, should be moved and managed without any reason at all?" *Quid est enim verius quam neminem esse oportere tam stulte arrogantem, ut in se mentem et rationem putet inesse, in cœlo mundoque non putet? Aut ea quæ vix summâ ingenii ratione comprehendat, nullâ ratione moveri putet?*

From what has been said, it is plain to me we have a more certain knowledge of the existence of a God, than of any thing our senses have not immediately discovered to us. Nay, I presume I may say, that we more certainly know that there is a God, than that there is any thing else without us. When I say "we know," I mean there is such a knowledge within our reach which we cannot miss, if we will but apply our minds to that as we do to several other inquiries.

7. *Our idea of a most perfect being, not the sole proof of a God.*—How far the idea of a most perfect being which a man may frame in his mind, does or does not prove the existence of a God, I will not here examine. For, in the different make of men's

tempers and application of their thoughts, some arguments prevail more on one, and some on another, for the confirmation of the same truth. But yet, I think this I may say, that it is an ill way of establishing this truth and silencing atheists, to lay the whole stress of so important a point as this upon that sole foundation: and take some men's having that idea of God in their minds (for it is evident some men have none, and some worse than none, and the most very different) for the only proof of a Deity; and out of an over-fondness of that darling invention, cashier, or at least endeavour to invalidate, all other arguments, and forbid us to hearken to those proofs, as being weak or fallacious, which our own existence and the sensible parts of the universe offer so clearly and cogently to our thoughts, that I deem it impossible for a considering man to withstand them. For I judge it as certain and clear a truth as can any where be delivered, that "the invisible things of God are clearly seen from the creation of the world, being understood by the things that are made, even his eternal power and Godhead." Though our own being furnishes us, as I have shown, with an evident and incontestable proof of a Deity; and I believe nobody can avoid the cogency of it who will but as carefully attend to it as to any other demonstration of so many parts; yet this being so fundamental a truth, and of that consequence that all religion and genuine morality depend thereon, I doubt not but I shall be forgiven by my reader if I go over some parts of this argument again, and enlarge a little more upon them.

8. *Something from eternity.*—There is no truth more evident than that something must be from eternity. I never yet heard of any one so unreasonable, or that could suppose so manifest a contradiction, as a time wherein there was perfectly nothing; this being of all absurdities the greatest, to imagine that pure nothing, the perfect negation and absence of all beings, should ever produce any real existence.

It being then unavoidable for all rational creatures to conclude that something has existed from eternity, let us next see what kind of thing that must be.

9. *Two sorts of beings cogitative and incogitative.*—There are but two sorts of beings in the world that man knows or conceives:—

First, Such as are purely material, without sense, perception, or thought, as the clippings of our beards and parings of our nails.

Secondly, Sensible, thinking, perceiving beings, such as we find ourselves to be; which, if you please, we will hereafter call "cogitative and incogitative beings;" which, to our present purpose, if for nothing else, are perhaps better terms than "material and immaterial."

10. *Incogitative being cannot produce a cogitative.*—If then ther

must be something eternal, let us see what sort of being it must be. And to that it is very obvious to reason, that it must necessarily be a cogitative being. For it is as impossible to conceive that ever bare incogitative matter should produce a thinking intelligent being, as that nothing should of itself produce matter. Let us suppose any parcel of matter eternal, great or small, we shall find it in itself able to produce nothing. For example : Let us suppose the matter of the next pebble we meet with, eternal, closely united, and the parts firmly at rest together; if there were no other being in the world, must it not eternally remain so, a dead, inactive lump? Is it possible to conceive it can add motion to itself, being purely matter, or produce any thing? Matter, then, by its own strength, cannot produce in itself so much as motion : the motion it has must also be from eternity, or else be produced and added to matter by some other being more powerful than matter: matter, as is evident, having not power to produce motion in itself. But let us suppose motion eternal too; yet matter, incogitative matter and motion, whatever changes it might produce of figure and bulk, could never produce thought. Knowledge will still be as far beyond the power of motion and matter to produce, as matter is beyond the power of nothing or nonentity to produce. And I appeal to every one's own thoughts, whether he cannot as easily conceive matter produced by nothing, as thought to be produced by pure matter, when before there was no such thing as thought or an intelligent being existing. Divide matter into as minute parts as you will, which we are apt to imagine a sort of spiritualizing or making a thinking thing of it; vary the figure and motion of it as much as you please; a globe, cube, cone, prism, cylinder, &c., whose diameters are but 1,000,000th part of a gry,* will operate no otherwise upon other bodies of proportionable bulk than those of an inch or foot diameter ; and you may as rationally expect to produce sense, thought, and knowledge, by putting together in a certain figure and motion gross particles of matter, as by those that are the very minutest that do any where exist. They knock, impel, and resist one another just as the greater do, and that is all they can do. So that, if we will suppose nothing first or eternal, matter can never begin to be : if we will suppose bare matter without motion, eternal motion can never begin to be : if we suppose only matter and motion first, or eternal, thought can never begin to be. For it is impossible to conceive that matter, either with or without motion,

---

* A gry is one-tenth of a line, a line one-tenth of an inch, an inch one-tenth of a philosophical foot, a philosophical foot one-third of a pendulum, whose diadroms, in the latitude of forty-five degrees, are each equal to one second of time, or one-sixtieth of a minute. I have affectedly made use of this measure here, and the parts of it, under a decimal division, with names to them ; because I think it would be of general convenience, that this should be the common measure in the commonwealth of letters.

could have originally in and from itself, sense, perception, and knowledge, as is evident from hence, that then sense, perception, and knowledge must be a property eternally inseparable from matter and every particle of it. Not to add, that though our general or specific conception of matter makes us speak of it as one thing, yet really all matter is not one individual thing, neither is there any such thing existing as one material being, or one single body, that we know or can conceive. And therefore, if matter were the eternal first cogitative being, there would not be one eternal infinite cogitative being, but an infinite number of eternal finite cogitative beings independent one of another, of limited force and distinct thoughts, which could never produce that order, harmony, and beauty, which is to be found in nature. Since, therefore, whatsoever is the first eternal being must necessarily be cogitative; and whatsoever is first of all things must necessarily contain in it, and actually have, at least, all the perfections that can ever after exist; nor can it ever give to another any perfection that it hath not, either actually in itself or at least in a higher degree: it necessarily follows, that the first eternal being cannot be matter.

11. *Therefore there has been an eternal wisdom.*—If, therefore, it be evident that something necessarily must exist from eternity, it is also as evident that that something must necessarily be a cogitative being: for it is as impossible that incogitative matter should produce a cogitative being, as that nothing, or the negation of all being, should produce a positive being or matter.

12. Though this discovery of the necessary existence of an eternal mind does sufficiently lead us into the knowledge of God, since it will hence follow that all other knowing beings that have a beginning must depend on him, and have no other ways of knowledge or extent of power than what he gives them; and therefore if he made those, he made also the less excellent pieces of this universe, all inanimate beings, whereby his omniscience, power, and providence will be established, and all his other attributes necessarily follow: yet, to clear up this a little farther, we will see what doubts can be raised against it.

13. *Whether material or no.*—First, Perhaps it will be said, that though it be as clear as demonstration can make it, that there must be an eternal being, and that being must also be knowing; yet, it does not follow but that thinking being may also be material. Let it be so; it equally still follows that there is a God. For if there be an eternal, omniscient, omnipotent being, it is certain that there is a God, whether you imagine that being to be material or no. But herein, I suppose, lies the danger and deceit of that supposition: there being no way to avoid the demonstration, that there is an eternal knowing Being, men devoted to matter would willingly have it granted that this knowing Being is material: and then letting slide out of their

minds, or the discourse, the demonstration whereby an eternal knowing Being was proved necessarily to exist, would argue all to be matter, and so deny a God, that is, an eternal cogitative Being; whereby they are so far from establishing, that they destroy, their own hypothesis. For if there can be, in their opinion, eternal matter without any eternal cogitative Being, they manifestly separate matter and thinking, and suppose no necessary connexion of the one with the other, and so establish the necessity of an eternal Spirit, but not of matter; since it has been proved already, that an eternal cogitative Being is unavoidably to be granted. Now, if thinking matter may be separated, the eternal existence of matter will not follow from the eternal existence of a cogitative Being, and they suppose it to no purpose.

14. *Not material: First, Because every particle of matter is not cogitative.*—But now let us see how they can satisfy themselves or others, that this eternal thinking Being is material.

First, I would ask them, whether they imagine that all matter, every particle of matter, thinks? This, I suppose, they will scarce say, since then there would be as many eternal thinking beings as there are particles of matter, and so an infinity of gods. And yet, if they will not allow matter as matter, that is, every particle of matter, to be as well cogitative as extended, they will have as hard a task to make out to their own reasons a cogitative being out of incogitative particles, as an extended being out of unextended parts, if I may so speak.

15. *Secondly, One particle alone of matter cannot be cogitative.*—Secondly, If all matter does not think, I next ask, whether it be only one atom that does so? This has as many absurdities as the other; for then this atom of matter must be alone eternal or not. If this alone be eternal, then this alone, by its powerful thought or will, made all the rest of matter. And so we have the creation of matter by a powerful thought, which is that the materialists stick at: for, if they suppose one single thinking atom to have produced all the rest of matter, they cannot ascribe that pre-eminency to it upon any other account than that of its thinking, the only supposed difference. But allow it to be by some other way which is above our conception, it must be still creation; and these men must give up their great maxim, *Ex nihilo nil fit.* If it be said, that "all the rest of matter is equally eternal as that thinking atom," it will be to say any thing at pleasure, though never so absurd: for to suppose all matter eternal, and yet one small particle in knowledge and power infinitely above all the rest, is without any the least appearance of reason to frame any hypothesis. Every particle of matter, as matter, is capable of all the same figures and motions of any other; and I challenge any one, in his thoughts, to add any thing else to one above another.

16. *Thirdly, A system of incogitative matter cannot be cogitative.*
—Thirdly, If then neither one peculiar atom alone can be this eternal thinking Being, nor all matter, as matter, *i. e.*, every particle of matter, can be it; it only remains that it is some certain system of matter duly put together, that is this thinking eternal Being. This is that which I imagine is that notion which men are aptest to have of God, who would have him a material being, as most readily suggested to them by the ordinary conceit they have of themselves and other men, which they take to be material thinking beings. But this imagination, however more natural, is no less absurd than the other: for, to suppose the eternal thinking Being to be nothing else but a composition of particles of matter, each whereof is incogitative, is to ascribe all the wisdom and knowledge of that eternal Being only to the juxtaposition of parts; than which nothing can be more absurd. For, unthinking particles of matter, however put together, can have nothing thereby added to them but a new relation of position, which it is impossible should give thought and knowledge to them.

17. *Whether in motion, or at rest.*—But further; this corporeal system either has all its parts at rest, or it is a certain motion of the parts wherein its thinking consists. If it be perfectly at rest, it is but one lump, and so can have no privileges above one atom.

If it be the motion of its parts on which its thinking depends, all the thoughts there must be unavoidably accidental and limited, since all the particles that by motion cause thought, being each of them in itself without any thought, cannot regulate its own motions, much less be regulated by the thought of the whole, since that thought is not the cause of motion, (for then it must be antecedent to it, and so without it,) but the consequence of it, whereby freedom, power, choice, and all rational and wise thinking or acting, will be quite taken away: so that such a thinking being will be no better nor wiser than pure blind matter, since to resolve all into the accidental unguided motions of blind matter, or into thought depending on unguided motions of blind matter, is the same thing; not to mention the narrowness of such thoughts and knowledge that must depend on the motion of such parts. But there needs no enumeration of any more absurdities and impossibilities in this hypothesis (however full of them it be) than that before mentioned; since, let this thinking system be all or a part of the matter of the universe, it is impossible that any one particle should either know its own or the motion of any other particle, or the whole know the motion of every particular; and so regulate its own thoughts or motions, or indeed have any thought resulting from such motion.

18. *Matter not co-eternal with an eternal Mind.*—Others would

have matter to be eternal, notwithstanding that they allow an eternal, cogitative, immaterial being. This, though it take not away the being of a God, yet since it denies one and the first great piece of his workmanship, the creation, let us consider it a little. Matter must be allowed eternal; why? Because you cannot conceive how it can be made out of nothing: why do you not also think yourself eternal? You will answer, perhaps, Because about twenty or forty years since you began to be. But if I ask you what that "you" is, which began then to be, you can scarce tell me. The matter whereof you are made began not then to be; for if it did, then it is not eternal; but it began to be put together in such a fashion and frame as makes up your body; but yet that frame of particles is not you, it makes not that thinking thing you are; (for I have now to do with one who allows an eternal, immaterial, thinking being, but would have unthinking matter eternal too;) therefore when did that thinking thing begin to be? If it did never begin to be, then have you always been a thinking thing from eternity: the absurdity whereof I need not confute till I meet with one who is so void of understanding as to own it. If, therefore, you can allow a thinking thing to be made out of nothing, (as all things that are not eternal must be,) why also can you not allow it possible for a material being to be made out of nothing by an equal power, but that you have the experience of the one in view, and not of the other; though, when well considered, creation of a spirit will be found to require no less power than the creation of matter. Nay, possibly, if we would emancipate ourselves from vulgar notions, and raise our thoughts, as far as they would reach, to a closer contemplation of things, we might be able to aim at some dim and seeming conception how matter might at first be made, and begin to exist, by the power of that eternal first Being; but to give beginning and being to a spirit would be found a more inconceivable effect of omnipotent power. But this being what would, perhaps, lead us too far from the notions on which the philosophy now in the world is built, it would not be pardonable to deviate so far from them, or to inquire so far as grammar itself would authorize, if the common settled opinion opposes it; especially in this place, where the received doctrine serves well enough to our present purpose, and leaves this past doubt, that, the creation or beginning of any one substance out of nothing being once admitted, the creation of all other, but the Creator himself, may, with the same ease, be supposed.

19. But you will say, "Is it not impossible to admit of the making any thing out of nothing, since we cannot possibly conceive it?" I answer, No: (1.) Because it is not reasonable to deny the power of an infinite Being because we cannot comprehend its operations. We do not deny other effects upon

this ground, because we cannot possibly conceive the manner of their production. We cannot conceive how any thing but impulse of body can move body; and yet that is not a reason sufficient to make us deny it possible, against the constant experience we have of it in ourselves, in all our voluntary motions, which are produced in us only by the free action or thought of our own minds; and are not nor can be the effects of the impulse or determination of the motion of blind matter, in or upon our bodies; for then it could not be in our power or choice to alter it. For example: my right hand writes whilst my left hand is still; what causes rest in one and motion in the other? Nothing but my will, a thought of my mind; my thought only changing, the right hand rests, and the left hand moves. This is matter-of-fact which cannot be denied: explain this, and make it intelligible, and then the next step will be to understand creation: for the giving a new determination to the motion of the animal spirits (which some make use of to explain voluntary motion) clears not the difficulty one jot, to alter the determination of motion being in this case no easier nor less than to give motion itself; since the new determination given to the animal spirits must be either immediately by thought, or by some other body put in their way by thought, which was not in their way before, and so must owe its motion to thought; either of which leaves voluntary motion as unintelligible as it was before. In the mean time, it is an overvaluing ourselves, to reduce all to the narrow measure of our capacities, and to conclude all things impossible to be done whose manner of doing exceeds our comprehension. This is to make our comprehension infinite, or God finite, when what he can do is limited to what we can conceive of it. If you do not understand the operations of your own finite mind, that thinking thing within you, do not deem it strange that you cannot comprehend the operations of that eternal, infinite Mind who made and governs all things, and whom the heaven of heavens cannot contain.

---

## CHAPTER XI.

### OF OUR KNOWLEDGE OF THE EXISTENCE OF OTHER THINGS.

1. *It is to be had only by sensation.*—The knowledge of our own being we have by intuition. The existence of a God reason clearly makes known to us, as has been shown.

The knowledge of the existence of any other thing, we can have only by sensation: for, there being no necessary connexion of real existence with any idea a man hath in his memory, nor of any other existence but that of God with the existence of any particular man, no particular man can know the existence of any other being, but only when by actual operating upon him it makes itself perceived by him. For, the having the idea of any thing in our mind no more proves the existence of that thing than the picture of a man evidences his being in the world, or the visions of a dream make thereby a true history.

2. *Instance whiteness of this paper.*—It is therefore the actual receiving of ideas from without that gives us notice of the existence of other things, and makes us know that something doth exist at that time without us which causes that idea in us, though perhaps we neither know nor consider how it does it : for it takes not from the certainty of our senses, and the ideas we receive by them, that we know not the manner wherein they are produced; *v. g.*, whilst I write this, I have, by the paper affecting my eyes, that idea produced in my mind which whatever object causes, I call "white;" by which I know that that quality or accident (*i. e.*, whose appearance before my eyes always causes that idea) doth really exist and hath a being without me. And of this the greatest assurance I can possibly have, and to which my faculties can attain, is the testimony of my eyes, which are the proper and sole judges of this thing; whose testimony I have reason to rely on as so certain that I can no more doubt, whilst I write this, that I see white and black, and that something really exists that causes that sensation in me, than that I write or move my hand; which is a certainty as great as human nature is capable of concerning the existence of any thing but a man's self alone and of God.

3. *This, though not so certain as demonstration, yet may be called "knowledge," and proves the existence of things without us.*—The notice we have by our senses of the existing of things without us, though it be not altogether so certain as our intuitive knowledge, or the deductions of our reason employed about the clear abstract ideas of our own minds; yet it is an assurance that deserves the name of knowledge. If we persuade ourselves that our faculties act and inform us right concerning the existence of those objects that affect them, it cannot pass for an ill-grounded confidence : for I think nobody can, in earnest, be so sceptical as to be uncertain of the existence of those things which he sees and feels. At least, he that can doubt so far, (whatever he may have with his own thoughts,) will never have any controversy with me : since he can never be sure I say any thing contrary to his opinion. As to myself, I think God has given me assurance enough of the existence of things without me; since, by their different application, I can produce in myself both pleasure and pain, which is one great concernment of my present state. This is certain, the confidence that our faculties do not herein deceive us is the greatest assurance we are capable of concerning the existence of material beings. For we cannot act any thing but by our faculties, nor talk of knowledge itself but by the help of those

faculties which are fitted to apprehend even what knowledge is. But, besides the assurance we have from our senses themselves, that they do not err in the information they give us of the existence of things without us, when they are affected by them, we are farther confirmed in this assurance by other concurrent reasons.

4. *First, Because we cannot have them but by the inlet of the senses.*—First, It is plain those perceptions are produced in us by exterior causes affecting our senses, because those that want the organs of any sense never can have the ideas belonging to that sense produced in their minds. This is too evident to be doubted: and therefore we cannot but be assured that they come in by the organs of that sense, and no other way. The organs themselves, it is plain, do not produce them; for then the eyes of a man in the dark would produce colours, and his nose smell roses in the winter: but we see nobody gets the relish of a pine-apple till he goes to the Indies where it is, and tastes it.

5. *Secondly, Because an idea from actual sensation and another from memory are very distinct perceptions.*—Secondly, Because sometimes I find that I cannot avoid the having those ideas produced in my mind: for though when my eyes are shut, or windows fast, I can at pleasure recall to my mind the ideas of light or the sun, which former sensations had lodged in my memory; so I can at pleasure lay by that idea, and take into my view that of the smell of a rose, or taste of sugar. But if I turn my eyes at noon towards the sun, I cannot avoid the ideas which the light or sun then produces in me. So that there is a manifest difference between the ideas laid up in my memory (over which, if they were there only, I should have constantly the same power to dispose of them, and lay them by at pleasure) and those which force themselves upon me and I cannot avoid having. And therefore it must needs be some exterior cause, and the brisk acting of some objects without me, whose efficacy I cannot resist, that produces those ideas in my mind, whether I will or no. Besides, there is nobody who doth not perceive the difference in himself between contemplating the sun as he hath the idea of it in his memory, and actually looking upon it: of which two his perception is so distinct, that few of his ideas are more distinguishable one from another: and therefore he hath certain knowledge that they are not both memory, or the actions of his mind and fancies only within him; but that actual seeing hath a cause without.

6. *Thirdly, Pleasure or pain, which accompanies actual sensation accompanies not the returning of those ideas without the external objects.*—Thirdly, Add to this, that many of those ideas are produced in us with pain, which afterwards we remember without the least offence. Thus the pain of heat or cold, when the idea of it is revived in our minds, gives us no disturbance; which

when felt, was very troublesome, and is again when actually repeated: which is occasioned by the disorder the external object causes in our bodies when applied to it. And we remember the pain of hunger, thirst, or the headache, without any pain at all; which would either never disturb us, or else constantly do it as often as we thought of it, were there nothing more but ideas floating in our minds, and appearances entertaining our fancies, without the real existence of things affecting us from abroad. The same may be said of pleasure accompanying several actual sensations; and, though mathematical demonstration depends not upon sense, yet the examining them by diagrams gives great credit to the evidence of our sight, and seems to give it a certainty approaching to that of demonstration itself. For it would be very strange that a man should allow it for an undeniable truth, that two angles of a figure which he measures by lines and angles of a diagram, should be bigger one than the other, and yet doubt of the existence of those lines and angles which, by looking on, he makes use of to measure that by.

7. *Fourthly, Our senses assist one another's testimony of the existence of outward things.*—Fourthly, Our senses, in many cases, bear witness to the truth of each other's report concerning the existence of sensible things without us. He that sees a fire may, if he doubt whether it be any thing more than a bare fancy, feel it too, and be convinced by putting his hand in it; which certainly could never be put into such exquisite pain by a bare idea or phantom, unless that the pain be a fancy too; which yet he cannot, when the burn is well, by raising the idea of it, bring upon himself again.

Thus I see, whilst I write this, I can change the appearance of the paper; and, by designing the letters, tell beforehand what new idea it shall exhibit the very next moment, barely by drawing my pen over it, which will neither appear (let me fancy as much as I will) if my hand stand still, or though I move my pen, if my eyes be shut; nor, when those characters are once made on the paper, can I choose afterwards but see them as they are; that is, have the ideas of such letters as I have made. Whence it is manifest that they are not barely the sport and play of my own imagination, when I find that the characters that were made at the pleasure of my own thoughts do not obey them; nor yet cease to be, whenever I shall fancy it, but continue to affect my senses constantly and regularly, according to the figures I made them. To which if we will add, that the sight of those shall, from another man, draw such sounds as I beforehand design they shall stand for, there will be little reason left to doubt that those words I write do really exist without me, when they cause a long series of regular sounds to affect my ears, which could not be the effect of my imagination, nor could my memory retain them in that order.

**8.** *This certainty is as great as our condition needs.*—But yet, if after all this any one will be so sceptical as to distrust his senses, and to affirm that all we see and hear, feel and taste, think and do, during our whole being, is but the series and deluding appearances of a long dream whereof there is no reality, and therefore will question the existence of all things or our knowledge of any thing; I must desire him to consider, that if all be a dream, then he doth but dream that he makes the question; and so it is not much matter that a waking man should answer him. But yet, if he pleases, he may dream that I make him this answer, that the certainty of things existing in *rerum natura*, when we have the testimony of our senses for it, is not only as great as our frame can attain to, but as our condition needs. For, our faculties being suited not to the full extent of being, nor to a perfect, clear, comprehensive knowledge of things free from all doubt and scruple, but to the preservation of us, in whom they are, and accommodated to the use of life, they serve to our purpose well enough, if they will but give us certain notice of those things which are convenient or inconvenient to us. For he that sees a candle burning, and hath experimented the force of its flame by putting his finger in it, will little doubt that this is something existing without him, which does him harm and puts him to great pain; which is assurance enough, when no man requires greater certainty to govern his actions by than what is as certain as his actions themselves. And if our dreamer pleases to try whether the glowing heat of a glass furnace be barely a wandering imagination in a drowsy man's fancy, by putting his hand into it, he may, perhaps, be awakened into a certainty, greater than he could wish, that it is something more than bare imagination. So that this evidence is as great as we can desire, being as certain to us as our pleasure or pain, *i. e.*, happiness or misery; beyond which we have no concernment either of knowing or being. Such an assurance of the existence of things without us, is sufficient to direct us in the attaining the good and avoiding the evil which is caused by them, which is the important concernment we have of being made acquainted with them.

**9.** *But reaches no farther than actual sensation.*—In fine, then, when our senses do actually convey into our understandings any idea, we cannot but be satisfied that there doth something at that time really exist without us which doth affect our senses, and by them give notice of itself to our apprehensive faculties, and actually produce that idea which we then perceive: and we cannot so far distrust their testimony as to doubt that such collections of simple ideas as we have observed by our senses to be united together, do really exist together. But this knowledge extends as far as the present testimony of our senses, employed about particular objects that do then affect them, and no farther. For if I saw such a collection of simple ideas as is wont to be called "man" existing together one minute since, and am now alone; I cannot be certain that the same man exists now, since there is no necessary connexion of his existence a minute since with his existence now: by a thousand ways he may cease to be, since I had the testimony of my senses for his existence. And if I cannot be certain that the man I saw last to-day is now in being, I can less be certain that he is so who hath been longer removed from my senses, and I have not seen since yesterday, or since the last year; and much less can I be certain of the existence of men that I never saw. And therefore, though it be highly probable that millions of men do now exist, yet, whilst I am alone writing this, I have not that certainty of it which we strictly call "knowledge;" though the great likelihood of it puts me past doubt, and it be reasonable for me to do several things upon the confidence that there are men (and men also of my acquaintance, with whom I have to do) now in the world: but this is but probability, not knowledge.

10. *Folly to expect demonstration in every thing.*—Whereby yet we may observe how foolish and vain a thing it is for a man of a narrow knowledge, who having reason given him to judge of the different evidence and probability of things, and to be swayed accordingly; how vain, I say, it is to expect demonstration and certainty in things not capable of it, and refuse assent to very rational propositions, and act contrary to very plain and clear truths, because they cannot be made out so evident as to surmount every the least (I will not say reason, but) pretence of doubting. He that in the ordinary affairs of life would admit of nothing but direct plain demonstration, would be sure of nothing in this world but of perishing quickly. The wholesomeness of his meat or drink would not give him reason to venture on it; and I would fain know what it is he could do upon such grounds as were capable of no doubt, no objection.

11. *Past existence is known by memory.*—As, when our senses are actually employed about any object, we do know that it does exist, so by our memory we may be assured that heretofore things that affected our senses have existed. And thus we have knowledge of the past existence of several things, whereof our senses having informed us, our memories still retain the ideas; and of this we are past all doubt so long as we remember well. But this knowledge also reaches no farther than our senses have formerly assured us. Thus, seeing water at this instant, it is an unquestionable truth to me that water doth exist; and remembering that I saw it yesterday, it will also be always true, and, as long as my memory retains it, always an undoubted proposition to me, that water did exist July 10th, 1688, as it will also be equally true that a certain number of very fine colours did exist, which at the same time I saw upon a bubble of that water: but being now quite out of the sight both of the water and bubbles

too, it is no more certainly known to me that the water doth now exist than that the bubbles or colours therein do so; it being no more necessary that water should exist to-day because it existed yesterday, than that the colours or bubbles exist to-day because they existed yesterday, though it be exceedingly much more probable, because water hath been observed to continue long in existence, but bubbles and the colours on them quickly cease to be.

12. *The existence of spirits not knowable.*—What ideas we have of spirits, and how we come by them, I have already shown. But though we have those ideas in our minds, and know we have them there, the having the ideas of spirits does not make us know that any such things do exist without us, or that there are any finite spirits, or any other spiritual beings but the eternal God. We have ground from revelation, and several other reasons, to believe with assurance that there are such creatures; but, our senses not being able to discover them, we want the means of knowing their particular existences. For we can no more know that there are finite spirits really existing by the idea we have of such beings in our minds, than by the ideas any one has of fairies or centaurs he can come to know that things answering those ideas do really exist.

And therefore concerning the existence of finite spirits, as well as several other things, we must content ourselves with the evidence of faith; but universal certain propositions concerning this matter are beyond our reach. For, however true it may be, *v. g.*, that all the intelligent spirits that God ever created do still exist, yet it can never make a part of our certain knowledge. These and the like propositions we may assent to as highly probable, but are not, I fear, in this state capable of knowing. We are not, then, to put others upon demonstrating, nor ourselves upon search of, universal certainty in all those matters wherein we are not capable of any other knowledge but what our senses give us in this or that particular.

13. *Particular propositions concerning existences are knowable.*— By which it appears that there are two sorts of propositions. (1.) There is one sort of propositions concerning the existence of any thing answerable to such an idea; as having the idea of an elephant, phœnix, motion, or an angel in my mind, the first and natural inquiry is, whether such a thing does any where exist. And this knowledge is only of particulars. No existence of any thing without us, but only of God, can certainly be known farther than our senses inform us. (2.) There is another sort of propositions, wherein is expressed the agreement or disagreement of our abstract ideas, and their dependence one on another. Such propositions may be universal and certain. So having the idea of God and myself, of fear and obedience, I cannot but be sure that God is to be feared and obeyed by me: and this proposition will

be certain concerning man in general, if I have made an abstract idea of such a species, whereof I am one particular. But yet this proposition, how certain soever, that men ought to fear and obey God, proves not to me the existence of men in the world, but will be true of all such creatures whenever they do exist: which certainty of such general propositions depends on the agreement or disagreement is to be discovered in those abstract ideas.

14. *And general propositions concerning abstract ideas.*—In the former case, our knowledge is the consequence of the existence of things producing ideas in our minds by our senses: in the latter, knowledge is the consequence of the ideas (be they what they will) that are in our minds, producing their general certain propositions. Many of these are called *æternæ veritates*, and all of them indeed are so; not from being written all or any of them in the minds of all men, or that they were any of them propositions in any one's mind till he, having got the abstract ideas, joined or separated them by affirmation or negation. But wheresoever we can suppose such a creature as man is, endowed with such faculties, and thereby furnished with such ideas, as we have, we must conclude he must needs, when he applies his thoughts to the consideration of his ideas, know the truth of certain propositions that will arise from the agreement or disagreement which he will perceive in his own ideas. Such propositions are therefore called "eternal truths," not because they are eternal propositions actually formed, and antecedent to the understanding that at any time makes them; nor because they are imprinted on the mind from any patterns that are any where of them out of the mind, and existed before; but because, being once made about abstract ideas so as to be true, they will, whenever they can be supposed to be made again at any time past or to come, by a mind having those ideas, always actually be true. For, names being supposed to stand perpetually for the same ideas, and the same ideas having immutably the same habitudes one to another, propositions concerning any abstract ideas that are once true must needs be eternal verities.

## CHAPTER XII.

### OF THE IMPROVEMENT OF OUR KNOWLEDGE.

1. *Knowledge is not from maxims.*—It having been the common received opinion amongst men of letters, that maxims were the foundation of all knowledge; and that the sciences were each of them built upon certain *præcognita*, from whence the understanding was to take its rise, and by which it was to conduct itself in its inquiries into the matters belonging to that science;

the beaten road of the Schools has been to lay down in the beginning one or more general propositions as foundations whereon to build the knowledge that was to be had of that subject. These doctrines thus laid down for foundations of any science were called "principles," as the beginnings from which we must set out, and look no farther backwards in our inquiries, as we have already observed.

2. (*The occasion of that opinion.*)—One thing which might probably give an occasion to this way of proceeding in other sciences was, as I suppose, the good success it seemed to have in mathematics, wherein men being observed to attain a great certainty of knowledge, these sciences came by pre-eminence to be called μαθήματα and μάθησις, "learning," or "things learned," thoroughly learned, as having, of all others, the greatest certainty, clearness, and evidence in them.

3. *But from the comparing clear and distinct ideas.*—But if any one will consider, he will (I guess) find that the great advancement and certainty of real knowledge, which men arrived to in these sciences, was not owing to the influence of these principles, nor derived from any peculiar advantage they received from two or three general maxims laid down in the beginning; but from the clear, distinct, complete ideas their thoughts were employed about, and the relation of equality and excess so clear between some of them, that they had an intuitive knowledge, and by that a way to discover it in others, and this without the help of those maxims. For I ask, is it not possible for a young lad to know that his whole body is bigger than his little finger but by virtue of this axiom, that "the whole is bigger than a part;" nor be assured of it till he has learned that maxim? Or cannot a country-wench know, that having received a shilling from one that owes her three, and a shilling also from another that owes her three, that the remaining debts in each of their hands are equal? Cannot she know this, I say, without she fetch the certainty of it from this maxim, that "if you take equals from equals the remainders will be equal;" a maxim which possibly she never heard or thought of? I desire any one to consider, from what has been elsewhere said, which is known first and clearest by most people—the particular instance or the general rule; and which it is that gives life and birth to the other. These general rules are but the comparing our more general and abstract ideas, which are the workmanship of the mind, made, and names given to them, for the easier despatch in its reasonings, and drawing into comprehensive terms and short rules its various and multiplied observations. But knowledge began in the mind, and was founded on particulars, though afterwards, perhaps, no notice be taken thereof; it being natural for the mind (forward still to enlarge its knowledge) most attentively to lay up those general notions, and make the proper use of them, which is to

disburden the memory of the cumbersome load of particulars. For I desire it may be considered what more certainty there is to a child, or any one, that his body, little finger and all, is bigger than his little finger alone, after you have given to his body the name "whole," and to his little finger the name "part," than he could have had before; or what new knowledge concerning his body can these two relative terms give him, which he could not have without them? Could he not know that his body was bigger than his little finger, if his language were yet so imperfect that he had no such relative terms as "whole" and "part?" I ask farther, When he has got these names, how is he more certain that his body is a whole and his little finger a part, than he was or might be certain, before he learned those terms, that his body was bigger than his little finger? Any one may as reasonably doubt or deny that his little finger is a part of his body, as that it is less than his body. And he that can doubt whether it be less, will as certainly doubt whether it be a part. So that the maxim, "The whole is bigger than a part," can never be made use of to prove the little finger less than the body, but when it is useless by being brought to convince one of a truth which he knows already. For he that does not certainly know that any parcel of matter, with another parcel of matter joined to it, is bigger than either of them alone, will never be able to know it by the help of these two relative terms, "whole" and "part," make of them what maxim you please.

4. *Dangerous to build upon precarious principles.*—But be it in the mathematics as it will, whether it be clearer that, taking an inch from a black line of two inches, and an inch from a red line of two inches, the remaining parts of the two lines will be equal: or that if you take equals from equals, the remainders will be equal: which, I say, of these two is the clearer and first known, I leave to any one to determine, it not being material to my present occasion. That which I have here to do is, to inquire whether, if it be the readiest way to knowledge to begin with general maxims, and build upon them, it be yet a safe way to take the principles which are laid down in any other science as unquestionable truths; and so receive them without examination, and adhere to them without suffering to be doubted of, because mathematicians have been so happy or so fair to use none but self-evident and undeniable. If this be so, I know not what may not pass for truth in morality, what may not be introduced and proved in natural philosophy.

Let that principle of some of the philosophers, that "all is matter, and that there is nothing else," be received for certain and indubitable, and it will be easy to be seen, by the writings of some that have revived it again in our days, what consequences it will lead us into. Let any one (with Polemo) take the world, or (with the Stoics) the æther or the sun, or (with Anaximenes) the air, to be God, and what a divinity, religion, and worship must we needs have! Nothing can be so dangerous as principles thus taken up without questioning or examination; especially if they be such as concern morality, which influences men's lives, and gives a bias to all their actions. Who might not justly expect another kind of life in Aristippus, who placed happiness in bodily pleasure? and in Antisthenes, who made virtue sufficient to felicity? And he who, with Plato, shall place beatitude in the knowledge of God, will have his thoughts raised to other contemplations than those who look not beyond this spot of earth, and those perishing things which are to be had in it. He that, with Archelaus, shall lay it down as a principle, that "right and wrong, honest and dishonest, are defined only by laws, and not by nature," will have other measures of moral rectitude and pravity than those who take it for granted that we are under obligations antecedent to all human constitutions.

5. *This is no certain way to truth.*—If therefore those that pass for principles are not certain (which we must have some way to know, that we may be able to distinguish them from those that are doubtful), but are only made so to us by our blind assent, we are liable to be misled by them; and, instead of being guided into truth, we shall, by principles, be only confirmed in mistake and error.

6. *But to compare clear complete ideas under steady names.*—But since the knowledge of the certainty of principles, as well as of all other truths, depends only upon the perception we have of the agreement or disagreement of our ideas, the way to improve our knowledge is not, I am sure, blindly, and with an implicit faith, to receive and swallow principles; but is, I think, to get and fix in our minds clear, distinct, and complete ideas, as far as they are to be had, and annex to them proper and constant names. And thus, perhaps, without any other principles, but barely considering those ideas, and, by comparing them one with another, finding their agreement and disagreement, and their several relations and habitudes, we shall get more true and clear knowledge by the conduct of this one rule, than by taking up principles, and thereby putting our minds into the disposal of others.

7. *The true method of advancing knowledge is, by considering our abstract ideas.*—We must therefore, if we will proceed as reason advises, adapt our methods of inquiry to the nature of the ideas we examine, and the truth we search after. General and certain truths are only founded in the habitudes and relations of abstract ideas. A sagacious and methodical application of our thoughts, for the finding out these relations, is the only way to discover all that can be put, with truth and certainty, concerning them, into general propositions. By what steps we are to proceed in these, is to be learned in the schools of the mathematicians who, from

very plain and easy beginnings, by gentle degrees, and a continued chain of reasonings, proceed to the discovery and demonstration of truths that appear at first sight beyond human capacity. The art of finding proofs, and the admirable methods they have invented for the singling out and laying in order those intermediate ideas that demonstratively show the equality or inequality of unapplicable quantities, is that which has carried them so far, and produced such wonderful and unexpected discoveries: but whether something like this, in respect of other ideas, as well as those of magnitude, may not in time be found out, I will not determine. This, I think, I may say, that if other ideas, that are the real as well as nominal essences of their species, were pursued in the way familiar to mathematicians, they would carry our thoughts farther, and with greater evidence and clearness, than possibly we are apt to imagine.

8. *By which morality also may be made clearer.*—This gave me the confidence to advance that conjecture which I suggest, chap. iii. sect. 18, vir., that morality is capable of demonstration as well as mathematics. For the ideas that ethics are conversant about, being all real essences, and such as, I imagine, have a discoverable connexion and agreement one with another; so far as we can find their habitudes and relations, so far we shall be possessed of certain, real, and general truths; and I doubt not but, if a right method were taken, a great part of morality might be made out with that clearness that could leave, to a considering man, no more reason to doubt than he could have to doubt of the truth of propositions in mathematics, which have been demonstrated to him.

9. *But knowledge of bodies is to be improved only by experience.*—In our search after the knowledge of substances, our want of ideas that are suitable to such a way of proceeding obliges us to a quite different method. We advance not here, as in the other, (where our abstract ideas are real as well as nominal essences,) by contemplating our ideas, and considering their relations and correspondencies; that helps us very little, for the reasons that in another place we have at large set down. By which, I think, it is evident that substances afford matter of very little general knowledge; and the bare contemplation of their abstract ideas will carry us but a very little way in the search of truth and certainty. What then are we to do for the improvement of our knowledge in substantial beings? Here we are to take a quite contrary course; the want of ideas of their real essences sends us from our own thoughts to the things themselves as they exist. Experience here must teach me what reason cannot: and it is by trying alone that I can certainly know what other qualities co-exist with those of my complex idea, *v. g.*, whether that yellow, heavy, fusible body I call "gold" be malleable or no; which experience (which way ever it prove in that particular

body I examine) makes me not certain that it is so in all or any
other yellow, heavy, fusible bodies, but that which I have tried.
Because it is no consequence one way or the other from my complex idea, the necessity or inconsistence of malleability hath no
visible connexion with the combination of that colour, weight,
and fusibility in any body. What I have said here of the
nominal essence of gold, supposed to consist of a body of such a
determinate colour, weight, and fusibility, will hold true, if
malleableness, fixedness, and solubility in *aqua regia* be added
to it. Our reasonings from these ideas will carry us but a little
way in the certain discovery of the other properties in those
masses of matter wherein all these are to be found. Because
the other properties of such bodies depending not on these, but
on that unknown real essence on which these also depend, we
cannot by them discover the rest; we can go no farther than the
simple ideas of our nominal essence will carry us, which is very
little beyond themselves; and so afford us but very sparingly
any certain, universal, and useful truths. For, upon trial, having
found that particular piece (and all others of that colour, weight,
and fusibility that I ever tried) malleable, that also makes now
perhaps a part of my complex idea, part of my nominal essence
of gold: whereby, though I make my complex idea, to which I
affix the name "gold," to consist of more simple ideas than
before; yet still, it not containing the real essence of any species
of bodies, it helps me not certainly to know (I say to *know*, perhaps it may be to *conjecture*) the other remaining properties of that
body, farther than they have a visible connexion with some or
all of the simple ideas that make up my nominal essence. For
example: I cannot be certain, from this complex idea, whether
gold be fixed or no; because, as before, there is no necessary
connexion or inconsistence to be discovered betwixt a complex
idea of a body, yellow, heavy, fusible, malleable; betwixt these,
I say, and fixedness, so that I may certainly know, that in whatsoever body these are found, there fixedness is sure to be. Here
again, for assurance, I must apply myself to experience; as far
as that reaches I may have certain knowledge, but no farther.

10. *This may procure us convenience, not science.*—I deny not
but a man accustomed to rational and regular experiments shall
be able to see farther into the nature of bodies, and guess righter
at their yet unknown properties, than one that is a stranger
to them: but yet, as I have said, this is but judgment and
opinion, not knowledge and certainty. This way of getting and
improving our knowledge in substances only by experience and
history, which is all that the weakness of our faculties in this
state of mediocrity which we are in in this world can attain to,
makes me suspect that natural philosophy is not capable of being
made a science. We are able, I imagine, to reach very little
general knowledge concerning the species of bodies and their

several properties. Experiments and historical observations we may have, from which we may draw advantages of ease and health, and thereby increase our stock of conveniences for this life; but beyond this I fear our talents reach not, nor are our faculties, as I guess, able to advance.

11. *We are fitted for moral knowledge and natural improvements.* —From whence it is obvious to conclude, that since our faculties are not fitted to penetrate into the eternal fabric and real essences of bodies, but yet plainly discover to us the being of a God, and the knowledge of ourselves, enough to lead us into a full and clear discovery of our duty and great concernment, it will become us, as rational creatures, to employ those faculties we have about what they are most adapted to, and follow the direction of nature, where it seems to point us out the way. For it is rational to conclude that our proper employment lies in those inquiries, and in that sort of knowledge which is most suited to our natural capacities, and carries in it our greatest interest, *i. e.*, the condition of our eternal estate. Hence I think I may conclude, that morality is the proper science and business of mankind in general, (who are both concerned and fitted to search out their *summum bonum*,) as several arts, conversant about several parts of nature, are the lot and private talent of particular men, for the common use of human life, and their own particular subsistence in this world. Of what consequence the discovery of one natural body and its properties may be to human life, the whole great continent of America is a convincing instance; whose ignorance in useful arts, and want of the greatest part of the conveniences of life, in a country that abounded with all sorts of natural plenty, I think, may be attributed to their ignorance of what was to be found in a very ordinary despicable stone, I mean the mineral of iron. And whatever we think of our parts or improvements in this part of the world, where knowledge and plenty seem to vie each with other; yet to any one that will seriously reflect on it, I suppose it will appear past doubt that, were the use of iron lost among us, we should in a few ages be unavoidably reduced to the wants and ignorance of the ancient savage Americans, whose natural endowments and provisions came no way short of those of the most flourishing and polite nations: so that he who first made known the use of that one contemptible mineral, may be truly styled "the father of arts and author of plenty."

12. *But must beware of hypotheses and wrong principles.*—I would not therefore be thought to disesteem or dissuade the study of nature. I readily agree, the contemplation of his works gives us occasion to admire, revere, and glorify their Author: and, if rightly directed, may be of greater benefit to mankind than the monuments of exemplary charity that have, at so great charge, been raised by the founders of hospitals and alms-houses.

He that first invented printing, discovered the use of the compass, or made public the virtue and right use of *kin-kina*, did more for the propagation of knowledge, for the supplying and increase of useful commodities, and saved more from the grave, than those who built colleges, work-houses, and hospitals. All that I would say is, that we should not be too forwardly possessed with the opinion or expectation of knowledge where it is not to be had, or by ways that will not attain it; that we should not take doubtful systems for complete sciences, nor unintelligible notions for scientifical demonstrations. In the knowledge of bodies, we must be content to glean what we can from particular experiments; since we cannot, from a discovery of their real essences, grasp at a time whole sheaves, and in bundles comprehend the nature and properties of whole species together. Where our inquiry is concerning co-existence, or repugnancy to co-exist, which by contemplation of our ideas we cannot discover, there experience, observation, and natural history must give us, by our senses and by retail, an insight into corporeal substances. The knowledge of bodies we must get by our senses, warily employed in taking notice of their qualities and operations on one another: and what we hope to know of separate spirits in this world, we must, I think, expect only from revelation. He that shall consider how little general maxims, precarious principles, and hypotheses laid down at pleasure have promoted true knowledge, or helped to satisfy the inquiries of rational men after real improvements; how little, I say, the setting out at that end has for many ages together advanced men's progress towards the knowledge of natural philosophy; will think, we have reason to thank those who, in this latter age, have taken another course, and have trod out to us, though not an easy way to learned ignorance, yet a surer way to profitable knowledge.

13. *The true use of hypotheses.*—Not that we may not, to explain any phenomena of nature, make use of any probable hypothesis whatsoever. Hypotheses, if they are well made, are at least great helps to the memory, and often direct us to new discoveries. But my meaning is, that we should not take up any one too hastily (which the mind, that would always penetrate into the causes of things and have principles to rest on, is very apt to do), till we have very well examined particulars, and made several experiments in that thing which we would explain by our hypothesis, and see whether it will agree to them all; whether our principles will carry us quite through, and not be as inconsistent with one phenomenon of nature as they seem to accommodate and explain another; and at least that we take care that the name of "principles" deceive us not, nor impose on us, by making us receive that for an unquestionable truth which is really, at best, but a very doubtful conjecture, such as are most (I had almost said all) of the hypotheses in natural philosophy.

**14.** *Clear and distinct ideas with settled names, and the finding of those which show their agreement or disagreement, are the ways to enlarge our knowledge.*—But whether natural philosophy be capable of certainty or no, the ways to enlarge our knowledge, as far as we are capable, seem to me, in short, to be these two:—

First, The first is to get and settle in our minds determined ideas of those things whereof we have general or specific names; at least of so many of them as we would consider and improve our knowledge in, or reason about. And if they be specific ideas of substances, we should endeavour also to make them as complete as we can; whereby I mean that we should put together as many simple ideas as, being constantly observed to co-exist, may perfectly determine the species; and each of those simple ideas, which are the ingredients of our complex ones, should be clear and distinct in our minds: for it being evident that our knowledge cannot exceed our ideas, as far as they are either imperfect, confused, or obscure, we cannot expect to have certain, perfect, or clear knowledge.

Secondly, The other is the art of finding out those intermediate ideas, which may show us the agreement or repugnancy of other ideas, which cannot be immediately compared.

**15.** *Mathematics an instance of it.*—That these two (and not the relying on maxims, and drawing consequences from some general propositions) are the right method of improving our knowledge in the ideas of other modes, besides those of quantity, the consideration of mathematical knowledge will easily inform us. Where, first, we shall find that he that has not a perfect and clear idea of those angles or figures of which he desires to know any thing, is utterly thereby uncapable of any knowledge about them. Suppose but a man not to have a perfect, exact idea of a right angle, a scalenum, or trapezium; and there is nothing more certain than that he will in vain seek any demonstration about them. Farther, it is evident that it was not the influence of those maxims which are taken for principles in mathematics, that hath led the masters of that science into those wonderful discoveries they have made. Let a man of good parts know all the maxims generally made use of in mathematics never so perfectly, and contemplate their extent and consequences as much as he pleases; he will, by their assistance, I suppose, scarce ever come to know that the square of the hypothenuse in a right-angled triangle is equal to the squares of the two other sides. The knowledge that "the whole is equal to all its parts;" and, "if you take equals from equals, the remainder will be equal," &c., helped him not, I presume, to this demonstration: and a man may, I think, pore long enough on those axioms without ever seeing one jot the more of mathematical truths. They have been discovered by the thoughts otherwise applied; the mind had other objects, other views before it, far different from those maxims, when it first got the knowledge of such kind of truths in mathematics; which men, well enough acquainted with those received axioms, but ignorant of their method who first made these demonstrations, can never sufficiently admire. And who knows what methods to enlarge our knowledge in other parts of science may hereafter be invented, answering that of algebra in mathematics, which so readily finds out ideas of quantities to measure others by, whose equality or proportion we could otherwise very hardly, or perhaps never come to know?

---

# CHAPTER XIII.

## SOME FARTHER CONSIDERATIONS CONCERNING OUR KNOWLEDGE.

1. *Our knowledge partly necessary, partly voluntary.*—Our knowledge, as in other things, so in this, has a great conformity with our sight, that it is neither wholly necessary, nor wholly voluntary. If our knowledge were altogether necessary, all men's knowledge would not only be alike, but every man would know all that is knowable; and if it were only voluntary, some men so little regard or value it, that they would have extreme little or none at all. Men that have senses cannot choose but receive some ideas by them; and if they have memory, they cannot but retain some of them; and if they have any distinguishing faculty, cannot but perceive the agreement or disagreement of some of them one with another; as he that has eyes, if he will open them by day, cannot but see some objects, and perceive a difference in them. But though a man with his eyes open in the light cannot but see, yet there be certain objects which he may choose whether he will turn his eyes to; there may be in his reach a book containing pictures and discourses, capable to delight and instruct him, which yet he may never have the will to open, never take the pains to look into.

2. *The application voluntary; but we know as things are, not as we please.*—There is also another thing in a man's power; and that is, though he turns his eyes sometimes towards an object, yet he may choose whether he will curiously survey it, and with an intent application endeavour to observe accurately all that is visible in it. But yet what he does see, he cannot see otherwise than he does. It depends not on his will to see that black which appears yellow; nor to persuade himself that what actually scalds him feels cold: the earth will not appear painted with flowers, nor the fields covered with verdure, whenever he has a mind to it: in the cold winter he cannot help seeing it white and hoary, if he will look abroad. Just thus is it with our understanding; all that is voluntary in our knowledge is the employing or with-

holding any of our faculties from this or that sort of objects, and a more or less accurate survey of them; but, they being employed, our will hath no power to determine the knowledge of the mind one way or other; that is done only by the objects themselves, as far as they are clearly discovered. And therefore as far as men's senses are conversant about external objects, the mind cannot but receive those ideas which are presented by them, and be informed of the existence of things without; and so far as men's thoughts converse with their own determined ideas, they cannot but in some measure observe the agreement and disagreement that is to be found amongst some of them, which is so far knowledge : and if they have names for those ideas which they have thus considered, they must needs be assured of the truth of those propositions which express that agreement or disagreement they perceive in them, and be undoubtedly convinced of those truths. For what a man sees, he cannot but see ; and what he perceives, he cannot but know that he perceives.

3. *Instance in numbers.*—Thus he that has got the ideas of numbers and hath taken the pains to compare one, two, and three to six, cannot choose but know that they are equal. He that hath got the idea of a triangle, and found the ways to measure its angles and their magnitudes, is certain that its three angles are equal to two right ones; and can as little doubt of that as of this truth, that "it is impossible for the same thing to be and not to be."

*In natural religion.*—He also that hath the idea of an intelligent but frail and weak being, made by and depending on another who is eternal, omnipotent, perfectly wise and good, will as certainly know that man is to honour, fear, and obey God, as that the sun shines when he sees it. For if he hath but the ideas of two such beings in his mind, and will turn his thoughts that way and consider them, he will as certainly find that the inferior, finite, and dependent is under an obligation to obey the supreme and infinite, as he is certain to find that three, four, and seven, are less than fifteen, if he will consider and compute those numbers; nor can he be surer in a clear morning that the sun is risen, if he will but open his eyes and turn them that way. But yet, these truths being never so certain, never so clear, he may be ignorant of either or all of them, who will never take the pains to employ his faculties, as he should, to inform himself about them.

## CHAPTER XIV.

### OF JUDGMENT.

**1.** *Our knowledge being short, we want something else.*—The understanding faculties being given to man, not barely for speculation, but also for the conduct of his life, man would be at a great loss if he had nothing to direct him but what has the certainty of true knowledge. For, that being very short and scanty, as we have seen, he would be often utterly in the dark, and in most of the actions of his life perfectly at a stand, had he nothing to guide him in the absence of clear and certain knowledge. He that will not eat till he has demonstration that it will nourish him, he that will not stir till he infallibly knows the business he goes about will succeed, will have little else to do but sit still and perish.

**2.** *What use to be made of this twilight state.*—Therefore, as God has set some things in broad daylight, as he has given us some certain knowledge, though limited to a few things in comparison, probably as a taste of what intellectual creatures are capable of, to excite in us a desire and endeavour after a better state; so, in the greatest part of our concernment, he has afforded us only the twilight, as I may so say, of probability, suitable, I presume, to that state of mediocrity and probationership he has been pleased to place us in here; wherein, to check our over-confidence and presumption, we might, by every day's experience, be made sensible of our short-sightedness and liableness to error; the sense whereof might be a constant admonition to us to spend the days of this our pilgrimage with industry and care in the search and following of that way which might lead us to a state of greater perfection: it being highly rational to think, even were revelation silent in the case, that as men employ those talents God has given them here, they shall accordingly receive their rewards at the close of the day, when their sun shall set, and night shall put an end to their labours.

**3.** *Judgment supplies the want of knowledge.*—The faculty which God has given man to supply the want of clear and certain knowledge, in cases where that cannot be had, is judgment: whereby the mind takes its ideas to agree or disagree; or, which is the same, any proposition to be true or false, without perceiving a demonstrative evidence in the proofs. The mind sometimes exercises this judgment out of necessity, where demonstrative proofs and certain knowledge are not to be had; and sometimes out of laziness, unskilfulness, or haste, even where demonstrative and certain proofs are to be had. Men often stay not warily to examine the agreement or disagreement of two ideas, which they are desirous or concerned to know; but, either incapable of such attention as is requisite in a long train of gradations, or impatient of delay, lightly cast their eyes on or wholly pass by the proofs; and so, without making out the demonstration, determine of the agreement or disagreement of two ideas, as it were, by a view of them as they are at a distance, and take it to be the one or the other, as seems most likely to them upon such a loose survey. This faculty of the mind, when it is exercised immediately about things, is called "judgment;" when about truths delivered in words, is most commonly called "assent" or "dissent:" which being the most usual way wherein the mind has occasion to employ this faculty, I shall, under these terms, treat of it as least liable in our language to equivocation.

4. *Judgment is the presuming things to be so without perceiving it.*—Thus the mind has two faculties conversant about truth and falsehood,—

First, Knowledge, whereby it certainly perceives, and is undoubtedly satisfied of the agreement or disagreement of any ideas.

Secondly, Judgment, which is the putting ideas together, or separating them from one another in the mind, when their certain agreement or disagreement is not perceived, but presumed to be so; which is, as the word imports, taken to be so before it certainly appears. And if it so unites or separates them as in reality things are, it is right judgment.

---

## CHAPTER XV.

### OF PROBABILITY.

1. *Probability is the appearance of agreement upon fallible proofs.* As demonstration is the showing the agreement or disagreement of two ideas by the intervention of one or more proofs, which have a constant, immutable, and visible connexion one with another; so probability is nothing but the appearance of such an agreement or disagreement by the intervention of proofs, whose connexion is not constant and immutable, or at least is not perceived to be so; but is, or appears for the most part to be so, and is enough to induce the mind to judge the proposition to be true or false, rather than the contrary. For example: In the demonstration of it, a man perceives the certain immutable connexion there is of equality between the three angles of a triangle, and those intermediate ones which are made use of to show their equality to two right ones; and so, by an intuitive knowledge of the agreement or disagreement of the intermediate ideas in each step of the progress, the whole series is continued with an evidence which clearly shows the agreement or disagreement of those three angles in equality to two right ones: and

thus he has certain knowledge that it is so. But another man, who never took the pains to observe the demonstration, hearing a mathematician, a man of credit affirm "the three angles of a triangle to be equal to two right ones," assents to it, *i. e.*, receives it for true. In which case the foundation of his assent is the probability of the thing, the proof being such as for the most part carries truth with it: the man on whose testimony he receives it not being wont to affirm any thing contrary to or besides his knowledge, especially in matters of this kind. So that that which causes his assent to this proposition, that "the three angles of a triangle are equal to two right ones," that which makes him take these ideas to agree without knowing them to do so, is the wonted veracity of the speaker in other cases, or his supposed veracity in this.

2. *It is to supply the want of knowledge.*—Our knowledge, as has been shown, being very narrow, and we not happy enough to find certain truth in every thing which we have occasion to consider, most of the propositions we think, reason, discourse, nay, act upon, are such as we cannot have undoubted knowledge of their truth; yet some of them border so near upon certainty, that we make no doubt at all about them, but assent to them as firmly, and act according to that assent as resolutely, as if they were infallibly demonstrated, and that our knowledge of them was perfect and certain. But, these being degrees herein, from the very neighbourhood of certainty and demonstration, quite down to improbability and unlikeliness, even to the confines of impossibility; and also degrees of assent from full assurance and confidence, quite down to conjecture, doubt, and distrust; I shall come now, (having, as I think, found out the bounds of human knowledge and certainty,) in the next place, to consider the several degrees and grounds of probability, and assent or faith.

3. *Being that which makes us presume things to be true before we know them to be so.*—Probability is likeliness to be true; the very notation of the word signifying such a proposition for which there be arguments or proofs to make it pass, or be received, for true. The entertainment the mind gives this sort of propositions is called "belief," "assent," or "opinion," which is the admitting or receiving any proposition for true, upon arguments or proofs that are found to persuade us to receive it as true, without certain knowledge that it is so. And herein lies the difference between probability and certainty, faith and knowledge, that in all the parts of knowledge there is intuition; each immediate idea, each step has its visible and certain connexion: in belief not so. That which makes me believe, is something extraneous to the thing I believe; something not evidently joined on both sides to, and so not manifestly showing the agreement or disagreement, of those ideas that are under consideration.

4. *The grounds of probability are two; conformity with our own*

*experience, or the testimony of other's experience.*—Probability, then, being to supply the defect of our knowledge, and to guide us where that fails, is always conversant about propositions whereof we have no certainty, but only some inducements to receive them for true. The grounds of it are, in short, these two following :—

First, The conformity of any thing with our own knowledge, observation and experience.

Secondly, The testimony of others, vouching their observation and experience. In the testimony of others, is to be considered, (1.) The number. (2.) The integrity. (3.) The skill of the witnesses. (4.) The design of the author, where it is a testimony out of a book cited. (5.) The consistency of the parts and circumstances of the relation. (6.) Contrary testimonies.

5. *In this, all the agreements*, pro *and* con, *ought to be examined before we come to a judgment.*—Probability wanting that intuitive evidence which infallibly determines the understanding, and produces certain knowledge, the mind, if it would proceed rationally, ought to examine all the grounds of probability, and see how they make more or less for or against any proposition, before it assents to or dissents from it; and upon a due balancing the whole, reject or receive it with a more or less firm assent proportionably to the preponderancy of the greater grounds of probability on one side or the other. For example :—

If I myself see a man walk on the ice, it is past probability, it is knowledge. But if another tells me he saw a man in England, in the midst of a sharp winter, walk upon water hardened with cold; this has so great conformity with what is usually observed to happen, that I am disposed, by the nature of the thing itself, to assent to it, unless some manifest suspicion attend the relation of that matter-of-fact. But if the same thing be told to one born between the tropics, who never saw nor heard of any such thing before, there the whole probability relies on testimony: and as the relators are more in number, and of more credit, and have no interest to speak contrary to the truth; so that matter-of-fact is like to find more or less belief; though to a man whose experience has been always quite contrary, and has never heard of anything like it, the most untainted credit of a witness will scarce be able to find belief: as it happened to a Dutch ambassador, who, entertaining the king of Siam with the particularities of Holland, which he was inquisitive after, amongst other things, told him, "that the water in his country would sometimes in cold weather be so hard that men walked upon it, and that it would bear-an elephant if he were there." To which the king replied, "Hitherto I have believed the strange things you have told me, because I look upon you-as a sober, fair man: but now I am sure you lie."

**6. *They being capable of great variety.*—**Upon these grounds depends the probability of any proposition: and as the conformity of our knowledge, as the certainty of observations, as the frequency and constancy of experience, and the number and credibility of testimonies do more or less agree or disagree with it, so is any proposition in itself more or less probable. There is another, I confess, which, though by itself it be no true ground of probability, yet is often made use of for one, by which men most commonly regulate their assent, and upon which they pin their faith more than anything else—and that is the opinion of others; though there cannot be a more dangerous thing to rely on, nor more likely to mislead one, since there is much more falsehood and error among men than truth and knowledge. And if the opinions and persuasions of others, whom we know and think well of, be a ground of assent, men have reason to be Heathens in Japan, Mahometans in Turkey, Papists in Spain, Protestants in England, and Lutherans in Sweden. But of this wrong ground of assent I shall have occasion to speak more at large in another place.

---

## CHAPTER XVI.

### OF THE DEGREES OF ASSENT.

**1. *Our assent ought to be regulated by the grounds of probability.*—**The grounds of probability we have laid down in the foregoing chapter, as they are the foundations on which our assent is built, so are they also the measure whereby its several degrees are or ought to be regulated: only we are to take notice, that whatever grounds of probability there may be, they yet operate no further on the mind, which searches after truth and endeavours to judge right, than they appear at least in the first judgment or search that the mind makes. I confess, in the opinions men have and firmly stick to in the world, their assent is not always from an actual view of the reasons that at first prevailed with them; it being in many cases almost impossible, and in most very hard, even for those who have very admirable memories, to retain all the proofs which upon a due examination made them embrace that side of the question. It suffices that they have once with care and fairness sifted the matter as far as they could; and that they have searched into all the particulars that they could imagine to give any light to the question, and with the best of their skill cast up the account upon the whole evidence: and thus, having once found on which side the probability appeared to them after as full and exact an inquiry as they can make, they lay up the conclusion in their memories as a truth they have discovered; and for the future they remain satisfied with the testimony of their memories, that this is the opinion that, by the proofs they have once seen of it, deserves such a degree of their assent as they afford it.

2. *These cannot always be actually in view, and then we must content ourselves with the remembrance that we once saw ground for such a degree of assent.*—This is all that the greatest part of men are capable of doing in regulating their opinions and judgments, unless a man will exact of them either to retain distinctly in their memories all the proofs concerning any probable truth, and that too in the same order and regular deduction of consequences in which they have formerly placed or seen them ; which sometimes is enough to fill a large volume upon one single question : or else they must require a man, for every opinion that he embraces, every day to examine the proofs: both which are impossible. It is unavoidable therefore that the memory be relied on in the case, and that men be persuaded of several opinions whereof the proofs are not actually in their thoughts ; nay, which perhaps they are not able actually to recall. Without this the greatest part of men must be either very sceptics, or change every moment, and yield themselves up to whoever, having lately studied the question, offers them arguments ; which, for want of memory, they are not able presently to answer.

3. *The ill consequence of this, if our former judgment were not rightly made.*—I cannot but own that men's sticking to their past judgment, and adhering firmly to conclusions formerly made, is often the cause of great obstinacy in error and mistake. But the fault is not, that they rely on their memories for what they have before well-judged, but because they judged before they had well examined. May we not find a great number (not to say, the greatest part) of men that think they have formed right judgments of several matters, and that for no other reason but because they never thought otherwise ? who imagine themselves to have judged right, only because they never questioned, never examined, their own opinions ? which is indeed to think they judged right, because they never judged at all: and yet these, of all men, hold their opinions with the greatest stiffness; those being generally the most fierce and firm in their tenets who have least examined them. What we once know, we are certain is so ; and we may be secure that there are no latent proofs undiscovered which may overturn our knowledge, or bring it in doubt. But in matters of probability, it is not in every case we can be sure that we have all the particulars before us that any way concern the question ; and that there is no evidence behind and yet unseen which may cast the probability on the other side, and outweigh all that at present seems to preponderate with us. Who almost is there that hath the leisure, patience, and means to collect together all the proofs concerning most of the opinions he has, so as safely to conclude that he hath a clear and full view, and

that there is no more to be alleged for his better information? And yet we are forced to determine ourselves on the one side or other. The conduct of our lives, and the management of our great concerns, will not bear delay; for those depend, for the most part, on the determination of our judgment in points wherein we are not capable of certain and demonstrative knowledge, and wherein it is necessary for us to embrace the one side or the other.

4. *The right use of it is mutual charity and forbearance.*—Since therefore it is unavoidable to the greatest part of men, if not all, to have several opinions, without certain and indubitable proofs of their truths; and it carries too great an imputation of ignorance, lightness, or folly, for men to quit and renounce their former tenets presently upon the offer of an argument which they cannot immediately answer and show the insufficiency of; it would, methinks, become all men to maintain peace and the common offices of humanity and friendship in the diversity of opinions, since we cannot reasonably expect that any one should readily and obsequiously quit his own opinion, and embrace ours with a blind resignation to an authority which the understanding of man acknowledges not. For, however it may often mistake, it can own no other guide but reason, nor blindly submit to the will and dictates of another. If he you would bring over to your sentiments be one that examines before he assents, you must give him leave at his leisure to go over the account again, and, recalling what is out of his mind, examine the particulars, to see on which side the advantage lies; and, if he will not think our arguments of weight enough to engage him anew in so much pains, it is but what we do often ourselves in the like case; and we should take it amiss if others should prescribe to us what points we should study: and if he be one who takes his opinions upon trust, how can we imagine that he should renounce those tenets which time and custom have so settled in his mind that he thinks them self-evident, and of an unquestionable certainty; or which he takes to be impressions he has received from God himself, or from men sent by him? How can we expect, I say, that opinions thus settled should be given up to the arguments or authority of a stranger or adversary? especially if there be any suspicion of interest or design, as there never fails to be where men find themselves ill-treated. We should do well to commiserate our mutual ignorance, and endeavour to remove it in all the gentle and fair ways of information, and not instantly treat others ill as obstinate and perverse because they will not renounce their own and receive our opinions, or at least those we would force upon them, when it is more than probable that we are no less obstinate in not embracing some of theirs. For where is the man that has uncontestable evidence of the truth of all that he holds, or of the falsehood of all he condemns; or can say, that he has

examined to the bottom all his own or other men's opinions? The necessity of believing without knowledge, nay, often upon very slight grounds, in this fleeting state of action and blindness we are in, should make us more busy and careful to inform ourselves than constrain others. At least those who have not thoroughly examined to the bottom all their own tenets, must confess they are unfit to prescribe to others, and are unreasonable in imposing that as truth on other men's belief which they themselves have not searched into, nor weighed the arguments of probability on which they should receive or reject it. Those who have fairly and truly examined, and are thereby got past doubt in all the doctrines they profess and govern themselves by, would have a juster pretence to require others to follow them; but these are so few in number, and find so little reason to be magisterial in their opinions, that nothing insolent and imperious is to be expected from them; and there is reason to think, that if men were better instructed themselves, they would be less imposing on others.

5. *Probability is either of matter-of-fact or speculation.*—But, to return to the grounds of assent, and the several degrees of it: we are to take notice that the propositions we receive upon inducements of probability are of two sorts; either concerning some particular existence, or, as it is usually termed, "matter-of-fact," which, falling under observation, is capable of human testimony· or else concerning things which, being beyond the discovery of our senses, are not capable of any such testimony.

6. *The concurrent experience of all other men with ours, produces assurance approaching to knowledge.*—Concerning the first of these, viz., particular matter-of-fact:—

First, Where any particular thing, consonant to the constant observation of ourselves and others in the like case, comes attested by the concurrent reports of all that mention it, we receive it as easily and build as firmly upon it as if it were certain knowledge; and we reason and act thereupon with as little doubt as if it were perfect demonstration. Thus, if all Englishmen, who have occasion to mention it, should affirm, that "it froze in England the last winter," or that "there were swallows seen there in the summer," I think a man could almost as little doubt of it as that "seven and four are eleven." The first, therefore, and highest degree of probability is, when the general consent of all men in all ages, as far as it can be known, concurs with a man's constant and never-failing experience in like cases, to confirm the truth of any particular matter-of-fact attested by fair witnesses; such are all the stated constitutions and properties of bodies, and the regular proceedings of causes and effects in the ordinary course of nature. This we call "an argument from the nature of things themselves:" for what our own and other men's constant observation has found always to be after the same manner, that we with reason conclude to be the effects of steady and regular causes, though they come not within the reach of our knowledge. Thus, that "fire warmed a man, made lead fluid, and changed the colour and consistency in wood or charcoal;" that "iron sunk in water, and swam in quicksilver:" these, and the like propositions about particular facts, being agreeable to our constant experience as often as we have to do with these matters, and being generally spoke of (when mentioned by others) as things found constantly to be so, and therefore not so much as controverted by any body, we are put past doubt that a relation affirming any such thing to have been, or any predication that it will happen again in the same manner, is very true. These probabilities rise so near to certainty that they govern our thoughts as absolutely, and influence all our actions as fully, as the most evident demonstration; and, in what concerns us, we make little or no difference between them and certain knowledge. Our belief thus grounded rises to assurance.

7. *Unquestionable testimony and experience for the most part produce confidence.*—Secondly, The next degree of probability is, when I find by my own experience, and the agreement of all others that mention it, a thing to be for the most part so; and that the particular instance of it is attested by many and undoubted witnesses; *v. g.*, history giving us such an account of men in all ages, and my own experience, as far as I had an opportunity to observe, confirming it, that most men prefer their private advantage to the public; if all historians that write of Tiberius say, that Tiberius did so, it is extremely probable. And in this case, our assent has a sufficient foundation to raise itself to a degree which we may call "confidence."

8. *Fair testimony, and the nature of the thing indifferent, produce also confident belief.*—Thirdly, In things that happen indifferently as "that a bird should fly this or that way," "that it should thunder on a man's right or left hand," &c., when any particular matter-of-fact is vouched by the concurrent testimony of unsuspected witnesses, there our assent is also unavoidable. Thus "that there is such a city in Italy as Rome; that about 1700 years ago there lived in it a man called Julius Cæsar; that he was a general, and that he won a battle against another called Pompey: this, though in the nature of the thing there be nothing for nor against it, yet being related by historians of credit, and contradicted by no one writer, a man cannot avoid believing it, and can as little doubt of it as he does of the being and actions of his own acquaintance, whereof he himself is a witness.

9. *Experience and testimonies clashing, infinitely vary the degrees of probability.*—Thus far the matter goes easy enough. Probability upon such grounds carries so much evidence with it that it naturally determines the judgment, and leaves us as little liberty to believe or disbelieve, as a demonstration does whether

we will know or be ignorant. The difficulty is, when testimonies contradict common experience, and the reports of history
and witnesses clash with the ordinary course of nature, or with
one another; there it is where diligence, attention, and exactness is required to form a right judgment, and to proportion the
assent to the different evidence and probability of the thing,
which rises and falls according as those two foundations of credibility, viz., common observation in like cases, and particular
testimonies in that particular instance, favour or contradict it.
These are liable to so great variety of contrary observations,
circumstances, reports, different qualifications, tempers, designs,
oversights, &c., of the reporters, that it is impossible to reduce
to precise rules the various degrees wherein men give their
assent. This only may be said in general, that as the arguments
and proofs, *pro* and *con*, upon due examination, nicely weighing
every particular circumstance, shall to any one appear upon the
whole matter, in a greater or less degree, to preponderate on
either side; so they are fitted to produce in the mind such different entertainment as we call "belief, conjecture, guess, doubt,
wavering, distrust, disbelief," &c.

10. *Traditional testimonies, the farther removed, the less their
proof.*—This is what concerns assent in matters wherein testimony is made use of; concerning which, I think it may not be
amiss to take notice of a rule observed in the law of England,
which is, "that though the attested copy of a record be good
proof, yet the copy of a copy, never so well attested, and by
never so credible witnesses, will not be admitted as a proof in
judicature." This is so generally approved as reasonable, and
suited to the wisdom and caution to be used in our inquiry after
material truths, that I never yet heard of any one that blamed
it. This practice, if it be allowable in the decisions of right and
wrong, carries this observation along with it, viz., "that any
testimony, the farther off it is from the original truth, the less
force and proof it has." The being and existence of the thing
itself, is what I call "the original truth." A credible man
vouching his knowledge of it, is a good proof: but if another
equally credible do witness it from his report, the testimony is
weaker; and a third that attests the hearsay of an hearsay, is
yet less considerable. So that, in traditional truths, each remove
weakens the force of the proof; and the more hands the tradition
has successively passed through, the less strength and evidence
does it receive from them. This I thought necessary to be taken
notice of, because I find amongst some men the quite contrary
commonly practised, who look on opinions to gain force by growing older; and what a thousand years since would not, to a
rational man, contemporary with the first voucher, have appeared
at all probable, is now urged as certain beyond all question, only
because several have since from him said it one after another.

Upon this ground, propositions, evidently false or doubtful enough in their first beginning, come by an inverted rule of probability to pass for authentic truths; and those which found or deserved little credit from the mouths of their first authors, are thought to grow venerable by age, and are urged as undeniable.

11. *Yet history is of great use.*—I would not be thought here to lessen the credit and use of history: it is all the light we have in many cases; and we receive from it a great part of the useful truths we have with a convincing evidence. I think nothing more valuable than the records of antiquity: I wish we had more of them, and more uncorrupted. But this truth itself forces me to say, that no probability can arise higher than its first original. What has no other evidence than the single testimony of one only witness, must stand or fall by his only testimony, whether good, bad, or indifferent; and though cited afterwards by hundreds of others, one after another, is so far from receiving any strength thereby that it is only the weaker. Passion, interest, inadvertency, mistake of his meaning, and a thousand odd reasons or capricious men's minds are acted by (impossible to be discovered), may make one man quote another man's words or meaning wrong. He that has but ever so little examined the citations of writers, cannot doubt how little credit the quotations deserve where the originals are wanting; and consequently how much less quotations of quotations can be relied on. This is certain, that what in one age was affirmed upon slight grounds, can never after come to be more valid in future ages by being often repeated. But the farther still it is from the original, the less valid it is; and has always less force in the mouth or writing of him that last made use of it, than in his from whom he received it.

12. *In things which sense cannot discover, analogy is the great rule of probability.*—The probabilities we have hitherto mentioned are only such as concern matter-of-fact, and such things as are capable of observation and testimony. There remains that other sort concerning which men entertain opinions with variety of assent, though the things be such that, falling not under the reach of our senses, they are not capable of testimony. Such are, (1.) The existence, nature, and operations of finite immaterial beings without us, as spirits, angels, devils, &c., or the existence of material beings, which, either from their smallness in themselves or remoteness from us, our senses cannot take notice of: as whether there be any plants, animals, and intelligent inhabitants in the planets and other mansions of the vast universe. (2.) Concerning the manner of operation in most parts of the works of nature; wherein, though we see the sensible effects, yet their causes are unknown, and we perceive not the ways and manner how they are produced. We see animals are generated, nourished and move; the loadstone draws iron; and the parts of a candle successively melting, turn into flame, and give us both light and heat. These

and the like effects we see and know; but the causes that operate, and the manner they are produced in, we can only guess and probably conjecture. For, these and the like coming not within the scrutiny of human senses, cannot be examined by them, or be attested by any body, and therefore can appear more or less probable only as they more or less agree to truths that are established in our minds, and as they hold proportion to other parts of our knowledge and observation. Analogy in these matters is the only help we have, and it is from that alone we draw all our grounds of probability. Thus, observing that the bare rubbing of two bodies violently one upon another produces heat, and very often fire itself, we have reason to think that what we call "heat" and "fire" consists in a violent agitation of the imperceptible minute parts of the burning matter. Observing likewise that the different refractions of pellucid bodies produce in our eyes the different appearances of several colours: and also that the different ranging and laying the superficial parts of several bodies, as of velvet, watered silk, &c., does the like; we think it probable that the colour and shining of bodies is in them nothing but the different arrangement and refraction of their minute and insensible parts. Thus finding in all parts of the creation, that fall under human observation, that there is a gradual connexion of one with another, without any great or discernible gaps between, in all that great variety of things we see in the world, which are so closely linked together that, in the several ranks of beings, it is not easy to discover the bounds betwixt them, we have reason to be persuaded that by such gentle steps things ascend upwards in degrees of perfection. It is a hard matter to say where sensible and rational begin, and where insensible and irrational end: and who is there quick-sighted enough to determine precisely which is the lowest species of living things, and which the first of those which have no life? Things, as far as we can observe, lessen and augment as the quantity does in a regular cone, where, though there be a manifest odds betwixt the bigness of the diameter at a remote distance, yet the difference between the upper and the under, where they touch one another, is hardly discernible. The difference is exceeding great between some men and some animals; but if we will compare the understanding and abilities of some men and some brutes, we shall find so little difference that it will be hard to say, that that of the man is either clearer or larger. Observing, I say, such gradual and gentle descents downwards in those parts of the creation that are beneath men, the rule of analogy may make it probable that it is so also in things above us and our observation; and that there are several ranks of intelligent beings, excelling us in several degrees of perfection, ascending upwards towards the infinite perfection of the Creator, by gentle steps and differences, that are every one at no great distance from the next to it. This sort of probability, which is the best conduct of rational experiments and the rise of hypothesis, has also its use and influence; and a wary reasoning from analogy leads us often into the discovery of truths and useful productions, which would otherwise lie concealed.

13. *One case where contrary experience lessens not the testimony.* —Though the common experience and the ordinary course of things have justly a mighty influence on the minds of men to make them give or refuse credit to any thing proposed to their belief; yet there is one case wherein the strangeness of the fact lessens not the assent to a fair testimony given of it. For, where such supernatural events are suitable to ends aimed at by Him who has the power to change the course of nature, there, under such circumstances, they may be the fitter to procure belief, by how much the more they are beyond or contrary to ordinary observation. This is the proper case of miracles; which, well attested, do not only find credit themselves, but give it also to other truths which need such confirmation.

14. *The bare testimony of revelation is the highest certainty.*— Besides those we have hitherto mentioned, there is one sort of propositions that challenge the highest degree of our assent, upon bare testimony, whether the thing proposed agree or disagree with common experience and the ordinary course of things or no. The reason whereof is, because the testimony is of such an one as cannot deceive nor be deceived, and that is of God himself. This carries with it assurance beyond doubt, evidence beyond exception. This is called by a peculiar name "revelation," and our assent to it, "faith;" which as absolutely determines our minds and as perfectly excludes all wavering, as our knowledge itself: and we may as well doubt of our own being as we can whether any revelation from God be true. So that faith is a settled and sure principle of assent and assurance, and leaves no manner of room for doubt or hesitation. Only we must be sure that it be a divine revelation, and that we understand it right: else we shall expose ourselves to all the extravagancy of enthusiasm, and all the error of wrong principles, if we have faith and assurance in what is not divine revelation. And therefore, in those cases, our assent can be rationally no higher than the evidence of its being a revelation, and that this is the meaning of the expressions it is delivered in. If the evidence of its being a revelation, or that this is its true sense, be only on probable proofs, our assent can reach no higher than an assurance or diffidence, arising from the more or less apparent probability of the proofs. But of faith and the precedency it ought to have before other arguments of persuasion, I shall speak more hereafter, where I treat of it as it is ordinarily placed, in contradistinction to reason; though, in truth, it be nothing else but an assent founded on the highest reason.

# CHAPTER XVII.

## OF REASON.

**1. *Various significations of the word "reason."***—The word "reason," in the English language, has different significations: sometimes it is taken for true and clear principles; sometimes for clear and fair deductions from those principles; and sometimes for the cause, and particularly the final cause. But the consideration I shall have of it here is in a signification different from all these; and that is, as it stands for a faculty in man; that faculty whereby man is supposed to be distinguished from beasts, and wherein it is evident he much surpasses them.

**2. *Wherein reasoning consists.***—If general knowledge, as has been shown, consists in a perception of the agreement or disagreement of our own ideas, and the knowledge of the existence of all things without us (except only of a God, whose existence every man may certainly know and demonstrate to himself from his own existence) be had only by our senses; what room then is there for the exercise of any other faculty but outward sense and inward perception? What need is there of reason? Very much; both for the enlargement of our knowledge and regulating our assent: for it hath to do both in knowledge and opinion, and is necessary and assisting to all our other intellectual faculties, and indeed contains two of them, viz., sagacity and illation. By the one it finds out, and by the other it so orders, the intermediate ideas as to discover what connexion there is in each link of the chain, whereby the extremes are held together; and thereby, as it were, to draw into view the truth sought for, which is that we call "illation" or "inference," and consists in nothing but the perception of the connexion there is between the ideas in each step of the deduction, whereby the mind comes to see either the certain agreement or disagreement of any two ideas, as in demonstration, in which it arrives at knowledge; or their probable connexion, on which it gives or withholds its assent, as in opinion. Sense and intuition reach but a very little way. The greatest part of our knowledge depends upon deductions and intermediate ideas: and in those cases where we are fain to substitute assent instead of knowledge, and take propositions for true without being certain they are so, we have need to find out, examine, and compare the grounds of their probability. In both these cases the faculty which finds out the means, and rightly applies them to discover certainty in the one and probability in the other, is that which we call "reason." For, as reason perceives the necessary and indubitable connexion of all the ideas or proofs one to another in each step of any demonstration that produces knowledge, so it likewise perceives the probable connexion of all the ideas or proofs one to another, in every step of a discourse to which it will think assent due. This is the lowest degree of that which can be truly called "reason." For, where the mind does not perceive this probable connexion, where it does not discern whether there be any such connexion or no, there men's opinions are not the product of judgment or the consequence of reason, but the effects of chance and hazard, of a mind floating at all adventures, without choice and without direction.

3. *Its four parts.*—So that we may in reason consider these four degrees: The first and highest is the discovering and finding out of proofs; the second, the regular and methodical disposition of them, and laying them in a clear and fit order, to make their connexion and force be plainly and easily perceived; the third is the perceiving their connexion; and the fourth, a making a right conclusion. These several degrees may be observed in any mathematical demonstration: it being one thing, to perceive the connexion of each part as the demonstration is made by another; another, to perceive the dependence of the conclusion on all the parts; a third, to make out a demonstration clearly and neatly one's self; and something different from all these, to have first found out those intermediate ideas or proofs by which it is made.

4. *Syllogism not the great instrument of reason.*—There is one thing more which I shall desire to be considered concerning reason; and that is, whether syllogism, as is generally thought, be the proper instrument of it, and the usefullest way of exercising this faculty. The causes I have to doubt are these:—

First, Because syllogism serves our reason but in one only of the fore-mentioned parts of it; and that is, to show the connexion of the proofs in any one instance and no more; but in this it is of no great use, since the mind can perceive such connexion where it really is as easily, nay perhaps better, without it.

If we will observe the actings of our own minds, we shall find that we reason best and clearest when we only observe the connexion of the proof, without reducing our thoughts to any rule of syllogism. And therefore we may take notice that there are many men that reason exceeding clear and rightly, who know not how to make a syllogism. He that will look into many parts of Asia and America, will find men reason there, perhaps, as acutely as himself, who yet never heard of a syllogism, nor can reduce any one argument to those forms: and I believe scarce any one ever makes syllogisms in reasoning within himself. Indeed, syllogism is made use of on occasion to discover a fallacy hid in a rhetorical flourish, or cunningly wrapped up in a smooth period; and, stripping an absurdity of the cover of wit and good language, show it in its naked deformity. But the weakness or fallacy of such a loose discourse it shows, by the artificial form it is put into, only to those who have thoroughly studied mode and figure, and have so examined the many ways that three propositions may be put together, as to know which of them does certainly conclude right, and which not, and upon what grounds it is that they do so. All who have so far considered syllogism as to see the reason why, in three propositions laid together in one form, the conclusion will be certainly right, but in another not certainly so, I grant are certain of the conclusion they draw from the premisses in the allowed modes and figures. But they who have not so far looked into those forms are not sure, by virtue of syllogism, that the conclusion certainly follows from the premises; they only take it to be so by an implicit faith in their teachers, and a confidence in those forms of argumentation: but this is still but believing, not being certain. Now, if of all mankind those who can make syllogisms are extremely few in comparison with those who cannot, and if of those few who have been taught logic there is but a very small number who do any more than believe that syllogisms in the allowed modes and figures do conclude right, without knowing certainly that they do so; if syllogisms must be taken for the only proper instrument of reason and means of knowledge; it will follow, that before Aristotle there was not one man that did or could know any thing by reason; and that, since the invention of syllogisms, there is not one of ten thousand that doth.

But God has not been so sparing to men to make them barely two-legged creatures, and left it to Aristotle to make them rational; *i.e.*, those few of them that he could get so to examine the grounds of syllogisms as to see that in above threescore ways that three propositions may be laid together, there are but about fourteen wherein one may be sure that the conclusion is right, and upon what ground it is that in these few the conclusion is certain, and in the other not. God has been more bountiful to mankind than so; he has given them a mind that can reason without being instructed in methods of syllogising: the understanding is not taught to reason by these rules; it has a native faculty to perceive the coherence or incoherence of its ideas, and can range them right without any such perplexing repetitions. I say not this any way to lessen Aristotle, whom I look on as one of the greatest men amongst the ancients; whose large views, acuteness and penetration of thought, and strength of judgment, few have equalled; and who, in this very invention of forms of argumentation, wherein the conclusion may be shown to be rightly inferred, did great service against those who were not ashamed to deny anything. And I readily own that all right reasoning may be reduced to his forms of syllogism. But yet I think, without any diminution to him, I may truly say, that they are not the only nor the best way of reasoning, for the leading of those into truth who are willing to find it, and desire to make the best use they may of their reason for the attainment of knowledge. And he himself, it is plain, found out some forms to be conclusive and others not, not by the forms themselves, but by the original way of knowledge, *i. e.*, by the visible agreement of ideas. Tell a country gentlewoman that the wind is south-west, and the weather louring and like to rain, and she will easily understand it is not safe for her to go abroad thin clad in such a day, after a fever: she clearly sees the probable connexion of all these, viz., south-west wind, and clouds, rain, wetting, taking cold, relapse, and danger of death, without tying them together in those artificial and cumbersome fetters of several syllogisms that clog and hinder the mind, which proceeds from one part to another quicker and clearer without them: and the probability which she easily perceives in things thus in their native state would be quite lost, if this argument were managed learnedly and proposed in mode and figure. For it very often confounds the connexion: and, I think, every one will perceive in mathematical demonstrations, that the knowledge gained thereby comes shortest and clearest without syllogisms.

Inference is looked on as the great act of the rational faculty; and so it is when it is rightly made: but the mind, either very desirous to enlarge its knowledge, or very apt to favour the sentiments it has once imbibed, is very forward to make inferences, and therefore often makes too much haste before it perceives the connexion of the ideas that must hold the extremes together.

To infer is nothing but, by virtue of one proposition laid down as true, to draw in another as true; *i.e.*, to see or suppose such a connexion of the two ideas of the inferred proposition. *V. g.*, let this be the proposition laid down, "Men shall be punished in another world," and from thence be inferred this other, "Then men can determine themselves." The question now is to know whether the mind has made this inference right or no; if it has made it by finding out the intermediate ideas, and taking a view of the connexion of them placed in a due order, it has proceeded rationally, and made a right inference. If it has done it without such a view, it has not so much made an inference that will hold, or an inference of right reason, as shown a willingness to have it be or be taken for such. But in neither case is it syllogism that discovered those ideas, or showed the connexion of them; for they must be both found out, and the connexion every where perceived, before they can rationally be made use of in syllogism: unless it can be said that any idea, without considering what connexion it hath with the two other, whose agreement should be shown by it, will do well enough in a syllogism, and may be taken at a venture for the *medius terminus* to prove any conclusion. But this nobody will say, because it is by virtue of the perceived agreement of the intermediate idea with the extremes, that the extremes are concluded to agree, and therefore each intermediate idea must be such as in the whole chain hath a visible connexion with those two it is placed between, or else thereby the conclusion cannot be inferred or drawn in; for wherever any link of the chain is loose and without connexion, there the whole strength of it is lost, and it hath no force to infer or draw in any thing.  In the instance above mentioned what is it shows the force of the inference, and consequently the reasonableness of it, but a view of the connexion of all the intermediate ideas that draw in the conclusion or proposition inferred ? *v. g.*, "Men shall be punished; God the punisher ; just punishment; the punished guilty; could have done otherwise; freedom; self-determination; " by which chain of ideas thus visibly linked together in train, *i. e.*, each intermediate idea agreeing on each side with those two it is immediately placed between, the ideas of men and self-determination appear to be connected; *i. e.*, this proposition, "Men can determine themselves," is drawn in or inferred from this, that "they shall be punished in the other world."  For here the mind, seeing the connexion there is between the idea of men's punishment in the other world and the idea of God punishing, between God punishing and the justice of the punishment, between justice of punishment and guilt, between guilt and a power to do otherwise, between a power to do otherwise and freedom, and between freedom and self-determination, sees the connexion between men and self-determination.

Now, I ask, whether the connexion of the extremes be not more clearly seen in this simple and natural disposition than in the perplexed repetitions and jumble of five or six syllogisms ? I must beg pardon for calling it "jumble" till somebody shall put these ideas into so many syllogisms, and then say that they are less jumbled, and their connexion more visible, when they are transposed and repeated, and spun out to a greater length in artificial forms than in that short, natural, plain order they are laid down in here, wherein every one may see it; and wherein they must be seen before they can be put into a train of syllogisms.  For the natural order of the connecting ideas must direct the order of the syllogisms, and a man must see the connexion of each intermediate idea with those that it connects, before he can with reason make use of it in a syllogism.  And when all those syllogisms are made, neither those that are nor those that are not logicians will see the force of the argumentation, *i. e.*, the connexion of the extremes, one jot the better.  [For those that are not men of art, not knowing the true forms of syllogism, nor the reasons of them, cannot know whether they are made in right and conclusive modes and figures or no, and so are not at all helped by the forms they are put into, though by them the natural order, wherein the mind could judge of their respective connexion, being disturbed, renders the illation much more uncertain than without them.]  And as for logicians themselves, they see the connexion of each intermediate idea with those it stands between, (on which the force of the inference depends,) as well before as after the syllogism is made, or else they do not see it at all.  For a syllogism neither shows nor strengthens the connexion of any two ideas immediately put together, but only by the connexion seen in them shows what connexion the extremes have one with another.  But what connexion the intermediate has with either of the extremes in that syllogism, that no syllogism does or can show.  *That* the mind only doth or can perceive, as they stand there in that juxtaposition, only by its own view, to which the syllogistical form it happens to be in gives no help or light at all; it only shows that if the intermediate idea agrees with those it is on both sides immediately applied to, then those two remote ones, or, as they are called "extremes," do certainly agree; and therefore the immediate connexion of each idea to that which it is applied to on each side, on which the force of the reasoning depends, is as well seen before as after the syllogism is made, or else he that makes the syllogism could never see it at all.  This, as has been already observed, is seen only by the eye, or the perceptive faculty of the mind, taking a view of them laid together in a juxtaposition; which view of any two it has equally whenever they are laid together in any proposition, whether that proposition be placed as a major or a minor, in a syllogism or no.

"Of what use, then, are syllogisms?"  I answer, Their chief and main use is in the Schools, where men are allowed, without shame, to deny the agreement of ideas that do manifestly agree; or out of the Schools, to those who from thence have learned, without shame, to deny the connexion of ideas which even to themselves is visible.  But to an ingenious searcher after truth, who has no other aim but to find it, there is no need of any such form to force the allowing of the inference; the truth and reasonableness of it is better seen in ranging of the ideas in a simple and plain order.  And hence it is that men, in their own inquiries after truth, never use syllogisms to convince themselves, [or, in teaching others, to instruct willing learners,] because, before they can put them into a syllogism, they must see the connexion that is between the intermediate idea and the two other ideas it is set between and applied to to show their agreement; and when they see that, they see whether the inference be good or no, and so syllogism comes too late to settle it.  For, to make use again of the former instance, I ask, whether the mind, considering the idea of justice placed as an intermediate idea between the punishment of men and the guilt of the punished (and till it does so consider it, the mind cannot make use of it as a *medius terminus*), does not as plainly see the force and strength of the inference as when it is formed into syllogism?  To show it in a very plain and easy example: Let *animal* be the intermediate idea, or *medius terminus*, that the mind makes use of to show the connexion of *homo* and *vivens;* I ask, whether the mind does not more readily and plainly see that connexion in the simple and proper position of the connecting idea in the middle, thus,

*Homo——Animal——Vivens,*

than in this perplexed one,

*Animal——Vivens——Homo——Animal?*

which is the position these ideas have in a syllogism, to show the connexion between *homo* and *vivens* by the intervention of *animal*.

Indeed, syllogism is thought to be of necessary use, even to the lovers of truth, to show them the fallacies that are often concealed in florid, witty, or involved discourses. But that this is a mistake, will appear if we consider that the reason why sometimes men who sincerely aim at truth, are imposed upon by such loose, and, as they are called, "rhetorical" discourses, is, that their fancies being struck with some lively metaphorical representations, they neglect to observe or do not easily perceive what are the true ideas upon which the inference depends. Now, to show such men the weakness of such an argumentation, there needs no more but to strip it of the superfluous ideas which, blended and confounded with those on which the inference depends, seem to show a connexion where there is none, or at least to hinder the discovery of the want of it; and then to lay the naked ideas on which the force of the argumentation depends in their due order; in which position the mind, taking a view of them, sees what connexion they have, and so is able to judge of the inference, without any need of a syllogism at all.

I grant that "mode" and "figure" is commonly made use of in such cases, as if the detection of the incoherence of such loose discourses were wholly owing to the syllogistical form; and so I myself formerly thought, till upon a stricter examination I now find, that laying the intermediate ideas naked in their due order, shows the incoherence of the argumentation better than syllogism; not only as subjecting each link of the chain to the immediate view of the mind in its proper place, whereby its connexion is best observed; but also because syllogism shows the incoherence only to those (who are not one of ten thousand) who perfectly understand "mode" and "figure," and the reason upon which those forms are established: whereas a due and orderly placing of the ideas upon which the inference is made makes every one, whether logician or not logician, who understands the terms and hath the faculty to perceive the agreement or disagreement of such ideas (without which, in or out of syllogism, he cannot perceive the strength or weakness, coherence or incoherence, of the discourse), see the want of connexion in the argumentation, and the absurdity of the inference.

And thus I have known a man unskilful in syllogism, who at first hearing could perceive the weakness and inconclusiveness of a long artificial and plausible discourse,' wherewith others better skilled in syllogism have been misled; and I believe there are few of my readers who do not know such. And indeed, if it were not so, the debates of most princes' councils and the business of assemblies would be in danger to be mismanaged, since those who are relied upon, and have usually a great stroke in them, are not always such who have the good-luck to be perfectly knowing in the forms of syllogism, or expert in mode and figure. And if syllogism were the only, or so much as the surest, way to detect the fallacies of artificial discourses, I do not think that all mankind, even princes in matters that concern their crowns and dignities, are so much in love with falsehood and mistake, that they would every where have neglected to bring syllogism into the debates of moment, or thought it ridiculous so much as to offer them in affairs of consequence; a plain evidence to me that men of parts and penetration, who were not idly to dispute at their ease, but were to act according to the result of their debates, and often pay for their mistakes with their heads or fortunes, found those scholastic forms were of little use to discover truth or fallacy, whilst both the one and the other might be shown, and better shown, without them to those who would not refuse to see what was visibly shown them.

Secondly, Another reason that makes me doubt whether syllogism be the only proper instrument of reason in the discovery of truth, is, that of whatever use mode and figure is pretended to be in the laying open of fallacy (which has been above considered), those scholastic forms of discourse are not less liable to fallacies than the plainer ways of argumentation; and for this I appeal to common observation, which has always found these artificial methods of reasoning more adapted to catch and entangle the mind than to instruct and inform the understanding. And hence it is that men, even when they are baffled and silenced in this scholastic way, are seldom or never convinced, and so brought over to the conquering side; they perhaps acknowledge their adversary to be the more skilful disputant, but rest nevertheless persuaded of the truth on their side; and go away, worsted as they are, with the same opinion they brought with them, which they could not do if this way of argumentation carried light and conviction with it, and made men see where the truth lay; and therefore syllogism has been thought more proper for the attaining victory in dispute, than for the discovery or confirmation of truth in fair inquiries : and if it be certain that fallacy can be couched in syllogisms, and it cannot be denied, it must be something else, and not syllogism, that must discover them.

I have had experience how ready some men are, when all the use which they have been wont to ascribe to anything is not allowed, to cry out, that I am for laying it wholly aside. But to prevent such unjust and groundless imputations, I tell them, that I am not for taking away any helps to the understanding in the attainment of knowledge; and if men skilled in and used to syllogisms find them assisting to their reason in the discovery of truth, I think they ought to make use of them. All that I aim at is, that they should not ascribe more to these forms than belongs to them; and think that men have no use, or not so full a use, of their reasoning faculty without them. Some eyes want spectacles to see things clearly and distinctly; but let not those that use them therefore say, nobody can see clearly without them: those who do so will be thought in favour of art (which perhaps they are beholding to) a little too much to depress and discredit nature. Reason, by its own penetration, where it is strong and exercised, usually sees quicker and clearer without syllogisms. If use of those spectacles has so dimmed its sight that it cannot without them see consequences or inconsequences in argumentation, I am not so unreasonable as to be against the using them. Every one knows what best fits his own sight; but let him not thence conclude all in the dark who use not just the same helps that he finds a need of.

5. *Helps little in demonstration, less in probability.*—But, however it be in knowledge, I think I may truly say, it is of far less or no use at all in probabilities. For, the assent there being to be determined by the preponderancy, after a due weighing of all the proofs with all circumstances on both sides, nothing is so unfit to assist the mind in that as syllogism; which, running away with one assumed probability, or one topical argument, pursues that till it has led the mind quite out of sight of the thing under consideration, and, forcing it upon some remote difficulty, holds it fast there entangled perhaps, and as it were manacled, in the chain of syllogisms, without allowing it the liberty, much less affording it the helps, requisite to show on which side, all things considered, is the greater probability.

6. *Serves not to increase our knowledge, but fence with it.*—But let it help us (as perhaps may be said) in convincing men of their errors and mistakes; (and yet I would fain see the man that was forced out of his opinion by dint of syllogism;) yet still it fails our reason in that part which, if not its highest perfection, is yet certainly its hardest task, and that which we most need its help in; and that is, the finding out of proofs, and making new discoveries. The rules of syllogism serve not to furnish the mind with those intermediate ideas that may show the connexion of remote ones. This way of reasoning discovers no new proofs, but is the art of marshalling and ranging the old ones we have already. The forty-seventh proposition of the first book of

Euclid is very true; but the discovery of it, I think, not owing to any rules of common logic. A man knows first, and then he is able to prove syllogistically: so that syllogism comes after knowledge; and then a man has little or no need of it. But it is chiefly by the finding out those ideas that show the connexion of distant ones, that our stock of knowledge is increased, and that useful arts and sciences are advanced. Syllogism, at best, is but the art of fencing with the little knowledge we have, without making any addition to it; and if a man should employ his reason all this way, he will not do much otherwise than he who, having got some iron out of the bowels of the earth, should have it beaten up all into swords, and put it into his servants' hands to fence with and bang one another. Had the king of Spain employed the hands of his people and his Spanish iron so, he had brought to light but little of that treasure that lay so long hid in the dark entrails of America. And I am apt to think, that he who shall employ all the force of his reason only in brandishing of syllogisms, will discover very little of that mass of knowledge which lies yet concealed in the secret recesses of nature; and which I am apt to think, native rustic reason (as it formerly has done) is likelier to open a way to and add to the common stock of mankind, rather than any scholastic proceeding by the strict rules of mode and figure.

7. *Other helps should be sought.*—I doubt not, nevertheless, but there are ways to be found to assist our reason in this most useful part; and this the judicious Hooker encourages me to say, who, in his *Eccl. Pol.* lib. i. sec. 6, speaks thus: " If there might be added the right helps of true art and learning (which helps, I must plainly confess, this age of the world, carrying the name of a learned age, doth neither much know nor generally regard), there would undoubtedly be almost as much difference in maturity of judgment between men therewith inured, and that which now men are, as between men that are now and innocents." I do not pretend to have found or discovered here any of those right helps of art this great man of deep thought mentions: but this is plain, that syllogism, and the logic now in use, which were as well known in his days, can be none of those he means. It is sufficient for me, if by a discourse, perhaps something out of the way (I am sure, as to me, wholly new and unborrowed), I shall have given occasion to others to cast about for new discoveries, and to seek in their own thoughts for those right helps of art which will scarce be found, I fear, by those who servilely confine themselves to the rules and dictates of others: for beaten tracks lead these sort of cattle (as an observing Roman calls them), whose thoughts reach only to imitation, *non quo eundum est, sed quo itur*. But I can be bold to say, that this age is adorned with some men of that strength of judgment and largeness of comprehension, that, if they would employ their thoughts on this subject,

could open new and undiscovered ways to the advancement of knowledge.

8. *We reason about particulars.*—Having here had an occasion to speak of syllogism in general, and the use of it in reasoning and the improvement of our knowledge, it is fit, before I leave this subject to take notice of one manifest mistake in the rules of syllogism; viz., "that no syllogistical reasoning can be right and conclusive but what has, at least, one general proposition in it;" as if we could not reason and have knowledge about particulars: whereas, in truth, the matter rightly considered, the immediate object of all our reasoning and knowledge is nothing but particulars. Every man's reasoning and knowledge is only about the ideas existing in his own mind, which are truly, every one of them, particular existences; and our knowledge and reasoning about other things is only as they correspond with those our particular ideas. So that the perception of the agreement or disagreement of our particular ideas, is the whole and utmost of all our knowledge. Universality is but accidental to it, and consists only in this, that the particular ideas about which it is are such as more than one particular thing can correspond with and be represented by. But the perception of the agreement or disagreement of any two ideas, and consequently our knowledge, is equally clear and certain, whether either, or both, or neither of those ideas be capable of representing more real beings than one, or no. One thing more I crave leave to offer about syllogism before I leave it, viz., May one not upon just ground inquire whether the form syllogism now has, is that which in reason it ought to have? For, the *medius terminus* being to join the extremes, *i. e.*, the intermediate ideas by its intervention, to show the agreement or disagreement of the two in question, would not the position of the *medius terminus* be more natural, and show the agreement or disagreement of the extremes clearer and better, if it were placed in the middle between them? which might be easily done by transposing the propositions, and making the *medius terminus* the predicate of the first, and the subject of the second. As thus;

*Omnis homo est animal,*
*Omne animal est vivens,*
*Ergo omnis homo est vivens.*

*Omne corpus est extensum et solidum,*
*Nullum extensum et solidum est pura extensio,*
*Ergo corpus non est pura extensio.*

I need not trouble my reader with instances in syllogisms whose conclusions are particular. The same reason holds for the same form in them as well as in the general.

9. Reason, though it penetrates into the depths of the sea and

earth, elevates our thoughts as high as the stars, and leads us through the vast spaces and large rooms of this mighty fabric, yet it comes far short of the real extent of even corporeal being, and there are many instances wherein it fails us: as,

*First, Reason fails us for want of ideas.*—First, It perfectly fails us where our ideas fail. It neither does nor can extend itself farther than they do. And therefore, wherever we have no ideas, our reasoning stops, and we are at an end of our reckoning: and if at any time we reason about words which do not stand for any ideas, it is only about those sounds and nothing else.

10. *Secondly, Because of obscure and imperfect ideas.*—Secondly, Our reason is often puzzled and at a loss because of the obscurity, confusion, or imperfection of the ideas it is employed about; and there we are involved in difficulties and contradictions. Thus, not having any perfect idea of the least extension of matter nor of infinity, we are at a loss about the divisibility of matter; but having perfect, clear, and distinct ideas of number, our reason meets with none of those inextricable difficulties in numbers, nor finds itself involved in any contradictions about them. Thus we, having but imperfect ideas of the operations of our minds, and of the beginning of motion or thought, how the mind produces either of them in us, and much imperfecter yet of the operation of God, run into great difficulties about free created agents, which reason cannot well extricate itself out of.

11. *Thirdly, For want of intermediate ideas.*—Thirdly, Our reason is often at a stand because it perceives not those ideas which could serve to show the certain or probable agreement or disagreement of any two other ideas: and in this some men's faculties far outgo others. Till algebra, that great instrument and instance of human sagacity, was discovered, men with amazement looked on several of the demonstrations of ancient mathematicians, and could scarce forbear to think the finding several of those proofs to be something more than human.

12. *Fourthly, Because of wrong principles.*—Fourthly, The mind, by proceeding upon false principles, is often engaged in absurdities and difficulties, brought into straits and contradictions without knowing how to free itself: and in that case it is in vain to implore the help of reason, unless it be to discover the falsehood and reject the influence of those wrong principles. Reason is so far from clearing the difficulties which the building upon false foundations brings a man into, that, if he will pursue it, it entangles him the more, and engages him deeper in perplexities.

13. *Fifthly, Because of doubtful terms.*—Fifthly, As obscure and imperfect ideas often involve our reason, so, upon the same ground, do dubious words and uncertain signs often, in discourses and arguings, when not warily attended to, puzzle men's reason, and bring them to a nonplus: but these two latter are our fault,

and not the fault of reason. But yet the consequences of them are nevertheless obvious; and the perplexities or errors they fill men's minds with are everywhere observable.

14. *Our highest degree of knowledge is intuitive, without reasoning.*—Some of the ideas that are in the mind, are so there that they can be by themselves immediately compared one with another: and in these the mind is able to perceive that they agree or disagree as clearly as that it has them. Thus the mind perceives that an arch of a circle is less than the whole circle, as clearly as it does the idea of a circle: and this therefore, as has been said, I call "intuitive knowledge," which is certain beyond all doubt, and needs no probation, nor can have any; this being the highest of all human certainty. In this consists the evidence of all those maxims which nobody has any doubt about, but every man (does not, as is said, only assent to, but) knows to be true, as soon as ever they are proposed to his understanding. In the discovery of and assent to these truths, there is no use of the discursive faculty, no need of reasoning, but they are known by a superior and higher degree of evidence. And such, if I may guess at things unknown, I am apt to think that angels have now, and the spirits of just men made perfect shall have in a future state, of thousands of things which now either wholly escape our apprehensions, or which our short-sighted reason has got some faint glimpse of, we in the dark grope after.

15. *The next is demonstration by reasoning.*—But though we have here and there a little of this clear light, some sparks of bright knowledge; yet the greatest part of our ideas are such, that we cannot discern their agreement or disagreement by an immediate comparing them. And in all these we have need of reasoning, and must, by discourse and inference, make our discoveries. Now, of these there are two sorts, which I shall take the liberty to mention here again.

First, Those whose agreement or disagreement, though it cannot be seen by an immediate putting them together, yet may be examined by the intervention of other ideas which can be compared with them. In this case, when the agreement or disagreement of the intermediate idea, on both sides, with those which we would compare, is plainly discerned, there it amounts to demonstration, whereby knowledge is produced; which, though it be certain, yet it is not so easy nor altogether so clear as intuitive knowledge; because in that there is barely one simple intuition, wherein there is no room for any the least mistake or doubt; the truth is seen all perfectly at once. In demonstration, it is true, there is intuition too, but not all together at once: for there must be a remembrance of the intuition of the agreement of the medium or intermediate idea with that we compared it with before, when we compare it with the other; and where there be many mediums, there the danger of the mistake is the greater. For, each agreement or disagreement of the ideas must be observed, and seen in each step of the whole train, and retained in the memory just as it is, and the mind must be sure that no part of what is necessary to make up the demonstration is omitted or overlooked. This makes some demonstrations long and perplexed, and too hard for those who have not strength of parts distinctly to perceive and exactly carry so many particulars orderly in their heads. And even those who are able to master such intricate speculations are fain sometimes to go over them again, and there is need of more than one review before they can arrive at certainty. But yet, where the mind clearly retains the intuition it had of the agreement of any idea with another, and that with a third, and that with a fourth, &c., there the agreement of the first and the fourth is a demonstration, and produces certain knowledge, which may be called "rational knowledge," as the other is "intuitive."

16. *To supply the narrowness of this, we have nothing but judgment upon probable reasoning.*—Secondly, There are other ideas whose agreement or disagreement can no otherwise be judged of but by the intervention of others which have not a certain agreement with the extremes, but an usual or likely one: and in these it is that the judgment is properly exercised, which is the acquiescing of the mind that any ideas do agree by comparing them with such probable mediums. This, though it never amounts to knowledge, no, not to that which is the lowest degree of it; yet sometimes the intermediate ideas tie the extremes so firmly together, and the probability is so clear and strong, that assent as necessarily follows it as knowledge does demonstration. The great excellency and use of the judgment is to observe right, and take a true estimate of the force and weight of each probability; and then casting them up all right together, choose that side which has the over-balance.

17. *Intuition, demonstration, judgment.*—Intuitive knowledge is the perception of the certain agreement or disagreement of two ideas immediately compared together.

Rational knowledge is the perception of the certain agreement or disagreement of any two ideas by the intervention of one or more other ideas.

Judgment is the thinking or taking two ideas to agree or disagree by the intervention of one or more ideas whose certain agreement or disagreement with them it does not perceive, but hath observed to be frequent and usual.

18. *Consequences of words, and consequences of ideas.*—Though the deducing one proposition from another, or making inferences in words, be a great part of reason, and that which it is usually employed about; yet the principal act of ratiocination is the finding the agreement or disagreement of two ideas one with another by the intervention of a third: as a man by a yard finds

two houses to be of the same length, which could not be brought together to measure their equality by juxtaposition. Words have their consequences as the signs of such ideas: and things agree or disagree as really they are; but we observe it only by our ideas.

19. *Four sorts of arguments.*—Before we quit this subject, it may be worth our while a little to reflect on four sorts of arguments that men in their reasonings with others do ordinarily make use of to prevail on their assent; or, at least, so to awe them as to silence their opposition.

*First*, Ad verecundiam.—First, The first is, to allege the opinions of men whose parts, learning, eminency, power, or some other cause, has gained a name and settled their reputation in the common esteem with some kind of authority. When men are established in any kind of dignity, it is thought a breach of modesty for others to derogate any way from it, and question the authority of men who are in possession of it. This is apt to be censured as carrying with it too much of pride, when a man does not readily yield to the determination of approved authors, which is wont to be received with respect and submission by others, and it is looked upon as insolence for a man to set up and adhere to his own opinion against the current stream of antiquity, or to put it in the balance against that of some learned doctor, or otherwise approved writer. Whoever backs his tenets with such authorities, thinks he ought thereby to carry the cause, and is ready to style it "impudence" in any one who shall stand out against them. This I think may be called *argumentum ad verecundiam*.

20. *Secondly*, Ad ignorantiam.—Secondly, another way that men ordinarily use to drive others, and force them to submit their judgments and receive the opinion in debate, is to require the adversary to admit what they allege as a proof, or to assign a better. And this I call *argumentum ad ignorantiam*.

21. *Thirdly*, Ad hominem.—Thirdly, A third way is to press a man with consequences drawn from his own principles or concessions. This is already known under the name of *argumentum ad hominem*.

22. *Fourthly*, Ad judicium.—Fourthly, The fourth is the using of proofs drawn from any of the foundations of knowledge or probability. This I call *argumentum ad judicium*. This alone of all the four brings true instruction with it, and advances us in our way to knowledge. For, (1.) It argues not another man's opinion to be right, because I, out of respect, or any other consideration but that of conviction, will not contradict him. (2.) It proves not another man to be in the right way, nor that I ought to take the same with him, because I know not a better. (3.) Nor does it follow that another man is in the right way because he has shown me that I am in the wrong. I may be modest, and

therefore not oppose another man's persuasion; I may be ignorant, and not be able to produce a better; I may be in an error,
and another may show me that I am so. This may dispose me
perhaps for the reception of truth, but helps me not to it; that
must come from proofs and arguments, and light arising from the
nature of things themselves, and not from my shamefacedness,
ignorance, or error.

23. *Above, contrary, and according to reason.*—By what has been
before said of reason, we may be able to make some guess at the
distinction of things, into those that are according to, above, and
contrary to reason. (1.) "According to reason" are such propositions whose truth we can discover by examining and tracing
those ideas we have from sensation and reflection, and by natural
deduction find to be true or probable. (2.) "Above reason"
are such propositions whose truth or probability we cannot by
reason derive from those principles. (3.) "Contrary to reason"
are such propositions as are inconsistent with or irreconcilable to
our clear and distinct ideas. Thus the existence of one God is
*according* to reason; the existence of more than one God is *contrary* to reason; the resurrection of the dead *above* reason.
Farther: as "above reason" may be taken in a double sense,
viz., either as signifying above probability, or above certainty,
so in that large sense also, "contrary to reason" is, I suppose,
sometimes taken.

24. *Reason and faith not opposite.*—There is another use of the
word "reason," wherein it is opposed to faith; which, though it
be in itself a very improper way of speaking, yet common use has
so authorized it, that it would be folly either to oppose or hope
to remedy it. Only I think it may not be amiss to take notice,
that, however faith be opposed to reason, faith is nothing but a
firm assent of the mind; which, if it be regulated, as is our duty,
cannot be afforded to any thing but upon good reason, and so
cannot be opposite to it. He that believes, without having any
reason for believing, may be in love with his own fancies; but
neither seeks truth as he ought, nor pays the obedience due to
his Maker, who would have him use those discerning faculties
he has given him to keep him out of mistake and error. He that
does not this to the best of his power, however he sometimes
lights on truth, is in the right but by chance; and I know not
whether the luckiness of the accident will excuse the irregularity
of his proceeding. This at least is certain, that he must be accountable for whatever mistakes he runs into; whereas he that
makes use of the light and faculties God has given him, and seeks
sincerely to discover truth by those helps and abilities he has,
may have this satisfaction in doing his duty as a rational creature,
that though he should miss truth, he will not miss the reward
of it; for he governs his assent right, and places it as he should,
who in any case or matter whatsoever believes or disbelieves

according as reason directs him. He that does otherwise, transgresses against his own light, and misuses those faculties which were given him to no other end but to search and follow the clearer evidence and greater probability. But since reason and faith are by some men opposed, we will so consider them in the following chapter.

———

## CHAPTER XVIII.

### OF FAITH AND REASON, AND THEIR DISTINCT PROVINCES.

1. *Necessary to know their boundaries.*—It has been above shown, (1.) That we are of necessity ignorant, and want knowledge of all sorts where we want ideas. (2.) That we are ignorant, and want rational knowledge where we want proofs. (3.) That we want general knowledge and certainty as far as we want clear and determined specific ideas. (4.) That we want probability to direct our assent in matters where we have neither knowledge of our own nor testimony of other men to bottom our reason upon.

From these things thus premised, I think we may come to lay down the measures and boundaries between faith and reason; the want whereof may possibly have been the cause, if not of great disorders, yet at least of great disputes, and perhaps mistakes, in the world: for till it be resolved how far we are to be guided by reason, and how far by faith, we shall in vain dispute and endeavour to convince one another in matters of religion.

2. *Faith and reason what, as contradistinguished.*—I find every sect, as far as reason will help them, make use of it gladly; and, where it fails them, they cry out, "It is matter of faith, and above reason." And I do not see how they can argue with any one, or ever convince a gainsayer, who makes use of the same plea, without setting down strict boundaries between faith and reason, which ought to be the first point established in all questions where faith has anything to do.

Reason therefore here, as contradistinguished to faith, I take to be the discovery of the certainty or probability of such propositions or truths which the mind arrives at by deduction made from such ideas which it has got by the use of its natural faculties, viz., by sensation or reflection.

Faith, on the other side, is the assent to any proposition, not thus made out by the deductions of reason, but upon the credit of the proposer, as coming from God in some extraordinary way of communication. This way of discovering truths to men we call "revelation."

3. *No new simple idea can be conveyed by traditional revelation.*—First, then, I say, that no man inspired by God can, by any

revelation, communicate to others any new simple ideas which they had not before from sensation or reflection: for, whatsoever impressions he himself may have from the immediate hand of God, this revelation, if it be of new simple ideas, cannot be conveyed to another, either by words or any other signs; because words, by their immediate operation on us, cause no other ideas but of their natural sounds; and it is by the custom of using them for signs that they excite and revive in our minds latent ideas, but yet only such ideas as were there before. For, words seen or heard recall to our thoughts those ideas only which to us they have been wont to be signs of; but cannot introduce any perfectly new and formerly unknown simple ideas. The same holds in all other signs, which cannot signify to us things of which we have before never had any idea at all.

Thus, whatever things were discovered to St. Paul when he was rapt up into the third heaven, whatever new ideas his mind there received, all the description he can make to others of that place is only this, that there are such things as "eye hath not seen, nor ear heard, nor hath it entered into the heart of man to conceive." And supposing God should discover to any one, supernaturally, a species of creatures inhabiting, for example, Jupiter or Saturn (for that it is possible there may be such, nobody can deny), which had six senses, and imprint on his mind the ideas conveyed to theirs by that sixth sense, he could no more by words produce in the minds of other men those ideas imprinted by that sixth sense, than one of us could convey the idea of any colour by the sounds of words into a man who, having the other four senses perfect, had always totally wanted the fifth of seeing. For our simple ideas, then, which are the foundation and sole matter of all our notions and knowledge, we must depend wholly on our reason, I mean, our natural faculties, and can by no means receive them, or any of them, from traditional revelation; I say, "traditional revelation," in distinction to original revelation. By the one I mean that first impression which is made immediately by God on the mind of any man, to which we cannot set any bounds; and by the other, those impressions delivered over to others in words, and the ordinary ways of conveying our conceptions one to another.

4. *Traditional revelation may make us know propositions knowable also by reason, but not with the same certainty that reason doth.* —Secondly, I say, that the same truths may be discovered and conveyed down from revelation, which are discoverable to us by reason and by those ideas we naturally may have. So God might, by revelation, discover the truth of any proposition in Euclid; as well as men, by the natural use of their faculties, come to make the discovery themselves. In all things of this kind there is little need or use of revelation, God having furnished us with natural and surer means to arrive at the knowledge of them. For,

whatsoever truth we come to the clear discovery of, from the knowledge and contemplation of our own ideas, will always be certainer to us than those which are conveyed to us by traditional revelation: for the knowledge we have that this revelation came at first from God, can never be so sure as the knowledge we have from the clear and distinct perception of the agreement or disagreement of our own ideas: *v. g.*, if it were revealed some ages since, that the three angles of a triangle were equal to two right ones, I might assent to the truth of that proposition upon the credit of the tradition that it was revealed: but that would never amount to so great a certainty as the knowledge of it upon the comparing and measuring my own ideas of two right angles, and the three angles of a triangle. The like holds in matter-of-fact, knowable by our senses: *v. g.*, the history of the deluge is conveyed to us by writings which had their original from revelation; and yet nobody, I think, will say he has as certain and clear a knowledge of the flood as Noah, that saw it, or that he himself would have had, had he then been alive and seen it. For he has no greater an assurance than that of his senses, that it is writ in the book supposed writ by Moses inspired; but he has not so great an assurance that Moses writ that book as if he had seen Moses write it. So that the assurance of its being a revelation is less still than the assurance of his senses.

5. *Revelation cannot be admitted against the clear evidence of reason.*—In propositions, then, whose certainty is built upon the clear perception of the agreement or disagreement of our ideas, attained either by immediate intuition, as in self-evident propositions, or by evident deductions of reason in demonstrations, we need not the assistance of revelation as necessary to gain our assent and introduce them into our minds; because the natural ways of knowledge could settle them there, or had done it already, which is the greatest assurance we can possibly have of any thing, unless where God immediately reveals it to us; and there too our assurance can be no greater than our knowledge is, that it is a revelation from God. But yet nothing, I think, can under that title shake or overrule plain knowledge, or rationally prevail with any man to admit it for true, in a direct contradiction to the clear evidence of his own understanding: for, since no evidence of our faculties by which we receive such revelations can exceed, if equal, the certainty of our intuitive knowledge, we can never receive for a truth any thing that is directly contrary to our clear and distinct knowledge: *v. g.*, the ideas of one body and one place do so clearly agree, and the mind has so evident a perception of their agreement, that we can never assent to a proposition that affirms the same body to be in two distant places at once, however it should pretend to the authority of a divine revelation, since the evidence, first, that we deceive not ourselves in ascribing it to God, secondly, that we understand it right, can

never be so great as the evidence of our own intuitive knowledge, whereby we discern it impossible for the same body to be in two places at once. And therefore no proposition can be received for divine revelation, or obtain the assent due to all such, if it be contradictory to our clear intuitive knowledge, because this would be to subvert the principles and foundations of all knowledge, evidence, and assent whatsoever: and there would be left no difference between truth and falsehood, no measures of credible and incredible in the world, if doubtful propositions shall take place before self-evident, and what we certainly know give way to what we may possibly be mistaken in. In propositions, therefore, contrary to the clear perception of the agreement or disagreement of any of our ideas, it will be in vain to urge them as matters of faith. They cannot move our assent under that or any other title whatsoever: for faith can never convince us of any thing that contradicts our knowledge, because, though faith be founded on the testimony of God (who cannot lie) revealing any proposition to us, yet we cannot have an assurance of the truth of its being a divine revelation greater than our own knowledge; since the whole strength of the certainty depends upon our knowledge that God revealed it, which, in this case, where the proposition supposed revealed contradicts our knowledge or reason, will always have this objection hanging to it, viz., that we cannot tell how to conceive that to come from God, the bountiful Author of our being, which, if received for true, must overturn all the principles and foundations of knowledge he has given us; render all our faculties useless; wholly destroy the most excellent part of his workmanship, our understandings; and put a man in a condition wherein he will have less light, less conduct, than the beast that perisheth. For if the mind of man can never have a clearer, and perhaps not so clear, evidence of any thing to be a divine revelation as it has of the principles of its own reason, it can never have a ground to quit the clear evidence of its reason, to give place to a proposition whose revelation has not a greater evidence than those principles have.

6. *Traditional revelation much less.*—Thus far a man has use of reason, and ought to hearken to it, even in immediate and original revelation, where it is supposed to be made to himself; but to all those who pretend not to immediate revelation, but are required to pay obedience, and to receive the truths revealed to others, which, by the tradition of writings or word of mouth, are conveyed down to them, reason has a great deal more to do, and is that only which can induce us to receive them. For, matter of faith being only divine revelation and nothing else, faith (as we use the word, called commonly "divine faith") has to do with no propositions but those which are supposed to be divinely revealed. So that I do not see how those who make revelation alone the sole object of faith can say that it is a matter of faith

and not of reason, to believe that such or such a proposition, to be found in such or such a book, is of divine inspiration; unless it be revealed that that proposition, or all in that book, was communicated by divine inspiration. Without such a revelation, the believing or not believing that proposition or book to be of divine authority can never be matter of faith, but matter of reason; and such as I must come to an assent to only by the use of my reason, which can never require or enable me to believe that which is contrary to itself: it being impossible for reason ever to procure any assent to that which to itself appears unreasonable.

In all things, therefore, where we have clear evidence from our ideas, and those principles of knowledge I have above mentioned, reason is the proper judge; and revelation, though it may, in consenting with it, confirm its dictates, yet cannot in such cases invalidate its decrees: nor can we be obliged, where we have the clear and evident sentence of reason, to quit it for the contrary opinion, under a pretence that it is matter of faith; which can have no authority against the plain and clear dictates of reason.

7. *Things above reason.* — But, Thirdly, there being many things wherein we have very imperfect notions, or none at all; and other things, of whose past, present, or future existence, by the natural use of our faculties, we can have no knowledge at all: these, as being beyond the discovery of our natural faculties and above reason, are, when revealed, the proper matter of faith. Thus, that part of the angels rebelled against God, and thereby lost their first happy state: and that the dead shall rise, and live again: these, and the like, being beyond the discovery of reason, are purely matters of faith, with which reason has, directly, nothing to do.

8. *Or not contrary to reason, if revealed, are matter of faith.* — But since God, in giving us the light of reason, has not thereby tied up his own hands from affording us, when he thinks fit, the light of revelation in any of those matters wherein our natural faculties are able to give a probable determination, revelation, where God has been pleased to give it, must carry it against the probable conjectures of reason; because the mind, not being certain of the truth of that it does not evidently know, but only yielding to the probability that appears in it, is bound to give up its assent to such a testimony, which, it is satisfied, comes from One who cannot err, and will not deceive. But yet it still belongs to reason to judge of the truth of its being a revelation, and of the signification of the words wherein it is delivered. Indeed, if any thing shall be thought revelation which is contrary to the plain principles of reason and the evident knowledge the mind has of its own clear and distinct ideas, there reason must be hearkened to as to a matter within its province: since a man can

never have so certain a knowledge that a proposition, which contradicts the clear principles and evidence of his own knowledge,
was divinely revealed, or that he understands the words rightly
wherein it is delivered, as he has that the contrary is true; and
so is bound to consider and judge of it as a matter of reason, and
not swallow it, without examination, as a matter of faith.

9. *Revelation, in matters where reason cannot judge, or but probably, ought to be hearkened to.*—First, Whatever proposition is
revealed, of whose truth our mind, by its natural faculties and
notions, cannot judge, that is purely matter of faith, and above
reason.

Secondly, All propositions whereof the mind, by the use of its
natural faculties, can come to determine and judge, from naturally
acquired ideas, are matter of reason; with this difference still,
that in those concerning which it has but an uncertain evidence,
and so is persuaded of their truth only upon probable grounds,
which still admit a possibility of the contrary to be true, without
doing violence to the certain evidence of its own knowledge, and
overturning the principles of all reason; in such probable propositions, I say, an evident revelation ought to determine our
assent even against probability. For where the principles of
reason have not evidenced a proposition to be certainly true or
false, their clear revelation, as another principle of truth and
ground of assent, may determine; and so it may be matter of
faith, and be also above reason, because reason, in that particular
matter, being able to reach no higher than probability, faith
gave the determination where reason came short, and revelation
discovered on which side the truth lay.

10. *In matters where reason can afford certain knowledge, that
is to be hearkened to.*—Thus far the dominion of faith reaches, and
that without any violence or hinderance to reason: which is not
injured or disturbed, but assisted and improved, by new discoveries of truth, coming from the eternal Fountain of all knowledge. Whatever God hath revealed is certainly true; no doubt
can be made of it. This is the proper object of faith: but whether
it be a divine revelation or no, reason must judge; which can
never permit the mind to reject a greater evidence to embrace
what is less evident, nor allow it to entertain probability in opposition to knowledge and certainty. There can be no evidence
that any traditional revelation is of divine original, in the words
we receive it, and in the sense we understand it, so clear and so
certain as that of the principles of reason: and therefore nothing
that is contrary to, and inconsistent with, the clear and self-evident
dictates of reason has a right to be urged or assented to as a
matter of faith, wherein reason hath nothing to do. Whatsoever
is divine revelation ought to over-rule all our opinions, prejudices,
and interests, and hath a right to be received with full assent:
such a submission as this of our reason to faith takes not away

the landmarks of knowledge; this shakes not the foundations of reason, but leaves us that use of our faculties for which they were given us.

11. *If the boundaries be not set between faith and reason, no enthusiasm or extravagancy in religion can be contradicted.*—If the provinces of faith and reason are not kept distinct by these boundaries, there will, in matter of religion, be no room for reason at all; and those extravagant opinions and ceremonies that are to be found in the several religions of the world will not deserve to be blamed; for to this crying up of faith in opposition to reason, we may, I think, in good measure, ascribe those absurdities that fill almost all the religions which possess and divide mankind. For men, having been principled with an opinion that they must not consult reason in the things of religion, however apparently contradictory to common sense and the very principles of all their knowledge, have let loose their fancies and natural superstition; and have been by them led into so strange opinions and extravagant practices in religion, that a considerate man cannot but stand amazed at their follies, and judge them so far from being acceptable to the great and wise God, that he cannot avoid thinking them ridiculous and offensive to a sober, good man. So that, in effect, religion, which should most distinguish us from beasts, and ought most peculiarly to elevate us as rational creatures above brutes, is that wherein men often appear most irrational, and more senseless than beasts themselves. *Credo quia impossibile est,* "I believe because it is impossible," might, in a good man, pass for a sally of zeal, but would prove a very ill rule for men to choose their opinions or religion by.

---

## CHAPTER XIX.

### OF ENTHUSIASM.

1. *Love of truth necessary.*—He that would seriously set upon the search of truth, ought in the first place, to prepare his mind with a love of it; for he that loves it not will not take much pains to get it, nor be much concerned when he misses it. There is nobody in the commonwealth of learning who does not profess himself a lover of truth; and there is not a rational creature that would not take it amiss to be thought otherwise of. And yet, for all this, one may truly say, there are very few lovers of truth for truth's sake, even amongst those who persuade themselves that they are so. How a man may know whether he be so in earnest, is worth inquiry: and I think there is this one unerring mark of it, viz., the not entertaining any proposition with greater assurance than the proofs it is built upon will warrant. Whoever

goes beyond this measure of assent, it is plain, receives not truth in the love of it; loves not truth for truth's sake, but for some other by-end. For, the evidence that any proposition is true (except such as are self-evident) lying only in the proofs a man has of it, whatsoever degrees of assent he affords it beyond the degrees of that evidence, it is plain all that surplusage of assurance is owing to some other affection, and not to the love of truth; it being as impossible that the love of truth should carry my assent above the evidence there is to me that it is true, as that the love of truth should make me assent to any proposition for the sake of that evidence which it has not that it is true; which is, in effect, to love it as a truth, because it is possible or probable that it may not be true. In any truth that gets not possession of our minds by the irresistible light of self-evidence, or by the force of demonstration, the arguments that gain it assent are the vouchers and gauge of its probability to us; and we can receive it for no other than such as they deliver it to our understandings. Whatsoever credit or authority we give to any proposition more than it receives from the principles and proofs it supports itself upon, is owing to our inclinations that way, and is so far a derogation from the love of truth as such; which, as it can receive no evidence from our passions or interests, so it should receive no tincture from them.

2. *A forwardness to dictate, from whence.*—The assuming an authority of dictating to others, and a forwardness to prescribe to their opinions, is a constant concomitant of this bias and corruption of our judgments: for how almost can it be otherwise, but that he should be ready to impose on others' belief who has already imposed on his own? Who can reasonably expect arguments and conviction from him in dealing with others, whose understanding is not accustomed to them in his dealing with himself? who does violence to his own faculties, tyrannizes over his own mind, and usurps the prerogative that belongs to truth alone, which is to command assent by only its own authority, *i.e.*, by and in proportion to that evidence which it carries with it.

3. *Force of enthusiasm.*—Upon this occasion I shall take the liberty to consider a third ground of assent, which, with some men, has the same authority and is as confidently relied on, as either faith or reason: I mean enthusiasm: which, laying by reason, would set up revelation without it; whereby in effect it takes away both reason and revelation, and substitutes in the room of it the ungrounded fancies of a man's own brain, and assumes them for a foundation both of opinion and conduct.

4. *Reason and revelation.*—Reason is natural revelation, whereby the eternal Father of light, and Fountain of all knowledge, communicates to mankind that portion of truth which he has laid within the reach of their natural faculties. Revelation is

natural reason enlarged by a new set of discoveries communicated by God immediately, which reason vouches the truth of by the testimony and proofs it gives that they come from God. So that he that takes away reason to make way for revelation, puts out the light of both; and does much-what the same as if he would persuade a man to put out his eyes, the better to receive the remote light of an invisible star by a telescope.

5. *Rise of enthusiasm.*—Immediate revelation being a much easier way for men to establish their opinions and regulate their conduct than the tedious and not always successful labour of strict reasoning, it is no wonder that some have been very apt to pretend to revelation, and to persuade themselves that they are under the peculiar guidance of heaven in their actions and opinions, especially in those of them which they cannot account for by the ordinary methods of knowledge and principles of reason. Hence we see that in all ages men, in whom melancholy has mixed with devotion, or whose conceit of themselves has raised them into an opinion of a greater familiarity with God, and a nearer admittance to his favour, than is afforded to others, have often flattered themselves with a persuasion of an immediate intercourse with the Deity, and frequent communications from the Divine Spirit. God, I own, cannot be denied to be able to enlighten the understanding by a ray darted into the mind immediately from the Fountain of light. This they understand he has promised to do; and who then has so good a title to expect it as those who are his peculiar people, chosen by him, and depending on him?

6. *Enthusiasm.*—Their minds being thus prepared, whatever groundless opinion comes to settle itself strongly upon their fancies, is an illumination from the Spirit of God, and presently of divine authority: and whatsoever odd action they find in themselves a strong inclination to do, that impulse is concluded to be a call or direction from heaven, and must be obeyed; it is a commission from above, and they cannot err in executing it.

7. This I take to be properly enthusiasm, which, though founded neither on reason nor divine revelation, but rising from the conceits of a warmed or overweening brain, works yet, where it once gets footing, more powerfully on the persuasions and actions of men than either of those two, or both together: men being most forwardly obedient to the impulses they receive from themselves; and the whole man is sure to act more vigorously where the whole man is carried by a natural motion. For, strong conceit, like a new principle, carries all easily with it, when got above common sense, and freed from all restraint of reason and check of reflection, it is heightened into a divine authority, in concurrence with our own temper and inclination.

8. *Enthusiasm mistaken for seeing and feeling.*—Though the odd opinions and extravagant actions enthusiasm has run men into

were enough to warn them against this wrong principle, so apt to misguide them both in their belief and conduct; yet the love of something extraordinary, the ease and glory it is to be inspired and be above the common and natural ways of knowledge, so flatters many men's laziness, ignorance, and vanity, that when once they are got into this way of immediate revelation, of illumination without search, and of certainty without proof and without examination, it is a hard matter to get them out of it. Reason is lost upon them; they are above it: they see the light infused into their understandings, and cannot be mistaken; it is clear and visible there like the light of bright sunshine; shows itself, and needs no other proof but its own evidence; they feel the hand of God moving them within, and the impulses of the Spirit, and cannot be mistaken in what they feel. Thus they support themselves, and are sure reason hath nothing to do with what they see and feel in themselves; what they have a sensible experience of, admits no doubt, needs no probation. Would he not be ridiculous who should require to have it proved to him, that the light shines, and that he sees it? It is its own proof, and can have no other. When the Spirit brings light into our minds, it dispels darkness. We see it as we do that of the sun at noon, and need not the twilight of reason to show it us. This light from heaven is strong, clear, and pure; carries its own demonstration with it; and we may as rationally take a glow-worm to assist us to discover the sun, as examine the celestial ray by our dim candle, reason.

9. This is the way of talking of these men: they are sure, because they are sure; and their persuasions are right, only because they are strong in them. For, when what they say is stripped of the metaphor of seeing and feeling, this is all it amounts to; and yet these similes so impose on them, that they serve them for certainty in themselves, and demonstration to others.

10. *Enthusiasm, how to be discovered.*—But, to examine a little soberly this internal light, and this feeling on which they build so much: these men have, they say, clear light, and they see; they have an awakened sense, and they feel: this cannot, they are sure, be disputed them. For when a man says he sees or he feels, nobody can deny it him that he does so. But here let me ask: This seeing, is it the perception of the truth of the proposition; or of this, that it is a revelation from God? This feeling, is it a perception of an inclination or fancy to do something, or of the Spirit of God moving that inclination? These are two very different perceptions, and must be carefully distinguished if we would not impose upon ourselves. I may perceive the truth of a proposition, and yet not perceive that it is an immediate revelation from God. I may perceive the truth of a proposition in Euclid, without its being or my perceiving it to be a revelation: nay, I may perceive I came not by this knowledge in a natural way, and so

may conclude it revealed, without perceiving that it is a revelation from God; because there be spirits which, without being divinely commissioned, may excite those ideas in me, and lay them in such order before my mind that I may perceive their connexion. So that the knowledge of any proposition coming into my mind, I know not how, is not a perception that it is from God; much less is a strong persuasion that it is true, a perception that it is from God, or so much as true. But, however it be called "light" and "seeing," I suppose it is at most but "belief" and "assurance;" and the proposition taken for a revelation is not such as they know to be true, but take to be true. For where a proposition is known to be true, revelation is needless: and it is hard to conceive how there can be a revelation to any one of what he knows already. If therefore it be a proposition which they are persuaded, but do not know, to be true, whatever they may call it, it is not seeing, but believing. For these are two ways whereby truth comes into the mind, wholly distinct, so that one is not the other. What I see, I know to be so by the evidence of the thing itself; what I believe, I take to be so upon the testimony of another: but this testimony I must know to be given, or else what ground have I of believing? I must see that it is God that reveals this to me, or else I see nothing. The question then here is, How do I know that God is the revealer of this to me; that this impression is made upon my mind by his Holy Spirit, and that therefore I ought to obey it? If I know not this, how great soever the assurance is that I am possessed with, it is groundless; whatever light I pretend to, it is but enthusiasm. For, whether the proposition supposed to be revealed be in itself evidently true, or visibly probable, or by the natural ways of knowledge uncertain, the proposition that must be well-grounded and manifested to be true is this, that God is the revealer of it; and that what I take to be a revelation is certainly put into my mind by him, and is not an allusion dropped in by some other spirit, or raised by my own fancy. For, if I mistake not, these men receive it for true because they presume God revealed it. Does it not then stand them upon to examine upon what grounds they presume it to be a revelation from God? Or else all their confidence is mere presumption; and this light they are so dazzled with, is nothing but an *ignis fatuus*, that leads them continually round in this circle: It is a revelation, because they firmly believe it; and they believe it, because it is a revelation.

11. *Enthusiasm fails of evidence, that the proposition is from God.*—In all that is of divine revelation, there is need of no other proof but that it is an inspiration from God: for he can neither deceive nor be deceived. But how shall it be known that any proposition in our minds is a truth infused by God; a truth that is revealed to us by him, which he declares to us, and therefore

we ought to believe? Here it is that enthusiasm fails of the evidence it pretends to. For, men thus possessed boast of a light whereby they say they are enlightened and brought into the knowledge of this or that truth. But if they know it to be a truth,'they must know it to be so either by its own self-evidence to natural reason, or by the rational proofs that make it out to be so. If they see and know it to be a truth either of these two ways, they in vain suppose it to be a revelation. For they know it to be true by the same way that any other man naturally may know that it is so, without the help of revelation. For thus all the truths, of what kind soever, that men uninspired are enlightened with, came into their minds and are established there. If they say they know it to be true because it is a revelation from God, the reason is good: but then it will be demanded, how they know it to be a revelation from God? If they say, By the light it brings with it, which shines bright in their minds, and they cannot resist; I beseech them to consider, whether this be any more than what we have taken notice of already, viz., that it is a revelation because they strongly believe it to be true. For all the light they speak of is but a strong, though ungrounded, persuasion of their own minds that it is a truth. For, rational grounds from proofs that it is a truth, they must acknowledge to have none; for then it is not received as a revelation but upon the ordinary grounds that other truths are received: and if they believe it to be true because it is a revelation, and have no other reason for its being a revelation but because they are fully persuaded, without any other reason, that it is true, they believe it to be a revelation only because they strongly believe it to be a revelation; which is a very unsafe ground to proceed on, either in our tenets or actions. And what readier way can there be to run ourselves into the most extravagant errors and miscarriages, than thus to set up fancy for our supreme and sole guide, and to believe any proposition to be true, any action to be right, only because we believe it to be so? The strength of our persuasions is no evidence at all of their own rectitude: crooked things may be as stiff and unflexible as straight; and men may be as positive and peremptory in error as in truth. How come else the untractable zealots in different and opposite parties? For if the light, which every one thinks he has in his mind, which in this case is nothing but the strength of his own persuasion, be an evidence that it is from God, contrary opinions may have the same title to be inspirations; and God will be not only the Father of lights, but of opposite and contradictory lights, leading men contrary ways; and contradictory propositions will be divine truths, if an ungrounded strength of assurance be an evidence that any proposition is a divine revelation.

12. *Firmness of persuasion, no proof that any proposition is from God.*—This can ot be otherwise whilst firmness of per-

suasion is made the cause of believing, and confidence of being in the right is made an argument of truth. St. Paul himself believed he did well, and that he had a call to it, when he persecuted the Christians, whom he confidently thought in the wrong; but yet it was he, and not they who were mistaken. Good men are men still liable to mistakes, and are sometimes warmly engaged in errors which they take for divine truths, shining in their minds with the clearest light.

13. *Light in the mind, what.*—Light, true light in the mind, is or can be nothing else but the evidence of the truth of any proposition; and if it be not a self-evident proposition, all the light it has, or can have, is from the clearness and validity of those proofs upon which it is received. To talk of any other light in the understanding, is to put ourselves in the dark, or in the power of the prince of darkness, and, by our own consent, to give ourselves up to delusion, to believe a lie: for if strength of persuasion be the light which must guide us, I ask, How shall any one distinguish between the delusions of Satan, and the inspirations of the Holy Ghost? He can transform himself into an angel of light. And they who are led by this son of the morning are as fully satisfied of the illumination, *i. e.*, are as strongly persuaded that they are enlightened by the Spirit of God, as any one who is so: they acquiesce and rejoice in it, are acted by it; and nobody can be more sure, nor more in the right (if their own strong belief may be judge), than they.

14. *Revelation must be judged of by reason.*—He therefore that will not give himself up to all the extravagancies of delusion and error, must bring this guide of his light within to the trial. God, when he makes the prophet, does not unmake the man; he leaves all his faculties in their natural state, to enable him to judge of his inspirations, whether they be of divine original or no. When he illuminates the mind with supernatural light, he does not extinguish that which is natural. If he would have us assent to the truth of any proposition, he either evidences that truth by the usual methods of natural reason, or else makes it known to be a truth which he would have us assent to by his authority, and convinces us that it is from him by some marks which reason cannot be mistaken in. Reason must be our last judge and guide in every thing. I do not mean that we must consult reason, and examine whether a proposition revealed from God can be made out by natural principles; and if it cannot, that then we may reject it: but consult it we must, and by it examine whether it be a revelation from God or no: and if reason finds it to be revealed from God, reason then declares for it as much as for any other truth, and makes it one of her dictates. Every conceit that thoroughly warms our fancies must pass for an inspiration, if there be nothing but the strength of our persuasions whereby to judge of our persuasions. If reason must not examine their

truth by something extrinsical to the persuasions themselves, inspirations and delusions, truth and falsehood, will have the same measure, and will not be possible to be distinguished.

15. *Belief no proof of revelation.*—If this internal light, or any proposition which under that title we take for inspired, be conformable to the principles of reason, or to the word of God, which is attested revelation, reason warrants it, and we may safely receive it for true, and be guided by it in our belief and actions: if it receive no testimony nor evidence from either of these rules, we cannot take it for a revelation or so much as for true, till we have some other mark that it is a revelation besides our believing that it is so. Thus we see, the holy men of old, who had revelations from God, had something else besides that internal light of assurance in their own minds to testify to them that it was from God. They were not left to their own persuasions alone, that those persuasions were from God, but had outward signs to convince them of the Author of those revelations. And when they were to convince others, they had a power given them to justify the truth of their commission from heaven, and by visible signs to assert the divine authority of a message they were sent with. Moses saw the bush burn without being consumed, and heard a voice out of it. This was something besides finding an impulse upon his mind to go to Pharaoh that he might bring his brethren out of Egypt; and yet he thought not this enough to authorize him to go with that message, till God, by another miracle of his rod turned into a serpent, had assured him of a power to testify his mission by the same miracle repeated before them whom he was sent to. Gideon was sent by an angel to deliver Israel from the Midianites; and yet he desired a sign to convince him that this commission was from God. These, and several the like instances to be found among the prophets of old, are enough to show that they thought not an inward seeing or persuasion of their own minds, without any other proof, a sufficient evidence that it was from God, though the scripture does not every where mention their demanding or having such proofs.

16. In what I have said, I am far from denying that God can or doth sometimes enlighten men's minds in the apprehending of certain truths, or excite them to good actions by the immediate influence and assistance of the Holy Spirit, without any extraordinary signs accompanying it. But in such cases too we have reason and scripture, unerring rules, to know whether it be from God or no. Where the truth embraced is consonant to the revelation in the written word of God, or the action conformable to the dictates of right reason or holy writ, we may be assured that we run no risk in entertaining it as such; because, though perhaps it be not an immediate revelation from God, extraordinarily operating on our minds, yet we are sure it is warranted by that revelation which he has given us of truth. But it is not

the strength of our private persuasion within ourselves that can warrant it to be a light or motion from heaven; nothing can do that but the written word of God without us, or that standard of reason which is common to us with all men. Where reason or scripture is express for any opinion or action, we may receive it as of divine authority; but it is not the strength of our own persuasions which can by itself give it that stamp. The bent of our own minds may favour it as much as we please; that may show it to be a fondling of our own, but will by no means prove it to be an offspring of heaven, and of divine original.

---

## CHAPTER XX.

### OF WRONG ASSENT, OR ERROR.

1. *Causes of error.*—Knowledge being to be had only of visible certain truth, error is not a fault of our knowledge, but a mistake of our judgment, giving assent to that which is not true.

But if assent be grounded on likelihood, if the proper object and motive of our assent be probability, and that probability consists in what is laid down in the foregoing chapters, it will be demanded, how men come to give their assents contrary to probability? For there is nothing more common than contrariety of opinions; nothing more obvious than that one man wholly disbelieves what another only doubts of, and a third steadfastly believes and firmly adheres to. The reasons whereof, though they may be very various, yet, I suppose, may be all reduced to these four: (1.) Want of proofs. (2.) Want of ability to use them. (3.) Want of will to use them. (4.) Wrong measures of probability.

2. *First, Want of proofs.*—First, By " want of proofs," I do not mean only the want of those proofs which are no where extant, and so are no where to be had; but the want even of those proofs which are in being, or might be procured. And thus men want proofs who have not the convenience or opportunity to make experiments and observations themselves, tending to the proof of any proposition; nor likewise the convenience to inquire into and collect the testimonies of others: and in this state are the greatest part of mankind who are given up to labour, and enslaved to the necessity of their mean condition, whose lives are worn out only in the provisions for living. These men's opportunity of knowledge and inquiry are commonly as narrow as their fortunes; and their understandings are but little instructed, when all their whole time and pains is laid out to still the croaking of their own bellies, or the cries of their children. It is not to be expected that a man who drudges on all his life in a laborious trade should be more knowing in the variety of

things done in the world, than a pack-horse, who is driven constantly forwards and backwards in a narrow lane and dirty road only to market, should be skilled in the geography of the country. Nor is it at all more possible, that he who wants leisure, books, and languages, and the opportunity of conversing with variety of men, should be in a condition to collect those testimonies and observations which are in being, and are necessary to make out many, nay, most of the propositions that, in the societies of men, are judged of the greatest moment: or to find out grounds of assurance so great, as the belief of the points he would build on them is thought necessary. So that a great part of mankind are, by the natural and unalterable state of things in this world, and the constitution of human affairs, unavoidably given over to invincible ignorance of those proofs on which others build, and which are necessary to establish those opinions. The greatest part of men, having much to do to get the means of living, are not in a condition to look after those of learned and laborious inquiries.

3. *Objection, " What shall become of those who want them ? " answered.*—What shall we say then? Are the greatest part of mankind, by the necessity of their condition, subjected to unavoidable ignorance in those things which are of greatest importance to them ? (for of these it is obvious to inquire). Have the bulk of mankind no other guide but accident and blind chance to conduct them to their happiness or misery? Are the current opinions and licensed guides of every country sufficient evidence and security to every man, to venture his greatest concernments on, nay, his everlasting happiness or misery? Or can those be the certain and infallible oracles and standards of truth which teach one thing in Christendom and another in Turkey? Or shall a poor countryman be eternally happy for having the chance to be born in Italy? or a day-labourer be unavoidably lost because he had the ill luck to be born in England? How ready some men may be to say some of these things I will not here examine; but this I am sure that men must allow one or other of these to be true, (let them choose which they please,) or else grant that God has furnished men with faculties sufficient to direct them in the way they should take, if they will but seriously employ them that way, when their ordinary vocations allow them the leisure. No man is so wholly taken up with the attendance on the means of living as to have no spare time at all to think of his soul, and inform himself in matters of religion. Were men as intent upon this as they are on things of lower concernment there are none so enslaved to the necessities of life, who might not find many vacancies that might be husbanded to this advantage of their knowledge.

4. *People hindered from inquiry.*—Besides those whose improvements and informations are straitened by the narrownes

of their fortunes, there are others whose largeness of fortune would plentifully enough supply books and other requisites for clearing of doubts and discovering of truth; but they are cooped in close by the laws of their countries, and the strict guards of those whose interest it is to keep them ignorant, lest, knowing more, they should believe the less in them. These are as far, nay, farther from the liberty and opportunities of a fair inquiry than those poor and wretched labourers we before spoke of: and, however they may seem high and great, are confined to narrowness of thought, and enslaved in that which should be the freest part of man, their understandings. This is generally the case of all those who live in places where care is taken to propagate the truth without knowledge, where men are forced, at a venture, to be of the religion of the country, and must therefore swallow down opinions, as silly people do empirics' pills, without knowing what they are made of, or how they will work, and have nothing to do but believe that they will do the cure; but in this are much more miserable than they, in that they are not at liberty to refuse swallowing what perhaps they had rather let alone, or to choose the physician to whose conduct they would trust themselves.

5. *Secondly, Want of skill to use them.*—Secondly, Those who want skill to use those evidences they have of probabilities, who cannot carry a train of consequences in their heads, nor weigh exactly the preponderancy of contrary proofs and testimonies, making every circumstance its due allowance, may be easily misled to assent to positions that are not probable. There are some men of one, some but of two syllogisms, and no more; and others that can but advance one step farther. These cannot always discern that side on which the strongest proofs lie, cannot constantly follow that which in itself is the more probable opinion. Now, that there is such a difference between men, in respect of their understandings, I think nobody, who has had any conversation with his neighbours, will question; though he never was at Westminster-hall or the Exchange on the one hand, nor at Alms-houses or Bedlam on the other: which great difference in men's intellectuals, whether it rises from any defect in the organs of the body particularly adapted to thinking; or in the dulness or untractableness of those faculties for want of use; or, as some think, in the natural differences of men's souls themselves; or some, or all of these together; it matters not here to examine: only this is evident, that there is a difference of degrees in men's understandings, apprehensions, and reasonings, to so great a latitude, that one may, without doing injury to mankind, affirm that there is a greater distance between some men and others in this respect than between some men and some beasts. But how this comes about is a speculation, though of great consequence, yet not necessary to our present purpose.

**6.** *Thirdly, Want of will to use them.*—Thirdly, There are another sort of people that want proofs, not because they are out of their reach, but because they will not use them; who, though they have riches and leisure enough, and want neither parts nor other helps, are yet never the better for them. Their hot pursuit of pleasure, or constant drudgery in business, engages some men's thoughts elsewhere; laziness and oscitancy in general, or a particular aversion for books, study, and meditation, keep others from any serious thoughts at all; and some, out of fear that an impartial inquiry would not favour those opinions which best suit their prejudices, lives, and designs, content themselves, without examination, to take upon trust what they find convenient and in fashion. Thus most men, even of those that might do otherwise, pass their lives without an acquaintance with, much less a rational assent to, probabilities they are concerned to know, though they lie so much within their view that, to be convinced of them, they need but turn their eyes that way. But we know some men will not read a letter which is supposed to bring ill news: and many men forbear to cast up their accounts, or so much as think upon their estates, who have reason to fear their affairs are in no very good posture. How men whose plentiful fortunes allow them leisure to improve their understandings, can satisfy themselves with a lazy ignorance, I cannot tell; but methinks they have a low opinion of their souls, who lay out all their incomes in provisions for the body, and employ none of it to procure the means and helps of knowledge; who take great care to appear always in a neat and splendid outside, and would think themselves miserable in coarse clothes, or a patched coat, and yet contentedly suffer their minds to appear abroad in a piebald livery of coarse patches, and borrowed shreds, such as it has pleased chance or their country tailor (I mean the common opinion of those they have conversed with) to clothe them in. I will not here mention how unreasonable this is for men that ever think of a future state, and their concernment in it, which no rational man can avoid to do sometimes; nor shall I take notice what a shame and confusion it is, to the greatest contemners of knowledge, to be found ignorant in things they are concerned to know. But this, at least, is worth the consideration of those who call themselves "gentlemen," that, however they may think credit, respect, power, and authority the concomitants of their birth and fortune, yet they will find all these still carried away from them by men of lower condition, who surpass them in knowledge. They who are blind will always be led by those that see, or else fall into the ditch: and he is certainly the most subjected, the most enslaved, who is so in his understanding. In the foregoing instances some of the causes have been shown of wrong assent, and how it comes to pass that probable doctrines are not always received with an assent proportionable to the reasons which are to be had for their probability : but hitherto we have considered only such probabilities whose proofs do exist, but do not appear to him who embraces the error.

7. *Fourthly, Wrong measures of probability, whereof.*—Fourthly, There remains yet the last sort, who, even where the real probabilities appear, and are plainly laid before them, do not admit of the conviction, nor yield unto manifest reasons, but do either ἐπέχειν, "suspend" their assent, or give it to the less probable opinion. And to this danger are those exposed who have taken up wrong measures of probability, which are, (1.) Propositions that are not in themselves certain and evident, but doubtful and false, taken up for principles. (2.) Received hypotheses. (3.) Predominant passions or inclinations. (4.) Authority.

8. *First, Doubtful propositions taken for principles.*—First, The first and firmest ground of probability is the conformity any thing has to our own knowledge; especially that part of our knowledge which we have embraced, and continue to look on as principles. These have so great an influence upon our opinions that it is usually by them we judge of truth, and measure probability, to that degree, that what is inconsistent with our principles is so far from passing for probable with us, that it will not be allowed possible. The reverence borne to these principles is so great, and their authority so paramount to all other, that the testimony not only of other men, but the evidence of our own senses, are often rejected when they offer to vouch any thing contrary to these established rules. How much the doctrine of innate principles, and that principles are not to be proved or questioned, has contributed to this, I will not here examine. This I readily grant, that one truth cannot contradict another; but, withal, I take leave also to say, that every one ought very carefully to beware what he admits for a principle, to examine it strictly, and see whether he certainly knows it to be true of itself by its own evidence, or whether he does only with assurance believe it to be so upon the authority of others: for he hath a strong bias put into his understanding, which will unavoidably misguide his assent, who hath imbibed wrong principles, and has blindly given himself up to the authority of any opinion in itself not evidently true.

9. There is nothing more ordinary than children's receiving into their minds* propositions (especially about matters of religion) from their parents, nurses, or those about them; which, being insinuated into their unwary as well as unbiassed understandings, and fastened by degrees, are at last (equally, whether true or false) riveted there, by long custom and education, beyond all possibility of being pulled out again. For, men, when they are grown up, reflecting upon their opinions, and finding those of this sort to be as ancient in their minds as their very memories,

---

* This is the reading of the fourth edition in folio.—EDIT.

not having observed their early insinuation, nor by what means they got them, they are apt to reverence them as sacred things, and not to suffer them to be profaned, touched, or questioned: they look on them as the *urim* and *thummim* set up in their minds immediately by God himself, to be the great and unerring deciders of truth and falsehood, and the judges to which they are to appeal in all manner of controversies.

10. This opinion of his principles (let them be what they will) being once established in any one's mind, it is easy to be imagined what reception any proposition shall find, how clearly soever proved, that shall invalidate their authority, or at all thwart with these internal oracles: whereas, the grossest absurdities and improbabilities, being but agreeable to such principles, go down glibly, and are easily digested. The great obstinacy that is to be found in men firmly believing quite contrary opinions, though many times equally absurd, in the various religions of mankind, are as evident a proof as they are an unavoidable consequence of this way of reasoning from received traditional principles. So that men will disbelieve their own eyes, renounce the evidence of their senses, and give their own experience the lie, rather than admit of any thing disagreeing with these sacred tenets. Take an intelligent Romanist, that from the very first dawning of any notions in his understanding, hath had this principle constantly inculcated, viz., that he must believe as the Church (*i. e.*, those of his communion) believes, or that the Pope is infallible; and this he never so as much heard questioned, till at forty or fifty years old he met with one of other principles: how is he prepared easily to swallow, not only against all probability, but even the clear evidence of his senses, the doctrine of transubstantiation! This principle has such an influence on his mind, that he will believe that to be flesh which he sees to be bread. And what way will you take to convince a man of any improbable opinion he holds, who, with some philosophers, hath laid down this as a foundation of reasoning, that he must believe his reason (for so men improperly call arguments drawn from their principles) against his senses? Let an enthusiast be principled that he or his teacher is inspired, and acted by an immediate communication of the Divine Spirit, and you in vain bring the evidence of clear reasons against his doctrine. Whoever therefore have imbibed wrong principles are not, in things inconsistent with these principles, to be moved by the most apparent and convincing probabilities, till they are so candid and ingenuous to themselves as to be persuaded to examine even those very principles, which many never suffer themselves to do.

11. *Secondly, Received hypotheses.*—Secondly, Next to these are men whose understandings are cast into a mould, and fashioned just to the size of a received hypothesis. The difference between these and the former is, that they will admit of matter-of-fact, and agree with dissenters in that; but differ only in assign

ing of reasons and explaining the manner of operation. These are not at that open defiance with their senses as the former; they can endure to hearken to their information a little more patiently; but will by no means admit of their reports in the explanation of things, nor be prevailed on by probabilities which would convince them that things are not brought about just after the same manner that they have decreed within themselves that they are. Would it not be an insufferable thing for a learned professor, and that which his scarlet would blush at, to have his authority of forty years' standing, wrought out of hard-rock Greek and Latin, with no small expense of time and candle, and confirmed by general tradition and a reverend beard, in an instant overturned by an upstart novelist? Can any one expect that he should be made to confess, that what he taught his scholars thirty years ago was all error and mistake, and that he sold them hard words and ignorance at a very dear rate? What probabilities, I say, are sufficient to prevail in such a case? And who ever, by the most cogent arguments, will be prevailed with to disrobe himself at once of all his old opinions, and pretences to knowledge and learning, which, with hard study, he hath all his time been labouring for, and turn himself out stark naked in quest afresh of new notions? All the arguments can be used will be as little able to prevail as the wind did with the traveller to part with his cloak, which he held only the faster. To this of wrong hypothesis may be reduced the errors that may be occasioned by a true hypothesis, or right principles, but not rightly understood. There is nothing more familiar than this. The instances of men contending for different opinions, which they all derive from the infallible truth of the scripture, are ar undeniable proof of it. All that call themselves Christians allow the text that says, Μετανοεῖτε, to carry in it the obligation to a very weighty duty. But yet, how very erroneous will one of their practices be, who, understanding nothing but the French, take this rule, with one translation, to be *Repentez-vous*, "Repent;" or with the other, *Faites pénitence*, "Do penance!"

12. *Thirdly, Predominant passions.*—Thirdly, Probabilities which cross men's appetites and prevailing passions, run the same fate. Let never so much probability hang on one side of a covetous man's reasoning, and money on the other, it is easy to foresee which will outweigh. Earthly minds, like mud walls, resist the strongest batteries; and though, perhaps, sometimes the force of a clear argument may make some impression, yet they nevertheless stand firm, keep out the enemy, truth, that would captivate or disturb them. Tell a man, passionately in love, that he is jilted; bring a score of witnesses of the falsehood of his mistress; it is ten to one but three kind words of hers shall invalidate all their testimonies. *Quod volumus, facilè credimus,* "What suits our wishes is forwardly believed," is, I suppose, what every one hath more than once experimented; and though

men cannot always openly gainsay or resist the force of manifest probabilities that make against them, yet yield they not to the argument; not but that is the nature of the understanding constantly to close with the more probable side, but yet a man hath a power to suspend and restrain its inquiries, and not permit a full and satisfactory examination, as far as the matter in question is capable, and will bear it to be made. Until that be done, there will be always these two ways left of evading the most apparent probabilities.

13. *The means of evading probabilities: First, Supposed fallacy.*—First, That the arguments being (as for the most part they are) brought in words, there may be a fallacy latent in them; and the consequences being, perhaps, many in train, they may be some of them incoherent. There are very few discourses so short, clear, and consistent, to which most men may not with satisfaction enough to themselves, raise this doubt, and from whose conviction they may not, without reproach of disingenuity or unreasonableness, set themselves free with the old reply, *Non persuadebis etiamsi persuaseris*, "Though I cannot answer, I will not yield."

14. *Secondly, Supposed arguments for the contrary.*—Secondly, Manifest probabilities may be evaded, and the assent withheld, upon this suggestion, that "I know not yet all that may be said on the contrary side. And therefore, though I be beaten, it is not necessary I should yield, not knowing what forces there are in reserve behind." This is a refuge against conviction, so open and so wide, that it is hard to determine when a man is quite out of the verge of it.

15. *What probabilities determine the assent.*—But yet there is some end of it; and a man, having carefully inquired into all the grounds of probability and unlikeliness, does his utmost to inform himself in all particulars fairly, and cast up the sum-total on both sides, may in most cases come to acknowledge, upon the whole matter, on which side the probability rests; wherein some proofs in matter of reason, being suppositions upon universal experience, are so cogent and clear, and some testimonies in matter-of-fact so universal, that he cannot refuse his assent. So that I think we may conclude, that in propositions where, though the proofs in view are of most moment, yet there are sufficient grounds to suspect that there is either fallacy in words, or certain proofs as considerable to be produced on the contrary side, their assent, suspense, or dissent, are often voluntary actions; but where the proofs are such as make it highly probable, and there is not sufficient ground to suspect that there is either fallacy of words (which sober and serious consideration may discover), nor equally valid proofs yet undiscovered latent on the other side (which also the nature of the thing may, in some cases, make plain to a considerate man), there, I think, a man who has weighed them can scarce refuse his assent to the side on which

the greater probability appears. Whether it be probable that a promiscuous jumble of printing-letters should often fall into a method and order which should stamp on paper a coherent discourse; or that a blind, fortuitous concourse of atoms, not guided by an understanding agent, should frequently constitute the bodies of any species of animals: in these and the like cases, I think, nobody that considers them can be one jot at a stand which side to take, nor at all waver in his assent. Lastly, When there can be no supposition (the thing in its own nature indifferent, and wholly depending upon the testimony of witnesses) that there is as fair testimony against as for the matter-of-fact attested, which by inquiry is to be learned; *v. g.*, whether there was, seventeen hundred years agone, such a man at Rome as Julius Cæsar: in all such cases, I say, I think it is not in any rational man's power to refuse his assent; but that it necessarily follows and closes with such probabilities. In other less clear cases, I think it is in a man's power to suspend his assent, and perhaps content himself with the proofs he has, if they favour the opinion that suits with his inclination or interest, and so stop from farther search. But that a man should afford his assent to that side on which the less probability appears to him, seems to me utterly impracticable, and as impossible as it is to believe the same thing probable and improbable at the same time.

16. *Where it is in our power to suspend it.*—As knowledge is no more arbitrary than perception, so, I think, assent is no more in our power than knowledge. When the agreement of any two ideas appears to our minds, whether immediately or by the assistance of reason, I can no more refuse to perceive, no more avoid knowing it, than I can avoid seeing those objects which I turn my eyes to and look on in daylight; and what, upon full examination, I find the most probable, I cannot deny my assent to. But though we cannot hinder our knowledge where the agreement is once perceived: nor our assent where the probability manifestly appears upon due consideration of all the measures of it; yet we can hinder both knowledge and assent by stopping our inquiry, and not employing our faculties in the search of any truth. If it were not so, ignorance, error, or infidelity could not in any case be a fault. Thus, in some cases, we can prevent or suspend our assent: but can a man, versed in modern or ancient history, doubt whether there be such a place as Rome, or whether there was such a man as Julius Cæsar? Indeed, there are millions of truths that a man is not, or may not think himself, concerned to know; as, whether our King Richard III. was crook-backed or no, or whether Roger Bacon was a mathematician or a magician. In these and suchlike cases, where the assent, one way or other, is of no importance to the interest of any one, no action, no concernment of his following or depending thereon, there it is not strange that the mind should give itself up to the common opinion, or render itself to the first comer. These and

the like opinions are of so little weight and moment, that, like motes in the sun, their tendencies are very rarely taken notice of. They are there as it were by chance, and the mind lets them float at liberty. But where the mind judges that the pro-position has concernment in it; where the assent or not assenting is thought to draw consequences of moment after it, and good or evil to depend on choosing or refusing the right side, and the mind sets itself seriously to inquire and examine the probability : there, I think, it is not in our choice to take which side we please, if manifest odds appear on either. The greater probability, I think, in that case, will determine the assent; and a man can no more avoid assenting or taking it to be true where he perceives the greater probability, than he can avoid knowing it to be true where he perceives the agreement or disagreement of any two ideas.

If this be so, the foundation of error will lie in wrong measures of probability; as the foundation of vice in wrong measures of good.

**17. *Fourthly, Authority.*—**Fourthly, The fourth and last wrong measure of probability I shall take notice of, and which keeps in ignorance or error more people than all the other together, is that which I have mentioned in the foregoing chapter : I mean the giving up our assent to the common received opinions, either of our friends or party, neighbourhood or country. How many men have no other ground for their tenets than the supposed honesty, or learning, or number of those of the same profession ? as if honest or bookish men could not err; or truth were to be established by the vote of the multitude ! Yet this, with most men, serves the turn. "The tenet has had the attestation of reverend antiquity; it comes to me with the passport of former ages, and therefore I am secure in the reception I give it; other men have been and are of the same opinion" (for that is all is said), "and therefore it is reasonable for me to embrace it." A man may more justifiably throw up cross and pile for his opinions, than take them up by such measures. All men are liable to error ; and most men are, in many points, by passion or interest, under temptation to it. If we could but see the secret motives that influenced the men of name and learning in the world, and the leaders of parties, we should not always find that it was the embracing of truth for its own sake that made them espouse the doctrines they owned and maintained. This at least is certain, there is not an opinion so absurd which a man may not receive upon this ground. There is no error to be named which has not had its professors: and a man shall never want crooked paths to walk in, if he thinks that he is in the right way, wherever he has the footsteps of others to follow.

**18. *Men not in so many errors as is imagined.*—**But, notwithstanding the great noise is made in the world about errors and opinions I must do mankind that right as to say, "There are not so many men in errors, and wrong opinions, as is commonly supposed." Not that I think they embrace the truth; but indeed, because, concerning those doctrines they keep such a stir about, they have no thought, no opinion at all. For if any one should a little catechize the greatest part of the partisans of most of the sects in the world, he would not find, concerning those matters they are so zealous for, that they have any opinions of their own : much less would he have reason to think that they took them upon the examination of arguments and appearance of probability. They are resolved to stick to a party that education or interest has engaged them in; and there, like the common soldiers of an army, show their courage and warmth as their leaders direct, without ever examining, or so much as knowing, the cause they contend for. If a man's life shows that he has no serious regard for religion, for what reason should we think that he beats his head about the opinions of his church, and troubles himself to examine the grounds of this or that doctrine? It is enough for him to obey his leaders, to have his hand and his tongue ready for the support of the common cause, and thereby approve himself to those who can give him credit, preferment, or protection in that society. Thus men become professors of, and combatants for, those opinions they were never convinced of, nor proselytes to; no, nor ever had so much as floating in their heads; and though one cannot say there are fewer improbable or erroneous opinions in the world than there are, yet this is certain, there are fewer that actually assent to them, and mistake them for truths, than is imagined.

## CHAPTER XXI.

### OF THE DIVISION OF THE SCIENCES.

1. *Three sorts.*—All that can fall within the compass of human understanding being either, First, The nature of things as they are in themselves, their relations, and their manner of operation: or, Secondly, That which man himself ought to do, as a rational and voluntary agent, for the attainment of any end, especially happiness: or, Thirdly, The ways and means whereby the knowledge of both the one and the other of these are attained and communicated: I think science may be divided properly into these three sorts:—

2. *First*, Physica.—First, The knowledge of things as they are in their own proper beings, their constitutions, properties, and operations, whereby I mean not only matter and body, but spirits also, which have their proper natures, constitutions, and operations, as well as bodies. This, in a little more enlarged sense of the word, I call, φυσικὴ, or, "natural philosophy." The end of this is bare speculative truth: and whatsoever can afford the mind of man any such falls under this branch, whether it be God him-

self, angels, spirits, bodies, or any of their affections, as number, and figure, &c.

3. *Secondly,* Practica.—Secondly, Πρακτική, the skill of right applying our own powers and actions for the attainment of things good and useful. The most considerable under this head is ethics, which is the seeking out those rules and measures of human actions which lead to happiness, and the means to practise them. The end of this is not bare speculation and the knowledge of truth ; but right, and a conduct suitable to it.

4. *Thirdly,* Σημιωτική.—Thirdly, The third branch may be called σημιωτική, or, the "doctrine of signs," the most usual whereof being words, it is aptly enough termed also λογική, "logic;" the business whereof is to consider the nature of signs the mind makes use of for the understanding of things, or conveying its knowledge to others. For, since the things the mind contemplates are none of them, besides itself, present to the understanding, it is necessary that something else, as a sign or representation of the thing it considers, should be present to it: and these are ideas. And because the scene of ideas that makes one man's thoughts cannot be laid open to the immediate view of another, nor laid up any where but in the memory, a no very sure repository ; therefore, to communicate our thoughts to one another, as well as record them for our own use, signs of our ideas are also necessary. Those which men have found most convenient, and therefore generally make use of, are articulate sounds. The consideration, then, of ideas and words as the great instruments of knowledge, makes no despicable part of their contemplation who would take a view of human knowledge in the whole extent of it. And perhaps, if they were distinctly weighed and duly considered, they would afford us another sort of logic and critic than what we have been hitherto acquainted with.

5. *This is the first division of the objects of knowledge.*—This seems to me the first and most general, as well as natural, division of the objects of our understanding. For a man can employ his thoughts about nothing but either the contemplation of things themselves for the discovery of truth; or about the things in his own power, which are his own actions, for the attainment of his own ends ; or the signs the mind makes use of, both in the one and the other, and the right ordering of them for its clearer information. All which three, viz., things as they are in themselves knowable, actions as they depend on us in order to happiness, and the right use of signs in order to knowledge, being *toto cœlo* different, they seemed to me to be the three great provinces of the intellectual world, wholly separate and distinct one from another.

# INDEX
## TO
# THE ESSAY ON
# THE HUMAN UNDERSTANDING.

# GREAT BOOKS IN PHILOSOPHY PAPERBACK SERIES

## ETHICS

| | |
|---|---|
| Aristotle—*The Nicomachean Ethics* | |
| Marcus Aurelius—*Meditations* | $8.95 |
| Jeremy Bentham—*The Principles of Morals and Legislation* | 5.95 |
| John Dewey—*The Moral Writings of John Dewey,* | 8.95 |
| *Revised Edition* (edited by James Gouinlock) | |
| Epictetus—*Enchiridion* | 10.95 |
| Immanuel Kant—*Fundamental Principles of the Metaphysic of Morals* | 3.95 |
| John Stuart Mill—*Utilitarianism* | 4.95 |
| George Edward Moore—*Principia Ethica* | 4.95 |
| Friedrich Nietzsche—*Beyond Good and Evil* | 8.95 |
| Bertrand Russell—*Bertrand Russell On Ethics, Sex, and Marriage* | 8.95 |
| (edited by Al Seckel) | |
| Benedict de Spinoza—*Ethics* and *The Improvement of the Understanding* | 18.95 |
| | 9.95 |

## SOCIAL AND POLITICAL PHILOSOPHY

| | |
|---|---|
| Aristotle—*The Politics* | |
| Mikhail Bakunin—*The Basic Bakunin: Writings, 1869–1871* | 7.95 |
| (translated and edited by Robert M. Cutler) | |
| Edmund Burke—*Reflections on the Revolution in France* | 10.95 |
| John Dewey—*Freedom and Culture* | 7.95 |
| G. W. F. Hegel—*The Philosophy of History* | 10.95 |
| Thomas Hobbes—*The Leviathan* | 9.95 |
| Sidney Hook—*Paradoxes of Freedom* | 7.95 |
| Sidney Hook—*Reason, Social Myths, and Democracy* | 9.95 |
| John Locke—*Second Treatise on Civil Government* | 11.95 |
| Niccolo Machiavelli—*The Prince* | 4.95 |
| Karl Marx/Frederick Engels—*The Economic and Philosophic* | 4.95 |
| *Manuscripts of 1844* and *The Communist Manifesto* | |
| John Stuart Mill—*Considerations on Representative Government* | 6.95 |
| John Stuart Mill—*On Liberty* | 6.95 |
| John Stuart Mill—*On Socialism* | 4.95 |
| John Stuart Mill—*The Subjection of Women* | 7.95 |
| Friedrich Nietzsche—*Thus Spake Zarathustra* | 4.95 |
| Thomas Paine—*Common Sense* | 9.95 |
| Thomas Paine—*Rights of Man* | 5.95 |
| Plato—*Plato on Homosexuality: Lysis, Phaedrus,* and *Symposium* | 7.95 |
| Plato—*The Republic* | 6.95 |
| | 9.95 |

## GREAT MINDS PAPERBACK SERIES

### ECONOMICS

| | |
|---|---|
| Charlotte Perkins Gilman—*Women and Economics:* | |
| *A Study of the Economic Relation between Women and Men* | 11.95 |
| Adam Smith—*Wealth of Nations* | 9.95 |

### RELIGION

| | |
|---|---|
| Desiderius Erasmus—*The Praise of Folly* | 9.95 |
| Thomas Henry Huxley—*Agnosticism and Christianity and Other Essays* | 10.95 |
| Ernest Renan—*The Life of Jesus* | 11.95 |
| Voltaire—*A Treatise on Toleration and Other Essays* | 8.95 |
| Andrew D. White—*A History of the Warfare* | |
| *of Science with Theology in Christendom* | 19.95 |

### SCIENCE

| | |
|---|---|
| Charles Darwin—*The Origin of Species* | 10.95 |
| Michael Faraday—*The Forces of Matter* | 8.95 |
| Galileo Galilei—*Dialogues Concerning Two New Sciences* | 9.95 |
| Ernst Haeckel—*The Riddle of the Universe* | 10.95 |
| William Harvey—*On the Motion of the Heart and Blood in Animals* | 9.95 |
| Julian Huxley—*Evolutionary Humanism* | 10.95 |

### HISTORY

| | |
|---|---|
| Edward Gibbon—*On Christianity* | 9.95 |
| Herodotus—*The History* | 13.95 |

### SOCIOLOGY

| | |
|---|---|
| Emile Durkheim—*Ethics and the Sociology of Morals* | |
| (translated with an introduction by Robert T. Hall) | 8.95 |

### LITERATURE

| | |
|---|---|
| Jonathan Swift—*A Modest Proposal and Other Satires* | |
| (with an introduction by George R. Levine) | 7.95 |
| H. G. Wells—*The Conquest of Time* (with an introduction by Martin Gardner) | 7.95 |

*(Prices subject to change without notice.)*